investigating the mind, brain, & behavior
AN INTRODUCTION TO PSYCHOLOGY

Third Edition

Compiled by

Justin M. Joffe and Julianne Krulewitz

Custom Edition for the University of Vermont

Taken from:

Research Stories for Introductory Psychology, Second Edition
by Larry Shaffer and Matthew R. Merrens

Psychology, Seventh Edition
by Carole Wade and Carol Tavris

Mastering the World of Psychology
by Samuel E. Wood, Ellen Green Wood and Denise Boyd

Development Through the Lifespan, Third Edition
by Laura E. Berk

Abnormal Psychology: Integrating Perspectives
by G. Terence Wilson, Peter E. Nathan, K. Daniel O'Leary and Lee Anna Clark

PEARSON

Custom Publishing

D1468262

Cover Art: *Psych Heads*, by Tom Rogers.

Taken from:

Research Stories for Introductory Psychology, Second Edition
by Larry Shaffer and Matthew R. Merrens
Copyright © 2004, 2001 by Pearson Education, Inc.
Published by Allyn and Bacon
Boston, Massachusetts 02116

Psychology, Seventh Edition
by Carole Wade and Carol Tavris
Copyright © 2003, 2000 by Pearson Education, Inc.
Published by Prentice Hall
Upper Saddle River, New Jersey 07458

Mastering the World of Psychology
by Samuel E. Wood, Ellen Green Wood and Denise Boyd
Copyright © 2004 by Pearson Education, Inc.
Published by Allyn and Bacon

Development Through the Lifespan, Third Edition
by Laura E. Berk
Copyright © 2004, 2001, 1998 by Pearson Education, Inc.
Published by Allyn and Bacon

Abnormal Psychology: Integrating Perspectives
by G. Terence Wilson, Peter E. Nathan, K. Daniel O'Leary and Lee Anna Clark
Copyright © 1996 by Allyn and Bacon
A Pearson Education Company

Printed in the United States of America
10 9 8 7 6 5 4 3 2 1

ISBN 0-536-32862-5

2006500255

AG/HA

Please visit our web site at *www.pearsoncustom.com*

PEARSON CUSTOM PUBLISHING
75 Arlington Street, Suite 300, Boston, MA 02116
A Pearson Education Company

To my brother; Edward Joffe, and my sister, Amelia Levin, with thanks for their constant and endless love, support, and generous hearts
—Justin

To mom and dad for helping me make my own path and to Brian for walking it with me. Love
—Julianne

CONTENTS

General Introduction   *1*

SECTION I   RESEARCH METHODOLOGY

Chapter One: Introduction   11

Chapter Two: Oh Rats!   33

Chapter Three: Psychics and scientists   45

Chapter Four: You're driving me crazy   55

Chapter Five: Hungry again? You can't be, you just had lunch   63

Chapter Six: Topless dancers bare all (to ethnographers)   75

SECTION II   BIOPSYCHOLOGY

Chapter Seven: Introduction   91

Chapter Eight: Grow your own . . . computer   145

Chapter Nine: Zipping Up the Genes   159

SECTION III   LEARNING, MEMORY, COGNITION

Chapter Ten: Introduction   171

Chapter Eleven: Being sick of the hospital   245

Chapter Twelve: Yoking Smoking   255

Chapter Thirteen: Stereotypes: A good thing in the cognitive toolkit   267

SECTION IV DEVELOPMENT

Chapter Fourteen: Introduction   277

Chapter Fifteen: The wolf in sheepdog's clothing   309

Chapter Sixteen: Now you see it, now you don't   319

Chapter Seventeen: Kids say the darndest things   331

Chapter Eighteen: Are your professors losing it? Not if they're using it   343

SECTION V SOCIAL AND PERSONALITY

Chapter Nineteen: Introduction   359

Chapter Twenty: Pants on fire   405

Chapter Twenty-One: Aggression breeds aggression   415

Chapter Twenty-Two: I'm OK, you're not   423

Chapter Twenty-Three: Just what I expected, you flirt!   435

Chapter Twenty-Four: You *will* do what you're told!   449

SECTION VI ABNORMAL BEHAVIOR AND THERAPY

Chapter Twenty-Five: Introduction   467

Chapter Twenty-Six: The SADdest time of the year   509

Chapter Twenty-Seven: Betting on the winners   519

Chapter Twenty-Eight: Show me the evidence   529

Chapter Twenty-Nine: To catch a cold   539

GENERAL INTRODUCTION: WHY THIS BOOK?

This book is the key component of a course that constitutes a new way of introducing students to psychology. We use it not to fill students with pieces of information gathered over decades of research but, instead, to help them learn to think like psychologists. This approach changes the introductory psychology course from a hurdle students have to jump to be admitted to more advanced courses (or to meet some curricular requirement) to one that serves two allied purposes:

- Developing skills that provide a foundation on which to build better understanding in more advanced courses, and
- Developing skills that can be used (whether or not a student takes any further psychology courses) to critically evaluate, both as consumers and taxpayers, claims made by psychologists about their wares.

A brief history of our experience with teaching introductory psychology is probably as good a way as any of explaining this book.

JOFFE'S TALE

In 1991 I took over the teaching of introductory psychology ("Psych 1") at the University of Vermont (UVM), a course I hadn't taught for many years (and never in Vermont). From 1991–1999 I taught this course in collaboration with another faculty member in a manner that is typical of large introductory college courses, both in psychology and in many other disciplines. An encyclopedic textbook (typically surveying the entire field in 700-plus pages, and accompanied by an intimidating myriad of ancillaries for both instructors and students such as instructors' manuals, test banks, study guides, CD-ROMS, web sites, etc.) constituted the "reading," and class meetings were occupied by lectures (ranging from conventional chalk-and-talk to power-point electronic fireworks). In our Psych 1 we used a range of guest lecturers to introduce students not just to the discipline of psychology but to the Department here at UVM, but in most other respects our course was pretty much like others.

My co-teacher through most of the 1990s, Professor James Rosen, and I believed that the lectures were mostly very good, the book excellent, the effort we expended enormous—and the students, on average, at best lukewarm about the course. Semester after semester we tried to make it more challenging and exciting—we added video and writing assignments and class demonstrations and discussion groups and peer advisors and extra-credit opportunities and a web page and whatever else we could think of to improve a large course without large numbers of additional instructors. Student evaluations went up a bit and down a bit, and too many students were saying that long lectures are boring, big classes are boring, psychology is boring. Even those who did very well on exams seemed to have acquired little more in the way of an education in the field of psychology than the ability to regurgitate trivial-pursuit details on multiple-choice exams. We seemed to be very far from producing students who were excited by the field and who had the tools to analyze claims skeptically, whether to provide important groundwork for analyzing research claims in more advanced psychology courses or to make them less gullible consumers of psychological claims and services (or both).

We searched hard and long for alternative ways of teaching psychology in a large introductory course. Eventually Linda Larrabee, the publisher's representative for the textbook we had been using, suggested we take a look at the way introductory psychology was being taught just across Lake Champlain from our campus in Burlington, at the State University of New York at Plattsburgh. A ferry ride is a pleasant prospect in springtime, and so Professor Rosen and I contacted the instructors involved and went to watch them teach a class. That is how we came to meet Professor Lary Shaffer, a Distinguished Teaching Professor and recipient of the SUNY Chancellor's Award for Excellence in Teaching, and Professor Matthew E. Merrens, a former chair of the Psychology Department at SUNY-Plattsburgh and also a recipient of the SUNY Chancellor's Award for Excellence in teaching.

The rest was, indeed, history.

We crossed the lake and watched them in action and came back convinced that here was a radically different and potentially far more effective way of introducing students to psychology, by engaging them actively in every class and teaching them to think like psychologists.

Our new course

We introduced our first "new improved" Psych 1 in the fall of 1999. We thought we had acquired a turnkey operation and that all it would involve would be reading the textbook (itself radically different in almost every way from conventional books—shorter, non-encyclopedic, not a survey, but summaries of 36 specific pieces of research) and carefully reviewing the instructors' materials before class.

We could not have been more wrong about the new course being a turnkey operation. I spent more time on this course in its first two semesters than I have on any two courses in my 40-some years of teaching, as we revised and rewrote almost all the instructors' materials. We worked very hard, but enjoyed it much more: attendance was way up, late arrivals and early departures almost a thing of the past, and student participation (they have no choice!) was at an unprecedented level. We had various complaints—some insightful, others less so—, but the level of bitterness underlying them had greatly declined.

We were fortunate indeed to have the help of a succession of graduate teaching fellows to help with the materials, the teaching, and the database. I am particularly grateful to those who helped us sail into unknown waters when we made the transition: these included Joshua Cooper, David Henehan, Mark Gorman, Amanda Barnett-Rhodes, Christina Weakland, and notably—because of the size of her contribution and her continuing involvement with the course—Julianne Krulewitz.

At first students' reactions to the course were not dramatically different. The Fall 1999 course evaluation data showed better instructor ratings than ever before on the course, but the overall evaluation, though at the better end of 10 years' worth of evaluations, was not as positive as we would have liked. Nevertheless we saw signs of success: we'd achieved evaluations at least as good as any in the previous 10 years despite the fact that we were, in effect, inventing the course as we went along—it wasn't just the first time we'd done it this way but that for many of the classes we were developing our lesson plans the night before—so the evaluations were (from this perspective) surprisingly good. Furthermore, we were not getting the handful of students we'd had in the past appending comments indicating a distressing level of bitterness and corrosive boredom. We still had our share of critical comments, but the extreme edge was absent.

During this intense but positive first year of our new Psych 1, we discovered things that we could change to improve the course further. Our impression, and a theme of student criticisms, was that there was too little variation in classes: every class period required students to hand in a brief report on the assigned chapter and to answer questions when called upon at random, the entire time being taken up with this question-and-answer format and the discussions that inevitably ensue from it. We agreed that a somewhat smaller number of writing assignments would achieve pretty much the same outcome but without the treadmill feel of papers being due every Monday, Wednesday, and Friday, and at the same time saw that this would leave us with some class time to add a component we found lacking, namely some context into which the students could fit the individual pieces of research described in each chapter of the book.

In the summer of 2000, with the help of funding from the University of Vermont's Center for Teaching and Learning (CTL), Julianne Krulewitz and a small team including James Rosen, Patti Cook, and me, worked to improve the materials we used: to add various components to enrich the classes—"mini-lectures," group discussions, writing assignments, a small amount of carefully selected video—, progressive increases in the level of critical thinking needed for answering the in-class questions, and so on. We thank the CTL for their support hope they will see this book as evidence that their support was worthwhile.

I hope it is clear from this brief history that there are two lots of people without whom this book would not exist—one is Lary Shaffer and Matthew R. Merrens, who invented the course and the kind of book we are emulating, the other Linda Larrabee, without whom we would not have found Shaffer and Merrens (neither the people nor the book!).

Lary Shaffer and Matt Merrens invented this way of teaching introductory psychology and wrote the initial book that is the core of the radically different way of teaching the course. They also provided us with the instructors' materials we started with. This book is not only modeled on their approach conceptually, it also contains a great deal of their original material. Marcie Mealia, of Allyn and Bacon publishers, has also given us help creating a new book. She suggested that in our search for overview chapters to introduce each section we should look at introductory chapters from more advanced textbooks in addition to chapters in introductory psychology texts. This helped us find material that best fitted our needs for this book.

My tale would be incomplete if I neglected to put on record the enormous help it has been having Julianne as my co-author. It is much more enjoyable having someone with whom to discuss the issues, decisions, difficulties, and good times that are part and parcel of doing a book of this kind, and from the time she agreed to become co-author my job has become easier and more enjoyable, and I know this is a better book in every way than it would have been without her involvement.

KRULEWITZ'S TALE

In the fall of 1999, about a month before beginning graduate school at UVM (and about a month after finishing college) I was informed that I would be a teaching assistant for Psych 1. As I soon discovered, this was an assignment that evoked apologetic head nods and sympathetic groans from many, if not most, senior graduate students and faculty members alike. To some, upon discovering that I had committed to not one, but two years as a Psych 1 teaching assistant, this seemed to be a fate worse than death (or at least really bad!). Not only was introductory psychology notorious among both students and faculty as being a class one just tried to survive—an obstacle to more relevant and interesting courses offered by the department—it was also going through a time of transition, and no one knew exactly how well, if at all, the "new improved Psych 1" would work.

Truth be told, even before hearing any of these grim stories from the "veterans" of Psych 1, I was a little nervous. How was I, with the ink barely dry on my diploma, supposed to teach hundreds of students each semester? Although I thought it possible (although not particularly probable) that the two professors I would be working with, both with decades of experience, could recite all the details from an introductory text, there was no way I could. And at this point, since lecturing to students seemed completely overwhelming, I certainly could not even begin to imagine engaging students in thoughtful discussion and critical thinking, the things that I really valued in education.

Thankfully, Psych 1 was nothing like I expected. In fact, those first days were some of the most exciting and enlightening days of teaching and learning I have ever experienced. I, along with fellow teaching assistants Joshua and Dave, professors Justin and James, and about 500 undergraduates each seemed to have this terrific epiphany: it is not about memorizing facts, it is about learning to think like a psychologist! As instructors, our job became to teach students how to approach psychology (and life) with a critical eye, how to evaluate research, and how to understand the value of good science. Each student's job was to take an active role in his or her education.

Now that memorization was no longer the main goal of Psych 1, now that students did not have to spend all their time frantically copying pages of notes, and now that instructors did not have to worry if the students were copying them correctly, there was time for all those things that I think are so important in higher education. We (the instructors and a class of 100–150 students) were discussing real psychology. We were all asking questions, searching for answers, and experiencing new ways of looking at the field.

As the semesters progressed we learned how to make our classes more interactive, more engaging, and more thoughtful. We evaluated our strengths and weaknesses, and developed new ways of approaching the major themes in psychology. From these evaluations, this book has emerged. We expect that in concert with class meetings, this book will give its readers a solid understanding of the major fields in psychology, exemplars of good research, and the tools they'll need to pursue an array of future endeavors. It is our hope, that with this new book, students will become even more passionate about psychology.

I am truly grateful to be taking part in the evolution of this course and this new book. From our first meeting those years ago, I saw Professor Joffe as a mentor. His desire to teach students is admirable. The effort he puts forth to make sure they actually learn is nothing short of amazing! To work with Justin, as a co-author is not just a great experience, it is an honor.

THE BOOK'S TALE

In the fall of 1999 we started using Shaffer and Merrens' *Research Stories for Introductory Psychology* as our textbook. The goal of this book was to help students understand the science of psychology and to facilitate the development of critical thinking skills. Rather than delivering the traditional overview of psychology (and all the dates, names, and facts that went along with it), Shaffer and Merrens' book focuses on describing a few representative research studies more completely. They retell actual research reports at an introductory level, taking care to elaborate on introductions, methods, and procedures, and to make complex statistical analyses understandable. Most importantly, this book provides a forum to evaluate research and cultivate the skills students can use to assess explanations of human behavior throughout their lives.

Why a new book?

Although we saw some improvements in student evaluations, attendance, and interest during the second year of teaching the course in a new way, we felt that the materials we were using lacked some features that could potentially enhance introductory psychology even more. There were several things we wanted to do that we knew would change the pristine Socratic purity of our Shaffer and

Merrens model but in our view would strengthen the course. These are the things we have done in this book:

- We have added overviews of fields in which the specific research projects fall so that students can relate the chapters on specific research studies to the wider context in which the research was done.

- We have organized this book so it provides a foundation for each of the six more specialized survey courses offered at our university (and which are common to the curriculum at many other schools as well). Students are introduced to (1) research methods, (2) biobehavioral psychology, (3) learning, memory, and cognition, (4) human development, (5) social and personality psychology, and (6) abnormal psychology and therapy.

- We have tried to select research that reflects the breadth of each field and covers some of its currently important sub-areas. Although we know that four research projects can do little more than scratch the surface of the work available in each of these areas, we are taking pains to insure that eventually each research chapter reflects a different and important sub-area of its particular field. (For example, in our biobehavioral section we intend to have research that covers brain physiology, neural plasticity, behavioral genetics, and evolutionary psychology).

- We are trying to insure that the research we summarize is of high quality and that individual chapters do not vary greatly in difficulty or clarity and that it covers topics that are likely to interest students.

- Because the major purpose of our course is to help students to understand behavior scientifically, perhaps most importantly we have tried to select only research that we believe clearly and accurately illustrates sound methodology.

In short, we needed a new textbook with overviews of the areas in which the selected research falls and with research "stories" chosen in a way that made them representative of the fields from which they were drawn. This version is a first approximation, and gradually we will substitute research chapters that help us better achieve our intentions.

Our story would be incomplete were we not to note a few other points. First, constructing this book has increased our admiration for Shaffer and Merrens' pioneering work by showing us just how hard it is to find suitable "research stories" and to rewrite them in a way that retains the integrity of the original work (that is, that summarizes research clearly and interestingly without "dumbing down" the material). Finding suitable research was the task where we found that we had most underestimated the difficulty: for each chapter we have completed to date we have had to look at the titles of over 200 articles, read the abstracts of 50–75, skim in their entirety about 20–30, and read carefully about 6–8.

In addition to thanking Shaffer and Merrens for their ideas and for the use of many of their research stories, we would like to express our gratitude to the other authors whose work appears in this book, work that we believe is well researched and written and that reflects enormous scholarly care and effort. Thank you, Berk, Wade, Tavris, Wood, Wood, Boyd, and Wilson, for these noteworthy contributions.

We are, of course, also indebted to each author whose research we have reviewed and rewritten, particularly authors of original articles who have commented on and helped clarify our presentations of their work, Bob Jacobs (whose work is described in Chapter 8) and Arthur P. Shimamura (Chapter 18). Their research exemplifies the solid theories and scientific methods we wish to teach our students.

We are grateful to colleagues who have taught sections of the course in the new way—Professors James Rosen, John Burchard, and Carol Miller—and who have put up with endless changes in instructors' materials and mysterious removals and replacements of chapters with patience and good humor, and who have frequently contributed helpful and constructive ideas.

Kim Brugger and Christina Oldham, our first editors at Pearson, harried us, heartened us, hurried us, helped us, and bought us dinner—we thank them for all these things (though not necessarily to the same degree for each), for their insight into what we are trying to do, and for accepting such an unusual project. They, and later Scott Salesses, helped us produce a key component of what we believe is an innovative way of introducing students to psychology.

Finally, we must thank all those Psych 1 students who took introductory psychology during its time of transition. In a manner of speaking, you were all generous contributors to our endeavor and mostly uncomplaining participants in what we might view as our own little experiment!

SECTION I
RESEARCH METHODOLOGY

CHAPTER 1

INTRODUCTION

Justin M. Joffe

Why do we do research—on the mind, brain, and behavior, or anything else for that matter? We humans, as a species, seem to be driven to try to understand the world around us, and research is a formal way of answering questions like "1) What's happening? 2) Is there a systematic (causal) effect? And 3) What is the causal mechanism or how does it work?" (Shavelson and Towne, 2004, p. 28).

The first step, then, is to describe something in the world, a "fact" that we find interesting and want to explain. Let's say we have information that children in smaller classes demonstrate better performance on achievement tests than children in larger classes. The next question might well be, does being in a smaller class cause the better performance? Shavelson and Towne (2004) discuss research carried out in Tennessee, in which 11,600 students in 79 schools were randomly assigned to three different classes: regular size (22–26 students), regular size with an aide, or small (13–17 students); this research showed that those in small classes outperformed students in both the other classes, and the research design (see discussion of "experiments" later in this chapter) leaves us confident that the reduced class size caused the better performance.

The question that then arises, the third question listed, is "How does it work?" "Was the effect due to an increase in the number and personal nature of teacher-student contacts or to less off-task student behavior . . . or to the level of student engagement . . . ?" (Shavelson and Towne, 2004, p. 29). I'm sure you can appreciate that answers to these questions are not simply interesting, but would be useful in finding effective ways to improve children's performance in school.

ANSWERING QUESTIONS SCIENTIFICALLY

Is a discipline considered to be a science because the information it provides is of high quality or very important? No, we base that decision on its *methods* of collecting and evaluating information. Scientific psychology (the kind we prefer) bases its conclusions (which are always tentative) not on speculation, intuition, the pronouncements of "authorities," or a vote, but on evidence collected according to a set of rules; its methods are empirical, which is to say that scientific psychology relies on the collection and evaluation of data.

The reason we have a set of rules is very similar to the reason we have rules of evidence in our legal system—to minimize errors, since the consequences of errors can be very serious.

The methodological rules themselves constitute claims that are subject to empirical testing. They should not be regarded as premises that need no empirical support; we should ask a question of them that can be answered empirically—do they work? That is, we can test the rules just as we use the rules to test assertions about why people behave the way they do. The research methods should not be decided by intuition, popularity, or fashion, but by an evaluation of evidence as to how useful they are.

The scientific methods that have developed over the past 500 years or so had their origins in the natural sciences (disciplines like physics, chemistry, and biology). These methods were adopted in the late 19th and early 20th Centuries—adopted and adapted to deal with subject matter that is often very different from that of the sciences in which the methods developed. Psychologists have been ambivalent about the appropriateness for their discipline of the hypothetico-deductive framework of modern science, possibly because parts of psychology appear to belong in the biological sciences, other parts in the social sciences. And it is the social sciences that have balked at attempts to confine them strictly to quantitative methods, methods based on the implicit belief that their subject matter is an objective reality that *the* scientific method can unveil, rather than a set of social constructions that require different methods of inquiry.

Conventional science, in simplified form, proceeds as follows:

1. We make an observation of relationships between events;

2. We invent a theory consistent with the observation, a theory that makes predictions about things we have not observed;

3. We test these predictions (hypotheses);

4. If the new observations are consistent with the predictions, we make additional predictions and test them. If the observations are partly or completely inconsistent with the predictions we modify the theory (or construct a new one if the old theory's predictions are frequently incorrect). We devise one that is consistent with all the observations we have made and that makes predictions about events we haven't already observed;

5. We go to step 3 and repeat the process.

For an hypothesis to be scientific it needs to state a relationship between variables that can be defined in terms of measurement operations. "Hunger causes rats to learn better" is a scientific hypothesis because we can operationally define both hunger (e.g., as measured by the number of hours the rats have been deprived of food) and learning (e.g., as the number of errors rats make in a maze, or the time they take to reach a goal-box containing food). "People who lead good lives go to heaven," on the other hand, is not; we might possibly get some agreement on what measures define a "good life," but we cannot operationalize and measure the hypothesized outcome, "going to heaven."

Another way of looking at this distinction between scientific and non-scientific hypotheses is to say that to be scientific an hypothesis must be, at least in principle, falsifiable. In other words there must be at least the possibility of an outcome that contradicts the prediction. So, for example, the hypothesis that "all birds can fly" is falsifiable, and is disproved when we observe an ostrich, but there is no possible observable or measurable event that would disprove the hypothesis about good people going to heaven.

Scientific psychology, by convention regarded as having become established in 1879 when Wilhelm Wundt set up the world's first psychology laboratory at the University of Leipzig, has always been very self-conscious about its methods. While physicists (for example) seem to have little need to ask whether or not what they do is scientific, psychologists seem perpetually to be asking the question. This may have to do with the maturity of the disciplines but it is more likely, we believe, due to differences in subject matter.

As Camic, Rhodes, and Yardley (2003) point out, what is real "is really not an issue for biologists or chemists as their 'subject' may be a diseased cell or a chemical interaction. When doing research involving people . . . the researcher and the participant are affected by each other and modify their responses, behaviors and perceptions based upon that interaction, and of course on events and histories prior to the interaction. This is the case whether one uses an interview or an experiment to collect data.

Yet in most of psychological research the psychologist-scientist controls the definition of reality and 'the threat to the social definitions of reality is neutralized by assigning an inferior . . . status . . . to all definitions existing outside the social universe' (Berger & Luckmann, 1966, p. 115). Those representations of research that exist outside of positivism and the experimental method are looked upon as inferior and are not taken as seriously by journal editors, funding sources, doctoral dissertation committees or faculty in psychology departments."

In other words, they are saying that in most psychological research there is no objective reality. Rather, there are multiple realities and "all knowledge is derived from the mental constructions of the members of a social system" (Reber, 1995, p. 157). Therefore, psychological phenomena cannot be explained and predicted by methods that primarily test hypotheses deduced from theories. Furthermore, psychological findings cannot be understood without recognizing that even the most scientific psychology contains subjective elements. Camic et al. (2003) say that because psychology has in many ways been modeled after sciences like biology and chemistry, research that does not follow the experimental methods of those sciences is considered unscientific and consequently, less important.

It is this difference in philosophy that most distinguishes two contrasting approaches to research—quantitative and qualitative—that we will examine in the next section. The many differences we can identify are less sharp than this fundamental difference in approach.

QUANTITATIVE AND QUALITATIVE RESEARCH

What distinguishes these two approaches to research? The most obvious answer, of course, is that quantitative data consist of numbers, qualitative of words. Trochim (2000), however, makes a convincing case that this is not a fundamental distinction between the two, insofar as qualitative data can readily be represented numerically (for example, we can classify sentences in terms of the themes they contain, count the number that refer to each theme, and so on); the old statistical saw—"whatever exists at all exists in some quantity"—seems to apply. Similarly, and more subtly, Trochim argues that "all quantitative data is based on qualitative judgment." He illustrates the point by discussing what it means when someone checks a number on a scale (where, say, "1" means you strongly disagree with a statement, "2" that you disagree, and so on, to "5" which means you strongly agree)—you can ask if the respondent understood the statement she was responding to, understood that the number chosen indicated agreement or disagreement, was thinking about it or just picking a number to get done rapidly, and so on. "All numerical information involves numerous judgments about what the number means," he concludes.

The difference between quantitative and qualitative research is sometimes characterized as follows: whereas quantitative research is well suited to finding ways of explaining and predicting behavior (and thoughts and emotions), it is not so well suited to understanding them. Quantitative research will, for example, give us the chemical composition of a substance (perhaps to enable us to synthesize it if we want to); qualitative research will tell us it smells like a rose. One of us used to tell students in a research methods course that if they wanted to understand people they would be better able to do so by reading poetry and novels than by studying psychology—but if they wished to predict behavior they should use quantitative designs. Qualitative approaches provide a somewhat more systematic approach to understanding than is usually adopted by poets and novelists. Both sets of information may be useful and informative and together give more complete information than either alone.

Many other distinctions between qualitative and quantitative research are also questionable. They represent distinctions between caricatures of the two and ignore the similarities and the overlap. However, just as a caricature drawing can capture something of a person's character even if it is not a fair and accurate representation of the person, the conventional distinctions between quantitative and qualitative methods can give a sense of how they differ. Consequently we have tabulated many of the distinctions made in order to give you some feeling for how the methods differ. When you look at these distinctions in Table 1.1, bear in mind two things:

- That most if not all of them overstate the differences between the two;
- That many comments oversimplify, and do not encompass all of the research although they may cover some of it. For example, the table cites "unnatural settings" as one of the weaknesses of quantitative research, but a lot of quantitative research is done in natural settings and there is nothing intrinsically natural about an interview, say, that might be used in qualitative research.

TABLE 1.1   Some Distinctions Between Qualitative and Quantitative Research

CHARACTERISTIC	QUANTITATIVE RESEARCH	QUALITATIVE RESEARCH
Aims	Explanation, prediction; test deductions from theory	Description, interpretation; build theory (inductive)
Research questions	Does A cause B?	What is A? B?
Focus	Narrow, concise	Broad, complex
Participants	Can be large numbers	Usually relatively small numbers
Research process	Established methods, defined variables, objective	More flexible, variables emerge in process, subjective
Data	Numbers	Words
Data analysis	Inferential statistics	Descriptive (or no) statistics
Research reports	Formal	More personal
Strengths	Rigor, generalizability of findings, control of variables	Deeper understanding, flexibility
Weaknesses	Inflexibility, unnatural context (e.g., laboratory)	Lack of generalizability, lack of control of variable
Fundamental beliefs	Objective, measurable reality	Multiple, constructed realities

Perhaps the best summary of all this is Blomeyer and Clemente's (2003) tongue-in-cheek example of the hypotheses and methods that would be involved in the two kinds of research:

> **Quantitative—**
> Hypothesis: All beans are alike.
> Null Hypothesis: No beans are different.
> Description of the method: First you count the beans then you tell how many.
>
> **Qualitative—**
> Research Questions: What is a bean?   What does it mean to be a bean?
>
> **Description of method**:   First you figure out what a bean is.   Then you examine it in the field.   Then you write a 200-page report.

More seriously, our impression is that the major difference between the two approaches, in addition to their philosophical position, lies not in their methods of data collection or the nature of the data itself, but in their methods of making sense of the information they collect, their methods of data analysis. These are sufficiently complex that we will not cover them in detail here. We will concentrate instead on quantitative methods, not because we wish to "privilege" them (as Camic et al. [2003] tell us is so often done) but because most of the studies described in detail in this book use them. We hope to include more research that uses qualitative methods in future editions of this book.

FOUR QUESTIONS ABOUT "HOW IT WORKS"

When we read research reports we not infrequently come across very different explanations of the same phenomena, different answers to the basic question, "How does it work?" Sometimes these explanations relate to what triggers a particular behavior, at other times they identify earlier events that affect the behavior, and once in a while the researcher makes statements about the purpose the behavior serves in the individual displaying it or even in the species studied. More rarely still we may find research that attempts to identify the factors in the evolutionary history of the species that affected the survival value of the behavior of interest.

These different explanations are not so much competitors (about which we'd ask, "Which is correct?") but rather complementary answers that together give us a far fuller explanation than any one alone. They are, of course, answers to different questions about determinants of behavior, questions that were systematically organized over 40 years ago by Nikolaas Tinbergen, the ethologist who was cowinner of the 1973 Nobel Prize for Physiology or Medicine.

Table 1.2 summarizes his scheme and suggests that two of the questions concern "causes" (what determines the behavior) and two concern "origins" or history. Two address what Tinbergen believed were explanations of *why* a behavior occurs, and two describe *how* it occurs. Let us look at each of them, starting with questions about how things happen.

The questions most frequently addressed in all fields of psychology concern immediate antecedents or mechanisms underlying behavior. We may ask questions about the effects of reward on rats in a Skinner box (see Chapter 11), about the brain mechanisms involved in memory (Chapter 5), or hundreds of other questions about what it is in our environment (which includes other people), in our physiology, including our brain, and in our thoughts and emotions that determines what we do. These are all questions about immediate antecedents.

Questions about the development of behavior are "How?" questions concerning origins. When we look at research methods we will see that two important variations on other experimental designs,

TABLE 1.2   Types of Questions About Behavior (Tinbergen, 1963)

	"HOW?" QUESTIONS	"WHY?" QUESTIONS
Questions about "Causes"	What are the immediate antecedents (i.e., the mechanism) of the behavior?	What is the adaptive significance of the behavior? **A.** What is its biological function (immediate effects)? **B.** What is its survival value? I.e., (how) do immediate functions affect reproductive success?
Questions about "Origins"	What is the developmental history of the behavior? (Factors in the history of the individual)	What is the evolutionary history of the behavior? (Factors in the history of the species)

longitudinal studies and cross-sectional ones, are particularly important for studying more distant antecedents of behavior, events from conception onward that may influence the way we are.

Assuming we do years of research and learn a good deal about how things work—about how pre-natal alcohol, say, can reduce learning ability in rats (Chapter 2), and how the way rewards affect the likelihood that people will stop smoking (Chapter 12), do we know all we want to know? For some pur-poses the answer may be yes, but many of us may also want to know something about why things work the way they do, and this is where Tinbergen's other two kinds of questions are relevant.

Questions about function, or adaptive significance, need to be looked at in two steps, the first being to ask, what immediate function (or functions) does the behavior serve? For example, a male bird's singing may discourage other males from coming too close, attract females, space out the bird population in an area so there is sufficient food, and so on. But the question that arises from the discov-ery of all its functions is, why do these functions need to be served? How do these immediate effects of the behavior affect the bird's likelihood of having offspring to pass on its genes? (As we will see in later chapters, reproductive success is the fundamental determinant of which genes increase in prevalence—and thus of which behaviors are more likely to be found in a population. Simply put, celibacy cannot be hereditary).

There are some points to note here. First, we should not assume conscious purpose in the organ-ism displaying the behavior of interest. It is misleading (or worse) to say something like "birds sing in order to attract mates and repel competitors." Second, we should not assume that all the behaviors we see serve the function of increasing reproductive success even if we can establish that they have immedi-ate beneficial effects. We need evidence of the purported effects on reproduction as well as on the immediate functions they serve.

Questions about evolutionary history are difficult to answer. Usually answers are based on infer-ences since there are no written records or videos of vast stretches of evolutionary time and so scenarios of conditions that determined why a particular behavior would have been useful in the distant past are often speculative. We might be able to infer things about food supply, features of the environment like temperature and vegetation, etc. from geological data, tree rings, and so on, but there is little direct evi-dence on what behaviors were advantageous. Observation of evolutionary changes over relatively short periods of time is by no means unknown, but it is rare—and exciting!

Years ago there was argument about which types of questions were more important and which were more scientific. It should be clear, however, that when we have evidence on all four types of ques-tions our knowledge will be much more complete.

"METHODS" AND "DESIGNS"

We have found that these two terms are often used interchangeably and seldom defined. This confuses our students and us, and so we want to make a distinction between them that we find helpful. By "meth-ods" we mean simply ways of collecting the information we want to examine. By "designs" we mean ways of organizing and examining information to describe, explain, or interpret it, or to generalize or predict from it.

The only author we have come across who explicitly makes a similar distinction is Laura Berk (2003), whose introductory chapter constitutes the introduction to Section IV of this book (our Chap-ter 16). Her distinction is similar to ours, and clear:

> *Research methods*—the specific activities of participants, such as taking tests, answering questionnaires, responding to interviews, or being observed.

> *Research designs*—overall plans for research studies that permit the best possible test of the investigator's hypothesis.

> Berk (2003), p. 27

Interestingly, given the similarity of our approach to this distinction, Berk classifies the *case study* as a research method, whereas we treat it as a research design (in which various methods can be employed). This probably indicates that the distinction between methods and designs is not as simple and clear as we would like it to be. Berg (2004) takes a similar position to ours: "The case study is not actually a data-gathering technique but a methodological approach that incorporates a number of data-gathering measures" (p. 251). We think that case studies can use one or more of a variety of methods to collect data (which can be qualitative or quantitative) and parts of the data generated can be organized to allow us to treat it in the same way as we would treat data from a quasi-experiment or a correlational study (designs that are explained later in this chapter).

We think it is possible that in principle any design could use any method, but in practice certain designs are far more likely to use some methods rather than others. Furthermore, we think that it is possible in principle at least to generate either quantitative or qualitative data (or both) using any design, and possibly any method. It is worth thinking about the extent to which this "going together" is a consequence of habit and how much it is built in to the nature of the research designs themselves; clarifying this may increase our ability to use the designs effectively.

There are advantages and drawbacks to each method and each design, and the pros and cons include variations in reliability—the degree to which we will get similar information from different observers or on different occasions—and validity—the extent to which we are confident that we are measuring what we think we are measuring (topics that we will discuss more fully later).

RESEARCH METHODS

Basic Research Methods

Simply stated, whatever kind of research you are doing there are three ways you can collect information about people, two of which can be used with other animals as well—you can watch them and note what they do (observation), ask them questions (self-report), or consult whatever records are available about them or their times (archival method). We look at these three major approaches and at some of the many variation in ways of observing, asking people about themselves, and so on.

A. Observation
  1. *Behavior:*
    • *Natural Situations:* Observation can be considered to be the oldest of scientific methods. Observations can be quantitative (e.g., recording how often something happens) or qualitative (comprising descriptions of what is happening). In most situations too much is happening to record everything, so almost inevitably some selection occurs. It is impossible to select what to observe without some theoretical guidance, however intuitive. Observations may be overt, when individuals know they are being observed, or covert, where they don't. Special instruments (e.g., video camera, tape-recorders, etc.) may be used.

      Observation can be done in natural settings (though it is not always easy to define what constitutes a natural setting, particularly for humans), in more structured settings (e.g., a naturally furnished room in a laboratory), or with some manipulation of the situation (e.g., to investigate if men are likely to hold doors open for women, you could watch until you had seen a number of natural occurrences of this, or you could get a woman to follow men into buildings and watch to see what happens).

    • *Tests:* These are ways of obtaining information about aptitudes (e.g., an IQ test) or abilities (e.g., musical or arithmetic skill, reaction time, learning). Usually ways of collecting *webct & Possible...*

what are the 3 basic research methods

information about personality, emotions, and motivation are also referred to as tests. We classify them as questionnaires (below) to make the point that they rely on self-report and this can be distinguished from behavior (such as doing arithmetic or playing the piano).

Some of the advantages and drawbacks of these and other methods are listed briefly in Table 1.3.

2. *Physiological Measures:* Physiological functions (e.g., heart-rate) are often studied when researchers are interested in topics like emotion. An advantage of such measures (compared to self-reports) is that it is far more difficult for people to change things like

TABLE 1.3 Research Methods—Some Advantages and Drawbacks

METHOD	ADVANTAGES	DRAWBACKS
OBSERVATION		
Behavior: Natural Situations	• Firsthand information, allowing description of behavior as it occurs • Behavior in natural environment, in response to everyday situations and events • Good place to start investigating little-investigated phenomena	• Difficult to control variables • Observation may be biased, expectations may distort observations • Hard to be unobtrusive, can't explain behavior • Inner states can only be inferred not seen. • Individuals may behave differently if they know they are being observed
Behavior: Tests	• Can achieve more precise measurements • More control of variables • Can obtain information on aptitudes, abilities	• Difficult to construct tests that are reliable and valid • Only limited control of variables • Behavior may be affected by the situation in unknown ways
Physiological Measures	• Precise and sophisticated measurements possible • Difficult to simulate or lie	• Interpretation of meaning of changes can be difficult • Some responses may be affected by the situation itself, not the variables manipulated
SELF-REPORT		
Interviews	• Individuals can reveal inner states that can't be seen • Information known only to interviewee can be elicited	• Answers may be distorted to present a positive (or negative) picture • Very time-consuming if done on a large scale • Interviewer characteristics may influence responses
Questionnaires	• Can quickly and inexpensively collect large amounts of information on large numbers of participants • Information on attitudes, opinions, feelings, and personality • Can readily track changes over time	• If sample unrepresentative or biased, cannot generalize • Responses may be inaccurate or untrue • Interviewer characteristics may influence responses • Poor questions can result in ambiguous answers (and thus produce unclear results)
ARCHIVES	• No effects of current researcher on behavior recorded • Provides information on past events that might otherwise be unavailable	• Records not always complete or accurate • Measures that would be more informative may not have been available when the information was recorded

brain waves or levels of hormones in their blood voluntarily than it is to answer a question in a way that presents one in a favorable light, or to perform badly on purpose when taking a test. On the other hand, we need to take precautions not to assume that a change in heart-rate, say, indicates guilt when it is seen in someone taking a "lie detector" test—it might well be due to some other emotion, such as fear of being wrongly convicted.

In the last 20 years or so, non-invasive techniques that enable us to get information about what the brain is doing when we feel certain emotions or do certain tasks have increased in sophistication and availability. (Non-invasive techniques are those that measure brain activity without having to open someone's skull and put electrodes or other devices in the brain itself). Neuroscientists use all kinds of high-tech (and expensive) machines to gain detailed information about changes in brain structure and function, including MRIs (magnetic resonance imaging), CT-scans (computerized axial tomography), and PET-scans (positron emission tomography). We will see information that can be obtained using such techniques when we look at some of the research in Section II, on biopsychology.

B. Self Report

1. *Interviews:* An interview may be highly structured or it may involve less structured narrative. It usually involves people responding orally to questions or talking about their thoughts on a topic. Group discussions can be used as well as individual interviews. Interviews, both individual and group, can vary considerably in structure. "Clinical interviews" might be very unstructured, with the interviewer asking questions that are largely based on answers to earlier questions, in order to explore issues that the patient raises that the interviewer considers important but could not have anticipated in advance. On the other hand, interviewers might use a set of questions that they follow with each interviewee except where a particular answer makes it sensible for them to skip some subsequent questions. (A simple example: If someone says they have never smoked, the interviewer does not ask questions about how many cigarettes a day, when they started, etc.—questions they would ask when people said they did smoke).

   Interviews can be a very time consuming way of gathering information, whether they are done individually or in groups (such as focus groups). On the other hand they can yield a wealth of information and usually have a degree of flexibility that other methods generally lack. Think of how much richer the information might be if you recorded people's answers to a question like "What do you think of the President's policy in Iraq?" than it would be if you had a questionnaire with a few statements to which people responded by indicating the extent to which they agreed or disagreed.

2. *Questionnaires:* These include "personality tests," measures of attitudes, opinions, and interests, questions about activities, and so on. Any set of questions or statements on any topic can constitute a questionnaire.

   When a structured list of questions is presented to large numbers of people we usually refer to the process as a *survey*. Surveys may be administered and responded to in writing or orally, face to face or over the phone. They enable us to obtain information (and a lot of it, if we wish) from large numbers of people fairly inexpensively. Some of the drawbacks of questionnaires are indicated in Table 1.3.

C. Archives

Data may be obtained by examining records comprised of information collected in a variety of ways (such as those described above) as well as census data, medical, legal, and financial records, newspapers, videotapes, etc.

RESEARCH DESIGNS

As we stated earlier, we see research designs as ways of organizing and examining information collected using one of the methods described above. Researchers seldom go about choosing methods, collecting information, and then thinking about how to examine it effectively (although one of the advantages of qualitative research is that much of the interpretation is determined by the nature of the information itself). More often, particularly in quantitative research, researchers consider simultaneously both the manner of collecting data and the ways of analyzing it.

Designs usually carry with them limitations on the methods with which the information collected can be organized and analyzed—statistically in the case of quantitative research, usually partly at least non-statistically in the case of qualitative research. Quantitative research imposes tighter restrictions (a smaller range of options) on suitable analyses than does qualitative research.

I. Basic Research Designs

1. *Experiment:* Participants are randomly assigned to groups that are treated differently in one or a few very specific ways—the researcher manipulates the *independent variable*. The researcher then assesses some attribute after manipulating the independent variable—that is, the researcher measures the *dependent variable*. If one group gets a specific treatment and others do not, usually the treated group is called the experimental group and other groups are called *control groups*. Conditions other than the independent variable are held as constant as possible for all groups so that results cannot be attributed to an uncontrolled or *confounding variables*. These constant conditions are called controls. If extraneous variables are well controlled, differences between the experimental and control groups can be interpreted as being caused by the independent variable.

   A simple example. If our hypothesis is that students who study more get better grades in introductory psychology, we could randomly assign 100 students to one of two groups. (There are a variety of ways to randomly assign participants to groups: e.g., we could toss a coin when each participant arrives at class, but that would risk our ending up with groups of unequal size. Instead we could put 100 pieces of paper in a box for students to draw from when they arrived; 50 would have "1" on them, meaning the individuals who drew them would be assigned to the experimental group, 50 "2," assigning individuals who drew them to the control group). The random assignment means we can be reasonably confident that on average the groups are not different to begin with in some important way that might affect their grades. Certainly both groups will have some smarter students and some less smart, some first years and some seniors, and so on. Members of each group are not clones, but the random assignment means that unless we are really unlucky we won't have one group with grade point averages (GPAs) of 3.8 and above and a second group with GPAs of less than 2.0, or one group of only women and one group of only men.

   Note that random assignment of participants to conditions, however desirable, is not essential to the design being regarded as an experiment. What is essential is the researcher's control of the variable of interest, the variable thought to be the cause of the effect of interest.

The next step in this example is simple in theory but would be virtually impossible in practice: to manipulate the independent variable, time studying, we might have all the members of one group study their textbook for three hours a day until the first exam, the second group only 15 minutes. We would statistically compare the two groups' scores on the first exam (the dependent variable) and if the group who studied more had significantly higher scores than the other group our hypothesis would be confirmed.

Three points to note: "statistically significant" doesn't necessarily mean important. By convention, a difference that is likely to happen 5 percent or less of the time by chance alone is called "significant"; the chance probability defines the word. The difference could be significant but relatively unimportant: for example, if the group who studied more had an average exam score only 2 points higher than the other group (on a test with 100 items), it might be difficult to convince other students to study that much more. The returns would not justify the effort, even if the difference were statistically significant.

Second, note that we say that the hypothesis was "confirmed," not "proved." Hypotheses, and the theories from which they are derived, are never proved. For one thing, there is always a possibility that the difference observed was due to chance—even if the probability is only one in a thousand. For another, there are many theories that might explain the same observation (or predict the same effect) and even if we have had confirmation of 50 predictions a theory makes it is always possible that the 51st prediction will be incorrect—then we might have to modify the theory or find a different one that predicts all 51 events we have observed; and that theory could be wrong on the 52nd prediction. Of course we have a lot of confidence in theories that make a great many accurate predictions, but great confidence is not the same as certainty.

Third, in an experiment we assign participants to groups randomly, but often these participants are not themselves a randomly selected sample of people from a larger population. Human research participants, for ethical and practical reasons, are volunteers, and it is possible (in some circumstances likely) that volunteers are different in some ways from people who do not volunteer. If other things are done the way they should be, the fact that the people are volunteers does not in itself affect our confidence that the manipulation of the independent variable caused the changes in the dependent variable. What it does affect is our confidence that the same thing will happen in the larger population from which our participants came. That is, if we show an effect (say) of alcohol consumption on grades in volunteers from an introductory psychology class, we cannot say with assurance that alcohol affects grades in such-and-such a way in students (or even in introductory psychology students). Without additional information we would not know whether or not non-volunteers have certain characteristics that determine that alcohol affects their grades in a different way from what we see in volunteers.

"Between" and "Within" subjects designs: In the examples we have used, different treatments are applied to different groups of participants, and when this happens we can refer to the research as a *"between subjects" experimental design*: it is the difference (if any) between different groups of participants that will confirm or disconfirm our predictions. We see an example of this kind of design in Chapter 2 ("Oh Rats!"). Sometimes we apply different treatments to the same group of participants, but at different times; one advantage of such a design is that differences on the two occasions cannot be attributed to differences (such as age, intelligence, income, etc.) between the two groups, because the same participants are tested under different conditions. We see an example of this kind of *"within subjects" experimental design* in Chapter 11 ("Being Sick of the Hospital").

Are experiments "unnatural? We usually think of experiments as being conducted in laboratories, and they often are. It is also possible and not unusual for researchers to manipulate variables in natural situations, something that increases the "external validity" of the research—that is, the confidence that similar findings would be obtained in real life situations.

2. *Quasi-experiment:* This term is used to describe a design in which participants achieve membership in different groups not as a result of random assignment but as a result of a characteristic they possess that is not under the experimenter's control; for example, gender, age, socioeconomic status, athletic ability, or ethnic identification are characteristics participants bring to the research, not attributes that are assigned to them by the researcher. A link may be found between one or more of these characteristics and some outcome variables, but cause and effect relationships are less certain.

To continue the studying-GPA example, we might ask students how much they studied each day rather than assigning them to high and low study-time groups. We could then look at the exam scores of those who studied more than three hours a day and compare them to the scores of those who studied 15 minutes a day or less. You can see that this is a little more practical than doing the experiment, but the convenience comes at a price. There is the risk of *confounding;* that is, there is a higher likelihood that the difference in the exam scores is attributable to something other than the time the students spent studying. Maybe the students who studied less partied more, and the difference in exam performance is due to their getting too little sleep. We are sure you can think of all sorts of other possibilities to explain the difference. The point is that we have far less confidence that the difference we found is due to the variable we investigated rather than to some other important way in which the two groups differed.

In a quasi-experiment (as you will read in Chapter 3) we do not have a true independent variable, one manipulated by the experimenter. Sometimes people call things like gender or GPA independent variables, but this is technically incorrect.

3. *Correlational study:* Correlational studies investigate the relationship between two variables. A correlation coefficient—the most commonly reported one is represented by the letter "r"—indicates the strength and direction (positive or negative) of the relationship between two variables. The number calculated can vary between −1.0 and +1.0, and the larger the number, regardless of whether it is positive or negative, the stronger the relationship.

When variables change in the same way, we have a positive correlation: when the one increases the other increases, or when one decreases the other decreases. For example, we might correlate hours of study with exam scores and find r = 0.41, indicating that students who studied more obtained better grades. Note that, as with a quasi-experiment, we still don't know if the difference is due to lack of sleep or lack of studying (or something else). Also note that we could analyze the data we collected (time spent studying, exam scores) as a quasi-experiment or a correlational study. Let's say we have scores for 200 students. We take all those who studied more than 3 hours a day (say 20 students), those who studied less than 15 minutes a day (say 40 students), and discard the rest. We then compare the exam scores of two groups statistically, and we have a quasi experiment (we could also have had a third group made up of students who studied 45–75 minutes a day, making for low, medium, and high groups; further variations are easy to think of).

Instead, we could correlate the study times and exam scores of all 200 students. A modest correlation might be all we would expect in most behavioral studies. This is because the outcomes of interest (like exam scores) are affected by many variables, and we would seldom expect a single variable (like time spent studying) to have a massive effect all on its own.

Had we calculated a correlation between amount of time people spent partying and exam score, we might have predicted a negative correlation, where an increase in the value of one variable is related to an decrease in the value of another (or vice versa). We might expect exam scores to be lower in people who party more (or we could say "as partying increases, exam scores decrease").

And, of course, two variables might be almost totally unrelated—people's social security numbers are unlikely to correlate highly with their exam scores, for example.

As with quasi-experiments, we need to be cautious about interpreting the relationships revealed by correlation coefficients. In the example here, we are not sure that increased study-time caused the students to get better grades. It could have been some other variable that affected both time spent studying and grades—like time partying, and its effect on amount of sleep. Here a third variable (not the two we measured) is causing changes in both the variables we measured. Again we do not have an independent variable, one manipulated by the experimenter, and we should not use the term to describe the variables studied. They can be called correlates or predictor variables or antecedent variables, but they are not independent variables.

We have seen an example of a third variable accounting for the differences in both the variables we measured, and this is one way we can get a significant correlation between variables without one causing changes in the other. It is also possible that one variable is causing changes in the other, but not in the direction we think—a correlation between grades and time spent watching TV could mean that watching TV (directly or indirectly) causes students to get poor grades. It could also mean the opposite—getting poor grades causes children to watch more TV (possibly because they dislike homework because of their poor grades).

We must always be cautious about interpreting relationships as causal (even when we have evidence from a very carefully controlled true experiment). In quasi-experiments there is a greater likelihood of confounds and in correlational studies a risk of both confounds and confusion about the direction of causation. However the statement that "correlation does not mean causation" should be critically examined rather than used as a mantra. Using it as a "rule" rather than as a guide implies that we draw conclusions in a somewhat mechanical way without benefit of reasoning. We believe that we can use our brains in determining to what extent a correlation between two variables indicates the presence of a causal relationship. If we can do two things, we can be reasonably confident about causal statements based on correlations. We need to:

- Exclude the likelihood that changes in our two variables, A and B, are attributable to changes in a third variable. Sometimes this can be done by reasoning, at other times by adducing related experimental evidence that shows changes similar to those seen in the correlational data. The effect of more stimulating environments on human brain anatomy, described in Chapter 7, was found in a study with several possible confounds that could account for changes, but data from rat experiments (with animals randomly assigned to groups and the independent variable manipulated by the experimenter) support the supposition that the stimulating environment caused the changes in the brain.

- Exclude the likelihood that causal direction is reversed, and that A causes changes in B rather than B causing changes in A. This is often possible if we know that one variable precedes rather than follows the other—if A occurs first and B later, it is unlikely that B causes A. The study of brain changes in taxi-drivers, described in Chapter 7, illustrates this.

If both these criteria are met, we have reasonable grounds for believing that changes in A cause changes in B. Indeed, it might be better to avoid this dichotomizing by clarifying what we mean by causation in the first place. As one of us has argued elsewhere, "If one takes the simplest approach [to causation], that variables have to be individually necessary and sufficient in order to be regarded as causal, one will find that very few causes have been identified in the biological and social sciences—or even in physics for that matter. In many cases we cannot claim that what we regard as a causal variable is either necessary or sufficient. In fact, we appear to recognize a causal relationship when we see that in the presence of a particular factor [variable] the probability of a certain outcome is increased and we have no reason to believe that both are dependent on a third variable" (Joffe, 1996, p. 205)—and this is the case whatever the research design.

4. *Case study:* A case study involves extensive observations of a few individuals. Data collection may include observing behavior, interviews, or record searching (archives). Case studies may be retrospective or prospective or both.

They are usually used

- when the behavior or situation of interest is so rare that other methods, involving larger groups of participants, are not possible, or
- when we want to describe and explore something or perhaps to develop rather than to test an hypothesis or make predictions or generalizations from our observations.

They have the strengths of qualitative studies (see Table 1.1), but are not the design of choice for testing hypotheses.

We might look at grades from previous years in a course, interview some of the students we could contact about their study habits, and attempt to see if there appeared to be a relationship between amount of time students studied and their exam scores. It certainly would not be our design of choice to test the hypothesis we were interested in but might well yield interesting insights into variables affecting exam performance and how they operate.

Table 1.4 summarizes some of the advantages and drawbacks of the research designs we have been discussing.

TABLE 1.4 Some Advantages and Drawbacks of Four Basic Research Designs

METHOD	ADVANTAGES	DRAWBACKS
1. Experiment	• Researcher controls independent variables and extraneous variables giving greater confidence in identification of cause and effect • Random assignment to groups limits likelihood of confounds	• Lab environment and manipulations can be artificial, and reduce extent to which results generalize to real world (not the case in field experiments) • Sometimes difficult to avoid experimenter effects (also in other designs) • Possible ethical problems (also in other designs) • Some real life variables (e.g., emotions) hard to duplicate artificially
2. Quasi-Experiment	• Can compare groups on attributes that cannot be manipulated experimentally (e.g., gender)	• Less confidence in cause-effect relationships • Possible confounds
3. Correlational Study	• Shows degree and direction of relationship between variables related • Basis for predictions	• Uncertainty about presence and direction of cause-effect relationship without additional evidence • Possible confounds
4. Case study	• Good source of hypotheses • In-depth information • Can shed light on rare conditions that are impractical or unethical to study in other ways • Compelling descriptions	• Important information may be missing • Memories may be selective or inaccurate • Cases may not be representative or typical • Lack generalizability • Subjectivity of observations, observer bias • Confounds

II. Research Designs: Variations

These are designs that are widely used in developmental psychology. They generally use one (or more) of the basic designs described above, but have additional features of importance.

1. *Longitudinal study:* A longitudinal study is one in which researchers follows a group composed of the same people across a period of the life span. Behavior is observed and/or measured at several time points. Longitudinal studies may cover a short time, such as a few weeks, or a long time, such as the entire life span. These studies often use quasi-experimental or correlational designs, but their defining characteristic is that the same people are studied repeatedly across time.

2. *Cross sectional study:* Like longitudinal studies, cross sectional studies are usually quasi-experiments or correlational studies used to study people of different ages to investigate developmental hypotheses. People of different ages are studied at about the same time, making the research easier and quicker to do than longitudinal studies but at a price in terms of possible confounds (especially "cohort effects," the effect of having grown up in circumstances particular to a given historical period—war, economic prosperity or adversity, etc.—not intrinsically related to age).

CONFIDENCE IN RESEARCH FINDINGS

It seems to us that what is important about research is not whether its methods are qualitative or quantitative or what specific design is used, but the extent to which the questions it asks are important and the degree to which there are good reasons to believe the answers it provides are correct. Note that we say "degree to which," not "whether or not" we can be confident about the results. Things are seldom totally clear-cut, and we mostly deal with degrees of confidence rather than a choice between concluding that "these findings are right" or "this research is wrong." Dichotomizing in this way would leave us sometimes throwing out the baby with the bathwater and other times being gullible. We strive for skepticism in the evaluation of research, not cynicism or gullibility.

(Questions about the importance or value of a specific piece of research are different from questions about its quality, and assessments probably far more subjective).

We addressed some things that affect quality in the process of looking at research designs and ways in which they diminish (or if badly done, increase) the likelihood that something other than the independent variable (in experiments) or the antecedent variables (in quasi-experiments and correlational studies) are responsible for the differences we observe.

In addition, the way participants are recruited and the circumstances and manner in which they are investigated affect our confidence in the *generalizability* of the findings: if we study only males, how confident can we be that the same effects will occur in females? If we study students, how confident can we be that our findings are applicable to a broader range of people—or even to students on a different campus? If we study people (or other animals) in a laboratory, how confident can we be that the relationships we observe between variables studied will hold in more natural settings? (The extent to which the situation in which data are collected resembles the real-life situation we are interested in applying the findings to is sometimes referred to as the "external validity" of the research).

Rats—and College Students

If you browse through a conventional introductory psychology textbook—the type that surveys the entire field in 700 pages or more—you may be struck by the amount of research that involves either rats or college students. These appear to be psychologists' favorite research participants. Now, as we joke in class, we probably can generalize from college students to humans, but a legitimate question that arises from animal research is, to what extent, if any, can we generalize from rodents, pigeons, non-human primates, etc. to humans?

Think about this: If your friendly pet mouse nibbled a piece of chocolate you gave her, immediately fell over writhing in apparent pain, and promptly died, would you eat the rest of that chocolate bar? If not, it might be because you believed that something that was highly toxic to a mouse might not be too good for a human (you!); that is, you'd behave as if you believed you could make a pretty strong generalization from a rodent to a human. For over 100 years psychologists have studied (among other things) sensation and perception, learning, social and sexual behavior, and brain-behavior relationships in rats, mice, dogs, cats, non-human primates, and other more exotic species, discovering principles and mechanisms that, in many cases, have not differed appreciably in humans. There are strict ethical requirements governing research on animals, but nonetheless there are many important research questions that can be tackled using animals that could not be investigated in humans. (See Chapter 2 for one example).

Believing that we can generalize to a reasonable extent from animals (I should say "non-human animals," but it begins to sound too pedantic) to humans is only one reason why psychologists and other scientists study animal behavior. A second reason we might study animal behavior might be quite simply because we are interested in the animals in their own right. There are hundreds (or even thousands) of species of animals that behave in interesting and intriguing ways, and plain curiosity or practical concerns (such as protecting ourselves) have motivated many scientists to spend lifetimes studying the behavior of different species.

A third category of reasons has to do with evolution. As Baker (2005) puts it:

All species, including humans, confront problems related to survival . . . (e.g., cognitive problems related to obtaining resources, surviving as a member of a social group), and there are diverse ways in which species solve these problems. Learning about how nonhuman species approach and solve these problems demonstrates the breadth and diversity of behavioral strategies that exist in living beings.

Understanding how evolution has shaped the abilities and limitations of other species helps us gain insight into the ways in which human behavior is subject to similar influeces.

Reliability and Validity

Another important aspect of research that affects our confidence in the findings is how good the measurements are, and this is usually assessed by looking at two features of measurements, reliability and validity (in quantitative research; there alternative criteria that parallel these in qualitative research).

Reliability: If you have a car that starts some mornings but not others, or a friend who sometimes fails to turn up when you have arranged to meet, you would probably describe both the car and the friend as "unreliable." When we describe a measurement process (often but not necessarily a "test" or "questionnaire," as defined earlier) as unreliable, we mean much the same thing.

If we claim to have a test that measures your math ability, you would expect it to give approximately the same results next week as this week, and if we told you this week that the test indicated that you have exceptional ability and next week, when you took it again, that your math ability was well below average, you would begin to doubt that we knew what we were talking about. We would say that the *test-retest reliability* is low, and not place much confidence in the findings.

Note three additional points:

- We might not regard the test as unreliable if your score improved considerably after you took several math courses, but differences between scores over a relatively short period of time or scores that fluctuated erratically for no apparent reason would probably lead us to discard it or to try to improve it.

- If the test was unreliable we would not have much confidence in its validity (the extent to which the test measures what it claims to measure—see below); the reason for this is subtle and implies that before we chose a measure of math ability (and thus operationally defined it) we had a concept of what it was, a concept that includes the notion that math ability doesn't fluctuate erratically from week to week.

- Tests are not either reliable or unreliable; they vary in how reliable they are. We usually assess and report reliability by calculating correlation coefficients.

Another kind of reliability has to do with agreement between observers who record behavior in some way—this is called *inter-observer reliability*. Let us say that two of you observe children in a playground and record the number of times you see aggressive behavior. If one of you reports many more instances than the other, we have a problem with the data. Whose count do we use? Neither person's of course. Instead we would probably do something on the lines of ensuring that we have a clear definition of what constitutes aggressive behavior and see if that improved agreement. Having two or more people independently observe events and using data only when there is a high level of agreement between the observers is important for quality control and our confidence in research findings.

Validity: If we told you we were going to base your grade in our course on the circumference of your wrist because it was a highly reliable measure you would quickly realize that reliability alone is not a sufficient reason for confidence in a measuring instrument. You might consider wrist circumference to be a poor measure of how much you had learned, and of course you would be right. Stated another way, it is an invalid measure—of learning, that is; it might just possibly be a valid measure of work done in a physical education class. The point is that a measure is a more or less valid measure of something in particular, not simply more or less valid in general. (And, as with reliability, it is a question of degree, not a question of a measure being valid or invalid).

There are at least three types of validity, some more complex than others.

Content validity refers to whether a test (for example) *looks* right. The wrist circumference measure fails this first test. In considering content validity we are concerned about the extent to which the content is reasonably representative of the area it is supposed to measure. A psychology test filled with questions about geology would obviously have low content validity; less obviously lacking in high validity might be a psychology test that had questions dealing only with learning and memory. Lack of content validity alone is an insufficient reason to discard a test. Sometimes a measure can have other kinds of validity even when the content is not obviously related to the concept being measured. In a personality test, for example, the measure might be better if the traits being assessed were not too obviously reflected in the questions, since when they are it is easier for people taking the test to fake their answers. People might not always answer questions honestly if they feel truthful answers might make them look bad.

A second type of validity, *criterion validity*, is sometimes referred to as predictive validity. The question asked of the test is, to what degree does it predict things about other aspects of personality or behavior that we believe should be related to what the test is measuring? For example, if I devise a test of managerial ability, if it has criterion validity we might expect higher-level managers to get higher scores (or for people with higher scores when they are hired to progress upwards in an organization faster than those with lower scores). Again, note that a test might be valid for one purpose but not for another, or for one group of people (probably similar to those who were used to develop and standardize the test) but not for another.

The most complex type of validity is that known as *construct validity*. Sometimes we devise tests to measure somewhat abstract concepts (like intelligence) that are referred to as hypothetical constructs (hence the term construct validity). Evaluating this kind of validity requires many studies looking at the relationship between the test score and a variety of related measures. Weiten (1998, pp. 243–344) gives an example that concerns the construct validity of a measure of the personality trait *extraversion*. It involves looking at a network of correlations (some positive, some negative, and some close to zero) between scores on the extraversion test and measures of other personality traits, including introversion, social discomfort, neuroticism, tolerance, sociability, and self-acceptance. The overall pattern "makes sense"—for example, extraversion is found to be negatively correlated with introversion and social discomfort (indicating that extraverted people are not introverted—surprise!—and are less uncomfortable in social situations), positively correlated with sociability and self-acceptance, and not correlated with responsibility or tolerance. As Weiten says, "it's the overall pattern of correlations that provides convincing (or unconvincing) evidence of a test's construct validity" (p. 344).

WHAT'S AHEAD

In subsequent sections of the book we discuss research in a variety of areas of psychology, but in all the areas our emphasis is on the concepts in this first section, those to do with the nature of the research enterprise. You will come across further discussions of research methods and designs, and of topics like reliability and validity. Whether the research is on biopsychology, learning, memory, cognition, development, social psychology, personality, abnormal psychology, or therapy, we will ask the same kinds of questions about it—questions concerning the appropriateness of the research design, the reliability and validity of the measures used, the rigor with which confounds are eliminated, and so on, questions that underpin the broader issue of the degree to which we can have confidence in the findings. If you read the general introduction to this book, you will readily see that this is in accord with our overall aim of helping you to learn to think like psychologists.

REFERENCES

Baker, S. C. (2005). Expanding our students' horizons: Incorporating a comparative perspective into psychology classes. *Excellence in Teaching*, January 2005, Vol. 7 [*http://PSYCHTEACHER@list.kennesaw.edu*].

Berg, B. L. (2004). *Qualitative research methods for the social sciences* (5th Ed.). Boston, MA: Pearson.

Berk, L. E. (2003). *Development through the lifespan* (3rd Ed.). Boston, MA: Allyn & Bacon.

Berger, P. L. and T. Luckmann (1966). *The social construction of reality: A treatise in thesociology of knowledge*. Garden City, NY: Doubleday.

Blomeyer, R. L. and R. Clemente (2003). The bean threads summary. *http://www.tltgroup.org/TailoredWebsites/OLNUCinc/BeanThreadsSummary.htm*

Camic, P. M., J. E. Rhodes, and L. Yardley (Eds.) (2003). *Qualitative research in psychology: Expanding perspectives in methodology and design*. Washington, DC: AmericanPsychological Association.

Joffe, J. M. (1996). Searching for the causes of the causes. *Journal of Primary Prevention*, *17*, 201–207.

Reber, A. S. (1995). *Dictionary of psychology*. London: Penguin.

Shavelson, R. J. and L. Towne (2004). What drives scientific research in education? Questions, not methods, should drive the enterprise. *APS Observer*, *17*, 27–30.

Tinbergen, N. (1963). On aims and methods in ethology. *Zeitschrift fur Tierpsychologie, 20*, 410–433.

Trochim, W. M. (2000) The research methods knowledge base (2nd Ed.). *http://trochim.human.cornell.edu/kb/index.htm*

Weiten, W. (1998). *Psychology: Themes and variations* (4th Ed.). Pacific Grove, CA: Brooks/Cole.

CHAPTER 2

OH RATS!¹

Material selected from:
Research Stories for Introductory Psychology,
Second Edition, by Lary Shaffer and Matthew R. Merrens

¹Incorporating the research of C. Kim, L. Kalynchuk, T. Kornecook, D. Mumby, N. Dadgar, J. Pinel, and J. Weinberg, "Object-Recognition and Spatial Learning and Memory in Rats Prenatally Exposed to Ethanol," 1997, *Behavioral Neuroscience, 111,* pp. 985–995.

If you ask most people, they will tell you that a psychology course is supposed to teach you to analyze peoples' minds. As a demonstration we are going to try to analyze your mind. This reading describes an experiment about rats. Now, here is what is on your mind:

"Rats! *Rats?* Let's see, (flip, flip, flip) how long *is* this chapter, anyway?"

or

"Rats! *Rats?* I wonder if the bookstore would still give me all my money back if I sold this stupid book and dropped this course. After all, the book has hardly been used."

or

"Rats! *Rats?* This is probably just some junk they put in the first chapter. The rest of the book must be about the unconscious and interesting stuff like that."

or

"Rats! *Rats?* Damn! I thought that this was going to be a cool course and now, one page into it, I am reading about **RATS**."

Did we read your mind? If we did, it was because we have common sense, rather than because we know about psychology. If we didn't, it shows that psychologists cannot read minds. Either way, there is no evidence here for mind reading. Hold that thought. You have only been reading this book for two minutes and you already may have learned something: people who tell you that they can read your mind are not psychologists. Psychologists know better than to say things like that.

Psychologists study behavior. Sometimes a lot can be learned about behavior from the study of rats. This chapter is really about behavior, not rats. Okay, so we lied when we implied that this chapter was about rats. If you were inclined to believe everything found in textbooks, then you have learned something else: textbooks sometimes lie. We will not lie to you (again) on purpose, but we may well lie accidentally. Psychology is a vital discipline and, as such, it is changing all the time. Although we intend to describe psychology as it is today, new research may alter current concepts, theories, or beliefs at any time.

STUDYING RATS

Because psychologists usually study behavior, rather than a particular organism, not all research in psychology involves the study of human beings. Sometimes other animals are used because the researcher really wants to know about the behavior of that animal, often to answer questions about its evolution or ecology. In other cases, nonhuman animals are used as participants because they are more convenient. Many studies of learning have used rats because they are economical to maintain in large animal colonies that have rows and rows of drawerlike cages. The researcher who could use rats as participants had easy access to research participants from the animal colonies that used to be part of psychology departments in most universities. The behavior under investigation in basic studies of learning can sometimes be so similar from species to species that it does not matter what type of animal is studied. Nonhuman animals have also been the participants of choice when researchers believed that a study was too dangerous for human participants. In this case, the researchers may want to know about humans, but believe that other animals are sufficiently similar to permit their findings to be applied to humans. The experiment with rats to be discussed below was one of these important investigations in which humans could not be used as research participants.

AN EXPERIMENT

In this book, we will use the word *experiment* in a very restricted and special sense. When most people speak of an experiment, they are talking about unsystematically trying something, as in: "I'm going to do an experiment to see if dogs like carrots." You toss the dog a piece of carrot. If he eats it, dogs are presumed to like carrots and if he spits it out, they dislike them. *One* dog in *one* state of hunger with *one* piece of carrot does not tell us much of anything about dogs and carrots. Alternatively, someone might say "I am going to do an experiment to see what will happen if I go to bed early tonight." Aside from all the problems of drawing conclusions based on one person doing something on one day, there is the additional problem that no particular outcome has been anticipated. In a real experiment, there is a clear statement about what is expected to happen as a result of the procedures. The experiment is a test of the correctness of this statement, called the *hypothesis*. In the example of going to bed early, there is no hypothesis. Nothing is being tested, so nothing important is likely to be learned. Going to bed early might be accompanied by a variety of outcomes, such as getting more sleep and feeling rested or waking up earlier and feeling tired the next day. In any event, there is little basis for the conclusion that going to bed early caused either of these—they might easily have happened regardless of bedtime.

C. Kwon Kim and a number of colleagues (Kim et al., 1997) did an experiment to demonstrate the effects of learning in rats that had been exposed to alcohol. We have chosen to discuss this particular study because of the importance of the question. In addition, it has the structural characteristics of a well-conducted experiment. First, we are going to do an overview of this experiment and then we will go back and highlight the features that permit this study to belong to the rarefied and elite class of research called the experiment. As with other studies discussed in this book, this one is important for its findings, but it is also important for its methods. For reasons that will become clear, not every scientific study can have all the procedural elements that are part of the experiment reported by Kim et al. (1997). Each of these elements is important to ensure that the conclusions drawn from the study are accurate.

THIS EXPERIMENT

Kim and coworkers obtained both female and male rats of a well-known genetic strain from a breeder. Because rats from the same strain are genetically quite similar, the differences found in the experiment were not likely to be the result of some genetic differences among the sample of rats in the study. The rats were all maintained in cages in a room that had controlled temperature and lighting. Here, again, an effort was made to avoid differences that might affect the outcome of the study. The males and females were housed together until the females became pregnant. Pregnancy in rats is indicated by the loss of a mucous vaginal plug. When the females lost this plug, it was known that they were on Day 1 of their pregnancy, and they were moved to individual cages.

At this point, each female was randomly assigned to one of three groups. Group E was fed a totally liquid diet—a sort of liquid rat chow—which contained adequate food but derived 36 percent of the calories from ethanol. Ethanol is the same kind of alcohol that is in beer, wine, and other alcohol-containing drinks. There were 21 rats in group E. A second group was called the *pair-fed*, or PF, group. This group was fed throughout pregnancy on a liquid diet that was the same as that of Group E, except that a sugarlike substance, maltose-dextrin, was substituted for the alcohol in their diets. This group was called pair-fed because each rat in this group was fed the same amount of liquid food (in grams per kilogram of body weight) as one of the Group E animals. Through its own consumption, each Group E animal determined how much a Group PF animal would be allowed to eat. In this way these two groups were directly comparable except that one group had alcohol as part of every meal and one did not. A third group of 21 pregnant females, Group C, for *control*, was fed usual rat food and water. The special diets of Group E and Group PF were replaced with standard rat chow and water on Day 22 of gestation. The rat pups were born on about Day 23.

There were no differences among the three groups of rats in the number of live or stillborn off-spring. On the day following birth, Group E and PF pups weighed less than Group C pups, but they caught up on subsequent days. By the time of birth, Group PF mothers weighed less than Group E or C mothers, but not alarmingly less. The weights of these mothers caught up and they were not different by Day 15 after birth. The mothers raised all the pups until they were weaned at 22 days old. Then the pups were housed in groups by litter and sex until testing began. One male rat from each litter was randomly selected for testing. These rats were called the *participants*. When the participants were 16 months old, their learning was tested in a maze task.

The Test Situation

Two different tests were conducted on these rats. One of these involved a visual discrimination task that we will not discuss further because it showed no significant differences among any of the participants. The other was a maze learning task called the Morris water maze. The Morris water maze was a large (180-cm-diameter × 60-cm-high) tank that was filled to the 22-cm level with water made opaque with nontoxic white paint. This opaque water was a maze because somewhere in it, 3–4 cm below the surface, there was a 12-cm-diameter circular platform. From trial to trial the platform remained in the same place within the maze. The other features of the research room also remained the same and could act as visual-orienting cues to help the rat in finding the invisible submerged platform on successive trials.

The rat was put in the maze and would swim around until it found the platform. Finding the platform was rewarding for the rats because they could stop swimming and climb up on it. The rat could not see the submerged platform; it had to find the platform in space. Once the rat had found it, learning was measured by putting the rat back in the water and timing how long it took to find the platform again. This measure is called *latency*. It is the amount of time it takes to perform a specific task. As learning progresses, we would expect the latency to get less and less as the rats learned the exact location of the platform and found it faster.

The researchers would place the rat in the maze and then retreat behind a screen so that the rat could no longer see them. While concealed behind the screen, the researchers watched the rats by means of a video monitor. The video monitor was connected to a video camera directly above the maze, permitting observations to be made without interfering with the swimming rat. Researchers watched the rat on the monitor and timed the latency for finding the platform. The experimenters who worked with the rats in the maze did not know which group the rats belonged to: Group E, PF, or C. Each trial in the maze began when a single rat was placed in one of four equally spaced positions around the rim of the pool. The start position was randomly selected from one of these four. Once started, the rat would swim until it found the platform. If it did not find the platform in 90 seconds, the trial was over and the rat was removed from the pool. Each rat was tested by giving it six trials a day on each of 10 days in a row. This kind of procedure is often called testing the animal in "blocks of six trials over 10 consecutive days."

The last two trials were different. On the 59th trial, the platform was raised up to the point where it was visible. The 59th trial was conducted to test whether some rats failed to find the platform in earlier trials because they were merely unable to respond to visual stimuli within the maze. The researchers believed that rats who had been exposed to prenatal alcohol had complex cognitive disabilities, not merely visual deficits. If they were correct, then all groups of rats would be expected to do well on Trial 59. On the 60th trial, the platform was removed, and the rat was allowed to search for it for one minute. On this trial, the data consisted of the number of times the rat swam directly over the area where the platform had been located. The researchers used a clever way to make a permanent record of the swimming path of the rat: they secured a piece of thin paper over the screen of the video monitor and traced the image of the moving rat with a marker as it swam about. The result was a tracing of the route taken by the swimming rat. The measure of success was called *annulus crossing*. An annulus is a ring. The rats were scored correct for each crossing of a ring drawn on the paper around the location where the platform used to be. The 60th trial was a test of the persistence of the rat in seeking the approximate location of the platform. *Persistence* was another behavioral outcome that might have been affected by prenatal exposure to alcohol, and Trial 60 was designed to investigate this possibility. The researchers did not expect to find differences among the rats in persistence at the task, but conducted Trial 60 to confirm this belief.

Results

Although all rats improved, the rats from the ethanol group had significantly longer latencies when the task was to find the hidden platform (see Figure 2.1a).

As always when behavior is measured, there was some variability. Looking in Figure 2.1b, for example, you can see that on Day 4, the ethanol group had shorter latencies than the other groups. Statistical analyses can help to determine if this particular data point is sufficiently important to be considered more than chance variation. Something accounted for this difference, and it might be interesting to know what it was, but, in the absence of that information, the overall trend is clearly one of longer latencies for the ethanol group.

Figure 2.2 shows what happened on Trial 59(2.2a), in which the platform was visible, and on Trial 60(2.2b), in which the platform was missing and the rats were swimming across the area where it had previously been found.

Although there might appear to be differences in latency making the ethanol group appear to be slower, these differences were so small that they were not statistically significant. Likewise, the numbers of annulus crossings when the platform was missing were also determined statistically to be no different from random or chance fluctuations in behavior. When differences are very small, statistical tests can help to determine if they are meaningful. In contrast, differences might merely be the result of small, ordinary, and unsystematic variations in behavior.

Discussion

Kim et al. (1997) concluded that prenatal exposure to alcohol could negatively influence the ability of rats to learn tasks involving the position of objects in space. Spatial learning may be different from some other kinds of learning that have been found to be less susceptible to the influence of prenatal alcohol exposure. This study supported the findings of a number of other studies of spatial learning and prenatal

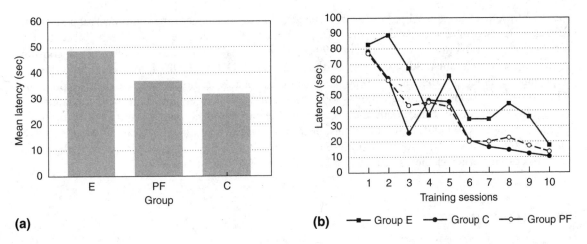

FIGURE 2.1   (a) Mean Latency to Find the Platform by Group (b) Latency to Find the Platform across Sessions

ethanol exposure. In contrast to the public perception, no one study "proves" anything for most scientists. Instead, it is recognized that all studies could have been more complete in some way. However, when a number of different studies by different researchers all point in the same direction, we may begin to have confidence in the overall findings. People who have training in science rarely talk about "proven" facts. That is the jargon used in advertisements and the news media. In contrast, when research outcomes are discussed, scientists acknowledge possible shortcomings by choosing words such as the findings *demonstrated* or *supported* the hypothesis that was being tested. The hypothesis in this study was that prenatal ethanol would affect later spatial learning in rats. It was supported.

These findings join an enormous body of research indicating the danger that maternal alcohol consumption poses to developing organisms. In humans, this is so well documented that it has a name: fetal alcohol syndrome, or FAS. This syndrome includes some superficial characteristics, such as widely

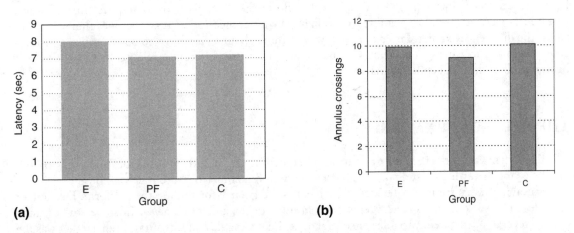

FIGURE 2.2   (a) Latency to Find the Visible Platform (b) Annulus Crossings at Site of the Missing Platform. Latency (in seconds) to find the visible platform in Trial 59 (a) and annulus crossings in searching for the missing platform in Trial 60 (b). None of the differences shown are statistically significant.

spaced eyes and a thin upper lip. However, it can also include permanent mental retardation and brain damage. Devastating effects such as low intelligence and poor judgment have been linked to FAS (Streissguth, Barr, Sampson, & Bookstein, 1994). How much alcohol is safe for a woman to consume during pregnancy? None (Astley, Clarren, Little, Sampson, & Daling, 1992). In thinking about this, it is important to remember that early in pregnancy women probably do not even know they are pregnant. The woman who stops drinking alcohol as soon as she knows she is pregnant is probably too late.

This study was an experiment and, as we noted, experiments contain a number of features that give us particular confidence in their findings. Because this is the first study in this book, we are going to dissect it and discuss these important components. In the rest of the book, we will be using these concepts to describe other studies, so you would be well advised to learn them now.

THE HYPOTHESIS

The hypothesis is the notion that the research is designed to test. In this case, it was that prenatal exposure to ethanol results in spatial learning deficits. Outside of science, *hypothesis* is often used to describe a wild guess about how something works. In scientific terms, a hypothesis is more serious than that. A scientist usually has a number of reasons to believe a hypothesis is correct before it is carefully tested. Past research or informal, less-structured observations may suggest correct hypotheses. Sometimes researchers will do pilot tests, which are incomplete versions of research that can be quickly done, to suggest the correctness of a hypothesis. Following pilot testing, a formal study may be undertaken. Usually scientists believe their hypotheses are correct, and they are trying to convince others by doing careful research to test their beliefs.

THE INDEPENDENT VARIABLE

The independent variable is the *difference* that is directly created or arranged by the experimenter. In this study, the independent variable was the difference in diet of the rat mothers: ethanol, maltose-dextrin, or rat chow. It is often said that the experimenter *manipulates* the independent variable. This literally means that the experimenters *handle* that part of the study. Conceptually, the researcher is trying to create one or a few differences to see what effects they will have on outcomes. In this study, researchers were as careful as possible to eliminate any differences other than the ones they wished to study, the differences in diet. Perhaps a good way to think about a variable is to consider its opposite, a constant. In an experiment, most things are held constant, so that differences in outcomes can be seen to be the result of the independent variable.

THE DEPENDENT VARIABLE

The dependent variable is the important measured outcome of the study. It is the measure of the particular behavior that is being studied. This name is easy to remember because it *depends* on the independent variable. In this study, a dependent variable was the latency for finding the platform. Dependent variables are also sometimes called dependent *measures* or dependent *outcomes*. In some studies there may be several independent variables or several dependent variables. In this study, prenatal diet was the independent variable but there were several dependent variables. Latency to find the submerged platform was one. Latency to find the platform when it was raised was another dependent measure. Annulus crossing was a third dependent outcome.

Usually a two-sentence description of a study can be constructed if you identify the independent and dependent variable. Identification of the variables in a study is the first step to understanding it. For example, in research about the effects of loud music on studying, the loud music would be the independent variable and some measure of study effectiveness—maybe a nice little quiz—would be the dependent variable. Once you have found the variables, you can begin to ask if these particular variables constitute an adequate test of the hypothesis.

OPERATIONAL DEFINITION

An operational definition is the definition of some psychological characteristic in terms of the way it is measured. For example, an IQ test result might be the operational definition of intelligence. In the study we have discussed in this chapter, latency was an operational definition of learning and the number of annulus crossings was the operational definition of persistence. One way to critically evaluate studies is to examine the operational definitions to see if they are adequate. For example, intelligence might be operationalized by asking people how smart they are. For most purposes, that operational definition would probably not be adequate.

RANDOM ASSIGNMENT

In this study, rat mothers were randomly assigned to Groups E, PF, and C. This means that any rat had an equal chance of ending up in any group. There was also another random process at work because among the litters of rat pups, one animal was randomly selected to be in the study. Any other method of assigning rats to groups might have resulted in some other characteristic of the rats playing a role in the dependent measure. The differences observed in the dependent variable were supposed to be the result of the differences the experimenter has manipulated. Random assignment to groups was the best way to ensure that the groups were not different before the independent variable was presented. For example, instead of random assignment, if the largest rat mothers were placed in Group C, the next largest in Group PF and the smallest in Group E, there would be no way to be sure that latencies observed in their pups were a result of alcohol exposure. In this case, latencies might also have been the result of maternal size.

No researcher would purposely assign all the big rats to one group, unless size was going to be studied as a variable. Nevertheless, the researcher wants to eliminate all systematic differences among animals in the groups to ensure that the only systematic difference remaining is the independent variable. The best way to achieve this is through random assignment to groups. Unless assignment is random, it is easy for an investigator to unknowingly introduce some kind of systematic differences into groups of participants. In a study like this, imagine that the rat parents arrived from the breeder in five crates, stacked one on top of another. Further imagine that the experimenters removed rats from the top crate, assigning them to Group E until Group E was full, then to Group PF, and last to Group C. This might be fine, but it might not. These rats were born and grew up in a rat colony. These colonies are racks of cages, usually five or six cages high and six or eight cages wide. Viewed from the front, the rat colony has the appearance of a rat apartment house, with each rat, or rat family, in its own little space. We do not know how the breeder decided which rat to put in which crate. The breeder might have loaded the crates by emptying cages in the top row of the rat colony first. Rats who had grown up in bottom cages might be behaviorally different than rats who grew up in top cages. You think this is far-fetched? Imagine growing up only being able to see people's knees. Unless this difference was to be the independent variable, a way to overcome it is to randomly assign rats to groups upon arrival at the lab where the experiment is to be conducted. Even if researchers think that such early experiences would make no difference, every effort is made to see that the only systematic difference between groups is the one created by the researcher: the independent variable.

Random assignment is not always possible. Nevertheless, part of thinking critically about research is being able to ask the right questions. If you were to read a study in which participants were not randomly assigned to groups, you should immediately begin to ask yourself about factors other than the independent variable, accidentally introduced into groups, that might have effects upon the dependent measures. Sometimes research articles do not say whether assignment to groups was random. When this happens, it is probably safest to conclude that they were not and to adjust your confidence in the findings accordingly.

Randomization may also appear in other aspects of a study. In this study, the swimming began at randomly assigned places in the pool. Something like a lottery was conducted ahead of time to determine where each rat would start. This was an additional attempt to remove bias. Imagine that two or three different experimenters are actually working with the rats in the pool. If one of them always starts the rats at the same location around the edge of the maze, this might influence the latency measure for these animals. If it also happened that this particular researcher started most of the rats from Group C, then the observed latencies might be merely a result of starting position, not the independent variable of alcohol exposure. This is another instance in which you can ask critical questions about studies. If some procedure was not randomized when you think it should have been, you might have less confidence in the findings.

"BLIND" STUDIES

Usually, if the participants in research did not know details, such as what group they were in or what the independent variable was, they were said to be *blind*. A study in which this is part of the procedure is sometimes called a *single-blind* study. If the participants were told what was going on in a study, there was an increased chance that their responses would be different, even unintentionally. In this study, the rat pups were not aware that other groups had been prenatally exposed to different things, so we somewhat facetiously suggest that this study qualifies to be thought of as single blind.

The term *blind experimenters* is used to indicate that the experimenters who actually worked with the participants did not know the group assignment of any particular participant. It is usually desirable that both the participants and the researchers who work with them in the experiment be prevented from discovering the details of group assignment or the nature of the independent variable. In a famous study, Robert Rosenthal (1973) gave students the task of teaching a rat to run a maze. The rats were randomly selected from a large group and given to individual students. However, some students were told that they had a smart rat and some were told that their rat was not very smart. Although the rats were really randomly assigned to student experimenters, the students who believed that their rats were smart ended up with rats who did better in the maze-learning task. Further study indicated that these students, without being aware of it, treated their rats differently. For example, they handled the rats more often, and this was associated with better maze performance. If experimenters can transmit their expectations to rats, it is probably even easier to do so with humans. For this reason, whenever possible, neither participants nor researchers should have knowledge that would allow them to react differently to the independent variable. When this is done a study is called *double blind*.

The American Psychological Association now discourages the use of the term *blind* because it considers this to be an insensitive label that is often easy to avoid. New studies in psychology are more likely to say that participants were *unaware* rather than *blind*. Nevertheless, the concepts of *single blind* and *double blind* are used in many other scientific fields and universally in older studies, so it is important that you understand what this means. There is a large section in the *Publication Manual* of the American

Psychological Association that offers guidelines designed to help authors to reduce bias in the language of research reports (American Psychological Association, 1994).

CONTROL GROUPS

You know by now that the independent variable is the difference that the experimenter handles, or manipulates. In order to see the effect of prenatal ethanol, it was essential to compare the behavior of some rats who were exposed to prenatal alcohol with some who were not exposed to it. The rats who were exposed to prenatal alcohol were called the experimental group, and any rats who were not exposed to prenatal alcohol were said to belong to *control groups*. Sometimes there are two or more control groups. In other research designs, participants can serve as their own control group by receiving one version of the independent variable at one time and another one later. In this study, both Group PF and Group C were control groups. The reason why there were two control groups may have been obvious to you as you read about the study. The experimental group had a liquid diet with alcohol as a component. If they had been compared only to Group C, the researchers would not know if the effects observed had been a result of alcohol compared to no alcohol, a solid diet compared to a liquid diet, or both. Group PF had a liquid diet but had no alcohol. The alcohol was replaced with a calorically equal substance in the diet of Group PF. To be sure that the quantity of liquid diet was the same in Group E and Group PF, each rat in Group PF was given the same amount of food as a rat chosen from Group E. This is called pair-feeding in this study, but a more general term for it is to say that the control group was *yoked* to the experimental group. A yoke is an old-fashioned wooden device that hitches two farm animals side by side so that they can pull a vehicle. The scientific use of this term means that the behavior of one participant determines what happens to another participant.

CAUSE AND EFFECT

The experiment is a very powerful way of testing hypotheses. However, it is often not possible to do an experiment. In that case, other scientific methods must be used. The advantage of a carefully conducted experiment is that it allows us to draw conclusions about cause and effect. One of the reasons why psychology exists is to find causes for behavior. The experiment is the only way to do this with any confidence. In our everyday lives, we do not generally require an experiment before we conclude that some event has caused a certain behavior. For example, if you are backing your car out of a parking space and hit a telephone pole, you may become angry. It is quite likely that the event of hitting the pole was the cause of your anger. We do not need to do an experiment in which a large group of randomly assigned people damages cars and another group does not in order to believe that accidents make us feel angry. This is not an important question. However, there are many important questions that psychology can address using the most powerful method yet developed for determining cause and effect: the experiment. Nonexperimental methods may tell us a great deal about behavior, but they should not be used to conclude that an independent variable is the cause of a dependent outcome or effect. As you will see, even true experiments are always limited in their scope, and we believe that conclusions about cause and effect from experiments should be made with appropriate caution.

There are many other scientific approaches discussed in this book, as well as a number of other experiments. As we will stress, these scientific methods are not perfect or flawless, but they are a great deal better than other approaches to knowledge such as hunches, guesses, intuitions, individual experiences, or the uncritical opinions of others.

RIGHTS OF RESEARCH PARTICIPANTS—THE ETHICAL ISSUE

There are committees in research institutions that examine each research proposal to ensure that the rights of the participants are considered. Even in research with rats, it is required that the research not be trivial and that the research design be sufficient to permit robust conclusions to be drawn. For humane reasons, researchers would have to describe what was going to happen to the rats at the conclusion of the research. The rights of research participants have been a major issue since the late 1960s and, as a result, it is now fairly difficult to do psychological research on any organisms. When the participants are people, the ethics of deception is an issue: is it fair to allow humans to participate in an experiment when they are not fully aware of the hypothesis?

Informed consent is now required before people can be research participants. People must be given quite a bit of information about what will happen to them in the study before they finally decide to participate. In some cases, this may mean that it is not possible to conduct an experiment in which the participants are unaware, or blind, to the conditions. It must also be made clear to participants that they are free to leave, without penalty, at any time during the experiment.

REFERENCES

American Psychological Association (1994). *Publication manual of the American Psychological Association* (4th ed.). Washington, DC: Author.

Astley, S. J., Clarren, S. K., Little, R. E., Sampson, P. D., & Daling, J. R. (1992). Analysis of facial shape in children gestationally exposed to marijuana, alcohol, and/or cocaine. *Pediatrics, 89,* 67–77.

Kim, C., Kalynchuk, L., Kornecook, T., Mumby, D., Dadgar, N., Pinel, J., & Weinberg, J. (1997). Object-recognition and spatial learning and memory in rats prenatally exposed to ethanol. *Behavioral Neuroscience, 111,* 985–995.

Rosenthal, R. (1973, September). The Pygmalion effect lives. *Psychology Today, 1,* 56–63.

Streissguth, A. P., Barr, H. M., Sampson, P. D., & Bookstein, F. L. (1994). Prenatal alcohol and offspring development: The first fourteen years. *Drug & Alcohol Dependence, 36,* 89–99.

CHAPTER 3

PSYCHICS AND SCIENTISTS[1]

Material selected from:
Research Stories for Introductory Psychology,
Second Edition, by Lary Shaffer and Matthew R. Merrens

---

[1]Incorporating the research of R. Wiseman, D. West, and R. Stemman, "An Experimental Test of Psychic Detection," 1996, *Journal of the Society for Psychical Research, 61,* pp. 34–45.

Do you know what this chapter is about? Then you must be psychic! (Or maybe you read the title.) This illustrates the main point of the chapter: although many people believe in psychic phenomena, there are also perfectly normal explanations for these seemingly paranormal happenings. There is no need to resort to unknown powers of the mind.

Many of us have had the experience of thinking about someone when the phone rings, and the phone call turns out to be from the person of whom we were thinking. Is this really *precognition*, the ability to predict the future through psychic means? It is possible to collect a little data to study this question. Keep a piece of paper near the phone and, each time it rings, guess who it is and write the guess down before answering. Circle the guesses that turn out to be correct. If someone in particular usually calls you at about the same time every day, you are likely to be correct in guessing his or her name because you would recognize the time he or she usually calls. Time of day explains those cases, so set them aside. The real test of your precognitive ability is to be able to correctly identify the unexpected callers. You will be correct once in a while just by chance. These unusual occasions on which you are correct are likely to be remembered clearly. The thousands of times you are not correct are forgotten; they are too ordinary to be memorable. Keeping a record will illustrate this for you, if you need illustration. The failure to remember thousands of disconfirming instances while remembering a few successes probably explains psychic precognitive identification of phone callers. The correct guesses are examples of coincidences.

Coincidence is a technical term that means that two events have occurred together either by accident or by chance. When someone you have not heard from in years phones you while you happen to be thinking of him or her, it is probably a coincidence. In order to think clearly about these things, you need to know that in a large set of events, coincidences are highly probable. They are almost *certain* to happen. Imagine that you have five unbiased coins. If you toss all five at once, the probability that they will all come up heads is 1 in 32, or about 3 percent. If you toss them 100 times, however, the probability of getting 5 heads at least once is 96 percent. It is almost certain to happen. Media reports often speak of "remarkable" coincidences as if they were unexpected. In a large series of events, coincidences are not unexpected or remarkable. If you receive about five phone calls a day you will have almost 10,000 calls in five years. With that many opportunities, it would not be at all surprising if you were to occasionally guess the correct identity of an unusual caller in advance.

Cable television and the Internet have many advertisements for psychics who claim to be able to use special powers to delve into your life and predict what will happen in the future. We believe that if they could really predict the future, they would be in Las Vegas predicting the future of roulette wheels and raking in the money. Of course, at the four dollars a minute they charge for talking to people on the phone, they are making $240.00 an hour, so they are not doing too badly. One of the best-known psychics in recent times was the late Jeanne Dixon. Some people believe that in 1956 she predicted the assassination of President Kennedy seven years before it happened. What she actually predicted was that the person, unknown to her, who won the 1960 election would "be assassinated or die in office, but not necessarily in the first term." This vague statement was a reasonable surmise given that seven of the early twentieth-century presidents either died in office (McKinley, Harding, Roosevelt), were very seriously ill (Wilson and Eisenhower), or experienced assassination attempts (Truman). It is also noteworthy that Jeanne Dixon failed to predict her own death in 1997.

The words *psi* and *parapsychology* are used as blanket terms to refer to unusual human processes of information or energy transfer, such as sensing or moving things, that are currently unexplained in terms of known physical, biological, or psychological mechanisms. This includes a variety of supposed happenings such as:

telepathy—knowing others' thoughts

psychokinesis—moving and otherwise affecting objects in the physical world through thought processes

clairvoyance—receiving information about remote events using pathways other than recognized sense organs

Some people who want to believe in psychic phenomena feel that the scientific community has somehow "ganged up" to suppress evidence of psi because it violates accepted theories or beliefs. This is not the case. There have been hundreds of research studies investigating paranormal phenomena, and nothing of substance has been found (Blackmore, 1996). Psi has not been rejected because it violates accepted scientific notions. It has been rejected as an explanation because there are plenty of ordinary rational explanations for the observed phenomena. The scientific arena is rigorous. Methods and procedures are scrutinized carefully before studies are accepted for publication. Yet, many initially unpopular ideas have passed the test of this scrutiny and have been accepted. Ideas such as continental drift and the circulation of the blood received acceptance in science because the evidence for them was compelling. At this point, there is no convincing evidence for psi. Magician James Randi, who has been a crusader in exposing fake psychics, offered $10,000 to anyone who could demonstrate psi in properly controlled conditions (Randi, 1982). He made this public offer in 1968 and has not yet had to pay the reward money. In a typical case of an attempt to win the prize money, a psychic claimed that he could use psychokinesis to turn the pages of a phone book without touching them. Randi gave him the chance to do so, but being a magician himself, Randi knew that these tricks are usually accomplished with small streams of compressed air emanating from somewhere, such as the psychic's sleeve. In what was to be a television demonstration of psychic page turning, Randi instituted a simple but elegant control. He scattered Styrofoam beads around the phone book, which would move at the slightest puff of air. The psychic walked around the book for 10 minutes sweating and scowling before claiming that bright lights were inhibiting his psychic powers (Gardner, 1989).

Although it may be widely believed that police use psychics in finding solutions to crime, the data available present a different picture. Sweat and Durm (1993) conducted a survey of police departments in the 50 largest cities in the United States. Although 17 percent of the police departments that responded said that they handled information from psychics "differently" than information from the general public, *all* police respondents noted that psychic information was no more helpful than information from the general public.

Psychics have frequently claimed to be able to use their powers to assist law enforcement agencies in the solution of baffling crimes (Nickell, 1994). The difficulty is that the reports are anecdotal. When scientists speak of *anecdotes*, they are referring to stories that people tell of personal experiences or hearsay. The intention is to use the story as evidence for some assertion about behavior. In this case, someone might say, "I heard about a psychic who was able to solve a murder that stumped the police." If you are thinking critically about this assertion, you should begin to question the source and the quality of the information. Psychics may make several vague and sometimes conflicting predictions about a crime. Once the real story of the crime is known, the correct predictions are remembered and the incorrect ones are forgotten (Hoebens, 1985; Rowe, 1993). This situation is very similar to the one we described concerning precognition and telephone calls. The rare instance that seems to confirm psi is remembered, and all the failures to confirm are forgotten.

An additional problem in evaluating the work of psychics in crime detection was identified by Lyons and Truzzi (1991). They pointed out that success in information about crimes should be measured against a baseline expectation. For example, a psychic may have told police that a person who suddenly disappeared is now dead, and this was later found to be accurate. In order to evaluate critically the extent of clairvoyant abilities, it would be necessary to know what percentage of people who suddenly disappear are later found to be dead. If this was a high-frequency outcome, then there may be nothing spectacular or important about the accuracy of the prediction. Anyone could have made it with no knowledge about the crime. If the psychic prediction referred to a highly unusual means of victim disposal, then it might have warranted more attention.

One of the earliest scientific investigations of psychic ability in crime detection involved four psychics who were shown photographs and objects that might have been related to crimes. Some of this material was evidence in criminal cases and some had nothing to do with any crimes. The psychics were asked to describe the crimes that might have involved the pictures and objects. The final report of this demonstration concluded that nothing of interest to police was produced by the psychics (Brink, 1960). Martin Reiser of the Los Angeles police department and his colleagues carried out a similar study with 12 psychics (Reiser, Ludwig, Saxe, & Wagner, 1979). Each psychic was presented with physical evidence from real crimes. The procedure was double blind: neither the psychics nor the experimenters knew anything about the crimes in advance. Psychics made predictions that were sorted into categories such as type of crime, victim, and suspect. These descriptions were compared with actual information about the crimes. The performance of the psychics was poor. On one crime, police had established 21 real facts. The psychics averaged 4 correct. On another, 33 facts were known and the psychics averaged 1.8 correct descriptions. Lyons and Truzzi (1991) have criticized this study and similar ones for methodological flaws. The data collected involved assessing a match or mismatch between each psychic statement and the key facts in the case. Other things that psychics said were simply discarded. For example, one crime involved the murder of a church historian. One of the psychics believed that the crime had something to do with a church, but there was no way in the data collection scheme to categorize this small, but accurate, assessment. Another methodological problem was that if psychics produced no information about a particular key fact, it was scored as a wrong response. This meant that, for example, not stating the sex of the victim was scored the same as saying the victim was male, when, in fact, she was female. These methodological issues might seem to put psychics at a disadvantage, thus lowering their scores and ignoring responses that did contain some correct information.

The research, which is the focus of this chapter, is from a study by Richard Wiseman, Donald West, and Roy Stemman (1996). They compared three self-proclaimed psychics against three college students in a test of psychic ability. One of their goals was to overcome shortcomings of earlier studies. The authors were contacted by a television production company that wanted to produce a program about psychic ability for a syndicated television series, *Arthur C. Clarke's Mysterious Universe*. The producers wanted to film a well-controlled test of psychic ability, and they were prepared to allow the psychologists to design the study and to specify the details of methodology to be followed.

PARTICIPANTS

Participants included three well-known psychics residing in Great Britain. One of these people had recently received considerable attention in the British news media because of claims that he had consistently and accurately predicted several crimes, terrorist attacks, and airplane disasters. He claimed that these predictions occurred in dreams. Although he had not been subjected to any formal assessment of accuracy, his local police department issued a statement saying he was "taken seriously," and that the information he provided was "acted upon immediately." The other two psychics in the study both worked as professional psychics. The participants in the other group for the study were three students recruited from the psychology department at the University of Hertfordshire. None of them claimed to have any psychic powers or any particular interest in solving crimes.

PROCEDURE

This study is an example of a research design called a quasi experiment. A difference between a quasi experiment and a true experiment is that the participants are not randomly assigned to groups. They cannot be, because they already belong to the groups to be studied before the research begins. In this case, they were either psychics or nonpsychics (students). Within psychology, opinions differ about whether or not this difference should be called an *independent variable*. There is no disagreement when this term is used to designate an experimental manipulation done to randomly assigned participants. Issues arise when the researcher does not create the input variable; rather it is already a characteristic of the participants before the beginning of the study. In the strictest sense, being a psychic or being a student is not an independent variable because the experimenter has not created it. We will adopt this strict sense. We do this not to be pedantic or picky, but because occasionally precision of thought and of phrasing is warranted. Unless there is an experimenter-created independent variable, no evidence has been produced for cause and effect. Often the main interest in behavior is to attempt to uncover causal components, and we believe that the somewhat common broad use of *independent variable* only clouds critical analysis of results. The only reason why we raise this issue is that published studies sometimes say that preexisting group characteristics, such as *gender* or *intelligence level*, are independent variables. Some statistical analyses also refer to preexisting group differences as independent variables. Although we allow that this is a judgment call, we are going to use the strict definition of an independent variable as something created by an experimenter. Instead, terms such as *predictors, antecedents, correlates,* or *participant variables* may be used to describe the relationship between group membership and outcomes measured in a quasi-experimental design.

The Essex Police Museum supplied three objects, each of which had been involved in a different actual crime. These objects were an old and rotting shoe belonging to a woman who had been murdered and buried, a deformed bullet recovered from the scene of a gunshot murder, and a red scarf that was used in a strangulation. Each of the crimes had been solved, and a great deal of detail was known about each one. Great care was taken to ensure that the people with whom the participants interacted in the lab had no knowledge of the crime. Sergeant Fred Feather, curator of the police museum, brought the objects to the lab, placed them on a table, and labeled them A, B, and C. He left the test area and waited in a distant part of the building while the tests were being conducted. The researcher who interacted with the participants during the tests knew nothing about the crimes or the objects. Participants were brought, one at a time, to the room where the objects were laying on a table. They were encouraged to handle the objects and to speak aloud any ideas, images, or thoughts that might be related to the crimes. They were told they could take as much time as they wished and could say as little or as much as they liked. During the test they were left alone in the room. With their full cooperation and knowledge, everything they said or did was filmed through a two-way mirror.

In advance, Sergeant Feather had supplied information for each of the crimes. This information permitted one of the researchers to construct six statements that were true of that particular crime, but untrue of the other crimes. These statements referred to specific aspects of the particular crime that were not likely to be true of crimes in general. This was done to eliminate correct answers from educated guessing that had nothing to do with psychic powers. For example, one might guess that a stabbing crime in a home occurred in the kitchen, because that is where most knives are kept. The three sets of 6 statements were combined and randomly ordered into a single list of 18 statements. Examples of these were:

> An accomplice involved
> Perpetrator aged in his twenties
> A link with milk
> Victim had only one son, aged four

After each participant was finished handling the objects and talking about them, one copy of the list of 18 crime descriptors was provided for each object. Participants were told that six of the statements were true for the crime associated with each object. Their task was to make check marks beside the six true statements for the particular crime connected with each object. They were allowed to take as much time as they wanted to complete this task. When they finished, they were ushered to a waiting area away from participants who had not yet been tested.

Results

The number of correctly identified statements for each participant, out of six possible, is shown in Figure 3.1.

The data in Figure 3.1 are the average number correct for each participant averaged across all three objects. The mean correct for the psychics as a group was 2.09 and for the student group it was 2.33. None of the means, individual or group, were statistically significantly different from the rest. The psychics did not appear to be better or worse than the students in identifying correct statements about crime objects.

Wiseman et al. (1996) wanted to be sure that the ability of the psychics was not underestimated by the methodology of the study. Choosing statements from a list did not take into account correct statements that the psychics might have made in handling and talking about the objects. To assess this qualitative information, a rater who was not involved in the test transcribed and separated each comment made by any of the participants. A list was made of all comments each participant made relating to a single crime. On this list, the order of these statements about each crime was randomized. These lists

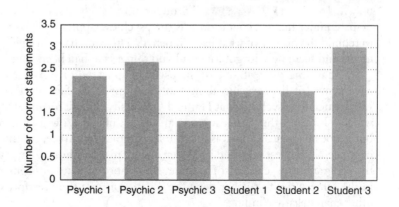

FIGURE 3.1 Participant's Identification of Statements.
Average number of correct statements selected by each participant for all three objects combined. The statements about a crime were chosen from a list of 18 statements, 6 of which were correct. Total possible correct was 6.

FIGURE 3.2   Comments Judged to Be Accurate. Average accuracy of unrestricted comments and statements made about crimes that were judged as being correct. Total possible correct was seven.

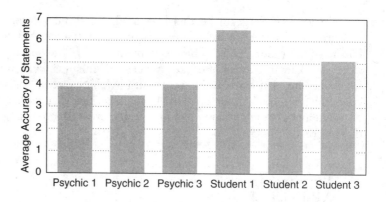

were then presented to two additional people, who had read about the crimes, acting as judges. The judges were asked to rate each of the statements about the crimes on a scale from 1 (very inaccurate) to 7 (very accurate). The ratings of the two judges for each participant were averaged and are shown in Figure 3.2.

The psychics made a total of 39 statements, and the students made 20 statements. There was no significant difference between the mean accuracy of the psychics and of the students (psychic mean = 3.83, student mean = 5.63). The reason why the accuracy level of these statements was so high is that many of the comments were obvious from the nature of the object. For example, one of the objects was a scarf and most of the comments correctly predicted that it had been used in a strangulation murder. A deformed bullet elicited comments such as "loud bang heard," "involved a shooting," and "looks like a squashed bullet." These are accurate, but unsurprising. Wiseman and his colleagues noted that no participant produced even one piece of information that would have been helpful to police in the investigation of the crimes.

DISCUSSION

The results in this study showed that the psychics were as unsuccessful as students at choosing correct statements about crimes. Neither group performed above the chance level. In addition a more qualitative analysis of free comments also showed the psychics performing at the same level as the students. After the study, all the participants were told about the findings. When presented with their results, none of the students thought that they had performed very well. However, all three psychics thought they had been "very successful." Throughout the study, the psychics appeared eager and willing to participate under the test conditions. As the psychics happily talked about their performances, they began to rebuild the history of what had happened. They emphasized small, vague, or somewhat correct statements and seemingly forgot they had said things that had been contradictory or wrong.

Following the test, one of the psychics appeared on a nationally televised talk show and said: "I have proved it [my psychic ability] in laboratories. In fact, only three weeks ago I did a test at the Department of Psychology at Hatfield University [The University of Hertfordshire in Hatfield, U.K.], which—I mean—they are just going around thinking 'How does he do this?' I don't know how I do it but it does happen." This was, of course, completely untrue. Nothing amazing or out of the ordinary happened in the test reported by Wiseman and his coauthors. The psychic's assertion was challenged on the program by psychologist Dr. Susan Blackmore and later Wiseman appeared on a different program in the same series to further deny the suggestion that the Hertfordshire test had resulted in anything other than negative findings.

Susan Blackmore (1996) spent years doing research on psi, working very hard to find evidence for psychic phenomena. The conclusion she drew from this work makes a fitting conclusion for this chapter, as well:

> I now know that the very idea of psi has got me nowhere. Parapsychology is often held up as the science of the future, the science that will tackle all those questions about the nature of mind or the farther reaches of human experience, the science that will force a new paradigm to topple the old and serve as a route to spirituality. But it does not deliver.

REFERENCES

Blackmore, S. J. (1996). *In search of the light: Adventures of a parapsychologist.* Buffalo, NY: Prometheus Books.

Brink, F. (1960). Parapsychology and police investigations. *International Criminal Police Review, 134,* 3–9.

Gardner, M. (1989). *How not to test a psychic: Ten years of remarkable experiments with Pavel Stepanek.* Buffalo, NY: Prometheus Books.

Hoebens, P. H. (1985). Reflections on psychic sleuths. In M. Truzzi and P. Kurtz (Eds.), *A skeptic's handbook of parapsychology.* Buffalo, NY: Prometheus Books.

Lyons, A., & Truzzi, M. (1991). *The blue sense.* New York: Warner Books.

Nickell, J. (1994). *Psychic sleuths: ESP and sensational cases.* Buffalo, NY: Prometheus Books.

Randi, J. (1982). *Flim flam: Psychics, ESP, unicorns and other delusions.* Buffalo, NY: Prometheus Books.

Reiser, M., Ludwig, L., Saxe, S., & Wagner, C. (1979). An evaluation of the use of psychics in the investigation of major crimes. *Journal of Police Science and Administration, 7,* 18–25.

Rowe, W. F. (1993). Psychic detectives: A critical examination. *Skeptical Inquirer, 17,* 159–165.

Sweat, J. A., & Durm, M. W. (1993). Psychics! Do police departments really use them? *Skeptical Inquirer, 17,* 148–158.

Wiseman, R., West, D., & Stemman, R. (1996). An experimental test of psychic detection. *Journal of the Society for Psychical Research, 61,* 34–45.

CHAPTER 4

YOU'RE DRIVING ME CRAZY[1]

Material selected from:
Research Stories for Introductory Psychology,
Second Edition, by Lary Shaffer and Matthew R. Merrens

---

[1]Incorporating the research of J. L. Deffenbacher, R. S. Lynch, E. R. Oetting, and D. A. Yingling, "Driving Anger: Correlates and a Test of State-Trait Theory," 2001, *Personality and Individual Differences, 31*, pp. 1321–1331.

On February 20, 1994, drivers—Michael Blodgett, 42, and Donald Graham, 54—became entangled in a disagreement while in traffic. After several miles of driving they pulled off the road and confronted each other. In the trunk of his car, Graham had a crossbow of the sort used for deer hunting. He retrieved it, pointed it at Blodgett, and killed him. In other incidents it is not unknown for people to give reasons for murder on the highways such as "He couldn't care less about the rest of us—he just kept blocking traffic." or "He practically ran me off the road—what was I supposed to do?" (American Automobile Association, 1997).

These are examples, admittedly extreme, of the phenomenon that has come to be called "road rage". Reports of road rage have become commonplace in all the news media. The reports are so common that a controversy has sprung up concerning the real frequency of road rage events. One of the issues involves the operational definition of road rage. A review of the news stories might suggest that any incident which takes place on or near a road is likely to be tagged with this label. If a car accidentally splashes mud on a pedestrian and the pedestrian responds by shouting and shaking a fist, is this road rage? Road rage is an attention-getting catchphrase and because the media are trying to get our attention, it is not surprising that road rage appears in so many news stories.

Ellison-Potter, Bell, and Defenbaker (2001) presented an approach to the problem of a more precise definition of road rage. They made a distinction between aggressive driving and road rage based partly upon legal terminology. Acts of aggressive driving include tailgating, horn honking, obscene gestures, and blocking the passing lane. Aggressive driving is a traffic offense. In contrast, road rage is a criminal offense. It includes such behaviors as assault with intent to cause bodily harm and, in the most extreme cases, attempted or actual homicide.

According to a 1997 report of the American Automobile Association, violent aggression has increased dramatically in recent years. For example, from 1990 to 1995 their data suggest a 51 percent increase in road violence. There were 10,037 incidents of road rage during that time period (American Automobile Association, 1997). These data were questioned on the webpage of The Atlantic (www. theatlantic.com) by science writer Michael Fumento. Fumento contended that the data may overstate incidents of aggressive driving and road rage because there is no law specifically against some of the behaviors involved and therefore police tickets have to be interpreted, not merely counted. In addition, the AAA data may not have taken sufficient account of the increased numbers of drivers on the road and of miles driven by these drivers.

CORRELATIONAL RESEARCH

Correlational study (handwritten margin note)

The last two chapters exposed you to two different research designs, the experiment and the quasi-experiment. A third type of research method that is very common in the study of human beings is the correlational study. The correlational approach to research looks at the relationship between variables under investigation. As you will see in reviewing the results of the research in this chapter, the findings are expressed in terms of a statistic called the correlation coefficient. The correlation coefficient is often symbolized by the lowercase letter r. A correlation coefficient gives two pieces of information about the relationship between variables: the strength of that relationship and its direction. The strength component of the correlation coefficient occurs on a scale ranging from –1.00 to +1.00. The closer the number is to 1.00 (+ or –), the stronger the magnitude of the relationship between variables. At maximum strength of $r = +1.00$ or $r = –1.00$ the relationship is perfect: if you know the magnitude of one variable you can perfectly predict the magnitude of the other. For example, if there are thirty students enrolled in a kindergarten class, there will be a perfect correlation between the number absent on Monday and the number attending school on Monday. If you know how many are absent, you can make perfect predictions about how many are present. As correlation coefficients approach zero it is likely that the variables studied have little relationship to one another and little predictive power. The relationship between hair length and IQ is probably near zero, as is the relationship between shoe size and family size.

The direction of the relationship is indicated by the sign (+ or –) of the correlation. Correlations that are negative reflect an inverse relationship between the two variables being measured. An inverse relationship means that as the measure of one variable increases, the measure of the other variable decreases (or vice versa). In contrast, a positive correlation means that both variables being assessed either increase together or decrease together. In other words, the sign (+ or –) tells you how the variables are related (directly or inversely). Table 4.1 provides an illustration of the range of correlation coefficients with qualitative descriptions of the strength of the correlations relationship at various points, while Table 4.2 presents some examples of variables that are likely to be correlated positively, negatively, or near zero.

As the absolute value of the number in the correlation coefficient increases, either toward –1.00 or +1.00, the strength of the relationship is greater. For example a correlation of –.86 is stronger than a

TABLE 4.1 The Range of Correlation Coefficients

APPROXIMATE CORRELATION STRENGTH	CORRELATION COEFFICIENT
Very strong	–1.0 to –.80
Strong	–.80 to –.60
Moderate	–.60 to –.30
Weak	–30 to –.10
No correlation	–.10 to +.10
Weak	+.10 to +.30
Moderate	+.30 to +.60
Strong	+.60 to +.80
Very strong	+.80 to +1.00

TABLE 4.2 Examples of Positive, Negative and No Correlation

STRONG POSITIVE CORRELATIONS
Study hours & grade point average
Calories consumed & body weight
Watching TV violence & engaging in aggressive behavior

STRONG NEGATIVE CORRELATIONS
Altitude & percentage of oxygen in air
Optimism & illness
Shyness & number of friendships

LITTLE OR NO CORRELATION
College ID number & grade point average
IQ in infancy & IQ in adulthood
Blood type & level of depression

correlation of +.59. After you have thought about this and looked at the examples in Table 4.2, test yourself by deciding whether the perfect correlation in the example of the kindergarten class above is positive or negative. Remember, the strength of the relationship is solely based on the number and not on the sign. Initially many students make the mistake of assuming a correlation with a positive sign is stronger than a negative one; again, the sign tells you about the direction of the relationship and the number tells you about how powerful it is. This means that as the number increases toward 1.00, in either a positive or negative direction, the strength of the relationship and therefore the predictive "power" is increased.

In real life the predictive power of strong correlations can be important because if you know the value of one variable, you can make a fairly good prediction about the value of the other. If I were the admissions director of a college and knew there was a strong positive relationship between a college entrance exam and final college grade point average, entrance exams would be a powerful tool for making admissions selection decisions. If I, as the admissions director, wanted solely to consider accepting students who would have high grade point averages at graduation, such an examination would be an excellent selection tool because of its predictive power.

Be aware that even a strong relationship between the two variables in correlational research does not ensure that those two variables are linked in a causal relationship. If there is a strong correlation between two variables, one may cause the other or there may be no causal relationship; even a strong correlation provides no evidence either way. Making causal assertions from correlational data is a very common error in everyday life. Just because there is a relationship, that does not necessarily mean that one factor causes the other. For example, the number of churches in a city and amount of criminal activity are positively correlated. If we were to make the assumption that these two measures are causally related then it would mean that churches are a breeding ground for crime or criminal activities leads to church construction. This example illustrates how a variable that is not being measured and is not under study can influence the two variables being studied. In this example, population is a likely "causal" factor that affects both the crime rate and the rate of church construction. Where population is large there are more churches and more crime. Other factors such as income and education levels may also contribute. Of course, it may be the case that two variables that are correlated do have a causal relationship, but a correlational approach alone does not provide evidence for a causal relationship. Strictly speaking, it takes an experimental design to explore causality; however, in some cases experimental designs cannot be used to study behavior. For example, the presumed link between smoking and cancer in humans is correlational because we cannot randomly assign humans to smoke or not. If we employed human participants in such an experimental study, our dependent variable, the data we would be collecting, would be symptoms of a disease that we, as researchers, initiated by placing participants in various smoking groups. This is obviously unethical. In this case, correlational research is better than nothing. If studies are repeated to gain more confidence in the findings, (a process called *replication*), the weight of evidence may begin to suggest casual links, even though they can not be confirmed without an experiment. As a general rule we think it is important to be very cautious about drawing causal conclusions based solely on simple correlational research designs.

RESEARCH ON DRIVING ANGER

It will not surprise you to learn that much of the past research on all types of driving anger has been conducted using archival data, such as court records, or by using surveys. However, there have been a handful of attempts to investigate driving anger with field studies. In these field studies researchers have typically set up a situation and then observed the behavior of drivers who encounter the setup. Diekmann, Jungbauer-Gans, Krassnig, and Lorenz (1996) created a situation in which German drivers were blocked by the researcher's car at a busy intersection. When the traffic light changed to green, the research car did not move and the researchers recorded the reactions of the driver immediately behind them. One of the interesting findings from this study was that the drivers of more expensive cars reacted more quickly with responses such as horn honking or light flashing. McGarva and Steiner (2000) did a somewhat similar study in North Dakota, only their drivers were students who volunteered to be in a study about "driving behavior." The participants were unaware that they were driving into a setup where they would be blocked. Their behavior while experiencing a blocking vehicle was recorded by a researcher riding with them. In the high status condition, it was found that participant drivers accelerated more quickly following provocation.

These bold researchers probably went about as far as it is possible to go in the design of field studies of driving anger. Stronger manipulations invoking more anger could present participants or researchers with unacceptable levels of risk. Another approach to a field study was taken by Deffenbacher, Lynch, Oetting, and Yingling (2001) in a correlational investigation of driving anger. Instead of directly observing the drivers, they asked drivers to observe themselves in naturally occurring situations that might invoke driving anger.

Participants

The participants were students from an upper-level psychology class. They volunteered to take part in the study and were rewarded with points amounting to a 1 percent increase in their final grade in the course. About 7 percent of the students in the class either chose not to participate or produced unusable data. In total, 61 men and 118 women participated. Ninety percent of them were white non-Hispanic.

Procedure

Four weeks into the semester participants were given driving logs to complete on each of three days of the following week. These logs contained structured items that participants used to report on their own driving. They recorded factors such as the amount of driving they did on an observation day and situations they encountered that produced anger on that day. They rated the anger on an intensity scale from zero (= no anger) to one hundred (= the most anger they had ever experienced.) They also indicated aggressive and risky behaviors they had performed by choosing them from a printed list. Aggressive behaviors were things such as angry gestures and swearing and risky behaviors were things such as speeding or drinking and driving.

Also at four weeks, the participants were given the short form of a psychological test called the Driving Anger Scale or DAS (Deffenbacher, Oetting, & Lynch, 1994). As you will see in subsequent chapters, psychological tests are also sometimes called "scales," "instruments," or "measures." The version of the DAS used in this study had 14 items. Although the items asked about different aspects of driving anger, the scale was considered to measure overall driving anger, rather than the specifics detailed by any particular question. In order to take the DAS, participants were asked to read short descriptions of driving events. They were supposed to imagine that these had happened to them and then they were asked to rate the severity of the anger that the situation would produce in them. They rated this anger intensity on a five point scale where 1 indicated "not at all" angry, 2 indicated "a little," 3 indicated "some," 4 indicated "much," and 5 indicated "very much." Examples of the individual items were things such as "A slow vehicle on a mountain road will not pull over and let people by," "Someone speeds up when you try to pass them," and "Someone backs right out in front of you without looking." (Deffenbacher, et al., 1994 p. 86).

Results

The data gathered from the three days of driving logs for each driver were averaged together. This would help to overcome the effects of a single, unusually bad incident. Responses collected on the driving logs were correlated with each other and with the responses from the DAS. Correlations between the Driving Anger Scale and the driving log responses are shown in Table 4.3.

TABLE 4.3   Correlations between Driving Anger as Measured by the Driving Anger Scale (DAS) and the Responses from Three Days of Driving Logs

DRIVING LOG MEASURE	CORRELATION (r) WITH DAS SCORE
Miles driven	−0.03
Frequency of driving	+0.04
Frequency of anger	+0.31
Intensity of anger	+0.40
Frequency of aggressive behavior	+0.28
Frequency of risky behavior	+0.23

There was almost no relationship between DAS score and the miles driven or frequency of driving. Driving farther or more often does not predict aggressive driving. There were moderate correlations between the DAS score and frequency of anger, as well as intensity of anger. It was expected that these correlations would be at least moderate because the DAS is designed to measure driver anger. Correlations were weaker between DAS score and frequency of aggressive behavior as well as frequency of risky behavior.

Although not shown in Table 4.3, strong correlations were found between a few of the items on the driving log. Frequency of aggressive behavior and frequency of anger were correlated $r = +0.69$. Frequency of aggressive behavior and intensity of anger were correlated $r = +0.62$. This suggests that the angry driver is also the aggressive driver. Because this relationship is what might be expected, it suggests that the driving log is accurately quantifying these responses. The correlation between frequency of risky behavior and frequency of aggressive behavior was $r = +0.43$. While this was only moderate, it makes the interesting suggestion that many drivers who are likely to drive at excess speed, for example, are also more likely to be aggressive.

In research about human behavior, correlations are not usually strong. There can be many things that might influence the behavior that is being studied. When a researcher selects only one of these factors, it should not be surprising that resulting correlations are less than perfect. We selected these particular data for discussion because there were a number of moderate to strong correlations. If you examine published studies in the psychology journals and look at the magnitude of correlations that are reported, you will sometimes find that conclusions are based on rather weak relationships. It is important to become a skeptical consumer of information. In everyday conversation, people will say "there is a correlation between" one thing and another. That statement has little meaning until you know the magnitude and the sign of the correlation. Literally, the only information carried in that statement is that the relationship is not zero.

RELIABILITY AND VALIDITY

In the discussion of the data about driving anger we noted that moderate to strong correlations were evidence that the measures were accurate. When there is evidence that measures are accurate, we say that they have a claim to validity. The term *validity* has a special technical meaning within psychology and it refers to accuracy. A measure is valid if it is accurate. Sometimes an entire piece of research may be said to have validity. Validity is often divided into two categories, *internal* and *external*. A study has internal validity if it thoroughly and rigorously tests the correctness of its hypothesis. Appropriateness of control conditions, operational definitions, and sample representativeness are examples of factors to consider in judging internal validity. To some extent, validity is a matter of opinion; however, a validity judgment is not merely some wild and crazy guess. In order to evaluate the validity of a study, one must carefully consider all aspects of the methodology, using the kinds of critical thinking skills that are discussed in this book. It is probably never the case that a study is either valid or not. More often, strengths and weaknesses have to be considered and a judgment is made which places the findings somewhere between absolute truth and complete lie.

The term *external validity* is used to indicate that the findings of a measure or an entire study can be generalized to the real world and do not merely apply to a contrived laboratory environment. The correlations between DAS outcomes and driving behavior in the real world are evidence for the external validity of the DAS.

There is a related concept called *reliability*. Reliability means repeatability. A measure would be considered reliable if it could be given twice and the outcome was the same. If a person took the Driving Anger Scale on Monday and again on Friday and the scores were the same or very similar, the DAS would be considered to be reliable. The same could be said for an entire study. If the replication of a study is conducted and the outcomes are the same, the study might be said to be reliable.

Although they are related concepts, it is important to understand that reliability and validity are not the same thing. If the fuel gauge on your car is stuck and always reads one-quarter of a tank, it is reliable, but not valid, except in the coincidental case where there really happens to be a quarter of a tank of fuel. This is an unusual example, but it illustrates the difference between reliability and validity. In psychology, reliability is often taken to be an indication of validity. Imagine that two observers are watching a behavior and collecting data about it. If their recordings are the same, or very similar, they are reliable and this reliability may also be taken as an indication of validity. We phrase this cautiously because it is possible that the observations are not valid because both observers may be observing inaccurately in the same way, but this would not be a typical case.

Probably few students ever read the preface to a textbook. We didn't when we were students. If you happened to read the preface to this book, you would have found out about our goals for your learning. In the simplest terms we want you to appreciate the value of scientific evidence, but we want you to be skeptical about claims that are made concerning behavior. For many of these assertions, there may be little or no evidence. Where evidence does exist, we would like you to be able to take some introductory steps at evaluating it. Often, this will mean evaluating the methodology used to collect the data. There is enormous variability in the quality of the information about behavior available to you. How much of it are you going to believe? This vast quantity of information is almost valueless to you unless you can evaluate the methodology and make a decision about the validity of the studies that underpin the information. To be able to make these judgments and to have a basis for making them is a precious skill that few people possess.

REFERENCES

American Automobile Association. (1997). *Aggressive driving, three studies*. Washington, DC: American Automobile Association Foundation for Traffic Safety.

Deffenbacher, J. L., Lynch, R. S., & Oetting, E. R. (1994). Development of a driving anger scale. *Psychological Reports*, 74, 83–91.

Deffenbacher, J. L., Lynch, R. S., Oetting, E. R., & Yingling, D. A. (2001). Driving Anger: Correlates and a Test of State-Trait Theory, *Personality and Individual Differences*, 31, 1321–1331.

Diekmann, A., Jungbauer-Gans, M., Krassnig, H., & Lorenz, S. (1996). *The Journal of Social Psychology, 136*, 761–768.

Ellison-Potter, P., Bell, P., & Deffenbacher, J. (2001). The effects of trait driving anger, anonymity and aggressive driving stimuli on aggressive driving behavior. *Journal of Applied Social Psychology, 31*, 431–443.

McGarva, A., & Steiner, M. (2000). Provoked driver aggression and status: a field study. *Transportation Research Part F, 3*, 167–179.

CHAPTER 5

HUNGRY AGAIN? YOU CAN'T BE, YOU JUST HAD LUNCH[1]

Justin M. Joffe

---

[1]Incorporating the research of P. Rozin, S. Dow, M. Moscovitch, and S. Rajaram (1998).

Ever been in an all-you-care-to-eat restaurant where the food was mouth-wateringly good? There are plates of shrimp, salads with delicious dressings, exotic fruits, cakes and pastries; dozens of dishes you really enjoy. You've paid, the food won't run out, you have plenty of time. Why do you stop eating?

Is this a dumb question? Possibly, but not as dumb as it might look at first. It seems easier to find a common-sense explanation for why we start a meal than why we end one, at least when it comes to common sense that stands up to scientific scrutiny. We eat because if we didn't we would die from lack of food, so it makes sense to have physiological processes that get us to start eating when we get hungry (that is, when our body needs fuel to carry out its metabolic activities and give our muscles and our brain the resources to do what we need to do).

But why do we stop? Common sense suggests it is because we are "full," but given the variations in intake of different people, even people of the same size and when consumption is measured when these people have been without food for the same time, it looks like the physiological mechanism or mechanisms underlying satiety (fullness) differ a great deal from one person to another. Two people of the same size who had the same breakfast at the same time may eat vastly different amounts of food at the all-you-care-to-eat restaurant, and this suggests that there is more going on to stop us eating than a straightforward physiological process. Why don't they feel full after more-or-less the same amount of food? We need to assume that the food is equally appealing to both of them, because otherwise we might be concerned that one eats less because she doesn't care for the food as much. (And that in turn would lead us into interesting territory about food preferences and where they come from, but let's leave that aside for the moment and assume there is a lot of food that both people find very tasty.)

Research on the factors that influence why we start and stop eating (and thus how much we consume) isn't of interest only because we want to solve the puzzle of how it all works. Given the extent of eating disorders and the increase in obesity in modern society in affluent countries, understanding things like "what causes humans to begin and end a meal?"—the title of the paper describing the research discussed in this chapter—might be of great help in understanding eating disorders and obesity, and provide us with clues to help treat and prevent such health-threatening conditions.

Physiologists and psychologists have been doing research on hunger—the "drive" postulated to underlie eating behavior—for over 100 years. This body of research provides a wealth of information about the role of both biological factors and psychological ones in determining when we eat, what we eat, and how much we eat. Researchers have identified areas of the brain that mediate starting of eating and cessation of eating and various hypotheses about what triggers these mechanisms have been investigated. Do we feel hungry because of contractions of the stomach, for example? In 1912 Walter Cannon, a renowned physiologist, reported an interesting case study that addressed this question.

Cannon's assistant at Harvard, A.L. Washburn (whose first names appear to be lost to history), "determined to become accustomed to the presence of a rubber tube in the oesophagus. Almost every day for several weeks W. [Washburn] introduced as far as the stomach a small tube, to the lower end of which was attached a soft-rubber balloon about 8 cm. in diameter. The tube was carried about each time for two or three hours. After this preliminary experience the introduction of the tube, and its presence in the gullet and stomach, were not at all disturbing" (Cannon and Washburn, 1912, p. 449). On days when observations were made Washburn would eat little or no breakfast and no lunch. At about 2 p.m. on those days he would swallow the balloon, which was then slightly inflated. Stomach contractions would put pressure on the balloon, and this squeezing would cause air to be pushed through the tube, and this in turn resulted in a mark being made on a recording device. "All these recording arrangements were out of W's sight; he sat with one hand at the key, ready, whenever the sensation of hunger was experienced, to make the current which moved the signal" (Cannon and Washburn, 1912, p. 449).

They found that contractions occurred about every two minutes and lasted on average about one minute. The contractions were usually near their maximum before Washburn pressed the key indicating he felt a hunger pang, and the pang decreased as the contraction faded. In other research, X-rays of the stomach taken before, during, and after a person's normal mealtime confirmed that people report hunger when the stomach shows contractions, suggesting that the signals from the stomach trigger the brain mechanisms controlling eating behavior.

Cannon and Washburn's case study is a nice illustration of the advantages of this research method—and its drawbacks. Wangensteen and Carlson (1931) came across a patient whose stomach had had to be surgically removed; the patient nevertheless felt hunger and ate normally. This later case study contradicts the inference that stomach contractions cause hunger, and was itself confirmed experimentally when Tsang (1938) showed that rats with their stomachs removed surgically nevertheless displayed food-related behaviors (such as increased activity around feeding time and maze learning for a food reward) no different from normal rats; they did eat more frequently, which is not surprising in an animal without a stomach.

Other researchers have looked for blood chemicals (such as glucose) and hormones that might play the part of triggering (and stopping) eating behavior by signaling parts of the hypothalamus in the brain. These mechanisms remain elusive, despite active research that continues partly in the hope of finding effective ways of preventing and treating obesity.

Pinpointing psychological factors involved in eating behavior has been no less difficult. Findings have been sometimes curious, and almost always intriguing. Our food preferences, for example, are influenced by physiological factors, with sweet and salty flavors being sought after everywhere in the world. However, the nature of the foods that satisfy these particular preferences vary enormously both across cultures (where one person's bug may easily be another person's gourmet delight) and from one person to another in a particular culture. Just think about which of your acquaintances think cold pizza is a breakfast treat and which think that those who like cold pizza for breakfast must suffer from neurological impairment of some sort.

Food preferences seem to come from our past, either the distant evolutionary past that shaped our physiological mechanisms or our individual experiences earlier in life (or not so much earlier in the case of taste aversions developed, for example, by overdosing on alcoholic beverages). But what about factors in the immediate present? Have you ever eaten a slice of pizza when you were not at all hungry just because your roommate ordered one and offered you a slice? Or sat down for dessert with a friend eating a full meal, "just to keep her company"? Or eaten a meal when you were not really hungry but it was dinnertime, and we are "supposed" to eat at mealtimes?

And, to return to the question at the beginning of this chapter, might it be external factors of some kind that lead you to stop eating even when you are not uncomfortably full and the food is delicious and abundant? Rozin, Dow, Moscovitch, and Rajaram (1998) precede the description of their research with a discussion of factors that regulate food intake "at the level of the meal." They briefly outline earlier work suggesting that in addition to physiological signals and palatability of food, psychological factors, including an appreciation of how recently we have eaten and how much we have eaten, may play an important role in determining when we start eating a meal and when we stop.

To oversimplify a little, it is as if we say to ourselves: "When did I last eat? It was a while ago, thus I am probably hungry." Or, "I have eaten recently. So I am probably not hungry." Or, "I have eaten a lot, so I am probably full." Of course we don't as a matter of routine think this way (although, on occasion we may well think something like "It's been hours since breakfast, I'm starving").

As Rozin et al. say, "it seems reasonable that for any particular meal, people stop either when they have finished what has been served or when they believe they have eaten a proper meal. On the other hand, people start eating when an appropriate occasion arises, as long as they do not remember having eaten very recently" (p. 392).

These hypotheses about initiation and termination of eating raise a variety of interesting questions; the one that Rozin et al. investigated in the paper under consideration is this: If I don't remember that I've just eaten a meal, will I eat another one if it is offered to me, even if it's only a very short time since I ate the first one?

RESEARCH DESIGN

The problem is, how do we attempt to answer a question like this empirically, rather than simply speculating? If you try to design an experiment, you will almost certainly find that there are all kinds of ethical constraints in doing the kind of research that would answer the question using humans. You might be able to devise a way of doing this with laboratory animals such as rats, but there might be difficulties in establishing that the rats did not recall just having had a meal. There may be ways of dealing with this difficulty, and I would recommend giving this some thought to see what the research would look like, and how confident you might be about the findings, if you could answer the question posed using our most powerful research design.

Rozin et al. investigated it using a very different research design, a case study. Case studies are descriptions of a very few people, indeed sometimes of just a single individual, with a particular characteristic or disorder, such as an injury to a particular area of the brain. Often the descriptions are based on very thorough and intensive observation and testing, and contain a wealth of detail that we could probably never collect on large groups of people. Given that case studies are usually undertaken to study conditions that are very rare, we are unlikely to have too many; in reality, the reverse is more likely to be the case. Indeed, case studies are often undertaken because the scarcity of people with the condition of interest and ethical prohibitions on deliberately creating the condition, make alternative, and more powerful, research methods impossible to use. And sometimes case studies are all one can get off the ground—Washburn volunteered to swallow a balloon, but there might be problems getting enough people to do so to run an experiment!

Case studies are often fascinating to read, providing the kind of detail that makes the individual studied very real, to the point sometimes where we feel we know the person concerned. Given that personal misfortunes like injury, disease, or terrible life experiences are often the things that make the people involved of interest to researchers, there is often considerable poignancy to the objective accounts—it is as if a friend suffered the disorder concerned. The "silver lining," if there is one, is that at least something of use to humankind emerges from an event that for the person concerned, and their friends and family, is nothing but tragic, such as a gunshot injury or a debilitating disease.

Case studies can often provide clues to causal relationships and insights into what sort of research might help go beyond describing a condition to establishing relationships between antecedents and consequences. On their own, however, they have serious limitations: how do we know that what we see in one or two individuals will apply to all or most of us?

disadvantages

Furthermore, the data collected in case studies can vary considerably in accuracy and objectivity, with information often coming from old medical records; these often contain more in the way of subjective verbal descriptions than quantified objective measures like test results. In addition, information of importance is often just unavailable, since it was not of sufficient interest at the time to note or record (and, perhaps, sophisticated tests of various sorts were just not available). Many of these deficiencies can be corrected for if data is collected proactively rather than sought out in old records, and if objective and quantifiable measures are obtained, rather than subjective verbal descriptions. Some earlier research in the area of memory and brain damage has features of the better kind of case study and the research we will look at in detail, that of Rozin and his colleagues, exemplifies some of the best practices in the design of case study research.

EARLIER RESEARCH

Some of the research on eating done prior to their own work that is cited by Rozin and his colleagues is from a pair of reports on a patient who is perhaps the most thoroughly studied person in medical history, a man known in the literature as "H.M." H.M. had brain surgery in 1953 at the age of 27 in an attempt to alleviate the problems of massive and severe epileptic seizures, a debilitating and dangerous disorder that had not improved with other forms of treatment. The operation, involving the removal of brain areas implicated in the seizures (the medial temporal lobes on both sides of the brain, and, importantly, the hippocampus), resulted in a major reduction in seizure activity, but also produced a condition known as anterograde amnesia, the characteristic feature of which is that a person cannot remember events that have happened since the time of the brain surgery (or brain damage). This is different from the kind of amnesia often depicted in movies and on TV, the kind called "retrograde," where the loss of memory is of events prior to the accident. The anterograde amnesia was almost complete in H.M.'s case, although his intellectual functioning is otherwise normal.

In the 50 years since his surgery, over 100 investigators have studied him, first at the Montreal Institute and, since 1966—in 1958 his parents and he moved to Connecticut—at the Massachusetts Institute of Technology (Corkin, 2002). The amount of information available on so many aspects of H.M.'s functioning, including his cognitive skills (such as language, perception, and memory) is staggering and intriguing, providing suggestions about the role of the temporal lobes in many aspects of cognitive and other functioning.

H.M.'s procedural memory is intact (he had no trouble dressing himself, or cleaning his teeth, and so on), he understands jokes that involve word play, can learn new visual-motor skills (like tracing the outline of a star when able to see his hand and pencil only in a mirror)—but he does not know how old he is nor what date it is, nor can he tell people much about events in his life much beyond his high-school years (a long time prior to the surgery). Detailed analysis of his ability to lay down new memories indicates that this ability is not entirely gone; it seems that frequently encountered images are remembered so that he does, for example, recognize himself in a mirror, and with prompting (such as being given a syllable of the person's first name) can name many public figures from the 1960s on (a period after his surgery and consequent amnesia). With faces from the 1920s and 30s his recognition is better than that of normal volunteers (Corkin, 2002).

If we want to answer Rozin's question—if I don't remember that I've just eaten a meal, will I eat another one if it is offered to me, even if it's only a very short time since I ate the first one?—H.M. would seem to be the man to study. Researchers studying H.M. in the 1980s reported that he showed no differences in his ratings of hunger (and thirst) before and after a meal and that he ate a second meal 1 minute after he had completed a first (Hebben, Corkin, Eichenbaum, and Shedlack, 1985).

Rozin et al. regarded one observation of one patient on one occasion as very limited, and so set out to study the question further by making multiple observations of two suitable patients.

METHOD

Participants

Paul Rozin and his colleagues had access to two patients, identified only as "R.H." and "B.R.," with "dense amnesia"—similar to that seen in H.M.—due to extensive damage to parts of the brain known as the hippocampus and the amygdala. The authors tell us that the damage to the brains of the two patients they investigated was "natural" as opposed to being the result of surgery as it was in H.M.'s case.

In case studies the performance of the individual of interest is often compared to that of normal people. Sometimes this is done implicitly—for example, we know that almost all normal adults know their age and when they ate their last meal, and we don't have to do research to tell us that people who do not know these things are unusual. In other cases we do need more subtle or precise information about "normal" people in order to determine if the case of interest is indeed different from them.

What is unusual in a case study is to find the researchers looking at controls who in fact enable us to rule out some of the confounds. Rozin et al. tested two other patients (J.C. and T.A.—yes, all these initials do make things a little confusing, and we'll make it simpler when we look in more detail at the people studied) who were, in effect, controls for the brain damage itself: both J.C. and T.A. had brain damage, but brain damage of a kind that did not produce the dense anterograde amnesia seen in R.H. and B.R. (and, in previous research, in the famous H.M.). If certain deficits or abnormalities are seen in the behavior of R.H. and B.R. that are not seen in J.C. and T.A. then presumably we can conclude that the abnormalities are not due to the brain damage alone, but rather to damage to particular brain areas.

Does this use of a pair of control participants make this design a small experiment or quasi-experiment? You need to think about this question, because it will give you a clearer idea of what constitutes an experiment, and that is not principally the number of participants involved. We do have, in psychology, research designs that enable reasonably confident statements to be made about causal relationships using only a single participant, the so-called "single-subject designs." Why, then, is Rozin et al.'s research, with its two participants with severe amnesia and two "controls" not characterized as an experiment or quasi-experiment?

In Rozin et al.'s research the question of confounds arises. That is, we have to ask whether other differences between the two pairs of patients can also be ruled out as the real causes of the abnormalities. This is a question that is always difficult to answer conclusively from case studies alone. You can make your own decision on this by examining the information available on all four patients, which is shown in Table 5.1, and by considering Rozin et al.'s arguments on the point, which I will summarize after we have looked at the procedures and findings.

As the table indicates, Rozin et al. had the opportunity to carry out tests on four patients with brain damage, two with damage to areas implicated in forming new memories and two with damage in other areas. If either of the two cases were asked about an event that had occurred as little as a minute previously he would have no recollection of it if something else had happened in that short time. The two controls, like most people, did not show this kind of profound lack of memory of very recent events.

Materials

Hunger rating scale: a written 9-point scale, with all the numbers defined verbally, ranging from 1 ("extremely full") to 9 ("extremely hungry") was used for all hunger ratings.

Meals: R.H., who lived alone, was interviewed about his food preferences and lunches he was offered were selected on this basis. B.R., an inpatient, was offered the hospital lunch served on the day he was tested. J.C. and T.A. were offered prepared meals. Details of meals are shown in Table 5.2.

TABLE 5.1   Information presented by Rozin et al. (1998) on the four patients they studied (R.H., B.R., J.C., and T.A.)

	CASE 1 (R.H.)	CASE 2 (B.R.)	CON 1 (J.C.)	CON 2 (T.A.)
Age at testing	48	59	54	57
Age at brain injury	ca 28	ca 58	ca 51	ca 55
Sex	Male	Male	Female	Male
Ethnicity/ Nationality	Black/American	White/Canadian	?/Canadian	?/Canadian
Education	BS	No information		
MRI results	Bilateral damage to hippocampus, hippocampal gyri, amygdala	Bilateral damage to medial temporal lobes (including hippocampus, amygdala), frontal areas	Not stated	Not stated
Cause of brain injury	Seizures of unknown cause	Herpes encephalitis	"Closed-head injury"	Stroke (right hemisphere)
Height	5' 6"	6' 1"	5' 2"	5' 7"
Weight	120 lbs	199 lbs	140 lbs	190 lbs
Sense of smell	Poor	Very poor	Not reported	Not reported
Other health issues	Lung cancer	Medication for seizures; partial gastrectomy 20 years earlier	Attentional problems; no others reported	Attentional problems; left side weakness (due to stroke)
Living situation	Lived alone	Neurological inpatient clinic	Not stated (outpatient)	Not stated (outpatient)
I.Q.	126	88	118	No data
Memory of recent events	Virtually none	Virtually none	"Reasonably intact"	"Reasonably intact"

Notes:

1. To make it easier to keep track of things, from here on I will refer to R.H. and B.R. as Case 1 and Case 2. These are the two people with the kind of brain damage that appears to be responsible for the "deep amnesia." I will refer to the participants who are the controls for the brain damage itself as Control 1 (Con 1 for short) (J.C.) and Con 2 (T.A.).
2. Age at onset of disorder: "ca" means I estimated the age from wording like "at the time of testing, he had suffered from a dense amnesic syndrome . . . for more than 20 years" or when a year is given for the time of brain damage but the year of testing is not stated.
3. MRI results refer to brain damage indicated by means of magnetic resonance imaging.

Procedures

The procedure was the same for each of the four participants, who were tested individually. Each session took place between 11:30 a.m. and 1:00 p.m., and sessions were held at varying intervals for the different participants, sometimes only a day apart but at other times as much as nearly four months apart.

TABLE 5.2   Meals offered to participants

SESSION	MEAL	CASE 1 (R.H.)	CASE 2 (B.R.)	CON 1 (J.C.)	CON 2 (T.A.)
1	1	Swanson TV dinner: turkey, peas, potatoes, applesauce (300–340 calories*); Apple juice	Hospital lunch: soup, cheese-rice casserole, bread & butter, salad, peas, applesauce, tea (537 cals)	Stouffer's Lean Cuisine: chicken, rice, string beans (216 cals); Water	Swanson TV dinner: Chicken, potatoes, corn, apple-crranberry crumb (420 cals); Water
	2	Same as Meal 1, Session 1	Same as Meal 1, Session 1	Same as Meal 1, Session 1	Same as Meal 1, Session 1
	3	Apple pie	Same as Meal 1, Session 1	—	—
2	1	Swanson veal parmigiana TV dinner (410 cals); Apple juice	Hospital lunch: soup, meatloaf, bread & butter, tomatoes, potatoes, beans, peaches, tea (703 cals)	President's Choice: vegetable lasagna (295 cals); Water	Same as Meal 1, Session 1
	2	Same as Meal 1 Session 2	Same as Meal 1, Session 2	Same as Meal 1, Session 2	Same as Meal 1, Session 1
	3	Same as Meal 1 Session 2	Same as Meal 1, Session 2	—	—
3	1	Same as Meal 1 Session 2	Hospital lunch soup, chicken, bread & butter, beets, mashed potatoes, salad, prunes, tea (672 cals):	—	—
	2	Same as Meal 3, Session 1	Same as Meal 1, Session 3	—	—
	3	Same as Meal 3, Session 1	Same as Meal 1, Session 3	—	—

*Strictly speaking, what we refer to in everyday language about food intake as "calories," are correctly "kilocalories" (1000 calories).

procedure

At the start of each session a researcher asked the participant to rate on the 9-point scale how hungry he or she felt; the scale was in front of the participant when he or she was asked to make the rating. After that, a meal was placed in front of the participant, who was told, "Here's lunch."

If participants stopped eating for a minute, they were asked if they were done. If they said yes, the plate was removed, otherwise it was left until they were finished, at which time participants were asked to rate their hunger again, using the same rating scale.

Then the researcher talked to the participant for 10–30 minutes and at that point they started again and did exactly what they had done before, offering a second and then, if that was accepted, a third meal. The sequence of procedures is summarized in Table 5.3.

TABLE 5.3 Sequence of events in each session

	CASES (3 SESSIONS)	CONTROLS (2 SESSIONS)
1	Hunger rating	Hunger rating
2	Meal 1	Meal 1
3	Hunger rating	Hunger rating
4	Conversation (10-30 mins)*	Conversation (10-30 mins)*
5	Hunger rating	Hunger rating
6	Meal 2	Meal 2
7	Hunger rating	Hunger rating
8	Conversation (10-30 mins)*	—
9	Hunger rating	—
10	Meal 3	—
11	Hunger rating	—

*If participant did not drink water he or she was asked to do so in order to reduce or eliminate aftertaste of food.

Results

The two people with amnesia (Case 1 and Case 2) showed little indication that they felt full after eating a meal. As can be seen in Table 5.4, on only one occasion did one of them reject a meal even when they had recently eaten one or two meals, and their ratings (Table 5.5) indicate that felt almost as hungry after eating a meal as before and that Case 1 (R.H.) was just as hungry after partly eating one or two meals as he was before eating at all. As the tables also indicate, the two Control participants did not show this pattern: both rejected a second meal and both rated their hunger considerably lower after a meal than before (on three of four occasions where before and after ratings were obtained).

TABLE 5.4 Meals eaten and meals accepted or rejected

SESSION	MEAL	CASE 1 (R.H.)	CASE 2 (B.R.)	CON 1 (J.C.)	CON 2 (T.A.)
1	1	Partly eaten	Eaten	Eaten	Eaten
	2	Partly eaten	Eaten	Rejected	Rejected
	3	Partly eaten	Rejected	—	—
2	1	Partly eaten	Eaten	Eaten	Eaten
	2	Partly eaten	Eaten	Rejected	Rejected
	3	Partly eaten	Stopped*	—	—
3	1	Partly eaten	Eaten	—	—
	2	Partly eaten	Eaten	—	—
	3	Partly eaten	Stopped*	—	—

*When B.R. (Case 2) accepted and started eating the third lunch he was stopped by the researcher, presumably because of health concerns. R.H. (Case 1) was allowed to eat as much as he wished of the third meal at each session because he had completed only part of some fairly small TV dinners. On two occasions he was offered a fourth meal and in both cases rejected it on the grounds that his "stomach was a little tight."

TABLE 5.5   Hunger ratings before and after meals (Participants rated their hunger on a 9-point scale from 1 ["extremely full"] to 9 ["extremely hungry"])

SESSION	MEAL	CASE 1 (R.H.)		CASE 2 (B.R.)		CON 1 (J.C.)		CON 2 (T.A.)	
		Before	After	Before	After	Before	After	Before	After
1	1	7	6	7	8	5	2	5	4
	2	7	7	2	5	1	*	3	*
	3	7	7	3	*	—		—	
2	1	7	6	6	5	7	2	7	3
	2	7	6	5	3	1	*	3	*
	3	7	6	5	*	—		—	
3	1	7	6	7	3	—		—	
	2	7	6.5	2	3	—		—	
	3	7	5	5	3	—		—	

*No "after" rating obtained because no meal was eaten.

Case 1 never mentioned that he had recently eaten when offered second and third lunches whereas Case 2 did mention this on all but one occasion. Both Control participants clearly knew they had recently eaten (one indicating surprise and amusement on being offered a second lunch, the other refusing politely but firmly).

Discussion

The answer to the question posed—if I don't remember that I've just eaten a meal, will I eat another one if it is offered to me, even if it's only a very short time since I ate the first one?—appears to be "yes." The two participants with severe amnesia accepted multiple meals and showed little change in their hunger ratings after eating.

Rozin et al. believe that their findings indicate that "memory of recent eating plays an important, but previously unappreciated, role in the onset and termination of meals by humans" (p. 394).

We know that both R.H. and B.R., the two cases, have profound memory loss and we see in the data presented that they are different from other people in accepting a second and even a third lunch a short time after eating a first meal; they also show little decline in their self-rated hunger after eating a meal and prior to eating a second or third one. However, how sure are we that it is the memory problem that is responsible for—causes, that is—the eating abnormalities? What else could perhaps be the cause?

Rozin et al. consider alternative explanations. Let us look at some of the alternatives they raise.

First, could the eating changes be attributable not to memory loss in itself, but simply to brain damage? Here we see the advantage of their having looked at the eating behavior of two control participants: J.C. and T.A. had brain damage too, but not to areas implicated in the laying down of new memories. In other word, it looks as if brain damage that does not produce severe amnesia does not produce the abnormalities of the onset and termination of eating. However, could it be that there were other differences in brain damage? Could the control participants have more of their brain intact and could it be the amount of the damage rather than the location of the damage that determines whether or not food intake will be affected? Case studies do not provide definitive answers to that question.

Second, could it be some effect of the brain damage in the two cases, other than the effect of the brain damage on memory, which accounts for the effects on eating? Effects on taste, for example, might alter eating behavior. Rozin et al. argue that this is unlikely because the details of damage in their two cases and in H.M. (the famous patient mentioned in the introduction) were different, even though overlapping areas were affected in all three cases. Furthermore, none of the three showed other eating abnormalities, such as eating "inappropriate" foods, that characterize damage to other brain mechanisms regulating eating.

Their arguments on the question of brain injury alone or injury causing effects on regulation of eating through other mechanisms make it plausible that it is the memory loss that accounts for the effects on eating, but not certain. That is a limitation of case studies.

Third, could the acceptance of meal after meal be due to the demand characteristics of the situation? This is an issue that arises frequently in research on humans. Are there aspects of the situation that bias the participant to act in certain ways, through participants either feeling some pressure to do what they think the researchers want or by the participants developing some kind of hypothesis about what is expected and, in effect, trying to please the researchers by doing what the participants think the researchers want? Rozin et al. consider this possibility and point out that although participants may have felt they needed to comply, (a) there was no pressure put on them to eat meals, and (b) the control participants who both, in fact, actually ate smaller first meals than one of the cases (see Table 5.2), never ate a second meal. In addition, both cases refused to answer some question they were asked in interviews and both refused to eat certain foods, indicating that they were not generally simply acting to please the researchers.

Rozin et al. also consider an issue that could be troublesome in accepting the interpretation that memory loss accounts for eating abnormalities, and that is the point mentioned in the results that Case 2 (B.R.) *did* recall having recently eaten on almost every occasion when he was offered a second or third lunch. The researchers argue that his memories were hazy and that, in any case, the recollection of having eaten should have resulted in refusals of meals not acceptance.

So, given the plausibility of the arguments based on the evidence presented that memory of having recently eaten a meal is an important determinant of when and how much we eat, does the same thing apply to us? How plausible is it to conclude that a major reason you don't eat lunch two or three times if it is offered to you again after you have eaten a meal is because you remember that you have already eaten? In short, how far can we generalize the findings of this research? Two people with serious brain damage causing profound amnesia accepted a second meal a short while after eating a first meal and a third meal a short time after that. Rozin et al. say they believe that "the amnesics in our study showed surprisingly normal relations to food, and . . . they can be considered reasonably normal with respect to food attitudes, except for the absence of recent conscious memory." In short, they believe that R.H. and B.R. are, except for their amnesia, pretty much like the rest of us.

REFERENCES

Cannon, W. B. & A. L. Washburn (1912) An explanation of hunger. *American Journal of Physiology, 29,* 441–454.

Corkin, S. (2002) What's new with the amnesic patient H. M.? *Nature Reviews Neuroscience, 3,* 153–160.

Hebben, N., S. Corkin, H. Eichenbaum, & K. Shedlack (1985) Diminished ability to interpret and report internal states after bilateral medial temporal resection: case H. M. *Behavioral Neuroscience, 99,* 1031–1039.

Rozin, P., S. Dow, M. Moscovitch, and S. Rajaram (1998). What causes humans to begin and end a meal? A role for memory for what has been eaten, as evidenced by a study of multiple meal eating in amnesic patients. *Psychological Science, 9,* 392–396.

Tsang, Y. C. (1938) Hunger motivation in gastrectomized rats. *Journal of Comparative Psychology, 26,* 1–17.

Wangensteen, O. H. & A. J. Carlson (1931). Hunger sensations in a patient after a total gastrectomy. *Proceedings of the Society for Experimental Biology, New York, 28,* 545–547.

CHAPTER 6

TOPLESS DANCERS BARE ALL (TO ETHNOGRAPHERS)[1]

Julianne Krulewitz

---

[1]Incorporating the research of W. E. Thompson, J. L. Harred, and B. E. Burks (2003).

Have you ever felt like you were not getting the respect you deserved? Maybe you sensed others were making judgments about you before they even got to know you or that they seemed to think they were better than you—more valued, more righteous, or more deserving than you. Maybe these people's attitudes about you seemed to be reflected in their behavior; maybe they gave you the cold shoulder or treated you unfairly.

Whether or not you've actually had these experiences, you can probably imagine how they might make you feel. You might become angry and upset, sad and withdrawn, or confused and defensive. You might try to deny the problem, or you might try to minimize your ostracism by hiding what you believe to be the source of the problem from others.

Hours of detailed interviews and observations (a research design referred to as an *ethnography*) revealed that women who strip for a living experience negative emotions similar to those of other stigmatized groups such as ethnic minorities, the obese, and the physically disabled (Crocker, Major, and Steele, 1998). Even topless dancers who claim they enjoy their jobs and offer many reasons why stripping is a good career say that being a topless dancer has caused them a great deal of anxiety and grief (Thompson, Harred, and Burks, 2003; Thompson and Harred, 1992). Many report that problems with relationships, future job opportunities, and in their day-to-day interactions with others stem from their work as dancers. In fact, although many topless dancers insist that they are proud of the work that they do, a large portion of them refrain from telling others, even people as close to them as a father or a boyfriend, that they dance topless for a living. Although the specific reasons why they withhold this information depend on the situation and certainly vary for each individual, one reason that so many women may not disclose their topless dancing is to avoid being stigmatized.

UNDERSTANDING STIGMA

In ancient Greece, the term *stigma* referred to some sort of sign (usually a mark that was cut or burned into the individual's body) the purpose of which was to display a less apparent defect that an individual possessed. People like slaves, criminals, and traitors were often branded with these stigmas so they could be more easily ostracized and avoided by others (Goffman, 1963). The meaning of stigma was reinterpreted by Christians to describe a bodily sign with religious meaning and then later was revised to refer to a visible indication of physical disorder. Many years later still, sociologist Erving Goffman developed the theory that any "person who is quite thoroughly bad, or dangerous, or weak" and who is "thus reduced in our minds from a whole and usual person to a tainted, discounted one," has become the target of stigmatization (Goffman, 1963, p. 3).

According to this more contemporary definition, a stigmatized individual is someone who possesses or is *thought* to possess some negative characteristic resulting in a flawed social identity (Crocker et al., 1998). In line with this definition (and in many ways with the original Greek definition as well) is the notion that a stigma is socially constructed. Although in some cases a stigma may be physically visible and unavoidable (e.g., skin of a certain tone) and in other cases, it may be concealable (e.g., sexual orientation), in all cases, it is our judgment of the characteristic in question that makes it stigmatizing or not. For example, although both extremely ugly people and extremely attractive people (which of course is in itself a value-based judgment) deviate from the norm, because attractiveness is valued in our society and ugliness is devalued, it is only stigmatizing to be ugly.

Of course, what is devalued in one context is not necessarily devalued in another. For instance, although being smart in middle school may precipitate the unfortunate label of geek or nerd, adults are often rewarded for their intelligence. Similarly, when surrounded by others who share the same devalued identity, an individual may not feel the same way as when he or she stands alone (e.g., being an African-American at a predominantly Caucasian school may evoke very different feelings than those felt at a more racially-diverse or predominantly black school). And while everybody may in fact be stigmatized in one situation or another (e.g., white men can't jump), members of some groups are certainly more prone to stigmatization than others (Crocker et al., 1998). Furthermore, individuals or groups who usually hold the more powerful positions in society are better able to combat the stigmatization they face than individuals or groups who do not have as many resources.

In general, individuals with devalued social identities are aware of their stigmatization (Crocker et al., 1998). As with many other difficult or distressing situations, stigmatized individuals may choose from a multitude of ways to deal with their problem. In some cases they may choose to ignore the stigma, disassociate themselves from those who devalue them, or pretend that their stigma does not exist. In others cases, they may try to face or even embrace the stigma. And in other cases still, they may try to transform their identity so it is no longer devalued. For example, imagine how a gay male living in our society may deal with his sexual orientation. He may choose to avoid thinking about being homosexual, steer clear of situations where homophobic individuals may be present, withhold information about his sexual orientation or even deny that he is gay. He may also "come out of the closet," and reveal his homosexuality or join a gay pride group. The way an individual chooses to cope with his or her stigma along with his or her success is influenced by a number of situational and individual-dependent factors (for a detailed explanation of these factors, see Crocker et al., 1998).

To gain a greater understanding of the techniques individuals with devalued social identities use to manage their stigma, topless dancers were interviewed and observed by a small team of researchers in the early 1990s and then again a decade later (Thompson, et al., 2003; Thompson and Harred, 1992). Although topless dancing is a multi-billion dollar industry, is sanctioned and controlled by the government, and is enjoyed by many upstanding citizens, Thompson and his colleagues determined that topless dancers remain members of a highly stigmatized group. As this ethnography reveals, like many other stigmas, this deviant career appears to dramatically affect the lives of these women in many ways.

RESEARCH DESIGN

As described in Chapter 1, qualitative research aims to establish a deep understanding of the individuals or population being studied and to develop a descriptive analysis of the emerging themes. To do this, researchers gather a great deal of detailed information about a specific topic in any one of a variety of ways such as observation or interviews. Because the goal of qualitative research is to capture the multiple, subjective realities that may exist, researchers often approach their research from a number of perspectives, analyze their data in a number of ways, and extend their investigation as needed.

One commonly used approach by qualitative researchers is ethnography. Though the definition varies depending on the specific time, context, and type of research being conducted, contemporary forms of ethnographies are generally described as being some set of formal techniques that are used to expose information about a given topic (Berg, 2004). Interestingly, ethnography can be considered a research method, a research design, or both, depending on whether it is the means by which data is collected (a method), it is used as a way of organizing and examining data (a design), or it is both the way information is gathered and the organizational plan. Consult chapter 1 for a more detailed discussion and additional examples of research methods and designs.

In any case, ethnography usually includes extensive fieldwork and detailed notes. Fieldwork may include, but is not limited to, covert and overt observation and participation, formal and informal interviewing, and the collection of documents and archival data. Information gathered in the field may initially be handwritten, filmed, or recorded and is then analyzed at a later date (Berg, 2004).

Like individuals conducting other forms of qualitative and quantitative research, an ethnographer must first determine what he or she is interested in researching, who to include in the sample, and how to collect data. Similar to researchers utilizing other research designs, ethnographers usually first become familiar with prior research, develop questions that build on these ideas, and determine how best to get the most accurate and thorough information. However, *unlike* many other types of research, there is an understanding (and often even an expectation) in ethnographic research that what and who is being studied will change as the study progresses. As one of the strengths of qualitative research is flexibility, ethnographers appreciate the necessity of constantly reassessing their motives and methods as they conduct their research.

After initial decisions about research design and methodology have been made, ethnographers must gain access to the field setting they wish to study. In many cases, "getting in" is one of the most difficult components of ethnographic research (Berg, 2004, p. 150). People are often reluctant to allow ethnographers into their group, area, or establishment and even when the researcher has been granted access by an authority (e.g., an administrator at an institution like a prison, mental hospital, or school) individuals are often reluctant to accept the researcher as a member of the group. To get the most out of their visits, ethnographers often attempt to establish trust by honestly stating their purpose and by developing relationships with members of the setting. Sometimes they seek out "gatekeepers," individuals such as a receptionist or secretary at a business or a bouncer at a club, to help them gain entry. Although in many cases not the highest-ranking members of the group, gatekeepers are often the ones who may make or break the ethnography. A gatekeeper who is willing to help may open many otherwise locked doors and may provide valuable information and opportunities while one who is not willing to help may have the opposite effect. Therefore, ethnographers often choose to negotiate "research bargains" with these gatekeepers as well as with more prominent members of the group (Berg, 2004, p. 160). They may also turn to one or more individuals who are willing to be guides or informants. In some instances they befriend an individual in the hopes that the relationship will "snowball" into a more general acceptance by the group and in other cases they establish a number of relationships at once (Berg, 2004, p. 151). For example, a researcher interested in sorority life might actually join a sorority, move in to the sorority house, and form friendships with one or more of her sisters.

Ethnographers may also choose to observe a setting without actually becoming part of it. If he or she was interested in understanding community members' attitudes about a particular local issue, the ethnographer might interview individual citizens and attend a series of community meetings. In other situations, it may be in the ethnographer's best interest to covertly study the group he or she wishes to know about. Ethnographers may withhold information about who they are, give false information, or use methods such as video and audio recordings to gather their data. Covert methods are often used when researchers do not think they will get accurate information if honest about their intentions, when detailed explanations are too cumbersome, or when they believe revealing their identities might be dangerous (Berg, 2004). For example, in a classic study on casual homosexual encounters, the researcher's decision to remain an anonymous voyeur enabled him to learn much more about the men's homosexual and heterosexual encounters than if he had approached men on their way into the public bathroom and asked for an interview (Humphrey, 1975 as cited in Berg, 2004). Deception does, of course, raise ethical issues that must be addressed by researchers before they embark on research in which they do not fully disclose their intentions to participants.

Once an ethnographer has gained entry, he or she must take care to nurture and maintain these needed relationships while at the same time, conducting detailed interviews with other group members, carefully observing interactions within the group and with outsiders, and recording all important information. Of course, since ethnography aims to observe settings and not necessarily change them, researchers take great care to have as little impact as possible on the individuals being studied. Because peoples' normal behavior is often altered when they know they are being observed (a phenomenon called the *Hawthorne Effect*[2]), ethnographers may try to become "invisible" to the individuals they are studying (Berg, 2004, p. 162). In some cases invisibility is literal (as is the case when researchers remain anonymous or watch a setting from afar) and in other cases it is more metaphorical. Invisibility increases over time as the researchers and the individuals they are studying become better acquainted and form relationships typical of the field setting. If a researcher behaves as a normal group member (e.g., becomes a "regular" at the local diner or works alongside others at the soup kitchen), individuals are much more likely to return to their normal interactions than if the researcher remains a distant outsider.

Although an ethnographer's invisibility increases his or her ability to develop meaningful relationships and consequently gather rich data in abundance, becoming invisible must be done with care to avoid potential dangers. In many cases, an invisible researcher may be mistaken for an actual group member and, as a result, be treated like one. For example, in Rosenhan's now famous psychiatric hospital study, he and his associates pretended to suffer from mild hallucinations. As a result, they were actually committed until they were able to convince doctors that their schizophrenia had gone into remission (Rosenhan, 1973). Although living among psychiatric patients for 5 to 52 days certainly enabled Rosenhan and his aides to collect rich data and accomplish their research goals, with an average stay of 19 days the researchers probably got a lot more than they bargained for!

An ethnographer who becomes invisible may also be considered "guilty by association" and face formidable consequences as a result. For example, imagine being an ethnographer studying a particular youth gang when the gang's rivals arrive. What would you do if you were studying the interactions between car thieves when the police showed up? Here, an ethnographer must choose between compromising his or her research and obeying the law. Along similar lines, invisibility may lead to learning more than an ethnographer has intended. In many cases, a trusted ethnographer may be privy to the group's plans. When the plan involves an upcoming fundraising event or a surprise birthday party, there is little problem, but when the plans include robbing a convenience store or threatening someone's life, the researcher has difficult decisions to make. Depending on formal agreements like confidentiality certificates and informal ones like a researcher's own sense of morality, he or she decides when the research needs to be interrupted or concluded and what other measures need to be taken (Berg, 2004).

Although invisibility and acceptance by the group may carry the potential for certain hazards, they also afford the ethnographer the opportunity to watch, listen, and learn much more than any outsider ever could. Good ethnographers learn to take in the physical setting from the beginning. Even if these first impressions do not make it into the ethnographer's final report, these early observations serve to familiarize the ethnographer with the setting and its inhabitants. As described earlier, because having one or more trusted informants is often imperative to gaining access to the rest of the group, researchers try to form these relationships early on. The more a researcher knows about the field setting and the group he or she is studying, the easier it is to locate subgroups within the field setting, to determine the questions that need to be asked, the appropriate time and place they should be posed, and what other resources will be needed to continue the ethnography.

In addition to observing the physical setting and asking questions, ethnographers also benefit from tracking the movements and interactions of those being studied. Watching daily routines as well as those activities that are out of the ordinary all provide useful information. Sometimes ethnographers will ask

---

[2]After a series of experiments at the Hawthorne works of the Western Electric Company designed to understand how different environmental changes to the workplace (like changes in the factory's lighting), could increase productivity resulted in positive changes in all conditions, researchers determined that it was the fact that they were being studied, not that their environment was being changed, that led workers to be more productive. (Mayo, 1933).

the individuals they are studying about their actions, at other times they will watch or listen from a distance (Berg, 2004). In fact, to an ethnographer, eavesdropping is a commonly used "trick of the trade."

Because ethnography aims to be a thorough and descriptive account of the people or setting being studied, researchers necessarily note what they have learned as they go along. Although one ethnographer's field notes may vary greatly from another's, there are four elements all notes generally include.

Cryptic Jottings

Cryptic jottings are notes taken while in the field (Berg, 2004). Because the researcher is busy listening, questioning, and interacting with others, these are usually just brief statements, drawings, or an unusual phrase or term that are used to trigger the researcher's memory at a later occasion when he or she has time to elaborate.

Detailed Descriptions

After the researcher has left the field, he or she generally writes more *detailed descriptions* of anything that he or she thinks may be important to the ethnography. These notes might include describing a room's colors, lighting, textures, smells, and general "feel." Fragments of conversations jotted down while in the field are rewritten to include as many phrases and ideas as can be remembered. Whenever possible these detailed descriptions will be verbatim. If the individual being observed had any noticeable features, such as a scar or a speech impediment, these will also be described in this extensive narrative (Berg, 2004).

Analytic Notes

Although ethnography attempts to provide a clear and accurate picture of the individuals being studied, this method also acknowledges and appreciates the ethnographer's voice. *Analytic notes*, or *observer comments*, are ideas that occur to researchers as they are writing detailed descriptions of their field-visit. They include the researchers' judgments about things they witnessed, connections that they make between the individuals being studied, and their theories for how or why something has happened the way it has.

Subjective Reflections

Ethnographers also make note of their own feelings and reactions toward experiences in the field. These *subjective reflections* often include comments such as how rewarding, scary, surprising, or angering a specific experience was (Berg, 2004).

To assure field notes will be accurately interpreted when reexamined, researchers make sure to distinguish between objective and subjective remarks. To make the sequence of events identifiable, they also note things like the date, time, and location. Finally, researchers attempt to use consistent shorthand for things like names and places throughout their field notes and are increasingly making use of available technology such as hand-held computers and audio recorders to increase the accuracy of their notes.

Once all the data have been collected and the field notes have been written and organized, ethnographers either conduct what is called *content analysis* (one of several ways of organizing data to show themes, topics, issues, and hypotheses that have emerged) or write a detailed narrative that reflects the information they learned during their field visits (for a detailed explanation of these processes see Berg, 2004). Just as technology has made note-taking more precise, sophisticated methodology and advanced statistics, as well as new computer software, has made many new ways of systematically classifying and interpreting data much more accessible.

PRIOR RESEARCH

In the early 1990s, Thompson and Harred (1992) interviewed over 40 women who danced topless for a living in a large Southwestern city. Through causal conversations, informal and formal interviews, and observations of the women at work, this ethnography revealed that although topless dancing carried little to no stigma while within the confines of the club, almost all of the participants felt their occupation was highly stigmatizing outside of the workplace. Waitresses, club managers, bartenders, and other current and former dancers corroborated the stories, comments, and concerns that were raised by the participating topless dancers. Even though all the dancers interviewed worked at relatively "high class" clubs that catered to middle and upper middle class businessmen and were supposedly law-abiding establishments, working at one of these "gentlemen's clubs" was considered by the dancers detrimental to retaining the community's respect and to future job opportunities (Thompson and Harred, 1992, p. 294).

Thompson and Harred's analysis revealed that dancers employed one of several tactics to avoid or overcome the stigma associated with topless dancing. In many cases, the women chose to disclose their profession only to a small group of people (i.e., coworkers and a few friends or family members) while keeping it a secret from most others. By "dividing their social worlds" they were able to develop a strong sense of identification and cohesion with the other dancers and at the same time escape being stigmatized by outsiders (Thompson and Harred, 1992, p. 302). Because many of the dancers were single mothers, supporting other members of their family, or were paying their way through school, they explained that although they did not really like their jobs, the paycheck compensated for the stigma they faced. Furthermore, many of the women interviewed maintained that not only is topless dancing harmless, but also that it is entertaining, therapeutic, and educational. These women went on to condemn the hypocrisy of the general public as well as many of the men who came to watch them dance.

METHOD

Ten years after their initial study, the ethnographers returned to the same Southwestern city to investigate any changes in the way topless dancing was perceived and in how topless dancers managed any stigma they felt (Thompson, Harred, and Burks, 2003). The city studied, with well over one million residents and approximately three million in the greater metropolitan area, is known for its large amount of adult entertainment. Research into the city's recent past revealed that despite its popularity, topless and other forms of nude dancing were considered just as deviant as they had been a decade earlier. In fact, as recent campaigns by the mayor and city council to crack down on what they considered to be immoral behavior had led to new ordinances, police raids, and health department inspections on clubs across the city, the ethnographers hypothesized the stigmatization of individuals working in this industry may have even increased (Thompson et al., 2003).

Participants

Three (two male and one female) ethnographers interviewed twenty-eight women who consented to discussing their careers as topless dancers at one of five "gentlemen's clubs" (Thompson et al., 2003). The participants ranged in age from 18[3] to 32 years old with a median age of 22.5.[4] A majority of the participants had at least one child. Twenty-two of the participants were White, three women identified as Black, two as Hispanic, and the remaining woman reported that she was Asian. Most of the women had graduated from high school and a number of them had also attended at least some college. The majority of the

---

[3]The authors noted that several of the women they interviewed looked like they were younger than 18.

[4]The median is a measure of central tendency that refers to the point at or below which 50% of the scores fall when the all of the numbers are positioned in numerical order (Howell, 1997).

women had been dancing between six months and two years, though it was one woman's first day on the job and another's fourteenth year. Although none of the women from Thompson et al.'s (1992) first study were re-interviewed, the researchers noted that the two groups of participants had a lot in common (Thompson et al., 2003). In fact, the only visible difference (at least of those that the researchers assessed) between the participants in the current study and those interviewed a decade earlier was in the prevalence of tattoos. The percentage of dancers with tattoos rose considerably from 10% in 1992 to 90% in 2003.

Setting

The five gentlemen's clubs included in this study were all considered among the city's finest. Three were clubs described in Thompson's earlier research and two were clubs that had opened subsequent to the previous study (Thompson et al., 2003). Each had an attractive appearance from the outside and offered customers such amenities as valet parking. Customers entered a small vestibule where they paid cover charges, could check coats, and when asked, show identification. Although the particular décor of the clubs varied, all had similar dark walls, carpets, and furniture and a brightly lit main stage as well as a number of smaller stages for dancers to perform on. The clubs also had full bar and food services. Some of the clubs also had "VIP" or "Champagne" rooms where a customer could supposedly pay for "anything" he[5] desired (Thompson et al., 2003, p. 558).

Typically, each woman danced several dances on the main stage and then moved from side stage to side stage until she had danced on them all. After her set was complete she would either join club patrons to solicit personal dances or free drinks (that she also earned money for) or she would return to the dressing room. Therefore at any given time there were a number of women dancing on the club's stages and circulating among the crowd. The ethnographers noted that although city ordinances prohibited dancers from removing their g-strings and from making physical contact with their clientele, these rules were rarely enforced, often broken, and sometimes even encouraged by club staff (Thompson et al., 2003).

Procedures

All interviews took place between the hours of 11:00 a.m. and 6:00 p.m., the "specialty hours" during which clubs tried to attract local businessmen. After gaining access to the clubs, the ethnographers conducted in-depth interviews with each of the participants.[6] They asked each woman a series of questions about her job and how it affected her life. Participants were encouraged to elaborate on any points they discussed and were also asked to provide any additional information they thought would be helpful. Consequently, the length of each conversation between ethnographer and participant varied greatly.

In addition to these formal interviews, Thompson et al. (2003) gathered insights from a number of other dancers, waitresses, hostesses, and club managers. By talking with these individuals informally and observing their interactions with the participants and with each other, the ethnographers were able to gain valuable insights into the way the dancers felt about themselves and how others perceived them.

RESULTS

Like their predecessors, the women interviewed by Thompson and his colleagues (2003) described their jobs as highly stigmatizing. Many of the dancers felt like others were making gross generalizations about them and other topless dancers they worked with.

---

[5]Although both men and women were free to patronize the clubs, as the title "Gentlemen's Club" implies, entertaining heterosexual men was main focus of each club.

[6]Ethnographers found open invitations to observe and interview the participants at work was more difficult than it had been a decade earlier due to more stringent municipal and organizational legislation.

As one said:
> They think we're loose and sluts just because we tittie dance. Well, maybe in some cases, they're right, some of these girls are sluts, but it's not fair to lump us all into one big group like that (Thompson et al., 2003, p. 553).

And as a second dancer described her experiences:
> The City Council and the cops think we're just like the prostitutes out on the street. They don't understand that we're decent girls just trying to make a living—and, they seem to forget that this is perfectly legal (Thompson et al., 2003, p. 563).

Disputing a powerful stereotype, another commented:
> Most people think we're just a bunch of wild girls who sleep around and do drugs. We're not like that. At least, I'm not (Thompson et al., 2003, p. 553).

Even non-dancing employees felt the repercussions of this stigma. One manager mentioned he would be shunned at "legitimate" restaurants after working at the gentleman's club and another employee said she withheld information about where she worked because people "might get the wrong idea" (as cited in Thompson et al., 2003, p. 553). To avoid being stereotyped as a slut, druggie, or as some other disreputable character and to bypass potential discrimination, many of the individuals interviewed revealed that although some of their acquaintances knew about their jobs, many did not. As described by the participants in Thompson et al.'s first study, "dividing social worlds" was apparently still a common practice among dancers and other employees as well.

Rationalization

Although many of the dancers kept their jobs a secret, it does not mean that they were not rationalizing why they danced to themselves and to the others who were part of their community (i.e., other club employees and the individuals they confided in). In fact, Thompson et al. (2003) discovered a distinct pattern of techniques that the women used to justify and explain their jobs. Some denied topless dancing was harmful, contrasting it to illegal and violent behaviors.

For example, one of the dancers argued:
> Every day there's people out there murdering, robbing, and raping people. We come in here behind closed doors and shake our tits for guys who pay to see us do it. What possible harm can come from that (Thompson et al., 2003, p. 562)?

Others did, however, comment that being a topless dancer had caused them personal harm. As one of the dancers interviewed put it, "This job takes something away from you—your dignity. It robs you of your heart and soul" (Thompson et al., 2003, p. 563).

And as a woman who had been dancing for 14 years said:
> …These other girls always say things, like "nobody gets hurt," and dancing topless is "harmless." Bullshit! It hurts the dancers. It takes something away from you—away from your soul. It makes you hard. You don't trust anybody, especially men. You can't have a real relationship with anybody. I think it destroys people. Not only the dancers, but I've seen men in here who blow their whole paychecks in one night. Don't tell me that doesn't hurt their wives and children…(Thompson et al., 2003, p. 563).

Despite the misgivings that some dancers expressed, most of the women interviewed countered that they were providing a legal, safe service that others had no right to stigmatize. As one dancer put it, "it's harmless fun, and even the loudest opponents [of these clubs] know it (Thompson et al., 2003, p. 562).

The ethnographers also noted that the dancers often condemned the very people who stigmatized them. Many dancers called the city council, the police, and many other members of the public "hypocrites".

One said:

…Half of 'em [the mayor, city council and police] would probably love to come in here and watch us dance. You should see the cops when they come in. They watch us dance for an hour or two before they bust anybody—and there's usually half a dozen of 'em at a time. How many cops does it take to write a ticket for lewd dancing to one or two harmless girls?

Another woman described how the morality some individuals espoused was inconsistent with their actions:

This crusade against topless clubs is such a bunch of crap. We have city council members, cops, professional athletes, and all kind of famous people come in here all the time. They have VIP cards and go to the private rooms so that nobody see them in here (Thompson et al., 2003, p. 562.).

Thompson et al.'s interviews also revealed that many of the women were not dancing to refute stereotypes or to highlight hypocrisy, but rather that they needed the job to help themselves and to help others. A number of the women said they were dancing to pay their way through school, to buy necessities, and to take care of children, partners, and parents. As one dancer said, "Almost all of us would rather be doing something else, but we're doing this to support our families" (Thompson et al., 2003, p. 565). According to accounts like this, escaping stigmatization was overshadowed by other more personal needs and altruistic goals.

Dissonance

As the ethnographers interpreted the words and actions of the women they interviewed, they noticed a number of discrepancies between the women's attitudes toward dancing topless and the behaviors they exhibited. For instance, even women who professed dancing was a good job disclosed that they would never want their daughters to follow in their footsteps. Many women expressed disdain and contempt towards the men they danced for and often flirted with at work. And even though the women were willing to bare all, dancing in front of strangers in almost no clothing, all but two used stage names. Thompson et al. (2003) conjectured that perhaps their participants were feeling something called cognitive or emotive dissonance.

Cognitive dissonance, first described by Leon Festinger in the 1950s, is based on the assumption that there is a pressure to be consistent. When people's attitudes are inconsistent with the way they are behaving, they feel uncomfortable. In order to relieve this discomfort, the individual tries to restore consistency. He or she does this either by changing his or her attitude, changing his or her behavior, or by minimizing the importance of the situation and its discordance (Festinger, 1957).[7]

In the case of the dancers in Thompson's study, reducing this dissonance was not an easy task. In fact, the only way that most of the women could relieve the distress it caused them was by projecting positive emotions that they did not feel and by separating their identities as topless dancers from their personal identities (as mothers, daughters, partners, and friends). For most, this was facilitated by a name change and a transformation in appearance and wardrobe. When exiting the stage, dancers left their pseudonyms, provocative dress, and overtly sexual behavior behind. In other words, by creating a

---

[7]In most cases, changing your attitude is easier than changing your behavior or making less of the dissonance. For example, as most will agree, it's easier to change your attitude about smoking ("smoking is not that bad for me" or "it won't affect me for years") than it is change your behavior (to quit smoking) or to ignore the relationship between your attitudes about smoking and your smoking behaviors ("smoking might be bad for me, but I don't smoke that much so I'll be okay").

second identity (i.e., name, personality, etc.) the women were able to justify their actions and diminish the dissonance they felt.

As the following example suggests, mediating the relationship between two conflicting identities is difficult:
> There's nothin' wrong with what I'm doin.' I love gettin' up here and shakin' my tits in front of these guys. It turns them on and it turns me on....Who am I kiddin'? That was Angel [her stage name] talking.' Hell, I'm a mother. I shouldn't even be in a place like this (Thompson et al., 2003, p. 566).

And as another dancer summed up:
> ...But when I go out there on that stage I quit being me and just start being Cheyenne [her stage name]. I guess you could say Cheyenne is my wild side. Don't get me wrong [she laughs] I'm not schizophrenic or have a split personality of anything, I just mean, when I come in this club, I quit being me and start being Cheyenne (Thompson et al., 2003, p. 566).

In addition to the dissonance and shifting of persona that the women expressed, Thompson and his colleagues observed this identity shift during their interviews. Even though women often approached the ethnographers scantily clad and making suggestive moves, once they realized their purpose (to talk to them about their experiences rather than watch them undress), they usually chose to retrieve more conservative clothing and to act less seductively. Together, these examples illuminate the way the women were trying to cope with their stigma and to reduce the emotional strain it added to their everyday lives.

DISCUSSION

Being a member of a devalued group can have profound effects on how you feel about yourself and on the opportunities available to you (Crocker, et al., 1998). In-depth observations and interviews of women who danced topless in Southwestern gentlemen's clubs revealed the extent to which an individual's occupation can be detrimental to her sense of self and her ability to command respect. This detailed ethnography exposed the dissonance that women feel when they choose to work in a "deviant" occupation and the steps they must take to control the negative repercussions of their career choice.

Although the advent of new technologies has made data collection and analysis easier, ethnography remains a complex, time-consuming, and arduous process. In addition to watching, listening and questioning, Thompson et al. (2003) have taken the time to understand the political and historical situation, observe the physical surroundings, and note even seemingly insignificant interactions between the many members of the group being studied. As a consequence, they have exposed information that would otherwise have remained undiscovered.

As to be expected, despite ethnographers' attempts to maintain a professional relationship with the population they study and retain clear goals throughout their research, many still find ending their research a difficult process (Berg, 2004). Breaking ties with participants who are otherwise neglected or stigmatized may be particularly hard for both researchers and the individuals they are studying. As with all grounded scientific research, however difficult, the costs of this research are outweighed by their benefits.

Thompson, Harred, and Burks' (2003) reliance on qualitative means to explore some of the important issues faced by topless dancers likely afforded them a more complete understanding of their participants' situations than quantitative research could expect to. Their thorough interviews and careful observations revealed that despite the legality and popularity of topless dancing, this practice evidently remains highly stigmatizing to those who take part in it.

REFERENCES

Berg, B. L. (2004). Qualitative research methods for the social sciences. Boston: Pearson, Allyn & Bacon.

Crocker, J., Major, B., and Steele, C. (1998). Social stigma. In D. T. Gilbert, S. T. Fiske, and L. Gardner, L. (Eds.), *The Handbook of Social Psychology: Vol. 2 (4ᵗʰ ed.)* (pp. 504–553). New York: McGraw-Hill.

Goffman, E. (1963). Stigma: Notes on the management of spoiled identity. New York: Simon & Schuster, Inc.

Howell, D. C. (1997). *Statistical methods for psychology (4ᵗʰ ed.)*. Belmont, C. A.: Duxbury Press, p. 35.

Festinger, L. (1957). A theory of cognitive dissonance. Stanford, CA: Stanford University Press.

Mayo, E. (1933). *The human problems of an industrial civilization*. New York: MacMillan.

Sykes, G. M. & Matza, D. (1957). Techniques of neutralization: A theory of delinquency. *American Sociological Review, 22*, 664–670.

Thompson, W. E., Harred, J. L., & Burks, B. E. (2003). Managing the stigma of topless dancing: a decade later. *Deviant Behavior, 24*, 551–570.

Thompson, W. E. & Harred, J. L. (1992). Topless dancers: Managing stigma in a deviant occupation. *Deviant Behavior: An Interdisciplinary Journal, 13*, 291–311.

SECTION II

BIOPSYCHOLOGY

CHAPTER 7

INTRODUCTION

Material selected from: *Psychology*,
Seventh Edition, by Wade & Tavris

EVOLUTION, GENES, AND BEHAVIOR

The tough-minded . . . respect difference. Their goal is a world made safe for differences. —RUTH BENEDICT

Think of all the ways that human beings are alike. Everywhere, no matter what their backgrounds or where they live, people love, work, argue, dance, sing, complain, and gossip. They rear families, celebrate marriages, and mourn losses. They reminisce about the past and plan for the future. They help their friends and fight their enemies. They smile with amusement, frown with displeasure, and glare in anger. *Where do all these commonalities come from?*

Think of all the ways that human beings differ. Some are extroverts, always ready to throw a party, make new friends, or speak up in a crowd; others are shy and introverted, preferring the safe and familiar. Some are trailblazers, ambitious and enterprising; others are placid, content with the way things are. Some take to book learning like a cat to catnip; others struggle in school but have lots of street smarts and practical know-how. Some are overwhelmed by even the most petty of problems; others remain calm and resilient in the face of severe difficulties. *Where do all these differences come from?*

For many years, psychologists addressing these questions tended to fall into two camps. On one side were the *nativists*, who emphasized genes and inborn characteristics, or *nature*; on the other side were the *empiricists*, who focused on learning and experience, or *nurture*. Edward L. Thorndike (1903), one of the leading psychologists of the early 1900s, staked out the first position when he claimed that "in the actual race of life . . . the chief determining factor is heredity." But in words that became famous, his contemporary, behaviorist John B. Watson (1925), insisted that experience could write virtually any message on the blank slate of human nature: "Give me a dozen healthy infants, well-formed, and my own specified world to bring them up in and I'll guarantee to take any one at random and train him to become any type of specialist I might select—doctor, lawyer, artist, merchant-chief and yes, even beggar-man and thief, regardless of his talents, penchants, tendencies, abilities, vocations, and race of his ancestors."

In this chapter, we focus mostly on the contribution of nature to our human commonalities and our individual differences, and on findings from two related areas. Researchers in **evolutionary psychology** emphasize the evolutionary mechanisms that might help explain commonalities in language learning, attention, perception, memory, sexual behavior, emotion, reasoning, and many other aspects of human psychology. Researchers in **behavioral genetics** study the contribution of heredity to individual differences in personality, mental ability, and other characteristics. You should keep in mind, however, that today no one argues in terms of nature *or* nurture; scientists understand that heredity and environment interact to produce not only our psychological traits but even most of our physical ones. Children can inherit a tendency to be nearsighted, for instance, but whether nearsightedness actually develops may depend on whether a child reads a lot or sits for hours staring at a TV set or computer monitor (Gwiazda et al., 1993). A teenager with a natural aptitude for sports may be more likely than other students to get on a school team and to get sports equipment as birthday presents, experiences that reward and encourage the development of that aptitude.

UNLOCKING THE SECRETS OF GENES

Let's begin by looking at what genes are and how they operate. **Genes,** the basic units of heredity, are located on **chromosomes,** rod-shaped structures found in the center (nucleus) of every cell of the body. Each sperm cell and each egg cell (ovum) contains 23 chromosomes, so when a sperm and egg unite at conception, the fertilized egg and all the body cells that eventually develop from it (except for sperm cells and ova) contain 46 chromosomes, arranged in 23 pairs.

Chromosomes consist of threadlike strands of **DNA (deoxyribonucleic acid)** molecules, and genes consist of small segments of this DNA. Each human chromosome contains thousands of genes, each with a fixed location. Collectively, all the genes together—current estimates put the number around 35,000, fewer than once thought—are referred to as the human **genome.** Many of these genes are found in other animals as well; others are uniquely human, setting us apart from chimpanzees, wasps, and plants. Many genes are inherited in the same form by everyone; others vary, contributing to our individuality.

Within each gene, four basic chemical elements of DNA—identified by the letters A, T, C, and G, and numbering in the thousands or even tens of thousands—are arranged in a particular order: for example, ACGTCTCTATA. . . . This sequence forms a code that helps determine the synthesis of one of the many proteins that affect virtually every aspect of the body, from its structure to the chemicals that keep it running.

Identifying even a single gene is a daunting task; biologist Joseph Levine and geneticist David Suzuki (1993) once compared it to searching for someone when all you know is that the person lives somewhere on Earth. Researchers must usually *clone* (produce copies of) several stretches of DNA on a chromosome, then use indirect methods to locate a given gene.

One method, which has been used to search for the genes associated with many physical and mental conditions, involves doing **linkage studies.** These studies take advantage of the tendency of genes lying close together on a chromosome to be inherited together across generations. The researchers start out by looking for **genetic markers,** DNA segments that vary considerably among individuals and whose locations on the chromosomes are already known. They then look for patterns of inheritance of these markers in large families in which a condition—say, depression or impulsive violence—is common. If a marker tends to exist only in family members who have the condition, then it can be used as a genetic landmark: The gene involved in the condition is apt to be located nearby on the chromosome, so the researchers have some idea where to search for it. The linkage method was used, for example, to locate the gene responsible for Huntington's disease, a fatal neurological disorder that affects motor control, intellectual functioning, and memory (Huntington's Disease Collaborative Research Group, 1993). Although in this instance only one gene was involved, the search took a decade of painstaking work.

In 2000, after years of heated competition, an international collaboration of researchers called the Human Genome Project and a private company, Celera Genomics, both announced that they had completed a rough draft of a map of the entire human genome. Using high-tech methods, the researchers were able to identify the sequence of nearly all 3 billion units of DNA (those A's, C's, T's, and G's) and to determine the boundaries between genes and how the genes are arranged on the chromosomes. This project has been enormously costly and time consuming, but it reflects the view among many scientists that the twenty-first century will be the century of the gene.

It is important to understand, however, that even when researchers locate a gene on a chromosome, they do not automatically know its role in physical or psychological functioning. Usually, locating a gene is just the first step in understanding what it does and how it works. Also, be wary of media

> **Thumbs Up!**
>
> Ask the members of your family, one person at a time, to clasp their hands together. Include aunts and uncles, grandparents—as many of your biological relatives as possible. Which thumb does each person put on top? About half of all people fold the left thumb over the right and about half fold the right thumb over the left, and these responses tend to run in families. Do your own relatives show one tendency over the other? (If your family is an adoptive one, of course, there is less chance of finding a trend.) Try the same exercise with someone else's family; do you get the same results? Even for behavior as simple as thumb folding, the details of how genes exert their effect remain uncertain (Jones, 1994).

reports implying that some gene is the *only* factor involved in a complex psychological ability or trait, such as intelligence or shyness. In 1998, for example, newspapers announced the discovery of a "worry gene." Don't worry about it. Unlike disorders such as Huntington's, most human traits—even such seemingly straightforward ones as height and eye color—are influenced by more than one gene pair. Psychological traits are especially likely to depend on multiple genes, with each one accounting for just a small part of the variance among people. Conversely, any single gene is apt to influence many different behaviors.

To make the picture even more complicated, when it comes to psychological qualities, genetic and environmental influences are inextricably intertwined. Thus, there is no simple, direct line between a single gene and any given behavior. New methods have been developed to tease out the small contribution that a specific gene is likely to make to a particular trait (Plomin & Crabbe, 2000), but at this point, all announcements of a "gene for this" or a "gene for that" should be viewed with extreme caution.

THE GENETICS OF SIMILARITY

One of the questions that opened this chapter was, how can we explain our human similarities—the experiences and behaviors that seem to be universal, such as loyalty to a family or clan, or the capacity for language? Evolutionary psychologists believe the answer lies partly in genetic dispositions that developed during the evolutionary history of our species. As British geneticist Steve Jones (1994) wrote, "Genetics is the key to the past. Every human gene must have an ancestor. . . . Each gene is a message from our forebears and together they contain the whole story of human evolution."

Evolution and Natural Selection

To read the messages from the past that are locked in our genes, we must first understand the nature of evolution itself. **Evolution** is basically a change in gene frequencies within a population, a change that typically takes place over many generations. As particular genes become more common in the population or less common, so do the characteristics they influence.

Why do gene frequencies in a population change? Why don't they stay put from one generation to another? One reason is that during the division of the cells that produce sperm and eggs, if an error occurs in the copying of the original DNA sequence, genes can spontaneously change, or *mutate*. In addition, during the formation of a sperm or an egg, small segments of genetic material cross over (exchange places) from one member of a chromosome pair to another, prior to the final cell division.

As genes spontaneously mutate and recombine during the production of sperm and eggs, new genetic variations—and therefore potential new traits—keep arising.

But that is only part of the story. According to the principle of **natural selection,** first formulated in general terms by the British naturalist Charles Darwin in *On the Origin of Species* (1859/1964), the fate of these genetic variations depends on the environment. (Darwin did not actually know about genes, as their discovery had not yet been widely publicized, but he realized that a species' characteristics must somehow be transmitted biologically from one generation to the next.)

The fundamental idea behind natural selection is this: If, in a particular environment, individuals with a genetically influenced trait tend to be more successful than other individuals in finding food, surviving the elements, and fending off enemies—and therefore better at staying alive long enough to produce offspring—their genes will become more and more common in the population. Their genes will have been "selected" by success, and over many generations, these genes may even spread throughout the species. In contrast, individuals whose traits are not as adaptive in the struggle for survival will not be as "reproductively fit": They will tend to die before reproducing, and therefore their genes, and the traits influenced by those genes, will become less and less common and eventually may even become extinct.

Scientists debate how gradually or abruptly such changes occur and whether competition for survival is always the primary mechanism of change. But they agree on the basic processes of evolution. Over the past century and a half, Darwin's ideas have been resoundingly supported by findings in anthropology, botany, and molecular genetics (Jones, 2000). Scientists have watched evolutionary developments occurring before their very eyes in organisms that change rapidly, such as microbes, insects, and various plants, and evolutionary principles such as natural selection now guide all of the biological sciences.

Evolutionary biologists often start with an observation about some characteristic and then try to account for it in evolutionary terms. For example, why do male peacocks have such fabulous and flamboyant feathers, whereas females look so drab and dull? Because during the evolution of peacocks, males who could put on the flashiest display got the attention of females, and such males therefore had a better chance of reproducing. In contrast, all females had to do was hang around and pick the guy with the fanciest feathers; they didn't even have to dress up.

Evolutionary psychologists work in the same way as biologists, but some take a slightly different tack: They start by asking what sorts of challenges human beings might have faced in their prehistoric past—having to decide which foods were safe to eat, for example, or needing to size up a stranger's intentions quickly. Then they draw inferences about the behavioral tendencies that might have been selected because they helped our forebears solve these survival problems and enhanced reproductive fitness. (They make no assumption about whether the behavior is adaptive or intelligent in the *present* environment.) Finally, they do research to see if those tendencies actually exist throughout the world.

For example, our ancestors' need to avoid eating poisonous or rancid food might have led eventually to an innate dislike for bitter tastes and rotten smells; those individuals who happened to be born with such dislikes would have stood a better chance of surviving long enough to reproduce. Similarly, it made good survival sense for our ancestors to develop an innate capacity for language and an ability to recognize faces and emotional expressions. But they would not have had much need for an innate ability to read or drive, inasmuch as books and cars had not yet been invented (Pinker, 1994).

For many evolutionary psychologists, a guiding assumption is that the human mind is not a general-purpose computer waiting to be programmed. Instead, they say, it developed as a collection of specialized and independent "modules" to handle specific survival problems, such as the need to find food or find a mate (Buss, 1995, 1999; Cosmides, Tooby, & Barkow, 1992; Mealey, 1996). A particular module may involve several dispersed but interconnected areas of the brain, just as a computer file can be fragmented on a disk (Pinker, 1997).

Critics worry that the idea of mental modules is no improvement over instinct theory, the once-popular notion in psychology that virtually every human activity and capacity, from cleanliness to cruelty, is innate. Frans de Waal (2001b), an evolutionary theorist who believes that someday all psychology departments will have a picture of Darwin hanging on the wall, has accused some of his colleagues of mistakenly assuming that if a trait exists, then it must be adaptive and must correspond to a mental module. This assumption, he points out, is incorrect: Male pattern baldness and pimples, for example, are not particularly adaptive! Some traits can even be costly; the problems that many people have with aching backs are no doubt an unfortunate consequence of our ability to walk on two feet. To understand our evolutionary legacy, de Waal argues, we must consider not just individual traits in isolation, but the whole package of traits that characterize the species. This is as true for psychological traits as for physical ones.

Those who subscribe to the modules approach respond that evidence from psychology and other disciplines can distinguish behavior that has a biological origin from behavior that does not. As Steven Pinker (1994) explains, if a mental module for some behavior exists, then neuroscientists should eventually discover the brain circuits or subsystems associated with it. Further, he adds, "When children solve problems for which they have mental modules, they should look like geniuses, knowing things they have not been taught; when they solve problems that their minds are not equipped for, it should be a long hard slog." Be careful, though, to avoid the common error of assuming that if something exists, it must be adaptive.

Innate Human Characteristics

Because of the way our species evolved, many abilities, tendencies, and characteristics are either present at birth in all human beings or develop rapidly as a child matures. These traits include not just the obvious ones, such as the ability to stand on two legs or to grasp objects with the forefinger and thumb, but also less obvious ones. Here are just a few examples:

1. *Infant reflexes.* Babies are born with a number of reflexes—simple, automatic responses to specific stimuli. For example, all infants will suck something put to their lips; by aiding nursing, this reflex enhances their chances of survival.

2. *An attraction to novelty.* Novelty is appealing to human beings and many other species. If a rat has had its dinner, it will prefer to explore an unfamiliar wing of a maze rather than the familiar wing where food is. Human babies reveal a surprising interest in looking at and listening to unfamiliar things—which, of course, includes most of the world. A baby will even stop nursing if someone new enters his or her range of vision.

3. *A desire to explore and manipulate objects.* All birds and mammals have this innate inclination. Primates, especially, like to "monkey" with things, taking them apart and scrutinizing the pieces, apparently for the sheer pleasure of it (Harlow, Harlow, & Meyer, 1950). Human babies shake rattles, bang pots, and grasp whatever is put into their tiny hands. For human beings, the natural impulse to handle interesting objects can be overwhelming, which may be one reason why the command "Don't touch" is so often ignored by children, museum-goers, and shoppers.

4. *An impulse to play and fool around.* Think of kittens and lion cubs, puppies and pandas, and all young primates, who will play with and pounce on each other all day until hunger or naptime calls. Play and exploration may be biologically adaptive because they help members of a species find food and other necessities of life and learn to cope with their environments. Indeed, the young of many species enjoy *practice play*, behavior that will be used for serious purposes when they are adults (Vandenberg, 1985). A kitten, for example, will stalk and attack a ball of yarn. In human beings, play teaches children how to get along with others and gives them a chance to practice their motor and linguistic skills (Pellegrini & Galda, 1993).

5. *Basic arithmetic skills.* Incredibly, by the age of only 1 week, infants show an understanding that a set of three items differs from a set of two items, indicating a rudimentary understanding of number. Of course, 1-week-old babies cannot count. However, they will spend more time looking at a novel set of three items after getting used to a set of two items, or vice versa, which means that they can recognize the difference. By 18 months, infants know that 4 is more than 3, which is more than 2, which is more than 1—suggesting that the brain is designed to understand "more than" and "less than" relationships for small numbers. Evolutionary psychologists believe that these and other fundamental arithmetic skills evolved because they were useful to our ancestors (Geary, 1995).

OUR HUMAN HERITAGE: LANGUAGE

Try to read this sentence aloud:

Kamaunawezakusomamanenohayawewenimtuwamaanasana.

Can you tell where one word begins and another ends? Unless you know Swahili, the syllables of this sentence will sound like gibberish.*

Well, to a baby learning its native tongue, *every* sentence must, at first, be gibberish. How, then, does an infant pick out discrete syllables and words from the jumble of sounds in the environment, much less figure out what the words mean and how to combine them? Is there something special about the human brain that allows a baby to discover how language works? Darwin thought so: Language, wrote Darwin (1874), is an instinctive ability unique to human beings. Many modern researchers think he was right.

The Nature of Language

To evaluate Darwin's claim, we must first appreciate that a **language** is not just any old communication system; it is a set of rules for combining elements that are inherently meaningless into utterances that convey meaning. The elements are usually sounds, but they can also be the gestures of American Sign Language (ASL) and other manual languages used by deaf and hearing-impaired people.

Some nonhuman animals are able to acquire aspects of language if they get help from their human friends. However, we seem to be the only species that acquires language naturally. Other primates use grunts, screeches, and gestures to warn each other of danger, attract attention, and express emotions, but the sounds are not combined to produce original sentences (at least, as far as anyone can tell). Bongo may make a sound of delight when he encounters food, but he cannot say, "The bananas in the next grove are a lot riper than the ones we ate last week and sure beat our usual diet of termites."

In contrast, language, whether spoken or signed, allows human beings to express and comprehend an infinite number of novel utterances, created on the spot. This ability is critical; except for a few fixed phrases ("How are you?" "Get a life!"), most of the utterances we produce or hear over a lifetime are new. For example, in this book you will find few, if any, sentences that you have read, heard, or spoken before in exactly the same form. Yet you can understand what you are reading, and you can produce new sentences of your own about the material.

Kama unaweza kusoma maneno haya, wewe ni mtu wa maana sana, in Swahili, means "If you can read these words, you are a remarkable person."

The Innate Capacity for Language

At one time, most psychologists assumed that children acquired language by imitating adults and paying attention when adults corrected their mistakes. Then along came linguist Noam Chomsky (1957, 1980), who argued that language was far too complex to be learned bit by bit, as one might learn a list of world capitals.

Children, said Chomsky, must not only figure out which sounds or gestures form words; they must also take the *surface structure* of a sentence—the way the sentence is actually spoken or signed—and infer an underlying *deep structure*—how the sentence is to be understood. For example, although "Mary kissed John" and "John was kissed by Mary" have different surface structures, any 5-year-old knows that the two sentences have essentially the same underlying meaning, in which Mary is the actor and John gets the kiss:

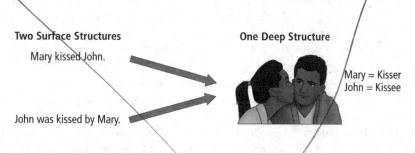

Two Surface Structures

Mary kissed John.

John was kissed by Mary.

One Deep Structure

Mary = Kisser
John = Kissee

Conversely, "Bill heard the trampling of the hikers," a single surface structure, can have two different underlying meanings: one in which the hikers are actors doing the trampling, and one in which they are the unfortunate objects of the trampling. Your ability to discern two different deep structures tells you that the sentence's meaning is ambiguous.

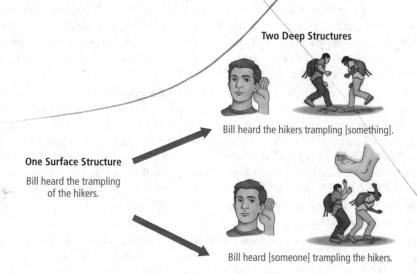

Two Deep Structures

Bill heard the hikers trampling [something].

Bill heard [someone] trampling the hikers.

One Surface Structure

Bill heard the trampling
of the hikers.

To transform surface structures into deep ones, said Chomsky, children must apply rules of grammar (*syntax*). These rules govern word order and other linguistic features that determine the role a word plays in a sentence (such as, say, kisser or kissee). Most people, even adults, cannot actually state the grammatical rules of their language (e.g., "In English, adjectives usually precede the noun they describe"), yet we are able to apply thousands of such rules without even thinking about it. No native speaker of English would say, "He threw the ball big."

Because no one actually teaches us grammar when we are toddlers, the human brain, Chomsky argued, must contain a **language acquisition device,** an innate mental module that allows young children to develop language if they are exposed to an adequate sampling of conversation; just as a bird is designed to fly, human beings are designed to use language. Another way of saying this is that children are born with a *universal grammar*—that is, their brains are sensitive to the core features common to all languages, such as nouns and verbs, subjects and objects, and negatives. These common features occur even in languages as seemingly different as Mohawk and English, or Okinawan and Bulgarian (Baker, 2001; Cinque, 1999; Pesetsky, 1999).

Over the years, linguists and *psycholinguists* (researchers who study the psychology of language) have gathered much evidence in support of the Chomskyan position:

1. ***Children in different cultures go through similar stages of linguistic development.*** For example, they will often form their first negatives simply by adding "no" or "not" at the beginning or end of a sentence ("No get dirty"); and at a later stage, they will use double negatives ("He don't want no milk"; "Nobody don't like me"), even when their language does not allow such constructions (Klima & Bellugi, 1966; McNeill, 1966).

2. ***Children combine words in ways that adults never would.*** They reduce a parent's sentence ("Let's go to the store!") to their own two-word version ("Go store!") and make many charming errors that an adult would not ("The alligator goed kerplunk"; "Daddy taked me"; "Hey, Horton heared a Who") (Ervin-Tripp, 1964; Marcus et al., 1992). Such errors, which linguists call *overregularizations*, are not random; they show that the child has grasped a grammatical rule (e.g., add the *t* or *d* sound to make a verb past tense, as in *walked* or *hugged*) and is merely overgeneralizing it (*taked*, *goed*).

3. ***Adults do not consistently correct their children's syntax, yet children learn to speak or sign correctly anyway.*** Learning explanations of language acquisition assume that children are rewarded for saying the right words and are punished for making errors. But parents do not stop to correct every error in their children's speech, so long as they can understand what the child is trying to say (Brown, Cazden, & Bellugi, 1969). Indeed, parents often *reward* children for incorrect statements! The 2-year-old who says "Want milk!" is likely to get it; most parents would not wait for a more grammatical (or polite) request.

4. ***Children not exposed to adult language may invent a language of their own.*** Deaf children who have never learned a standard language, either signed or spoken, have made up their *own* sign languages, and across cultures, these languages show similarities in sentence structure (Goldin-Meadow & Mylander, 1998). The most astounding case comes from Nicaragua, where a group of deaf children of hearing parents, sent to two special schools, eventually created a home-grown but grammatically complex sign language that is unrelated to Spanish (Senghas & Coppola, 2001). Scientists have had a unique opportunity to observe the evolution of this language as it developed from a few simple signs to a full-blown linguistic system.

5. ***Infants as young as 7 months can derive simple linguistic rules from a string of sounds.*** If babies are repeatedly exposed to artificial "sentences" with an ABA pattern, such as "Ga ti ga" or "Li na li," until they get bored, they will then prefer new sentences with an ABB pattern (such as "Wo fe fe") over new sentences with an ABA pattern (such as "Wo fe wo"). (They indicate this preference by looking longer at a flashing light associated with the novel pattern than one associated with the familiar pattern.) Conversely, when the original sentences have an ABB structure, babies will prefer novel ones with an ABA structure. These responses suggest to many researchers that babies can discriminate the different types of structures (Marcus et al., 1999). Astonishingly, this ability emerges even before they can understand or produce any words.

A Grammar Test Everyone Can Pass

How would you complete these sentences, spoken aloud?

This morning I saw one sik. Later I saw two more _____.
This morning I saw one wug. Later I saw two more _____.
This morning I saw one litch. Later I saw two more _____.

Think about the sounds you added to these nonsense words; they differed, didn't they? In English, the plural form of most nouns depends on the last sound of the singular form. The precise rules are quite complicated, yet every speaker of English has an implicit knowledge of them and will correctly add an s sound to rat to make rats, a z sound to *rag* to make *rags*, and an *iz* sound to *radish* to make *radishes*. (The only exceptions are people with a rare genetic disorder, as described in the text.) When 5- and 6-year-olds are asked for the plural versions of nonsense words, they easily apply the appropriate rules (Berko, 1958). Such evidence has helped to convince many psychologists that human beings have an innate ability to infer the rules of grammar.

Chomsky's ideas so revolutionized thinking about language and human nature that some linguists refer to the initial publication of his ideas as The Event (Rymer, 1993). Chomsky changed the questions researchers asked about language development, and even the terms they used (language "acquisition" replaced language "learning"). Although Chomsky himself avoided the evolutionary implications of his argument, others maintain that an innate facility for language evolved in human beings because it permitted our ancestors to convey precise information about time, space, objects, and events, and to negotiate alliances that were necessary for survival (Pinker, 1994).

The next logical step might be to identify the specific brain modules and genes that contribute to our ability to acquire language. Clues come from a large three-generation British family with a rare genetic disorder that prevents normal language acquisition. Family members who are affected with this disorder have pronunciation problems and also have trouble applying grammatical rules for changing tenses or constructing plurals—rules that normal children learn easily and unconsciously. For example, they can learn the distinction between *mice* and *mouse* but they cannot learn the general rule about adding an s, z, or iz sound to make a noun plural, as in *bikes* (s), *gloves* (z), and *kisses* (iz). Instead, they must learn each plural as a separate item, and they make many errors (Gopnik & Goad, 1997; Matthews, 1994).

Linkage studies recently led British researchers to a mutation in a specific gene that seems to contribute to this syndrome, possibly by orchestrating the activity of other genes during prenatal brain development (Lai et al., 2001). Scientists are still debating whether the gene's ultimate influence is on pronunciation, specific grammar circuits in the brain, or some general intellectual or perceptual process necessary for speech or language. Nonetheless, this research is an important first step in isolating possible genetic influences on language.

Learning and Language

Despite the evidence for Chomsky's view, some theorists still give experience a greater role. Using computers, they have been able to design *neural networks*, mathematical models of the brain that can "learn" some aspects of language, such as regular and irregular past-tense verbs, without the help of a language acquisition device or preprogrammed rules. Neural networks simply adjust the connections among hypothetical "neurons" in response to incoming data, such as repetitions of a word in its past tense form. The success of these computer models, say their designers, suggests that children, too, may be able to acquire linguistic features without getting a head start from inborn brain circuits (Rodriguez, Wiles, & Elman, 1999; Rumelhart & McClelland, 1987). Some theorists argue that instead of inferring grammatical rules, children learn the probability that any given word or syllable will follow another—something that infants as young as eight months are able to do (Saffran, Aslin, & Newport, 1996; Seidenberg, 1997). In this view, infants are more like statisticians than grammarians.

Even theorists who emphasize an inborn grammatical capacity acknowledge that in any behavior as complex as language, nurture must also play a role. Although there are commonalities in language acquisition around the world, there are also some major differences. This means that language does not merely unfold biologically but also depends on the environment (Gopnik, Choi, & Baumberger, 1996; Slobin, 1985, 1991).

Further, although most children have the capacity to acquire language from mere exposure to it, parents help things along. They may not go around correcting their children's speech all day, but neither do they ignore their children's errors. For example, when a child makes a mistake or produces a clumsy sentence, parents almost invariably respond by recasting the sentence or expanding its elements ("Monkey climbing!" "Yes, the monkey is climbing the tree") (Bohannon & Stanowicz, 1988). In turn, children are more likely to imitate adult recasts and expansions, suggesting that they are learning from them (Bohannon & Symons, 1988). It is likely, therefore, that language development depends on both biological readiness and social experience. Some aspects of language imply a genetic capacity for acquiring grammatical rules. But children may also learn, from experience, the statistical patterns among words, as well as irregular constructions (Marcus, 1999; Pinker, 1999).

The importance of both heredity and the environment is apparent in the tragic cases of abandoned and abused children who have been completely isolated from normal social interaction until late childhood. After they are rescued, these children may learn words and be able to use simple sentences, but they rarely speak normally or catch up grammatically. Such sad evidence suggests the existence of a biologically determined *critical period* in language development during the first few years of life or possibly the first decade (Curtiss, 1977; Lenneberg, 1967; Tartter, 1986). During these make or break years, children need exposure to language and opportunities to practice their emerging linguistic skills in conversation with others.

OUR HUMAN HERITAGE: COURTSHIP AND MATING

Most psychologists agree that the evolutionary history of our species has made certain kinds of learning either difficult or easy. Most acknowledge that simple behaviors, such as smiling or a preference for sweet tastes, resemble instincts, behaviors that are relatively uninfluenced by learning and that occur in all members of the species. And most agree that human beings inherit some of their cognitive, perceptual, emotional, and linguistic capacities. But social scientists disagree heartily about whether biology and evolution can help account for complex social customs, such as warfare, cooperation, and altruism (the willingness to help others). Nowhere is this disagreement more apparent than in debates over the origins of male–female differences in sexual behavior, so we are going to focus on that endlessly fascinating topic.

Evolution and Sexual Strategies

In 1975, one of the world's leading experts on ants, Edward O. Wilson, published a little book that had a big impact. It was titled *Sociobiology: The New Synthesis*, the "synthesis" being the application of biological principles to the social and sexual customs of both nonhuman animals and human beings. **Sociobiology** became a popular topic for researchers and the public, generating great controversy.

Sociobiologists contend that evolution has bred into each of us a tendency to act in ways that maximize our chances of passing on our genes, and to help our close biological relatives, with whom we share many genes, do the same. In this view, just as nature has selected physical characteristics that have proved adaptive, so it has selected psychological traits and social customs that aid individuals in propagating their genes. Customs that enhance the odds of such transmission survive in the form of kinship bonds, dominance arrangements, taboos against female adultery, and many other aspects of social life.

In addition, sociobiologists believe that because the males and females of most species have faced different kinds of survival and mating problems, the sexes have evolved to differ profoundly in aggressiveness, dominance, and sexual strategies (Symons, 1979; Trivers, 1972). In many species, they argue, it is adaptive for males to compete with other males for access to young and fertile females, and to try to win and then inseminate as many females as possible. The more females a male mates with, the more genes he can pass along. (The human record in this regard was achieved by a man who fathered 899 children [Daly & Wilson, 1983]. What else he did with his time is unknown.) But according to sociobiologists, females need to shop for the best genetic deal, as it were, because they can conceive and bear only a limited number of offspring. Having such a large biological investment in each pregnancy, females cannot afford to make mistakes. Besides, mating with a lot of different males would produce no more offspring than staying with just one. So females try to attach themselves to dominant males who have resources and status and are likely to have "superior" genes.

The result of these two opposite sexual strategies, in this view, is that males generally want sex more often than females do; males are often fickle and promiscuous, whereas females are devoted and faithful; males are drawn to sexual novelty and even rape, whereas females want stability and security; males are relatively undiscriminating in their choice of sexual partners, whereas females are cautious and choosy; and males are competitive and concerned about dominance, whereas females are less so.

Evolutionary psychologists generally agree with these conclusions, but they differ from sociobiologists in some respects. One difference is that sociobiologists often study nonhuman species and argue by analogy, but most evolutionary psychologists consider such analogies to be simplistic and misleading. For example, because male scorpion flies force themselves on females, sociobiologists have drawn an analogy between this behavior and human rape, and have concluded that human rape must have the same evolutionary origins (Thornhill & Palmer, 2000). But this analogy does not bear scrutiny. Human rape has many motives, including, among others, revenge, sadism, and conformity to peer pressure. It is often committed by high-status men who could easily find consenting sexual partners, and all too frequently its victims are children or the elderly, who do not reproduce. In general, therefore, evolutionary psychologists rely less on comparisons with other species than sociobiologists do, focusing instead on commonalities in human mating and dating practices around the world.

Evolutionary psychologists and sociobiologists also disagree on some theoretical matters that are beyond the scope of our discussion here. Nevertheless, both groups emphasize the evolutionary origins of many human sex differences that appear to be universal, or at least very common. In one massive project, 50 scientists studied 10,000 people in 37 cultures located on six continents and five islands (Buss, 1994). Around the world, they found, men are more violent than women and more socially dominant. They are more interested in the youth and beauty of their sexual partners, presumably because youth is associated with fertility (see Figure 7.1). They are more sexually jealous and possessive, presumably because males can never be 100 percent sure that their children are really theirs genetically. They are quicker than women to have sex with partners they don't know well and more inclined toward polygamy and promiscuity, presumably so that their sperm will be distributed as widely as possible. Women, in contrast, tend to emphasize the financial resources or prospects of a potential mate, his status, and his willingness to commit to a relationship. Many studies have reported similar results (Bailey et al., 1994; Buss, 1996; Buunk et al., 1996; Daly & Wilson, 1983; Mealey, 2000; Sprecher, Sullivan, & Hatfield, 1994).

FIGURE 7.1   Preferred Age in a Mate. In most societies, men say they prefer to marry women younger than themselves, whereas women prefer men who are older (Buss, 1995). Evolutionary psychologists attribute these preferences to male concern with a partner's fertility and female concern with a partner's material resources and status. When the man is much older than the woman, people rarely comment, but when the woman is older, people take notice.

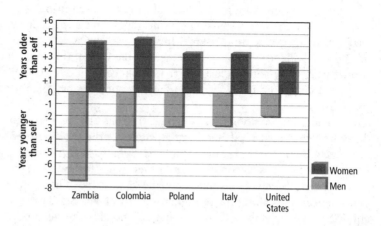

Culture and the "Genetic Leash"

Sociobiological and evolutionary views of sex differences have become enormously popular. Newsmagazines regularly run cover stories about the supposed evolutionary advantages for males of sowing their seeds far and wide and the supposed evolutionary advantages for females of finding a man with a good paycheck.

But critics—including some evolutionary theorists—argue that current evolutionary explanations of infidelity and monogamy are based on simplistic *stereotypes* of gender differences. The actual behavior of humans and other animals often fails to conform to images of sexually promiscuous males and coy, choosy females (Barash & Lipton, 2001; Birkhead, 2001; Fausto-Sterling, 1997; Hrdy, 1994). In species after species—birds, fish, and mammals, including human beings—females are sexually ardent and often have many male partners. The female's sexual behavior does not seem to depend only on the goal of being fertilized by the male: Females have sex when they are not ovulating and even when they are already pregnant. And in many species, from penguins to primates, males do not just mate and run. They stick around, feeding the infants, carrying them on their backs, and protecting them against predators (Hrdy, 1988; Snowdon, 1997).

These findings have sent evolutionary theorists scurrying to figure out the evolutionary benefits of female promiscuity and male nurturance. For example, by having many partners, perhaps a female increases the number of males who will support her offspring. This motive is quite explicit among the Barí people of Venezuela. A man who impregnates a woman is considered the child's primary father. But if she takes a lover during her pregnancy (an approved practice), he is considered a secondary father, and he is expected to supply mother and baby with extra food (Beckerman et al., 1998).

Critics, however, argue that all evolutionary explanations, whether of female fidelity or female promiscuity, are inadequate when applied to human beings, because human sexual behavior is so amazingly varied and changeable. Cultures range from those in which women have many children to those in which they have very few, from those in which men are intimately involved in child rearing to those in which they do nothing at all, from those in which women may have many lovers to those in which women may be killed for having sex outside of marriage (Hatfield & Rapson, 1996). In many places, the chastity of a potential mate is much more important to men than to women; but in other places, it is important to both sexes—or to neither one (see Figure 7.2). Sexual attitudes and practices also vary tremendously within a culture, from extremely traditional to extremely unconventional, as is immediately apparent to anyone surveying the panorama of sexual attitudes and behaviors within the United States and Canada (Laumann et al., 1994; Levine, 2002).

FIGURE 7.2   Attitudes Toward Chastity. In many places, men care more about a partner's chastity than women do, as evolutionary psychologists would predict. But culture has a powerful impact on these attitudes, as this graph shows. Notice that in China, both sexes prefer a partner who has not yet had intercourse, whereas in Sweden, chastity is a nonissue. (From Buss, 1995.)

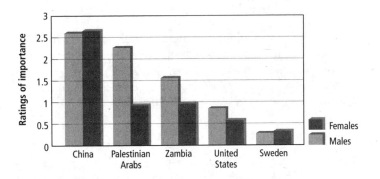

On questionnaires, when people (usually undergraduates) are asked to rank the qualities they most value in a potential mate, sex differences appear, just as evolutionary theory would predict (Kenrick et al., 2001). However, *both* sexes usually rank kindness, intelligence, and understanding over physical qualities or financial status. Plenty of women are not attracted to rich men, nor are all men attracted to stereotypically beautiful women.

Finally, a serious problem with the prevailing evolutionary view of mate selection is that our prehistoric ancestors, unlike the undergraduates in these studies, did not exactly have 5,000 fellow students to choose from. They lived in small bands, and if they were lucky they might get to choose between Urp and Ork, and that's about it; they could not hold out for some knockout or millionaire down the road. Because there wasn't a great range of potential partners to choose from, there would have been no need for the development of the kinds of sexual strategies described by evolutionary theorists (Hazan & Diamond, 2000). Instead, evolution might have instilled in us a tendency to select a mate based on similarity (the person's genes are like our own) and proximity (the person is around a lot). Indeed, similarity and proximity are among the strongest predictors today of the mates people actually choose, whatever they may say on questionnaires.

Debate over these matters can become quite heated because of worries that evolutionary arguments will be used to justify social and political inequalities and even violent behavior. In the past, evolutionary ideas have been used to promote *social Darwinism*, the notion that the wealthy and successful are more "reproductively fit" than other people. Such arguments have also led some people to conclude that men, with less investment in child rearing and more interest in status and dominance, are destined to control business and politics. Edward Wilson (1975) thinks so. "Even with identical education and equal access to all professions [for both sexes]," he wrote, "men are likely to continue to play a disproportionate role in political life, business, and science." This is not a message that people who hope for gender equality welcome!

Ultimately, what evolutionary scientists and their critics are quarreling about is the relative power of biology and culture. In *On Human Nature* (1978), Wilson argued that genes hold culture on a leash. The big question, replied paleontologist Stephen Jay Gould (1987), is how long and tight is that leash? Is it too tight to allow much change, or is it long enough to permit many possible customs? To sociobiologists, the leash is short and tight. To evolutionary psychologists, it is elastic enough to permit culture to modify evolved biological tendencies, although those tendencies can be pretty powerful (Kenrick & Trost, 1993). To critics of both sociobiology and evolutionary psychology, cultural variations mean that no single, genetically determined sexual strategy exists for human beings. What evolution has bestowed on us, they say, is an amazingly flexible brain. Therefore, in matters of sex and love, as in all other human behaviors, the leash is long and flexible.

THE GENETICS OF DIFFERENCE

We have been focusing on the origins of human similarities. We turn now to the second great issue in the nature–nurture debate: the origins of the differences among us. We begin with a critical discussion of what it means to say that a trait is "heritable." Then, to illustrate how behavioral geneticists study differences among people that might be influenced by genes, we will examine in detail a single, complex issue: the genetic contribution to intelligence.

The Meaning of Heritability

Suppose you want to measure flute-playing ability in a large group of music students, so you have some independent raters assign each student a score, from 1 to 20. When you plot the scores, you find that some people are what you might call melodically disadvantaged and should forget about a musical career; others are flute geniuses; and the rest fall somewhere in between. What causes the variation in this group of students? Why are some so musically talented and others so inept? Are these differences primarily genetic, or are they the result of experience and motivation?

To answer such questions, behavioral geneticists compute a statistic called **heritability,** which gives an estimate of the *proportion of the total variance in a trait that is attributable to genetic variation within a group.* Because the heritability of a trait is expressed as a proportion (such as .60, or 60/100), the maximum value it can have is 1.0 (equivalent to "100 percent of the variance"). Height is highly heritable; that is, within a group of equally well-nourished individuals, most of the variation among them will be accounted for by their genetic differences. In contrast, table manners have low heritability because most variation among individuals is accounted for by differences in upbringing. Our guess is that flute-playing ability—and musical ability in general—falls somewhere in the middle. Differences in the ability to correctly perceive musical pitch and melody appear to be highly heritable; some people, it seems, really are born with a "tin ear" (Drayna et al., 2001). Nonetheless, musical training can enhance normal musical ability, and lack of musical training can keep a person with normal ability from tuning in to the nuances of music.

Many people hold completely mistaken ideas about heritability. But as genetic findings pour in, the public will need to understand this concept more than ever. You cannot understand the nature–nurture issue without understanding the following important facts about heritability:

1. *An estimate of heritability applies only to a particular group living in a particular environment.* Heritability may be high in one group and low in another. Suppose that all of the children in Community A are affluent, eat plenty of high-quality food, have kind and attentive parents, and go to the same top-notch schools. Because their environments are similar, any intellectual differences among them will have to be due largely to their genetic differences. In other words, mental ability in this group will be highly heritable. In contrast, the children in Community B are rich, poor, and in between. Some of them have healthy diets; others live on fatty foods and cupcakes. Some attend good schools; others go to inadequate ones. Some have doting parents, and some have unloving and neglectful ones. These children's intellectual differences could be due to their environmental differences, in which case the heritability of intelligence for this group will be low.

2. *Heritability estimates do not apply to individuals, only to variations within a group.* You inherited half your genes from your mother and half from your father, but your *combination* of genes has never been seen before and will never be seen again (unless you have an identical twin). You also have a unique history of family relationships, intellectual training, and life experiences. It is impossible to know just how your genes and your personal history have interacted to produce the person you are today. For example, if you are a great flute player, no one can say whether your ability is mainly a result of inherited

musical talent, living all your life in a family of devoted flute players, a private obsession that you acquired at age 6 when you saw the opera *The Magic Flute*—or a combination of all three. For one person, genes may make a tremendous difference in some aptitude or disposition; for another, the environment may be far more important. Scientists can only study the extent to which differences among people *in general* are explained by their genetic differences.

3. ***Even highly heritable traits can be modified by the environment.*** Although height is highly heritable, malnourished children may not grow to be as tall as they would with sufficient food, and children who eat an extremely nutritious diet may grow up to be taller than anyone thought they could. Hair color is genetically determined, but a trip to a hair stylist can transform you from a brunette to a blond, or vice versa. The same principle applies to psychological traits, although biological determinists sometimes fail to realize this. They argue, for example, that because IQ is highly heritable, IQ and school achievement cannot be boosted much (Herrnstein & Murray, 1994). But even if the first part of the statement is true, the second part does not necessarily follow, as we will see.

Computing Heritability

Scientists have no way to estimate the heritability of a trait or behavior directly, so they must *infer* it by studying people whose degree of genetic similarity is known. You might think that the simplest approach would be to compare blood relatives within families; everyone knows about families that are famous for some talent or trait. But family traits do not tell us much because close relatives usually share environments as well as genes. If Carlo's parents and siblings all love lasagna, that does not mean a taste for lasagna is heritable! The same applies if everyone in Carlo's family has a high IQ, is mentally ill, or is moody.

A better approach is to study adopted children (e.g., Loehlin, Horn, & Willerman, 1996; Plomin & DeFries, 1985). Such children share half their genes with each birth parent, but they grow up in a different environment, apart from their birth parents. On the other hand, they share an environment with their adoptive parents and siblings, but not their genes:

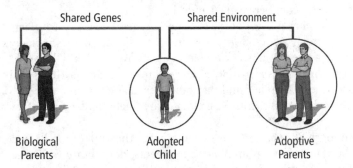

Shared Genes   Shared Environment

Biological Parents   Adopted Child   Adoptive Parents

Researchers can compare correlations between the traits of adopted children and those of their biological and adoptive relatives and can use the results to compute an estimate of heritability.

Another approach is to compare identical twins with fraternal twins. **Identical (monozygotic) twins** develop when a fertilized egg (zygote) divides into two parts that then develop as two separate embryos. Because the twins come from the same fertilized egg, they share all their genes. (Identical twins may be slightly different at birth, however, because of differences in the blood supply to the two fetuses or other chance factors.) In contrast, **fraternal (dizygotic) twins** develop when a woman's ovaries release two eggs instead of one and each egg is fertilized by a different sperm. Fraternal twins are wombmates, but they are no more alike genetically than any other two siblings (they share, on average, only half their genes), and they may be of different sexes.

Behavioral geneticists can estimate the heritability of a trait by comparing groups of same-sex fraternal twins with groups of identical twins. The assumption is that if identical twins are more alike than fraternal twins, then the increased similarity must be due to genetic influences.

Perhaps, however, identical twins are treated differently than fraternal twins. People may treat identical twins, well, identically—or they may go to the other extreme, emphasizing the twins' differences. To avoid these problems, investigators have studied identical twins who were separated early in life and reared apart. (Until recently, adoption policies and attitudes toward births out of wedlock permitted such separations to occur.) In theory, separated identical twins share all their genes but not their environments. Any similarities between them should be primarily genetic and should permit a direct estimate of heritability.

OUR HUMAN DIVERSITY: THE CASE OF INTELLIGENCE

Behavioral–genetics research has transformed our understanding of many aspects of behavior that were once explained solely in psychological terms (Plomin et al., 2001). Sometimes the findings have been reassuring, such as the discovery that overweight is not just a matter of "failed willpower" or "repressed anger" but also involves genetic tendencies. Some findings, such as the discovery that some mental illnesses have a genetic component, have been accepted readily. But other findings have inflamed political passions and upset people. No topic has aroused more controversy than the nature of intelligence.

Genes and Individual Differences

In heritability studies, the usual measure of intellectual functioning is an **intelligence quotient,** or **IQ** score. Scores on an IQ test reflect how a child has performed compared with other children of the same age, or how an adult has performed compared with other adults. The average score for each age group is arbitrarily set at 100. The distribution of scores in the population approximates a normal bell-shaped curve, with scores near the average (mean) most common and very high or very low scores rare. Two-thirds of all test-takers score between 85 and 115.

Most psychologists believe that IQ tests measure a general quality that affects all aspects of mental ability, but the tests have many critics. Some argue that intelligence comes in many varieties, more than are captured by a single score. Others argue that IQ tests are culturally biased, tapping mostly those abilities that depend on experiences in a middle-class environment and favoring white people over people of other ethnicities. For now, keep in mind that most heritability estimates apply only to those mental skills that affect IQ test scores and that these estimates are likely to be more valid for some groups than for others.

Despite these important qualifications, it is clear that the kind of intelligence that produces high IQ scores is highly heritable. For children and adolescents, heritability estimates average around .50; that is, about half of the variance in IQ scores is explainable by genetic differences (Chipuer, Rovine, & Plomin, 1990; Devlin, Daniels, & Roeder, 1997; Plomin, 1989). For adults, the estimates are higher—in the .60 to .80 range (Bouchard, 1995; McClearn et al., 1997; McGue et al., 1993).

In studies of twins, the scores of identical twins are always much more highly correlated than those of fraternal twins, a difference that reflects the influence of genes. In fact, the scores of identical twins reared *apart* are more highly correlated than those of fraternal twins reared *together*, as you can see in Figure 7.3. In adoption studies, the scores of adopted children are more highly correlated with those of their birth parents than with those of their biologically unrelated adoptive parents; the higher the birth parents' scores, the higher the child's score is likely to be. As adopted children grow into adolescence, the correlation between their IQ scores and those of their biologically unrelated

FIGURE 7.3 Correlations in Siblings' IQ Scores. The IQ scores of identical twins are highly correlated, even when they are reared apart. The figures represented in this graph are based on average correlations across many studies (Bouchard & McGue, 1981).

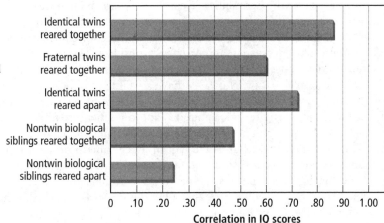

family members diminishes; and in adulthood, the correlation falls to *zero* (Bouchard, 1997b; Scarr, 1993; Scarr & Weinberg, 1994).

Just a few years ago, a research team led by psychologist Robert Plomin identified the first marker for a gene that might influence performance on IQ tests (Chorney et al., 1998). DNA analysis showed that one form of the gene occurred twice as often in groups of children with very high IQ scores as in groups of children with average scores. But the gene accounted for less than 2 percent of the variance among individuals, which translates to about 4 IQ points.

Since then, a few other genes that may influence cognitive ability have been identified (Fisher et al., 1999; Hill et al., 1999). Each of these genes—if confirmed—is likely to contribute just a tiny piece to the puzzle of genetic variation. Special methods, beyond the scope of this book, are now being used in research with animals and humans to try to track down these and other genes that might be involved in intellectual performance, mental disorders, and personality traits, and to figure out just how those genes might produce their effects (Plomin & Crabbe, 2000).

Overall, the research on the heritability of IQ-test performance is pretty impressive. But remember: If heredity accounts for only part of why people differ in their IQ scores, then the environment (and random errors in measurement) must account for the rest.

The Question of Group Differences

If genes influence individual differences in intelligence, do they also help account for differences between groups, as many people assume? Unfortunately, the history of this issue has been marred by ethnic, class, and gender prejudice. As Stephen Jay Gould (1996) noted, genetic research has often been bent to support the belief that some groups are destined by "the harsh dictates of nature" to be subordinate to others. Because this issue has enormous political and social importance, we are going to examine it closely.

Most of the focus has been on black–white differences in IQ, because African-American children score, on average, some 10 to 15 points lower than do white children. (We are talking about *averages;* the distributions of scores for black children and white children overlap considerably.) A few psychologists have proposed a genetic explanation of this difference (Jensen, 1969, 1981; Rushton, 1988). In their much-discussed book *The Bell Curve: Intelligence and Class Structure in American Life* (1994), the late psychologist Richard Herrnstein and conservative political theorist Charles Murray cited heritability studies to imply that the gap in IQ scores between the average white and the average black child can never be closed.

You can see why heritability research provokes much more controversy than does research on, say, the sex lives of sea lions. Racists have used theories of genetic differences between groups to justify their own hatreds, and politicians have used them to argue for cuts in programs that would benefit blacks and other minorities. Herrnstein and Murray themselves concluded that there was little point in spending money trying to raise the IQs of low-scoring children.

Genetic explanations, however, have a fatal flaw: They use heritability estimates based mainly on white samples to estimate the role of heredity in *group* differences, a procedure that is not valid. This problem sounds pretty technical, but it is not too difficult to understand, so stay with us.

Consider, first, not people but tomatoes. Suppose you have a bag of tomato seeds that vary genetically; all things being equal, some will produce tomatoes that are puny and tasteless, and some will produce tomatoes that are plump and delicious. Now you take a bunch of these seeds in your left hand and another bunch from the same bag in your right hand. Though one seed differs genetically from another, there is no *average* difference between the seeds in your left hand and those in your right. You plant the left hand's seeds in pot A, with some enriched soil that you have doctored with nitrogen and other nutrients, and you plant the right hand's seeds in pot B, with miserable, depleted soil from which you have extracted nutrients. You sing to pot A and put it in the sun; you ignore pot B and leave it in a dark corner.

When the tomato plants grow, they will vary *within* each pot in terms of height, the number of tomatoes produced, and the size of the tomatoes, purely because of genetic differences. But there will also be an average difference between the plants in pot A and those in pot B: The plants in pot A will be healthier and bear more tomatoes. This difference *between* pots is due entirely to the different soils and the care that has been given to them—even though the heritability of the *within*-pot differences is 100 percent (Lewontin, 1970). The same is true for real plants, by the way; if you take identical, cloned plants and grow them at different elevations, they will develop differently (Lewontin, 2001).

The same principle applies to people as to tomatoes. Although intellectual differences *within* groups are at least partly genetic in origin, that does not mean differences *between* groups are genetic. Blacks and whites do not grow up, on the average, in the same "pots" (environments). Because of a long legacy of racial discrimination and de facto segregation, black children, as well as Latino and other minority children, often receive far fewer nutrients—literally, in terms of food, and figuratively, in terms of education, encouragement by society, and intellectual opportunities. Ethnic groups also differ in countless cultural ways that affect their performance on IQ tests. And negative stereotypes about ethnic groups may cause members of these groups to doubt their own abilities, become anxious and self-conscious, and perform more poorly than they otherwise would on tests.

Doing good research on the origins of group differences in IQ is extremely difficult in the United States, where racism affects the lives of even affluent, successful African-Americans (Cose, 1994; Parker, 1997; Staples, 1994). However, the handful of studies that have overcome past methodological problems fail to reveal any genetic differences between blacks and whites in whatever it is that IQ tests measure. For example, one study found that children fathered by black and white American soldiers in Germany after World War II and reared in similar German communities by similar families did not differ significantly in IQ (Eyferth, 1961). Another showed that degree of African ancestry (which can be roughly estimated from skin color, blood analysis, and genealogy) is not related to measured intelligence, as a genetic theory of black–white differences would predict (Scarr et al., 1977). And white and black infants do equally well on a test that measures their preference for novel stimuli, a predictor of later IQ scores (Fagan, 1992).

An intelligent reading of the research on intelligence, therefore, does not direct us to conclude that differences among cultural, ethnic, or national groups are permanent, genetically determined, or signs of any group's innate superiority. On the contrary, the research suggests that we should make sure that all children grow up in the best possible soil, with room for the smartest and the slowest to find a place in the sun.

The Environment and Intelligence

By now you may be wondering what kinds of experiences hinder intellectual development and what kinds of environmental "nutrients" promote it. Here are some of the influences associated with reduced mental ability:

- *Poor prenatal care.* If a pregnant woman is malnourished, contracts infections, takes certain drugs, smokes, drinks excessively, or is heavily exposed to pollutants, her child is at risk of having learning disabilities and a lower IQ.

- *Malnutrition.* The average IQ gap between severely malnourished and well-nourished children can be as high as 20 points (Stoch & Smythe, 1963; Winick, Meyer, & Harris, 1975).

- *Exposure to toxins.* Lead, for example, can damage the nervous system, producing attention problems, lower IQ scores, and poorer school achievement (Needleman et al., 1996). Many children in the United States are exposed to dangerous levels of lead from dust, contaminated soil, lead paint, and old lead pipes, and the concentration of lead in black children's blood is 50 percent higher than in white children's (Lanphear et al., 2002).

- *Stressful family circumstances.* Factors that predict reduced intellectual competence include a father who does not live with the family, a mother with a history of mental illness, limited parental work skills, and a history of stressful events during the child's early life (Sameroff et al., 1987). On average, each risk factor reduces a child's IQ score by 4 points. Children with seven risk factors score more than *30 points lower* than those with no risk factors.

In contrast, a healthy and stimulating environment can raise mental performance, sometimes dramatically (Guralnick, 1997; Ramey & Ramey, 1998). In one longitudinal study called the Abecedarian Project, inner-city children who got lots of mental enrichment at home and in child care or school, starting in infancy, had much better school achievement than did children in a control group (Campbell & Ramey, 1995).

Perhaps the best evidence for the importance of environmental influences on intelligence is the fact that IQ scores in developed countries have been climbing steadily for at least three generations (Flynn, 1987, 1999) (see Figure 7.4). Genes in these countries cannot possibly have changed enough to account for this rise in scores. The causes are still being debated, but most cognitive psychologists believe they include improvements in education, an increasing emphasis on the skills required by technology, and better nutrition (Neisser, 1998).

FIGURE 7.4   Climbing IQ Scores. Raw scores on IQ tests have been rising in developed countries for many decades, at a rate much too steep to be accounted for by genetic changes. Because test norms are periodically readjusted to set the average score at 100, most people are unaware of the increase. On this graph, average scores are calibrated according to 1989 norms. As you can see, performance was much lower in 1918 than in 1989. (Adapted from Horgan, 1995.)

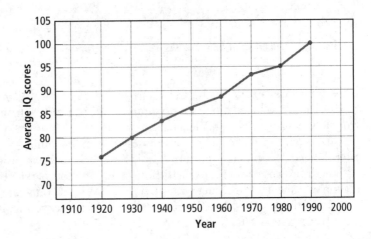

We see, then, that although heredity may provide the range of a child's intellectual potential—a Homer Simpson can never become an Einstein—many other factors affect where in that range the child will fall.

IN PRAISE OF HUMAN VARIATION

This chapter opened with two questions: What makes us alike as human beings, and why do we differ? Today, a prevalent but greatly oversimplified answer is: It's all in our genes. Genes, it's claimed, make men sexually adventurous and women sexually choosy. You either "have" a gene for smartness, musical ability, math genius, friendliness, or any other trait, or you don't. When researchers announced that they might have found a gene involved in mouse intelligence, *Time* magazine lost no time in putting the news on its cover with the headline "The IQ Gene?" (September 13, 1999). In this climate, many people who believe in the importance of learning, opportunities, and experience feel that they must take an equally oversimplified position: Genes don't matter at all.

As we have seen, however, heredity and environment always interact to produce the unique mixture of qualities that make up a human being. Moreover, once genetic and environmental influences become a part of us, they blend and become indistinguishable. We can no more speak of genes, or of the environment, "causing" personality or intelligence than we can speak of butter, sugar, or flour individually causing the taste of a cake (Lewontin, Rose, & Kamin, 1984). Many people do speak that way, however, out of a desire to make things clearer than they actually are, and sometimes to justify prejudices about ethnicity, gender, or class.

An unstated assumption in many debates about nature and nurture is that the world would be a better place if certain kinds of genes prevailed. This assumption overlooks the fact that nature loves genetic diversity, not similarity. The ability of any species to survive depends on such diversity. If every penguin, porpoise, or person had exactly the same genetic strengths and weaknesses, these species could not survive changes in the environment; a new virus, or a change in weather, would wipe out the entire group. With diversity, at least some penguins, porpoises, or people have a good chance of making it.

When we see the world through an evolutionary lens, we realize that psychological diversity is adaptive, too. Each of us has something valuable to contribute, whether it is artistic talent, academic ability, creativity, social skill, athletic prowess, a sense of humor, mechanical aptitude, practical wisdom, a social conscience, or the energy to get things done. In our complicated, fast-moving world, all of these qualities are needed. The challenge, for any society, is to promote the potential of each of its members.

NEURONS, HORMONES, AND THE BRAIN

It's amazing to think that the body feeds the brain sugar and amino acids, and what comes out is poetry and pirouettes.

—ROBERT COLLINS

After suffering damage to the front part of the right side of the brain, a stroke patient in Zurich, Switzerland, developed a puzzling symptom. Although the left side of his body was weak and he had trouble seeing objects in his left field of vision, what concerned him most was the blandness of the hospital food. In fact, he had become obsessed with fine dining—a phenomenon his neuropsychologist later dubbed "gourmand syndrome." In his diary, the patient wrote, "It is time for . . . a good sausage with hash browns or some spaghetti Bolognese, or risotto and a breaded cutlet, nicely decorated, or a scallop of game in cream sauce with spaetzle. . . . What a connoisseur I am, and now I am dried-up here, just like in the desert. Where is the next oasis?" After recovering, he quit his job as a political journalist and became a food columnist (Regard & Landis, 1997).

Another brain-injured man, who had been in a nearly fatal car crash in Arizona, gradually emerged from a five-month coma. With great effort, he relearned to speak, read, work at his computer, and get around in a wheelchair. Before the accident, he had managed to hold down a job as a special-education teacher while working on a doctorate. Afterwards, however, his behavior became increasingly erratic and strange. One morning he telephoned the police to report that he had lost a cereal bowl (Winslade, 1998).

A former English teacher and poet had a tumor in a part of the brain that processes the expressive qualities of speech, such as rhythm and intonation. Although she could understand words and sentences perfectly well, she could not tell whether a speaker was indignant, cheerful, or dejected unless she carefully analyzed the person's facial expressions and gestures. She was deaf to the emotional nuances of speech, the variations of tone and cadence that can move a listener to laughter, tears, or outrage. But she had one skill that many people lack. Because she could not be swayed by verbal theatrics or tone of voice, she could easily spot a liar (Sacks, 1985).

These fascinating cases, and thousands like them, teach us that the modest-looking 3-pound organ inside our skulls is the bedrock of all behavior and mental activity. When injury or disease affects the brain's functioning, life is inevitably changed, either physically or mentally. Sometimes the changes are subtle and even benign, as in the case of "gourmand syndrome." All too often, though, they are not.

Neuropsychologists, along with neuroscientists from other disciplines, study the brain and the rest of the nervous system in hopes of gaining a better understanding of human and animal behavior. In this chapter, we will examine the structure of the brain and the rest of the nervous system as background for our later discussions of these and other topics.

At this moment, your own brain, assisted by other parts of your nervous system, is busily taking in these words. Whether you are excited, curious, or bored, your brain is registering some sort of emotional reaction. As you continue reading, your brain will (we hope) store away much of the information in this chapter. Later on, your brain may enable you to smell a flower, climb the stairs, greet a friend, solve a personal problem, or chuckle at a joke. But the brain's most startling accomplishment is its knowledge that it is doing all these things. This self-awareness makes brain research different from the study of anything else in the universe. Scientists must use the cells, biochemistry, and circuitry of their own brains to understand the cells, biochemistry, and circuitry of brains in general.

Because the brain is the site of consciousness, people disagree about what language to use in discussing it. If we say that your brain stores events or registers emotions, we imply a separate "you" that is "using" that brain. But if we leave "you" out of the picture and just say the brain does these things, we risk implying that brain mechanisms alone explain behavior, which is untrue; we lose sight of the person—and the motives, choices, and personality traits that shape behavior. No one has ever been able to resolve this dilemma.

William Shakespeare called the brain "the soul's frail dwelling house." Actually, this miraculous organ is more like the main room in a house filled with many alcoves and passageways—the "house" being the nervous system as a whole. Before we can understand the windows, walls, and furniture of this house, we need to become acquainted with the overall floor plan. It's a pretty technical plan, which means that you will be learning many new terms, but you will need to know these terms in order to understand how biological psychologists go about explaining psychological topics.

THE NERVOUS SYSTEM: A BASIC BLUEPRINT

The function of a nervous system is to gather and process information, produce responses to stimuli, and coordinate the workings of different cells. Even the lowly jellyfish and the humble worm have the beginnings of such a system. In very simple organisms that do little more than move, eat, and eliminate wastes, the "system" may be no more than one or two nerve cells. In human beings, who do such complex things as dance, cook, and take psychology courses, the nervous system contains billions of cells. Scientists divide this intricate network into two main parts: the central nervous system and the peripheral (outlying) nervous system.

The Central Nervous System

The **central nervous system (CNS)** receives, processes, interprets, and stores incoming sensory information—information about tastes, sounds, smells, color, pressure on the skin, the state of internal organs, and so forth. It also sends out messages destined for muscles, glands, and internal organs. The CNS is usually conceptualized as having two components: the brain, which we will consider in detail later, and the **spinal cord.** The spinal cord is actually an extension of the brain. It runs from the base of the brain down the center of the back, protected by a column of bones (the spinal column), and it acts as a bridge between the brain and the parts of the body below the neck.

The spinal cord produces some behaviors on its own, without any help from the brain. These *spinal reflexes* are automatic, requiring no conscious effort. For example, if you accidentally touch a hot iron, you will immediately pull your hand away, even before your brain has had a chance to register what has happened. Nerve impulses bring a message to the spinal cord (hot!), and the spinal cord immediately sends out a command via other nerve impulses, telling muscles in your arm to contract and to pull your hand away from the iron. (Reflexes above the neck, such as sneezing and blinking, involve the lower part of the brain, rather than the spinal cord.)

The neural circuits underlying many spinal reflexes are linked to neural pathways that run up and down the spinal cord, to and from the brain. Because of these connections, reflexes can sometimes be influenced by thoughts and emotions. An example is erection in men, a spinal reflex that can be inhibited by anxiety or distracting thoughts, and initiated by erotic thoughts. Some reflexes can be brought under conscious control. If you concentrate, you may be able to keep your knee from jerking when it is tapped, as it normally would. Similarly, most men can learn to voluntarily delay ejaculation, another spinal reflex.

The Peripheral Nervous System

The **peripheral nervous system (PNS)** handles the central nervous system's input and output. It contains all portions of the nervous system outside the brain and spinal cord, right down to the nerves in the tips of the fingers and toes. If your brain could not collect information about the world by means of a peripheral nervous system, it would be like a radio without a receiver. In the peripheral nervous system, *sensory nerves* carry messages from special receptors in the skin, muscles, and other internal and external sense organs to the spinal cord, which sends them along to the brain. These nerves put us in touch with both the outside world and the activities of our own bodies. *Motor nerves* carry orders from the central nervous system to muscles, glands, and internal organs. They enable us to move, and they cause glands to contract and to secrete substances, including chemical messengers called *hormones.*

Scientists further divide the peripheral nervous system into two parts: the somatic (bodily) nervous system and the autonomic (self-governing) nervous system. The **somatic nervous system,** sometimes called the *skeletal nervous system,* consists of nerves that are connected to sensory receptors—cells that enable you to sense the world—and also to the skeletal muscles that permit voluntary action. When you feel a bug on your arm, or when you turn off a light or write your name, your somatic system is active. The **autonomic nervous system** regulates the functioning of blood vessels, glands, and internal (visceral) organs such as the bladder, stomach, and heart. When you see someone you have a crush on, and your heart pounds, your hands get sweaty, and your cheeks feel hot, you can blame your autonomic nervous system.

The autonomic nervous system is itself divided into two parts: the **sympathetic nervous system** and the **parasympathetic nervous system.** These two parts work together, but in opposing ways, to adjust the body to changing circumstances (see Figure 7.5). The sympathetic system acts like the accelerator of a car, mobilizing the body for action and an output of energy. It makes you blush, sweat, and breathe more deeply, and it pushes up your heart rate and blood pressure. When you are in a situation that requires you to fight, flee, or cope, the sympathetic nervous system whirls into action.

FIGURE 7.5 The Autonomic Nervous System. In general, the sympathetic division of the autonomic nervous system prepares the body to expend energy, and the parasympathetic division restores and conserves energy. Sympathetic nerve fibers exit from areas of the spinal cord shown in red in this illustration; parasympathetic fibers exit from the base of the brain and from spinal cord areas shown in green.

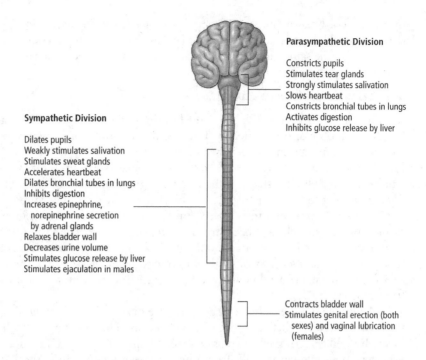

Parasympathetic Division

Constricts pupils
Stimulates tear glands
Strongly stimulates salivation
Slows heartbeat
Constricts bronchial tubes in lungs
Activates digestion
Inhibits glucose release by liver

Sympathetic Division

Dilates pupils
Weakly stimulates salivation
Stimulates sweat glands
Accelerates heartbeat
Dilates bronchial tubes in lungs
Inhibits digestion
Increases epinephrine,
  norepinephrine secretion
  by adrenal glands
Relaxes bladder wall
Decreases urine volume
Stimulates glucose release by liver
Stimulates ejaculation in males

Contracts bladder wall
Stimulates genital erection (both
  sexes) and vaginal lubrication
  (females)

The parasympathetic system is more like a brake: It does not stop the body, but it does tend to slow things down or keep them running smoothly. It enables the body to conserve and store energy. If you have to jump out of the way of a speeding motorcyclist, sympathetic nerves increase your heart rate. Afterward, parasympathetic nerves slow it down again and keep its rhythm regular.

COMMUNICATION IN THE NERVOUS SYSTEM

The blueprint we just described provides only a general idea of the nervous system's structure. Now let's turn to the details.

The nervous system is made up in part of **neurons,** or *nerve cells.* Neurons are the brain's communication specialists, transmitting information to, from, and within the central nervous system. They are held in place by **glia,** or *glial cells* (from the Greek for "glue"), which make up 90 percent of the brain's cells.

For a long time, people thought that glial cells merely provided scaffolding for the more important and exciting neurons. We now know, however, that glial cells have many vital functions: They provide the neurons with nutrients, insulate them, protect the brain from toxic agents, and remove cellular debris when neurons die. Glial cells also communicate chemically with each other and with neurons, and without them, neurons probably could not function effectively (Gallo & Chittajallu, 2001; Netting, 2001). For example, one kind of glial cell, shaped like a star, appears to give neurons the go-ahead to construct and maintain connections called *synapses* and to start "talking" to each other (Ullian et al., 2001). Without glial cells, then, neurons could not do their job. In coming years, we will be learning a great deal more about the still poorly understood role of glial cells in learning, memory, and other processes.

At present, however, much more is known about neurons. Although often called the building blocks of the nervous system, in structure neurons are more like snowflakes than blocks, exquisitely delicate and differing from one another greatly in size and shape. In the giraffe, a neuron that runs from the spinal cord down the animal's hind leg may be 9 feet long! In the human brain, neurons are microscopic. No one is sure how many neurons the human brain contains, but a typical estimate is 100 billion, about the same number as there are stars in our galaxy—and some estimates go much higher.

The Structure of the Neuron

As you can see in Figure 7.6, a neuron has three main parts: *dendrites*, a *cell body*, and an *axon*. The **dendrites** look like the branches of a tree; indeed, the word *dendrite* means "little tree" in Greek. Dendrites act like antennas, receiving messages from as many as 10,000 other nerve cells and transmitting these messages toward the cell body. They also do some preliminary processing of those messages. The **cell body,** which is shaped roughly like a sphere or a pyramid, contains the biochemical machinery for keeping the neuron alive. It also plays the key role in determining whether the neuron should "fire"—that is, transmit a message to other neurons—depending on inputs from other neurons. The **axon** (from the Greek for "axle") transmits messages away from the cell body to other neurons or to muscle or gland cells. Axons commonly divide at the end into branches, called *axon terminals*. In adult human beings, axons vary from only 4 thousandths of an inch to a few feet in length. Dendrites and axons give each neuron a double role: As one researcher put it, a neuron is first a catcher, then a batter (Gazzaniga, 1988).

Many axons, especially the larger ones, are insulated by a surrounding layer of fatty material called the **myelin sheath,** which is derived from glial cells. This covering is divided into segments that make it look a little like a string of link sausages (see Figure 7.6 again). One purpose of the myelin sheath is to prevent signals in adjacent cells from interfering with each other. Another, as we will see shortly, is to speed up the conduction of neural impulses. In individuals with multiple sclerosis, loss of myelin causes erratic nerve signals, leading to loss of sensation, weakness or paralysis, lack of coordination, or vision problems.

In the peripheral nervous system, the fibers of individual neurons (axons and sometimes dendrites) are collected together in bundles called **nerves,** rather like the lines in a telephone cable. The human body has 43 pairs of peripheral nerves; one nerve from each pair is on the left side of the body, and the other is on the right. Most of these nerves enter or leave the spinal cord, but 12 pairs in the head, the *cranial nerves,* connect directly to the brain.

FIGURE 7.6 The Structure of a Neuron. Incoming neural impulses are received by the dendrites of a neuron and are transmitted to the cell body. Outgoing signals pass along the axon to terminal branches.

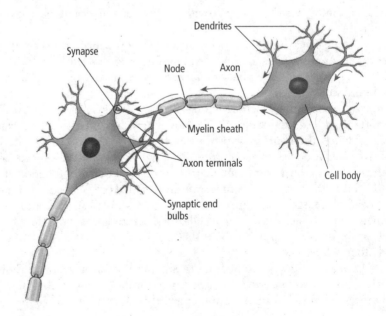

Neurons in the News

Until recently, neuroscientists assumed that if neurons in the central nervous system were injured or damaged, they could never regenerate (grow back). But then the conventional wisdom got turned upside down. Animal studies showed that severed axons in the spinal cord *can* regrow if you treat them with certain nervous-system chemicals (Schnell & Schwab, 1990). Researchers are now working to fine-tune this process, and are hopeful that regenerated axons will someday enable people with spinal-cord injuries to use their limbs again.

Another entrenched assumption also recently bit the dust. Scientists used to think that in mammals no new CNS cells were produced after infancy. This assumption was accepted as dogma throughout most of the twentieth century, despite evidence challenging it (Gross, 2000). But then Canadian neuroscientists, working with mice, immersed immature cells from the animal's brains in a growth-promoting protein and showed conclusively that these cells could give birth to new neurons, in a process called **neurogenesis.** What astonished the scientists even more, the new neurons then continued to divide and multiply (Reynolds & Weiss, 1992). One of the researchers, Samuel Weiss, said that this result "challenged everything I had read; everything I had learned when I was a student" (quoted in Barinaga, 1992).

Since then, scientists have discovered that the human brain and other body organs also contain such cells, which are now usually referred to as **stem cells,** or sometimes *precursor cells.* These, too, give rise to new neurons when treated in the laboratory. And stem cells involved in learning and memory seem to divide and mature throughout adulthood—a discovery of tremendous promise for human well-being. The evidence comes primarily from studies of rodents and monkeys, but also from a small autopsy study of five elderly people (Erikkson, 1998; Gage et al., 1998; Gould et al., 1998; Gould, Reeves, et al., 1999). Animal studies suggest that we have some control over the generation of stem cells, because physical and mental exercise promote the production and survival of new cells (Gould, Beylin, et al., 1999; Kempermann, Brandon, & Gage, 1998; van Praag, Kempermann, & Gage, 1999). One of the researchers, psychologist Elizabeth Gould, commented, "It is a classic case of 'use it or lose it'" (quoted in the *Los Angeles Times*, February 23, 1999). On the other hand, stress can inhibit the production of new cells (Gould et al., 1998), and nicotine can kill them (Berger, Gage, & Vijayarqhavan, 1998).

Stem-cell research is one of the hottest areas in biology and neuroscience, and also one of the most hotly debated. In the United States, federal funding for basic stem-cell research has faced strong resistance by antiabortion activists. The reason: Scientists prefer working with cells from aborted fetuses and from embryos that are a few days old, which consist of just a few cells. Embryonic stem cells, which are usually taken from "extra" embryos about to be discarded by fertility clinics, are especially useful because they can differentiate into any type of cell, from neurons to kidney cells, whereas those from adults are far more limited and are also harder to keep alive.

Currently, American researchers who rely on federal funding must get their embryonic cells from only a few, already established sources. But scientists and patient-advocacy groups feel it is important for this research to continue and expand, because transplanted stem cells may eventually help people recover from damage or disease in the brain and spinal cord, as well as other parts of the body. In the meantime, scientists are making progress in prodding stem cells taken from adult organs, such as bone marrow and skin, to transform themselves into brain cells (Brazelton et al., 2000; Toma et al., 2001; Woodbury et al., 2000). One team working with rats has reported positive results using umbilical cord cells (Sanchez-Ramos et al., 2001). Another team has even grown living cells from precursor cells taken from the brains of human cadavers (Palmer et al., 2001)! It is not yet clear, however, whether such cells will be usable in therapeutic applications.

Every year brings more incredible findings about neurons, findings that only a short time ago would have seemed like science fiction. A long road lies ahead, and many daunting technical hurdles remain to be overcome before these findings yield practical benefits. Eventually, however, new treatments for medical and psychological disorders may be among the most stunning contributions of this line of basic biological research.

How Neurons Communicate

Neurons do not directly touch each other, end to end. Instead, they are separated by a minuscule space called the *synaptic cleft*, where the axon terminal of one neuron nearly touches a dendrite or the cell body of another. The entire site—the axon terminal, the cleft, and the covering membrane of the receiving dendrite or cell body—is called a **synapse.** Because a neuron's axon may have hundreds or even thousands of terminals, a single neuron may have synaptic connections with a great many others. As a result, the number of communication links in the nervous system runs into the trillions or perhaps even the quadrillions.

When we are born, most of these synapses have not yet formed, but during infancy new synapses proliferate at a great rate. Throughout life, axons and dendrites continue to grow, and tiny projections on dendrites, called *spines*, increase in size and number, producing more complex connections among the brain's nerve cells. Just as new learning and stimulating environments promote the production of new neurons, they also produce the greatest increases in synaptic complexity (Diamond, 1993; Greenough & Anderson, 1991; Greenough & Black, 1992; Rosenzweig, 1984). Throughout life, too, unused synaptic connections are "pruned away" as cells or their branches die and are not replaced. Thus, the brain's circuits are continually changing in response to information, challenges, and changes in the environment.

This remarkable *plasticity* (flexibility) may help explain why people with brain damage sometimes experience amazing recoveries—why individuals who cannot recall simple words after a stroke may be speaking normally within a matter of months, and why patients who cannot move an arm after a head injury may regain full use of it after physical therapy. Their brains have rewired themselves to adapt to the damage (Liepert et al., 2000)!

Neurons speak to one another, or in some cases to muscles or glands, in an electrical and chemical language. When a nerve cell is stimulated, a change in electrical potential occurs between the inside and the outside of the cell. The physics of this process involves the sudden, momentary inflow of positively charged sodium ions across the cell's membrane, followed by the outflow of positively charged potassium ions. The result is a brief change in electrical voltage, called an **action potential,** which produces an electrical current or impulse.

If an axon is unmyelinated, the action potential at each point in the axon gives rise to a new action potential at the next point; thus, the action potential travels down the axon somewhat as fire travels along the fuse of a firecracker. But in myelinated axons, the process is a little different. Conduction of a neural impulse beneath the sheath is impossible, in part because sodium and potassium ions cannot cross the cell's membrane except at the breaks (nodes) between the myelin's "sausages." Instead, the action potential "hops" from one node to the next. (More specifically, positively charged ions flow down the axon at a very fast rate, causing regeneration of the action potential at each node.) This arrangement allows the impulse to travel faster than it could if the action potential had to be regenerated at every point along the axon. Nerve impulses travel more slowly in babies than in older children and adults because when babies are born, the myelin sheaths on their axons are not yet fully developed.

When a neural impulse reaches the axon terminal's buttonlike tip, it must get its message across the synaptic cleft to another cell. At this point, *synaptic vesicles*, tiny sacs in the tip of the axon terminal, open and release a few thousand molecules of a chemical substance called a **neurotransmitter.** Like sailors carrying a message from one island to another, these molecules then diffuse across the synaptic cleft.

When they reach the other side, the neurotransmitter molecules bind briefly with *receptor sites*, special molecules in the membrane of the receiving neuron's dendrites (or sometimes cell body), fitting these sites much as a key fits a lock. Changes occur in the receiving neuron's membrane, and the ultimate effect is either *excitatory* (a voltage shift in a positive direction) or *inhibitory* (a voltage shift in a negative direction), depending on which receptor sites have been activated. If the effect is excitatory, the probability that the receiving neuron will fire increases; if it is inhibitory, the probability decreases.

Inhibition in the nervous system is extremely important. Without it, we could not sleep or coordinate our movements. Excitation of the nervous system would be overwhelming, producing convulsions.

What any given neuron does at any given moment depends on the net effect of all the messages being received from other neurons. Only when the cell's voltage reaches a certain threshold will it fire. Thousands of messages, both excitatory and inhibitory, may be coming into the cell. The receiving neuron must essentially average them, but how it does this, and how it "decides" whether to fire, is still not well understood. The ultimate neural message in the brain depends on the rate at which individual neurons are firing, how many are firing, what types of neurons are firing, where the neurons are located, and the degree of synchrony among different neurons. It does *not* depend on how strongly the individual neurons are firing, however, because a neuron always either fires or it doesn't. Like the turning on of a light switch, the firing of a neuron is an *all-or-none* event.

Chemical Messengers in the Nervous System

The nervous system "house" would remain forever dark and lifeless without chemical couriers such as the neurotransmitters. Let's look more closely now at these substances, and at two other types of chemical messengers: endorphins and hormones.

Neurotransmitters: Versatile Couriers. As we have seen, neurotransmitters make it possible for one neuron to excite or inhibit another. Neurotransmitters exist not only in the brain, but also in the spinal cord, the peripheral nerves, and certain glands. Through their effects on specific nerve circuits, these substances can affect mood, memory, and well-being. The nature of the effect depends on the level of the neurotransmitter, its location, and the type of receptor it binds with. Hundreds of substances are known or suspected to be neurotransmitters, and the number keeps growing. Here are a few of the better-understood neurotransmitters and some of their known or suspected effects:

- *Serotonin* affects neurons involved in sleep, appetite, sensory perception, temperature regulation, pain suppression, and mood.
- *Dopamine* affects neurons involved in voluntary movement, learning, memory, emotion, and, possibly, response to novelty.
- *Acetylcholine* affects neurons involved in muscle action, cognitive functioning, memory, and emotion.
- *Norepinephrine* affects neurons involved in increased heart rate and the slowing of intestinal activity during stress, and neurons involved in learning, mem-ory, dreaming, waking from sleep, and emotion.
- *GABA (gamma-aminobutyric acid)* functions as the major inhibitory neurotransmitter in the brain.
- *Glutamate* functions as the major excitatory neurotransmitter in the brain. It is released by about 90 percent of the brain's neurons during excitation. Star-shaped glial cells then "mop up" the excess to prevent overstimulation.

Harmful effects can occur when neurotransmitter levels are too high or too low. Low levels of serotonin and norepinephrine have been associated with severe depression. Abnormal GABA levels have been implicated in sleep and eating disorders and in convulsive disorders, including epilepsy (Bekenstein & Lothman, 1993). People with Alzheimer's disease—a devastating condition that leads to memory loss, personality changes, and eventual disintegration of all physical and mental abilities—lose brain cells responsible for producing acetylcholine, and this deficit may help account for their memory problems. A loss of cells that produce dopamine is responsible for the tremors, rigidity, and weakness that characterize Parkinson's disease. In multiple sclerosis, immune cells produce an overabundance of glutamate, which damages or kills the glial cells that normally make myelin (Werner, Pitt, & Raine, 2001).

We want to warn you, however, that pinning down the relationship between neurotransmitter abnormalities and behavioral or physical abnormalities is extremely tricky. Each neurotransmitter plays multiple roles, and the functions of different substances often overlap. Further, it is always possible that something about a disorder leads to abnormal neurotransmitter levels, instead of the other way around. Although drugs that boost or decrease levels of particular neurotransmitters are sometimes effective in treating disorders, that does not necessarily mean that abnormal neurotransmitter levels are *causing* the disorders. After all, aspirin can relieve a headache, but headaches are not caused by a lack of aspirin!

Many of us regularly ingest things that affect our own neurotransmitters. For example, most recreational drugs produce their effects by blocking or enhancing the actions of neurotransmitters. So do some herbal remedies. St. John's wort, which many people take for depression, prevents the cells that release serotonin from reabsorbing excess molecules that have remained in the synaptic cleft; as a result, serotonin levels rise. Many people do not realize that such remedies, because they affect the nervous system's biochemistry, can interact with other medications and can be harmful in high doses. Even ordinary foods can influence the availability of neurotransmitters in the brain.

Endorphins: The Brain's Natural Opiates. Another intriguing group of chemical messengers is known collectively as *endogenous opioid peptides,* or more popularly as **endorphins.** Endorphins have effects similar to those of natural opiates; that is, they reduce pain and promote pleasure. They are also thought to play a role in appetite, sexual activity, blood pressure, mood, learning, and memory. Some endorphins function as neurotransmitters, but most act primarily by altering the effects of neurotransmitters—for example, by limiting or prolonging those effects.

Endorphins were identified in the early 1970s. Candace Pert and Solomon Snyder (1973) were doing research on morphine, a pain-relieving and mood-elevating opiate derived from heroin, which is made from poppies. They found that morphine works by binding to receptor sites in the brain. This seemed odd. As Snyder later recalled, "We doubted that animals had evolved opiate receptors just to deal with certain properties of the poppy plant" (quoted in Radetsky, 1991). Pert and Snyder reasoned that if opiate receptors exist, then the body must produce its own internally generated, or *endogenous,* morphinelike substances, which they named "endorphins." Soon they and other researchers confirmed this hypothesis.

Endorphin levels seem to shoot up when an animal or a person is afraid or under stress. This is no accident; by making pain bearable in such situations, endorphins give a species an evolutionary advantage. When an organism is threatened, it needs to do something fast. Pain, however, can interfere with action: A mouse that pauses to lick a wounded paw may become a cat's dinner; a soldier who is overcome by an injury may never get off the battlefield. But, of course, the body's built-in system of counteracting pain is only partly successful, especially when painful stimulation is prolonged.

A link may also exist between endorphins and the pleasures of social contact. When young puppies, guinea pigs, and chicks are injected with low doses of either morphine or endorphins, the animals show much less distress than usual when separated from their mothers. (In all other respects, they behave normally.) The morphine or endorphins seem to provide a biochemical replacement for the mother, or, more precisely, for the endorphin surge presumed to occur during contact with her. Conversely, when young guinea pigs and chicks received a chemical that *blocks* the effects of opiates, their crying increases (Panksepp et al., 1980). These findings suggest that endorphin-stimulated euphoria may be a child's initial motive for seeking affection and cuddling—that, in effect, a child attached to a parent is a child addicted to love.

Hormones: Long-Distance Messengers. **Hormones,** which make up the third class of chemical messengers, are produced primarily in **endocrine glands.** They are released directly into the bloodstream, which carries them to organs and cells that may be far from their point of origin. Hormones have dozens of jobs, from promoting bodily growth to aiding digestion to regulating metabolism.

Neurotransmitters and hormones are not always chemically distinct; the two classifications are like social clubs that admit some of the same members. A particular chemical, such as norepinephrine, may belong to more than one classification, depending on where it is located and what function it is performing. Nature has been efficient, giving some substances more than one task to perform.

The following hormones, among others, are of particular interest to psychologists:

1. **Melatonin,** which is secreted by the *pineal gland*, deep within the brain, helps to regulate daily biological rhythms and promotes sleep.

2. **Adrenal hormones,** which are produced by the *adrenal glands* (organs that are perched right above the kidneys), are involved in emotion and stress. These hormones also rise in response to nonemotional conditions, such as heat, cold, pain, injury, burns, and physical exercise, and in response to some drugs, such as caffeine and nicotine. The outer part of each adrenal gland produces *cortisol*, which increases blood-sugar levels and boosts energy. The inner part produces *epinephrine* (popularly known as adrenaline) and *norepinephrine*. When adrenal hormones are released in your body, activated by the sympathetic nervous system, they increase your arousal level and prepare you for action. Adrenal hormones also enhance memory.

3. **Sex hormones,** which are secreted by tissue in the gonads (testes in men, ovaries in women), and also by the adrenal glands, include three main types, all occurring in both sexes but in differing amounts and proportions in males and females after puberty. *Androgens* (the most important of which is *testosterone*) are masculinizing hormones produced mainly in the testes but also in the ovaries and the adrenal glands. Androgens set in motion the physical changes males experience at puberty—for example, a deepened voice and facial and chest hair—and cause pubic and underarm hair to develop in both sexes. Testosterone also influences sexual arousal in both sexes. *Estrogens* are feminizing hormones that bring on physical changes in females at puberty, such as breast development and the onset of menstruation, and that influence the course of the menstrual cycle. *Progesterone* contributes to the growth and maintenance of the uterine lining in preparation for a fertilized egg, among other functions. Estrogens and progesterone are produced mainly in the ovaries but also in the testes and the adrenal glands.

   Researchers are now studying the possible involvement of sex hormones in behavior not linked to sex or reproduction. For example, estrogens appear to promote the formation of synapses in certain brain areas, and although the evidence has not been entirely consistent, many researchers now believe that these hormones may contribute to learning and memory (Maki & Resnick, 2000; Sherwin, 1998a; Wickelgren, 1997). But the most common belief about the nonsexual effects of sex hormones—that fluctuating levels of estrogen and progesterone make most women "emotional" before menstruation—has not been borne out by research.

Table 7.1 summarizes the three types of brain chemicals we have discussed, and their effects.

MAPPING THE BRAIN

We come now to the main room of the nervous system "house": the brain. A disembodied brain stored in a formaldehyde-filled container is unexciting, a putty-colored, wrinkled glob of tissue that looks a little like an oversized walnut. It takes an act of imagination to envision this modest-looking organ writing *Hamlet*, discovering radium, or inventing the paper clip.

TABLE 7.1   Nervous-System Chemicals and Their Effects

TYPE	FUNCTION	EFFECTS	WHERE PRODUCED	EXAMPLES
Neurotransmitters	Enable neurons to excite or inhibit each other	Diverse, depending on which circuits are activated or suppressed	Brain, spinal cord, peripheral nerves, certain glands	Serotonin, dopamine, norepinephrine
Endorphins	Usually modulate the effects of neurotransmitters	Reduce pain, promote pleasure; also linked to learning, memory, and other functions	Brain, spinal cord	(Several varieties, not discussed in this text)
Hormones	Affect functioning of target organs and tissues	Dozens, ranging from promotion of digestion to regulation of metabolism	Primarily in endocrine glands	Epinephrine, norepinephrine, estrogens, androgens

In a living person, of course, the brain is encased in a thick protective vault of bone. How, then, can scientists study it? One approach is to study patients who have had a part of the brain damaged or removed because of disease or injury. Another, called the *lesion method*, involves damaging or removing sections of brain in animals, then observing the effects.

The brain can also be probed with devices called *electrodes*. Some electrodes are coin-shaped and are simply pasted or taped onto the scalp. They detect the electrical activity of millions of neurons in particular regions of the brain and are widely used in research and medical diagnosis. The electrodes are connected by wires to a machine that translates the electrical energy from the brain into wavy lines on a moving piece of paper or visual patterns on a screen. That is why electrical patterns in the brain are known as "brain waves." Different wave patterns are associated with sleep, relaxation, and mental concentration.

A brain-wave recording is called an **electroencephalogram (EEG).** A standard EEG is useful but not very precise because it reflects the activities of many cells at once. "Listening" to the brain with an EEG machine is like standing outside a sports stadium: You know when something is happening, but you can't be sure what it is or who is doing it. Fortunately, computer technology can be combined with EEG technology to get a clearer picture of brain activity patterns associated with specific events and mental processes; the computer suppresses all the background "noise," leaving only the pattern of electrical response to the event being studied.

For even more precise information, researchers use *needle electrodes*, very thin wires or hollow glass tubes that can be inserted into the brain, either directly in an exposed brain or through tiny holes in the skull. Only the skull and the membranes covering the brain need to be anesthetized; the brain itself, which processes all sensation and feeling, paradoxically feels nothing when touched. Therefore, a human patient or an animal can be awake and not feel pain during the procedure. Needle electrodes can be used both to record electrical activity from the brain and to stimulate the brain with weak electrical currents. Stimulating a given area often results in a specific sensation or movement. *Microelectrodes* are so fine that they can be inserted into single cells.

A more recently devised method of stimulating the brain, **transcranial magnetic stimulation (TMS),** involves delivering a large current through a wire coil placed on a person's head. The current produces a magnetic field about 40,000 times greater than the earth's natural magnetic field (Travis, 2000). This procedure causes neurons under the coil to fire. It can be used to produce motor responses (say, a twitch in the thumb or a knee jerk) and can also be used by researchers to temporarily inactivate an area and observe the effects on behavior—functioning, in effect, as a "virtual" (and temporary) lesion method. The drawback is that when neurons fire, they cause many other neurons to become active too, so it is often hard to tell which neurons are critical for a particular task. Still, TMS has produced some important findings—for example, that a brain area involved in processing visual patterns is also active when a person merely imagines the stimulus (Kosslyn et al., 1999). TMS has also been used to treat depression.

Since the mid-1970s, many other amazing doors to the brain have opened. The **PET scan (positron-emission tomography)** goes beyond anatomy to record biochemical changes in the brain as they are happening. One type of PET scan takes advantage of the fact that nerve cells convert glucose, the body's main fuel, into energy. A researcher can inject a patient with a glucoselike substance that contains a harmless radioactive element. This substance accumulates in brain areas that are particularly active and are consuming glucose rapidly. The substance emits radiation, which is a telltale sign of activity, like cookie crumbs on a child's face. The radiation is detected by a scanning device, and the result is a computer-processed picture of biochemical activity on a display screen, with different colors indicating different activity levels. Other kinds of PET scans measure blood flow or oxygen consumption, which also reflect brain activity.

PET scans, which were originally designed to diagnose abnormalities, have produced evidence that certain brain areas in people with emotional disorders are either unusually quiet or unusually active. But PET technology can also show which parts of the brain are active during ordinary activities and emotions. It lets researchers see which areas are busiest when a person hears a song, recalls a sad memory, works on a math problem, or shifts attention from one task to another.

Another technique, **MRI (magnetic resonance imaging),** allows the exploration of "inner space" without injecting chemicals. Powerful magnetic fields and radio frequencies are used to produce vibrations in the nuclei of atoms making up body organs, and the vibrations are then picked up as signals by special receivers. A computer analyzes the signals, taking into account their strength and duration, and converts them into a high-contrast picture of the organ. An ultrafast version of MRI, called *functional MRI*, picks up magnetic signals from blood that has given up its oxygen to active brain cells. It can capture brain changes many times a second as a person performs a task, such as reading a sentence or solving a puzzle.

Table 7.2 summarizes the methods we have discussed. Still other scanning methods are becoming available with each passing year. Some even produce a moving picture that shows ongoing changes in the brain. These methods have allowed neuroscientists to correlate activity in specific brain areas with everything from mathematical calculations to moral reasoning to spiritual meditation. A word of caution, though: Brain scans alone do not tell us precisely what is happening inside a person's head, either mentally or physiologically. They tell us *where* things happen, but not *how* they happen—for example, how different circuits connect up to produce behavior. Enthusiasm for technology has produced a mountain of findings, but also many unwarranted conclusions about "brain centers" or "critical circuits" for this or that behavior. One scientist (cited in Wheeler, 1998) drew this analogy: A researcher scans the brains of gum-chewing volunteers, finds out which parts of their brains are active, and concludes that he or she has found the brain's "gum-chewing center"!

Descriptive studies using brain scans, then, are just a first step in understanding brain processes. Nonetheless, they are an exciting first step, providing initial clues to what goes on in the brain when we think and feel. The brain can no longer hide from researchers behind the fortress of the skull. It is now possible to get a clear visual image of our most enigmatic organ without so much as lifting a scalpel.

TABLE 7.2   Windows on the Brain

METHOD	WHAT IS LEARNED
Case studies of persons with brain damage	How damage to or loss of neural circuits affects behavior and cognition
Lesion studies with animals	How damage to or loss of neural circuits affects behavior
EEGs	Patterns of electrical activity in the brain
Needle electrodes and microelectrodes	More precise information about electrical activity in small groups of neurons or single neurons
Transcranial magnetic stimulation (TMS)	What happens behaviorally when a brain area is temporarily inactivated
PET scans	Visually displayed information about areas that are active or quiet during an activity or response, and about changes associated with disorders
MRI	Images of brain structure
Functional MRI	Visually displayed information about areas that are active or quiet during an activity or response, and about changes associated with disorders

A WALK THROUGH THE BRAIN

Most modern brain theories assume that different brain parts perform different (though overlapping) tasks. This concept, known as **localization of function,** goes back at least to Joseph Gall (1758–1828), the Austrian anatomist who thought that personality traits were reflected in the development of specific areas of the brain. Gall's theory of *phrenology* was completely wrong-headed (if you'll pardon the pun), but his general notion of specialization in the brain had merit.

To learn about what the major brain structures do, let's take an imaginary stroll through the brain. Pretend, now, that you have shrunk to a microscopic size and that you are wending your way through the "soul's frail dwelling house," starting at the lower part, just above the spine. Figure 7.7 shows the major structures we will encounter along our tour; you may want to refer to it as we proceed. Keep in mind, though, that our descriptions will necessarily be quite general, and that in any activity—feeling an emotion, having a thought, performing a task—many different structures are involved.

The Brain Stem

We begin at the base of the skull with the **brain stem,** which began to evolve some 500 million years ago in segmented worms. The brain stem looks like a stalk rising out of the spinal cord. Pathways between the spinal cord and upper areas of the brain pass through the brain stem's two main structures: the medulla and the pons. The **pons** is involved in (among other things) sleeping, waking, and dreaming. The **medulla** is responsible for bodily functions that do not have to be consciously willed, such as breathing and heart rate. Hanging has long been used as a method of execution because when it breaks the neck, nervous pathways from the medulla are severed, stopping respiration.

FIGURE 7.7   The Human Brain. This cross-section depicts the brain as if it were split in half. The view is of the inside surface of the right half, and shows the structures described in the text.

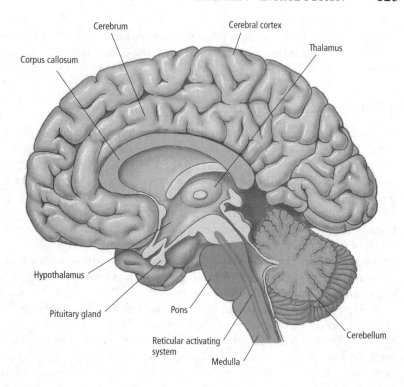

Extending upward from the core of the brain stem is the **reticular activating system (RAS).** This dense network of neurons, which extends above the brain stem into the center of the brain and has connections with areas that are higher up, screens incoming information and arouses the higher centers when something happens that demands their attention. Without the RAS, we could not be alert or perhaps even conscious.

The Cerebellum

Standing atop the brain stem and looking toward the back part of the brain, we see a structure about the size of a small fist. It is the **cerebellum,** or "lesser brain," which contributes to a sense of balance and coordinates the muscles so that movement is smooth and precise. If your cerebellum were damaged, you would probably become exceedingly clumsy and uncoordinated. You might have trouble using a pencil, threading a needle, or even walking. In addition, this structure is involved in remembering certain simple skills and acquired reflexes (Daum & Schugens, 1996; Krupa, Thompson, & Thompson, 1993). Evidence has accumulated that the cerebellum, which was once considered just a motor center, also plays a part in higher cognitive tasks, such as analyzing sensory information, solving problems, and understanding words (Fiez, 1996; Gao et al., 1996; Müller, Courchesne, & Allen, 1998).

The Thalamus

Deep in the interior of the brain, roughly at its center, we can see the **thalamus,** the busy traffic officer of the brain. As sensory messages come into the brain, the thalamus directs them to higher centers. For example, the sight of a sunset sends signals that the thalamus directs to a vision area, and the sound of an oboe sends signals that the thalamus sends on to an auditory area. The only sense that completely bypasses the thalamus is the sense of smell, which has its own private switching station, the *olfactory bulb*.

The olfactory bulb lies near areas involved in emotion. Perhaps that is why particular odors—the smell of fresh laundry, gardenias, a steak sizzling on the grill—often rekindle memories of important personal experiences.

The Hypothalamus and the Pituitary Gland

Beneath the thalamus sits a structure called the **hypothalamus** (*hypo* means "under"). It is involved in drives associated with the survival of both the individual and the species—hunger, thirst, emotion, sex, and reproduction. It regulates body temperature by triggering sweating or shivering, and it controls the complex operations of the autonomic nervous system. It also contains the biological clock that controls the body's daily rhythms.

Hanging down from the hypothalamus, connected to it by a short stalk, is a cherry-sized endocrine gland called the **pituitary gland.** The pituitary is often called the body's "master gland" because the hormones it secretes affect many other endocrine glands. The master, however, is really only a supervisor. The true boss is the hypothalamus, which sends chemicals to the pituitary that tell it when to "talk" to the other endocrine glands. The pituitary, in turn, sends hormonal messages out to these glands.

Many years ago, in a study that became famous, James Olds and Peter Milner reported finding "pleasure centers" in the hypothalamus (Olds, 1975; Olds & Milner, 1954). Olds and Milner trained rats to press a lever in order to get a buzz of electricity delivered through tiny electrodes. Some rats would press the bar thousands of times an hour, for 15 or 20 hours at a time, until they collapsed from exhaustion. When they revived, they went right back to the bar. When forced to make a choice, the hedonistic rodents opted for electrical stimulation over such temptations as water, food, and even an attractive rat of the other sex that was making provocative gestures. Today, however, researchers believe that brain stimulation activates complex neural pathways rather than discrete "centers," and that changes in neurotransmitter levels are involved. Moreover, controversy exists about just how to interpret the rats' responses (which, by the way, do not occur in people when their brains are stimulated in the same way). Were the rats really feeling pleasure, or just some kind of craving or compulsion?

The hypothalamus, along with the two structures we are about to come to, has often been considered to belong to a loosely interconnected set of structures called the **limbic system,** shown in Figure 7.8.

FIGURE 7.8   The Limbic System. Structures of the limbic system play an important role in memory and emotion. The text describes two of these structures, the amygdala and the hippocampus. The hypothalamus is also often included as part of the limbic system.

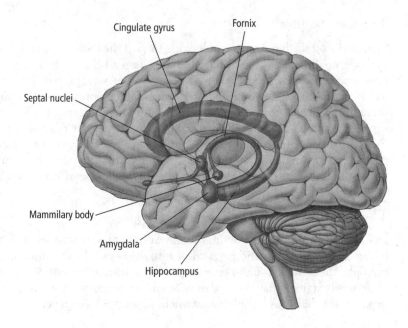

Cingulate gyrus

Fornix

Septal nuclei

Mammilary body

Amygdala

Hippocampus

(*Limbic* comes from the Latin for "border": These structures form a sort of border between the higher and lower parts of the brain.) Some anatomists also include parts of the thalamus in this system. Structures in this region are heavily involved in emotions, such as rage and fear, that we share with other animals (MacLean, 1993). The usefulness of speaking of the limbic system as an integrated set of structures is currently in dispute, because these structures also have other functions, and because parts of the brain outside of the limbic system are involved in emotion. However, the term "limbic system" is still in wide use among researchers, so we thought you should know it.

The Amygdala

The **amygdala** (from the ancient Greek word for "almond") appears to be responsible for evaluating sensory information, quickly determining its emotional importance, and contributing to the initial decision to approach or withdraw from a person or situation. For example, it instantly assesses danger or threat. The amygdala also plays an important role in mediating anxiety and depression; PET scans find that depressed and anxious patients show increased neural activity in this structure (Davidson et al., 1999; Drevets, 2000).

The Hippocampus

Another important area traditionally classified as "limbic" is the **hippocampus,** which has a shape that must have reminded someone of a sea horse, for that is what its name means. This structure compares sensory information with what the brain has learned to expect about the world. When expectations are met, it tells the reticular activating system to "cool it." There's no need for neural alarm bells to go off every time a car goes by, a bird chirps, or you feel your saliva trickling down the back of your throat!

The hippocampus has also been called the "gateway to memory." It enables us to form spatial memories so that we can accurately navigate through our environment (Maguire et al., 2000). And, along with adjacent brain areas, it enables us to form new memories about facts and events—the kind of information you need to identify a flower, tell a story, or recall a vacation trip. The information is then stored in the cerebral cortex, which we will be discussing shortly. For example, when you recall meeting someone yesterday, various aspects of the memory—information about the person's greeting, tone of voice, appearance, and location—are probably stored in different locations in the cortex (Damasio et al., 1996; Squire, 1987). But without the hippocampus, the information would never get to these destinations (Mishkin et al., 1997; Squire & Zola-Morgan, 1991).

We know about the "gateway" function of the hippocampus in part from research on brain-damaged patients with severe memory problems. The case of one man, known to researchers as H. M., is probably the most intensely studied in the annals of medicine (Corkin, 1984; Corkin et al., 1997; Milner, 1970; Ogden & Corkin, 1991). In 1953, when H. M. was 27, surgeons removed most of his hippocampus, along with part of the amygdala. The operation was a last-ditch effort to relieve H. M.'s severe and life-threatening epilepsy. People who have epilepsy, a neurological disorder that has many causes and takes many forms, often have seizures. Usually, the seizures are brief, mild, and controllable by drugs, but in H. M.'s case, they were unrelenting and uncontrollable.

The operation did achieve its goal: Afterward, the young man's seizures were milder and could be managed with medication. His memory, however, had been affected profoundly. Although H. M. continued to recall most events that had occurred before the operation, he could no longer remember new experiences for much longer than 15 minutes; they vanished like water down the drain. With sufficient practice, H. M. could acquire new manual or problem-solving skills, such as playing tennis or solving a puzzle, but he could not remember the training sessions in which he learned these skills. He would read the same magazine over and over without realizing it. He could not recall the day of the week, the year, or even his last meal. Most scientists attribute these deficits to an inability to form new memories for long-term storage.

Today, many years later, H. M., now elderly, will occasionally recall an unusually emotional event, such as the assassination of someone named Kennedy. He sometimes remembers that both his parents are dead, and he knows he has memory problems. But, according to Suzanne Corkin, who has studied H. M. extensively, these "islands of remembering" are the exceptions in a vast sea of forgetfulness. This good-natured man still does not know the scientists who have studied him for decades. He thinks he is much younger than he is, and he can no longer recognize a photograph of his own face; he is stuck in a time warp from the past.

The Cerebrum

At this point in our tour, the largest part of the brain still looms above us. It is the cauliflower-like **cerebrum,** where the higher forms of thinking take place. The complexity of the human brain's circuitry far exceeds that of any computer in existence, and much of its most complicated wiring is packed into this structure. Compared with many other creatures, we humans may be ungainly, feeble, and thin-skinned, but our well-developed cerebrum enables us to overcome these limitations and creatively control our environment (and, some would say, to mess it up).

The cerebrum is divided into two separate halves, or **cerebral hemispheres,** connected by a large band of fibers called the **corpus callosum.** In general, the right hemisphere is in charge of the left side of the body and the left hemisphere is in charge of the right side of the body. As we will see shortly, the two hemispheres also have somewhat different tasks and talents, a phenomenon known as **lateralization.**

The Cerebral Cortex. Working our way right up through the top of the brain, we find that the cerebrum is covered by several thin layers of densely packed cells known collectively as the **cerebral cortex.** Cell bodies in the cortex, as in many other parts of the brain, produce a grayish tissue; hence the term *gray matter.* In other parts of the brain (and in the rest of the nervous system), long, myelin-covered axons prevail, providing the brain's *white matter.* Although the cortex is only about 3 millimeters thick, it contains almost three-fourths of all the cells in the human brain. The cortex has many deep crevasses and wrinkles, which enable it to contain its billions of neurons without requiring us to have the heads of giants—heads that would be too big to permit us to be born. In other mammals, which have fewer neurons, the cortex is less crumpled; in rats, it is quite smooth.

Lobes of the Cortex. On each cerebral hemisphere, deep fissures divide the cortex into four distinct regions, or lobes (see Figure 7.9):

- The **occipital lobes** (from the Latin for "in back of the head") are at the lower back part of the brain. Among other things, they contain the *visual cortex*, where visual signals are processed. Damage to the visual cortex can cause impaired visual recognition or blindness.

- The **parietal lobes** (from the Latin for "pertaining to walls") are at the top of the brain. They contain the *somatosensory cortex*, which receives information about pressure, pain, touch, and temperature from all over the body. The areas of the somatosensory cortex that receive signals from the hands and the face are disproportionately large because these body parts are particularly sensitive. Parts of the parietal lobes are also involved in attention and various mental operations.

- The **temporal lobes** (from the Latin for "pertaining to the temples") are at the sides of the brain, just above the ears, behind the temples. They are involved in memory, perception, and emotion, and they contain the *auditory cortex*, which processes sounds. An area of the left temporal lobe known as *Wernicke's area* is involved in language comprehension.

FIGURE 7.9   Lobes of the Cerebrum. Deep fissures divide the cortex of each cerebral hemisphere into four regions.

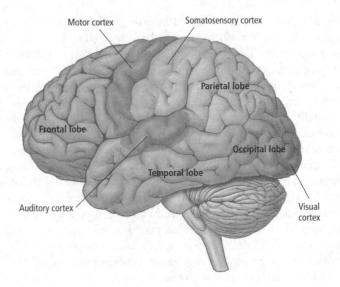

- The **frontal lobes,** as their name indicates, are located toward the front of the brain, just under the skull in the area of the forehead. They contain the *motor cortex*, which issues orders to the 600 muscles of the body that produce voluntary movement. In the left frontal lobe, a region known as *Broca's area* handles speech production. During short-term memory tasks, areas in the frontal lobes are especially active (Goldman-Rakic, 1996). The frontal lobes are also involved in emotion, and in the ability to make plans, think creatively, and take initiative.

Because of their different functions, the lobes of the cerebral cortex tend to respond differently when stimulated. If a surgeon applied electrical current to your somatosensory cortex in the parietal lobes, you would probably feel a tingling in the skin or a sense of being gently touched. If your visual cortex in the occipital lobes were electrically stimulated, you might report a flash of light or swirls of color. And, eerily, many areas of your cortex, when stimulated, would do nothing at all; these "silent" areas are sometimes called the *association cortex*, because they are involved in higher mental processes.

Experiences at different times of your life can affect how specific areas in the cortical lobes are organized. For example, functional MRI studies show that bilingual people who learned both of their languages in early childhood tend to use a single, uniform Broca's area when generating complex sentences in the two languages. But in people who learned a second language during adolescence, Broca's area is divided into two distinct regions, one for each language (Kim et al., 1997). The explanation may be that the brain's wiring process for language production occurs differently in childhood than it does later on.

Psychologists are especially interested in the forwardmost part of the frontal lobes, the *prefrontal cortex*. This area barely exists in mice and rats and takes up only 3.5 percent of the cerebral cortex in cats and about 7 percent in dogs, but it accounts for fully 29 percent of the cortex in human beings.

Scientists have long known that the frontal lobes, and the prefrontal cortex in particular, must have something to do with personality. The first clue appeared in 1848, when a bizarre accident drove an inch-thick, 3½-foot-long iron rod clear through the head of a young railroad worker named Phineas Gage. The rod (which is still on display at Harvard University, along with Gage's skull) entered beneath the left eye and exited through the top of the head, destroying much of the prefrontal cortex (H. Damasio et al., 1994). Miraculously, Gage survived this trauma and, by most accounts, he retained the ability to speak, think, and remember. But his friends complained that he was "no longer Gage." In a sort of Jekyll-and-Hyde transformation, he had changed from a mild-mannered, friendly, efficient worker into a foul-mouthed, ill-tempered, undependable lout who could not hold a steady job or stick to a plan. His employers had to let him go, and he was reduced to exhibiting himself as a circus attraction.

Today, there is some controversy about the exact details of this sad incident. For example, no one is really sure what Gage was like before his accident; perhaps the doctors exaggerated the extent of his personality transformation (Macmillan, 2000). But many other cases of brain injury, whether from stroke or trauma, support the conclusion that most scientists draw from the Gage case: that parts of the frontal lobes are involved in social judgment, rational decision making, and the ability to set goals and to make and carry through plans (Klein & Kihlstrom, 1998). Like Gage, people with damage in these areas sometimes mismanage their finances, lose their jobs, and abandon their friends. As neurologist Antonio Damasio (1994) wrote, "Observing social convention, behaving ethically, and, in general, making decisions advantageous to one's survival and progress, require both knowledge of rules and strategies and the integrity of specific brain systems." Interestingly, the mental deficits that characterize damage to these areas are accompanied by a flattening out of emotion and feeling, which suggests that normal emotions are necessary for everyday reasoning and the ability to learn from mistakes.

The frontal lobes also govern the ability to do a series of tasks in the proper sequence and to stop doing them at the proper time. The pioneering Soviet psychologist Alexander Luria (1980) studied many cases in which damage to the frontal lobes disrupted these abilities. One man observed by Luria kept trying to light a match after it was already lit. Another planed a piece of wood in the hospital carpentry shop until it was gone, and then went on to plane the workbench!

Table 7.3 summarizes the major parts of the brain and their primary functions.

TABLE 7.3   Functions Associated with the Major Brain Structures

The functions listed here are just some of those that have been linked with these structures.

STRUCTURE	FUNCTIONS
Brain stem	
Pons	Sleeping, waking, dreaming
Medulla	Automatic functions such as breathing, heart rate
Reticular activating system (RAS) (extends into center of the brain)	Screening of incoming information, arousal of higher centers, consciousness
Cerebellum	Balance, muscular coordination, memory for simple skills and learned reflexes, possible involvement in more complex mental tasks
Thalamus	Relay of impulses from higher centers to the spinal cord, and of incoming sensory information (except for olfactory sensations) to other brain centers
Hypothalamus	Behaviors necessary for survival, such as hunger, thirst, emotion, reproduction; regulation of body temperature; control of autonomic nervous system

(continued)

Study

TABLE 7.3   Functions Associated with the Major Brain Structures (continued)

STRUCTURE	FUNCTIONS
Pituitary gland	Under direction of the hypothalamus, secretion of hormones that affect other glands
Amygdala	Initial evaluation of sensory information to determine its importance; mediation of anxiety and depression
Hippocampus	Comparison of sensory information with expectations, modulation of the RAS; formation of new memories about facts and events
Cerebrum (including cerebral cortex)	Higher forms of thinking
Occipital lobes	Visual processing
Parietal lobes	Processing of pressure, pain, touch, temperature
Temporal lobes	Memory, perception, emotion, hearing, language comprehension
Frontal lobes	Movement, short-term memory, planning, setting goals, creative thinking, initiative, social judgment, rational decision making, speech production

THE TWO HEMISPHERES OF THE BRAIN

We have seen that the cerebrum is divided into two hemispheres that control opposite sides of the body. Although similar in structure, these hemispheres have somewhat separate talents, or areas of specialization.

Split Brains: A House Divided

In a normal brain, the two hemispheres communicate with one another across the corpus callosum, the bundle of fibers that connects them. Whatever happens in one side of the brain is instantly flashed to the other side. What would happen, though, if the two sides were cut off from one another?

In 1953, Ronald E. Myers and Roger W. Sperry took the first step toward answering this question by severing the corpus callosum in cats. They also cut parts of the nerves leading from the eyes to the brain. Normally, each eye transmits messages to both sides of the brain. After this procedure, a cat's left eye sent information only to the left hemisphere and its right eye sent information only to the right hemisphere.

At first, the cats did not seem to be affected much by this drastic operation. But Myers and Sperry showed that something profound had happened. They trained the cats to perform tasks with one eye blindfolded; for example, a cat might have to push a panel with a square on it to get food but ignore a panel with a circle. Then the researchers switched the blindfold to the cat's other eye and tested the animal again. Now the cats behaved as if they had never learned the trick. Apparently, one side of the brain did not know what the other side was doing. It was as if the animals had two minds in one body. Later studies confirmed this result with other species, including monkeys (Sperry, 1964).

In all the animal studies, ordinary behavior, such as eating and walking, remained normal. Encouraged by this finding, a team of surgeons decided in the early 1960s to try cutting the corpus callosum in patients with debilitating, uncontrollable epilepsy. In severe forms of this disease, disorganized electrical activity spreads from an injured area to other parts of the brain. The surgeons reasoned that cutting the connection between the two halves of the brain might stop the spread of electrical activity from one side to the other. The surgery was done, of course, for the sake of the patients, who were desperate, but as a bonus, scientists would be able to find out what happens what each cerebral hemisphere can do when it is quite literally cut off from the other.

The results of this *split-brain surgery* generally proved successful. Seizures were reduced and sometimes disappeared completely. In their daily lives, split-brain patients did not seem much affected by the fact that the two hemispheres were incommunicado. Their personalities and intelligence remained intact; they could walk, talk, and in general lead normal lives. Apparently, connections in the undivided deeper parts of the brain kept body movements and other functions normal. But in a series of ingenious studies, Sperry and his colleagues (and later other researchers) showed that perception and memory had been affected, just as they had been in the earlier animal research. In 1981, Sperry won a Nobel Prize for his work.

It was already known that the two hemispheres are not mirror images of each other. In most people, language is largely handled by the left hemisphere; thus, a person who suffers brain damage because of a stroke—a blockage in or rupture of a blood vessel in the brain—is much more likely to have language problems if the damage is in the left side than if it is in the right. Sperry and his colleagues wanted to know: How would splitting the brain affect language and other abilities?

To understand this research, you must know how nerves connect the eyes to the brain. (The human patients, unlike Myers and Sperry's cats, did not have these nerves cut.) If you look straight ahead, everything in the left side of the scene before you—the "visual field"—goes to the right half of your brain, and everything in the right side of the scene goes to the left half of your brain. This is true for both eyes.

The procedure was to present information only to one or the other side of the patients' brains. In one early study, the researchers took photographs of different faces, cut them in two, and pasted different halves together (Levy, Trevarthen, & Sperry, 1972). The reconstructed photographs were then presented on slides. The person was told to stare at a dot on the middle of the screen, so that half the image fell to the left of this point and half to the right. Each image was flashed so quickly that the person had no time to move his or her eyes. When the patients were asked to say what they had seen, they named the person in the right part of the image. But when they were asked to point with their left hands to the face they had seen, they chose the person in the left side of the image. Further, they claimed they had noticed nothing unusual about the original photographs! Each side of the brain saw a different half-image and automatically filled in the missing part. Neither side knew what the other side had seen.

Tap, Tap, Tap

Have a right-handed friend tap on a paper with a pencil held in the right hand, for one minute. Then have the person do the same with the left hand, using a fresh sheet of paper. Finally, repeat the procedure, having the person talk at the same time as tapping. For most people, talking will decrease the rate of tapping—but more for the right hand than for the left, probably because both activities involve the same hemisphere, and there is "competition" between them. (Left-handed people vary more in terms of which hemisphere is dominant for language, so the results for them will be more variable.)

Why did the patients name one side of the picture but point to the other? Speech centers are usually in the left hemisphere. When the person responded with speech, it was the left side of the brain doing the talking. When the person pointed with the left hand, which is controlled by the right side of the brain, the right hemisphere was giving its version of what the person had seen.

In another study, the researchers presented slides of ordinary objects and then suddenly flashed a slide of a nude woman. Both sides of the brain were amused, but because only the left side has speech, the two sides responded differently. When the picture was flashed to one woman's left hemisphere, she laughed and identified it as a nude. When it was flashed to her right hemisphere, she said nothing but began to chuckle. Asked what she was laughing at, she said, "I don't know . . . nothing . . . oh—that funny machine." The right hemisphere could not describe what it had seen, but it reacted emotionally, just the same (Gazzaniga, 1967).

The Two Hemispheres: Allies or Opposites?

The split-brain operation is still being performed, and split-brain patients continue to be studied. Research on left–right differences is also being done with people whose brains are intact (Springer & Deutsch, 1998). Electrodes and brain scans are used to measure activity in the left and right hemispheres while people perform different tasks. The results confirm that nearly all right-handed people and a majority of left-handers process language mainly in the left hemisphere. The left side is also more active during some logical, symbolic, and sequential tasks, such as solving math problems and understanding technical material.

Because of its cognitive talents, many researchers refer to left hemisphere *dominance*. They believe that the left hemisphere usually exerts control over the right hemisphere. One well-known split-brain researcher, Michael Gazzaniga (1983), once argued that without help from the left side, the right side's mental skills would probably be "vastly inferior to the cognitive skills of a chimpanzee." He and others also believe that a mental "module" in the left hemisphere is constantly trying to explain actions and emotions generated by brain parts whose workings are nonverbal and outside of awareness.

You can see in split-brain patients how the left hemisphere concocts such explanations. In one classic example, a picture of a chicken claw was flashed to a patient's left hemisphere, a picture of a snow scene to his right. The task was to point to a related image for each picture from an array, with a chicken the correct choice for the claw and a shovel for the snow scene. The patient chose the shovel with his left hand and the chicken with his right. When asked to explain why, he responded (with his left hemisphere) that the chicken claw went with the chicken, and the shovel was for cleaning out the chicken shed. The left brain had seen the left hand's response but did not know about the snow scene, so it interpreted the response by using the information it did have (Gazzaniga, 1988).

Other researchers, including Sperry (1982), have rushed to the right hemisphere's defense. The right side, they point out, is no dummy. It is superior in problems requiring spatial–visual ability, the ability you use to read a map or follow a dress pattern, and it excels in facial recognition and the ability to read facial expressions. It is active during the creation and appreciation of art and music. It recognizes nonverbal sounds, such as a dog's barking. The right brain also has some language ability. Typically, it can read a word briefly flashed to it and can understand an experimenter's instructions. In a few split-brain patients, right-brain language ability has been well developed, showing that individual variation exists in brain lateralization. In one unusual case, a left-handed patient could not read aloud words flashed to her right hemisphere, yet she retained the ability to write them down (Baynes et al., 1998).

Some researchers have also credited the right hemisphere with having a cognitive style that is intuitive and holistic, in contrast to the left hemisphere's more rational and analytic mode. Over the years, this idea has been oversold by books and programs that promise to make people more creative by making them more "right-brained." But the differences between the two hemispheres are relative, not absolute—a matter of degree. In most real-life activities, the two sides cooperate naturally, with each making a valuable contribution. For example, mathematical ability involves not only areas in the left frontal lobe, but also areas in both the left and the right parietal lobes. The former are needed to compute exact sums using language ("2 times 5 is 10"), and the latter are needed for using visual or spatial imagery, such as a mental "number line," to estimate quantity or magnitude ("6 is closer to 9 than to 2") (Dehaene et al., 1999).

Be cautious, then, about thinking of the two sides as two "minds." As Sperry (1982) himself once noted, "The left-right dichotomy . . . is an idea with which it is very easy to run wild."

TWO STUBBORN ISSUES IN BRAIN RESEARCH

If you have mastered the definitions and descriptions in this chapter, you are prepared to read popular accounts of advances in neuropsychology. But many questions remain about how the brain works, and we will end this chapter with two of them.

Where Is the Self?

When we think about the remarkable blob of tissue in our heads that allows us to remember, to dream, and to think—the blob that can make our existence a hideous nightmare when it is damaged or diseased—we are led, inevitably, to a question that has been pondered for thousands of years: Where, exactly, is the self?

When you say, "I am feeling unhappy," your amygdala, your serotonin receptors, your endorphins, and all sorts of other brain parts and processes are active, but who, exactly, is the "I" doing the feeling? When you say, "I've decided to have a hot dog instead of a hamburger" who is the "I" doing the choosing? When you say, "My mind is playing tricks on me," who is the "me" watching your mind play those tricks, and who is it that's being tricked? Isn't the self observing itself a little like a finger pointing at its own tip?

Most religions resolve the problem by teaching that an immortal self or soul exists entirely apart from the mortal brain. But modern brain scientists usually consider mind to be a matter of matter. They may have personal religious convictions about a soul, or a spiritual response to the awesome complexity and interconnectedness of nature, but most assume that what we call "mind," "consciousness," "self-awareness," or "subjective experience" can be explained in physical terms as a product of the cerebral cortex.

Our conscious sense of a unified self may even be an illusion. Neurologist Richard Restak (1983, 1994) has noted that many of our actions and choices occur without any direction by a conscious self. He concludes that "the brains of all creatures are probably organized along the lines of multiple centers and various levels." Cognitive scientist Daniel Dennett (1991) suggests that the brain or mind consists of independent brain parts that deal with different aspects of thought and perception, constantly conferring with each other and revising their "drafts" of reality. Likewise, Michael Gazzaniga (1985, 1998) proposes that the brain is organized as a loose confederation of independent modules, or mental systems, all working in parallel. Most of these modules operate without our conscious awareness. As we saw, Gazzaniga believes that one verbal module, an "interpreter" (usually in the left hemisphere), is constantly coming up with theories to explain the actions, moods, and thoughts of the other modules. The result is the sense of a unified self.

Interestingly, the idea that the brain consists of modules and that the self is an illusion is consistent with the teachings of many Eastern spiritual traditions. Buddhism, for example, teaches that the self is not a unified "thing" but rather a collection of thoughts, perceptions, concepts, and feelings that shift and change from moment to moment. To Buddhists, the unity and the permanence of the self are a mirage. Such notions are contrary, of course, to what most people in the West, including psychologists, have always believed about their "selves."

The mind-brain puzzle has plagued philosophers for thousands of years. Even in these days of modern technology, details about the neural circuits responsible for our sense of self remain hazy. Many researchers believe that the frontal lobes play a critical role, but not all accept the idea of modules. And no one understands yet how the inner life of the mind, or our sense of subjective experience, is linked to the physical processes of the brain. Some brain-injured patients who, like H. M., are unable to store new memories about their experiences can nonetheless describe what kind of person they have been since the brain damage occurred (Klein & Kihlstrom, 1998). Where in the brain does this capacity to reflect on one's own personality reside?

Over a century ago, William James (1890/1950) described the "self-as-knower," the inner sense we all have of being a distinct person who thinks, feels, and acts. Psychologists, neuroscientists, cognitive scientists, and philosophers all hope to learn more about how our brains and nervous systems give rise to the self-as-knower. What do you think about the existence and location of your "self" . . . and who, by the way, is doing the thinking? Think about it!

Are There "His" and "Hers" Brains?

A second stubborn issue concerns the existence of sex differences in the brain. Historically, findings on male–female brain differences have often flip-flopped in a most suspicious manner, a result of the biases of the observers rather than the biology of the brain (Shields, 1975). For example, in the 1960s, scientists speculated that women were more "right-brained" and men were more "left-brained," which supposedly explained why men were "rational" and women "intuitive." Then, when the virtues of the right hemisphere were discovered, such as creativity and artistic ability, some researchers decided that men were more right-brained. But it is now clear that the abilities popularly associated with the two sexes do not fall neatly into the two hemispheres of the brain. The left side is more verbal (presumably a "female" trait), but it is also more mathematical (presumably a "male" trait). The right side is more intuitive ("female"), but it is also more spatially talented ("male").

To evaluate the issue of sex differences in the brain intelligently, we need to ask two questions: Do male and female brains differ physically? And if so, what, if anything, does this difference have to do with behavior?

Let's consider the first question. Many anatomical and biochemical sex differences have been found in animal brains, especially in areas related to reproduction. And of course, we would expect to find male–female brain differences that are related to the regulation of sex hormones and other aspects of reproduction in human beings, too. But many researchers want to know whether there are differences that affect how men and women think or behave—and here, the picture is murkier.

For example, in 1982, an autopsy study of 14 human brains reported an average sex difference in the size and shape of the *splenium*, a small section at the end of the corpus callosum, the bundle of fibers dividing the cerebral hemispheres (de Lacoste-Utamsing & Holloway, 1982). This finding quickly made its way into newspapers, magazines, and even textbooks, before anyone had replicated it. But a decade later, a thorough review of the literature found that the 1982 results were an anomaly: Two very early studies (in 1906 and 1909) found that the splenium was *larger* in men, and 21 later studies found no sex difference at all (Byne, 1993). Similarly, a Canadian analysis of 49 studies found only trivial differences between the two sexes, differences that paled in comparison with the huge individual variations *within* each sex (Bishop & Wahlsten, 1997). These findings, unlike the 1982 results, never made the headlines.

Researchers have also looked for sex differences in other ways, such as by examining the density of neurons in specific areas. One team, examining nine autopsied brains, found that the women had an average of 11 percent more cells in areas of the cortex associated with the processing of auditory information; in fact, all of the women had more of these cells than did any of the men (Witelson, Glazer, & Kigar, 1994).

Other researchers have used brain scans to search for average sex differences in brain activity when people work on particular tasks. In one highly publicized study (Shaywitz et al., 1995), 19 men and 19 women were asked to say whether pairs of nonsense words rhymed, a task that required them to process and compare sounds. MRI scans showed that in both sexes an area at the front of the left hemisphere was activated. But in 11 of the women and none of the men, the corresponding area in the right hemisphere was also active. In a more recent MRI study, 10 men and 10 women listened to a John Grisham thriller being read aloud. Both men and women showed activity in the left temporal lobe, but women also showed some activity in the right temporal lobe (Phillips et al., 2001).

These findings, along with many others, provide evidence for a sex difference in lateralization: For some types of tasks, especially those involving language, men seem to rely more heavily on one side of the brain whereas women tend to use both sides. Such a difference could help explain why left-hemisphere damage is less likely to cause language problems in women than in men after a stroke (Inglis & Lawson, 1981; McGlone, 1978).

Many other intriguing sex differences have been reported—for example, that female brains have a higher proportion of gray matter than men's do (Gur et al., 1999), and that men use the right side of the amygdala while storing memories of an emotionally upsetting film whereas women use the left side (Cahill et al., 2001). In the coming years, research may reveal additional anatomical and information-processing differences in the brains of males and females. But even if sex differences exist, we are still left with our second question: *What do the differences mean for the behavior or personality traits of men and women in real life?*

Some popular writers have been quick to assume that brain differences explain, among other things, women's allegedly superior intuition, women's love of talking about feelings and men's love of talking about sports, women's greater verbal ability, men's edge in math ability, and why men won't ask for directions when they're lost. But there are at least three problems with these conclusions:

1. *These supposed gender differences are stereotypes;* in each case, the overlap between the sexes is greater than the difference between them. Even when differences are statistically significant they are often quite small in practical terms (Hyde, 2000).

2. *A biological difference does not necessarily have implications for behavior or performance.* In the rhyme-judgment study, for example, both sexes did equally well, despite the differences in their MRIs. And in the emotional-film study, the two sexes reported comparable emotional reactions and had similar memories for the films' content. As for how brain differences might be related to more general abilities, speculations are as plentiful as ants at a picnic, but at present they remain just that—speculations. As one writer noted, differences between men's and women's brains "are few, they are slight; we don't know what causes them, and in many cases we don't know what they do" (Blum, 1997).

3. *Sex differences in the brain could be the result rather than the cause of behavioral differences.* Experiences in life are constantly sculpting the circuitry of the brain, affecting the way brains are organized and how they function—and males and females often have different experiences. Thus, in discussing the results of the listening study, one of the researchers noted that "We don't know if the difference is because of the way we're raised, or if it's hard-wired in the brain" (quoted in Hotz, 2000).

In sum, the answer to our second question, whether physical differences are linked to behavior, is: "No one really knows." It is important to keep an open mind about new findings on sex differences in the brain, but because the practical significance of these findings (if any) is not yet clear, it is also important to be cautious and aware of how such results might be exaggerated and misused.

THE LESSON OF EINSTEIN'S BRAIN

The study of the brain illuminates the capacities we all share as human beings—thought, language, memory, emotion. And yet each brain is unique, not only because a unique genetic package is present in each of us at birth, but also because a lifetime of experiences, nutrients, and sensations is constantly altering the brain's biochemistry and neural networks. Roger Sperry (1982) said it well: "The individuality inherent in our brain networks makes that of fingerprints or facial features gross and simple by comparison."

Thus, if you are a string musician, the area in your brain associated with music production is likely to be larger than that of nonmusicians; and the earlier in life you started to play, the larger it becomes (Jancke, Schlaug, & Steinmetz, 1997). If you are a cab driver, the area in your hippocampus responsible for visual representations of the environment is likely to be larger than average (Maguire et al., 2000). And, as we saw earlier, if you became bilingual in childhood, a single part of your Broca's area probably handles both languages, but if you learned a second language later in life you will probably have a separate part for each.

Because experience affects the brain, it is often hard to tease out cause-and-effect relationships between the brain and ability. For example, some people have hoped that examining parts of Einstein's brain would tell us what was special enough about it to make "Einstein" a synonym for "genius." We do know that geniuses are in all likelihood born with brains that differ in some way from other people's. A few years ago, Canadian researchers reported that a parietal area crucial for mathematical thought, three-dimensional imagery, and other mental processes was wider in Einstein's brain than in "normal" brains (Witelson et al., 1999). Might this explain Einstein's brilliance? Perhaps so. But it is also possible that a lifetime of "brain work" bulked up Einstein's parietal area. We may never know, by studying a single brain of even the greatest genius, how much his brain shaped his life, and how much his life shaped his brain.

The study of our most miraculous organ, the brain, helps us understand the abilities we all rely on and the memories and emotions that make us human. But analyzing a human being in terms of physiology alone is like analyzing the Taj Mahal solely in terms of the materials that were used to build it. Even if we could monitor every cell and circuit of the brain, we would still need to understand the circumstances, thoughts, and cultural rules that affect whether we are gripped by hatred, consumed by grief, lifted by love, or transported by joy.

REFERENCES

Bailey, J. M., Gaulin, S., Agyei, Y., & Gladue, B. A. (1994). Effects of gender and sexual orientation on evolutionarily relevant aspects of human mating psychology. *Journal of Personality and Social Psychology, 66*, 1081–1093.

Baker, M. C. (2001). *The atoms of language: The mind's hidden rules of grammar*. New York: Basic Books.

Barash, D. P., & Lipton, J. E. (2001). *The myth of monogamy: Fidelity and infidelity in animals and people*. New York: W. H. Freeman.

Barinaga, M. (1992). Challenging the "no new neurons" dogma. *Science, 255*, 1646.

Baynes, K., Eliassen, J. C., Lutsep, H. L., & Gazzaniga, M. S. (1998). Modular organization of cognitive systems masked by interhemispheric integration. *Science, 280*, 902–905.

Beckerman, S., Lizarralde, R., Ballew, C., et al. (1998). The Barí partible paternity project: Preliminary results. *Current Anthropology, 39*, 164–167.

Bekenstein, J. W., & Lothman, E. W. (1993). Dormancy of inhibitory interneurons in a model of temporal lobe epilepsy. *Science, 259*, 97–100.

Berger, F., Gage, F. H., & Vijayaraghavan, S. (1998). Nicotinic receptor-induced apoptotic cell death of hippocampal progenitor cells. *Journal of Neuroscience, 18,* 6871–6881.

Berko, J. (1958). The child's learning of English morphology. *Word, 14,* 150–177.

Birkhead, T. (2001). *Promiscuity: An evolutionary history of sperm competition.* Cambridge, MA: Harvard University Press.

Bishop, K. M., & Wahlsten, D. (1997). Sex differences in the human corpus callosum: Myth or reality? *Neuroscience and Biobehavioral Reviews, 21,* 581–601.

Blum, D. (1997). *Sex on the brain: The biological differences between men and women.* New York: Viking.

Bohannon, J. N., & Stanowicz, L. (1988). The issue of negative evidence: Adult responses to children's language errors. *Developmental Psychology, 24,* 684–689.

Bohannon, J. N., & Symons, V. (1988). *Conversational conditions of children's imitation.* Paper presented at the biennial Conference on Human Development, Charleston, South Carolina.

Bouchard, T. J., Jr. (1995). Nature's twice-told tale: Identical twins reared apart—what they tell us about human individuality. Paper presented at the annual meeting of the Western Psychological Association, Los Angeles.

Bouchard, T. J., Jr. (1997b). IQ similarity in twins reared apart: Findings and responses to critics. In R. J. Sternberg & E. Grigorenko (eds.), *Intelligence: Heredity and environment.* New York: Cambridge University Press.

Bouchard, T. J., Jr., & McGue, M. (1981). Familial studies of intelligence: A review. *Science, 212,* 1055–1058.

Brazelton, T. R., Rossi, F. M., Keshet, G. I.; & Blau, H. M. (2000). From marrow to brain: expression of neuronal phenotypes in adult mice. *Science, 290,* 1775–1779.

Brown, R., Cazden, C., & Bellugi, U. (1969). The child's grammar from I to III. In J. P. Hill (ed.), *Minnesota Symposium on Child Psychology* (Vol. 2). Minneapolis: University of Minnesota Press.

Buss, D. M. (1994). *The evolution of desire: Strategies of human mating.* New York: Basic Books.

Buss, D. M. (1995). Evolutionary psychology: A new paradigm for psychological science. *Psychological Inquiry, 6,* 1–30.

Buss, D. M. (1996). Sexual conflict: Can evolutionary and feminist perspectives converge? In D. M. Buss & N. Malamuth (eds.), *Sex, power, conflict: Evolutionary and feminist perspectives.* New York: Oxford University Press.

Buss, D. M. (1999). *Evolutionary psychology: The new science of the mind.* Boston: Allyn and Bacon.

Buunk, B., Angleitner, A., Oubaid, V., & Buss, D. M. (1996). Sex differences in jealousy in evolutionary and cultural perspective: Tests from the Netherlands, Germany, and the United States. *Psychological Science, 7,* 359–363.

Byne, W. (1993). Sexual orientation and brain structure: Adding up the evidence. Paper presented at the annual meeting of the International Academy of Sex Research, Pacific Grove, CA.

Cahill, L., Haier, R. J., White, N. S., et al. (2001). Sex-related differences in amygdala activity during emotionally influenced memory storage. *Neurbiology of Learning and Memory, 75,* 1–9.

Campbell, F. A., & Ramey, C. T. (1995). Cognitive and school outcomes for high risk students at middle adolescence: Positive effects of early intervention. *American Educational Research Journal, 32,* 743–772.

Chipuer, H. M.; Rovine, M. J.; & Plomin, R. (1990). LISREL modeling: Genetic and environmental influences on IQ revisited. *Intelligence, 14,* 11–29.

Chomsky, N. (1957). *Syntactic structures.* The Hague, Netherlands: Mouton.

Chomsky, N. (1980). Initial states and steady states. In M. Piatelli-Palmerini (ed.), *Language and learning: The debate between Jean Piaget and Noam Chomsky.* Cambridge, MA: Harvard University Press.

Chorney, M. J., Chorney, K., Seese, N., et al. (1998). A quantitative trait locus associated with cognitive ability in children. *Psychological Science, 9,* 159–166.

Cinque, G. (1999). *Adverbs and functional heads: A cross-linguistic approach.* New York: Oxford University Press.

Corkin, S. (1984). Lasting consequences of bilateral medial temporal lobectomy: Clinical course and experimental findings in H. M. *Seminars in Neurology, 4,* 249–259.

Corkin, S., Amaral, D. G., Gonzalez, R. G., et al. (1997). H. M.'s medial temporal lobe lesion: Findings from magnetic resonance imaging. Journal of *Neuroscience, 17,* 3964–3979.

Cose, E. (1994). *The rage of a privileged class.* New York: HarperCollins.

Cosmides, L., Tooby, J., & Barkow, J. H. (1992) Introduction: Evolutionary psychology and conceptual integration. In J. H. Barkow, L. C., & J. Tooby (eds.), *The adapted mind: Evolutionary psychology and the generation of culture.* New York: Oxford University Press.

Curtiss, S. (1977). *Genie: A psycholinguistic study of a modern-day "wild child."* New York: Academic Press.

Daly, M., & Wilson, M. (1983). *Sex, evolution, and behavior* (2nd ed.). Belmont, CA: Wadsworth.

Damasio, A. R. (1994). *Descartes' error: Emotion, reason, and the human brain*. New York: Grosset/Putnam.

Damasio, H., Grabowski, T. J., Frank, R., et al. (1994). The return of Phineas Gage: Clues about the brain from the skull of a famous patient. *Science, 264*, 1102–1105.

Damasio, H. G., Thomas J., Tranel, D., et al. (1996). A neural basis for lexical retrieval. *Nature, 380*, 499–505.

Darwin, C. (1859). *On the origin of species*. [A facsimile of the first edition, edited by Ernst Mayer, 1964.] Cambridge, MA: Harvard University Press.

Darwin, C. (1874). *The descent of man and selection in relation to sex* (2nd ed.). New York: Hurst.

Daum, I., & Schugens, M. M. (1996). On the cerebellum and classical conditioning. *Psychological Science, 5*, 58–61.

Davidson, R. J., Abercrombie, H., Nitschke, J. B., & Putnam, K. (1999). Regional brain function, emotion, and disorders of emotion. *Current Opinion in Neurobiology, 9*, 228–234.

de Lacoste-Utamsing, C., & Holloway, R. L. (1982). Sexual dimorphism in the human corpus callosum. *Science, 216*, 1431–1432.

de Waal, F. (2001b). Inevitability of evolutionary psychology and the limitations of adaptationism: Lessons from the other primates. Invited address at the annual meeting of the American Psychological Association, San Francisco.

Dehaene, S., Spelke, E., Pinel, P., et al. (1999). Sources of mathematical thinking: Behavioral and brain-imaging evidence. *Science, 284*, 970–974.

Dennett, D. C. (1991). *Consciousness explained*. Boston: Little, Brown.

Devlin, B., Daniels, M., & Roeder, K. (1997). The heritability of IQ. *Nature, 388*, 468–471.

Diamond, M. C. (1993, Winter–Spring). An optimistic view of the aging brain. *Generations, 17*, 31–33.

Drayna, D., Manichaikul, A., de Lange, M., et al. (2001). Genetic correlates of musical pitch recognition in humans. *Science, 291*, 1969–1972.

Drevets, W. C. (2000). Neuroimaging studies of mood disorders. *Biological Psychiatry, 48*, 813–829.

Eriksson, P. S., Perfilieva, E., Bjork-Eriksson, T., et al. (1998). Neurogenesis in the adult human hippocampus. *Nature Medicine, 4*, 1313–1317.

Ervin-Tripp, S., (1964). Imitation and structural change in children's language. In E. H. Lenneberg (ed.), *New directions in the study of language*. Cambridge, MA: MIT Press.

Eyferth, K., (1961). [The performance of different groups of the children of occupation forces on the Hamburg-Wechsler Intelligence Test for Children.] *Archiv für die Gesamte Psychologie, 113*, 222–241.

Fagan, J. F., III (1992). Intelligence: A theoretical viewpoint. *Current Directions in Psychological Science, 1*, 82–86.

Fausto-Sterling, A., (1997). Beyond difference: A biologist's perspective. *Journal of Social Issues, 53*, 233–258.

Fiez, J. A. (1996). Cerebellar contributions to cognition. *Neuron, 16*, 13–15.

Fisher, P. J., Turic, D., McGuffin, P., et al. (1999). DNA pooling identifies QTLs for general cognitive ability in children on chromosome 4. *Human Molecular Genetics, 8*, 915–922.

Flynn, J. R. (1987). Massive IQ gains in 14 nations: What IQ tests really measure. *Psychological Bulletin, 95*, 29–51.

Flynn, J. R. (1999). Searching for justice: the discovery of IQ gains over time. *American Psychologist, 54*, 5–20.

Gage, F. H., Kempermann, G., Palmer, T. D., et al. (1998). Multipotent progenitor cells in the adult dentate gyrus. *Journal of Neurobiology, 36*, 249–266.

Gallo, V., & Chittajallu, R. (2001). Unwrapping glial cells from the synapse: What lies inside? *Science, 292*, 872–873.

Gao, J-H., Parsons, L. M.; Bower, J. M., et al. (1996). Cerebellum implicated in sensory acquisition and discrimination rather than motor control. *Science, 272*, 545–547.

Gazzaniga, M. S. (1967). The split brain in man. *Scientific American, 217*(2), 24–29.

Gazzaniga, M. S. (1983). Right hemisphere language following brain bisection: A 20-year perspective. *American Psychologist, 38*, 525–537.

Gazzaniga, M. S. (1985). *The social brain: Discovering the networks of the mind*. New York: Basic Books.

Gazzaniga, M. S. (1988). *Mind matters*. Boston: Houghton Mifflin.

Gazzaniga, M. S. (1998). *The mind's past*. Berkeley, CA: University of California Press.

Geary, D. C. (1995). Reflections of evolution and culture in children's cognition: Implications for mathematical development and instruction. *American Psychologist, 50*, 24–37.

Goldin-Meadow, S., & Mylander, C. (1998). Spontaneous sign systems created by deaf children in two cultures. *Nature, 391*, 279–281.

Goldman-Rakic, P. S. (1996). Opening the mind through neurobiology. Invited address at the annual meeting of the American Psychological Association, Toronto, Canada.

Gopnik, M., Choi, S., & Baumberger, T. (1996). Cross-linguistic differences in early semantic and cognitive development. *Cognitive Development, 11,* 197–227.

Gopnik, M., & Goad, H. (1997). What underlies inflectional error patterns in genetic dysphasia? *Journal of Neurolinguistics, 10,* 109–137.

Gould, E., Beylin, A., Tanapat, P., et al. (1999). Learning enhances adult neurogenesis in the hippocampal formation. *Nature Neuroscience, 2,* 260–265.

Gould, E., Reeves, A. J., Graziano, M. S. A., & Gross, C. G. (1999). Neurogenesis in the neocortex of adult primates. *Science, 286,* 548–552.

Gould, E., Tanapat, P., McEwen, B. S., et al. (1998). Proliferation of granule cell precursors in the dentate gyrus of adult monkeys is diminished by stress. *Proceedings of the National Academy of Science, 95,* 3168–3171.

Gould, S. J. (1987). *An urchin in the storm.* New York: W. W. Norton.

Gould, S. J. (1996). *The mismeasure of man* (rev. ed.). New York: Norton.

Greenough, W. T., & Anderson, B. J. (1991). Cerebellar synaptic plasticity: Relation to learning vs. neural activity. *Annals of the New York Academy of Sciences, 627,* 231–247.

Greenough, W. T., & Black, J. E. (1992). Induction of brain structure by experience: Substrates for cognitive development. In M. Gunnar & C. A. Nelson (eds.), *Behavioral developmental neuroscience: Vol. 24. Minnesota Symposia on Child Psychology.* Hillsdale, NJ: Erlbaum.

Gross, C. G. (2000). Neurogenesis in the adult brain: death of a dogma. *Nature Review of Neuroscience, 1,* 67–73.

Gur, R. C., Turetsky, B. I., Matsui, M., et al. (1999). Sex differences in brain gray and white matter in healthy young adults: correlations with cognitive performance. *Journal of Neuroscience, 19,* 4065–4072.

Guralnick, M. J. (ed.) (1997). *The effectiveness of early intervention.* Baltimore: Brookes.

Gwiazda, J., Thorn, F., Bauer, J., & Held, R. (1993). Emmetropization and the progression of manifest refraction in children followed from infancy to puberty. *Clinical Vision Sciences, 8,* 337–344.

Harlow, H. F., Harlow, M. K., & Meyer, D. R. (1950). Learning motivated by a manipulation drive. *Journal of Experimental Psychology, 40,* 228–234.

Hatfield, E., & Rapson, R. L. (1996). *Love and sex: Cross-cultural perspectives.* Boston: Allyn & Bacon.

Hazan, C., & Diamond, L. M. (2000). The place of attachment in human mating. *Review of General Psychology, 4,* 186–204.

Herrnstein, R. J., & Murray, C. (1994). *The bell curve: Intelligence and class structure in American life.* New York: Free Press.

Hill, L., Craig, I. W., Ball, D. M., et al. (1999). DNA pooling and dense marker maps: A systematic search for genes for cognitive ability. *NeuroReport, 10,* 843–848.

Hotz, R. L. (2000, November 29). Women use more of brain when listening, study says. *Los Angeles Times,* A1, A18–19.

Hrdy, S. B. (1988). Empathy, polyandry, and the myth of the coy female. In R. Bleier (ed.), *Feminist approaches to science.* New York: Pergamon.

Hrdy, S. B. (1994). What do women want? In T. A. Bass (ed.), *Reinventing the future: Conversations with the world's leading scientists.* Reading, MA: Addison-Wesley.

Huntington's Disease Collaborative Research Group (1993). A novel gene containing a trinucleotide repeat that is expanded and unstable on Huntington's disease chromosomes. *Cell, 72,* 971–983.

Hyde, J. S. (2000). A gendered brain? [Review of *Sex and cognition,* by D. Kimura.] *Journal of Sex Research, 37,* 191.

Inglis, J., & L., J. S. (1981). Sex differences in the effects of unilateral brain damage on intelligence. *Science, 212,* 693–695.

James, W. (1890/1950). *Principles of psychology* (Vol. 1). New York: Dover.

Jancke, L.; Schlaug, G., & Steinmetz, H. (1997). Hand skill asymmetry in professional musicians. *Brain and Cognition, 34,* 424–432.

Jensen, A. R. (1969). How much can we boost IQ and scholastic achievement? *Harvard Educational Review, 39,* 1–123.

Jensen, A. R. (1981). *Straight talk about mental tests.* New York: Free Press.

Jones, S. (1994). *The language of genes.* New York: Anchor/Doubleday.

Jones, S. (2000). *Darwin's ghost: "The Origin of Species" updated.* New York: Random House.

Kempermann, G., Brandon, E. P., & Gage, F. H. (1998). Environmental stimulation of 120/SvJ mice causes increased cell proliferation and neurogenesis in the adult dentate gyrus. *Current Biology, 8,* 939–942.

Kenrick, D. T., Sundie, J. M., Nicastle, L. D., & Stone, G. O. (2001). Can one ever be too wealthy or too chaste? Searching for nonlinearities in mate judgment. *Journal of Personality and Social Psychology, 80,* 462–471.

Kenrick, D. T., & Trost, M. R. (1993). The evolutionary perspective. In A. E. Beall & R. J. Sternberg (eds.), *The psychology of gender.* New York: Guilford Press.

Kim, K. H. S., Relkin, N. R., Lee, K-M., & Hirsch, J. (1997). Distinct cortical areas associated with native and second languages. *Nature, 388,* 171–174.

Klein, S. B., & Kihlstrom, J. F. (1998). On bridging the gap between social-personality psychology and neuropsychology. *Personality and Social Psychology Review, 2,* 228–242.

Klima, E. S., & Bellugi, U. (1966). Syntactic regularities in the speech of children. In J. Lyons & R. J. Wales (eds.), *Psycholinguistics papers.* Edinburgh, Scotland: Edinburgh University Press.

Kosslyn, S. M., Pascual-Leone, A., Felician, O., et al. (1999). The role of area 17 in visual imagery: convergent evidence from PET and rTMS. *Science, 284,* 167–170.

Krupa, D. J., Thompson, J. K., & Thompson, R. F. (1993). Localization of a memory trace in the mammalian brain. *Science, 260,* 989–991.

Lai, C. S. L., Fisher, S. E., Hurst, J. A.; et al. (2001). A forkhead-domain gene is mutated in a severe speech and language disorder. *Nature, 413,* 519–523.

Lanphear, B. P., Hornung, R., Ho, M., et al. (2002). Environmental lead exposure during early childhood. *Journal of Pediatrics, 140,* 49–47.

Laumann, E. O., & Gagnon J. H. (1995). A sociological perspective on sexual action. In R. G. Parker & J. H. Gagnon (eds.), *Conceiving sexuality: Approaches to sex research in a postmodern world.* New York: Routledge.

Laumann, E. O., Gagnon, J. H., Michael, R. T., & Michaels, S. (1994). *The social organization of sexuality.* Chicago: University of Chicago Press.

Lenneberg, E. H. (1967). *Biological foundations of language.* New York: Wiley.

Levine, J., & Suzuki, D. (1993). *The secret of life: Redesigning the living world.* Boston: WGBH Educational Foundation.

Levine, J. (2002). *Harmful to minors.* Minneapolis: University of Minnesota Press.

Levy, J., Trevarthen, C., & Sperry, R. W. (1972). Perception of bilateral chimeric figures following hemispheric deconnection. *Brain, 95,* 61–78.

Lewontin, R. C. (1970). Race and intelligence. *Bulletin of the Atomic Scientists, 26*(3), 2–8.

Lewontin, R. C. (2001, March 5). Genomania: A disorder of modern biology and medicine. Invited address at the University of California, Los Angeles.

Lewontin, R. C., Rose, S., & Kamin, L. J. (1984). *Not in our genes: Biology, ideology, and human nature.* New York: Pantheon.

Liepert, J., Bauder, H., Miltner, W. H., et al. (2000). Treatment-induced cortical reorganization after stroke in humans. *Stroke, 31,* 1210–1216.

Loehlin, J. C., Horn, J. M., & Willerman, L. (1996). Heredity, environment, and IQ in the Texas adoption study. In R. J. Sternberg & E. Grigorenko (eds.), *Intelligence: Heredity and environment.* New York: Cambridge University Press.

Luria, A. R. (1980). *Higher cortical functions in man* (2nd rev. ed.). New York: Basic Books.

MacLean, P. (1993). Cerebral evolution of emotion. In M. Lewis & J. M. Haviland (eds.), *Handbook of emotions.* New York: Guilford Press.

Macmillan, M. (2000). *An odd kind of fame: Stories of Phineas Gage.* Cambridge: MIT Press, 2000.

Maguire, E. A., Gadian, D. G., Johnsrude, I. S., et al. (2000). Navigation-related structural change in the hippocampi of taxi drivers. *Proceedings of the National Academy of Sciences, 97,* 4398–4403.

Maki, P. M., & Resnick, S. M. (2000). Longitudinal effects of estrogen replacement therapy on PET cerebral blood flow and cognition. *Neurobiology of Aging, 21,* 373–383.

Marcus, G. F. (1999). *The algebraic mind.* Cambridge, MA: MIT Press.

Marcus, G. F., Pinker, S., Ullman, M, et al. (1992). Overregularization in language acquisition. *Monographs of the Society for Research in Child Development, 57* (Serial No. 228), 1–182.

Marcus, G. F., Vijayan, S., Rao, S. B., & Vishton, P. M. (1999). Rule learning by seven-month-old infants. *Science, 283,* 77–80.

Matthews, J. (ed.) (1994). *McGill working papers in linguistics* (Vol. 10 [1 & 2]). [Special Issue: Linguistic aspects of familial language impairment.] Montreal, Quebec: McGill University.

McClearn, G. E., Johanson, B., Berg, S., et al. (1997). Substantial genetic influence on cognitive abilities in twins 80 or more years old. *Science, 176,* 1560–1563.

McGlone, J. (1978). Sex differences in functional brain asymmetry. *Cortex, 14,* 122–128.

McGue, M., Bouchard, T. J., Jr., Iacono, W. G., & Lykken, D. T. (1993). Behavioral genetics of cognitive ability: A life-span perspective. In R. Plomin & G. E. McClearn (eds.), *Nature, nurture, and psychology.* Washington, DC: American Psychological Association.

McNeill, D. (1966). Developmental psycholinguistics. In F. L. Smith & G. A. Miller (eds.), *The genesis of language: A psycholinguistic approach.* Cambridge, MA: MIT Press.

Mealey, L. (1996). Evolutionary psychology: The search for evolved mental mechanisms underlying complex human behavior. In J. P. Hurd (ed.), *Investigating the biological foundations of human morality* (Vol. 37). Lewiston, NY: Edwin Mellen Press.

Mealey, L. (2000). *Sex differences: Developmental and evolutionary strategies.* San Diego: Academic Press.

Milner, B. (1970). Memory and the temporal regions of the brain. In K. H. Pribram & D. E. Broadbent (eds.), *Biology of memory.* New York: Academic Press.

Mishkin, M., Suzuki, W. A., Gadian, D. G., & Vargha-Khadem, F. (1997). Hierarchical organization of cognitive memory. *Philosophical Transactions of the Royal Society of London, B: Biological Science, 352,* 1461–1467.

Müller, R-A., Courchesne, E., & Allen, G. (1998). The cerebellum: So much more. [Letter.] *Science, 282,* 879–880.

Needleman, H. L., Riess, J. A., Tobin, M. J., et al. (1996). Bone lead levels and delinquent behavior. *Journal of the American Medical Association, 275,* 363–369.

Neisser, U. (ed.) (1998). *The rising curve: Long-term gains in IQ and related measures.* Washington, DC: American Psychological Association.

Netting, J. (2001, April 7). Gray matters: Neurons get top billing, but lesser-known brain cells also star. *Science News, 159,* 222–223.

Ogden, J. A., & Corkin, S. (1991). Memories of H. M. In W. C. Abraham, M. C. Corballis, & K. G. White (eds.), *Memory mechanisms: A tribute to G. V. Goddard.* Hillsdale, NJ: Erlbaum.

Olds, J. (1975). Mapping the mind onto the brain. In F. G. Worden, J. P. Swazy, & G. Adelman (eds.), *The neurosciences: Paths of discovery.* Cambridge, MA: Colonial Press.

Olds, J., & Milner, P. (1954). Positive reinforcement produced by electrical stimulation of septal area and other regions of the rat brain. *Journal of Comparative and Physiological Psychology, 47,* 419–429.

Palmer, T. D., Schartz, P. H., Taupin, P., et al. (2001). Cell culture. Progenitor cells from human brain after death. *Nature, 411,* 42–43.

Panksepp, J. (1998). Attention deficit hyperactivity disorders, psychostimulants, and intolerance of childhood playfulness: A tragedy in the making? *Current Directions in Psychological Science, 7,* 91–98.

Parker, G. M. (1997). *Trespassing: My sojourn in the halls of privilege.* Boston: Houghton Mifflin.

Pellegrini, A. D., & Galda, L. (1993). Ten years after: A reexamination of symbolic play and literacy research. *Reading Research Quarterly, 28,* 163–175.

Pert, C. B., & Snyder, S. H. (1973). Opiate receptor: Demonstration in nervous tissue. *Science, 179,* 1011–1014.

Pesetsky, D. (1999). Introduction to symposium: "Grammar: What's innate?" Paper presented at the annual meeting of the American Association for the Advancement of Science, Anaheim.

Phillips, M. D., Lowe, M. J., Lurito, J. T., et al. (2001). Temporal lobe activation demonstrates sex-based differences during passive listening. *Radiology, 220,* 202–207.

Pinker, S. (1994). *The language instinct: How the mind creates language.* New York: Morrow.

Pinker, S. (1997). *How the mind works.* New York: Norton.

Pinker, S. (1999). *Words and rules: The ingredients of language.* New York: Basic Books.

Plomin, R. (1989). Environment and genes: Determinants of behavior. *American Psychologist, 44,* 105–111.

Plomin, R., & Crabbe, J. (2000). DNA. *Psychological Bulletin, 126,* 806–828.

Plomin, R., & DeFries, J. C. (1985). *Origins of individual differences in infancy: The Colorado Adoption Project.* New York: Academic Press.

Plomin, R., DeFries, J. C., McClearn, G. E., & McGuffin, P. (2001). *Behavioral genetics* (4th ed.). New York: Worth.

Radetsky, P. (1991, April). The brainiest cells alive. *Discover, 12,* 82–85, 88, 90.

Ramey, C. T., & Ramey, S. L. (1998). Early intervention and early experience. *American Psychologist, 53,* 109–120.

Regard, M., & Landis, T. (1997). "Gourmand syndrome": Eating passion associated with right anterior lesions. *Neurology, 48,* 1185–1190.

Restak, R. (1983, October). Is free will a fraud? *Science Digest, 91*(10), 52–55.

Restak, R. M. (1994). *The modular brain.* New York: Macmillan.

Reynolds, B. A., & Weiss, S. (1992). Generation of neurons and astrocytes from isolated cells of the adult mammalian central nervous system. *Science, 255,* 1707–1710.

Rodriguez, P., Wiles, J., & Elman, J. L. (1999). A recurrent neural network that learns to count. *Connection Science, 11,* 5–40.

Rosenzweig, M. R. (1984). Experience, memory, and the brain. *American Psychologist, 39,* 365–376.

Rumelhart, D. E., & McClelland, J. L. (1987). Learning the past tenses of English verbs: Implicit rules or parallel distributed processing. In B. MacWhinney (ed.), *Mechanisms of language acquisition.* Hillsdale, NJ: Erlbaum.

Rumelhart, D. E., McClelland, J. L.; & the PDP Research Group (1986). *Parallel distributed processing: Explorations in the microstructure of cognition* (Vols. 1 and 2). Cambridge, MA: MIT Press.

Rymer, R. (1993). *Genie: An abused child's flight from silence.* New York: HarperCollins.

Sacks, O. (1985). *The man who mistook his wife for a hat and other clinical tales.* New York: Simon & Schuster.

Saffran, J. R., Aslin, R. N., & Newport, E. L. (1996). Statistical learning by 8-month-old infants. *Science, 274,* 1926–1928.

Sameroff, A. J., Seifer, R., Barocas, R., et al. (1987). Intelligence quotient scores of 4-year-old children: Social-environmental risk factors. *Pediatrics, 79,* 343–350.

Sanchez-Ramos, J. R., Song, S., Kamath, S. G., et al. (2001). Expressioon of neural markers in human umbilical cord blood. *Experimental Neurology, 171,* 109–115.

Scarr, S. (1993). Biological and cultural diversity: The legacy of Darwin for development. *Child Development, 64,* 1333–1353.

Scarr, S., & Weinberg, R. A. (1994). Educational and occupational achievement of brothers and sisters in adoptive and biologically related families. *Behavioral Genetics, 24,* 301–325.

Scarr, S., Pakstis, A. J., Katz, S. H., & Barker, W. B. (1977). Absence of a relationship between degree of white ancestry and intellectual skill in a black population. *Human Genetics, 39,* 69–86.

Schnell, L., & Schwab, M. E. (1990, January 18). Axonal regeneration in the rat spinal cord produced by an antibody against myelin-associated neurite growth inhibitors. *Nature, 343,* 269–272.

Seidenberg, M. S. (1997). Language acquisition and use: Learning and applying probabilistic constraints. *Science, 275,* 1599–1603.

Senghas, A., & Coppola, M. (2001). Children creating language: How Nicaraguan Sign Language acquired a spatial grammar. *Psychological Science, 12,* 323–328.

Shaywitz, B. A., Shaywitz, S. E., Pugh, K. R., et al. (1995). Sex differences in the functional organization of the brain for language. *Nature, 373,* 607–609.

Sherwin, B. B. (1998a). Estrogen and cognitive functioning in women. *Proceedings of the Society for Experimental Biological Medicine, 217,* 17–22.

Shields, S. A. (1975). Functionalism, Darwinism, and the psychology of women: A study in social myth. *American Psychologist, 30,* 739–754.

Slobin, D. I. (ed.) (1985). *The cross-linguistic study of language acquisition* (Vols. 1 and 2). Hillsdale, NJ: Erlbaum.

Slobin, D. I. (ed.) (1991). *The cross-linguistic study of language acquisition* (Vol. 3). Hillsdale, NJ: Erlbaum.

Snowdon, C. T. (1997). The "nature" of sex differences: Myths of male and female. In P.A. Gowaty (ed.), *Feminism and evolutionary biology.* New York: Chapman and Hall.

Sperry, R. W. (1964). The great cerebral commissure. *Scientific American, 210*(1), 42–52.

Sperry, R. W. (1982). Some effects of disconnecting the cerebral hemispheres. *Science, 217,* 1223–1226.

Springer, S. P., & Deutsch, G. (1998). Left brain, right brain: *Perspectives from cognitive neuroscience.* New York: Freeman.

Squire, L. R. (1987). *Memory and the brain.* New York: Oxford University Press.

Squire, L. R., & Zola-Morgan, S. (1991). The medial temporal lobe memory system. *Science, 253,* 1380–1386.

Staples, B. (1994). *Parallel time.* New York: Pantheon.

Stoch, M. B., & Smythe, P. M. (1963). Does undernutrition during infancy inhibit brain growth and subsequent intellectual development? *Archives of Diseases in Childhood, 38,* 546–552.

Symons, D. (1979). *The evolution of human sexuality.* New York: Oxford University Press.

Tartter, V. C. (1986). *Language processes*. New York: Holt, Rinehart and Winston.

Thorndike, E. L. (1903). *Educational psychology*. New York: Columbia University Teachers College.

Thornhill, R., & Palmer, C. T. (2000). *A natural history of rape: Biological bases of sexual coercion*. Cambridge, MA: MIT Press.

Toma, J. G., Akhavan, M., Frenandes, K. J., et al. (2001). Isolation of multipotent adult stem cells from the dermis of mammalian skin. *Nature Cell Biology, 3*, 778–784.

Travis, J. (2000). Snap, crackle, and feel good? Magnetic fields that map the brain may also treat its disorders. *Science News*.

Trivers, R. (1972). Parental investment and sexual selection. In B. Campbell (ed.), *Sexual selection and the descent of man*. New York: Aldine de Gruyter.

Ullian, E. M., Sapperstein, S. K., Christopherson, K. S., & Barres, B. A. (2001). Control of synapse number by glia. *Science, 291*, 657–661.

van Praag, H., Kempermann, G., & Gage, F. H. (1999). Running increases cell proliferation and neurogenesis in the adult mouse dentate gyrus. *Nature Neuroscience, 2*, 266–270.

Vandenberg, B. (1985). Beyond the ethology of play. In A. Gottfried & C. C. Brown (eds.), *Play interactions*. Lexington, MA: Lexington Books.

Watson, J. B. (1925). *Behaviorism*. New York: Norton.

Werner, P., Pitt, D., & Raine, C. S. (2001). Multiple sclerosis: altered glutamate homeostasis in lesions correlates with aligodendrocyte and axonal damage. Annals of Neurology, 50, 169–180.

Wheeler, D. L. (1998, September 11). Neuroscientists take stock of brain-imaging studies. *Chronicle of Higher Education*, A20–A21.

Wickelgren, I. (1997). Estrogen stakes claim to cognition. *Science, 276*, 675–678.

Wilson, E. O. (1975). *Sociobiology: The new synthesis*. Cambridge, MA: Belknap/Harvard University Press.

Wilson, E. O. (1978). *On human nature*. Cambridge, MA: Harvard University Press.

Winick, M., Meyer, K. K., & Harris, R. C. (1975). Malnutrition and environmental enrichment by early adoption. *Science, 190*, 1173–1175.

Winslade, W. J. (1998). *Confronting traumatic brain injury: Devastation, hope, and healing*. New Haven: Yale University Press.

Witelson, S. F., Glazer, I. I., & Kigar, D. L. (1994). Sex differences in numerical density of neurons in human auditory association cortex. *Society for Neuroscience Abstracts, 30* (Abstr. No. 582.12).

Witelson, S., Kigar, D. L., & Harvey, T. (1999). The exceptional brain of Albert Einstein. *Lancet, 353*, 2149–2153.

Woodbury, D., Schwarz, E. J, Prockop, D. J.; & Black, I. B. (2000). Adult rat and human bone marrow stromal cells differentiate into neurons. *Journal of Neuroscience Research, 61*, 364–370.

CHAPTER 8

GROW YOUR OWN . . . COMPUTER[1]

Justin M. Joffe

---

[1]Incorporating the research of B. Jacobs, M. Schall, and A.B. Scheibel (1993).

The brain is often compared to a computer, and often the comparison implies that the brain isn't as good as a reasonably high-end desktop. I suppose that if you limit the comparison to logic, a good computer might win. A lot of research on human cognition indicates that there are built-in inaccuracies in some of our reasoning and in the way we recall past events. These biases often make very good sense insofar as they are a trade off between speed of processing and accuracy, and in our evolutionary past it may often have been better for us to jump to conclusions than to be eaten by a predator, but nevertheless these kinds of pressures to survive and reproduce have not directly affected the "reasoning" powers of computers.

If we made the comparison on something like intelligence, however, I think the brain might beat out the computer—how often have you yelled at your e-mail for not realizing that you had typed the right address, even though it lacked the dot? An intelligent person would have realized whom you were writing to and not returned an error message. And an intelligent word processor would not let me write, "I went two the cafeteria four coffee," even if all the words are spelled correctly.

Both of these decisions, about the relative bias and intelligence of brains and computers, are judgment calls. There are also more objective measures of the similarities and differences that may be of interest. Take the capacity of the hardware: the human brain probably has about 100 billion neurons (nerve cells) though estimates range as high as 200 billion. The Society for Neuroscience's web site says that if you were to count the 100 billion neurons in the brain, and counted at the rate of one neuron per second, it would take you about 3,171 years to complete the job (*http://web.sfn.org/*—an excellent place to look for information on the brain). Each neuron has connections (synapses) with an average of about 10,000 other cells and the approximately 10 billion neurons in the cerebral cortex are estimated to have a total of 60 *trillion* synapses.

How does this compare to a computer in terms of memory capacity, processing power, and processing speed? There are too many ways of looking at these questions to deal with here without losing track of the main issue, but if you are interested you can spend a fascinating hour or two by typing the words "brain" and "computer" into a search engine on your computer. At the very least we might agree that computers do not rewire themselves, but (as the work described in this chapter indicates) brains do (Jacobs, 2003).

The feature of the brain most relevant to the research we will look at in this chapter is its "plasticity," and this is something it does not share with computers. In my opinion, that is—I am sure many people could argue a case for computers having plasticity. I think you have to stretch the meaning of the term to cover the things the brain does in this regard.

Plasticity refers to the brain's capacity to grow and change, particularly to the ability it has to compensate to some extent for damage to an area by transferring the lost functions to other areas of the brain and to grow more neurons in areas where they are needed due to demands placed on a person. We will look at examples of two kinds of evidence: (a) Research showing that when parts of the brain that normally mediate functions are damaged other parts take over; (b) Work indicating that when demands are placed on functions the brain can allocate more resources and even grow more neurons to handle the functions involved. (We will not look at the normal changes in the brain during the prenatal period and early childhood, called "developmental plasticity".)

RESEARCH ON PLASTICITY

First, some of the research findings on compensation for losses. Parts of the brain can be damaged or destroyed in a variety of ways, including accidents, gunshot wounds, strokes, tumors, other diseases, and surgery. Generally, compensation for damage is greater when damage occurs early (say up to about age 10) than when it occurs later in life. Data supporting the hypothesis that brain areas can take on different functions to their normal ones comes from experimental research on non-human animals, and from clinical studies of people with brain damage.

Patterson, Varga-Khadem, and Polkey (1989) studied two girls who, at age 15, had had one side of their brain removed to treat terrible seizures due to a rare brain disease known as Rasmussen's syndrome. This case study constituted a kind of mini-experiment, since one girl had to have her right cerebral hemisphere removed, the other her left. Language is normally mediated in the left hemisphere (this is the case in 96% of people), so one might expect little effect of the loss of the right hemisphere on reading skills like word recognition, naming letters, and reading words, which is what the experimenters investigated. On the other hand, one would expect substantial loss of function if the left hemisphere were removed. In fact, the girl with the intact left hemisphere performed well on all the tests. The other girl, however, with only a right hemisphere, had difficulty with some of the tasks (for example, she could not produce a word to rhyme with a word she was given, even in the case of simple words like "cat," and had difficulty naming printed words). The findings of most interest, however, were those indicating the extent to which her right hemisphere alone was capable of handling language tasks. In fact, the girl's ability to function linguistically was studied before the decision was made to remove her left hemisphere, since a total loss of language skills might have been judged to be worse than the debilitating seizures the surgery was intended to cure. On three occasions her left hemisphere was anaesthetized, and on one occasion her right; the test results were complex, but it was found that total loss of speech occurred only when her right hemisphere was anaesthetized. It seems that language functions had, to some extent at least, been transferred from her impaired left hemisphere to her intact right one even prior to the surgery.

Later, Muller and collaborators (1999) reported on brain functioning in patients who had suffered damage to their left hemisphere either early in life (onset before the age of 5 of—in most cases—epilepsy) compared to others who had lesions later (onset after the age of 20 of problems involving—in most of these cases—a type of brain tumor). It was already known that the right hemisphere is more active during language processing in adults with left hemisphere damage than in adults with unimpaired left hemispheres, and Muller et al. were interested in determining whether this effect would be stronger in patients with damage occurring in early development. Previously, data from animal research and some case studies had shown that plasticity might be greater earlier in development. Their interest was in brain function rather than structure, so they used PET scans. Positron Emission Tomography is a technique of measuring the radioactivity emitted by cells when positively charged particles (positrons) undergo radioactive decay; a computer puts together a picture of this, giving us an image that shows the amount of the blood flow or metabolic activity that is taking place in various parts of the brain under different conditions.

When people without brain lesions listen to sentences (language perception), considerably more activity is seen in parts of the left hemisphere than in the same parts of the right. The average activity in the same regions in the 10 adults with later-onset lesions was about the same on the left and the right, and the activity in these areas in those patients with early onset lesions was reversed—there was more activity in the right hemisphere than in the left. When brain activity was measured while participants were repeating sentences read to them (language production), similar changes were seen but not in all brain areas looked at. The authors concluded that reorganization of brain function following lesions involves, among other things, "regions that are not normally involved in a given function" becoming involved, and that the degree of reorganization—plasticity—is greater when the damage occurs earlier. Such plasticity is not limited to early development, though, and some older adults who suffer lesions due to strokes recover the lost functions to some degree, presumably because intact brain areas take over from the areas lost.

NORMAL BRAINS

What then happens in a *normal* brain when greater than normal demands are placed on some of its areas? For example, if sensory systems such as sight or hearing are missing, what can the brain do to improve functioning of other systems that may help people compensate for the missing senses? Evidence from people who are born blind or deaf, or who become so in infancy, reveals interesting and important adaptations, and the findings are in line with experimental research on cats blinded or deafened at birth: blinded cats have more of their cortex used in hearing than normal cats and are better at locating sounds in their environments (Rauscheker and Kniepert, 1994), whereas those deafened show activity in response to visual stimuli in areas of the brain usually involved in hearing (Rebillard, Carlier, Rebillard, and Pujol, 1977). Studies of blind and deaf humans (reviewed by Bosworth and Dobkins, 1999) show similar use of areas of the brain not needed for processing missing sensory processes to process information from other senses, such as visual brain areas processing sounds and touch or auditory areas being used for sight. Bosworth and Dobkins themselves found differences in the brain organization connected with processing visual movement, a skill of use to deaf people in communicating fluently in sign language. Deaf people did much better when such information was in the right visual field, suggesting that their left hemisphere has become specialized for movement detection, whereas in people with intact hearing it is specialized for spoken language. In short, the left hemisphere is dominant for language in both deaf and hearing people, but for the former the specialization involves motion detection not spoken language.

But does this kind of thing happen in humans and non-humans with normal intact brains *and* sense organs, or is plasticity found only in response to unusual and severe challenges like blindness and brain lesions? For over 50 years we have known that enriching environments during early development improves cognitive skills. Rats that grow up in stimulating environments, containing features like wheels, ladders to climb, objects to explore, and so on learn mazes much faster than rats reared in "normal" impoverished laboratory cages (e.g., Forgays and Forgays, 1952). Then, about a decade later, researchers began looking at the question of whether the environments and experiences that improved learning ability affected the brain in some way, as one might predict—for how else would their cognitive skill be improved?

ENVIRONMENT AND BRAIN STRUCTURE AND FUNCTION

A group of researchers at the University of California at Berkely did extensive research on the effects of living in enriched environments on rats' brains. This group, including Edward Bennett, Marion Diamond, David Krech, and Mark Rosenzweig demonstrated that the brains of rats that lived in enriched environments for various periods of time and at different ages showed considerable changes in both anatomy and chemistry. Summarizing much of the work done over many years, Diamond (2002) notes that there were increases in the thickness and weight of the cerebral cortex (attributable to various changes, including increased size of neurons, increased number and length of dendrites, and increased numbers of glial cells) as well as changes in various brain chemicals. These changes increase the number of connection and probably underlie the improved learning skills of the rats. These and related findings of chemical and anatomical plasticity were a surprise to those holding traditional views of brain development: until modern evidence was available the widespread assumption was that the brain changed little after its development in young organisms, except perhaps for loss of cells and deterioration as we age.

How do we study effects of environmental factors on the brains of humans? We could probably justify *enriching* children's environments (placing extra mobiles above babies' cribs or more toys in pre-school classrooms would probably not raise ethical concerns) but what would we do about a control group? Could we justify placing one group of babies (or college students!) in a featureless, boring, unstimulating environment for a period of months or even years? The answer should be obvious, and perhaps stimulate you to think about the rat experiments: which rats should we see as the experimental group, and which as the controls?

Researchers' ingenuity comes to our rescue here: in addition to studying changes in the brain attributable to naturally occurring life experiences of different kinds, they have looked at differences in the brains of people who have lived in environments that differ naturally in some perhaps important ways.

The first line of research has produced some interesting findings, strongly supporting the general hypothesis that the brain can reorganize itself in response to environmental demands in ways that increase its efficacy in processing information. For example, have you ever watched a skilled violinist, and wondered whether she has a brain that is different from yours that enables her to do such complex manual tasks so effectively? She probably does, but you could probably compete if you were willing to devote the time to it. The practice that improves your playing skills will also improve (and almost certainly is attributable to) the amount of your cerebral cortex (the number of nerve cells, in other words) that is devoted to the fingers you need to play the violin.

Using a method of studying the brain by measuring magnetic fields (a technique called magnetic source imaging) researchers can determine how the cerebral cortex's functions are organized without surgery or other techniques that might be dangerous or uncomfortable. When Elbert, Pantev, Wienbruch, Rockstroh, and Taub (1995) used this technique to see how much of the cortex was devoted to representation of the fingers, they found that the area devoted to the fingers of the left hand of string players was larger than it was in controls. The effect was least evident in the thumb (used far less than the fingers) and "no such differences were observed for the representations of the right hand digits" (remember that a string instrument player uses the left hand for far more finger movements than the right hand). They found that the effect was greater in people who had started playing before the age of 12 than in those who learned when they were older, but changes occurred in older people too. "These results," they say "suggest that the representation of different parts of the body in the primary somatosensory cortex of humans depends on use and changes to conform to the current needs and experiences of the individual" (p. 305).

Thus we see that the changes in the use of brain areas found in people born blind or deaf occur also in those without sensory losses. And this evidence is bolstered by data from a different source—taxi drivers. In some major cities (though not all, as unfortunate travelers will tell you) aspirant taxi drivers have to pass exacting tests of their knowledge of the topography of the city; they really have to know their way around before they get a license to drive a cab. In London (England), a large and complex city with hardly a rectangular city block on its map, and with one way systems and all the other facilities of modern road systems (apparently intended to cause early deaths in drivers due to stress), it takes would-be taxi drivers an average of two years to acquire "The Knowledge" needed to pass the police examinations. Maguire and her collaborators (2000) hypothesized, on the basis of other research, including that on brain changes in musicians, that there would be changes in brain structure in healthy human brains of people with "extensive experience of spatial navigation" (p. 4398), namely London taxi drivers.

Using a measurement technique based on an imaging technique known as Magnetic Resonance Imaging (MRI), they found significant enlargement in an area of the brain associated with memory, including spatial memory (the posterior hippocampus), in 16 London taxi drivers with an average of over 14 years in the business; their brains were compared with those of healthy males who did not drive taxis. And in the taxi drivers the size of this brain area on the right side of the brain but not on the left was significantly (and positively) correlated with the amount of time they had spent driving taxis. Another part of the same brain area, the anterior hippocampus, was significantly smaller in the taxi drivers, but there were no other differences between their brains and those of the controls. The researchers suggest that these reciprocal changes (an increase in the size of one area and a decrease in the size of a neighboring area) indicate "a relative redistribution of gray matter in the hippocampus" (p. 4402)— what's needed for spatial function is appropriated from a neighboring area—and that a "mental map" of the city is stored in the posterior hippocampus, which needs more space to accommodate it. This suggestion is contrary to the more widely accepted notion that the hippocampus is more important in the formation of new memories than in long-term storage (think about H.M., described in the chapter "Hungry Again").

The correlations of changes in the hippocampi with the length of time men had been driving taxis argue against reverse causation, the notion that people with larger posterior hippocampi are more likely to choose to become taxi drivers. In those with little experience the brain area is little different from men who do not drive taxis, in those with more experience the difference is greater. Interestingly, the hippocampal area that was enlarged in taxi drivers was enlarged about equally on both sides of the brain, but the correlations with years spent as a taxi driver (which increased size of the posterior hippocampus and decreased that of the anterior) was found only in the right hippocampus, the side the researchers had earlier found to be activated when drivers were asked to recall complicated routes from one part of the city to another.

Does more general environmental enrichment of the type we described briefly, which affects the size and chemistry of various brain areas in rodents and which is correlated with improved learning ability, have an effect on the structure or function of the human brain? This is essentially the question that Jacobs, Schall, and Scheibel set out to answer. They focused on the area of the brain known to be very important in mediating the comprehension of language and the production of meaningful speech, the portion of the left temporal lobe known as Wernicke's area (named after the neurologist who first explicated its role in language); the same brain structures in the right hemisphere are not called Wernicke's area. This region was chosen partly because the kinds of general experiences the researchers were interested in were those relating to a person's intellectual and verbal life, which they assumed to be roughly reflected in the amount of education the person has had.

Jacobs et al. chose dendritic branching as their major dependent measure for a variety of reasons. In the first place, dendritic branching is affected by various forms of stimulation and experience, and earlier studies had shown increases in dendritic branching in rat brains after rats had been trained in mazes; intriguingly, if rats learned a reaching task with one paw, only one side of the brain showed changes; the hemisphere serving the untrained paw was unaffected (Greenough, Larson, and Withers, 1985). Furthermore, dendrites are a likely candidate for changes in cognitive functioning: recall that almost all the input to a nerve cell is through its dendrites, so that increases in dendritic complexity increase the number of connections a neuron has, and in effect increase the computing power of the system.

The researchers thus set out to "extend the environmental enrichment paradigm to humans" (p. 98). They hypothesized that someone with a "more active verbal/intellectual life" would have "more complex dendritic systems than an individual with less verbal/intellectual interaction" (p. 98).

METHOD

Participants

The research we are looking at is of a kind where participants might better be labeled "subjects." The brain tissue studied came from autopsies on people who had died in the Los Angeles area from a variety of causes. The subjects ranged in age from 18 (a traffic accident victim) to 79 (death from heart disease). Most (15) were Caucasian, three (two women and one man) were African-American, and there was one Hispanic man and one Armenian man. All the people were right handed and their brain tissue was included only if it showed no signs of neurological problems and if there had not been a delay of more than 24 hours between death and post-mortem, unless the cadaver had been refrigerated after death and the brain tissue appeared to be in good condition (fewer than 10 percent of available brains met these criteria). Characteristics of the subjects are shown in Table 8.1. All information came from autopsy reports, medical records, and telephone calls to next of kin if needed information could not be ascertained from the other sources.

Procedures

Blocks of tissue were removed from the same areas of the right and left hemispheres of the 20 brains. Tissue samples were coded to prevent experimenter bias and the source of the tissue was identified only after the data had been entered into the computer. Then the tissue was stained, sliced into very thin sections using a special machine, and the slices mounted on microscope slides. Individual neurons (including the cell body, the axon, and the dendrites) were then drawn to scale using a device known as a

TABLE 8.1 Characteristics of the subjects studied: numbers of people in each category

	MEN	WOMEN	AVERAGE AGE (YEARS)
Education[1]			
<HS	3	0	62.7
HS	3	6	46.7
UNI	4	4	49.0
TOTAL	**10**	**10**	**Men: 52.2 (range 18–78)** **Women: 47.8 (range 20–79)**
Cause of death			
Accident	2	0	32
Leukemia	1	3	36
Liver failure	1	2	34
Heart-related	2	4	62
Other[2]	4	1	64

1 "< HS" = Had not graduated from High School
   "HS" = High school diploma but less than 2 years of college
   "UNI" = More than 2 years of college, including college graduates
2 Includes various cancers, pneumonia, sepsis

"camera lucida." This is an optical instrument that projects an image onto a sheet of paper so it can be traced; the device can be attached to a microscope for drawing cells placed under the microscope.[2]

In this way the researchers were able to obtain drawings of 20 intact neurons per brain (10 from each hemisphere). When these drawings were entered into a computer, very precise measures of dendrites could be obtained for each neuron:

1. Total length (TL): the sum of the lengths of all the dendritic segments; the values reported for various groups are adjusted to take into account the size of the groups.
2. Average length (AL): TL divided by the number of segments.
3. Number of segments (NS): the number of dendritic segments.

We thus have a design we can characterize as a two (hemispheres) by two (sexes) by three (levels of education) design. If we do the arithmetic, we see that they measured 400 neurons: 10 from each hemisphere (= 20 neurons) of 10 men and 10 women (= 20 brains). They could also distinguish between segments close to where the dendrite starts out from the cell body, which probably formed earlier in the development of the neuron, and segments (branches) seen further out, which are probably dendrites that developed later.

RESULTS

They found that each neuron they studied had an average of four dendrites; there were a total of 1610 dendrites in the 400 neurons they examined, and a total of 16,697 segments for statistical analysis (an average of over 40 dendritic segments per neuron, a figure that may give you some idea of the complexity of the neuron). Approximately half the dendrites were from women (827), half from men (783), half from the left hemisphere (809), half from the right (801).

Changes with Age

In their first paper based on these data the researchers reported primarily on age-related changes in dendrites (Jacobs and Scheibel, 1993). They found significant differences between their younger group (six women and four men, all under 50, with an average age of 34.5 years) and their older one (four women and six men, all over 50, and averaging 65.5 years) in both total and average dendritic length, which decreased with age; on both measures the correlations between age and length were significant (−0.44 for total length and −0.69 for average length). The decrease in length was more pronounced in branches further from the cell body. There were no significant age-related changes in dendritic number however, and the correlation (0.23) was not significant.

Jacobs and Scheibel note that there is a lot of variability in these age-related changes and the oldest subject, a 79 year-old woman, had dendritic values well above average. They also note that the data are from a cross-sectional study and that "the observed dendritic changes revealed trends that were neither inevitable nor absolute" (p. 93). The considerable variability in the measures was one of the reasons they looked at variables like gender and education that might contribute to the big differences from one person to another, and these are the focus of the second paper they wrote, the paper that is the main source of the material for this chapter.

[2]The technique is far more complex than my brief summary indicates. If you are interested, consult Jacobs and Scheibel (1993) for many more fascinating details of what they did. In more recent work the camera lucida is replaced with a program called "Neurolucida" that allows the cells to be traced directly onto a computer (Jacobs, 2003).

Left Vs Right Hemisphere

The measures for each of the two hemispheres are shown in Table 8.2.

On average, dendrites in the left hemisphere were longer than those in the right, but the differences were small and, as you can see from the last column in the table, inconsistent.

Women Vs Men

Differences between the brains of women and men are shown in Table 8.3.

Women had more dendritic segments than men, and both the total and average lengths of segments were greater. This sex difference was small but consistent across age; other research shows sex differences as early as age 9.

TABLE 8.2   Number and length of dendrites in the left and right hemispheres of the 10 women and 10 men

	LEFT HEMISPHERE	RIGHT HEMISPHERE	RIGHT AS PERCENTAGE OF LEFT	NUMBER OF WOMEN/MEN WITH LEFT VALUES > RIGHT
Number of Segments (NS)	425	410	96.5	7/6 (= 13/20)
Total Length (TL)*	26371	25424	96.4	6/6 (= 12/20)
Average Length (AL)*	62.10	61.98	99.8	3/5 (=8/20)

*Length is measured in microns (millionths of a meter—25,400 microns would be about 1 inch).

NS: the number of dendritic segments
TL: the sum of the lengths of all the dendritic segments
AL: TL divided by the number of segments

TABLE 8.3   Number and length of dendrites in brains of 10 women and 10 men

	WOMEN	MEN	MEN AS PERCENTAGE OF WOMEN
Number of Segments (NS)	857	813	94.9
Total Length (TL)*	54177	49414	91.2
Average Length (AL)*	63.20	60.82	96.2

*Length is measured in microns (millionths of a meter—25,400 microns would be about 1 inch).

NS: the number of dendritic segments
TL: the sum of the lengths of all the dendritic segments
AL: TL divided by the number of segments

Education

Dendritic measures in relation to level of education are shown in Table 8.4.

All three measures show increases with increasing educational level. People who had graduated from high school had about 5 percent more dendritic segments than those who had not, and people with more than 2 years of college had about 4 percent more than the high school graduates. The change with increasing levels of education is even greater when dendritic length is examined: total length is 19 percent higher in high school graduates and 27% higher in those with 2 years or more of college than it is in people who had not graduated from high school. As the last row of Table 8.4 indicates, the effects were consistent, with the total length of almost all the people in the UNI group above the overall average.

Discussion

As we see in Table 8.2, the differences between the two hemispheres in number and length of dendrites is neither as large nor as consistent as one might expect, given that the brain area studied in the left hemisphere is Wernicke's area, the area that mediates language comprehension. The absence of larger differences cannot be attributed to other variable (like age or sex) since the tissue from the two hemispheres is from the same people. However, as Jacobs et al. point out, there is variation from person to person in exactly which parts of the cortex are involved in particular functions, so that without other evidence we cannot be certain that the tissue examined was serving the same function in each individual.

The sex differences (Table 8.3) are consistent and similar to dendritic differences found in rats and monkeys and in accord with research showing greater cerebral activity in women (as measured by PET scans and MRIs, for example). Could these differences be due to something other than gender? In other words, do the women and men differ in some other way that might account for the differences? The finding of a relationship between dendritic length and age might make us suspect that the sex

TABLE 8.4   Number and length of dendrites in brains of people of different educational levels

	< HS+	HS+	UNI+
Number of women/men	0/3	6/3	4/4
Number of Segments (NS)	787	827	861
Total Length (TL)*	43397	51695	55057
Average Length (AL)*	55.17	62.48	63.92
Number of individuals with TL values greater than the average TL	0	4	7

*Length is measured in microns (millionths of a meter—25,400 microns would be about 1 inch)
+< HS: Had not graduated from High School
+HS: High school diploma but less than 2 years of college
+UNI = More than 2 years of college, including college graduates

NS: the number of dendritic segments
TL: the sum of the lengths of all the dendritic segments
AL: TL divided by the number of segments

differences could be the result of age differences, but a look at the age data in Table 8.1 may lead us to conclude that the women and men are fairly well matched on this variable.

The largest and most consistent effects are seen in looking at the data on educational level, with increase in all measures in people with more formal education (Table 8.4). Could these differences be attributable to some other variable? Here the picture is not as clear as it is with sex differences, since the group with the lowest educational level contained only three people, all of them men, and with an average age over 13 years more than that of the next oldest group (Table 8.1). The authors suggest that age and sex might account, at least partly, for the differences between the lowest educational level group and the other two groups. However, the differences between the high school graduates (HS) and those with 2 years or more of college (UNI) are not obviously due to other differences: the groups are similar in average age, and sex differences would reduce the differences since there are more women (who have higher dendritic values than men) in the HS group (6/9) than in the UNI group (4/8).

Jacobs et al. make two important additional points about education. First, whatever the short-term effects of attending college might be on dendrites, it is unlikely that they would last for a long time unless a person's work and other interests were of a kind that stimulated dendritic growth throughout life. They had available to them some information on the occupations and general lifestyles of people whose brains they studied, and looking at this found that women with higher than average total dendritic length tended to be "more occupationally and socially active" (p. 108), while men in manual labor jobs had dendritic lengths below the group average (except for one who had been to graduate school).

The second point they raise is one that we frequently encounter when we cannot carry out a true experiment (with random assignment to groups and experimenter control of the independent variable): is the difference in the brains of those with more education attributable to the educational experience (including the greater intellectual stimulation that may characterize the work and lifestyles of those with more education)? Or could it be that people with more complex dendritic systems in their brains are more likely to attend college, to graduate, to go on to graduate school? This is where the experimental research on animals may help us come to a conclusion; when rats are randomly assigned to more complex and stimulating environments we see similar changes in their brains to those seen in people with more years of formal education, and we know that the rats did not choose the environment they lived in.

Jacobs et al. conclude that their results support what has long been known in animals: "dendritic systems proliferate in response to active interaction with novel and challenging environments" (p. 109).

The brain demonstrates considerable plasticity throughout life. In the case of damage it has a capacity to transfer functions to areas that normally do not serve those functions, in the case of challenge it has the capacity to increases the size of areas devoted to frequently used skills and the complexity of the neural systems in those areas.

So read another chapter, write a summary, discuss it with friends. You will improve your grades—and grow your brain!

REFERENCES

Bosworth, R. G. & K. R. Dobkins (1999) Left-hemisphere dominance for motion processing in deaf signers. *Psychological Science, 10,* 256–262.

Diamond, M. C. (2002) Response of the brain to enrichment. http://www.newhorizons.org/neuro/diamond_brain_response.htm

Elbert, T., C. Pantev, C. Wienbruch, B. Rockstroh, & E. Taub (1995). Increased cortical representation of the fingers of the left hand in string players *Science, 270,* 305–307.

Forgays, D. G & J. W. Forgays (1952) The nature of the effect of free-environmental experience in the rat. *Journal of Comparative and Physiological Psychology, 45,* 322–328.

Greenough, W. T., J. R. Larson, & G. S. Withers (1985) Effects of unilateral and bilateral training in a reaching task on dendritic branching of neurons in the rat motor-sensory forelimb cortex. *Behavioral Neurology and Biology, 44,* 301–314.

Jacobs, B. (2003). Personal communication.

Jacobs, B., M. Schall, and A. B. Scheibel (1993). A quantitative dendritic analysis of Wernicke's area in humans. II. Gender, hemispheric, and environmental factors. *The Journal of Comparative Neurology, 327,* 97–111.

Jacobs B. & A. B. Scheibel (1993) A quantitative dendritic analysis of Wernicke's area in human. I. Lifespan changes. *The Journal of Comparative Neurology, 327,* 83–96.

Krech, D., M. M. Rosenzweig, & E. Bennett (1960) Effects of environmental complexity and training on brain chemistry. *Journal of Comparative and Physiological Psychology, 53,* 509–519.

Maguire, E. A., D. G. Gadian, I. S. Johnsrude, C. D. Good, J. Ashburner, R. S. J. Frackowiak, & C. D. Frith (2000) Navigation-related structural change in the hippocampi of taxi drivers. *Proceedings of the National Academy of Sciences, 97,* 4398–4403.

Muller, R.-A., R. D. Rothermel, M. E. Behen, O. Muzik, P. K. Chakraborty, & H. T. Chugani (1999) Language organization in patients with early and late left-hemisphere lesion: a PET study. *Neuropsychologia, 37,* 545–557.

Patterson, K., F. Varga-Khadem, & C. E. Polkey (1989) Reading with one hemisphere. *Brain, 112,* 39–63.

Rauscheker, J. P. & U. Kniepert (1994) Auditory localization behavior in visually deprived cats. *European Journal of Neuroscience, 61,* 149–160.

Rebillard, G., E. Carlier, M. Rebillard, & R. Pujol (1977) Enhancement of visual responses in the primary visual cortex of the cat after early destruction of cochlear receptors. *Brain Research, 129,* 162–164.

CHAPTER 9

ZIPPING UP THE GENES[1]

Material selected from:
Research Stories for Introductory Psychology,
Second Edition, by Lary Shaffer and Matthew R. Merrens

---

[1]Incorporating the research of T. Bouchard and M. McGue, "Genetic and Rearing Environmental Influences on Adult Personality: An Analysis of Adopted Twins Reared Apart," 1990, *Journal of Personality*, *58*, pp. 263–292.

Where does personality come from? The readings about personality in this book have each, in their own way, tried to provide some answers to this question. As you will come to understand, there is no single source of personality; rather, it is part of a complex interaction among many factors. We wish it was possible to give you simple answers, but, for this question, simple answers are wrong answers. One of the differences that has been found between high school students and upper-level college students is that the college students are better able to deal with multiple answers to a single question (Perry, 1981). High school seems to prepare students to seek THE answer, whereas the college experience seems to help people understand that this is often too simple. The style of thinking exhibited by high school students has been called *dichotomous thinking*. They are likely to see the world in terms of dichotomies; that is, they see the world as being either one thing or another. A national sports figure may be either a god or pond scum, not a realistic mix of attributes of all sorts. In the distant past, the field of psychology thought in the same way as a high school kid: mind *or* body and nature *or* nurture are examples of discarded dichotomies. Psychology now takes a multidetermined approach to areas where dichotomous thinking was once common. As an example of this, genes are now appreciated as a component of behavior acting in concert with many other influences.

THE MEASUREMENT OF VARIABILITY

In trying to find out where personality comes from, we are really asking why some people have different personalities from others; why there are so many differences in personality. Usually, the question is about a particular trait: why are some people so optimistic and some so pessimistic? Differences among people can be measured with a statistic called the *variance*. Variance is a measure of the differences that can be found within a particular trait among members of some group. If you have taken a course on statistics you may know how to calculate the variance, but the calculation of it is not required for the understanding of this chapter.

If you line up a group of 12-year-olds, you will be able to see considerable variation in the extent of their physical development. A statistical measure of that variability, such as the variance, would yield a high score for physical development within that group. To take a behavioral example, the variance in juvenile delinquency would probably be quite high within most junior high schools. Some kids would commit many delinquent acts, some would commit none, and there would be a group in the middle.

There would be quite a bit of variability, so the value of the variance would be high. Variance can only be measured within some specific group. It may be possible to imagine measuring the variance for juvenile delinquency for U.S. kids in all junior high schools, but practically speaking, we could not. To do that would involve assessing the delinquency of each individual kid. Usually, if you are interested in the variance of some population (such as all kids in the United States) you will try to take a *representative* sample of the population and assume that the variance of that sample is similar to the population. If the sample is large, a random sample will probably be representative. With small samples, representativeness is more difficult to achieve, even with random selection.

The same applies to personality traits. The variance must be obtained from studying a particular group. We cannot know what the variance is for optimism within the United States, but we might be able to estimate it with research samples that were representative of the entire country. These samples can be difficult to construct but if they are large and carefully selected, they can yield good estimates of the variation within a large population.

SOURCES OF VARIABILITY

An important comparison can be made here between life sciences, including psychology, and some of the physical sciences. In physical sciences, variability is often largely the result of errors made in the scientific procedures. Imagine a simple demonstration of the physics of falling objects. If you want to know the speed at which objects fall you might drop 10 bricks, one at a time, from a tall building and have a friend measure the falling time of each brick with a stopwatch. Variability might be introduced because you dropped some bricks end first and some side first. Perhaps a few times the bricks hit window ledges on the way down. The human who is timing the fall of the bricks may also introduce some variability because he might not be paying full attention to the task after a number of bricks had fallen. This variability found in brick falling would be the result of errors and imprecision.

In psychology, variability may also be the result of error and imprecision but, much more importantly, the variability may reflect important real differences among people. For example, the driving ability of elderly people has been shown to deteriorate as the people get older, partially because of slowing of reaction time (Hakamies-Blomqvist, Johansson, & Lundberg, 1996). This variability is more than measurement error—some people are better drivers than others. In psychology, the variability is usually more than error—it can be the main focus of the study. Among people, differences are usually more interesting than similarities. If we were to tell you that all of the kids in a particular classroom have IQs that are about average, you might think "So what?" In contrast, if we were to tell you that there was a classroom in which some kids had very low IQs and some kids had high IQs, then you immediately have a question for psychological science: Why are these kids different? This could also be phrased, "What accounts for the variance in IQ in this classroom?" Either way, it is the same question.

The answer to the question, "Where does personality come from?" requires a clear understanding of the nature of variability within a group. The variance is one measure of this variability. We believe you can understand this, no matter how skilled or unskilled you are in statistics. Statistics are an important part of measurement in psychology, but at the introductory level it is probably more important to understand the concepts than it is to understand the math.

Once variability itself is grasped, the next step in finding out where personality comes from is to ask how much of the variability of a trait within a group is the result of the variability in any one specific factor. We might ask, for example, how much of the variance in a personality trait is accounted for by variability in genes, parenting, schooling, nutrition, or socioeconomic status. Note we are *not* asking how *much* of personality is accounted for by each factor. Rather, we are saying that we can measure personality, find a range of variation in that trait, and find out how much of the *variation* in the personality trait is the result of the variation in some other specific factor (see Figure 9.1). The research and statistical methods exist to enable us to answer this question.

FIGURE 9.1 Illustration of Variance.
(a) Optimism for Group A. (b) Optimism for Group B. Imagine that these are data on samples of students who have been selected from two classrooms, Group A from one class and Group B from another. Both have been given a pencil-and-paper optimism scale designed to measure their outlook about life. It is easy to see that there is more variation in Group B than in Group A. It would be interesting to do a larger study to find out why the members of Group A are so similar. The study we would do would ask why Group A has less variability than Group B. It would also ask what is the source of this variance. Perhaps, for example, the scores in Group B also have considerable variance, and the people who are not very optimistic, Judy, Katy and Jeanne, are doing poorly in the class. As you can see, one way to approach this problem would be to calculate correlations between grades and optimism score. That might explain some of the variance. If Group A is a small class where students get a lot of individual attention and Group B is a large class, this might also explain some of the variance. You can, perhaps, think of other factors that might explain some of the variance.

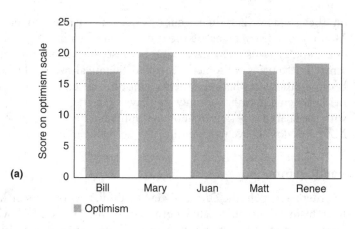

(a)

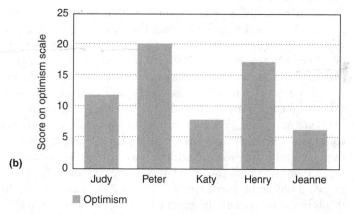

(b)

You should be able to guess that no one factor such as genes, parenting, or school will ever account for 100 percent of the variance in a psychological trait or a behavior. Nevertheless, some factors have been shown to account for rather large amounts of measured variation. You may be surprised to learn that for personality, painstaking research has indicated that a large amount of the variance is the result of variation in genetic factors. With proper research methods, to be discussed below, it is possible to find out how much of the variation is the result of individual nongenetic components and how much is the result of genes. The amount of variance in a trait that is the result of genetic factors is called the *heritability* of that trait.

TWINS

The usual way to approach the measurement of heritability in a human population is to measure the trait in question among individuals of known genetic relatedness—fathers and sons, siblings, half-siblings, cousins, or other relatives. A team of scientists at the University of Minnesota has been working on the heritability question for a number of years. Rather than relying on other family members who may share only small amounts of genetic material, this team has concentrated on twins. There are two kinds of twins, dizygotic and monozygotic. Dizygotic (DZ) twins are the result of two eggs being fertilized at the same time by two different sperm (*di* means two and a *zygote* is a fertilized egg). These individuals are no more closely related genetically than any other siblings. This means that they share, on the average, half their genes. They just happen to have been conceived at the same time. Monozygotic (MZ) twins are the result of one fertilized egg splitting into two individuals (*mono* means one and a *zygote* is a fertilized egg). Because they came from one zygote, their genetic material is the same. These twins are sometimes called "identical twins." They are interesting as research participants because differences between them cannot be caused by genes—their genes are the same. The similarities between MZ twins certainly *may* have a genetic explanation, but they may also have something to do with the shared experiences and environments that are usual for MZ twins. Again, *similarities* between MZ twins do *not* have to result only from their shared genes.

Participants

In order to sort out the effects of genetic influences on personality, Thomas Bouchard and the research team from Minnesota located a group of twins, MZ and DZ, who had been separated early in life and raised apart in different environments. These were called *MZA* and *DZA*, short for *MZ apart* and *DZ apart* (Tellegen et al., 1988).

If personality measures of monozygotic twins raised apart show strong correlations, we might be able to conclude the similarities are the result of genetic influences. The dizygotic twins in this study form a very important control group. The dizygotic twins share no more genes than ordinary brothers or sisters. On the average, this is 50 percent. If the DZAs show about half as much similarity as the MZAs in personality, then we have some additional evidence for the role of genes in personality.

It might seem that it would be difficult to find many separated twins and, once found, some of these twins might not want to be studied. The research team from Minnesota found that, indeed, separated twins are quite rare. However, with hard work, quite a number of pairs were located. Bouchard and his colleagues noted that the twins seemed to enjoy being studied. The Minnesota team worked hard to make the lab visits of all twins interesting and worthwhile so that they would remain in the study (Lykken, 1982).

Twins do not always know if they are MZ or DZ. In everyday life, this decision is usually made based on physical appearance: if the twins look quite similar, they are assumed to be MZ twins. Clearly this is not good enough for genetic research, because some DZ twins may appear to be quite similar, in the same way that nontwin siblings may sometimes look quite a bit alike. Bouchard and McGue verified the MZ and DZ status of all twins in the study by testing blood samples to examine a variety of indicators of genetic relatedness. In addition, they examined fingerprints and other physical indices. Given these measures, the probability that a DZ pair would end up misclassified as an MZ pair in this research was less than 1 in 1,000.

Participants were 45 MZA pairs and 26 DZA pairs. In a study such as this, it is very important to know how much contact the twins had with each other. In a perfect study, the twins would have been separated at birth and would not have been reunited until after personality had been assessed. However, real life does not produce this situation very often. Nevertheless, Bouchard and McGue were able to assure themselves that their twin pairs had been apart for a sufficiently long enough time so that shared environmental conditions were unlikely to account for personality. Extensive interviews were conducted to collect information on the length of time that had passed before the twins were separated and on the amount of time they had spent together after they were reunited. The mean values for separation time are found in Table 9.1. This table also shows the range for each mean. The range is the lowest score in the group and the highest score in the group. It is a fairly crude measure of variability because if there is one individual with an extreme score, that person will distort one end of the range. If you look at the means and at the ranges together, you can get a better picture of the variability than you will get from looking at one or the other alone. For example, one MZA twin pair was together for 48.7 months before they were separated, but that could not be typical of many other MZA pairs, or the mean for the whole group would be higher than 5.1 months.

Total contact months shown in Table 9.1 is the amount of time before separation combined with the amount of contact twins experienced after reunion.

TABLE 9.1   Means and Ranges for Age and Contact in MZA and DZA Twins

	AGE	% FEMALES	MONTHS PRIOR TO SEPARATION	YEARS PRIOR TO CONTACT REUNION	TOTAL CONTACT MONTHS
MZA (N = 45)					
Mean	41.0	65.2	5.1	30.0	26.5
Range	19 to 68		0 to 48.7	.5 to 64.7	.3 to 284.5
DZA* (N = 26)					
Mean	42.0	75.0	12.7	37.3	13.1
Range	25 to 61		.1 to 54.8	17 to 57.9	.2 to 54.2

*There were three opposite sex sets of twins in the DZA sample.

Procedure

When the twins were brought to the Minnesota lab, they engaged in about 50 hours of medical and psychological assessment. The researchers were interested in collecting as much information as possible on them because this may have been the last research of this kind to be done. Adoption agencies are now very reluctant to separate twins. In contrast, this was commonly done when the people in this study were children. Although we are primarily presenting information about personality, quite a bit of other information has been collected about twins by the Minnesota researchers (Lykken, Bouchard, McGue, & Tellegen, 1993).

The personality measure used by Bouchard and McGue was the California Psychological Inventory, or CPI. The CPI is a widely used personality test, probably selected because it has been shown to be a valid measure of personality. The form of the CPI that was used had 480 items designed to measure "aspects and attributes of interpersonal behavior that are to be found in all cultures and societies, and that possess a direct relationship to … social interactions." In addition, Bouchard and McGue asked the twins to assess their rearing environment using the Family Environment Scale, or FES. The FES is a self-report questionnaire made up of a wide range of statements about family environments. The twins' spouses were used as a comparison control group to ensure that the twins were not in some way different in personality simply because they were separated twins. The spouses were useful for this comparison because they were not twins, and they had not been separated from siblings.

Results

The combined CPI scores of all MZA twins look about the same as the scores for all DZA twins combined. The combined scores for a few of the CPI scales are shown in Table 9.2.

These scores are not different than those found for typical adults, nor were they different from those found for the control group of spouses of twins. In terms of personality, as a group, the twins looked about like the rest of us. As a group, MZA and DZA twins were also similar for the Family Environment Scale measures. On FES family variables such as cohesion, expressiveness, conflict, independence, achievement orientation, intellectual-cultural orientation, active-recreational orientation, moral/religious orientation, organization, and control, the two groups of twins were not different. Both MZA and DZA samples were similar to the FES scores of the group of nonadopted spouses, suggesting that any effects seen were not merely the result of having been raised in an adoptive home.

The twins were separated early in life. When comparisons were made within a pair of twins, the data from the FES showed that there was no reason to think that their adoptive environments were

TABLE 9.2 Examples of Mean CPI Scores for MZA-Combined and DZA-Combined Samples

SCALE ON CPI	MEAN MZA	MEAN DZA
Dominance	25.5	24.2
Sociability	22.5	19.5
Self-acceptance	19.4	18.3
Tolerance	20.7	20.0
Responsibility	26.9	26.2
Self-control	30.1	30.0
Flexibility	9.3	8.1

particularly similar. Obviously, if both twins of a pair are placed in highly similar adoptive homes, similarity between twins in adulthood could be a result of home characteristics, shared genes, or both. Correlations were calculated for the Family Environment Scale ratings of each twin pair. High correlations would mean that the different adoptive homes were quite similar in family interaction style. Only a few of these correlations were significantly different from zero, suggesting that the adoptive homes were not very similar when one member of a twin pair was compared to the other twin in the pair.

In contrast, the members of a twin pair, particularly the MZA pairs, showed fairly strong correlations for personality when one twin was compared to the other. Table 9.3 shows some examples of correlations for MZA pairs and DZA pairs. A third column shows the heritability for the listed factors. These heritabilities have been calculated from the twin data in this study and represent, as you will remember, the proportion of variability that is the result of genetic factors. Heritability may range from zero—where there is no genetic influence, to a theoretical 1.00—where genes are the only source of observed variation.

The difference between correlations for MZA twins and DZA twins is striking, and the heritabilities range around .5, suggesting that about half of the variation observed in the personalities of these people was a result of genetic factors. A few personality traits not shown in Table 9.3 had lower heritability, such as *communality* (=.104) and *flexibility* (=.051) but these were rare.

TABLE 9.3 Examples of Correlations for MZA and DZA Twins and Heritabilities for California Psychological Inventory Scales

CPI SCALE	CORRELATION FOR MZA	CORRELATION FOR DZA	HERITABILITY*
Dominance	.53	.24	.541
Capacity for status	.60	.39	.652
Self-acceptance	.62	.11	.616
Well-being	.59	.17	.583
Responsibility	.48	.34	.626
Socialization	.53	.39	.577
Self-control	.68	−.28	.612
Tolerance	.55	.22	.602
Good impression	.53	−.19	.464
Achieve via conformance	.44	.02	.414
Achieve via independence	.62	.25	.665

*Note: Be careful not to confuse heritability with the correlation coefficients. Although the arrangement of the digits is superficially similar, they are very different measures. Heritability is the proportion of variance for a particular trait that is the result of genetic factors.

Statistical Significance

In psychology, the numerical results of studies are usually assessed with some sort of statistical analysis to help the reader decide how much confidence to put in the findings. In order to understand the basics of these statistical analyses, imagine an exercise in which you consult a table of random numbers of the type often found in the back of statistics books. This table consists of long columns of numbers generated by some sort of random process, such as drawing numbers from a hat. Next, you randomly select ten of these random numbers from one column and ten other random numbers from another column in the table. Calculate an arithmetic mean for each of the two columns. It is likely that the means will be at least slightly different because, after all, the numbers were selected at random. The difference between the means in this case is a direct result of chance factors because all the numbers were random in the first place.

Now imagine that you have conducted a little psychology experiment and you have two columns of scores from the measure that is your dependent variable. You calculate the arithmetic mean for each column and you find that the means are slightly different. You need to know if that difference is the result of your independent variable or if it is the result of chance factors. In this case, *chance factors* could be a number of things that you did not control, such as how much sleep your participants had the night before the study, whether they were hungry or not, how interested they were in the study, and other things like that. If the difference between the means for your dependent variable was only the result of uncontrolled chance variation, your finding is meaningless.

There is no way to be absolutely sure whether an outcome in an experiment is a result of chance factors or the independent variable. However, statistical tests can assess how likely it is that the outcome is the result of chance, and that is the way these tests are used in science. The result of a statistical test is a statement indicating the probability that a difference—such as the difference between two means—is the result of chance. Scientists have arbitrarily decided on a probability level at which they are willing to agree that differences measured are not considered to be the result of chance. This arbitrary level is a probability of 5 percent. If the statistical test shows that there is only a 5 percent or lower probability that the difference is the result of chance factors, scientists are willing to assume that the difference was the result of the research manipulation, not other, uncontrolled, events. The notation that is used to indicate this is $p < .05$, meaning the probability is less than 5 percent that differences are the result of chance. Perhaps needless to say, smaller probabilities are also accepted as indications that differences are not the result of chance. Probabilities such as $p < .01$, $p < .001$, and $p < .0001$ may commonly be found in research reports. These and any others indicating a 5 percent or smaller likelihood of chance are called *statistically significant* findings. This term is reserved for probabilities of chance at 5 percent or lower. Above 5 percent, such as $p < .06$ or $p < .10$, findings should be considered statistically non significant. Sometimes this is abbreviated in research reports as *NS*, for *not significant*.

For the data in Table 9.3, the researchers conducted a statistical test to determine if the heritabilities were significantly greater than zero. Zero heritability would mean that none of the observed variance was the result of genetic factors. All of the heritabilities shown in Table 9.3 were statistically significantly greater than zero.

Discussion

This is not an isolated finding. Research with other personality assessments (Tellegen et al., 1988) and with other groups in other countries (Rose, Koskenvuo, Kaprio, Langinvainio, & Sarna, 1988) have found substantially the same thing. Bouchard and McGue note that our intuitive estimates of the effects of environmental factors in personality are often inflated. Although we have not presented the data for MZ twins reared together, you may be quite surprised to learn that MZ twins show about the same levels of personality correlations when reared together as when reared apart. Summing up the literature, Bouchard and McGue say, "We are led to what must for some seem a rather remarkable conclusion: The degree of MZ twin resemblance on self-reported personality characteristics does not appear to depend upon whether the twins are reared together or apart, whether they are adolescent or adult, in what industrialized country they reside ... degree of personality similarity between reared-apart and reared-together twins suggests that common familial environmental factors do not have a substantial influence upon adult personality."

If 50 percent of the variance in personality is accounted for by genes, what about the rest? As in the introductory example involving falling bricks, some of it will be a result of error in measurement and other unsystematic factors. One twin may have had more rest than the other on the day of testing. The personality test questions may mean slightly different things to different members of a twin pair.

Aside from heritability and error, Bouchard and McGue conclude that most of the rest of the variance is accounted for by idiosyncratic environmental factors. Idiosyncratic factors are those that are different from one person to the next, even from one twin to the next. One way to understand these factors is to think about your own experience compared to that of other people raised in what may be naïvely called "the same environment." If you had siblings, you may be able to use them as examples; if not, think of a group setting such as a schoolroom. Individual homes and schools may seem like the *same* environment for the kids in them, but the current thinking in psychology suggests this is not the case. As Sandra Scarr (1992) pointed out, the actual experience of these contexts varies greatly from one individual to the next because, among other reasons, different people elicit or evoke different responses from the so-called *same* situations. Many of us may remember being hunted down and punished for specific behaviors while siblings and classmates seemed to get away with the same behavior. Perhaps when others told the teacher that the dog had eaten their homework, the teacher expressed concern for them. When you said the same thing, the teacher yelled at you and expressed concern for your dog. On the flip side, many of us will also remember having a special relationship with a teacher, very different from that person's relations with our classmates. Parents may love all their kids, but the kids get treated differently from one another. These are the idiosyncratic factors that can make a superficially similar environment into a very different place for each individual.

So, after all this, where does personality come from? You will now recognize that there is no easy answer to this question. Bouchard and McGue have demonstrated that genetics play a considerable role in personality differences among people. This is likely to be one reason why, as in other personality chapters in this book, personality seems to be quite consistent across situations and over parts of the life span. Does this mean that personality cannot change? No. We will have more complete answers to this question when we understand more about the idiosyncratic environmental factors that also seem to be involved in personality. The first step in that understanding has been a big one. It has involved the acceptance of the idea that personality is not merely the result of learning *or* biology. Whatever the future holds for this line of research, it is already clear that there are important things going on down there in your genes.

REFERENCES

Bouchard, T., & McGue, M. (1990). Genetic and rearing environmental influences on adult personality: An analysis of adopted twins reared apart. *Journal of Personality, 58,* 263–292.

Hakamies-Blomqvist, L., Johansson, K., & Lundberg, C. (1996). Medical screening of older drivers as a traffic safety measure: A comparative Finnish-Swedish Evaluation study. *Journal of the American Geriatrics Society, 44,* 650–653.

Lykken, D. (1982). Research with twins: The concept of emergenesis. *Psychophysiology, 19,* 361–373.

Lykken, D. T., Bouchard, T. J., McGue, M., & Tellegen, A. (1993). Heritability of interests: A Twin Study. *Journal of Applied Psychology, 78,* 649–661.

Perry, W. G. (1981). Cognitive and ethical growth. In A. Chickering (Ed.), *The Modern American College* (pp. 76–116). San Francisco: Jossey-Bass.

Rose, R. J., Koskenvuo, M., Kaprio, J., Langinvainio, H., & Sarna, S. (1988). Shared genes, shared experiences and similarity of personality: Data from 14,288 adult Finnish co-twins. *Journal of Personality and Social Psychology, 54,* 161–171.

Scarr, S. (1992). Developmental theories for the 1990s: Developmental and individual differences. *Child Development, 63,* 1–19.

Tellegen, A., Lykken, D. T., Bouchard, T. J., Jr., Wilcox, K. J., Segal, N. L., & Rich, S. (1988). Personality similarity in twins reared apart and together. *Journal of Personality and Social Psychology, 54,* 1031–1039.

SECTION III

LEARNING, MEMORY, COGNITION

CHAPTER 10

INTRODUCTION

Material selected from:
Mastering the World of Psychology,
by Wood, Wood & Boyd

LEARNING

If you have a dog, you may be able to relate to Michael and Lori's story:

One day, their dog Jake decided he preferred to stay indoors at night, rather than be put into the backyard, as had been the rule since he was a puppy. He got his way by hiding in the house before Michael and Lori went to bed at night. Wanting to get as many hours of sleep as possible, Michael and Lori began a nightly ritual—going through the house, looking for Jake in closets and under the beds, and calling his name. But he never came when they called him at bedtime, and they were rarely able to find him.

Jake had associated their calling him at that time with being put outside before he was ready.

Then, when the spirit moved him (usually in the middle of the night), Jake would leap onto their bed, awakening Michael and Lori. After many sleepless nights, they were desperate for a solution to the problem.

Then, one day, when they were opening a can of soup, Jake raced through the house and slid to a stop in front of his bowl. He had learned to associate the sound of the can opener with food. So, Michael and Lori decided to conduct an experiment. Instead of calling Jake before bedtime, they began turning on the can opener when they were ready to put Jake out. The deception worked; the dog came running every time he heard the can opener. Michael and Lori felt a bit guilty about tricking Jake. Nevertheless, by applying simple learning principles, these dog owners were finally able to get a good night's rest.

Learning may be defined as a relatively permanent change in behavior, knowledge, capability, or attitude that is acquired through experience and cannot be attributed to illness, injury, or maturation. Several parts of this definition need further explanation. First, defining learning as a "relatively permanent change" excludes temporary changes that could result from illness, fatigue, or fluctuations in mood. Second, referring to a change that is "acquired through experience" excludes some readily observable changes in behavior that occur as a result of brain injuries or certain diseases. Also, certain observable changes that occur as individuals grow and mature have nothing to do with learning. For example, technically speaking, infants do not *learn* to crawl or walk. Basic motor skills and the maturational plan that governs their development are a part of the genetically programmed behavioral repertoire of every species.

CLASSICAL CONDITIONING

Pavlov and Classical Conditioning

Ivan Pavlov (1849–1936) organized and directed research in physiology at the Institute of Experimental Medicine in St. Petersburg, Russia, from 1891 until his death 45 years later. He conducted classic experiments on the physiology of digestion, which won him a Nobel Prize in 1904—the first time this honor went to a Russian. In the course of his research, Pavlov designed a machine that could collect saliva from a dog's mouth. Quite by accident, Pavlov observed drops of saliva collecting in the machine's containers when the dogs heard the footsteps of the laboratory assistants coming to feed them. How could an involuntary response such as salivation come to be associated with sounds that preceded feeding? Pavlov spent the rest of his life studying this question.

Classical conditioning is a form of learning in which an association is formed between one stimulus and another. A stimulus (plural, *stimuli*) is any event or object in the environment to which an organism responds. In Jake's case, the sound of a can opener became associated with food. Similarly, humans learn to respond in specific ways to a variety of words and symbols. Adolf Hitler, the IRS, Santa Claus, and the American flag are just names and symbols, but they tend to evoke strong emotional responses because of their associations. People's lives are profoundly influenced by the associations learned through classical conditioning, sometimes referred to as *respondent conditioning*, or *Pavlovian conditioning*.

Pavlov (1927/1960) used tones, bells, buzzers, lights, geometric shapes, electric shocks, and metronomes in his conditioning experiments. In a typical experiment, food powder was placed in the dog's mouth, causing salivation. Because dogs do not need to be conditioned to salivate to food, the salivation is an unlearned response, or **unconditioned response (UR).** Any stimulus, such as food, that without learning will automatically elicit, or bring forth, an unconditioned response is called an **unconditioned stimulus (US).**

Unconditioned Stimulus (US)		*Unconditioned Response (UR)*
food	→	salivation
loud noise	→	startle
light in eye	→	contraction of pupil
puff of air in eye	→	eyeblink response

Pavlov demonstrated that dogs could be conditioned to salivate to a variety of stimuli never before associated with food. During the conditioning process, the researcher would present a neutral stimulus such as a musical tone shortly before placing food powder in the dog's mouth. The food powder would cause the dog to salivate. Pavlov found that after the tone and food were paired many times, usually 20 or more, the tone alone would elicit salivation (Pavlov, 1927/1960, p. 385). Pavlov called the tone the learned stimulus, or **conditioned stimulus (CS),** and he called salivation after the tone the learned response, or **conditioned response (CR).** (See Figure 10.1.)

In a modern view of classical conditioning, the conditioned stimulus can be thought of as a signal that the unconditioned stimulus will follow (Schreurs, 1989). In Pavlov's experiment, the tone became a signal that food would follow shortly. So, the signal (conditioned stimulus) gives advance warning, and the organism (animal or person) is prepared with the proper response (conditioned response), even before the unconditioned stimulus arrives (Gallistel & Gibbon, 2000).

Because the conditioned stimulus serves as a signal for the unconditioned stimulus, conditioning takes place fastest if the conditioned stimulus occurs shortly before the unconditioned stimulus. It takes place more slowly or not at all when the two stimuli occur at the same time. The ideal time between the presentations of the conditioned and the unconditioned stimuli is about ½ second, but this time varies according to the type of response being conditioned and the nature and intensity of the conditioned stimulus and the unconditioned stimulus (see Wasserman & Miller, 1997).

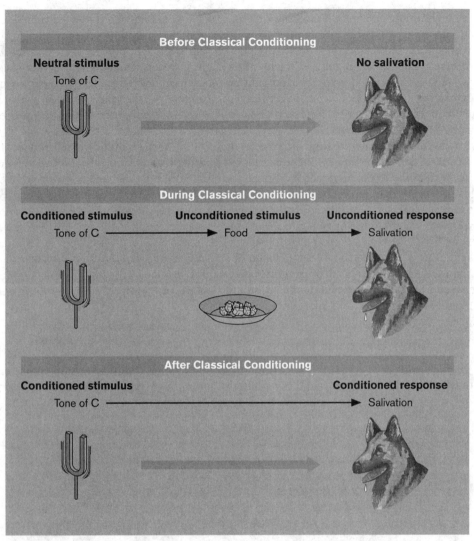

FIGURE 10.1   Classically Conditioning a Salivation Response. A neutral stimulus (a tone) elicits no salivation until it is repeatedly paired with the unconditioned stimulus (food). After many pairings, the neutral stimulus (now called the conditioned stimulus) alone produces salivation. Classical conditioning has occurred.

Further, conditioned stimuli may be linked together to form a series of signals, a process called **higher-order conditioning.** For example, think about what happens when you have to have some kind of blood test. Typically, you sit in a chair next to a table on which the nurse prepares materials such as needles, syringes, and such. Next, some kind of constricting device is tied around your arm, and the nurse pats on the surface of your skin until a vein becomes visible. Each step in the sequence tells you that the unavoidable needle "stick" and the pain (largely the result of reflexive muscle tension) that follows is coming. The stick itself is the unconditioned stimulus to which you reflexively respond. But all the steps that precede it are conditioned stimuli that cause you to anticipate the pain of the stick itself. And with each successive step, your muscles respond to your anxiety by contracting a bit more in anticipation of the stick, a conditioned response.

After conditioning an animal to salivate to a tone, what would happen if you continued to sound the tone but no longer paired it with food? Pavlov found that without the food, salivation to the tone became weaker and weaker and then finally disappeared altogether—a process known as **extinction.** After the response had been extinguished, Pavlov allowed the dog to rest and then brought it back to the laboratory. He found that the dog would again salivate to the tone. Pavlov called this recurrence **spontaneous recovery.** But the spontaneously recovered response was weaker and shorter in duration than the original conditioned response. Figure 10.2 shows the rate of responses during the processes of extinction and spontaneous recovery.

Pavlov also found that a tone similar to the original conditioned stimulus would produce the conditioned response (salivation), a phenomenon called **generalization.** But the salivation decreased as the tone became less similar to the original conditioned stimulus, until the tone became so different that the dog would not salivate at all. Once the tone became sufficiently different, the dog exhibited **discrimination;** that is, it had learned to respond only to tones within a certain range.

It is easy to see the value of generalization and discrimination in daily life. For instance, if you enjoyed being in school as a child, you probably feel more positive about your college experiences than your classmates who enjoyed school less. Because of generalization, we do not need to learn a conditioned response to every stimulus that may differ only slightly from an original one. Further, discriminating between the odors of fresh and spoiled milk will spare you an upset stomach. Discriminating between a rattlesnake and a garter snake could save your life.

John Watson, Little Albert, and Peter

In 1919, John Watson (1878–1958) and his assistant, Rosalie Rayner, conducted a now-infamous study to prove that fear could be classically conditioned. In the laboratory, Rayner presented an 11-month-old

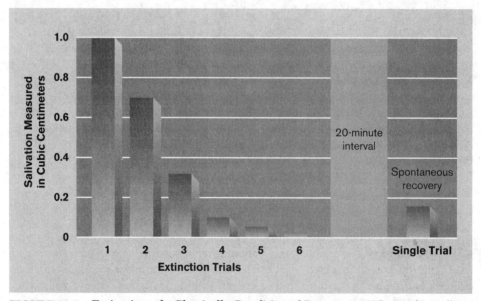

FIGURE 10.2   Extinction of a Classically Conditioned Response. When a classically conditioned stimulus (the tone) was presented in a series of trials without the unconditioned stimulus (the food), Pavlov's dogs salivated less and less until there was virtually no salivation. But after a 20-minute rest, one sound of the tone caused the conditioned response to reappear in a weakened form (producing only a small amount of salivation), a phenomenon Pavlov called spontaneous recovery. (Data from Pavlov, 1927/1960, p. 58.)

infant, known as Little Albert, with a white rat. As Albert reached for the rat, Watson struck a steel bar with a hammer just behind Albert's head. This procedure was repeated, and Albert "jumped violently, fell forward and began to whimper" (Watson & Rayner, 1920, p. 4). A week later, Watson continued the experiment, pairing the rat with the loud noise five more times. Then, at the sight of the white rat alone, Albert began to cry (see Figure 10.3). Moreover, when Albert returned to the laboratory 5 days later, the fear had generalized to a rabbit, a dog, a fur coat, Watson's hair, and a Santa Claus mask. After 30 days Albert made his final visit to the laboratory. His fears were still evident, although they were somewhat less intense. Watson concluded that conditioned fears "persist and modify personality throughout life" (Watson & Rayner, 1920, p. 12).

Although Watson had formulated techniques for removing conditioned fears, Albert and his family moved away before they could be tried on him. Since Watson apparently knew that Albert would be leaving the area before these fear-removal techniques could be applied, he clearly showed a disregard for the child's welfare. Fortunately, the American Psychological Association now has strict ethical standards for the use of human and animal participants in research experiments and would not sanction an experiment such as Watson's.

Some of Watson's ideas for removing fears were excellent and laid the groundwork for some behavior therapies used today. Three years after his experiment with Little Albert, Watson and a colleague, Mary Cover Jones (1924), found 3-year-old Peter, who, like Albert, was afraid of white rats. He was also afraid of rabbits, a fur coat, feathers, cotton, and a fur rug. Peter's fear of the rabbit was his strongest fear, and this became the target of Watson's fear-removal techniques.

Peter was brought into the laboratory, seated in a high chair, and given candy to eat. A white rabbit in a wire cage was brought into the room but kept far enough away from Peter that it would not upset him. Over the course of 38 therapy sessions, the rabbit was brought closer and closer to Peter, who continued to enjoy his candy. Occasionally, some of Peter's friends were brought in to play with the rabbit at a safe distance from Peter so that he could see firsthand that the rabbit did no harm. Toward the end of Peter's therapy, the rabbit was taken out of the cage and eventually put in Peter's lap. By the final session, Peter had grown fond of the rabbit. What is more, he had lost all fear of the fur coat, cotton, and feathers, and he could tolerate the white rats and the fur rug.

So far, we have considered classical conditioning primarily in relation to Pavlov's dogs and Watson's human research participants. How is classical conditioning viewed today?

FIGURE 10.3   The Conditioned Fear Response. Little Albert's fear of a white rat was a conditioned response that was generalized to other stimuli, including a rabbit and, to a lesser extent, a Santa Claus mask.

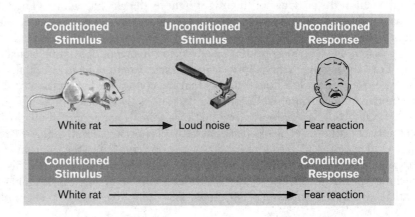

CONTEMPORARY VIEWS OF CLASSICAL CONDITIONING

Pavlov viewed classical conditioning as a mechanical process that resulted in a conditioned reflex more or less automatically. Beginning in the late 1960s, though, researchers began to discover exceptions to some of the general principles Pavlov identified.

The Cognitive Perspective

Psychologist Robert Rescorla (1967, 1968, 1988; Rescorla & Wagner, 1972) was able to demonstrate that the critical element in classical conditioning is not the repeated pairing of the conditioned stimulus and the unconditioned stimulus. Rather, the important factor is whether the conditioned stimulus provides information that enables the organism to reliably predict the occurrence of the unconditioned stimulus. Using rats as his subjects, Rescorla used a tone as the conditioned stimulus and a shock as the unconditioned stimulus. For one group of rats, the tone and shock were paired 20 times—the shock always occurred during the tone. The other group of rats likewise received a shock 20 times while the tone was sounding, but this group also received 20 shocks that were not paired with the tone. Only the first group, for which the tone was a reliable predictor of the shock, developed the conditioned fear response to the tone. The second group showed little evidence of conditioning, because the shock was just as likely to occur without the tone as with it. In other words, for this group, the tone provided no additional information about the shock.

Biological Predispositions

According to Martin Seligman (1972), most common fears "are related to the survival of the human species through the long course of evolution" (p. 455). Seligman (1970) has suggested that humans and other animals are prepared to associate only certain stimuli with particular consequences. One example of this preparedness is the tendency to develop a **taste aversion**—the intense dislike and/or avoidance of a particular food that has been associated with nausea or discomfort. For example, experiencing nausea and vomiting after eating, say, a hotdog can be enough to condition a long-lasting taste aversion to hotdogs.

In a classic study of the role played by classical conditioning in the development of a taste aversion, Garcia and Koelling (1966) exposed rats to a three-way conditioned stimulus: a bright light, a clicking noise, and flavored water. For one group of rats, the unconditioned stimulus was being exposed to either X rays or lithium chloride, either of which produces nausea and vomiting several hours after exposure; for the other group, the unconditioned stimulus was an electric shock to the feet. The rats that were made ill associated the flavored water with the nausea and avoided it at all times, but they would still drink unflavored water when the bright light and the clicking sound were present. The rats receiving the electric shock continued to prefer the flavored water over unflavored water, but they would not drink at all in the presence of the bright light or the clicking sound. The rats in one group associated nausea only with the flavored water; those in the other group associated electric shock only with the light and the sound.

Garcia and Koelling's research established two exceptions to traditional ideas of classical conditioning. First, the finding that rats formed an association between nausea and flavored water ingested several hours earlier contradicted the principle that the conditioned stimulus must be presented shortly before the unconditioned stimulus. The finding that rats associated electric shock only with noise and light and nausea only with flavored water revealed that animals are apparently biologically predisposed to make certain associations and that associations between any two stimuli cannot be readily conditioned.

Other research on conditioned taste aversions has led to the solution of practical problems such as helping cancer patients. Bernstein and colleagues (Bernstein, 1985; Bernstein et al., 1982) devised a technique to help cancer patients avoid developing aversions to desirable foods. A group of cancer patients were given a novel-tasting, maple-flavored ice cream before chemotherapy. The nausea caused by the treatment resulted in a taste aversion to the ice cream. The researchers found that when an unusual or unfamiliar food becomes the "scapegoat," or target, for taste aversion, other foods in the patient's diet may be protected, and the patient will continue to eat them regularly. So, cancer patients should refrain from eating preferred or nutritious foods prior to chemotherapy. Instead, they should be given an unusual-tasting or unfavored food shortly before treatment. As a result, they are less likely to develop aversions to foods they normally eat and, in turn, more likely to maintain their body weight during treatment.

Classical Conditioning in Everyday Life

Many of our emotional responses—positive and negative—result from classical conditioning. You may have a fear, or phobia, that was learned through classical conditioning. For example, many people who have had painful dental work develop a dental phobia. Not only do they come to fear the dentist's drill, but they develop anxiety in response to a wide range of stimuli associated with it—the dentist's chair, the waiting room, or even the building where the dentist's office is located. Neuroscientists have learned that this kind of fear conditioning is associated with both the amygdala and the hippocampus (Anagnostaras et al., 2000).

Through classical conditioning, environmental cues associated with drug use can become conditioned stimuli and later produce the conditioned responses of drug craving (Field & Duka, 2002; London et al., 2000). Consequently, drug counselors strongly urge recovering addicts to avoid any cues (people, places, and things) associated with their past drug use. Relapse is far more common in those who do not avoid such associated environmental cues. This observation helps explain why the American soldiers who used heroin heavily in Vietnam had only a 7% addiction rate when they returned to the United States, where they no longer encountered many of the environmental cues associated with use of the drug (Basic Behavioral Science Task Force, 1996).

Businesspeople wine and dine customers, hoping that they and their product or service will elicit the same positive response as the pleasant setting and fine food. Advertisers seek to classically condition consumers when they show products along with great-looking models or celebrities or in situations where people are enjoying themselves. Advertisers reason that if the "neutral" product is associated with people, objects, or situations consumers particularly like, then in time the product will elicit a similarly positive response. Pavlov found that presenting the tone just before the food was the most efficient way to condition salivation in dogs. Television advertisements, too, are most effective when the products are presented before the beautiful people or situations are shown (van den Hout & Merckelbach, 1991).

Research indicates that even the immune system is subject to classical conditioning (Ader, 1985; Ader & Cohen, 1982, 1993; Exton et al., 2000). In a classic study of this kind, Robert Ader was conducting an experiment with rats, conditioning them to avoid saccharin-sweetened water. Immediately after drinking the sweet water (which rats consider a treat), the rats were injected with a tasteless drug (cyclophosphamide) that causes severe nausea. The conditioning worked, and from that time on, the rats would not drink the sweet water, whether or not they had received the drug. Attempting to reverse the conditioned response, Ader force-fed the sweet water to the rats for many days; later, unexpectedly, many of them died. Ader was puzzled, because the sweet water was in no way lethal. Checking further into the properties of the tasteless drug, Ader learned that it suppresses the immune system. A few doses of an immune-suppressing drug paired with sweetened water had produced a conditioned response. As a result, the sweet water alone continued to suppress the immune system, causing the rats to die. Ader and Cohen successfully repeated the experiment with strict controls to rule out other explanations. How far-reaching the power of classical conditioning must be if a neutral stimulus such as sweetened water can produce effects similar to those of a powerful drug! And not only can classically conditioned stimuli suppress the immune system, they can be used to boost it as well (Exton et al., 2000; Markovic et al., 1993).

Recent research (Stanton, 2000) suggests that three basic components of learning are involved in classical conditioning: sensorimotor, affective (emotional), and cognitive components. Even the simplest of conditioned responses, such as the eyeblink reflex, involves all three of these learning components. The sensorimotor component of learning results in the eyeblink itself and is handled by neural circuits in the brain's cerebellum. The affective component of learning encodes the conditioned "fear" and depends on the neural circuitry of the amygdala. The cognitive component of learning consists of all higher-order learning and memory processes. It forms a representation of the entire conditioning episode, including the relationship between the conditioned stimulus and the unconditioned stimulus and the context (environment) in which conditioning occurs. The neural circuitry handling this cognitive component of learning is in the hippocampus (Stanton, 2000; Green & Woodruff-Pak, 2000).

Research indicates that the amygdala is involved in the conditioning of emotions such as fear. However, memories of such conditioning are stored in other areas of the brain, even though the neural circuits in the amygdala produce the intense emotions that occur with fear conditioning (Lehmann et al., 2000; Vazdarjanova, 2000). An intact hippocampus is also essential to the conditioning of emotions (Anagnostaras et al., 2000). The cerebellum is the essential brain structure for motor (movement) conditioning and also the storage site for the memory traces formed during such conditioning (Steinmetz, 2000; Thompson et al., 2000).

OPERANT CONDITIONING

Thorndike and the Law of Effect

Based on his studies of *trial-and-error learning* in cats, dogs, chicks, and monkeys, American psychologist Edward Thorndike (1874–1949) formulated several laws of learning, the most important being the law of effect (Thorndike, 1911/1970). The **law of effect** states that the consequence, or effect, of a response determines whether the tendency to respond in the same way in the future will be strengthened or weakened. Responses closely followed by satisfying consequences are more likely to be repeated. Thorndike (1898) insisted that it was "unnecessary to invoke reasoning" to explain how the learning took place.

In Thorndike's best-known experiments, a hungry cat was placed in a wooden box with slats, which was called a *puzzle box*. It was designed so that the animal had to manipulate a simple mechanism—pressing a pedal or pulling down a loop—to escape and claim a food reward just outside the box. The cat would first try to squeeze through the slats; when these attempts failed, it would scratch, bite, and claw inside the box. In time, the cat would accidentally trip the mechanism, which would open the door and release it. Each time, after winning freedom and claiming the food reward, the cat was returned to the box. After many trials, the cat learned to open the door almost immediately after being placed in the box. Thorndike's law of effect formed the conceptual starting point for B. F. Skinner's work in operant conditioning.

B. F. Skinner and Operant Conditioning

Burrhus Frederic Skinner (1904–1990) became fascinated at an early age by the complex tricks he saw trained pigeons perform at country fairs. He was also interested in constructing mechanical devices and in collecting an assortment of animals, which he kept as pets. These interests were destined to play a major role in his later scientific achievements (Bjork, 1993). Following a failed attempt at becoming a writer after graduating from college, Skinner began reading the books of Pavlov and Watson. He became so intrigued that he entered graduate school at Harvard and completed his PhD in psychology in 1931. Like Watson, Skinner believed that the causes of behavior are in the environment and do not result from inner mental events such as thoughts, feelings, or perceptions. Rather, Skinner claimed that these inner mental events are themselves behaviors, and like any other behaviors, are shaped and determined by environmental forces. Although Skinner's social theories generated controversy, little controversy exists about the significance of his research on operant conditioning.

In **operant conditioning,** the consequences of behavior are manipulated in order to increase or decrease the frequency of a response or to shape an entirely new response. Behavior that is reinforced—followed by rewarding consequences—tends to be repeated. A **reinforcer** is anything that strengthens or increases the probability of the response it follows.

Operant conditioning permits the learning of a broad range of new responses. For example, humans can learn to modify their brain-wave patterns through operant conditioning if they are given immediate positive reinforcement for the brain-wave changes that show the desired direction of change. Such operantly conditioned changes can result in better performance on motor tasks and faster responses on a variety of cognitive tasks (Pulvermüller et al., 2000).

Shaping, a technique Skinner used, is particularly effective in conditioning complex behaviors. With shaping, rather than waiting for the desired response to occur and then reinforcing it, a researcher (or parent or animal trainer) reinforces any movement in the direction of the desired response, gradually guiding the responses closer and closer to the ultimate goal. The series of more closely matching responses are known as **successive approximations.**

Skinner designed a soundproof apparatus, commonly called a **Skinner box,** with which he conducted his experiments in operant conditioning. One version of the box is equipped with a lever or bar that a rat presses to gain a reward of food pellets or water from a dispenser. A record of the animal's bar pressing is registered on a device called a *cumulative recorder,* also invented by Skinner. Through the use of shaping, a rat in a Skinner box is conditioned to press a bar for rewards. It may be rewarded first for simply turning toward the bar. The next reward comes only when the rat moves closer to the bar; each step closer to the bar is rewarded. Next, the rat must touch the bar to receive a reward. Finally, it is rewarded only when it presses the bar.

Shaping—rewarding successive approximations of the desired response—has been used effectively to condition complex behaviors in people as well as other animals. Parents may use shaping to help their children develop good table manners, praising them each time they show an improvement. Teachers often use shaping with disruptive children, reinforcing them at first for very short periods of good behavior and then gradually expecting them to work productively for longer and longer periods. Through shaping, circus animals have learned to perform a wide range of amazing feats and pigeons have learned to bowl and play Ping-Pong.

You have seen that responses followed by reinforcers tend to be repeated and that responses no longer followed by reinforcers will occur less and less frequently and eventually die out. In operant conditioning, **extinction** occurs when reinforcers are withheld. A rat in a Skinner box will eventually stop pressing a bar when it is no longer rewarded with food pellets. The process of spontaneous recovery, which we discussed in relation to classical conditioning, also occurs in operant conditioning. A rat whose bar pressing has been extinguished may again press the bar a few times when it is returned to the Skinner box after a period of rest.

Skinner conducted many of his experiments with pigeons placed in a specially designed Skinner box. The box contained small illuminated disks that the pigeons could peck to receive bits of grain from a food tray. Using this technique, Skinner found that **generalization** occurs in operant conditioning. A pigeon reinforced for pecking at a yellow disk is likely to peck at another disk similar in color. The less similar a disk is to the original color, the lower the rate of pecking will be.

Discrimination in operant conditioning involves learning to distinguish between a stimulus that has been reinforced and other stimuli that may be very similar. Discrimination develops when the response to the original stimulus is reinforced but responses to similar stimuli are not reinforced. For example, to encourage discrimination, a researcher would reinforce the pigeon for pecking at the yellow disk but not for pecking at the orange or red disk. Pigeons have even been conditioned to discriminate between a cubist-style Picasso painting and a Monet with 90% accuracy. However, they weren't able to tell a Renoir from a Cezanne ("Psychologists' pigeons . . . ," 1995).

Certain cues come to be associated with reinforcement or punishment. For example, children are more likely to ask their parents for a treat when the parents are smiling than when they are frowning.

A stimulus that signals whether a certain response or behavior is likely to be rewarded, ignored, or punished is called a **discriminative stimulus.** If a pigeon's pecking at a lighted disk results in a reward but pecking at an unlighted disk does not, the pigeon will soon be pecking at the lighted disk but not at the unlighted one. The presence or absence of the discriminative stimulus—in this case, the lighting of a disk—will control whether the pecking takes place.

Why do children sometimes misbehave with a grandparent but not with a parent, or make one teacher's life miserable yet behave like model students for another? The children may have learned that in the presence of some people (the discriminative stimuli), their misbehavior will almost certainly lead to punishment, but in the presence of certain other people, it may be overlooked, or even rewarded.

Reinforcement

Reinforcement is a key concept in operant conditioning and may be defined as any event that strengthens or increases the probability of the response that it follows. There are two types of reinforcement: positive and negative. **Positive reinforcement,** roughly the same thing as a reward, refers to any pleasant or desirable consequence that, if applied after a response, increases the probability of that response. Many employees will work hard for a raise or a promotion, salespeople will increase their efforts to get awards and bonuses, students will study to get good grades, and children will throw temper tantrums to get candy or ice cream. In these examples, the raises, promotions, awards, bonuses, good grades, candy, and ice cream are positive reinforcers.

Just as people engage in behaviors to get positive reinforcers, they also engage in behaviors to avoid or escape aversive, or unpleasant, stimuli. With **negative reinforcement,** a person's or animal's behavior is reinforced by the termination or avoidance of an aversive stimulus. If you find that a response successfully ends an aversive stimulus, you are likely to repeat it. You will turn on the air conditioner to terminate the heat and will get out of bed to turn off a faucet and end the annoying "drip, drip, drip." Heroin addicts will do almost anything to obtain heroin to terminate their painful withdrawal symptoms. In these instances, negative reinforcement involves putting an end to the heat, the dripping faucet, and the withdrawal symptoms.

Responses that end discomfort and those that are followed by rewards are likely to be strengthened or repeated because both lead to a more desirable outcome. Some behaviors are influenced by a combination of positive and negative reinforcement. If you eat a plateful of rather disgusting leftovers to relieve intense hunger, you are eating solely to remove hunger, a negative reinforcer. But if your hunger is relieved by a delicious dinner at a fine restaurant, both positive and negative reinforcement have played a role: Your hunger has been removed, and the dinner has been a reward in itself.

A **primary reinforcer** is one that fulfills a basic physical need for survival and does not depend on learning. Food, water, sleep, and termination of pain are examples of primary reinforcers. And sex is a powerful reinforcer that fulfills a basic physical need for survival of the species. Fortunately, learning does not depend solely on primary reinforcers. If that were the case, people would need to be hungry, thirsty, or sex-starved before they would respond at all. Much observed human behavior occurs in response to secondary reinforcers. A **secondary reinforcer** is acquired or learned by association with other reinforcers. Some secondary reinforcers (money, for example) can be exchanged at a later time for other reinforcers. Praise, good grades, awards, applause, attention, and signals of approval such as a smile or a kind word are all examples of secondary reinforcers.

Initially, Skinner conditioned rats by reinforcing each bar-pressing response with a food pellet. Reinforcing every correct response, known as **continuous reinforcement,** is the most efficient way to condition a new response. However, after a response has been conditioned, partial or intermittent reinforcement is more effective in maintaining or increasing the rate of response. **Partial reinforcement** is operating when some but not all responses are reinforced.

Partial reinforcement results in a greater resistance to extinction than does continuous reinforcement (Lerman et al., 1996). This result is known as the *partial reinforcement effect.* There is an inverse relationship between the percentage of responses that have been reinforced and resistance to extinction. That is, the lower the percentage of responses that are reinforced, the longer extinction will take when reinforcement is withheld. The strongest resistance to extinction ever observed occurred in one experiment in which pigeons were conditioned to peck at a disk. Holland and Skinner (1961) report that "after the response had been maintained on a fixed ratio of 900 and reinforcement was then discontinued, the pigeon emitted 73,000 responses during the first $4\frac{1}{2}$ hours of extinction" (p. 124).

Schedules of Reinforcement

Partial reinforcement may be administered according to different **schedules of reinforcement.** Different schedules produce distinct rates and patterns of responses, as well as varying degrees of resistance to extinction when reinforcement is discontinued (see Figure 10.4). The two basic types of schedules are ratio and interval schedules. *Ratio schedules* require that a certain number of responses be made before one of the responses is reinforced. With *interval schedules,* a given amount of time must pass before a reinforcer is administered. These types of schedules are further subdivided into fixed and variable categories.

On a **fixed-ratio schedule,** a reinforcer is given after a fixed number of nonreinforced responses. If the fixed ratio is set at 30 responses (FR-30), a reinforcer is given after 30 correct responses. Examples are payments to factory workers according to the number of units produced and to migrant farm workers for each bushel of fruit they pick. A fixed-ratio schedule is a very effective way to maintain a high response rate, because the number of reinforcers received depends directly on the response rate. The faster people or animals respond, the more reinforcers they earn and the sooner they earn them. When large ratios are used, people and animals tend to pause after each reinforcement but then return to the characteristic high rate of responding.

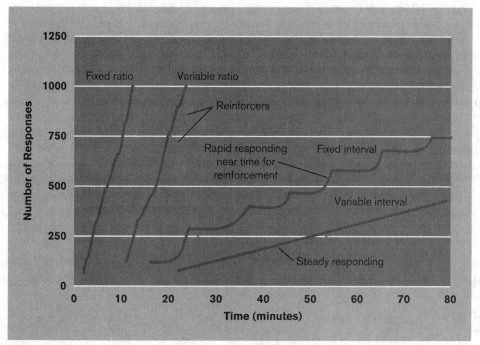

FIGURE 10.4   Four Types of Reinforcement Schedules. Skinner's research revealed distinctive response patterns for four partial-reinforcement schedules (the reinforcers are indicated by the diagonal marks). The ratio schedules, based on the number of responses, yielded a higher response rate than the interval schedules, which are based on the amount of time elapsed between reinforcers.

The pauses after reinforcement that occur with a high fixed-ratio schedule normally do not occur with the **variable-ratio schedule.** On a variable-ratio schedule, a reinforcer is given after a varying number of nonreinforced responses based on an average ratio. With a variable ratio of 30 responses (VR-30), people might be reinforced first after 10 responses, then after 50, then again after 30 responses, and so on. They cannot predict exactly what number of responses will be reinforced, but, in this example, reinforcement is averaging 1 in 30. Variable-ratio schedules result in higher, more stable rates of responding than fixed-ratio schedules. Skinner (1953) reports that on this schedule "a pigeon may respond as rapidly as five times per second and maintain this rate for many hours" (p. 104). The best example of the power of the variable-ratio schedule is found in the gambling casino. Slot machines, roulette wheels, and most other games of chance pay on this type of schedule. In general, the variable-ratio schedule produces the highest response rate and the most resistance to extinction.

On a **fixed-interval schedule,** a specific time interval must pass before a response is reinforced. For example, on a 60-second fixed-interval schedule (FI-60), a reinforcer is given for the first correct response that occurs 60 seconds after the last reinforced response. People working on salary are reinforced on the fixed-interval schedule. Unlike ratio schedules, reinforcement on interval schedules does not depend on the number of responses made, only on the one correct response made after the time interval has passed. Characteristic of the fixed-interval schedule is a pause or a sharp decline in responding immediately after each reinforcement and a rapid acceleration in responding just before the next reinforcer is due.

Variable-interval schedules eliminate the pause after reinforcement that is typical with fixed-interval schedules. On a **variable-interval schedule,** a reinforcer is given after the first correct response following a varying time of nonreinforced responses based on an average time. Rather than being given every 60 seconds, for example, a reinforcer might be given after a 30-second interval, with successive reinforcers following after 90-, 45-, and 75-second intervals. But the average time elapsing between reinforcers would be 60 seconds (VI-60). This schedule maintains remarkably stable and uniform rates of responding, but the response rate is typically lower than that with ratio schedules, because reinforcement is not tied directly to the number of responses made. Random drug testing in the workplace is an excellent example of application of the variable-interval schedule and appears to be quite effective. Table 10.1 summarizes the characteristics of the four types of schedules of reinforcement.

Factors other than the schedule of reinforcement influence the operant conditioning process. For example, as the magnitude of reinforcement increases, acquisition of a response is faster, the rate of

TABLE 10.1   Reinforcement Schedules Compared

SCHEDULE OF REINFORCEMENT	RESPONSE RATE	PATTERN OF RESPONSES	RESISTANCE TO EXTINCTION
Fixed-ratio schedule	Very high	Steady response with low ratio. Brief pause after each reinforcement with very high ratio.	The higher the ratio, the more resistance to extinction.
Variable-ratio schedule	Highest response rate	Constant response pattern, no pauses.	Most resistance to extinction.
Fixed-interval schedule	Lowest response rate	Long pause after reinforcement, followed by gradual acceleration.	The longer the interval the more resistance to extinction.
Variable-interval schedule	Moderate	Stable, uniform response.	More resistance to extinction than fixed-interval schedule with same average interval.

responding is higher, and resistance to extinction is greater (Clayton, 1964; Dallery et al., 2001; Katz et al., 2002). In addition, the longer the delay in reinforcement, the more slowly a response is acquired (Church, 1989; Mazur, 1993). The motivation of the learner contributes as well. Skinner found that when food is the reinforcer, a hungry animal will learn faster than a full animal. To maximize motivation, he used rats that had been deprived of food for 24 hours and pigeons that were maintained at 75–80% of their normal body weight.

Punishment

Punishment is the opposite of reinforcement. Punishment lowers the probability of a response by following it with an aversive, or unpleasant, consequence. However, punishment can be accomplished by either adding an unpleasant stimulus or removing a pleasant stimulus. The added unpleasant stimulus might take the form of criticism, a scolding, a disapproving look, a fine, or a prison sentence. The removal of a pleasant stimulus might consist of withholding affection and attention, suspending a driver's license, or taking away a privilege such as watching television.

It is common to confuse punishment and negative reinforcement because both involve an unpleasant stimulus, but there is a big difference between the two. Punishment may involve adding an aversive stimulus, but with negative reinforcement, an aversive stimulus is terminated or avoided. Moreover, the two have opposite effects: Unlike punishment, negative reinforcement increases the probability of a desired response by removing an unpleasant stimulus when the correct response is made. "Grounding" can be used as either punishment or negative reinforcement. If a teenager fails to clean her room after many requests to do so, her parents could ground her for the weekend—a punishment. An alternative approach would be to use negative reinforcement—to tell her she is grounded until the room is clean. Which approach is more likely to be effective?

A number of potential problems are associated with the use of punishment:

1. According to Skinner, *punishment does not extinguish an undesirable behavior; rather, it suppresses that behavior when the punishing agent is present.* But the behavior is apt to continue when the threat of punishment is removed and in settings where punishment is unlikely. If punishment (imprisonment, fines, and so on) reliably extinguished unlawful behavior, there would be fewer repeat offenders in the criminal justice system.

2. *Punishment indicates that a behavior is unacceptable but does not help people develop more appropriate behaviors.* If punishment is used, it should be administered in conjunction with reinforcement or rewards for appropriate behavior.

3. *The person who is severely punished often becomes fearful and feels angry and hostile toward the punisher.* These reactions may be accompanied by a desire to retaliate or to avoid or escape from the punisher and the punishing situation. Many runaway teenagers leave home to escape physical abuse. Punishment that involves a loss of privileges is more effective than physical punishment and engenders less fear and hostility (Walters & Grusec, 1977).

4. *Punishment frequently leads to aggression.* Those who administer physical punishment may become models of aggressive behavior—people who demonstrate aggression as a way of solving problems and discharging anger. Children of abusive, punishing parents are at greater risk than other children of becoming aggressive and abusive themselves (Widom, 1989).

If punishment can lead to such problems, what can be done to discourage undesirable behavior? Many psychologists believe that removing the rewarding consequences of the behavior is the best way to extinguish an undesirable or problem behavior. According to this view, parents should extinguish a child's temper tantrums not by punishment, but by never giving in to the child's demands during a tantrum. A parent might best extinguish problem behavior performed merely to get attention by ignoring it and giving attention to more appropriate behavior. Sometimes, simply explaining why a certain behavior is not appropriate is all that is required to extinguish it. Using positive reinforcement such as praise will make good behavior more rewarding for children. This approach brings with it the attention that children want and need—attention that often comes only when they misbehave. Table 10.2 summarizes the differences between reinforcement and punishment.

Making Punishment More Effective

It is probably unrealistic to believe that punishment can be dispensed with entirely. If a young child runs into the street, puts a finger near an electrical outlet, or reaches for a hot pan on the stove, a swift punishment may save the child from a potentially disastrous situation. Research has revealed several factors that influence the effectiveness of punishment: its timing, its intensity, and the consistency of its application (Parke, 1977).

1. *Punishment is most effective when it is applied during the misbehavior or as soon afterward as possible.* Interrupting the problem behavior is most effective because doing so abruptly halts its rewarding aspects. The longer the delay between the response and the punishment, the less effective the punishment is in suppressing the response (Camp et al., 1967). When there is a delay, most animals do not make the connection between the misbehavior and the punishment. With humans, however, if the punishment must be delayed, the punisher should remind the perpetrator of the incident and explain why the behavior was inappropriate.

2. *Ideally, punishment should be of the minimal severity necessary to suppress the problem behavior.* Animal studies reveal that the more intense the punishment, the greater the suppression of the undesirable behavior (Church, 1963). But the intensity of the punishment should match the seriousness of the misdeed. Unnecessarily severe punishment is likely to produce the negative side effects mentioned earlier. Yet, if the initial punishment is too mild, it will have no effect. Similarly, gradually increasing the intensity of the punishment is not effective; the perpetrator will gradually adapt to it, and the unwanted behavior will persist (Azrin & Holz, 1966). At a minimum, if a behavior is to be suppressed,

TABLE 10.2   The Effects of Reinforcement and Punishment

REINFORCEMENT (INCREASES OR STRENGTHENS A BEHAVIOR)	PUNISHMENT (DECREASES OR SUPRESSES A BEHAVIOR)
Adding a pleasant stimulus (positive reinforcement) Presenting food, money, praise, attention, or other rewards.	**Adding an aversive stimulus** Delivering a pain-producing or otherwise aversive stimulus, such as a spanking or an electric shock.
Subtracting an aversive stimulus (negative reinforcement) Removing or terminating some pain-producing or otherwise aversive stimulus, such as an electric shock.	**Subtracting a pleasant stimulus** Removing some pleasant stimulus or taking away privileges, such as TV watching, use of automobile.

the punishment must be more punishing than the misbehavior is rewarding. In human terms, a $200 ticket is more likely to suppress the urge to speed than a $2 ticket.

A person who wishes to apply punishment must understand that the purpose of punishment is not to vent anger but rather to modify behavior. Punishment meted out in anger is likely to be more intense than necessary to bring about the desired result.

3. *To be effective, punishment must be applied consistently.* A parent cannot ignore misbehavior one day and punish the same act the next. And both parents should react to the same misbehavior in the same way. An undesired response will be suppressed more effectively when the probability of punishment is high. Would you be tempted to speed if you saw a police car in your rear-view mirror?

Culture and Punishment

Punishment has been used throughout recorded history to control and suppress people's behavior. It is administered when important values, rules, regulations, and laws are violated. But not all cultures share the same values or have the same laws regulating behavior. U.S. citizens traveling in other countries need to be aware of how different cultures view and administer punishment. A memorable incident—widely publicized when it occurred a decade ago and still relevant today—revealed sharp differences in concepts of crime and punishment between the United States and Singapore.

In 1994, Michael Fay, an 18-year-old American living in Singapore, was arrested and charged with 53 counts of vandalism, including the spray painting of dozens of cars. He was fined approximately $2,000, sentenced to 4 months in jail, and received four lashes with a rattan cane, an agonizingly painful experience. In justifying their system of punishment, the officials in Singapore were quick to point out that their city, about the same size as Los Angeles, is virtually free of crime—few murders, rapes, beatings, or robberies. Among Americans, sentiment about the caning was mixed. Some, including Michael's parents, viewed it as barbarous and cruel. But many Americans (51% in a CNN poll) expressed the view that caning might be an effective punishment under certain circumstances.

Escape and Avoidance Learning

Learning to perform a behavior because it terminates an aversive event is called *escape learning*, and it reflects the power of negative reinforcement. Taking aspirin to relieve a pounding headache is an example of an escape behavior. *Avoidance learning*, in contrast, depends on two types of conditioning: classical and operant. Through classical conditioning, an event or condition comes to signal an aversive state. For example, a child may associate an increase in the volume of his parent's voice with an impending punishment. Because of such associations, people may engage in behaviors to avoid the anticipated aversive consequences. So, the child stops an unacceptable behavior when his parent, in a louder-than-usual voice, tells him to do so, in order to avoid the punishment that is sure to follow.

Many avoidance behaviors occur in response to phobias. Students who have had a bad experience speaking in front of a class may begin to fear any situation that involves speaking before a group. Such students may avoid taking courses that require class presentations or taking leadership roles that necessitate public speaking. Avoiding such situations prevents them from suffering the perceived dreaded consequences. But the avoidance behavior is negatively reinforced and thus is strengthened through operant conditioning. Maladaptive avoidance behaviors are very difficult to extinguish, because people never give themselves a chance to learn that the dreaded consequences probably will not occur or that they are greatly exaggerated.

There is an important exception to the ability of humans and other animals to learn to escape or avoid aversive situations: **Learned helplessness** is a passive resignation to aversive conditions learned by repeated exposure to aversive events that are inescapable and unavoidable. The initial experiment on learned helplessness was conducted by Overmeier and Seligman (1967). Dogs in the experimental group were strapped into harnesses from which they could not escape and were exposed to electric shocks. Later, these same dogs were placed in a box with two compartments separated by a low barrier. The dogs then experienced a series of trials in which a warning signal was followed by an electric shock administered through the box's floor. However, the floor was electrified only on one side, and the dogs could have escaped the electric shocks simply by jumping the barrier. Surprisingly, the dogs did not do so. Dogs in the control group had not previously experienced the inescapable shock and behaved in an entirely different manner; they quickly learned to jump the barrier when the warning signal sounded, thus escaping the shock. Seligman (1975) later reasoned that humans who have suffered painful experiences they could neither avoid nor escape may also experience learned helplessness. Then, having experienced this helplessness, they may simply give up and react to disappointment in life by becoming inactive, withdrawn, and depressed (Seligman, 1991).

Applications of Operant Conditioning

Operant conditioning has numerous applications. For example, the principles of operant conditioning are used effectively to train animals that help physically challenged people lead more independent lives. Dogs and monkeys have been trained to help people who are paralyzed or confined to wheelchairs, and, of course, for years, seeing-eye dogs have been trained to assist the blind.

Biofeedback, a procedure in which people learn to consciously control autonomic functions such as heart rate, is another important application of operant conditioning principles. Biofeedback devices have sensors that monitor slight changes in these physiological responses and then amplify and convert the changes into visual or auditory signals. Thus, people can see or hear evidence of internal processes, and by trying out various strategies (thoughts, feelings, or images), they can learn which ones routinely increase, decrease, or maintain a particular level of activity. Biofeedback has been used to regulate heart rate and to alleviate migraine and tension headaches, gastrointestinal disorders, asthma attacks, anxiety tension states, epileptic seizures, sexual dysfunctions, and neuromuscular disorders due to cerebral palsy, spinal-cord injuries, and stroke (Kalish, 1981; L. Miller, 1989; N. E. Miller, 1985).

Behavior modification is a method of changing behavior through a systematic program based on the principles of operant conditioning. Many institutions—schools, mental hospitals, homes for youthful offenders, and prisons—have used behavior modification programs with varying degrees of success. One type of behavior modification program is a **token economy**—a program that motivates socially desirable behavior by reinforcing it with tokens. The tokens (poker chips or coupons) may later be exchanged for desired goods such as candy or cigarettes and privileges such as weekend passes, free time, or participation in desired activities. Token economies have been used effectively in mental hospitals to encourage patients to attend to grooming, to interact with other patients, and to carry out housekeeping tasks (Ayllon & Azrin, 1965, 1968). They have also been used in schools in an effort to encourage students to increase desirable behaviors such as reading books. However, the results of more than 100 studies suggest that the overuse of tangible rewards may have certain long-term negative effects, such as undermining people's intrinsic motivation to regulate their own behavior (Deci et al., 1999).

Before moving on to cognitive learning, review the basic components of classical and operant conditioning in Table 10.3.

COGNITIVE LEARNING

According to cognitive theorists, **cognitive processes**—thinking, knowing, problem solving, remembering, and forming mental representations—are critically important to a more complete, more comprehensive view of learning than that provided by the conditioning theories.

TABLE 10.3 Classical and Operant Conditioning Compared

CHARACTERISTICS	CLASSICAL CONDITIONING	OPERANT CONDITIONING
Type of association	Between two stimuli	Between a response and its consequence
State of subject	Passive	Active
Focus of attention	On what precedes response	On what follows response
Type of response typically involved	Involuntary or reflexive response	Voluntary response
Bodily response typically involved	Internal responses; emotional and glandular reactions	External responses; muscular and skeletal movement and verbal responses
Range of responses	Relatively simple	Simple to highly complex
Responses learned	Emotional reactions; fears, likes, dislikes	Goal-oriented responses

Insight and Latent Learning

In his book *The Mentality of Apes* (1925), Wolfgang Köhler (1887–1967) describes an experiment in which he hung a bunch of bananas inside a cage containing chimps but overhead, out of reach of the apes; boxes and sticks were left in the cage. Köhler observed the chimps' unsuccessful attempts to reach the bananas by jumping up or swinging sticks at them. Eventually the chimps solved the problem by piling the boxes one on top of the other until they could reach the bananas, as if it had come to them in a flash of **insight.** They seemed to have suddenly discovered the relationship between the sticks or boxes and the bananas. Köhler insisted that insight, rather than trial-and-error learning, accounted for the chimps' successes, because they could easily repeat the solution and transfer this learning to similar problems. Humans often learn through insight, as you may have experienced if you have had a sudden "Aha! Now I understand!" moment when trying to solve some type of problem.

Edward Tolman (1886–1959) maintained that **latent learning,** like insight, could occur without reinforcement (Tolman, 1932). A classic experimental study by Tolman and Honzik (1930) supports this position. Three groups of rats were placed in a maze daily for 17 days. The first group always received a food reward at the end of the maze. The second group never received a reward, and the third group did not receive a food reward until the 11th day. The first group showed a steady improvement in performance over the 17-day period. The second group showed slight, gradual improvement. The third group, after being rewarded on the 11th day, showed a marked improvement the next day and from then on, outperformed the rats that had been rewarded daily. The rapid improvement of the third group indicated to Tolman that latent learning had occurred—that the rats had actually learned the maze during the first 11 days.

The rats in Tolman's experiment did learn something before reinforcement and without exhibiting any evidence of learning by overt, observable behavior. But what did they learn? Tolman concluded that the rats had learned to form a **cognitive map,** a mental representation or picture, of the maze but had not demonstrated their learning until they were reinforced. In later studies, Tolman showed how rats quickly learn to rearrange learned cognitive maps and find their way through increasingly complex mazes with ease.

Observational Learning

The earlier discussion of operant conditioning described how people and other animals learn by directly experiencing the consequences, positive or negative, of their behavior. But must people experience rewards and punishment firsthand in order to learn? Not according to Albert Bandura (1986), who contends that many behaviors or responses are acquired through observational learning, or, as he now calls it, *social-cognitive learning*. **Observational learning,** sometimes called **modeling,** results when people observe the behavior of others and note the consequences of that behavior. And observational learning is not restricted to humans. Monkeys, for example, learn specific fears by observing other monkeys (Cook et al., 1985).

The person who demonstrates the behavior or whose behavior is imitated is called the **model.** Parents, movie stars, and sports personalities can be powerful models. The effectiveness of a model is related to his or her status, competence, and power. Other important factors are the age, sex, attractiveness, and ethnicity of the model. Whether learned behavior is actually performed depends largely on whether the observed model is rewarded or punished for the behavior and whether the observer expects to be rewarded for the behavior (Bandura, 1969, 1977). Research has also shown that observational learning is improved when several sessions of observation (watching the behavior) precede attempts to perform the behavior and are then repeated in the early stages of practicing it (Weeks & Anderson, 2000).

But repetition alone isn't enough to cause an observer to learn from a model: An observer must be physically and cognitively capable of performing the behavior in order to learn it. In other words, no matter how much time you devote to watching Jennifer Capriati play tennis or Tiger Woods play golf, you won't be able to acquire skills like theirs unless you possess physical talents equal to theirs. Similarly, it is doubtful that a kindergartener will learn geometry from watching her 10th-grade brother do his homework.

Emotional responses are often acquired through observational learning. For instance, Gerull and Rappe (2002) found that toddlers whose mothers expressed fear at the sight of rubber snakes and spiders displayed significantly higher levels of fear of these objects when tested later than did toddlers in a control group whose mothers had not expressed such fears. Conversely, children who see "a parent or peer behaving nonfearfully in a potentially fear-producing situation may be 'immunized' " to feeling fear when confronted with a similar frightening situation later (Basic Behavioral Science Task Force, 1996, p. 139).

Bandura suspected that aggressive behavior is particularly likely to be copied as a result of observational learning and that aggression and violence on TV programs, including cartoons, tend to increase aggression in children. One of his classic studies involved three groups of preschool children. Children in one group individually observed an adult model punching, kicking, and using a mallet to hit a 5-foot, inflated plastic "Bobo Doll," while uttering aggressive phrases (Bandura et al., 1961, p. 576). Children in the second group observed a nonaggressive model who ignored the Bobo Doll and sat quietly assembling Tinker Toys. Children in the third group (the control group) were placed in the same setting with no adult present. Later, each child was observed through a one-way mirror. Children exposed to the aggressive model imitated much of the aggression and also engaged in significantly more nonimitative aggression than did children in either of the other two groups. Children who had observed the nonaggressive model showed less aggressive behavior than did children in the control group.

A further study compared the degree of aggression in children following exposure to (1) a live aggressive model, (2) a filmed version of the episode, and (3) a film depicting an aggressive cartoon character using the same aggressive behaviors in a fantasylike setting (Bandura et al., 1963). A control group was not exposed to any of the three aggressive models. The groups exposed to the aggressive models used significantly more aggression than the control group. The researchers concluded that "of the three experimental conditions, exposure to humans on film portraying aggression was the most influential in eliciting and shaping aggressive behavior" (p. 7).

Bandura's research provided the impetus for studying the effects of televised violence and aggression in both cartoons and regular programming. Researchers have also shown in a variety of ways—including carefully controlled laboratory experiments with children, adolescents, and young adults—that violent video games increase aggressive behavior (Anderson & Bushman, 2001). Moreover, the effects of media violence are evident across a wide range of categories: music, music videos, advertising, and the Internet (Villani, 2001).

Watching excessive violence gives people an exaggerated view of the pervasiveness of violence in society, while making them less sensitive to the victims of violence. Media violence also encourages aggressive behavior in children by portraying aggression as an acceptable and effective way to solve problems and by teaching new forms of aggression (Wood et al., 1991).

Some have argued that when televised violence is followed by appropriate consequences, such as arrest, children may learn not to engage in aggression. However, experimental research has demonstrated that children do not process information about consequences in the same way adults do (Krcmar & Cooke, 2001). Children appear to judge the rightness or wrongness of an act of violence in terms of provocation; that is, they believe that violence as retaliation is morally acceptable, even if it is punished by an authority figure.

However, just as children imitate the aggressive behavior they observe on television, they also imitate the prosocial, or helping, behavior they observe. Programs such as *Mister Rogers' Neighborhood* and *Sesame Street* have been found to have a positive influence on children.

MEMORY

"Shut up, or I'll cut you," Jennifer's attacker warned her as he held the knife against her throat. Just moments before, Jennifer had screamed as the man grabbed her, threw her down on the bed, and pinned her hands behind her. Now, feeling the pain of the knife's sharp point on her throat, she knew he meant what he said. But she steeled herself to study the rapist—his facial features, scars, tattoos, voice, mannerisms—vowing to herself that she would remember the man well enough to send him to prison.

Hours after her ordeal, Jennifer Thompson viewed police photos of potential suspects, searching for that of her rapist—his pencil-thin moustache, eyebrows, nose, and other features. She then selected a composite photo that looked like the rapist. A week later, she viewed six suspects holding cards numbered 1 to 6. Jennifer looked at suspect number 5 and announced with total confidence, "That's the man who raped me."

The man was Ronald Cotton, who had already served a year and a half in prison for attempted sexual assault. In court, Thompson was unshakably confident, so sure that this man had raped her. Cotton was nervous and frightened. His alibis didn't check out, and a piece missing from one of his shoes resembled a piece found at the crime scene. But it was the confident, unwavering testimony of the only eyewitness, Jennifer Thompson, that sealed his fate. The jury found him guilty and sentenced him to life in prison, just as Thompson had hoped.

"God knows I'm innocent," said Cotton, and he vowed to prove it somehow.

Remarkably, after Cotton had been in prison for more than a year, a new inmate, Bobby Poole, convicted of a series of brutal rapes, joined him at his work assignment in the kitchen. When Cotton told Poole that he had been convicted of raping Jennifer Thompson, Poole laughed and bragged that Cotton was doing some of his time.

Finally, after Cotton had served 11 years, law professor Richard Rosen heard his story and agreed to help him. Rosen knew that DNA tests could be performed that were far more sophisticated than those that had been available 11 years earlier. It was Cotton's DNA samples that cleared him of the crime. Poole's DNA samples, however, proved that he had raped Thompson.

After being proved innocent and released from prison, Ronald Cotton talked with and forgave Jennifer Thompson, who had falsely accused him. Cotton is now married with a beautiful daughter, Raven. With Thompson's help, he got a six-figure settlement from the state government. (Adapted from O'Neil, 2000.)

Does this case simply reflect the rare and unusual in human memory, or are memory errors common occurrences? This and many other questions you may have about memory will be answered in this chapter.

REMEMBERING

The Three Processes in Memory

The act of remembering requires three processes: encoding, storage, and retrieval (see Figure 10.5). The first process, **encoding,** involves transforming information into a form that can be stored in memory. For example, if you met someone named Will at a party, you might associate his name with that of the actor Will Smith. The second memory process, **storage,** involves keeping or maintaining information in memory. The final process, **retrieval,** occurs when information stored in memory is brought to mind. Calling Will by name the next time you meet him shows that you have retrieved his name from memory.

Physiological changes must occur during a process called **consolidation,** which allows new information to be stored in memory for later retrieval. These physiological changes require the synthesis of protein molecules (Lopez, 2000). Until recently, conventional wisdom held that the process of consolidation had to occur only once for each item memorized. But as we will see later in the chapter, in the section on the causes of forgetting, some seemingly consolidated memories can be induced to disappear (Nader et al., 2000).

The Three Memory Systems

How are memories stored? According to one widely accepted view, the *Atkinson-Shiffrin model*, there are three different, interacting memory systems, known as sensory, short-term, and long-term memory (Atkinson & Shiffrin, 1968; Broadbent, 1958). We will examine each of these three memory systems, which are shown in Figure 10.6.

As information comes in through the senses, virtually everything you see, hear, or otherwise sense is held in **sensory memory,** but only for the briefest period of time. Exactly how long does visual sensory memory last? For a fraction of a second, glance at the three rows of letters shown below and then close your eyes. How many of the items can you recall?

X   B   D   F
M   P   Z   G
L   C   N   H

Most people can recall correctly only four or five of the items when they are briefly presented. Does this indicate that visual sensory memory can hold only four or five items at a time? To find out, researcher George Sperling (1960) briefly flashed 12 items, as shown above, to participants. Immediately upon turning off the display, he sounded a high, medium, or low tone that signaled the participants

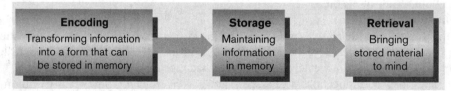

FIGURE 10.5   The Processes Required in Remembering. The act of remembering requires successful completion of all three of these processes: encoding, storage, and retrieval.

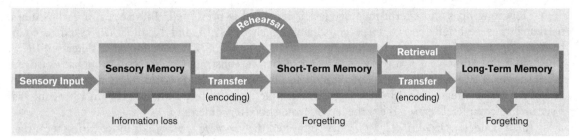

FIGURE 10.6 The Three Memory Systems. According to the Atkinson-Shiffrin model, there are three separate memory systems: sensory memory, short-term memory, and long-term memory.

to report only the top, middle, or bottom row of items. Before they heard the tone, the participants had no way of knowing which row they would have to report. Yet Sperling found that, when the participants could view the letters for $\frac{15}{1000}$ to $\frac{1}{2}$ second, they could report correctly all the items in any row nearly 100% of the time. But the items fade from sensory memory so quickly that during the time it takes to report three or four of the items, the other eight or nine have already disappeared.

Auditory sensory memory lasts about 2 seconds (Klatzky, 1980). You may have the sense that words are echoing in your mind after someone stops speaking to you. This phenomenon is the result of the relatively long time that auditory information remains in sensory memory, compared to visual information. Thus, your brain has much more time to attend to sounds and to move information about them to the next phase of processing.

From sensory memory, information moves to **short-term memory.** Whatever you are thinking about right now is in your short-term memory. Unlike sensory memory, which holds virtually the exact sensory stimulus, short-term memory usually codes information according to sound (Conrad, 1964). The letter T is coded as the sound "tee," not as the shape T. In addition, short-term memory has a very limited capacity—about seven (plus or minus two) different items or bits of information at one time. When short-term memory is filled to capacity, displacement can occur (just as you start to lose things when the top of your desk becomes overcrowded!). In **displacement,** each new incoming item pushes out an existing item, which is then forgotten.

One way to overcome the limitation on the capacity of short-term memory to seven or so bits of information is to use a technique that George A. Miller (1956), a pioneer in memory research, calls *chunking*—organizing or grouping separate bits of information into larger units, or chunks. A *chunk* is an easily identifiable unit such as a syllable, a word, an acronym, or a number (Cowan, 1988). For example, the numbers 5 2 9 7 3 1 2 5 can be chunked as 52 97 31 25, giving short-term memory the easier task of dealing with four chunks of information rather than eight separate bits.

Anytime you chunk information on the basis of knowledge stored in long-term memory—in other words, by associating it with some kind of meaning—you increase the effective capacity of short-term memory (Lustig & Hasher, 2002). And when you increase the effective capacity of short-term memory, you are more likely to transfer information to long-term memory. (*Hint:* The headings and subheadings in textbook chapters are labels for manageable chunks of information. You will remember more of a chapter if you use them as organizers for your notes and as cues to recall chapter information when you are reviewing for an exam.)

Items in short-term memory are lost in less than 30 seconds unless you repeat them over and over to yourself. This process is known as **rehearsal.** But rehearsal is easily disrupted. Distractions that are stressful are especially likely to disrupt short-term memory. And a threat to survival certainly does so, as researchers showed when they pumped the odor of a feared predator, a fox, into a laboratory where rats were performing a task requiring short-term memory (Morrison et al., 2002; Morrow et al., 2000).

How long does short-term memory last if rehearsal is prevented? In a series of early studies, participants were briefly shown three consonants (such as H, G, and L) and then asked to count backward by threes from a given number (for example, 738, 735, 732, ...) (Peterson & Peterson, 1959). After intervals lasting from 3 to 18 seconds, participants were instructed to stop counting backward and recall the three letters. Following a delay of 9 seconds, the participants could recall an average of only one of the three letters. After 18 seconds, there was practically no recall whatsoever. An 18-second distraction had completely erased the three letters from short-term memory.

Allan Baddeley (1990, 1992, 1995) has suggested that *working memory* is a more fitting term than short-term memory. In other words, this memory system is where you *work on* information to understand it, remember it, use it to solve a problem, or to communicate with someone. Research shows that the prefrontal cortex is the primary area of the brain responsible for working memory (Courtney et al., 1997; Rao et al., 1997).

Some of the information in short-term memory makes its way into long-term memory. **Long-term memory,** the type of memory most people are referring to when they use the word "memory," is each individual's vast storehouse of permanent or relatively permanent memories. There are no known limits to the storage capacity of long-term memory, and long-term memories can last for years, some of them for a lifetime. Long-term memory holds all the knowledge you have accumulated, the skills you have acquired, and the memories of your past experiences. Information in long-term memory is usually stored in verbal form, although visual images, sounds, and odors can be stored there, as well.

But how did this vast store of information make its way from short-term memory into long-term memory? Sometimes, through mere repetition or rehearsal, a person is able to transfer information into long-term memory. Your teachers may have used a drilling technique to try to cement the multiplication tables and other material in your long-term memory. Another approach is **elaborative rehearsal.** The goal of this strategy is to relate new information to information already in your long-term memory (Symons & Johnson, 1997). For example, you might remember the French word *maison* (house) by relating it to the English word *mansion* (a type of house). Forming such associations, especially if they are personally relevant, increases your chances of retrieving new information later. Figure 10.7 summarizes the three memory systems.

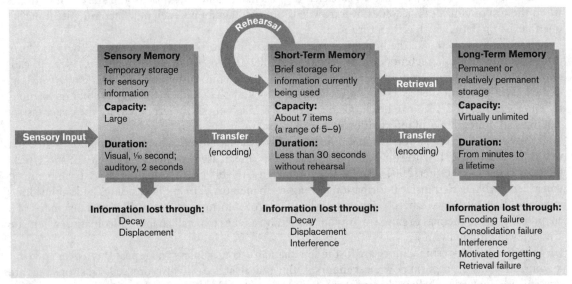

FIGURE 10.7 Characteristics of and Processes Involved in the Three Memory Systems. The three memory systems differ in what and how much they hold and for how long they store it. (From Peterson & Peterson, 1959.)

There are two main subsystems within long-term memory. The first, **declarative memory** (also called *explicit memory*), stores information that can be brought to mind in the form of words or images and then stated, or declared. **Episodic memory** is the part of declarative memory that holds memories of events as they have been subjectively experienced (Wheeler et al., 1997). It is somewhat like a mental diary, recording the episodes of your life—the people you have known, the places you have seen, and the experiences you have had. **Semantic memory,** the second part of declarative memory, is memory for general knowledge, or objective facts and information. In other words, semantic memory is a mental dictionary or encyclopedia of stored knowledge.

The second subsystem of long-term memory, **nondeclarative memory** (also called *implicit memory*), consists of motor skills, habits, and simple classically conditioned responses (Squire et al., 1993). Acquired through repetitive practice, motor skills include such things as eating with a fork, riding a bicycle, and driving a car. Although acquired slowly, once learned, these skills become habit, are quite reliable, and can be carried out with little or no conscious effort. Figure 10.8 shows the subsystems of long-term memory.

The Levels-of-Processing Model

Not all psychologists support the notion of three memory systems. Craik and Lockhart (1972) propose instead a **levels-of-processing model.** They suggest that whether people remember an item for a few seconds or a lifetime depends on how deeply they process the information. With the shallowest levels of processing, a person is merely aware of the incoming sensory information. Deeper processing takes place only when the person does something more with the information, such as forming relationships, making associations, attaching meaning to a sensory impression, or engaging in active elaborations on new material. However, the deeper levels of processing that establish a memory also require background knowledge, so that lasting connections can be formed between the person's existing store of knowledge and the new information (Willoughby et al., 2000).

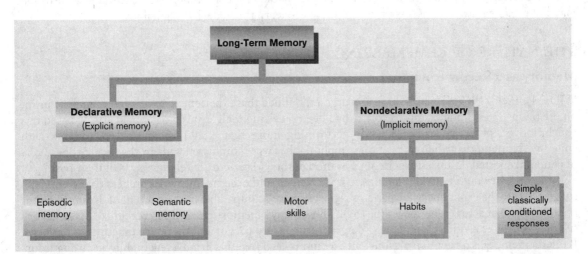

FIGURE 10.8   Subsystems of Long-Term Memory. Declarative memory can be divided into two parts: episodic memory, which stores memories of personally experienced events, and semantic memory, which stores facts and information. Nondeclarative memory consists of motor skills acquired through repetitive practice, habits, and simple classically conditioned responses.

Three Kinds of Memory Tasks

Psychologists have used three main types of tasks to measure memory retention: recall, recognition, and the relearning method. In **recall,** a person must produce required information by searching memory without the help of **retrieval cues**—the stimuli or bits of information that aid in the retrieval of particular information from long-term memory. Trying to remember someone's name, recalling items on a shopping list, and answering fill-in-the-blank and essay items on exams are all recall tasks. Often, serial recall (recalling items in a certain order) is easier than free recall (recalling items in any order) because in serial recall, each letter, word, or number may serve as a cue for the one that follows. Indeed, research suggests that, in free-recall tasks, order associations are more resistant to distractions than meaningful associations (Howard, 2002).

Recognition is exactly what the word implies. A person simply recognizes something as familiar—a face, a name, a taste, a melody. Recent brain-imaging studies have discovered that the hippocampus plays an extensive role in memory tasks involving recognition, but the degree of hippocampal activity varies for different tasks. When the task is recognizing famous faces, widespread brain activity takes place in both hemispheres, involving the prefrontal and temporal lobes and including the hippocampus and surrounding hippocampal region. Less widespread brain activity is observed during the recognition of recently encoded faces or the encoding of faces seen for the first time (Henson et al., 2002). Studies with monkeys having brain damage limited to the hippocampal region also show that this region is essential for normal recognition tasks (Teng et al., 2000; Zola et al., 2000).

There is yet another way to measure memory retention that is even more sensitive than recognition. With the **relearning method,** or the *savings method*, retention is expressed as the percentage of time saved when material is relearned, compared with the time required to learn the material originally. Suppose it took you 40 minutes to memorize a list of words, and 1 month later you were tested, using recall or recognition. If you could not recall or recognize a single word, would this mean that you had absolutely no memory of anything on the test? Or could it mean that the recall and recognition methods were not sensitive enough to pick up what little information you may have stored? How could a researcher measure a remnant of this former learning? Using the relearning method, a researcher could time how long it took you to relearn the list of words. If it took 20 minutes to relearn the list, this would represent a 50% savings compared to the original learning time of 40 minutes. College students demonstrate the relearning method each semester when they study for comprehensive final exams. Relearning material for a final exam takes less time than it took to learn the material originally.

THE NATURE OF REMEMBERING

Memory as a Reconstruction

Wilder Penfield (1969), a Canadian neurosurgeon, claimed that experiences leave a "permanent imprint on the brain . . . as though a tape recorder had been receiving it all" (p. 165). Penfield (1975) based this conclusion on observations made while performing more than 1,100 operations on patients with epilepsy. He found that when parts of the temporal lobes were stimulated with an electrical probe, 3.5% of patients reported flashback experiences, as though they were actually reliving parts of their past.

After reviewing Penfield's findings, Ulrich Neisser and other memory researchers (Neisser, 1967) suggested that the experiences the patients reported were "comparable to the content of dreams," rather than the recall of actual experiences (p. 169). Thus, today's memory researchers recognize that memory seldom works like a video cassette recorder, capturing every part of an experience exactly as it happens. Rather a memory is a **reconstruction**—an account pieced together from a few highlights, using information that may or may not be accurate (Loftus & Loftus, 1980). Put another way, remembering "is not so much like reading a book as it is like writing one from fragmentary notes" (Kihlstrom, 1995, p. 341). As a result, memory is quite often inaccurate, and recall is, even for people with the most accurate memories, partly truth and partly fiction.

An early memory researcher, Englishman Sir Frederick Bartlett (1886–1969), suggested that memory is influenced by **schemas**—integrated frameworks of knowledge stored in long-term memory. Schemas aid in processing large amounts of material because they provide frameworks into which people can incorporate new information and experience. For example, if you have taken a course in the past that included discussion of psychoanalytic theory, information about Freud and other psychoanalysts will be easier for you to learn than it will be for students who have no prior knowledge of psychoanalytic theory. Your prior knowledge is organized into schemas that provide "shelves" on which to store the new information.

Schemas can also distort memory, though. When you witness an event, your schemas may cause you to omit some facts about what actually occurred or to add non-factual details. Schema-based distortion can also occur when people alter the memory of an event or an experience in order to fit their beliefs, expectations, logic, or prejudices. The tendency to distort often causes gross inaccuracies in what people remember. For instance, people often distort memories of their own lives in the positive direction. Bahrick and others (1996) found that 89% of college students accurately remembered the A's they earned in high school, but only 29% accurately recalled the D's.

We are very likely to alter or distort what we see or hear to make it fit with what we believe should be true.

Eyewitness Testimony

As the story at the beginning of this section suggests, eyewitness testimony is highly subject to error. In fact, most memory experts say that it should always be viewed with caution (Loftus, 1979). Nevertheless, it does play a vital role in the U.S. justice system. Says Loftus (1984), "We can't afford to exclude it legally or ignore it as jurors. Sometimes, as in cases of rape, it is the only evidence available, and it is often correct" (p. 24).

Fortunately, eyewitness mistakes can be minimized. Eyewitnesses to crimes often identify suspects from a lineup. If shown photographs of a suspect before viewing the lineup, eyewitnesses may mistakenly identify that suspect in the lineup because the person looks familiar. Research suggests that it is better to have an eyewitness first describe the perpetrator and then search for photos matching that description than to have the eyewitness start by looking through photos and making judgments as to their similarity to the perpetrator (Pryke et al., 2000).

The composition of the lineup is also important. Other individuals in a lineup must resemble the suspect in age and body build and must certainly be of the same race. Even then, if the lineup does not contain the perpetrator, eyewitnesses may identify the person who most closely resembles him or her (Gonzalez et al., 1993). Eyewitnesses are less likely to make errors if a sequential lineup is used, that is, if the participants in the lineup are viewed one after the other, rather than simultaneously (Loftus, 1993a). Some police officers and researchers prefer a "showup"—a procedure that involves presenting only one suspect and having the witness indicate whether that person is the perpetrator. There are fewer misidentifications with a showup, but also more failures in making positive identifications (Wells, 1993).

Eyewitnesses are more likely to identify the wrong person if the person's race is different from their own. According to Egeth (1993), misidentifications are approximately 15% higher in cross-race than in same-race identifications. Misidentification is also somewhat more likely to occur when a weapon is used in a crime. The witnesses may pay more attention to the weapon than to the physical characteristics of the criminal (Steblay, 1992).

Even questioning witnesses after a crime can influence what they later remember. Because leading questions can substantially change a witness's memory of an event, it is critical that the interviewers ask neutral questions (Leichtman & Ceci, 1995). Misleading information supplied to the witness after the event can result in erroneous recollections of the actual event, a phenomenon known as the *misinformation effect* (Kroll et al., 1988; Loftus & Hoffman, 1989). Loftus (1997) and her students have conducted "more than 20 experiments involving over 20,000 participants that document how exposure to misinformation induces memory distortion" (p. 71). Furthermore, after eyewitnesses have repeatedly recalled information, whether accurate or inaccurate, they become even more confident when they testify in court because the information is so easily retrieved (Shaw, 1996). And the confidence eyewitnesses have in their testimony is not necessarily an indication of its accuracy (Loftus, 1993a; Sporer et al., 1995). In fact, eyewitnesses who perceive themselves to be more objective have more confidence in their testimony, regardless of its accuracy, and they are more likely to include incorrect information in their verbal descriptions (Geiselman et al., 2000).

Recovering Repressed Memories

Perhaps because of the frequency of such cases in novels, on television, and in movies, recent studies have found that many people in the United States believe that unconscious memories of abuse can lead to serious psychological disorders (Stafford & Lynn, 2002). Such beliefs have also been fostered by self-help books such as *The Courage to Heal*, published in 1988, by Ellen Bass and Laura Davis. This best-selling book became the "bible" for sex abuse victims and the leading "textbook" for some therapists who specialized in treating them. Bass and Davis not only sought to help survivors who remembered having suffered sexual abuse, but also reached out to people who had no memory of any sexual abuse and tried to help them determine whether they might have been abused. These authors suggested that "if you are unable to remember any specific instances . . . but still have a feeling that something abusive happened to you, it probably did" (p. 21). They offered a definite conclusion: "If you think you were abused and your life shows the symptoms, then you were" (p. 22). And they freed potential victims of sexual abuse from the responsibility of establishing any proof: "You are not responsible for proving that you were abused" (p. 37).

However, many psychologists are skeptical, claiming that the "recovered" memories are actually false memories created by the suggestions of therapists. Critics point out that numerous studies have shown that traumatic memories are rarely, if ever, repressed (e.g., Bowers & Farvolden, 1996; Merckelbach et al., 2003). Moreover, they maintain that "when it comes to a serious trauma, intrusive thoughts and memories of it are the most characteristic reaction" (p. 359). According to Loftus (1993b), "the therapist convinces the patient with no memories that abuse is likely, and the patient obligingly uses reconstructive strategies to generate memories that would support that conviction" (p. 528). Repressed-memory therapists believe, however, that healing hinges on their patients' being able to recover the repressed memories.

Critics further charge that recovered memories of sexual abuse are suspect because of the techniques therapists usually use to uncover them: hypnosis and guided imagery. As you have learned, hypnosis does not improve the accuracy of memory, only the confidence that what one remembers is accurate.

Can merely imagining experiences lead people to believe that those experiences actually happened to them? Yes, according to some studies. Many research participants who are instructed to imagine that a fictitious event happened do, in fact, develop a false memory of the imagined event (Hyman & Pentland, 1996; Hyman et al., 1995; Loftus & Pickrell, 1995; Worthen & Wood, 2001).

False childhood memories can also be experimentally induced. Garry and Loftus (1994) were able to implant a false memory of being lost in a shopping mall at 5 years of age in 25% of participants aged 18 to 53, after verification of the fictitious experience by a relative. Repeated exposure to suggestions of false memories can create those memories (Zaragoza & Mitchell, 1996).

Critics are especially skeptical of recovered memories of events that occurred in the first few years of life. The hippocampus, which is vital in the formation of episodic memories, is not fully developed then, and neither are the areas of the cortex where memories are stored (Squire et al., 1993). Furthermore, young children, who are still limited in language ability, do not store memories in categories that are accessible to adults. Accordingly, Widom and Morris (1997) found that memories of abuse are better when the victimization took place between the ages of 7 and 17 than when it occurred in the first 6 years of life.

The American Psychological Association (1994), the American Psychiatric Association (1993c), and the American Medical Association (1994) have issued status reports on memories of childhood abuse. The position of all three groups is that current evidence supports the possibilities that repressed memories exist *and* that false memories can be constructed in response to suggestions of abuse. This position suggests that recovered memories of abuse should be verified independently before they are accepted as facts. Taking such a position is critically important. False memories are easily formed. And, once formed, they are often relied on with great confidence (Dodson et al., 2000; Henkel et al., 2000).

Flashbulb Memories

We probably all remember where we were and what we were doing when we heard about the tragic events of September 11, 2001. This type of extremely vivid memory is called a **flashbulb memory** (Bohannon, 1988). Brown and Kulik (1977) suggest that a flashbulb memory is formed when a person learns of an event that is very surprising, shocking, and highly emotional. You might have a flashbulb memory of receiving the news of the death or serious injury of a close family member or a friend.

Several studies suggest that flashbulb memories are not as accurate as people believe them to be. Neisser and Harsch (1992) questioned university freshmen about the Challenger disaster the morning after the space shuttle exploded in 1986. When the same students were questioned again 3 years later, one-third gave accounts that differed markedly from those given initially, even though they were extremely confident of their recollections. Further, flashbulb memories appear to be forgotten at about the same rate and in the same ways as other kinds of memories (Curci et al., 2001).

Memory and Culture

Sir Frederick Bartlett (1932) believed that some impressive memory abilities operate within a social or cultural context and cannot be understood as a pure process. He stated that "both the manner and matter of recall are often predominantly determined by social influences" (p. 244). Studying memory in a cultural context, Bartlett (1932) described the amazing ability of the Swazi people of Africa to remember the slight differences in individual characteristics of their cows. One Swazi herdsman, Bartlett claimed, could remember details of every cow he had tended the year before. Such a feat is less surprising when you consider that the key component of traditional Swazi culture is the herds of cattle the people tend and depend on for their living. Do the Swazi people have superior memory powers? Bartlett asked young Swazi men and young European men to recall a message consisting of 25 words. The Swazi had no better recall ability than the Europeans.

Among many of the tribal peoples in Africa, the history of the tribe is preserved orally. Thus, an oracle, or specialist, must be able to encode, store, and retrieve huge volumes of historical data (D'Azevedo, 1982). Elders of the Iatmul people of New Guinea are also said to have committed to memory the lines of descent for the various clans of their people stretching back for many generations (Bateson, 1982). The unerring memories of the elders for these kinship patterns are used to resolve disputed property claims (Mistry & Rogoff, 1994).

Barbara Rogoff, an expert in cultural psychology, maintains that such phenomenal, prodigious memory feats are best explained and understood in their cultural context (Rogoff & Mistry, 1985). The tribal elders perform their impressive memory feats because it is an integral and critically important part of the culture in which they live. Most likely, their ability to remember lists of nonsense syllables would be no better than your own.

Studies examining memory for locations among a tribal group in India, the Asur, who do not use artificial lighting of any kind, provide further information about the influence of culture on memory (Mishra & Singh, 1992). Researchers hypothesized that members of this group would perform better on tests of memory for locations than on conventional tasks used by memory researchers. This is because, lacking artificial lights, the Asur have to remember locations so that they can move around in the dark without bumping into things. When the Asur people were tested, they did indeed remember locations better than word pairs.

In classic research, cognitive psychologists have also found that people more easily remember stories set in their own culture than those set in others. In one of the first of these studies, researchers told a story about a sick child to women in the United States and to Aboriginal women in Australia (Steffensen & Calker, 1982). Participants were randomly assigned to groups for whom story outcomes were varied. In one version, the girl got well after being treated by a physician. In the other, a traditional native healer was called in to help the girl. Aboriginal participants better recalled the story with the native healer, and American participants were more accurate in their recall of the story in which a physician treated the girl.

FACTORS INFLUENCING RETRIEVAL

The Serial Position Effect

If you were introduced to a dozen people at a party, you would most likely recall the names of the first few individuals you met and the last one or two, but forget many of the names of those in between. The reason is the **serial position effect**—the finding that, for information learned in sequence, recall is better for items at the beginning and the end than for items in the middle of the sequence.

Information at the beginning of a sequence is subject to the **primacy effect**—it is likely to be recalled because it already has been placed in long-term memory. Information at the end of a sequence is subject to the **recency effect**—it has an even higher probability of being recalled because it is still in short-term memory. The poorer recall of information in the middle of a sequence occurs because that information is no longer in short-term memory and has not yet been placed in long-term memory. The serial position effect lends strong support to the notion of separate systems for short-term and long-term memory (Postman & Phillips, 1965).

Environmental Context and Memory

Have you ever stood in your living room and thought of something you needed from your bedroom, only to forget what it was when you got there? Did the item come to mind when you returned to the living room? Tulving and Thompson (1973) suggest that many elements of the physical setting in which a person learns information are encoded along with the information and become part of the memory. If part or all of the original context is reinstated, it may serve as a retrieval cue. That is why returning to the living room elicits the memory of the object you intended to get from the bedroom. In fact, just visualizing yourself in the living room might do the trick (Smith, 1979). (Next time you're taking a test and having difficulty recalling something, try visualizing yourself in the room where you studied!)

Godden and Baddeley (1975) conducted one of the early studies of context and memory with members of a university scuba diving club. Participants memorized a list of words when they were either 10 feet underwater or on land. They were later tested for recall of the words in the same or in a different environment. Words learned underwater were best recalled underwater, and words learned on land were best recalled on land. In fact, when the scuba divers learned and recalled the words in the same context, their scores were 47% higher than when the two contexts were different (see Figure 10.9). More recent studies have found similar context effects (e.g., Bjorklund et al., 2000).

Odors can also supply powerful and enduring retrieval cues for memory. In a study by Morgan (1996), participants were placed in isolated cubicles and exposed to a list of 40 words. They were instructed to perform a cognitive task using the words but were not asked to remember them. Then, back in the cubicle 5 days later, participants were unexpectedly tested for recall of the 40 words. Experimental participants who experienced a pleasant odor during the initial task and again when tested 5 days later had significantly higher recall than control participants who did not experience the odor at either time.

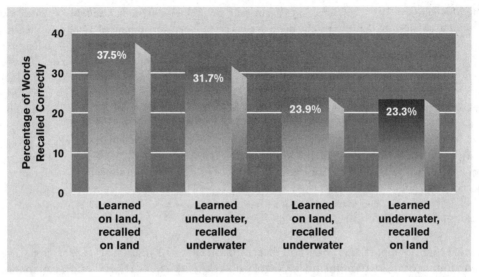

FIGURE 10.9 **Context-Dependent Memory.** Godden and Baddeley showed the strong influence of environmental context on recall. Scuba divers who memorized a list of words, either on land or underwater, had significantly better recall in the same physical context in which the learning had taken place. (Data from Godden & Baddeley, 1975.)

The State-Dependent Memory Effect

People tend to recall information better if they are in the same internal emotional state as they were when the information was encoded; psychologists call this the **state-dependent memory effect.** Anxiety appears to affect memory more than other emotions. For example, when researchers exposed college students to spiders and/or snakes while they were learning lists of words, the students recalled more words when the creatures were also present during tests of recall (Lang et al., 2001).

Adults who are clinically depressed tend to recall more of their negative life experiences (Clark & Teasdale, 1982) and are likely remember their parents being unloving and rejecting (Lewinsohn & Rosenbaum, 1987). Moreover, a review of 48 studies revealed a significant relationship between depression and memory impairment. Recognition and recall were more impaired in younger depressed patients than in older ones (Burt et al., 1995). But as depression lifts, the tendency toward negative recall and the memory impairment reverse themselves.

BIOLOGY AND MEMORY

Brain Damage

Researchers are finding specific locations in the brain that house and mediate functions and processes in memory. One important source of information comes from people who have suffered memory loss resulting from damage to specific brain areas. One especially important case is that of H.M., a man who suffered from such severe epilepsy that, out of desperation, he agreed to a radical surgical procedure. The surgeon removed the part of H.M.'s brain believed to be causing his seizures, the medial portions of both temporal lobes—the amygdala and the **hippocampal region,** which includes the hippocampus itself and the underlying cortical areas. It was 1953, and H.M. was 27 years old.

After his surgery, H.M. remained intelligent and psychologically stable, and his seizures were drastically reduced. But unfortunately, the tissue cut from H.M.'s brain housed more than the site of his seizures. It also contained his ability to use working memory to store new information in long-term memory. Though the capacity of his short-term memory remained the same, and he remembers the events of his life stored well before the operation, H.M. suffers from **anterograde amnesia.** He has not been able to remember a single event that has occurred since the surgery. And though H.M. turned 75 in 2001, as far as his conscious long-term memory is concerned, it was still 1953 and he was still 27 years old.

Surgery affected only H.M.'s declarative, long-term memory—his ability to store facts, personal experiences, names, faces, telephone numbers, and the like. But researchers were surprised to discover that he could still form nondeclarative memories; that is, he could still acquire skills through repetitive practice although he could not remember having done so. For example, since the surgery, H.M. has learned to play tennis and improve his game, but he has no memory of ever having played. (Adapted from Milner, 1966, 1970; Milner et al., 1968.)

Animal studies support the conclusion that the parts of H.M.'s brain that were removed are critical to the functioning of short-term memory (Ragozzino et al., 2002). Moreover, other patients who have suffered similar brain damage show the same types of memory loss (Squire, 1992). Recent research supports the hypothesis that the hippocampus is especially important in forming episodic memories (Eichenbaum, 1997; Gluck & Myers, 1997; Spiers et al., 2001). Semantic memory, however, depends not only on the hippocampus, but also on other parts of the hippocampal region underlying it (Vargha-Khadem et al., 1997). Consequently, many researchers argue that neurological bases for episodic and semantic memory are entirely separate (e.g., Tulving, 2002).

One interesting study (Maguire et al., 2000) suggests that the hippocampus may also support navigational skills by helping to create intricate neural spatial maps. MRI scans revealed that the rear (posterior) region of the hippocampus of London taxi drivers was significantly larger than that of participants in a matched control group whose living did not depend on navigational skills. In addition, the longer the time spent as a taxi driver, the greater the volume of the posterior hippocampus. Similarly, in many birds and small mammals, the volume of the hippocampus increases seasonally, as navigational skills for migration and spatial maps showing where food is hidden become critical for survival (Clayton, 1998; Colombo & Broadbent, 2000). Moreover, animal studies show that the hippocampus also plays an important role in the reorganization of previously learned spatial information (Lee & Kesner, 2002).

Neuronal Changes in Memory

The first close look at the nature of memory in single neurons was provided by Eric Kandel and his colleagues, who traced the effects of learning and memory in the sea snail *Aplysia* (Dale & Kandel, 1990). Using tiny electrodes implanted in several single neurons in the sea snail, the researchers mapped the neural circuits that are formed and maintained as the animal learns and remembers. They also discovered the different types of protein synthesis that facilitate short-term and long-term memory (Sweatt & Kandel, 1989). Kandel won a Nobel Prize in 2000 for his work. But the studies of learning and memory in *Aplysia* reflect only simple classical conditioning, which forms a type of nondeclarative memory. Other researchers studying mammals report that physical changes occur in the neurons and synapses in regions of the brain involved in declarative memory (Lee & Kesner, 2002).

Most neuroscientists believe that **long-term potentiation (LTP)**—an increase in the efficiency of neural transmission at the synapses that lasts for hours or longer—is the physiological process that underlies the formation of memories (Bliss & Lomo, 2000; Martinez & Derrick, 1996; Nguyen et al., 1994). (To potentiate means "to make potent or to strengthen.") Research demonstrating that blocking LTP interferes with learning supports their hypothesis. For instance, Davis and colleagues (1992) gave rats enough of a drug that blocks certain receptors to interfere with their performance in a maze-running task and discovered that LTP in the hippocampus of the rats was also disrupted. In contrast, Riedel (1996) found that LTP is enhanced and memory is improved when a drug that excites those same receptors is administered to rats shortly after maze training.

Hormones and Memory

The strongest and most lasting memories are usually those fueled by emotion. Research by Cahill and McGaugh (1995) suggests that there may be two pathways for forming memories—one for ordinary information and another for memories that are fired by emotion. When a person is emotionally aroused, the adrenal glands release the hormones adrenalin (epinephrine) and noradrenaline (norepinephrine) into the bloodstream. Long known to be involved in the "fight or flight" response, these hormones enable humans to survive, and they also help to establish powerful and enduring memories of the circumstances surrounding threatening situations. Such emotionally laden memories activate the amygdala (known to play a central role in emotion) and other parts of the memory system. Emotional memories are lasting memories, and this may be the most important factor in explaining the intensity and durability of flashbulb memories.

Other hormones may have important effects on memory. Excessive levels of the stress hormone *cortisol*, for example, have been shown to interfere with memory in patients who suffer from diseases of the adrenal glands, the site of cortisol production (Jelicic & Bonke, 2001). Furthermore, people whose bodies react to experimenter-induced stressors, such as forced public speaking, by releasing higher-than-average levels of cortisol perform less well on memory tests than those whose bodies release lower-than-average levels in the same situations (Al'absi et al., 2002).

FORGETTING

Ebbinghaus and the First Experimental Studies on Forgetting

Hermann Ebbinghaus (1850–1909) conducted the first experimental studies on learning and memory. He (1885/1964) conducted his studies on memory using 2,300 *nonsense syllables*—combinations of letters that can be pronounced but have no meaning, such as LEJ, XIZ, LUK, and ZOH—as his material and himself as the only participant. He carried out all of his experiments at about the same time of day in the same surroundings, eliminating all possible distractions. Ebbinghaus memorized lists of nonsense syllables by repeating them over and over at a constant rate of 2.5 syllables per second, marking time with a metronome or a ticking watch. He repeated a list until he could recall it twice without error, a point that he called *mastery*.

Ebbinghaus recorded the amount of time or the number of trials it took to memorize his lists to mastery. Then, after different periods of time had passed and forgetting had occurred to some extent, he recorded the amount of time or number of trials needed to relearn the same list to mastery. Ebbinghaus compared the time or trials required for relearning with those of the original learning and then computed the percentage of time saved—the *savings score*. The percentage of savings represented the percentage of the original learning that remained in memory.

Ebbinghaus learned and relearned more than 1,200 lists of nonsense syllables to discover how rapidly forgetting occurs. Figure 10.10 shows his famous *curve of forgetting*, which consists of savings scores at various time intervals after the original learning. The curve of forgetting shows that the largest amount of forgetting occurs very quickly, but after that forgetting tapers off. If Ebbinghaus retained information as long as a day or two, very little more of it would be forgotten even a month later. When researchers measured psychology students' retention of names and concepts, they found that the pattern of forgetting was similar to Ebbinghaus's curve. Forgetting of names and concepts was rapid over the first several months, leveled off in approximately 36 months, and remained about the same for the next 7 years (Conway et al., 1991).

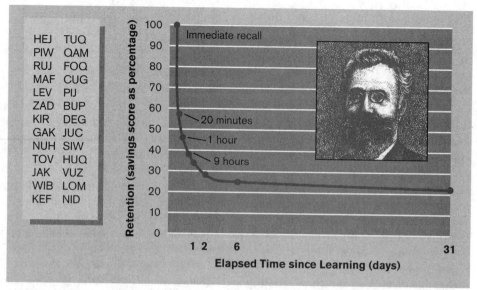

FIGURE 10.10   Ebbinghaus's Curve of Forgetting. After memorizing lists of nonsense syllables similar to those on the left, Ebbinghaus measured his retention after varying intervals of time using the relearning method. Forgetting was most rapid at first, as shown by his retention of only 58% after 20 minutes and 44% after 1 hour. Then the rate of forgetting tapered off, with a retention of 34% after 1 day, 25% after 6 days, and 21% after 31 days. (Data from Ebbinghaus, 1885/1964.)

The Causes of Forgetting

There are many reasons why people fail to remember. Often, however, when people say they cannot remember, they have not actually forgotten. Instead, the inability to remember may be a result of **encoding failure**—the fact that the information never entered long-term memory in the first place.

In your lifetime you have seen thousands of pennies, but unless you are a coin collector, you probably have not encoded the details of a penny's appearance. After studying a large group of participants, Nickerson and Adams (1979) reported that few people could reproduce a penny from recall. In fact, only a handful of participants could even recognize a drawing of a real penny when it was presented along with incorrect drawings.

Decay theory, probably the oldest theory of forgetting, assumes that memories, if not used, fade with time and ultimately disappear entirely. The term *decay* implies a change in the "neural trace" or physiological record, of the experience. According to this theory, the neural trace may decay or fade within seconds, days, or much longer periods of time. Most psychologists now accept the notion of decay, or fading of the neural trace, as a cause of forgetting in sensory and short-term memory but not in long-term memory. There does not appear to be a gradual, inevitable decay of the long-term memory trace. In one study, Harry Bahrick and others (1975) found that after 35 years, participants could recognize 90% of their high school classmates' names and photographs—the same percentage as for recent graduates.

A major cause of forgetting that affects people every day is **interference.** Whenever you try to recall any given memory, two types of interference can hinder the effort, as shown in Figure 10.11. *Proactive interference* occurs when information or experiences already stored in long-term memory hinder the ability to remember newer information (Underwood, 1957). For example, Isabel's romance with her new boyfriend, José, got off to a bad start when she accidentally called him Dave, her former

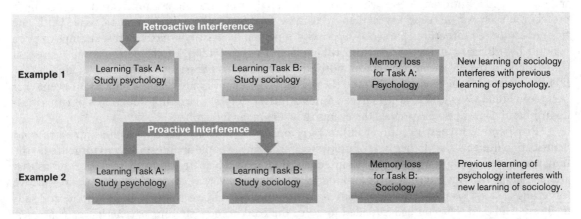

FIGURE 10.11 Retroactive and Proactive Interference. As shown in Example 1, retroactive interference occurs when new learning hinders the ability to recall information learned previously. As shown in Example 2, proactive interference occurs when prior learning hinders new learning.

boyfriend's name. *Retroactive interference* happens when new learning interferes with the ability to remember previously learned information. The more similar the new learning is to the previous learning, the more interference there is. For example, when you take a psychology class, it may interfere with your ability to remember what you learned in your sociology class, especially with regard to theories (for example, psychoanalytic theory) that are shared by the two disciplines but applied and interpreted differently. To minimize interference, you can follow a learning activity with sleep and arrange learning time so that you do not study similar subjects back to back.

Recall from earlier in the chapter that *consolidation* is the process by which encoded information is stored in memory. When a disruption in this process occurs, a long-term memory usually does not form. **Consolidation failure** can result from anything that causes a person to lose consciousness—a car accident, intoxication, a blow to the head, a grand mal seizure, or an electroconvulsive shock treatment given for severe depression. Memory loss of the experiences that occurred shortly before the loss of consciousness is called **retrograde amnesia.**

Nader and a team of researchers (Nader et al., 2000) demonstrated that conditioned fears in rats can be erased by infusing into the rats' brains a drug that prevents protein synthesis (such synthesis is necessary for memory consolidation). Rats experienced a single pairing of a tone (the conditioned stimulus) and a foot shock (the unconditioned stimulus). Later, the rats were exposed to the sound of the tone alone (the conditioned stimulus) and showed a fear response of "freezing" (becoming totally immobile as if paralyzed by fright). Clearly, the rats remembered the feared stimulus. Twenty-four hours later, the rats were again exposed to the tone alone, and it elicited fear, causing them to freeze. Immediately, the drug anisomycin, which prevents protein synthesis in the brain, was infused into the rats' amygdala (the part of the brain that processes fear responses). After the drug was infused, the rats were shocked again, but they showed no fear response (freezing) when the tone was sounded. The rats in the study had already consolidated the memory of the fear, but it was completely wiped out after the drug prevented protein synthesis from occurring. This means that fear memories, once activated, must be "reconsolidated," or they may disappear. This finding has positive implications. If fear memories can be activated and then wiped out with drugs that prevent protein synthesis, a new therapy may be on the horizon for people who suffer from debilitating fears (Nader et al., 2000).

Of course, there are occasions when people may prefer to avoid remembering—times when they want to forget. Earlier in the chapter, we discussed the possibility that people may repress memories of traumatic events. But even people who have not suffered severe trauma use **motivated forgetting** to protect themselves from experiences that are painful, frightening, or otherwise unpleasant. With one form of motivated forgetting, known as *suppression*, a person makes a conscious, active attempt to put a painful, disturbing, or anxiety- or guilt-provoking memory out of mind, but the person is still aware that the event occurred. With another type of motivated forgetting—**repression**—unpleasant memories are literally removed from consciousness, and the person is no longer aware that the unpleasant event ever occurred (Freud, 1922). People who have **amnesia** (memory loss) that is not due to loss of consciousness or brain damage have repressed the events they no longer remember.

Prospective forgetting, forgetting to carry out some intended action—such as going to your dentist appointment—is another type of motivated forgetting. People are most likely to forget to do the things they view as unimportant, unpleasant, or burdensome. They are less likely to forget things that are pleasurable or important to them (Winograd, 1988). However, as you probably know, prospective forgetting isn't always motivated by a desire to avoid something. Have you ever arrived home and suddenly remembered that you had intended to go to the bank to deposit your paycheck? In such cases, prospective forgetting is more likely to be the result of interference or consolidation failure.

Endel Tulving (1974) claims that much of what people call forgetting is really an inability to locate the needed information in memory—as in the *tip-of-the-tongue (TOT) phenomenon* (Brown & McNeil, 1966). Surely you have experienced trying to recall a name, a word, or some other bit of information, knowing what you are searching for almost as well as your own name. You're on the verge of recalling the word or name, perhaps aware of the number of syllables and the beginning or ending letter of the word. It's on the tip of your tongue, but it just won't quite come out.

IMPROVING MEMORY

Organizing material to be learned is a tremendous aid to memory. One way of organizing a textbook chapter is to make an outline; another is to associate important concepts with the psychologists who proposed or discovered them.

Do you still remember the words to songs that were popular when you were in high school? Can you recite many of the nursery rhymes you learned as a child even though you haven't heard them in years? You probably can because of **overlearning.** Research suggests that people remember material better and longer if they overlearn it—that is, if they practice or study beyond the minimum needed to barely learn it (Ebbinghaus, 1885/1964). A pioneering study in overlearning by Krueger (1929) showed substantial long-term gains for participants who engaged in 50% and 100% overlearning. Furthermore, overlearning makes material more resistant to interference and is perhaps the best insurance against stress-related forgetting. So, the next time you study for a test, don't stop studying as soon as you think you know the material. Spend another hour or so going over it, and you will be surprised at how much more you will remember.

Most students have tried cramming for examinations, but spacing study over several different sessions is generally more effective than **massed practice**—learning in one long practice session without rest periods (Glover & Corkill, 1987). You will remember more from less total study time if you space your study over several sessions. Long periods of memorizing make material particularly subject to interference and often result in fatigue and lowered concentration. Also, when you space your practice, you probably create a new memory that may be stored in a different place, thus increasing your chance for recall. The spacing effect applies to learning motor skills as well as to learning facts and information. Music students can tell you that it is better to practice for half an hour each day, every day, than to practice many hours in a row once a week.

Many students simply read and reread their textbook and notes when they study for an exam. Research over many years shows that you will recall more if you increase the amount of recitation you use as you study. For example, it is better to read a page or a few paragraphs and then recite what you have just read. Then continue reading, stop and recite again, and so on. In a classic study, A. I. Gates (1917) tested groups of students who spent the same amount of time in study, but who spent different percentages of that time in recitation and rereading. Participants recalled two to three times more if they increased their recitation time up to 80% and spent only 20% of their study time rereading.

COGNITION, LANGUAGE, AND CREATIVITY

Can you imagine a person being able to control an artificial limb almost as precisely as a real limb by using brain power alone? Researcher John Chapin and colleagues (Taylor et al., 2002; Whitehouse, 2000) have accomplished just that. First, researchers used computer-controlled equipment to "record" on a microchip the electrical activity in a motor neuron in the brain of a rat when one of the rat's limbs was moved. Then, duplicate microchips were implanted in the brains of rats in early experiments and in those of humans in later studies. The microchips enabled both rat and human amputees to control robotic limbs, using their own brains, with the same speed and accuracy as they could natural limbs. Moreover, their movement skills improved with practice, just as with natural limbs (König & Verschure, 2002).

Clearly, many of the achievements of computer technology are impressive, but can computers really think? The answer hinges, of course, on how *thinking* is defined. Today's supercomputers far outclass any human in mathematical computation and search-and-match activity. But some experts point out that even supercomputers do not really think on their own. After all, computers can do only what human programmers instruct them to do. So the real question is not whether computers think, but what is it about human thinking and intelligence that has allowed us to develop machines that can mimic the mental processes that enable us to acquire, store, and use information—collectively referred to by psychologists as **cognition?**

IMAGERY AND CONCEPTS

Can you imagine hearing a recording of your favorite song or someone calling your name? In doing such a thing, you take advantage of your own ability to use mental **imagery**—that is, to represent or picture a sensory experience. In an early survey of 500 adults conducted by McKellar (1972), 97% said they had visual images; 93% reported auditory images (imagine your psychology professor's voice); 74% claimed to have motor imagery (imagine raising your hand); 70%, tactile or touch images (imagine rubbing sandpaper); 67%, gustatory images (imagine the taste of a dill pickle); and 66%, olfactory images (imagine smelling a rose). Not only can we form a mental image of an object, but we can manipulate and move it around mentally, much as we would if we were actually holding and looking at the object (Cooper & Shepard, 1984; Farah, 1995; Kosslyn & Sussman, 1995).

Studies measuring participants' regional cerebral blood flow (rCBF) while they are engaged in imaging have shown that verbal descriptions of objects activate regions of the brain known to be involved in higher-level visual processing (Mellet et al., 2000). And research examining the brain's responses to stimuli indicate that the same areas are activated when we hear a sound as when we imagine hearing a sound (Cho & Lee, 2001). Brain-imaging studies also show that the same regions in the motor cortex and related areas that are involved in the physical movements required for rotation of objects are very active during mental imaging of such activity, although the cerebellum is more active during actual performance than during visualization (Lotze et al., 1999; Richter et al., 2000).

Fortunately, human thinking is not limited to conjuring up images of sights, sounds, touches, tastes, and smells. We are capable of conceptualizing as well. A **concept** is a mental category used to represent a class or group of objects, people, organizations, events, situations, or relations that share common characteristics or attributes. *Furniture, tree, student, college,* and *wedding* are all examples of concepts. As fundamental units of thought, concepts are useful tools that help us to order our world and to think and communicate with speed and efficiency.

Thanks to our ability to use concepts, we are not forced to consider and describe everything in great detail before we make an identification. If you see a hairy, brown-and-white, four-legged animal with its mouth open, tongue hanging out, and tail wagging, you recognize it immediately as a representative of the concept *dog*. *Dog* is a concept that stands for a class of animals that share similar characteristics or attributes, even though they may differ in significant ways. Great Danes, dachshunds, collies, Chihuahuas, and other breeds—you recognize all these varied creatures as fitting into the concept *dog*. Moreover, the concepts we form do not exist in isolation, but rather in hierarchies. For example, dogs represent one subset of the concept *animal;* at a higher level, animals are a subset of the concept *living things*. Thus, concept formation has a certain logic to it.

Psychologists identify two basic types of concepts: formal (also known as artificial) concepts and natural (also known as fuzzy) concepts. A **formal concept** is one that is clearly defined by a set of rules, a formal definition, or a classification system. Most of the concepts we form and use are **natural concepts,** acquired not from definitions but through everyday perceptions and experiences. A leading cognition researcher, Eleanor Rosch, and her colleagues studied concept formation in its natural setting and concluded that in real life, natural concepts (such as *fruit*, *vegetable*, and *bird*) are somewhat fuzzy, not clear-cut and systematic (Rosch, 1973, 1978).

Many formal concepts are acquired in school. For example, we learn that an equilateral triangle is one in which all three sides are the same size. We acquire many natural concepts through experiences with examples, or positive instances of the concept. When children are young, parents may point out examples of a car—the family car, the neighbor's car, cars on the street, and pictures of cars in books. But if a child points to some other type of moving vehicle and says "car," the parent will say, "No, that's a truck," or "This is a bus." *Truck* and *bus* are negative instances, or nonexamples, of the concept *car*. After experience with positive and negative instances of the concept, a child begins to grasp some of the properties of a car that distinguish it from other wheeled vehicles.

How do we use concepts in our everyday thinking? One view suggests that, in using natural concepts, we are likely to picture a **prototype** of the concept—an example that embodies its most common and typical features. Your *bird* prototype is more likely to be robin or a sparrow than either a penguin or a turkey: Those birds can fly, while penguins and turkeys can't. Nevertheless, both penguins and turkeys are birds. So not all examples of a natural concept fit it equally well. This is why natural concepts often seem less clear-cut than formal ones. Nevertheless, the prototype most closely fits a given natural concept, and other examples of the concept most often share more attributes with that prototype than with the prototype of any other concept.

A more recent theory of concept formation suggests that concepts are represented by their **exemplars**—individual instances, or examples, of a concept that are stored in memory from personal experience (Estes, 1994). So, if you work with penguins or turkeys every day, your exemplar of *bird* might indeed be a penguin or a turkey. By contrast, most people encounter robins or sparrows far more often than penguins or turkeys (except the roasted variety!). Thus, for the majority of people, robins or sparrows are exemplars of the *bird* concept.

DECISION MAKING

Decision making is the process of considering alternatives and choosing among them. Decisions are influenced by many factors, including values, interests, life goals, experiences, and knowledge. There are several strategies we use when making decisions.

The Additive Strategy

Suppose you wanted to rent an apartment starting next semester. How would you go about deciding among different apartments? You could use the **additive strategy**—a decision-making approach in which each alternative is rated on each of the important factors affecting the decision and the alternative with the highest overall rating is chosen. Two important factors in choosing where to live are location and price. So, your goal would be to find an apartment in a safe location near where you work or attend school that is within your price range.

A variation on the additive strategy is *elimination by aspects* (Tversky, 1972). With this approach, the factors on which the alternatives are to be evaluated are ordered from most important to least important. Any alternative that does not satisfy the most important factor is automatically eliminated. The process of elimination continues as each factor is considered in order. The alternative that survives is the one chosen. For example, if the most important factor for your apartment search was that the maximum rent you could afford was $800 per month, then you would automatically eliminate all the apartments that rented for more than that. Then, if the second most important factor was availability of parking, you would look at the list of apartments that cost $800 or less per month and weed out those without appropriate parking. You would then continue with your third most important factor and so on, until you had trimmed the list down.

Heuristics

Sometimes we make decisions based on **heuristics**—rules of thumb that are derived from experience and used in decision making and problem solving, although there is no guarantee of their accuracy or usefulness. For instance, decision making is quite likely to be influenced by how quickly and easily information affecting or related to the decision comes to mind—that is, how readily available that information is in memory. The cognitive rule of thumb that the probability of an event or the importance assigned to it is based on its availability in memory is known as the **availability heuristic.** Any information affecting a decision, whether it is accurate or not, is more likely to be considered if it is readily available. In 1998, Oprah Winfrey was sued by a group of cattle ranchers for comments made on her show about "mad cow disease" and the possibility that it made eating hamburgers too risky. In other words, the cattle ranchers were blaming Oprah for establishing an availability heuristic that led viewers to decide not to eat their product.

Another common heuristic used in decision making, in judging people, or in predicting the probability of certain events is the representativeness heuristic. The **representativeness heuristic** is a thinking strategy based on how closely a new object or situation is judged to resemble or match an existing prototype of that object or situation (Pitz & Sachs, 1984). The representativeness heuristic is an effective decision-making strategy that can lead to good decisions if the instance selected truly matches the appropriate prototype.

However, the representativeness heuristic can mislead as well. Suppose you were playing a coin-tossing game in which you had to predict whether the outcome of each toss would be heads or tails. Let's say the first five coin tosses came up heads. What would you predict the next toss to be? Many people would predict tails to be more likely on the next toss, because a sample of coin tosses should be approximately 50% heads. Thus, a tail is long overdue, they reason. Nevertheless, the next toss is just as likely to be a head as a tail. After 100 coin tosses, the proportions of heads and tails should be about equal, but for each individual coin toss, the probability still remains 50–50.

Framing

Framing refers to the way information is presented so as to emphasize either a potential gain or a potential loss as the outcome. To study the effects of framing on decision making, Kahneman and Tversky (1984) presented the following options to a group of participants. Which program would you choose?

The United States is preparing for the outbreak of a dangerous disease, which is expected to kill 600 people. There have been designed two alternative programs to combat the disease. If program A is adopted, 200 people will be saved. If program B is adopted, there is a one-third probability that all 600 will be saved and a two-thirds probability that no people will be saved.

The researchers found that 72% of the participants selected the "sure thing" of program A over the "risky gamble" of program B. Now consider the options as they were reframed:

If program C is adopted, 400 people will die. If program D is adopted, there is a one-third probability that nobody will die and a two-thirds probability that all 600 people will die.

Which program did you choose? Of research participants given this version of the problem, 78% chose program D. A careful reading will reveal that program D has exactly the same consequences as program B in the earlier version. How can this result be explained? The first version of the problem was framed to focus attention on the number of lives that could be saved. And when people are primarily motivated to achieve gains (save lives), they are more likely to choose a safe option over a risky one, as 72% of the participants did. The second version was framed to focus attention on the 400 lives that would be lost. When trying to avoid losses, people appear much more willing to choose a risky option, as 78% of the participants were.

Framing has numerous practical applications to decision making. Customers are more readily motivated to buy products if they are on sale than if they are simply priced lower than similar products to begin with. As a result, customers focus on what they save (a gain) rather than on what they spend (a loss). People seem more willing to purchase an $18,000 car and receive a $1,000 rebate (a gain) than to simply pay $17,000 for the same car. Heuristics can be effective and efficient cognitive techniques, but they can also lead to errors in perceptions and decisions.

PROBLEM SOLVING

We all face problems—great and small—that we must solve. **Problem solving** refers to thoughts and actions required to achieve a desired goal that is not readily attainable. How would you go about solving the problem described in Table 10.4?

How did you choose to solve the problem? Some people examine the problem carefully and devise a strategy—such as placing the 1 or the 7 in the middle box because each has only one forbidden

TABLE 10.4   Number Cross Problem

Insert the numbers 1 through 7 in the seven boxes, one digit to a box, in such a way that no consecutive numbers are next to each other horizontally, vertically, or diagonally. Several solutions are possible.

Answers:

consecutive number (2 or 6) to avoid. Many people, however, simply start placing the numbers in the boxes and then change them around when a combination doesn't work. This approach, called **trial and error,** involves trying one solution after another, in no particular order, until hitting on the answer by chance. Even nonhuman animals use trial and error. However, other techniques are far more effective and less time-consuming.

Another major problem-solving method is the algorithm (Newell & Simon, 1972). An **algorithm** is a systematic, step-by-step procedure that guarantees a solution to a problem of a certain type if the algorithm is appropriate and is executed properly. Formulas used in mathematics and sciences are algorithms. Another type of algorithm is a systematic strategy for exploring every possible solution to a problem until the correct one is reached. In some cases, millions or even billions or more possibilities may have to be considered before the solution is found. Computers are programmed to solve many problems using algorithms because, with a computer, an accurate solution is guaranteed and millions of possible solutions can be tried in a few seconds.

Many problems do not lend themselves to solution by algorithms, however. Suppose you were a contestant on *Wheel of Fortune*, trying to solve this missing-letter puzzle:

P _ Y _ _ _ L _ _ Y.

An exhaustive search algorithm would be out of the question—even Vanna White's smile would fade long before the nearly 9 billion possibilities could be considered. An easier way to solve such problems is by using a heuristic. Using a heuristic does not guarantee success but offers a promising way to attack a problem and arrive at a solution. The missing-letter puzzle is easily solved through a simple heuristic that makes use of your existing knowledge of words (prefixes, roots, suffixes). You can supply the missing letters and spell out PSYCHOLOGY.

One heuristic that is effective for solving some problems is **working backwards,** sometimes called the *backward search*. This approach starts with the solution, a known condition, and works back through the problem. Once the backward search has revealed the steps to be taken and their order, the problem can be solved.

Another popular heuristic strategy is **means–end analysis,** in which the current position is compared with a desired goal, and a series of steps is formulated and then taken to close the gap between the two (Sweller & Levine, 1982). Many problems are large and complex and must be broken down into smaller steps or subproblems before a solution can be reached. If your professor assigns a term paper, for example, you probably do not simply sit down and write it. You must first determine how you will approach the topic, research the topic, make an outline, and then write the sections over a period of time. At last, you will be ready to assemble the complete term paper, write several drafts, and put the finished product in final form before handing it in and receiving your A.

The **analogy heuristic**—applying a solution used for a past problem to a current problem that has many similar features—is another problem-solving strategy. Situations with many features in common are said to be *analogous*. When faced with a new problem to solve, you can look for commonalities between the new problem and problems you have solved before and then apply a strategy similar to one that has worked in the past. For example, if your car is making strange sounds and you take it to an auto mechanic, the mechanic may be able to diagnose the problem by analogy—the sounds your car is making are comparable to sounds heard before and associated with a particular problem.

Impediments to Problem Solving

Sometimes we face problems that seem to defy solution despite our best efforts. We lack the relevant knowledge or experience to solve some problems and have insufficient material resources to solve others. In some cases, though, we are hampered in our efforts to solve problems in daily life because of

functional fixedness—the failure to use familiar objects in novel ways to solve problems. We tend to see objects only in terms of their customary functions. Just think of all the items you use daily—tools, utensils, and other equipment—that help you perform certain functions. Often, the normal functions of such objects become fixed in your thinking so that you do not consider using them in new and creative ways.

Suppose you wanted a cup of coffee, but the glass carafe for your coffeemaker was broken. If you suffered from functional fixedness, you might come to the conclusion that there was nothing you could do to solve your problem at that moment. But, rather than thinking about the object or utensil that you don't have, think about the function that it needs to perform. What you need is something to catch the coffee, not necessarily the specific type of glass carafe that came with the coffeemaker. Could you catch the coffee in a bowl or cooking utensil, or even in coffee mugs?

Another impediment to problem solving, similar to functional fixedness but much broader, is mental set. **Mental set** is a mental rut in one's approach to solving problems, the tendency to continue to use the same old method even though another approach might be better. Perhaps you hit on a way to solve a problem once in the past and continue to use the same technique in similar situations, even though it is not highly effective or efficient. People are much more susceptible to mental set when they fail to consider the special requirements of a problem. Not surprisingly, the same people who are subject to mental set are also more likely to have trouble with functional fixedness when they attempt to solve problems (McKelvie, 1984).

Artificial Intelligence and Robotics

Artificial intelligence, or AI, refers to the programming of computer systems to simulate human thinking in solving problems and in making judgments and decisions. However, computers cannot, as humans can, take exceptions into account, consider the context, or make countless other interpretations as they "think." They cannot execute many of the tasks that humans perform with ease, such as recognizing a particular face or interpreting a slurred, indistinct word in a conversation (Lenat, 1995).

Researchers hope to make artificial intelligence programs that will more closely approximate human thinking by devising computer systems based on an understanding of how neurons in certain parts of the brain are connected and how the connections develop (Buonomano & Merzenich, 1995; Hinton et al., 1995). Computer systems that are intended to mimic the human brain are called **neural networks.** Like those in the brain, connections in a computer neural network can be strengthened or weakened as a result of experience. Computer-based voice recognition systems used in a variety of commercial settings are supported by such neural networks. But unlike humans, such computer systems cannot understand the subtleties of language—tone of voice, quality of nonverbal behavior, or even level of politeness (Peterson, 1993).

One area in which human cognition has been applied to develop technological marvels is **robotics**—the science of automating human and animal functions. In some cases, robotics have made it possible to manipulate variables in experiments that previously could be investigated only in correlational studies. Scientists studying the mating behavior of bowerbirds, for example, observed the females of the species repeatedly crouching during the attraction phase of mating (Patricelli et al., 2002). To examine the crouching variable in an experiment, they built a robotic version of a female bowerbird whose crouching actions could be remotely controlled. By systematically exposing male bowerbirds to crouching and noncrouching behavior and by varying the amount and frequency of crouching, they were able to learn that males use females' crouching behavior as cues to initiate displays of their colorful plumage.

Experiments involving robotic birds may seem far removed from any kind of practical application. However, projects such as this one help scientists and engineers learn more about how to build and program robots to behave much like their living counterparts. Consequently, the technology needed to use robotics to improve human life is expanded. Indeed, the potential for robotics to improve life is tremendous—the robotic limbs described at the beginning of the chapter are just one example.

LANGUAGE

Language is a means of communicating thoughts and feelings, using a system of socially shared but arbitrary symbols (sounds, signs, or written symbols) arranged according to rules of grammar. Language expands our ability to think because it allows us to consider abstract concepts—such as justice—that are not represented by physical objects. Further, thanks to language, we can share our knowledge and thoughts with one another in an extremely efficient way. Thus, whether spoken, written, or signed, language is our most important cognitive tool.

The Structure of Language

Psycholinguistics is the study of how language is acquired, produced, and used and how the sounds and symbols of language are translated into meaning. Psycholinguists use specific terms for each of the five basic components of language.

The smallest units of sound in a spoken language—such as *b* or *s* in English—are known as **phonemes.** Three phonemes together form the sound of the word *cat: c* (which sounds like *k*), *a*, and *t*. Combinations of letters that form particular sounds are also phonemes, such as the *th* in *the* and the *ch* in *child.* The same phoneme may be represented by different letters in different words; this occurs with the *a* in *stay* and the *ei* in *sleigh.* And the same letter can serve as different phonemes. The letter *a*, for example, is sounded as four different phonemes in *day, cap, watch,* and *law.*

Morphemes are the smallest units of meaning in a language. A few single phonemes serve as morphemes, such as the article *a* and the personal pronoun *I.* The ending *-s* gives a plural meaning to a word and is thus a morpheme in English. Many words in English are single morphemes—*book, word, learn, reason,* and so on. In addition to root words, morphemes may also be prefixes (such as *re-* in *relearn*) or suffixes (such as *-ed* to show past tense, as in *learned*). The single morpheme *reason* becomes a dual morpheme in *reasonable.* The morpheme *book* (singular) becomes two morphemes in *books* (plural).

Syntax is the aspect of grammar that specifies the rules for arranging and combining words to form phrases and sentences. The rules of word order, or syntax, differ from one language to another. For example, an important rule of syntax in English is that adjectives usually come before nouns. So English speakers refer to the residence of the U.S. President as "the White House." In Spanish, in contrast, the noun usually comes before the adjective, and Spanish speakers say *"la Casa Blanca,"* or "the House White."

Semantics refers to the meaning derived from morphemes, words, and sentences. The same word can have different meanings depending on how it is used in sentences: "I don't mind." "Mind your manners." "He has lost his mind." Or consider another example: "Loving to read, the young girl read three books last week." Here, the word *read* is pronounced two different ways and, in one case, is the past tense.

Finally, **pragmatics** is the term psycholinguists use to refer to aspects of language such as *intonation*, the rising and falling patterns that are used to express meaning. For example, think about how you would say the single word *cookie* to express each of the following meanings: "Do you want a cookie?" or "What a delicious looking cookie!" or "That's a cookie." The subtle differences reflect your knowledge of the pragmatic rules of English; for example, questions end with a rising intonation, while statements end with a falling intonation. Pragmatic rules also come into play when you speak in one way to your friend and another to your professor. That is, the social rules associated with language use are also included in pragmatics.

Animal Language

Ask people what capability most reliably sets humans apart from all other animal species, and most will answer language. And for good reason. As far as scientists know, humans are the only species to have developed this rich, varied, and complex system of communication. As early as 1933 and 1951, researchers attempted to teach chimpanzees to speak by raising the chimps in their homes. These experiments failed because the vocal tract in chimpanzees and the other apes is not adapted to human speech, so researchers turned to sign language. Psychologists Allen and Beatrix Gardner (1969) took in a 1-year-old chimp named Washoe and taught her sign language. Washoe learned signs for objects and certain commands, such as *flower, give me, come, open,* and *more.* By the end of her fifth year, she had mastered about 160 signs (Fleming, 1974).

Psychologist David Premack (1971) taught another chimp, Sarah, to use an artificial language he developed. Its symbols consisted of magnetized chips of various shapes, sizes, and colors. Premack used operant conditioning techniques to teach Sarah to select the magnetic chip representing a fruit and place it on a magnetic language board. The trainer would then reward Sarah with the fruit she had requested. Sarah mastered the concepts of similarities and differences, and eventually she could signal whether two objects were the same or different with nearly perfect accuracy (Premack & Premack, 1983). Even more remarkable, Sarah could view a whole apple and a cut apple and, even though she had not seen the apple being cut, could match the apple with the utensil needed to cut it—a knife.

At the Yerkes Primate Research Center at Emory University, a chimp named Lana participated in a computer-controlled language training program. She learned to press keys imprinted with geometric symbols that represented words in an artificial language called Yerkish. Researcher Sue Savage-Rumbaugh and a colleague (1986; Rumbaugh, 1977) varied the location, color, and brightness of the keys, so Lana had to learn which symbols to use no matter where they were located. One day, her trainer Tim had an orange that she wanted. Lana had available symbols for many fruits—apple, banana, and so on—but none for an orange. Yet there was a symbol for the color orange. So Lana improvised and signaled, "Tim give apple which is orange." Impressive!

But was humanlike language being displayed in these studies with primates? Not according to Herbert Terrace (1979, 1981), who examined the research of others and conducted his own. Terrace and coworkers taught sign language to a chimp they called Nim Chimpsky (after the famed linguist Noam Chomsky) and reported Nim's progress from the age of 2 weeks to 4 years. Nim learned 125 symbols, which is respectable, but does not amount to language, according to Terrace (1985, 1986). Terrace believed that chimps like Nim and Washoe were simply imitating their trainers and making responses to get reinforcers, according to the laws of operant conditioning, not the laws of language. Finally, Terrace suggested that the studies with primates were probably influenced by experimenter bias; trainers might unconsciously tend to interpret the behavior of the chimps as more indicative of progress toward developing language than it really was. However, Terrace had not heard of Kanzi when he expressed his skepticism.

The most impressive performance in language training so far is that of a pygmy chimpanzee, Kanzi, who developed an amazing ability to communicate with his trainers without any formal training. During the mid-1980s, researchers had taught Kanzi's mother to press symbols representing words. Her progress was not remarkable; but her infant son Kanzi, who stood by and observed her during training, was learning rapidly (thanks to observational learning). When Kanzi had a chance at the symbol board, his performance quickly surpassed that of his mother and of every other chimp the researchers had tested.

Kanzi demonstrated an advanced understanding (for chimps) of spoken English and could respond correctly even to new commands, such as "Throw your ball to the river," or "Go to the refrigerator and get out a tomato" (Savage-Rumbaugh, 1990; Savage-Rumbaugh et al., 1992). By the time Kanzi was 6 years old, a team of researchers who worked with him had recorded more than 13,000 "utterances" and reported that Kanzi could communicate using some 200 different geometric symbols (Gibbons, 1991). Kanzi could press symbols to ask someone to play chase with him and even ask two others to play chase while he watched. And if Kanzi signaled someone to "chase" and "hide," he was insistent that his first command, "chase," be done first (Gibbons, 1991). Kanzi was not merely responding to nearby trainers whose actions or gestures he might have copied. He responded just as well when requests were made over earphones so that no one else in the room could signal to him purposely or inadvertently.

Do such seemingly remarkable feats indicate that chimps are capable of using anything close to human language? Impressive as Kanzi's accomplishments seem to be, Premack firmly maintains that it is unlikely that animals are capable of language. They can be taught to signal, to choose, and to solve some problems, but mere strings of words spoken, written, or signed do not amount to language unless they are structured grammatically.

Most animal species studied by language researchers are limited to motor responses such as sign language, gestures, using magnetic symbols, or pressing keys on symbol boards. But these limitations do not extend to some bird species such as parrots, which are capable of making humanlike speech sounds. One remarkable case is Alex, an African gray parrot that not only mimics human speech but seems to do so intelligently. Able to recognize and name various colors, objects, and shapes, Alex answers questions about them in English. Asked "Which object is green?" Alex easily names the green object (Pepperberg, 1991, 1994b). And he can count as well. When asked such questions as "How many red blocks?" Alex answers correctly about 80% of the time (Pepperberg, 1994a).

Research with sea mammals such as whales and dolphins has established that they apparently use complicated systems of grunts, whistles, clicks, and other sounds to communicate within their species (Herman, 1981; Savage-Rumbaugh, 1993). Researchers at the University of Hawaii have trained dolphins to respond to fairly complex commands requiring an understanding of directional and relational concepts. Dolphins can learn to pick out an object and put it on the right or left of a basket, for example, and comprehend such commands as "in the basket" and "under the basket" (Chollar, 1989).

Language and Thinking

If language is unique to humans, then does it drive human thinking? Does the fact that you speak English mean that you reason, think, and perceive your world differently than does someone who speaks Spanish, or Chinese, or Swahili? According to one hypothesis presented about 50 years ago, it does. Benjamin Whorf (1956) put forth his **linguistic relativity hypothesis,** suggesting that the language a person speaks largely determines the nature of that person's thoughts. According to this hypothesis, people's worldview is constructed primarily by the words in their language. As proof, Whorf offered his classic example. The languages used by the Eskimo people have a number of different words for snow— "*apikak*, first snow falling; *aniv*, snow spread out; *pukak*, snow for drinking water"—while the English-speaking world has but one word, *snow* (Restak, 1988, p. 222). Whorf claimed that such a rich and varied selection of words for various snow types and conditions enabled Eskimos to think differently about snow than do people whose languages lack such a range of words.

Eleanor Rosch (1973) tested whether people whose language contains many names for colors would be better at thinking about and discriminating among colors than people whose language has only a few color names. Her participants were English-speaking Americans and the Dani, members of a remote tribe in New Guinea whose language has only two names for colors—*mili* for dark, cool colors and *mola* for bright, warm colors. Rosch showed members of both groups single-color chips of 11 colors—black, white, red, yellow, green, blue, brown, purple, pink, orange, and gray—for 5 seconds each. Then, after 30 seconds, she had the participants select the 11 colors they had viewed from an assortment of 40 color chips. Did the Americans outperform the Dani participants, for whom brown, black, purple, and blue are all *mili*, or dark? No. Rosch found no significant differences between the Dani and the Americans in discriminating, remembering, or thinking about those 11 basic colors. Rosch's study did not support the linguistic relativity hypothesis.

Clearly, however, it would be a mistake to go too far in the opposite direction and assume that language has no influence on how people think. Thought both influences and is influenced by language, and language appears to reflect cultural differences more than it determines them (Pinker, 1994; Rosch, 1987). For example, consider the generic use of the pronoun *he* to refer to people in general. If your professor says, "I expect each student in this class to do the best he can," does this announcement mean the same to males and females? Not according to research conducted by Gastil (1990), in which participants read sentences worded in three different forms.

Studies confirm that the generic *he* is not interpreted very generically. It is interpreted heavily in favor of males (Hamilton, 1988; Henley, 1989; Ng, 1990). If this were not the case, the following sentence would not seem unusual at all: Like other mammals, man bears his offspring live.

Bilingualism

Most native-born Americans speak only one language, English. But a sizeable minority are *bilingual*, that is, they speak both English and another language. Indeed, in the United States today, there are between 30 and 35 million people aged 5 and older for whom English is a second language. Among the languages spoken at home by these people, Spanish is by far the leader (used by 17–18 million people). Following Spanish, other languages spoken in many U.S. homes are French (by under 2 million people), German (a little over 1.5 million), Italian (1.4 million), and Chinese (1.3 million) (U.S. Bureau of the Census, 2001).

Most linguists are convinced that being bilingual has many advantages (Genesee, 1994). For example, in Canada, where most students study both French and English, bilingual students are said to score higher on aptitude and math tests than their counterparts who speak only one language (Lambert et al., 1993). But what about the effect of learning two languages on the process of language development itself? Research suggests that there are both advantages and disadvantages to learning two languages early in life.

One of the benefits is that, among preschool and school-age children, bilingualism is associated with better *metalinguistic skills*, the capacity to think about language (Bialystok et al., 2000; Mohanty & Perregaux, 1997). In addition, most bilingual children display greater ability than monolingual children in focusing attention on language tasks (Bialystok & Majumder, 1998). And bilingual children seem to more easily grasp the connection between sounds and symbols than do their monolingual peers (Bialystok, 1997; Oller et al., 1998).

On the downside, infants in bilingual homes reach some milestones later than those learning a single language. For example, bilingual infants' vocabularies are as large as those of monolingual infants, but the words they know are divided between two languages (Patterson, 1998). Consequently, they are behind monolingual infants in word knowledge, no matter which language is considered, a difference that persists into the school years. And even in adulthood, bilingualism is sometimes associated with decreased efficiency in memory tasks involving words (Gollan & Silverberg, 2001; McElree et al., 2000). However, bilinguals appear to develop compensatory strategies that allow them to make up for these inefficiencies. Consequently, bilinguals often perform such memory tasks just as accurately as monolinguals do, though they may respond more slowly.

Research further indicates that bilingual children who are equally fluent in both of their languages encounter few, if any, learning problems in school (Vuorenkoski et al., 2000). Similarly, teens and adults who are equally fluent in two languages demonstrate few, if any, differences in efficiency of verbal memory (McElree et al., 2000). However, most children do not attain equal fluency in both languages. As a result, they tend to think more slowly in the language in which they have lower fluency (Chincotta & Underwood, 1997). When the language in which they are less fluent is the language in which they are schooled, they are at risk for learning problems (Thorn & Gathercole, 1999). Further, in adulthood, these "unbalanced" bilinguals are more likely than monolinguals or bilinguals with equal fluency in both languages to display reduced speed and accuracy on verbal memory tasks (McElree et al., 2000).

The one clear advantage to learning two languages earlier in life is that people who are younger when they learn a second language are far more likely to be able to speak it with an appropriate accent (McDonald, 1997). One reason for this difference between early and late language learners may have to do with slight variations in neural processing in Broca's area, the area of the brain that controls speech production. Research by Kim and others (1997) suggests that bilinguals who learned their second language early (younger than age 10 or 11) rely on the same patch of tissue in Broca's area for both of the languages they speak. But in bilinguals who were older when they learned their second language, two different sections of Broca's area are active while language tasks are being performed—one section for the first language learned and another for the second. Yet the two sections are very close, only ⅓ inch apart.

Language and the Brain

What parts of the brain are key in processing language? Paulesu and colleagues (2000) used PET (positron emission tomography) scans to view activity in areas of the brains of Italian and English speakers while they read aloud a list of words and nonwords. The PET scans of all participants in this study revealed heightened activity in a widespread area of the brain known to be associated with reading, as was expected. But the new information that the researchers uncovered is that the brain activity in three regions varied according to the speaker's native language. Compared with the English speakers, the Italian speakers showed greater brain activity in an upper area of the left temporal lobe when reading words and nonwords. English speakers showed increased brain activity in the left frontal lobe and in an upper region of the left temporal lobe when reading nonwords. The researchers explained the cross-linguistic difference in terms of characteristics of the two languages. Italian has few spelling inconsistencies; a particular combination of letters almost always represents the same sound. By contrast, English includes many combinations of letters—such as *ough*—that can have several different pronunciations (*cough*, *bough*, *though*, and so on). Consequently, processing written language requires the involvement of different brain areas in the two languages.

But what about semantics and syntax? Two brain areas that are important for processing these aspects of language are Broca's area and Wernicke's area. The role of Broca's area was long believed to be largely restricted to the physical production of speech. But a recent brain-imaging study (Ni et al., 2000) revealed that Broca's area was highly activated when participants were processing errors in syntax, such as the wrong usage in the sentence "Trees can grew." Other research has confirmed the role of Broca's area in syntactic processing (Dogil et al., 2002). Further, both Wernicke's area and part of the cerebellum are activated when people make judgments about the grammatical characteristics of language.

THE NATURE OF INTELLIGENCE

The Search for a Useful Definition of Intelligence

First, let's ask the most obvious question: What is intelligence? A task force of experts from the American Psychological Association (APA) defined **intelligence** as an individual's "ability to understand complex ideas, to adapt effectively to the environment, to learn from experience, to engage in various forms of reasoning, and to overcome obstacles by taking thought" (Neisser et al., 1996, p. 77). Nevertheless, no concept in psychology has been at the center of more public policy debates and more scientific disagreement than intelligence (Moffitt et al., 1993). Is intelligence a single, general capability, or are there multiple types of intelligence? Is intelligence influenced more by heredity or by environment? Is it fixed or changeable, culture-free or culture-bound? The nature of intelligence continues to be hotly debated.

English psychologist Charles Spearman (1863–1945) observed that people who are bright in one area are usually bright in other areas as well. In other words, they tend to be generally intelligent. Spearman (1927) came to believe that intelligence is composed of a general ability that underlies all intellectual functions. Spearman concluded that intelligence tests tap this *g factor*, or general intelligence, and a number of *s* factors, or specific intellectual abilities. Spearman's influence can be seen in those intelligence tests, such as the Stanford–Binet, that yield one IQ score to indicate the level of general intelligence.

Another early researcher in testing, Louis L. Thurstone (1938), rejected Spearman's notion of general intellectual ability, or *g* factor. After analyzing the scores of many participants on some 56 separate ability tests, Thurstone identified seven **primary mental abilities:** verbal comprehension, numerical ability, spatial relations, perceptual speed, word fluency, memory, and reasoning. He maintained that all intellectual activities involve one or more of these primary mental abilities. Thurstone and his wife, Thelma G. Thurstone, developed their Primary Mental Abilities Tests to measure these seven abilities. Thurstone believed that a single IQ score obscured more than it revealed. He suggested that a profile showing relative strengths and weaknesses on the seven primary mental abilities would provide a more accurate picture of a person's intelligence.

Some theorists, instead of searching for the factors that underlie intelligence, propose that there are different types of intelligence. For example, Harvard psychologist Howard Gardner (1983) denies the existence of a *g* factor. Instead he proposes eight independent and equally important forms of intelligence, as shown in Figure 10.12. Gardner's theory "has enjoyed wide popularity, especially among educators, but [his] ideas are based more on reasoning and intuition than on the results of empirical research studies" (Aiken, 1997, p. 196). Still, Gardner's theory has provided psychologists, educators, and others who are interested in intelligence with a helpful way of describing and discussing the varying kinds of abilities people have.

Psychologist Robert Sternberg (1985a, 1986a) has formulated a **triarchic theory of intelligence,** which, as the term *triarchic* implies, proposes that there are three types of intelligence. Sternberg claims that traditional IQ tests measure only one type—*componential intelligence*—which is strongly correlated with success in school. A second type—*experiential intelligence*—is reflected in creative thinking and problem solving. People with high experiential intelligence are able to solve novel problems, deal with unexpected challenges, and find creative ways to perform common daily tasks. A third type—*contextual intelligence*, or practical intelligence—might be equated with common sense or "street smarts." People with high contextual intelligence are survivors who capitalize on their strengths, compensate for their

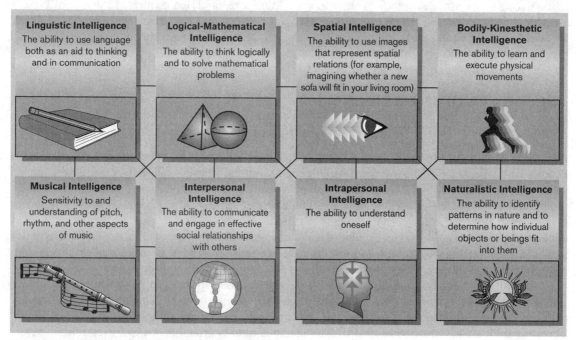

FIGURE 10.12   Gardner's Eight Frames of Mind

weaknesses, and adapt well to their environment. People who have succeeded in spite of hardships and adverse circumstances probably have a great deal of contextual intelligence.

Sternberg and his associates are developing a promising new intelligence test that measures all three types of abilities (Sternberg et al., 2001). Moreover, Sternberg's ideas have become popular among educators. Several studies have shown that instruction based on the idea that traditional tests and curricula tap into only one of the three types of intelligence can be effective with students who are low achievers (Grogorenko et al., 2002). In such interventions, teachers emphasize the practical relevance of formal academic knowledge and help students apply it to real-world problems.

MEASURING INTELLIGENCE

The first successful effort to measure intelligence resulted not from a theoretical approach, but as a practical means of solving a problem. In 1903, the French government formed a special commission to look for a way of assessing the intellectual potential of individual school children. One of the commission members, Alfred Binet (1857–1911), with the help of his colleague, psychiatrist Theodore Simon, developed a variety of tests that eventually became the first intelligence test, the *Binet–Simon Intelligence Scale*, first published in 1905.

The Binet–Simon Scale used a type of score called *mental* age. A child's mental age was based on the number of items she or he got right as compared with the average number right for children of various ages. In other words, if a child's score equaled the average for 8-year-olds, the child was assigned a mental age of 8, regardless of her or his chronological age (age in years). To determine whether children were bright, average, or retarded, Binet compared the children's mental and chronological ages. A child who was mentally 2 years ahead of his or her chronological age was considered bright; one who was 2 years behind was considered retarded. But there was a flaw in Binet's scoring system. A 4-year-old with a mental age of 2 is far more retarded than a 12-year-old with a mental age of 10. How could a similar degree of retardation at different ages be expressed?

German psychologist William Stern (1914) provided an answer. In 1912, he devised a simple formula for calculating an index of intelligence—*the intelligence quotient.* But it was American psychologist Lewis M. Terman, a professor at Stanford University, who perfected this new way of scoring intelligence tests. In 1916, Terman published a thorough revision of the Binet–Simon scale, consisting of items adapted for use with American children. Terman also established new **norms,** or age-based averages, based on the scores of large numbers of children. Within 3 years, 4 million American children had taken Terman's revision, known as the *Stanford–Binet Intelligence Scale.* It was the first test to make use of Stern's concept of the **intelligence quotient (IQ)**. (Terman also introduced the abbreviation *IQ.*) Terman's formula for calculating an IQ score was

$$\frac{\text{Mental Age}}{\text{Chronological Age}} \times 100 = IQ$$

For example,

$$\frac{14}{10} \times 100 = 140 \text{ (superior IQ)}$$

The highly regarded Stanford–Binet is an individually administered IQ test for those aged 2 to 23. It contains four subscales: verbal reasoning, quantitative reasoning, abstract visual reasoning, and short-term memory. An overall IQ score is derived from scores on the four subscales, and the test scores correlate well with achievement test scores (Laurent et al., 1992). Intelligence testing became increasingly popular in the United States in the 1920s and 1930s, but it quickly became obvious that the

Stanford–Binet was not useful for testing adults. The original IQ formula could not be applied to adults, because at a certain age people achieve maturity in intelligence. According to the original IQ formula, a 40-year-old with the same IQ test score as the average 20-year-old would be considered mentally retarded, with an IQ of only 50. Obviously, something was wrong with the formula when applied to populations of all ages.

In 1939, psychologist David Wechsler developed the first successful individual intelligence test for adults, designed for those aged 16 and older. Scores are based on how much an individual deviates from the average score for adults rather than on mental and chronological ages. The original test has been revised, restandardized, and renamed the *Wechsler Adult Intelligence Scale (WAIS-R)* and is one of the most widely used psychological tests. The test contains both verbal and performance (nonverbal) subtests, which yield separate verbal and performance IQ scores as well as an overall IQ score. This is a key difference from the Stanford–Binet, which yields a single IQ score. Wechsler also published the *Wechsler Intelligence Scale for Children (WISC-R)* and the *Wechsler Preschool and Primary Scale of Intelligence (WPPSI)*, which is normed for children aged 4 to 6½. One advantage of the Wechsler scales is their ability to identify intellectual strengths in nonverbal areas as well as verbal ones. Wechsler also believed that differences in a person's scores on the various verbal and performance subtests could be used for diagnostic purposes.

Individual intelligence tests such as the Stanford–Binet and the Wechsler scales must be given to one person at a time by a qualified professional. For testing large numbers of people in a short period of time (often necessary due to budget limitations), group intelligence tests are the answer. Group intelligence tests such as the *California Test of Mental Maturity*, the *Cognitive Abilities Test*, and the *Otis–Lennon Mental Ability Test* are widely used.

Requirements of Good Tests

If your watch gains 6 minutes one day and loses 3 or 4 minutes the next day, it is not reliable. You want a watch you can rely on to give the correct time day after day. Like a watch, an intelligence test must have **reliability;** the test must consistently yield nearly the same score when the same person is tested and then retested on the same test or an alternative form of the test. The higher the correlation between the two scores, the more reliable the test.

Tests can be highly reliable but worthless if they are not valid. **Validity** is the ability or power of a test to measure what it is intended to measure. For example, a thermometer is a valid instrument for measuring temperature; a bathroom scale is valid for measuring weight. But no matter how reliable your bathroom scale is, it will not take your temperature. It is valid only for weighing.

Aptitude tests are designed to predict a person's probable achievement or performance at some future time. Selecting students for admission to college or graduate schools is based partly on the predictive validity of aptitude tests such as the Scholastic Assessment Test (SAT), the American College Testing Program (ACT), and the Graduate Record Examination (GRE). How well do SAT scores predict success in college? Moderately, at best. The correlation between SAT scores and the grades of first year college students is about .40 (Linn, 1982).

Once a test is proven to be valid and reliable, the next requirement is **standardization.** There must be standard procedures for administering and scoring the test. Exactly the same directions must be given, whether written or oral, and the same amount of time must be allowed for every test taker. But even more important, standardization means establishing norms by which all scores are interpreted. A test is standardized by administering it to a large sample of people representative of those who will be taking the test in the future. The group's scores are analyzed, and then the average score, standard deviation, percentile rankings, and other measures are computed. These comparative scores become the norms used as the standard against which all other scores on that test are measured.

The Range of Intelligence

You may have heard the term *bell curve* and wondered just exactly what it is. When large populations are measured on intelligence or physical characteristics such as height and weight, the frequencies of the various scores or measurements usually conform to a *bell-shaped* distribution known as the *normal curve*—hence the term *bell curve*. The majority of the scores cluster around the mean (average). The more scores deviate from the mean (that is, the farther away from it they fall), either above or below, the fewer there are. And the normal curve is perfectly symmetrical; that is, there are just as many cases above as below the mean. The average IQ test score for all people in the same age group is arbitrarily assigned an IQ score of 100. On the Wechsler intelligence tests, approximately 50% of the scores are in the average range, between 90 and 110. About 68% of the scores fall between 85 and 115, and about 95% fall between 70 and 130. Some 2% of the scores are above 130, which is considered superior, and about 2% fall below 70, in the range of mental retardation (see Figure 10.13).

But what does it mean to have a "superior" IQ? In 1921, to try to answer this question, Lewis Terman (1925) launched a longitudinal study, now a classic, in which 1,528 gifted students were selected and measured at different ages throughout their lives. Tested on the Stanford–Binet, the participants— 857 males and 671 females—had unusually high IQs, ranging from 135 to 200, with an average of 151. Terman's early findings put an end to the myth that mentally superior people are more likely to be physically inferior. In fact, Terman's gifted participants excelled in almost all the abilities he studied— intellectual, physical, emotional, moral, and social. Terman also exploded many other myths about the

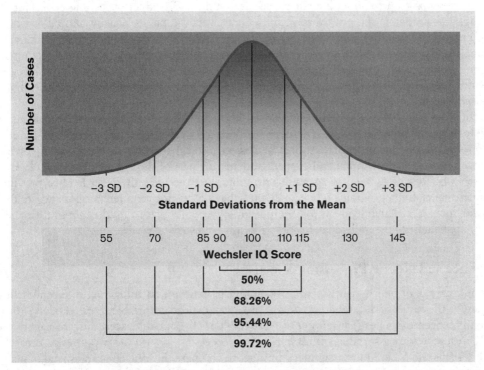

FIGURE 10.13   The Normal Curve. When a large number of test scores are compiled, they are typically distributed in a normal (bell-shaped) curve. On the Wechsler scales, the average, or mean, IQ score is set at 100. As the figure shows, about 68% of the scores fall between 15 IQ points (1 standard deviation) above and below 100 (from 85 to 115), and about 95.5% of the scores fall between 30 points (2 standard deviations) above and below 100 (from 70 to 130).

mentally gifted (Terman & Oden, 1947). For example, you may have heard the saying that there is a thin line between genius and madness. Actually, Terman's gifted group enjoyed better mental health than the general population. And Terman's participants earned more academic degrees, achieved higher occupational status and higher salaries, were better adjusted both personally and socially, and were healthier than their less mentally gifted peers. However, most women at that time did not pursue careers outside of the home, so the findings related to occupational success applied primarily to the men. Terman (1925) concluded that "there is no law of compensation whereby the intellectual superiority of the gifted is offset by inferiorities along nonintellectual lines" (p. 16). The Terman study continues today, with the surviving participants in their 80s or 90s. In a report on Terman's study, Shneidman (1989) states its basic findings—that "an unusual mind, a vigorous body, and a relatively well-adjusted personality are not at all incompatible" (p. 687).

At the opposite end of the continuum from Terman's sample are the 2% of the U.S. population whose IQ scores are in the range of **mental retardation.** There are many causes of mental retardation, including brain injuries, chromosomal abnormalities such as Down syndrome, chemical deficiencies, and hazards present during fetal development. And studies continue to document the enduring mental deficits produced by early exposure to lead (Garavan et al., 2000; Morgan et al., 2000). Individuals are not classified as mentally retarded unless (1) their IQ score is below 70 and (2) they have a severe deficiency in everyday adaptive functioning—the ability to care for themselves and relate to others (Grossman, 1983). There are degrees of retardation from mild to profound. Individuals with IQs ranging from 55 to 70 are considered mildly retarded; from 40 to 54, moderately retarded; from 25 to 39, severely retarded; and below 25, profoundly retarded. Mildly retarded individuals are able to acquire academic skills such as reading up to about a sixth-grade level and may be able to become economically self-supporting. The academic skills of those with moderate retardation are usually limited to the first- or second-grade level; these individuals can learn self-care skills and often function well in sheltered work environments. People with severe levels of retardation typically are unable to acquire academic skills but can communicate verbally and learn habits such as brushing their teeth. At the profound level of retardation, individuals usually learn only rudimentary motor skills and limited self-help skills such as feeding themselves.

Before the late 1960s, mentally retarded children in the United States were educated almost exclusively in special schools. Since then, there has been a movement toward **inclusion**—or educating mentally retarded students in regular schools. Inclusion, also called *mainstreaming*, may involve placing these students in classes with nonhandicapped students for part of the day or in special classrooms in regular schools. Resources spent on training programs for the mentally retarded are proving to be sound investments. Such programs rely heavily on behavior modification techniques and are making it possible for some retarded individuals to become employed workers earning the minimum wage or better. Everyone benefits—the individual, his or her family, and society as well.

Intelligence and Neural Processing Speed

A growing number of neuroscientists and psychologists believe that individual differences in intelligence may be the result of differences in neural processing speed, a variable that has been shown to be strongly influenced by genes (Luciano et al., 2001, 2003). Presumably, according to this hypothesis, higher IQ test scores are associated with faster neural processing. To test the hypothesis, researchers are using PET scans and other brain-imaging techniques to compare the efficiency and speed of neural processing in people with a range of intelligence levels. Other researchers, using reaction-time tasks such as measuring the amount of time required for a participant to identify or classify objects, have also found that processing speed is related to intelligence (Fry & Hale, 1996; Neisser et al., 1996). But researchers find it challenging to distinguish neural processing time from physical reaction time (Brody, 1992). For example, a participant must decide whether two objects flashed on a screen are the same or different and then respond physically by pushing one of two buttons, labeled "S" and "D." Consequently, the time taken for the mental task (processing speed) may be affected by the time needed for the physical task (reaction time), and that physical factor may have nothing to do with intelligence.

A research technique that measures inspection time is a better way to gauge processing speed (Deary & Stough, 1996; Scheuffgen et al., 2000). A typical inspection-time task is shown in Figure 10.14. An image of the incomplete stimulus, part (a), is flashed to the participant very briefly and then immediately masked by a stimulus that covers it, part (b). The participant then is asked whether the longer side of the original stimulus appeared on the left or the right. Of course, the experiment is very simple, but the relevant factor is how much inspection time (from a few hundred milliseconds to 10 milliseconds or less) is needed for a participant to consistently achieve a given level of accuracy—say, 75% or 85%. The shorter the inspection time, the greater the "speed of intake of information" (Deary & Stough, 1996). Is inspection time (perceptual speed) related to intelligence? Apparently so. Deary and Stough claim that "inspection time is, to date, the only single information-processing index that accounts for approximately 20% of intelligence-test variance" (p. 599). Even so, experts in intelligence still lack a sufficient understanding of the relationship between inspection time and intelligence (Brody, 1992).

THE IQ CONTROVERSY

Intelligence testing has become a major growth industry. And many Americans have come to believe that a "magical" number—an IQ score, a percentile rank, or some other derived score—unfailingly portrays a person's intellectual capacity, ability, or potential. It is true that studies indicate that intelligence test scores are related to a wide range of social outcomes, including achievement test scores, job performance, income, social status, and years of education completed (Neisser et al., 1996), and they are fairly good predictors of academic performance (grades). However, abuses occur when a score on an intelligence or aptitude test is the only, or even the major, criterion for admitting individuals to various educational programs. Intelligence tests do not measure attitude and motivation, critical ingredients of success. Many people are admitted to educational programs who probably should not be, while others are denied admission who could profit from the programs and possibly make significant contributions to society.

Early categorization based solely on IQ scores can doom children to slow-track educational programs that are not appropriate for them. Many poor and minority children (particularly those for whom English is a second language) and visually or hearing impaired children have been erroneously placed in special education programs. IQ tests predicted that they were not mentally able to profit from regular classroom instruction. There would be no problem if IQ test results were consistently accurate, but in fact they are not.

One criticism that continues to plague advocates of IQ testing is the suggestion that minority children and those for whom English is a second language are at a disadvantage when they are assessed on

FIGURE 10.14   A Typical Inspection-Time Task
(From Deary & Stough, 1996.)

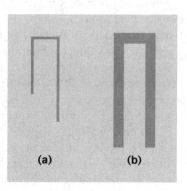

conventional tests because their cultural backgrounds differ from that assumed by the tests' authors. In response, attempts have been made to develop **culture-fair intelligence tests** designed to minimize cultural bias. The questions do not penalize individuals whose cultural experience or language differs from that of the mainstream or dominant culture.

A new testing technique called *dynamic assessment* represents a different approach to moderating the effects of cultural bias on IQ scores. In dynamic assessment, examinees are taught the goal and format of each IQ subtest before actually being tested. The rationale behind the technique is that children from middle-class backgrounds have more experience with testing procedures than do children from low-income homes, and they better understand that the goal of testing is to demonstrate competency. Thus, the goal of dynamic assessment is to provide children from disadvantaged backgrounds with the same skills middle-class children bring to the testing situation, thereby improving their scores. And the assumptions of this technique appear to be valid: Studies of dynamic assessment show that it significantly increases the number of minority children who achieve above-average IQ scores (Lidz & Macrine, 2001)

The Heritability of IQ Scores

The most vocal area of disagreement concerning intelligence has been the **nature–nurture controversy,** the debate over whether intelligence is primarily the result of heredity or environment. Englishman Sir Francis Galton (1874) initiated this debate, which has raged for more than 100 years, and coined the term. After studying a number of prominent families in England, Galton concluded that intelligence was inherited. Hereditarians agree with Galton, claiming that intelligence is largely inherited—the result of nature. Environmentalists, on the other hand, insist that it is influenced primarily by one's environment—the result of nurture. Most psychologists now agree that both nature and nurture contribute to intelligence, but they continue to debate the proportions contributed by each.

Behavioral genetics is a field of research that investigates the relative effects of heredity and environment on behavior and ability (Plomin et al., 1997). One of the primary methods used by behavioral geneticists is the **twin study method,** in which researchers study *identical twins* (monozygotic twins, who have exactly the same genes) and *fraternal twins* (dizygotic twins, who are no more alike genetically than other siblings) to determine how much they resemble each other on a variety of characteristics. If identical twins raised apart (that is, in different environments) are more alike than fraternal twins raised together (that is, in the same environment), then genes are assumed to contribute more strongly than environment to the particular trait being studied. **Heritability** is an index of the degree to which a characteristic is estimated to be influenced by heredity. Figure 10.15 shows estimates of the proportional contributions of genetic and environmental factors to intelligence. Some research using the **adoption study method,** comparing children to both their adoptive and biological parents, also supports the assertion that genes strongly influence IQ scores.

Minnesota is the site of the most extensive U.S. study of identical and fraternal twins. The Minnesota Center for Twin and Adoption Research has assembled the *Minnesota Twin Registry*, which in 1998 included over 10,000 twin pairs (Bouchard, 1998). Since 1979, researchers at the center, headed by Thomas Bouchard, have studied about 60 pairs of fraternal twins and 80 pairs of identical twins who were reared apart. Of all the traits Bouchard and his colleagues studied, the most heritable trait turned out to be intelligence. Bouchard (1997) reports that various types of twin studies have consistently yielded heritability estimates of .60 to .70 for intelligence.

Not all researchers agree with Bouchard's heritability estimate for intelligence. Combining data from a number of twin studies, Plomin and others (1994) found the heritability estimate for general intelligence to be .52. Similar findings emerged from analyses of dozens of adoption studies and twin studies involving over 10,000 pairs of twins. These analyses concluded that the heritability of general cognitive ability is about .50 (McClearn et al., 1997; Plomin, 2003). Psychologists who consider environmental factors to be the chief contributors to differences in intelligence also take issue with

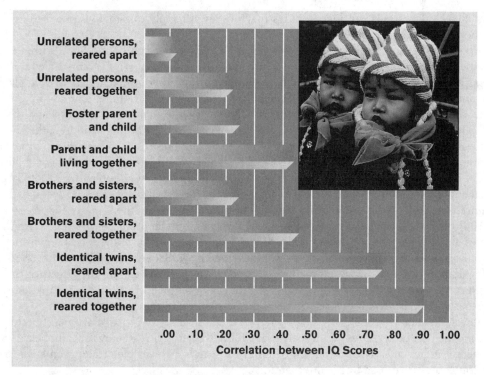

FIGURE 10.15   Correlations between the IQ Scores of Persons with Various Relationships.   The more closely related two individuals are, the more similar their IQ scores tend to be. Thus, there is a strong genetic contribution to intelligence. (Based on data from Bouchard & McGue, 1981; Erlenmeyer-Kimling & Jarvik, 1963.)

Bouchard's findings. They claim that most separated identical twins are raised by adoptive parents who have been matched as closely as possible to the biological parents. This fact, the critics say, could account for the similarity in IQ. In response to his critics, Bouchard (1997) has pointed out that children who are not related biologically but are raised in the same home are no more similar in intelligence once they reach adulthood than complete strangers.

Adding support to the nature side of the debate, adoption studies reveal that children adopted shortly after birth have IQs more closely resembling those of their biological parents than those of their adoptive parents. The family environment has an influence on IQ early in life, but that influence seems to diminish. Twin and adoption studies indicate that for people in adulthood, genes are most closely correlated with IQ (Loehlin et al., 1988, 1989; McCartney et al., 1990; Plomin & Rende, 1991). In fact, the influence of genes seems to increase predictably as people age: There is a heritability of .30 in infancy, .40 in childhood, .50 in adolescence, and about .60 in adulthood (McGue et al., 1993). But does this mean that intelligence is immune to the effects of environment?

Environmental Effects on IQ

Clearly, the high degree of similarity in the intelligence scores of identical twins who have been reared apart makes a strong case for the powerful influence of genes. But even Bouchard and his colleagues (1990) caution against trying to generalize their findings to people raised in disadvantaged environments. Bouchard (1997) states: "A child raised in crushing poverty by illiterate parents is unlikely to score well on IQ tests, no matter what his mental inheritance. ... Twin studies tend to attract few subjects in such dire straits, so their findings may not always apply to people exposed to extremes of deprivation or privilege" (p. 56).

Several studies indicate that IQ test scores are not fixed but can be modified with an enriched environment. Several decades ago, Sandra Scarr and Richard Weinberg (1976) studied 130 African American and interracial children who had been adopted by highly educated, upper-middle-class White American families; 99 of the children had been adopted in the first year of life. The adoptees were fully exposed to middle-class cultural experiences and vocabulary, the "culture of the tests and the school" (p. 737). How did the children perform on IQ and achievement tests? For these children, the 15-point IQ gap between Blacks and Whites that had been observed by some researchers was bridged by an enriched environment. Compared to an average IQ score of 90, which would be expected had these children been reared by their biological parents, the average IQ score of the 130 adoptees was 106.3. And their achievement test scores were slightly above the national average, not below. On the average, the earlier the children were adopted, the higher their IQs. The mean IQ score of the 99 early adoptees was 110.4, about 10 IQ points above the average for White Americans. Similarly, studies in France also show that IQ scores and achievement are substantially higher when children from lower-class environments are adopted by middle- and upper-middle-class families (Duyme, 1988; Schiff and Lewontin, 1986).

In addition to these encouraging adoption studies, research examining the effects of early childhood interventions on the IQ scores of children from poor families clearly indicates that early educational experiences can affect IQ scores. Some of the best known of these interventions have been carried out by developmental psychologist Craig Ramey of the University of North Carolina (Burchinal et al., 1997; Campbell & Ramey, 1994; Campbell et al., 2001; Ramey, 1993; Ramey & Campbell, 1987). And unlike many studies of early interventions, Ramey's research involves true experiments—so it is clear that the outcomes are caused by the interventions.

In one of Ramey's programs (Campbell and Ramey, 1994), 6- to 12-month-old infants of low-IQ, low-income mothers were randomly assigned to either an intensive 40-hour-per-week day-care program that continued throughout the preschool years or a control group that received only medical care and nutritional supplements. When the children reached school age, half in each group (again based on random assignment) were enrolled in a special after-school program that helped their families learn how to support school learning with educational activities at home. Ramey followed the progress of the children in all four groups through age 12, giving them IQ tests at various ages. Those who participated in the infant and preschool program scored higher on IQ tests than peers who received either no intervention or only the school-aged intervention. Perhaps more important, during the elementary school years, about 40% of the control group participants had IQ scores classified as borderline or retarded (scores below 85), compared with only 12.8% of those who were in the infant program. Further, more recent research shows that the cognitive advantage enjoyed by the infant intervention groups has persisted into adulthood (Campbell et al., 2001). Ramey's work clearly shows that the environment has great potential to influence IQ scores.

Historical evidence also suggests that environmental factors have a strong influence on IQ scores. Americans and similarly advantaged populations all over the world have gained about 3 IQ points per decade since 1940. James Flynn (1987, 1999; Dickens & Flynn, 2001) analyzed 73 studies involving some 7,500 participants ranging in age from 12 to 48 and found that "every Binet and Wechsler [standardization group] from 1932 to 1978 has performed better than its predecessor" (Flynn, 1987, p. 225). This consistent improvement in IQ scores over time is known as the *Flynn effect* (Holloway, 1999). The average IQ in Western industrialized nations is currently about 15 IQ points higher than it was 50 years ago. Regarding the Black–White IQ gap among U.S. adults, Flynn (1987) asserts that "the environmental advantage Whites enjoy over Blacks is similar to what Whites (adults) of today enjoy over their own parents or grandparents of 50 years ago" (p. 226).

It should not be surprising that enriched environments alter traits that are highly heritable. Consider the fact that American and British adolescents are 6 inches taller on average than their counterparts a century and a half ago (Tanner, 1990). Height has the same heritability (.90) today as it did in the mid-19th century. So this tremendous average gain in height of 6 inches is entirely attributable to environmental influences: better health, better nutrition, and so on. The highest heritability estimates for intelligence are far lower than those for height. It seems clear, then, that environmental influences have the power to affect intelligence and achievement. For example, poverty affects nutrition, and research clearly shows that malnutrition, especially early in life, can harm intellectual development (Brown & Pollitt, 1996; Grogorenko, 2003).

Gender Differences in Cognitive Abilities

Concerning gender differences in cognitive abilities, there are two important points to keep in mind: First, the differences within each gender are greater than the differences between the genders. Second, even though gender differences in cognitive abilities have been generally small on average, there tends to be more variation in such abilities among males than among females—that is, the range of test scores is typically greater for males.

Researchers Janet Hyde and Marcia Linn (1988) examined 165 studies reporting test results on verbal ability for approximately 1.5 million males and females. But they found no significant gender differences in verbal ability. Hedges and Nowell (1995) analyzed the results of the National Assessment of Educational Progress, which has tested a representative sample of 70,000 to 100,000 American school-children, aged 9, 13, and 17, annually in reading comprehension, writing, math, and science. The researchers compared the achievement of the 17-year-olds from 1971 through 1992 and reported that females outperformed males in reading and writing, while males did better in science and math. Although average gender differences were small, there was one prominent exception: "Females performed substantially better than males in writing every year" (p. 44). Furthermore, Hedges and Nowell reported that more males than females were near the bottom of the distribution, not only in writing, but in reading comprehension as well. Finally, in high school, girls are generally more fluent verbally than boys are (Halpern, 1992) and do considerably better in spelling (Lubinsky & Benbow, 1992).

But do males have the edge in math? In one of the largest studies conducted to date on gender differences in mathematics, Hyde and others (1990) analyzed 100 studies, which together represented test results for more than 3 million participants. They found no significant gender difference in the understanding of mathematical concepts among the various age groups. Although females did slightly better in mathematical problem solving in elementary and middle school, males scored moderately higher in high school and college. Benbow and Stanley (1980, 1983) found a significant male superiority in a select segment of the population—the brightest of the bright in mathematics ability. On the math portion of the SAT, twice as many boys as girls scored above 500, and 13 times as many scored above 700. Hedges and Nowell (1995) reported that twice as many boys as girls were in the top 3% of the Project Talent Mathematics total scale, and seven times as many boys were in the top 1%.

Parents often expect boys to do better than girls in math (Lummis & Stevenson, 1990). Such expectations may become a *self-fulfilling prophecy*, leading girls to lack confidence in their math ability and to decide not to pursue advanced math courses (Eccles & Jacobs, 1986). A report by the American Association of University Women Education Foundation provided evidence that many science teachers and some math teachers, as well, tend to pay noticeably more attention to boys than to girls (Chira, 1992). Such treatment may discourage girls with math or science aptitude from choosing careers in these areas.

Some psychologists think that males' higher math achievement test scores are the result of superior spatial abilities. Researchers have found that, in general, males tend to perform somewhat better than females on tests of spatial skills (Kimura, 1992; Linn & Hyde, 1989; Linn & Peterson, 1985). This gender difference has been found on some but not all of the various spatial tasks (Geary, 1996; Kimura, 1992). Some research has shown that spatial abilities appear to be enhanced by prenatal exposure to high levels of androgens (Berenbaum et al., 1995). However, this finding does not minimize the role of social experiences and expectations in shaping children's abilities and interests.

Cultural Beliefs, Expectations, Effort, and Academic Achievement

In a classic study of cross-cultural differences in achievement, Stevenson and others (1986) compared the math ability of randomly selected elementary school children from three comparable cities—Taipei in Taiwan, Sendai in Japan, and Minneapolis in the United States. By the fifth grade, the Asian students were outscoring the Americans by about 15 points in math ability. And the Asian superiority held firmly from the highest to the lowest achievement levels. Of the lowest 100 students in math achievement, 67 were Americans; of the top 100, only 1 was. The Japanese children scored the highest of the three groups in fifth grade, and even the lowest-scoring Japanese classes did better than the top-scoring classes in the United States.

How can such differences in achievement for children from different cultures be explained? Research carried out by Stevenson and others (1990) suggests that cultural beliefs and practices may be a major factor in explaining the gap in math ability. Their research was conducted with first and fifth graders from the same three cities as in the math comparison study, a total of 1,440 students (480 from each of the three countries). The children were tested in reading and mathematics and interviewed along with their mothers. In a follow-up study 4 years later, the first graders (now fifth graders) were tested again, and they and their mothers were interviewed once more. Stevenson and his colleagues (1990) reported that the Chinese and Japanese mothers considered academic achievement to be the *most important pursuit of their children*, whereas American parents did not value it as a central concern. The Asian, but not the American, families structured their home activities to promote academic achievement as soon as their first child started elementary school.

More importantly, perhaps, the Asian parents downplayed the role of innate ability in school achievement. Instead, they emphasized the value of hard work and persistence (Stevenson, 1992). American parents, in contrast, believed more firmly in genetic limitations on ability and achievement. Such a belief has devastating effects, according to Stevenson, who states, "When parents believe success in school depends for the most part on ability rather than effort, they are less likely to foster participation in activities related to academic achievement" (p. 73). Also, American mothers tended to overestimate the cognitive abilities of their children, but the Chinese and Japanese mothers did not. Asian mothers held higher standards for their children and also gave more realistic assessments of their children's abilities (see Figure 10.16).

In follow-up studies, Stevenson and others (1993) found that the achievement gap between Asian and American students persisted over a 10-year period. Differences in high school achievement were explained in part by the fact that the American students spent more time working at part-time jobs and socializing than their Asian counterparts did, a finding confirmed by several other cross-cultural researchers (Fuligni & Stevenson, 1995; Larson & Verma, 1999).

But are Asian students more likely than students in the United States to be depressed, nervous, stressed, and heavily burdened by pressures to maintain academic excellence? One large cross-cultural study comparing 11th-grade students from Japan, Taiwan, and the United States did find a correlation between achievement in mathematics and psychological distress—but, surprisingly, for the American students, not the Asian students (Crystal et al., 1994). Moreover, contrary to popular belief, adolescent suicide rates are lower in Japan than in the United States.

Why should high-achieving American students, but not Asian students, pay a price in terms of psychological distress? The researchers found that Asian teenagers typically enjoy support and encouragement for their academic achievement from family and peers alike. In contrast, high-achieving teenagers in the United States are torn between studying hard to excel academically and pursuing nonacademic social interests. Such interests may be strongly encouraged by their peers and often by parents who want their children to be "well-rounded." Which of these two cultural tendencies is more likely to maximize the development of one's intellectual potential? Perhaps the answer to the stunning record of academic achievement of Asian students lies not in their genes, but in the cultural values that nurture them.

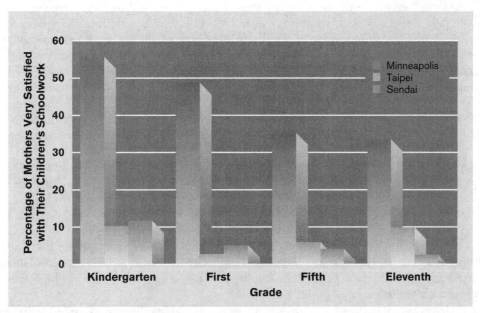

FIGURE 10.16   Ramey's Infant Intervention. In the Ramey study, children were randomly assigned in infancy to an experimental group with special day care (the "full intervention" group) or to a control group. From kindergarten through third grade, half of each group received supplementary family support, and the other half did not. The difference in IQ between the intervention and control groups remained statistically significant even at age 12. (From Campbell & Ramey, 1994.)

EMOTIONAL INTELLIGENCE

Daniel Goleman (1995) claims that success in life is more markedly influenced by emotional intelligence than by IQ. **Emotional intelligence** refers to a set of capabilities that are separate from IQ but necessary for success in life—in the workplace, in intimate personal relations, and in social interactions. Research supports this view, showing that emotional intelligence is unrelated to IQ scores (Lam & Kirby, 2002; Van der Zee et al., 2002). Moreover, scores on tests of emotional intelligence predict both academic and social success (Rozell et al., 2002). For these reasons, emotional intelligence has become an important concept in psychology.

The foundation of emotional intelligence is *self-knowledge*. It involves an awareness of emotions, an ability to manage those emotions, and self-motivation. Awareness of one's own emotions—recognizing and acknowledging feelings as they happen—is at the very heart of emotional intelligence. It means being aware not only of moods, but of thoughts about those moods as well. Those who are able to monitor their feelings as they arise are more likely to be able to manage them rather than being ruled by them.

Managing emotions does not mean suppressing them, any more than it means giving free rein to every feeling and impulse. As Goleman (1995) puts it, "The goal is balance, not emotional suppression: every feeling has its value and significance. A life without passion would be a dull wasteland of neutrality, cut off and isolated from the richness of life itself" (p. 56). Thus, to manage emotions is to express them in an appropriate manner and not let them get out of control. For example, if not tempered with reason, uncontrolled anger can lead to rage and violence. People high in emotional intelligence have learned how to regulate their moods and not let anger, boredom, or depression ruin their day (or their lives). You manage your emotions when you do something to cheer yourself up, soothe your own hurts, reassure yourself, or otherwise temper an inappropriate or out-of-control emotion.

Self-motivation refers to an aspect of self-control that enables a person to get moving and pursue worthy goals, persist at tasks even when frustrated, and resist the temptation to act on impulse. Resisting impulsive behavior is, according to Goleman (1995), "the root of all emotional self-control" (p. 81). Indeed, of all the attributes of emotional intelligence, the ability to postpone immediate gratification and to persist in working toward some greater future gain is most closely related to success—whether one is trying to get a college degree, build a business, or even stay on a diet. One researcher has found that 4-year-old children who mastered the art of delaying instant gratification in order to advance toward some greater future goal are "far superior as students" later, when they graduate from high school, than are four-year-olds who were not able to resist the impulse to satisfy their immediate wishes (Shoda et al., 1990).

The interpersonal aspects of emotional intelligence are sensitivity to and understanding of others' emotions and the ability to handle relationships. Two components of emotional intelligence that are prerequisites for handling relationships are (1) the ability to manage one's own emotions and (2) *empathy*, or the ability to perceive, understand, and relate to the emotions of others. These two components combine to produce the ability to respond appropriately to emotions in others. And this, Goleman (1995) maintains, is the very center of the art of handling relationships. But he does not mean "handling" in an autocratic, dominating sense. People who handle relationships well, says Goleman, are able to shape encounters, "to mobilize and inspire others to thrive in intimate relationships, to persuade and influence, to put others at ease" (p. 113).

Although it is not one of the five main domains of emotional intelligence identified by Salovey and Mayer (1990), *optimism* appears to be a component of emotional intelligence. People who are optimistic have a "strong expectation in general [that] things will turn out all right in life" (p. 88). The most significant aspect of optimism in the context of emotional intelligence is the way in which optimists explain their successes and failures. When optimists fail, they attribute their failure to something in the situation that can be changed. Thus, they believe that by trying harder, they can succeed the next time. But when pessimists fail, they blame themselves and attribute their failure to some personal characteristic or flaw that cannot be changed.

CREATIVITY

Creativity can be thought of as the ability to produce original, appropriate, and valuable ideas and/or solutions to problems. Some psychologists go beyond this basic definition and suggest that creative people have the ability to see connections between objects or ideas that are rarely noticed by the noncreative. In fact one of the first tests of creativity, the *Remote Associates Test*, tapped into this aspect of creativity (Mednick & Mednick, 1967).

Research indicates that there is a modest correlation between creativity and IQ. Highly creative people tend to be well above average in intelligence, but in the upper IQ ranges (over 120) there seems to be little correlation between IQ and creativity (Barron & Harrington, 1981). Moreover, genuine creativity rarely appears in the form of sudden flashes (Haberlandt, 1997). For the most part, creative ideas that come to conscious awareness have been incubating for some time. One theorist has suggested that there are four basic stages in the creative problem-solving process (Goleman et al., 1992):

1. *Preparation*—searching for information that may help solve the problem

2. *Incubation*—letting the problem "sit" while the relevant information is digested; perhaps the most important part of the process; takes place below the level of awareness

3. *Illumination*—being suddenly struck by the right solution

4. *Translation*—transforming the new insight into useful action

Psychologists studying exceptionally creative individuals (e.g., Bloom et al., 1985) have learned that they share a number of characteristics that distinguish them from less creative individuals. For one, they have a great deal of expertise in a specific area that has been built up over years of disciplined study and practice. Creative individuals are also open to new experiences and ideas, even those that may seem quite odd to others; moreover, they seem to be inherently curious and inquisitive (Sternberg, 1985a). Creative people also tend to be independent thinkers who are less influenced by the opinions of others than their less creative counterparts are. Perhaps because of their independence, creative individuals are more likely to be motivated by the anticipation, excitement, and enjoyment of their work than by a desire to please others. Finally, creative endeavor requires hard work and persistence in the face of failure. For instance, Albert Einstein published 248 papers on his theory of relativity before it was finished, and Mozart, when he died at age 35, had created 609 musical compositions (Haberlandt, 1997).

REFERENCES

Ader, R. (1985). CNS immune systems interactions: Conditioning phenomena. *Behavioral and Brain Sciences, 9,* 760–763.

Ader, R., & Cohen, N. (1982). Behaviorally conditioned immunosuppression and murine systemic Lupus erythematosus. *Science, 215,* 1534–1536.

Ader, R., & Cohen, N. (1993). Psychoneuroimmunology: Conditioning and stress. *Annual Review of Psychology, 44,* 53–85.

Aiken, L. R. (1997). *Psychological testing and assessment* (9th ed.). Boston: Allyn & Bacon.

Al'absi, M., Hugdahl, K., & Lovallo, W. (2002). Adrenocortical stress responses and altered working memory performance. *Psychophysiology, 39,* 95–99.

American Medical Association. (1994). Report of the Council on Scientific Affairs: Memories of childhood abuse. CSA Report 5-A-94.

American Psychiatric Association. (1993). *Statement approved by the Board of Trustees, December 12, 1993.* Washington, DC: Author.

American Psychological Association. (1994). *Interim report of the APA Working Group on Investigation of Memories of Childhood Abuse.* Washington, DC: Author.

Anagnostaras, S. B., Joseelyn, S. A., Frankland, P. W., & Silva, A. J. (2000). Computer-assisted behavioral assessment of Pavlovian fear conditioning in mice. *Learning & Memory, 7,* 48–57.

Anderson, C., & Bushman, B. (2001). Effects of violent video games on aggressive behavior, aggressive cognition, aggressive affect, physiological arousal, and prosocial behavior: A meta-analytic review of the scientific literature. *Psychological Science, 12,* 353–359.

Atkinson, R. C., & Shiffrin, R. M. (1968). Human memory: A proposed system and its controlled processes. In K. W. Spence & J. T. Spence (Eds.), *The psychology of learning and motivation* (Vol. 2, pp. 89–195). New York: Academic.

Ayllon, T., & Azrin, N. H. (1965). The measurement and reinforcement of behavior of psychotics. *Journal of the Experimental Analysis of Behavior, 8,* 357–383.

Ayllon, T., & Azrin, N. (1968). *The token economy: A motivational system for therapy and rehabilitation.* New York: Appleton-Century-Crofts.

Azrin, N. H., & Holtz, W. C. (1966). Punishment. In W. K. Honig (Ed.), *Operant behavior: Areas of research and application.* New York: Appleton-Century-Crofts.

Baddeley, A. (1990). *Human memory.* Boston: Allyn & Bacon.

Baddeley, A. (1992). Working memory. *Science, 255,* 556–559.

Baddeley, A. D. (1995). Working memory. In M. S. Gazzaniga (Ed.), *The cognitive neurosciences.* Cambridge, MA: MIT Press.

Bahrick, H. P., Bahrick, P. O., & Wittlinger, R. P. (1975). Fifty years of memory for names and faces: A cross-sectional approach. *Journal of Experimental Psychology: General, 104,* 54–75.

Bahrick, H. P., Hall, L. K., & Berger, S. A. (1996). Accuracy and distortion in memory for high school grades. *Psychological Science, 7,* 265–271.

Bandura, A. (1969). *Principles of behavior modification.* New York: Holt, Rinehart & Winston.

Bandura, A. (1977). *Social learning theory.* Englewood Cliffs, NJ: Prentice-Hall.

Bandura, A. (1986). *Social functions of thought and action: A social-cognitive theory.* Englewood Cliffs, NJ: Prentice-Hall.

Bandura, A., Ross, D., & Ross, S. A. (1961). Transmission of aggression through imitation of aggressive models. *Journal of Abnormal and Social Psychology, 63,* 575–582.

Bandura, A., Ross, D., & Ross, S. A. (1963). Imitation of film-mediated aggressive models. *Journal of Abnormal and Social Psychology, 66,* 3–11.

Barron, F., & Harrington, D. M. (1981). Creativity, intelligence, and personality. *Annual Review of Psychology, 32,* 439–476.

Bartlett, F. C. (1932). *Remembering: A study in experimental and social psychology.* London: Cambridge University Press.

Basic Behavioral Science Task Force of the National Advisory Mental Health Council. (1996). Basic behavioral science research for mental health: Perception, attention, learning, and memory. *American Psychologist, 51,* 133–142.

Bass, E., & Davis, L. (1988). *The courage to heal.* New York: Harper & Row.

Bateson, G. (1982). Totemic knowledge in New Guinea. In U. Neisser (Ed.), *Memory observed: Remembering in natural contexts.* San Francisco: W. H. Freeman.

Benbow, C. P., & Stanley, J. C. (1980). Sex differences in mathematical ability: Fact or artifact? *Science, 210,* 1262–1264.

Benbow, C. P., & Stanley, J. C. (1983). Sex differences in mathematical reasoning ability: More facts. *Science, 222,* 1029–1031.

Berenbaum, S. A., Korman, K., & Leveroni, C. (1995). Early hormones and sex differences in cognitive abilities. *Learning and Individual Differences, 7,* 303–321.

Bernstein, I. L. (1985). Learned food aversions in the progression of cancer and its treatment. *Annals of the New York Academy of Sciences, 443,* 365–380.

Bernstein, I. L., Webster, M. M., & Bernstein, I. D. (1982). Food aversions in children receiving chemotherapy for cancer. *Cancer, 50,* 2961–2963.

Bialystok, E. (1997). Effects of bilingualism and biliteracy on children's emerging concepts of print. *Developmental Psychology, 33,* 429–440.

Bialystok, E., & Majumder, S. (1998). The relationship between bilingualism and the development of cognitive processes in problem solving. *Applied Psycholinguistics, 19,* 69–85.

Bialystok, E., Shenfield, T., & Codd, J. (2000). Languages, scripts, and the environment: Factors in developing concepts of print. *Developmental Psychology, 36,* 66–76.

Bjork, D. W. (1993). *B. F. Skinner: A life.* New York: Basic Books.

Bjorklund, D. F., Cassel, W. S., Bjorklund, B. R., Brown, R. D., Park, C. L., Ernst, K., & Owen, F. A. (2000). Social demand characteristics in children's and adults' memory and suggestibility: The effect of different interviewers on free recall and recognition. *Applied Cognitive Psychology, 14,* 421–433.

Bliss, T. V., & Lomo, T. (2000). Plasticity in a monosynaptic cortical pathway. *Journal of Physiology, 207,* 61.

Bloom, B. S. (Ed.). (1985). *Developing talent in young people.* New York: Ballantine.

Bohannon, J. N., III. (1988). Flashbulb memories for the Space Shuttle disaster: A tale of two theories. *Cognition, 29,* 179–196.

Bouchard, T. J., Jr. (1997, September/October). Whenever the twain shall meet. *The Sciences, 37,* 52–57.

Bouchard, T. J., Jr. (1998, May 13). Personal communication.

Bouchard, T. J., Jr., Lykken, D. T., McGue, M., Segal, N. L., & Tellegen, A. (1990). Sources of human psychological differences: The Minnesota study of twins reared apart. *Science, 250,* 223–228.

Bouchard, T. J., Jr., & McGue, M. (1981). Familial studies of intelligence: A review. *Science, 212,* 1055–1058.

Bowers, K. S., & Farvolden, P. (1996). Revisiting a century-old Freudian slip-from suggestion disavowed to the truth repressed. *Psychological Bulletin, 119,* 355–380.

Broadbent, D. E. (1958). *Perception and communication.* New York: Pergamon Press.

Brown, J. L., Pollitt, E. (1996). Malnutrition, poverty and intellectual development. *Scientific American, 224.* 38–43.

Brown, R., & Kulik, J. (1977). Flashbulb memories. *Cognition, 5,* 73–99.

Brown, R., & McNeil, D. (1966). The "tip of the tongue" phenomenon. *Journal of Verbal Learning and Verbal Behavior, 5,* 325–337.

Buonomano, D. V., & Merzenich, M. M. (1995). Temporal information transformed into a spatial code by a neural network with realistic properties. *Science, 267,* 1028–1030.

Burchinal, M., Campbell, F., Bryant, D., Wasik, B., & Ramey, C. (1997). Early intervention and mediating processes in cognitive performance of children of low-income African American families. *Child Development, 68,* 935–954.

Burt, D. B., Zembar, M. J., & Niederehe, G. (1995). Depression and memory impairment: A meta-analysis of the association, its pattern, and specificity. *Psychological Bulletin, 117*, 285–305.

Cahill, L., & McGaugh, J. (1995). A novel demonstration of enhanced memory associated with emotional arousal. *Consciousness and Cognition, 4*, 410–421.

Camp, D. S., Raymond, G. A., & Church, R. M. (1967). Temporal relationship between response and punishment. *Journal of Experimental Psychology, 74*, 114–123.

Campbell, F. A., & Ramey, C. T. (1994). Effects of early intervention on intellectual and academic achievement: A follow-up study of children from low-income families. *Child development, 65*, 684–698.

Campbell, F., Pungello, E., Miler-Johnson, S., Burchinal, M., & Ramey, C. (2001). The development of cognitive and academic abilities: Growth curves from an early childhood educational experiment. *Developmental Psychology, 37*, 231–242.

Chincotta, D., & Underwood, G. (1997). Estimates, language of schooling and bilingual digit span. *European Journal of Cognitive Psychology, 9*, 325–348.

Chira, S. (1992, February 12). Bias against girls is found rife in schools, with lasting damage. *The New York Times*, pp. A1–A23.

Cho, K. (2001). Chronic "jet lag" produces temporal lobe atrophy and spatial cognitive deficits. *Nature Neuroscience, 4*, 567–568.

Cho, K., Ennaceur, A., Cole, J., & Kook Suh, C. (2000). Chronic jet lag produces cognitive deficits. *Journal of Neuroscience, 20*, RC66.

Chollar, S. (1989). Conversation with the dolphins. *Psychology Today, 23*, 52–57.

Church, R. M. (1963). The varied effects of punishment on behavior. *Psychological Review, 70*, 369–402.

Church, R. M. (1989). Theories of timing behavior. In S. P. Klein & R. Mowrer (Eds.), *Contemporary learning theories: Instrumental conditioning theory and the impact of biological constraints on learning*. Hillsdale, NJ: Erlbaum.

Clark, D. M., & Teasdale, J. D. (1982). Diurnal variation in clinical depression and accessibility of memories of positive and negative experiences. *Journal of Abnormal Psychology, 91*, 87–95.

Clayton, K. N. (1964). T-maze choice learning as a joint function of the reward magnitudes for the alternatives. *Journal of Comparative and Physiological Psychology, 58*, 333–338.

Clayton, N. S. (1998). Memory and the hippocampus in foodstoring birds: A comparative approach. *Neuropharmacology, 37*, 441–452.

Colombo, M., & Broadbent, N. (2000). Is the avian hippocampus a functional homologue of the mammalian hippocampus? *Neuroscience and Biobehavioral Reviews, 24*, 465–484.

Conrad, R. (1964). Acoustic confusions in immediate memory. *British Journal of Psychology, 55*, 75–84.

Conway, M. A., Cohen, G., & Stanhope, N. (1991). On the very long-term retention of knowledge acquired through formal education: Twelve years of cognitive psychology. *Journal of Experimental Psychology: General, 120*, 395–409.

Cook, M., Mineka, S., Wolkenstein, B., & Laitsch, K. (1985). Observational conditioning of snake fear in unrelated rhesus monkeys. *Journal of Abnormal Psychology, 94*, 591–610.

Cooper, L. A., & Shepard, R. N. (1984). Turning something over in the mind. *Scientific American, 251*, 106–114.

Courtney, S. M., Ungerleider, L. G., Keil, K., & Haxby, J. V. (1997). Transient and sustained activity in a distributed neural system for human working memory. *Nature, 386*, 608–611.

Cowan, N. (1988). Evolving conceptions of memory storage, selective attention, and their mutual constraints within the human information-processing system. *Psychological Bulletin, 104*, 163–191.

Craik, F. I. M., & Lockhart, R. S. (1972). Levels of processing: A framework for memory research. *Journal of Verbal Learning and Verbal Behavior, 11*, 671–684.

Crystal, D. S., Chen, C., Fulligni, A. J., Stevenson, H. W., Hsu, C-C., Ko, H-J., Kitamura, S., & Kimura, S. (1994). Psychological maladjustment and academic achievement: A cross-cultural study of Japanese, Chinese, and American high school students. *Child Development, 65*, 738–753.

Curci, A., Luminet, O., Finkenaeur, C., & Gisler, L. (2001). Flashbulb memories in social groups: A comparative test-retest study of the memory of French president Mitterrand's death in a French and a Belgian group. *Memory, 9*, 81–101.

Dale, N., & Kandel, E. R. (1990). Facilitatory and inhibitory transmitters modulate spontaneous transmitter release at cultured *Aplysia* sensorimotor synapses. *Journal of Physiology, 421*, 203–222.

Dallery, J., Silverman, K., Chutuape, M., Bigelow, G., & Stitzer, M. (2001). Voucher-based reinforcement of opiate plus cocaine abstinence in treatment-resistant methadone patients: Effects of reinforcer magnitude. *Experimental & Clinical Psychopharmacology, 9,* 317–325.

Davis, S., Butcher, S. P., & Morris, R. G. M. (1992). The NMDA receptor antagonist D-2-amino-5-phosphonopentanoate (D-AP5) impairs spatial learning and LTP in vivo at intracerebral concentrations comparable to those that block LTP in vitro. *Journal of Neuroscience, 12,* 21–34.

D'Azevedo, W. A. (1982). Tribal history in Liberia. In U. Neisser (Ed.), *Memory observed: Remembering in natural contexts.* San Francisco: W. H. Freeman.

Deary, I. J., & Stough, C. (1996). Intelligence and inspection time: Achievements, prospects, and problems. *American Psychologist, 51,* 599–608.

Deci, E. L., Koestner, R., & Ryan, R. M. (1999). A meta-analytic review of experiments examining the effects of extrinsic rewards on intrinsic motivation. *Psychological Bulletin, 125,* 627–668.

Dickens, W., & Flynn, R. (2001). Heritability estimates versus large environmental effects: The IQ paradox resolved. *Psychological Review, 108,* 346–369.

Dodson, C. S., Koutstaal, W., & Schacter, D. L. (2000). Escape from illusion: Reducing false memories. *Trends in Cognitive Sciences, 4,* 391–397.

Dogil, G., Ackerman, H., Grodd, W., Haider, H., Kamp, H., Mayer, J., Riecker, A., & Wildgruber, D. (2002). The speaking brain: A tutorial introduction to fMRI experiments in the production of speech, prosody, and syntax. *Journal of Neurolinguistics, 15,* 59–90.

Duyme, M. (1988). School success and social class: An adoption study. *Developmental Psychology, 24,* 203–209.

Ebbinghaus, H. E. (1964). *Memory: A contribution to experimental psychology* (H. A. Ruger & C. E. Bussenius, Trans.). New York: Dover. (Original work published 1885)

Eccles, J. S., & Jacobs, J. E. (1986). Social forces shape math attitudes and performance. *Signs, 11,* 367–389.

Egeth, H. E. (1993). What do we not know about eyewitness identification? *American Psychologist, 48,* 577–580.

Eichenbaum, H. (1997). Declarative memory: Insights from cognitive neurobiology. *Annual Review of Psychology, 48,* 547–572.

Estes, W. K. (1994). *Classification and cognition.* New York: Oxford University Press.

Exton, M. S., von Auer, A. K., Buske-Kirschbaum, A., Stockhorst, U., Göbel, U., & Schedlowski, M. (2000). Pavlovian conditioning of immune function: Animal investigation and the challenge of human application. *Behavioural Brain Research, 110,* 129–141.

Farah, M. J. (1995). The neural bases of mental imagery. In M. S. Gazzaniga (Ed.), *The cognitive neurosciences.* Cambridge, MA: MIT Press.

Field, M., & Duka, T. (2002). Cues paired with a low dose of alcohol acquire conditioned incentive properties in social drinkers. *Psychopharmacology, 159,* 325–334.

Fixx, J. F. (1978). *Solve It! A perplexing profusion of puzzles.* New York: Doubleday.

Fleming, J. D. (1974, July). Field report: The state of the apes. *Psychology Today,* pp. 31–46.

Freud, S. (1922). *Beyond the pleasure principle.* London: International Psychoanalytic Press.

Fry, A. F., & Hale, S. (1996). Processing speed, working memory, and fluid intelligence. *Psychological Science, 7,* 237–241.

Fuligni, A. J., & Stevenson, H. W. (1995). Time use and mathematics achievement among American, Chinese, and Japanese high school students. *Child Development, 66,* 830–842.

Gallistel, C. R., & Gibbon, J. (2000). Time, rate, and conditioning. *Psychological Review, 107,* 289–344.

Galton, F. (1874). *English men of science: Their nature and nurture.* London: Macmillan.

Garavan, H., Morgan, R. E., Levitsky, D. A., Hermer-Vasquez, L., & Strupp, B. J. (2000). Enduring effects of early lead exposure: Evidence for a specific deficit in associative ability. *Neurotoxicology and Teratology, 22,* 151–164.

Garcia, J., & Koelling, A. (1966). Relation of cue to consequence in avoidance learning. *Psychonomic Science, 4,* 123–124.

Gardner, H. (1983). *Frames of mind: The theory of multiple intelligence.* New York: Basic Books.

Gardner, R. A., & Gardner, B. T. (1969). Teaching sign language to a chimpanzee. *Science, 165,* 664–672.

Garry, M., & Loftus, E. R. (1994). Pseudomemories without hypnosis. *International Journal of Clinical and Experimental Hypnosis, 42,* 363–373.

Gastil, J. (1990). Generic pronouns and sexist language: The oxymoronic character of masculine generics. *Sex Roles, 23,* 629–643.

Gates, A. I. (1917). Recitation as a factor in memorizing. *Archives of Psychology, 40.*

Geary, D. C. (1996). Sexual selection and sex differences in mathematical abilities. *Behavioral and Brain Sciences, 19,* 229–284.

Geiselman, R. E., Schroppel, T., Tubridy, A., Konishi, T., & Rodriguez, V. (2000). Objectivity bias in eye witness performance. *Applied Cognitive Psychology, 14,* 323–332.

Genesee, F. (1994). Bilingualism. In V. S. Ramachandran (Ed.), *Encyclopedia of human behavior* (Vol. 1, pp. 383–393). San Diego, CA: Academic.

Gerull, F., & Rappe, R. (2002). Mother knows best: The effects of maternal modelling on the acquisition of fear and avoidance behavior in toddlers. *Behaviour Research & Therapy, 40,* 279–287.

Gibbons, A. (1991). Déjà vu all over again: Chimp-language wars. *Science, 251,* 1561–1562.

Glover, J. A., & Corkill, A. J. (1987). Influence of paraphrased repetitions on the spacing effect. *Journal of Educational Psychology, 79,* 198–199.

Gluck, M. A., & Myers, C. E. (1997). Psychobiological models of hippocampal function in learning and memory. *Annual Review of Psychology, 48,* 481–514.

Godden, D. R., & Baddeley, A. D. (1975). Context-dependent memory in two natural environments: On land and underwater. *British Journal of Psychology, 66,* 325–331.

Goleman, D. (1995). *Emotional intelligence.* New York: Bantam.

Goleman, D., Kaufman, P., & Ray, M. (1992). *The creative spirit.* New York: Dutton.

Gollan, T., & Silverberg, N. (2001). Tip-of-the-tongue states in Hebrew-English bilinguals. *Bilingualism: Language and Cognition, 4,* 63–83.

Gonzalez, R., Ellsworth, P. C., & Pembroke, M. (1993). Response biases in lineups and showups. *Journal of Personality and Social Psychology, 64,* 525–537.

Green, J. T., & Woodruff-Pak, D. S. (2000). Eyeblink classical conditioning: Hippocampal formation is for neutral stimulus associations as cerebellum is for association-response. *Psychological Bulletin, 126,* 138–158.

Grogorenko, E. (2003). Intraindividual fluctuations in intellectual functioning: Selected links between nutrition and the mind. In R. Sternberg, J. Lautrey, & T. Lubart (Eds.), *Models of intelligence: International perspectives.* Washington, DC: American Psychological Association.

Grogorenko, E., Jarvin, L., & Sternberg, R. (2002). School-based tests of the triarchic theory of intelligence: Three settings, three samples, three syllabi. *Contemporary Educational Psychology, 27,* 167–208.

Grossman, H. J. (Ed.). (1983). *Manual on terminology and classification in mental retardation.* Washington, DC: *American Association on Mental Deficiency.*

Haberlandt, D. (1997). *Cognitive psychology* (2nd ed.). Boston: Allyn & Bacon.

Halpern, D. F. (1992). *Sex differences in cognitive abilities* (2nd ed.). Hillside, NJ: Erlbaum.

Hamilton, M. C. (1988). Using masculine generics: Does generic "he" increase male bias in the user's imagery? *Sex Roles, 19,* 785–789.

Harris, L. J., & Blaiser, M. J. (1997). Effects of a mnemonic peg system on the recall of daily tasks. *Perceptual and Motor Skills, 84,* 721–722.

Hedges, L. B., & Nowell, A. (1995). Sex differences in mental test scores, variability, and numbers of high-scoring individuals. *Science, 269,* 41–45.

Henkel, L. A., Franklin, N., & Johnson, M. K. (2000). Cross-modal source monitoring confusions between perceived and imagined events. *Journal of Experimental Psychology: Learning, Memory, and Cognition, 26,* 321–335.

Henley, N. M. (1989). Molehill or mountain? What we know and don't know about sex bias in language. In M. Crawford & M. Gentry (Eds.), *Gender and thought: Psychological perspectives.* New York: Springer-Verlag.

Henson, R., Shallice, T., Gorno-Tempini, M., & Dolan, R. (2002). Face repetition effects in implicit and explicit memory as measured by fMRI. *Cerebral Cortex, 12,* 178–186.

Herman, L. (1981). Cognitive characteristics of dolphins. In L. Herman (Ed.), *Cetacean behavior.* New York: Wiley.

Hinton, G. E., Dayan, P., Frey, B. J., & Neal, R. M. (1995). The "wake-sleep" algorithm for unsupervised neural networks. *Science, 268,* 1158–1161.

Holland, J. G., & Skinner, B. F. (1961). *The analysis of behavior.* New York: McGraw-Hill.

Holloway, M. (1999, January). Flynn's effect. *Scientific American, 280,* 37–38.

Howard, M. (2002). When does semantic similarity help episodic retrieval? *Journal of Memory & Language, 46,* 85–98.

Hyde, J. S. Fenema, E., & Lamon, S. J. (1990). Gender differences in mathematics performance: A meta-analysis. *Psychological Bulletin, 107*, 139–155.

Hyde, J. S., & Linn, M. C. (1988). Gender differences in verbal ability: A meta-analysis. *Psychological Bulletin, 104*, 53–69.

Hyman, I. E., Jr., Husband, T. H., & Billings, E. J. (1995). False memories of childhood. *Applied Cognitive Psychology, 9*, 181–197.

Hyman, I. E., Jr., & Pentland, J. (1996). The role of mental imagery in the creation of false childhood memories. *Journal of Memory and Language, 35*, 101–117.

Jelicic, M., & Bonke, B. (2001). Memory impairments following chronic stress? A critical review. *European Journal of Psychiatry, 15*, 225–232.

Jones, M. C. (1924). A laboratory study of fear: The case of Peter. *Pedagogical Seminary, 31*, 308–315.

Kahneman, D., & Tversky, A. (1984). Choices, values, and frames. *American Psychologist, 39*, 341–350.

Kalish, H. I. (1981). *From behavioral science to behavior modification.* New York: McGraw-Hill.

Katz, E., Robles-Sotelo, E., Correia, C., Silverman, K., Stitzer, M., & Bigelow, G. (2002). The brief abstinence test: Effects of continued incentive availability on cocaine abstinence. *Experimental & Clinical Psychopharmacology, 10*, 10–17.

Kihlstrom, J. F. (1995). The trauma-memory argument. *Consciousness and Cognition, 4*, 65–67.

Kim, K. H. S., Relkin, N. R., Lee, K-M., & Hirsch, J. (1997). Distinct cortical areas associated with native and second languages. *Nature, 388*, 171–174.

Kimura, D. (1992). Sex differences in the brain. *Scientific American, 267*, 118–125.

Klatzky, R. L. (1980). *Human memory: Structures and processes* (2nd ed.). New York: W. H. Freeman.

Köhler, W. (1925). *The mentality of apes* (E. Winter, Trans.). New York: Harcourt Brace Jovanovich.

König, P., & Verschure, F. M. J. (2002). Neurons in action. *Science, 296*, 1817–1818.

Kosslyn, S. M., & Sussman, A. L. (1995). Roles of imagery in perception: Or, there is no such thing as immaculate perception. In M. S. Gazzaniga (Ed.), *The cognitive neurosciences.* Cambridge, MA: MIT Press.

Krcmar, M., & Cooke, M. (2001). Children's moral reasoning and their perceptions of television violence. *Journal of Communication, 51*, 300–316.

Kroll, N. E. A., Ogawa, K. H., & Nieters, J. E. (1988). Eyewitness memory of the importance of sequential information. *Bulletin of the Psychonomic Society, 26*, 395–398.

Krueger, W. C. F. (1929). The effect of overlearning on retention. *Journal of Experimental Psychology, 12*, 71–81.

Lam, L., & Kirby, S. (2002). Is emotional intelligence an advantage? An exploration of the impact of emotional and general intelligence on individual performance. *Journal of Social Psychology, 142*, 133–143.

Lambert, W. E., Genesee, F., Holobow, N., & Chartrand, L. (1993). Bilingual education for majority English-speaking children. *European Journal of Psychology Education, 8*, 3–22.

Lang, A., Craske, M., Brown, M., & Ghaneian, A. (2001). Fear-related state dependent memory. *Cognition & Emotion, 15*, 695–703.

Larson, R., & Verma, S. (1999). How children and adolescents spend time across the world: Work, play, and developmental opportunities. *Psychological Bulletin, 125*, 701–736.

Laurent, J., Swerdik, M., & Ryburn, M. (1992). Review of validity research on the Stanford-Binet Intelligence Scale: Fourth Edition. *Psychological Assessment, 4*, 102–112.

Lee, I., & Kesner, R. (2002). Differential contribution of NMDA receptors in hippocampal subregions to spatial working memory. *Nature Neuroscience, 5*, 162–168.

Lehmann, H., Treit, D., & Parent, M. B. (2000). Amygdala lesions do not impair shock-probe avoidance retention performance. *Behavioral Neuroscience, 114*, 1107–1116.

Leichtman, M. D., & Ceci, S. J. (1995). The effects of stereotypes and suggestions on preschoolers' reports. *Developmental Psychology, 31*, 568–578.

Lenat, D. B. (1995, September). Artificial intelligence. *Scientific American, 273*, 80–82.

Lerman, D. C., & Iwata, B. A. (1996). Developing a technology for the use of operant extinction in clinical settings: An examination of basic and applied research. *Journal of Applied Behavior Analysis, 29*, 345–382.

Lerman, D. C., Iwata, B. A., Shore, B. A., & Kahng, S. W. (1996). Responding maintained by intermittent reinforcement: Implications for the use of extinction with problem behavior in clinical settings. *Journal of Applied Behavior Analysis, 29*, 153–171.

Lewinsohn, P. M., & Rosenbaum, M. (1987). Recall of parental behavior by acute depressives, remitted depressives, and nondepressives. *Journal of Personality and Social Psychology, 52*, 611–619.

Lidz, C., & Macrine, S. (2001). An alternative approach to the identification of gifted culturally and linguistically diverse learners: The contribution of dynamic assessment. *School Psychology International, 22*, 74–96.

Linn, M. C., & Hyde, J. S. (1989). Gender, mathematics, and science. *Educational Researcher, 18*, 17–27.

Linn, M. C., & Peterson, A. C. (1985). Emergence and characterization of sex differences in spatial ability: A meta-analysis. *Child Development, 56*, 1479–1498.

Linn, R. L. (1982). Ability testing: Individual differences, prediction, and differential prediction. In A. K. Wigdor & W. R. Garner (Eds.), *Ability testing: Uses, consequences, and controversies* (Part II). Washington, DC: National Academy Press.

Loftus, E. F. (1979). *Eyewitness testimony.* Cambridge, MA: Harvard University Press.

Loftus, E. F. (1984, February). Eyewitnesses: Essential but unreliable. *Psychology Today,* pp. 22–27.

Loftus, E. F. (1993a). Psychologists in the eyewitness world. *American Psychologist, 48*, 550–552.

Loftus, E. F. (1993b). The reality of repressed memories. *American Psychologist, 48*, 518–537.

Loftus, E. F. (1997). Creating false memories. *Scientific American, 277*, 71–75.

Loftus, E. F., & Hoffman, H. G. (1989). Misinformation and memory: The creation of new memories. *Journal of Experimental Psychology: General, 118*, 100–104.

Loftus, E. F., Loftus, G. R. (1980). On the permanence of stored information in the human brain. *American Psychologist, 35*, 409–420.

Loftus, E. F., & Pickrell, J. (1995). The formation of false memories. *Psychiatric Annals, 25*, 720–725.

London, E. D., Ernst, M., Grant, S., Bonson, K., & Weinstein, A. (2000). Orbitofrontal cortex and human drug abuse: Functional imaging. *Cerebral Cortex, 10*, 334–342.

Lopez, J. C. (2000). Shaky memories in indelible ink. *Nature Reviews Neuroscience, 1*, 6–7.

Lotze, M., Montoya, P., Erb, M., Hulsmann, E., Flor, H., Klose, U., Birbaumer, N., & Grodd, W. (1999). Activation of cortical and cerebellar motor areas during executed and imagined hand movements: An fMRI study. *Journal of Cognitive Neuroscience, 11*, 491–501.

Lubinsky, D., & Benbow, C. P. (1992). Gender differences in abilities and preferences among the gifted: Implications for the math science pipeline. *Current Directions in Psychological Science, 1*, 61–66.

Luciano, M., Wright, M., Smith, G., Geffen, G., Geffen, L., & Martin, N. (2001). Genetic covariance among measures of information processing speed, working memory, and IQ. *Behavior Genetics, 31*, 581–592.

Luciano, M., Wright, M., Smith, G., Geffen, G., Geffen, L., & Martin, N. (2003). Genetic covariance between processing speed and IQ. In R. Plomin, J. DeFries, I. Craig, & P. McGuffin (Eds.), *Behavioral genetics in the postgenomic era* (pp. 163–182). Washington, DC: American Psychological Association.

Lummis, M., & Stevenson, H. W. (1990). Gender differences in beliefs about achievement: A cross-cultural study. *Developmental Psychology, 26*, 254–263.

Lustig, C., & Hasher, L. (2002). Working memory span: The effect of prior learning. *American Journal of Psychology, 115*, 89–101.

Maguire, E. A., Gadian, D. G., Johnsrude, I. S., Good, C. D., Ashburner, J., Frackowiak, R. S. J., & Frith, C. D. (2000). Navigation-related structural change in the hippocampi of taxi drivers. *Proceedings of the National Academy of Science, 97*, 4398–4403.

Markovic, B. M., Dimitrijevic, M., & Jankovic, B. D. (1993). Immunomodulation by conditioning: Recent developments. *International Journal of Neuroscience, 71*, 231–249.

Martinez, J. L., Jr., & Derrick, B. E. (1996). Long-term potentiation and learning. *Annual Review of Psychology, 47*, 173–203.

Mazur, J. E. (1993). Predicting the strength of a conditioned reinforcer: Effects of delay and uncertainty. *Current Directions in Psychological Science, 2*(3), 70–74.

McClearn, G. E., Johansson, B., Berg, S., Pedersen, N. J., Ahern, F., Petrill, S. A., & Plomin, R. (1997). Substantial genetic influence on cognitive abilities in twins 80 or more years old. *Science, 276*, 1560–1563.

McDonald, J. L. (1997). Language acquisition: The acquisition of linguistic structure in normal and special populations. *Annual Review of Psychology, 48*, 215–241.

McElree, B., Jia, G., & Litvak, A. (2000). The time course of conceptual processing in three bilingual populations. *Journal of Memory & Language, 42*, 229–254.

McKellar, P. (1972). Imagery from the standpoint of introspection. In P. W. Sheehan (Ed.), *The function and nature of imagery* (pp. 36–63). New York: Academic Press.

McKelvie, S. J. (1984). Relationship between set and functional fixedness: A replication. *Perceptual and Motor Skills, 58,* 996–998.

Mednick, S. A., & Mednick, M. T. (1967). *Examiner's manual, Remote Associates Test.* Boston: Houghton-Mifflin.

Mellet, E., Tzourio-Mazoyer, N., Bricogne, S., Mazoyer, B., Dennis, M., & Kosslyn, S. M. (2000). Functional anatomy of high-resolution visual mental imagery. *Journal of Cognitive Neuroscience, 12,* 98–109.

Merckelbach, H., Kekkers, T., Wessel, I., & Roefs, A. (2003). Dissociative symptoms and amnesia in Dutch concentration camp survivors. *Comprehensive Psychiatry, 44,* 65–69.

Miller, G. A. (1956). The magical number seven, plus or minus two: Some limits on our capacity for processing information. *Psychologic Review, 63,* 81–97.

Miller, L. (1989, November). What biofeedback does (and doesn't) do. *Psychology Today,* pp. 22–23.

Miller, N. E. (1985, February). Rx: Biofeedback. *Psychology Today,* pp. 54–59.

Milner, B. (1970). Memory and the medial temporal regions of the brain. In K. H. Pribram & D. E. Broadbent (Eds.), *Biology of memory.* New York: Academic Press.

Milner, B., Corkin, S., & Teuber, H. L. (1968). Further analysis the hippocampal amnesic syndrome: 14-year follow-up study of H. M. *Neuropsychologia, 6,* 215–234.

Milner, B. R. (1966). Amnesia following operation on the temporal lobes. In C. W. M. Whitty & O. L. Zangwill (Eds.), *Amnesia* (pp. 109–133). London: Butterworth.

Mishra, R., & Smith, T. (1992). Memories of Asur children for locations and pairs of pictures. *Psychological Studies, 37,* 38–46.

Mistry, J., & Rogoff, B. (1994). Remembering in cultural context. In W. J. Lonner & R. Malpass (Eds.), *Psychology and culture* (pp. 139–144). Boston: Allyn & Bacon.

Moffitt, T. E., Caspi, A., Harkness, A. R., & Silva, P. A. (1993). The natural history of change in intellectual performance: Who changes? How much? Is it meaningful? *Journal of Child Psychology and Psychiatry, 34,* 455–506.

Mohanty, A., & Perregaux, C. (1997). Language acquisition and bilingualism. In J. Berry, P. Dasen, & T. Saraswathi (Eds.), *Handbook of cross-cultural psychology. Vol. 2: Basic processes and human development.* Boston: Allyn & Bacon.

Morgan, C. L. (1996). Odors as cues for the recall of words unrelated to odor. *Perceptual and Motor Skills, 83,* 1227–1234.

Morgan, R. E., Levitsky, D. A., & Strupp, B. J. (2000). Effects of chronic lead exposure on learning and reaction time in a visual discrimination task. *Neurotoxicology and Teratology, 22,* 337–345.

Morrison, P., Allardyce, J., & McKane, J. (2002). Fear knot: Neurobiological disruption of long-term memory. *British Journal of Psychiatry, 180,* 195–197.

Morrow, B. A., Roth, R. H., & Elsworth, J. D. (2000). TMT, a predator odor, elevates mesoprefontal dopamine metabolic activity and disrupts short-term working memory in the rat. *Brain Research Bulletin, 52,* 519–523.

Nader, K., Schafe, G. E., & Le Doux, J. E. (2000). Fear memories require protein synthesis in the amygdala for reconsolidation after retrieval. 722–726.

Neisser, U. (1967). *Cognitive Psychology.* New York: Appleton-Century-Crofts.

Neisser, U., Boodoo, G., Bouchard, T. J., Jr., Boykin, A. W., Brody, N., Ceci, S. J., Halpern, D. F., Loehlin, J. C., Perloff, R., Sternberg, R. J., & Urbina, S. (1996). Intelligence: Knowns and unknowns. *American Psychologist, 51,* 77–101.

Neisser, U., & Harsch, N. (1992). Phantom flashbulbs: False recollections of hearing the news about Challenger. In E. Winograd & U. Neisser (Eds.), *Affect and accuracy in recall: Studies of "flashbulb" memories* (pp. 9–31). New York: Cambridge University Press.

Newell, A., & Simon, H. A. (1972). *Human problem solving.* Englewood Cliffs, NJ: Prentice-Hall.

Ng, S. H. (1990). Androcentric coding of man and his in memory by language users. *Journal of Experimental Social Psychology, 26,* 455–464.

Nguyen, P. V., Abel, T., & Kandel, E. R. (1994). Requirement of a critical period of transcription for induction of a late phase of LTP. *Science, 265,* 1104–1107.

Ni., W., Constable, R. T., Menci, W. E., Pugh, K. R., Fulbright, R. K., & Shaywitz, S. E. (2000). An event-related neuroimaging study distinguishing form and content in sentence processing. *Journal of Cognitive Neuroscience, 12,* 120–133.

Nickerson, R. S., & Adams, M. J. (1979). Long-term memory for a common object. *Cognitive Psychology, 11,* 287–307.

Oller, D., Cobo-Lewis, A., & Eilers, R. (1998). Phonological translation in bilingual and monolingual children. *Applied Psycholinguistics, 19,* 259–278.

O'Neil, H. (2000, September 28). A perfect witness. *St. Louis Post-Dispatch,* p. A8.

Overmeier, J. B., & Seligman, M. E. P. (1967). Effects of inescapable shock upon subsequent escape and avoidance responding. *Journal of Comparative and Physiological Psychology, 67,* 28–33.

Parke, R. D. (1977). Some effects of punishment on children's behavior—revisited. In E. M. Heterington, E. M. Ross, & R. D. Parke (Eds.), *Contemporary readings in child psychology.* New York: McGraw-Hill.

Patricelli, G., Uy, J., Walsh, G., & Borgia, G. (2002). Male displays adjusted to female's response. *Nature, 415,* 279–280.

Patterson, J. (1998). Expressive vocabulary of bilingual toddlers: Preliminary findings. *Electronic Multicultural Journal of Communication Disorders, 1,* Retrieved April 11, 2001, from www.asha.ucf.edu/patterson.html

Paulesu, E., McCrory, E., Fazio, L., Menoncello, N., Brunswick, N., Cappa, S. F., et al. (2000). A cultural effect on brain function. *Nature Neuroscience, 3,* 91–96.

Pavlov, I. P. (1960). *Conditioned reflexes: An investigation of the physiological activity of the cerebral cortex* (G. V. Anrep, Trans.). New York: Dover. (Original translation published 1927).

Penfield, W. (1969). Consciousness, memory, and man's conditioned reflexes. In K. Pribram (Ed.), *On the biology of learning* (pp. 129–168). New York: Harcourt Brace Jovanovich.

Penfield, W. (1975). *The mystery of the mind: A critical study of consciousness and the human brain.* Princeton, NJ: Princeton University Press.

Pepperberg, I. M. (1991, Spring). Referential communication with an African grey parrot. *Harvard Graduate Society Newsletter,* 1–4.

Pepperberg, I. M. (1994a). Numerical competence in an African gray parrot (Psittaqcus erithacus). *Journal of Comparative Psychology, 108,* 36–44.

Pepperberg, I. M. (1994b). Vocal learning in grey parrots (*Psittacus erithacus*): Effects of social interaction, reference, and context. *The Auk, 111,* 300–314.

Peterson, I. (1993). Speech for export: Automating the translation of spoken words. *Science News, 144,* 254–255.

Peterson, L. R., & Peterson, M. J. (1959). Short-term retention of individual verbal items. *Journal of Experimental Psychology, 58,* 193–198.

Pinker, S. (1994). *The language instinct: How the mind creates language.* New York: Morrow.

Pitz, G. F., & Sachs, N. J. (1984). Judgment and decision: Theory and application. *Annual Review of Psychology, 35,* 139–163.

Plomin, R. (2003). General cognitive ability. In R. Plomin, J. DeFries, I. Craig, & P. McGuffin (Eds.), *Behavioral genetics in the postgenomic era* (pp. 183–202). Washington, DC: American Psychological Association.

Plomin, R., DeFries, J. C., McClearn, G. E., & Rutter, M. (1997). *Behavioral genetics* (3rd ed.). New York: Freeman.

Plomin, R., Owen, M. J., & McGuffin, P. (1994). The genetic basis of complex human behaviors. *Science, 264,* 1733–1739.

Plomin, R., & Rende, R. (1991). Human behavioral genetics. *Annual Review of Psychology, 42,* 161–190.

Postman, L., & Phillips, L. W. (1965). Short-term temporal changes in free recall. *Quarterly Journal of Experimental Psychology, 17,* 132–138.

Premack, D. (1971). Language in chimpanzees. *Science, 172,* 808–822.

Premack, D., & Premack, A. J. (1983). *The mind of an ape.* New York: Norton.

Pryke, S., Lindsay, R. C. L., & Pozzulo, J. D. (2000). Sorting mug shots: Methodological issues. *Applied Cognitive Psychology, 14,* 81–96.

Psychologists' pigeons score 90 pct. picking Picasso. (1995, May 7). *St. Louis Post-Dispatch,* p. 2A.

Pulvermüller, F., Mohr, B., Schleichert, H., & Veit, R. (2000). Operant conditioning of left-hemispheric slow cortical potentials and its effect on word processing. *Biological Psychology, 53,* 177–215.

Ragozzino, M., Detrick, S., & Kesner, R. (2002). The effects of prelimbic and infralimbic lesions on working memory for visual objects in rats. *Neurobiology of Learning & Memory, 77,* 29–43.

Ramey, C. (1993). A rejoinder to Spitz's critique of the Abecedarian experiment. *Intelligence, 17,* 25–30.

Ramey, C., & Campbell, F. (1987). The Carolina Abecedarian project. An educational experiment concerning human maleability. In J. J. Gallagher & C. T. Ramey (Eds.), *The malleability of children* (pp. 127–140). Baltimore: Brookes.

Rao, S. C., Rainer, G., & Miller, E. K. (1997). Integration of what and where in the primate prefrontal cortex. *Science, 276,* 821–824.

Rescorla, R. A. (1967). Pavlovian conditioning and its proper control procedures. *Psychological Review, 74,* 71–80.

Rescorla, R. A. (1968). Probability of shock in the presence and absence of CS in fear conditioning. *Journal of Comparative and Physiological Psychology, 66,* 1–5.

Rescorla, R. A. (1988). Pavlovian conditioning: It's not what you think it is. *American Psychologist, 43,* 151–160.

Rescorla, R. A., & Wagner, A. R. (1972). A theory of Pavlovian conditioning: Variations in the effectiveness of reinforcement and nonreinforcement. In A. Black & W. F. Prokasy (Eds.), *Classical conditioning: II. Current research and theory.* New York: Appleton.

Restak, R. (1988). *The mind.* Toronto: Bantam.

Richter, W., Somorjai, R., Summers, R., Jarmasz, M., Ravi, S., Menon, J. S., et al. (2000). Motor area activity during mental rotation studied by time-resolved single-trial fMRI. *Journal of Cognitive Neuroscience, 12,* 310–320.

Riedel, G. (1996). Function of metabotropic glutamate receptors in learning and memory. *Trends in Neurosciences, 19,* 219–224.

Roediger, H. L., III, & McDermott, K. B. (1995). Creating false memories: Remembering words not presented in lists. *Journal of Experimental Psychology: Learning, Memory, and Cognition, 21,* 803–814.

Rogolf, B., & Mistry, J. (1985). Memory development in cultural context. In M. Pressley & C. Brainerd (Eds.), *The cognitive side of memory development.* New York: Springer-Verlag.

Rosch, E. H. (1973). Natural categories. *Cognitive Psychology, 4,* 328–350.

Rosch, E. H. (1978). Principles of categorization. In E. H. Rosch & B. Lloyd (Eds.), *Cognition and categorization.* Hillsdale, NJ: Erlbaum.

Rosch, E. H. (1987). Linguistic relativity. *Et Cetera, 44,* 254–279.

Rozell, E., Pettijohn, C., & Parker, R. (2002). An empirical evaluation of emotional intelligence: The impact on management development. *Journal of Management Development, 21,* 272–289.

Rumbaugh, D. M. (1977). *Language learning by a chimpanzee: The Lana project.* New York: Academic Press.

Salovey, P., & Mayer, J. D. (1990). Emotional intelligence. *Imagination, cognition, and personality, 9,* 185–211.

Savage-Rumbaugh, E. S. (1986). *Ape language.* New York: Columbia University Press.

Savage-Rumbaugh, E. S. (1990). Language acquisition in a nonhuman species: Implications for the innateness debate. *Developmental Psychology, 26,* 599–620.

Savage-Rumbaugh, E. S. (1993). Language learnability in man, ape, and dolphin. IN H. L. Roitblat, L. M. Herman, & P. E. Nachtigall (Eds.), *Language and communication: Comparative perspectives. Comparative cognition and neuroscience* (pp. 457–484). Hillsdale, NJ: Erlbaum.

Savage-Rumbaugh, E. S., Sevcik, R. A., Brakke, K. E., & Rumbaugh, D. M. (1992). Symbols: Their communicative use, communication, and combination by bonobos (Pan paniscus). In L. P. Lipsitt & C. Rovee-Collier (Eds.). *Advances in infancy research* (Vol. 7, pp. 221–278). Norwood, NJ: Ablex.

Scarr, S., & Weinberg, R. (1976). The influence of "family background" on intellectual attainment. *American Sociological Review, 43,* 674–692.

Scheuffgen, K., Happé, F., Anderson, M., & Frith, U. (2000). High "intelligence," low "IQ"? Speed of processing and measured IQ in children with autism. *Developmental Psychopathology, 12,* 183–190.

Schiff, M., & Lewontin, R. (1986). *Education and class: The irrelevance of IQ genetic studies.* Oxford, England: Clarendon.

Schreurs, B. G. (1989). Classical conditioning of model systems: A behavioral review. *Psychobiology, 17,* 145–155.

Seligman, M. E. P. (1970). On the generality of the laws of learning. *Psychological Review, 77,* 406–418.

Seligman, M. E. P. (1972). Phobias and preparedness. In M. E. P. Seligman & J. L. Hager (Eds.), *Biological boundaries of learning.* Englewood Cliffs, NJ: Prentice Hall.

Seligman, M. E. P. (1975). *Helplessness: On depression, development and death.* San Francisco: Freeman.

Seligman, M. E. P. (1991). *Learned optimism.* New York: Knopf.

Shaw, J. S. III. (1996). Increases in eyewitness confidence resulting from postevent questioning. *Journal of Experimental Psychology: Applied, 2,* 126–146.

Shneidman, E. (1989). The Indian summer of life: A preliminary study of septuagenarians. *American Psychologist, 44,* 684–694.

Shneidman, E. S. (1994). Clues to suicide, reconsidered. *Suicide and Life-Threatening Behavior, 24,* 395–397.

Shoda, Y., Mischel, W., & Peake, P. K. (1990). Predicting adolescent cognitive and self-regulatory competencies from preschool delay of gratification. *Developmental Psychology, 26*, 978–986.

Skinner, B. F. (1953). *Science and human behavior.* New York: Macmillan.

Spearman, C. (1927). *The abilities of man.* New York: Macmillan.

Sperling, G. (1960). The information available in brief visual presentations. *Psychological Monographs: General and Applied, 74*, Whole No. 498, 1–29.

Spiers, H., Maguire, E., & Burgess, N. (2001). Hippocampal amnesia. *Neurocase, 7*, 357–382.

Sporer, S. L., Penrod, S., Read, D., & Cutler, B. (1995). Choosing, confidence, and accuracy: A meta-analysis of the confidence-accuracy relation in eyewitness identification studies. *Psychological Bulletin, 118*, 315–327.

Squire, L. R. (1992). Memory and the hippocampus: A synthesis from findings with rats, monkeys, and humans. *Psychological Review, 99*, 195–231.

Squire, L. R., Knowlton, B., & Musen, G. (1993). The structure and organization of memory. *Annual Review of Psychology, 44*, 453–495.

Stafford, J., & Lynn, S. (2002). Cultural scripts, memories of childhood abuse, and multiple identities: A study of role-played enactments. *International Journal of Clinical & Experimental Hypnosis, 50*, 67–85.

Stanton, M. E. (2000). Multiple memory systems, development and conditioning. *Behavioural Brain Research, 110*, 25–37.

Steblay, N. M. (1992). A meta-analytic review of the weapon focus effect. *Law and Human Behavior, 16*, 413–424.

Steffensen, M., & Calker, L. (1982). Intercultural misunderstandings about health care: Recall of descriptions of illness and treatments. *Social Science and Medicine, 16*, 1949–1954.

Steinmetz, J. E. (2000). Brain substrates of classical eyeblink conditioning: A highly localized but also distributed system. *Behavioural Brain Research, 110*, 13–24.

Sternberg, R., Castejon, J., Prieto, M., Hautamacki, J., & Grogorenko, E. (2001). Confirmatory factor analysis of the Sternberg Triarchic Abilities Test in three international samples: An empirical test of the triarchic theory of intelligence. *European Journal of Psychological Assessment, 17*, 1–16.

Stern, W. (1914). *The psychological methods of testing intelligence.* Baltimore: Warwick and York.

Sternberg, R. J. (1985a). *Beyond IQ: A triarchic theory of human intelligence.* New York: Cambridge University Press.

Sternberg, R. J. (1986a). *Intelligence applied: Understanding and increasing your intellectual skills.* San Diego: Harcourt Brace Jovanovich.

Stevenson, H. W. (1992). Learning from Asian schools. *Scientific American, 267*, 70–76.

Stevenson, H. W. Chen, C., & Lee, S. Y. (1993). Mathematics achievement of Chinese, Japanese, and American children: Ten years later. *Science, 259*, 53–58.

Stevenson, H. W., Lee, S. Y., Chen, C., Stigler, J. W., Hsu, C. C., & Kitamura, S. (1990). Contexts of achievement. *Monographs of the Society for Research in Child Development, 55*(1–2, Serial No. 221).

Stevenson, H. W., Lee, S. Y., & Stigler, J. W. (1986). Mathematics achievement of Chinese, Japanese, and American children. *Science, 231*, 693–699.

Sweatt, J. D., & Kandel, E. R. (1989). Persistent and transcriptionally dependent increase in protein phosphorylation in long-term facilitation of Aplysia sensory neurons. *Nature, 339*, 51–54.

Sweller, J., & Levine, M. (1982). Effects of goal specificity on means-end analysis and learning. *Journal of Experimental Psychology: Learning, Memory, and Cognition, 8*, 463–474.

Symons, C. S., & Johnson, B. T. (1997). The self-reference effect in memory: A meta-analysis. *Psychological Bulletin, 121*, 371–394.

Tanner, J. M. (1990). *Fetus into man* (2nd ed.). Cambridge MA: Harvard University Press.

Taylor, D. M., Helms Tillery, S. J., & Schwartz, A. B. (2002). Direct cortical control of 3D neuroprosthetic devices. *Science, 296*, 1829–1832.

Teng, E., Stefanacci, L., Squire, L. R., & Zola, S. M. (2000). Contrasting effects on discrimination learning after hippocampal lesions and conjoint hippocampal-caudate lesions in monkeys. *Journal of Neuroscience, 20*, 3853–3863.

Terman, L. M. (1925). *Genetic studies of genius, Vol. 1: Mental and physical traits of a thousand gifted children.* Stanford, CA: Stanford University Press.

Terman, L. M., & Oden, M. H. (1947). *Genetic studies of genius, Vol. 4: The gifted child grows up.* Stanford, CA: Stanford University Press.

Terrace, H. S. (1979, November). How Nim Chimpski changed my mind. *Psychology Today*, 65–76.

Terrace, H. S. (1981). A report to an academy. *Annals of the New York Academy of Sciences, 364*, 115–129.

Terrace, H. S. (1985). In the beginning was the "name." *American Psychologist, 40*, 1011–1028.

Terrace, H. S. (1986). *Nim: A chimpanzee who learned sign language.* New York: Columbia University Press.

Thompson, R. F., Swain, R., Clark, R., & Shinkman, P. (2000). Intracerebellar conditioning—Brogden and Gantt revisited. *Behavioural Brain Research, 110*, 2–11.

Thorn, A., & Gathercole, S. (1999). Language-specific knowledge and short-term memory in bilingual and non-bilingual children. *Quarterly Journal of Experimental Psychology: Human Experimental Psychology, 52A*, 303–324.

Thorndike, E. (1989). Some experiments on animal intelligence. *Science, 7*(181), 818–824.

Thorndike, E. L. (1970). *Animal intelligence: Experimental studies.* New York: Macmillan. (Original work published 1911).

Thurstone, L. L. (1938). *Primary mental abilities.* Chicago: University of Chicago Press.

Tolman, E. C. (1932). *Purposive behavior in animals and men.* New York: Appleton-Century-Crofts.

Tolman, E. C., & Honzik, C. H. (1930). Introduction and removal of reward, and maze performance in rats. *University of California Publications in Psychology, 4*, 257–275.

Tulving, E. (1974). Cue-dependent forgetting. *American Scientist, 62*, 74–82.

Tulving, E. (2002). Episodic memory: From mind to brain. *Annual Review of Psychology, 53*, 1–25.

Tulving, E., & Thompson, D. M. (1973). Encoding specificity and retrieval processes in episodic memory. *Psychological Review, 80*, 352–373.

Tversky, A. (1972). Elimination by aspects: A theory of choice. *Psychological Review, 79*, 281–299.

Underwood, B. J. (1957). Interference and forgetting. *Psychological Review, 64*, 49–60.

U.S. Bureau of the Census. (2001). *Statistical abstract of the United States.* Washington, DC: U.S. Government Printing Office.

van den Hout, M., & Merckelbach, H. (1991). Classical conditioning: Still going strong. *Behavioural Psychotherapy, 19*, 59–79.

Van der Zee, K., Thijs, M., & Schakel, L. (2002). The relationship of emotional intelligence with academic intelligence and the Big Five. *European Journal of Personality, 16*, 103–125.

Vargha-Khadem, F., Gadian, D. G., Watkins, D. E., Connelly, A., Van Paesschen, W., & Mishkin, M. (1997). Differential effects of early hippocampal pathology on episodic and semantic memory. *Science, 277*, 376–380.

Vazdarjanova, A. (2000). Does the basolateral amygdala store memories for emotional events? *Trends in Neurosciences, 23*, 345–346.

Villani, S. (2001). Impact of media on children and adolescents: A 10-year review of the research. *Journal of the American Academy of Child & Adolescent Psychiatry, 40*, 392–401.

Vuorenkoski, L., Kuure, O., Moilanen, I., & Peninkilampi, V. (2000). Bilingualism, school achievement, and mental well-being: A follow-up study of return migrant children. *Journal of Child Psychology & Psychiatry & Allied Disciplines, 41*, 261–266.

Walters, C. C., & Grusec, J. E. (1977). *Punishment.* San Francisco: Freeman.

Wasserman, E. A., & Miller, R. R. (1997). What's elementary about associative learning? *Annual Review of Psychology, 48*, 573–607.

Watson, J. B., & Rayner, R. (1920). Conditioned emotional reactions. *Journal of Experimental Psychology, 3*, 1–14.

Weeks, D. L., & Anderson, L. P. (2000). The interaction of observational learning with overt practice: Effects on motor skill learning. *Acta Psychologia, 104*, 259–271.

Wells, G. L. (1993). What do we know about eyewitness identification? *American Psychologist, 48*, 553–571.

Wheeler, M. A., Stuss, D. T., & Tulving, E. (1997). Toward a theory of episodic memory: The frontal lobes and autonoetic consciousness. *Psychological Bulletin, 121*, 331–354.

Whitehouse, D. (2000). Rats control robot arm with brain power alone [on-line]. Retrieved from http://www.robotbooks.com/robot-rats.htm

Whorf, B. L. (1956). Science and linguistics. In J. B. Carroll (Ed.), *Language, thought, and reality: Selected writings of Benjamin Lee Whorf.* Cambridge, MA: MIT Press.

Widom, C. S. (1989). Does violence beget violence? A critical examination of the literature. *Psychological Bulletin, 106*, 3–28.

Widom, C. S., & Morris, S. (1997). Accuracy of adult recollections of childhood victimization: Part 2: Childhood sexual abuse. *Psychological Bulletin, 9*, 34–46.

Willoughby, T., Wood, E., McDermott, C., & McLaren, J. (2000). Enhancing learning through strategy instruction and group interaction: Is active generation of elaborations critical? *Applied Cognitive Psychology, 14*, 19–30.

Winograd, E. (1988). Some observations on prospective remembering. In M. M. Gruneberg, P. E. Morris, & R. N. Sykes (Eds.), *Practical aspects of memory: Current research and issues: Vol. 1* (pp. 348–353). Chichester, England: John Wiley & Sons.

Wood, W., Wong, F. Y., & Chachere, J. G. (1991). Effects of media violence on viewers' aggression in unconstrained social interaction. *Psychological Bulletin, 109*, 371–383.

Worthen, J., & Wood, V. (2001). Memory discrimination for self-performed and imagined acts: Bizarreness effects in false recognition. *Quarterly Journal of Experimental Psychology, 54A*, 49–67.

Zaragoza, M. S., & Mitchell, K. J. (1996). Repeated exposure to suggestion and the creation of false memories. *Psychological Science, 7*, 294–300.

Zola, S. M., Squire, L. R., Teng, E., Stenfanacci, L., Buffalo, E. A., & Clark, R. E. (2000). Impaired recognition memory in monkeys after damage limited to the hippocampal region. *Journal of Neuroscience, 20*, 451–463.

CHAPTER 11

BEING SICK OF THE HOSPITAL[1]

Material selected from:
Research Stories for Introductory Psychology,
Second Edition, by Lary Shaffer and Matthew R. Merrens

---

[1]Incorporating the research of D. H. Bovbjerg, W. H. Redd, L. A. Maier, J. C. Holland, L. M. Lesko, D. Niedzwiecki, S. C. Rubin, and T. B. Hakes, "Anticipatory Immune Suppression and Nausea in Women Receiving Cyclic Chemotherapy for Ovarian Cancer," 1990, *Journal of Consulting and Clinical Psychology, 58*, pp. 153–157.

Usually, people go to the hospital when they are ill. This chapter considers the reverse: the learning process through which the hospital, and the treatment associated with it, can make people sick. When you first consider a hospital making people sick, you may be tempted to focus on the food, which is stereotypically considered to be bad. In defense of the food, it is not like Mommy makes, but it is exactly what Mommy *would* make if she had to feed 1,000 or more people, many of whom are on highly specialized diets.

Because we are not talking about the food, what is it about a hospital that can make people sick? First, we need to be clear about what we mean by "sick." We mean *sick*, physically sick; sick in a way that can be measured using the kinds of assessments available to contemporary medicine. It is important to be precise about this; we are talking about the kind of illness that is technically called *somatoform* illness. Sometimes the older label for this disorder, *psychosomatic illness*, is used in popular media to mean an imaginary illness, one that has no physical basis. That is not correct. In a somatoform illness, a person really has observable symptoms but, unlike other illnesses, the cause is not some obvious disease organism, such as a virus or a bacterium. This is not to suggest the causes of somatoform illness are mystical or unknowable. The causes of somatoform disorders are just as concrete as viruses and bacteria. In the case to be discussed here, no one would argue about the concreteness of the causes: the hospital was made of concrete. We are doing more than playing with words. The research to be discussed has shown that a hospital, in all its concrete and glass glory, can make people sick.

In order to understand how this can happen, we have to follow a path that connects the hospital to the illness through a process of learning. The special kind of learning that was implicated in this example is called classical conditioning, or Pavlovian conditioning, after its discoverer, Ivan Pavlov (1849–1936). We will briefly consider Pavlov's work before returning to the illustration of somatoform illness. There are at least two reasons for this detour. First, you should know a few things about Pavlov. Although we try to focus on contemporary psychology in this book, there are a few examples of psychological phenomena that are so well known that they are familiar to any educated person. Pavlov's work is one of these. It is an important model, or way of thinking, about certain types of events in psychology. These models are sometimes called paradigms (pronounced *pair-ah-dimes*). A second and perhaps more compelling reason is that the hospital illustration, and many other examples from life, cannot be understood without a clear understanding of the Pavlovian paradigm.

GOING TO THE DOGS

Initially Pavlov did not seek to find out about somatoform illness, or even about learning. Pavlov lived and worked in Russia and was educated as a physiologist. He studied at the University of St. Petersburg, a center of intellectual life in a largely agrarian country, which otherwise had high levels of illiteracy. In this setting, Pavlov was aware of the privilege afforded by a university education. As a young man he was very much influenced by the study of reflexes. Reflexes were considered to be automatic responses to stimuli, responses that did not require any conscious thought or planning. With some slight refinement, this basic definition is still used today. The physiologists of Pavlov's student days considered reflexes to be the basic building blocks of behavior. Complex behaviors were presumed to be made of reflexes, in the same way that a brick wall is made of bricks. In particular, Pavlov was greatly impressed by the work of Sechenov, the professor of physiology at St. Petersburg. Sechenov believed that all physical acts were reflexes and that the study of reflexes would move psychology away from philosophy and "the deceitful voice of consciousness [to] positive facts or points of departure that can be verified at any time by experiment" (quoted from Frolov, 1938, p. 6). Clearly, the scientific establishment of the time felt some uncertainty about the emerging field of psychology and wished its approach and content to be more like that of other sciences. So do we.

Pavlov worked for many years studying digestive physiology. He approached digestion by observing it in animals who were alive and who were functioning as normally as possible. He developed masterful surgical techniques for collecting and studying saliva and gastric juices from the stomach. Pavlov even augmented his meager research budget by selling gastric juice from dogs to the general public as a supposed aid for stomach problems (Babkin, 1940). This stuff did not turn out to be a miracle cure and probably tasted just as you might imagine it would. If anything, its sales bring credit to Pavlov's ability to sell his ideas to others.

In 1904 Pavlov was awarded the Nobel Prize for his research on digestion. Pavlov's formal speech on the occasion of the award spoke little about digestion but, rather, presented some other observations he had made while doing the digestion research. The observations he recounted took him to the forefront of psychology. He retains this position today, almost 100 years later.

In his work on the digestive processes of dogs, Pavlov had perfected a little operation in which a cut was made in the dog's cheek, allowing a tube to be introduced through the cheek and into the salivary duct. A glass vial at the end of this tube collected and measured the saliva produced in response to various stimuli (see Figure 11.1).

AN UNEXPECTED OBSERVATION

Pavlov was interested in studying the amount and timing of saliva production in response to various foods. Salivation was clearly a reflex because it did not have to be consciously turned on or off; it was an automatic response to food being placed in the dog's mouth. However, in the course of this work, Pavlov noticed dogs often salivated before the food was in the mouth. The dogs salivated when they saw food, when they saw a food bowl, or even when they heard the footsteps of laboratory personnel at feeding time. At first these responses were considered no more than nuisances that interfered with the study of digestion (Anokhin, 1971). Over time, Pavlov and his coworkers came to realize they had observed something very important. Because the stimulus for these salivary responses was not the usual stimulus, food in the mouth, something unusual was happening. Pavlov came to understand that he had observed a basic kind of learning.

Pavlov developed some terminology for describing this situation and, with slight modification, his descriptions continue to be used today. In the situation Pavlov described, the food is called the *unconditioned stimulus* (UCS) and the salivation is the *unconditioned response* (UCR). The word *conditioned* merely means learned, so when you are attempting to decode a situation using Pavlovian terms, you may find it

FIGURE 11.1   Classical Conditioning Apparatus Similar to That Used by Pavlov

helpful to substitute the word *learned* whenever you read the word *conditioned*. If you do this, it becomes a straightforward task to put a situation into Pavlovian terms. An *unconditioned* stimulus should always result in a particular *unconditioned* response without any learning, as that is the definition of *unconditioned*. Think of these responses to stimuli as reflexes. They are unlearned and automatic, requiring no thought or planning. If food is put in your mouth, you salivate. You do not have to plan or think about the response. You do not need to learn how to do this. If we were to pop a balloon right behind you, you would make a startle response—this is another example of an unconditioned stimulus and an unconditioned response. Yet another one: if you touch a hot iron you will pull your hand away quickly. In each of these examples, the stimulus is called the UCS (unconditioned stimulus) and the response is called the UCR (unconditioned response).

Pavlov's dogs experienced a repeated pairing of some other stimuli with the unconditioned stimulus (food). For example, each time a dog was given food—the UCS—this food was paired with the footsteps of a laboratory worker bringing it. After a number of pairings, the dogs learned that footsteps signaled the approach of food. Once this was learned, the saliva would begin to flow in response to the sound of the footsteps. In this new pairing of stimulus and response, the footsteps and the saliva were called, respectively, the *conditioned stimulus* and the *conditioned response*, or the CS and the CR. They were called the *conditioned stimulus* and the *conditioned response* because they were learned: the dog learned to make this response to a new stimulus. One way to diagrammatically represent this can be found in Figure 11.2.

When you are trying to analyze a Pavlovian or classical conditioning situation into its elements, you can use four guidelines to check your analysis:

1. The UCR and the CR will be responses—something that the organism does. The UCS and the CS will be stimuli, usually something in the environment, such as food or footsteps.
2. The UCR will be the organism's reflexive response, one that requires no learning. If the response has to be learned, it is not a UCR. By this logic, you should expect the same UCR to follow a particular UCS in all the members of a particular species.

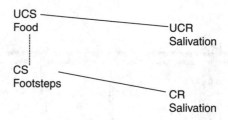

FIGURE 11.2   Pavlovian Analysis of Salivation

3. The stimulus that will become the CS should not lead to the response being studied until it has been paired with the UCS. Footsteps only resulted in salivation when repeatedly paired with the UCS, the food. Sometimes many pairings are required for classical conditioning; sometimes few are sufficient.
4. The UCR and the CR will appear to be the same behavior. The difference between them is that in one instance the response is not learned and in the other case the response is learned. The difference between the UCR and the CR is how behavior came to be produced by a stimulus: not learned or learned.

If you survey a number of sources that discuss classical conditioning, you may be surprised at how many give examples that contain errors because they do not pass these little tests. Probably the fourth guideline, similarity of UCR and CR, is the most often violated.

As a footnote to Pavlov's work, popular culture usually remembers the CS as a bell, not footsteps. Pavlov's early work on conditioning used a variety of stimuli for the CS including footsteps, a metronome, a variety of tones, and some visual stimuli.

Not all learning involves Pavlovian conditioning. In spite of the importance of the Pavlovian paradigm, it is quite restricted because it requires an unlearned association as the basis for subsequent learning. Although subsequent studies identified so-called higher-order conditioning in which an additional stimulus is paired with an already established CS, classical conditioning has to start with an unlearned association. Once you understand the components of the Pavlovian paradigm, you should quickly be able to determine if classical conditioning is at work in behavior you observe. Learning to play basketball, for example, has little if anything to do with classical conditioning. It is much better explained by the imitation of behavior and the resulting rewards, such as the ball going through the hoop or the cheers of others.

Probably the only way for you to thoroughly understand classical conditioning is for you to use the terms we have described and to try to apply them to new examples. When you can do this for novel examples, you own this concept. To give you a start, try to do a Pavlovian analysis, identifying the UCS, UCR, CS, and CR, in the following situation:

Imagine that you live in an old building with problematic plumbing. If you are in the shower and someone in the bathroom next door flushes the toilet, the cold water disappears from your shower. You feel the water temperature go from pleasantly warm to scalding, and you jump out of the shower. After a few experiences with this situation, you jump out when you hear the next-door toilet flush. Once you have assigned classical conditioning terms, you can check your Pavlovian analysis against Figure 11.3.

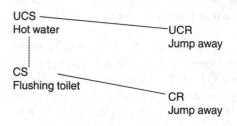

FIGURE 11.3   Pavlovian Analysis of Jumping Away from Hot Water

So much for dogs and toilets. You should, by now have a sufficient grasp of the concepts of classical conditioning to allow us to discuss the work of Dana Bovbjerg and colleagues about hospitals making people sick (Bovbjerg et al., 1990). It has been known since the 1980s that cancer patients who receive chemotherapy often experience two side effects of the treatment: nausea and suppression of the immune system (DeVita, Hellman, & Rosenberg, 1985). These outcomes were first noticed shortly after the treatment. However, some patients showed more puzzling symptoms of nausea or vomiting *before* each treatment. This was called Anticipatory Nausea and Vomiting, or ANV. Between one-quarter and three-quarters of patients were troubled by ANV. ANV seemed to be triggered by things as diverse as the sight of the clinic, the sound of a nurse's voice, or even the mere thought of treatment.

A number of clinical studies investigated ANV and the conclusions pointed to classical conditioning (Redd, 1989). If you want to test your ability to analyze this example in Pavlovian terms, stop here, look away, and do so before we give you the answer. The toxic drugs that are used in chemotherapy (UCS) make people feel nauseated (UCR). The hospital (CS) is constantly paired with the drug treatment (UCS) until the hospital (CS) itself makes people feel nauseated (CR). This is diagrammed in Figure 11.4.

The effects of this classical conditioning are so powerful that hospitals can still nauseate some former patients years after chemotherapy has ended (Cella, Pratt, & Holland, 1986). This fits with other research, which has shown that for many animals classical conditioning has long-lasting effects when feeling ill was the CR (see, for example, Gustafson, Garcia, Hawkins, & Rusinak, 1974).

The study by Bovbjerg et al. (1990) further investigated ANV and, in addition, sought evidence that anticipatory immune suppression (AIS) was also taking place in cancer patients. Immune suppression is the name given to a number of physiological responses that result in depressed functioning of the immune system. The immune system is the body's way of recognizing and dealing with disease organisms. When the immune system function decreases before some event, in this case chemotherapy, it is called Anticipatory Immune Suppression or AIS. AIS has been the subject of a number of other research studies because of its importance to clinical medicine (see, for example, Kiecolt-Glaser & Glaser, 1988).

PARTICIPANTS

Thirty-six patients were identified who had all undergone surgical treatment for ovarian cancer. These women also met other criteria for being participants, including: they had not been treated with chemotherapy for any prior illness, their treatment plan called for chemotherapy, they had already received at least three treatments, and they lived within a 2-hour driving time of the hospital where the chemotherapy was being given. Twenty-seven of the original 36 eligible women agreed to be in the study. Of these 27, 7 had to be dropped for a variety of reasons including eventual change of their chemotherapy treatment and difficulty in drawing blood from their veins.

PROCEDURES

During the course of the study, an appointment was made for a home visit at least 3 days before chemotherapy treatments. Blood was drawn for later analysis in order to assess immune system functioning. During the home visits, an experienced research technician administered some rating instruments

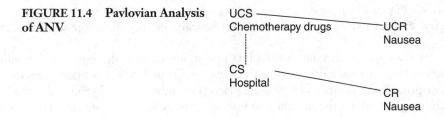

FIGURE 11.4 Pavlovian Analysis of ANV

UCS — Chemotherapy drugs ⟍ UCR Nausea

CS Hospital ⟍ CR Nausea

called *scales*. On one scale, patients were asked to rate their current level of nausea. They rated this by choosing a number from a visual scale in which numbers were arranged as if they were numbers on a thermometer. This is called a visual analog scale, or VAS. The VAS is a useful tool for the quantification of feelings. Turning subjective states into numbers makes it possible to deal with the data quantitatively by computing averages and drawing graphs. The amount of anxiety being experienced was recorded on a questionnaire, the Spielberger State-Trait Anxiety Inventory, or STAI, as well as by asking for a single assessment on another visual analog scale. These two anxiety measures were used so that one could be a reliability check for the other. Measures of anxiety can be imprecise, and having more than one was a way of boosting confidence in the results of the study.

Later, when participants arrived at the hospital, the anxiety measures were repeated. Participants were asked to recall and rate past feelings of nausea at three times before chemotherapy: the previous evening, on awakening the morning of chemotherapy, and immediately before chemotherapy was administered. Another sample of blood was drawn just before chemotherapy. The independent variable in this part of the study was the setting: home or hospital. The dependent measures were the ratings of anxiety, nausea, and analysis of immune functioning. This part of the study is a so-called *within-subjects* design. It is an experiment, but unlike some other experiments, the participants are their own control group. We saw this research design in the previous chapter. The same participants are exposed to two different situations, in this case, home and hospital.

RESULTS

Biochemical analyses of blood samples taken at home and at the hospital showed that there was not much suppression of the immune system at home. However, by the time the participants had arrived at the hospital, their blood samples showed biochemical indicators of immune function that were statistically significantly lower than in the home blood samples ($p < .001$). Lower immune function indicated that the immune response was worse. Sixteen of the 20 patients elected to receive some sedative drugs upon arrival at the hospital, prior to blood drawing. To ensure that these sedatives were not responsible for immune suppression, a separate statistical analysis was performed on the patients who did not wish to have any sedatives. The patients who had no sedatives also showed immune suppression, suggesting that sedatives were not suppressing the immune system. Although the researchers might have preferred to have no sedatives given to any of the participants in the study, it is important to understand that these "participants" were also people. In older studies the participants were usually referred to as *subjects*. This terminology is still used in phrases such as *within subjects design*, where no reference is made to specific people. The American Psychological Association now suggests that authors avoid the impersonal term *subjects* in the preparation of research reports (American Psychological Association, 1994). The word *subjects* is sterile, and one might forget that these participants were women, each recovering from surgical treatment of a frightening disease. It speaks very well of them that they were willing to participate in research and to tolerate additional procedures in the home and hospital in order to help advance scientific understanding.

The measures of anxiety, the Spielberger State-Trait Anxiety Inventory and the visual scale (VAS), both indicated higher levels of anxiety in the hospital than at home ($p = .036$; $p < .001$). In addition, the visual scale for nausea indicated that anticipatory nausea was a greater problem in the hospital than at home ($p = .008$) (see Figure 11.5).

In summary, levels of all three symptoms were statistically significantly lower at home than in the hospital.

Although, as a group, the women showed immune suppression in the hospital, five individuals within the group did not. An additional data analysis was performed in which these five women were considered as one group and the other women were placed in another group. In this quasi-experimental analysis, immune suppression was the variable that was being investigated by comparing the groups; one

FIGURE 11.5   Degree of Symptoms Reported by Chemotherapy Patients at Home and in the Hospital

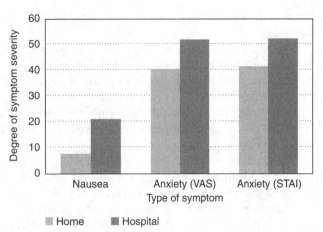

group had it and one group did not. Nausea and anxiety continued to be outcome measures. The finding was that there were no significant differences between the anxiety measures when the AIS group was compared to the non-AIS group. Both groups were anxious in the hospital. This can be interpreted as meaning that the subjective feelings of anxiety were not always linked to immune suppression. This was important because it indicated that anxiety was not always associated with immune suppression. It follows that finding ways to lower the anxiety felt by these women would not be expected to also help them with immune suppression. Anxiety and immune suppression are separate responses to the situation.

In contrast, in this analysis, the patients who had immune suppression also reported higher levels of nausea in the hospital than those who had no immune suppression ($p = .04$). In this case it seems possible that, because these symptoms are linked, dealing with one of them might help to treat the other. The discovery of a link of some sort can point the way to future research that may find causal links.

DISCUSSION

Bovbjerg et al. (1990) acknowledge their debt to studies of laboratory animals that pointed the way to this research. Lab animals can be used in studies that would not be ethically acceptable for human participants. It might be interesting to know what types of stimuli, other than hospitals, can serve as conditioned stimuli for immune suppression but ethics rightly limit research manipulations that can be performed on humans.

The sample in the Bovbjerg et al. (1990) study is small and the validity of the conclusions could be enhanced by replications on other groups of people. All science is tentative, particularly when studies report findings that have not been observed before. Nevertheless, this study was carefully conducted, and its findings make some important suggestions about anticipatory nausea and vomiting (ANV) and anticipatory immune suppression (AIS). In particular, it appears that increased anxiety is not, by itself, responsible for AIS. It is known that people undergoing stressful life events may show immune suppression (Kiecolt-Glaser & Glaser, 1988). In this study, however, small-group analysis suggested that anxiety did not always accompany immune suppression. If this finding were to be confirmed by other studies, it might lead to the practical suggestion that counseling to relieve anxiety would not be expected to help chemotherapy patients avoid AIS.

Both ANV and AIS were seen in this study in response to the hospital environment. Probably the best explanation for this was that they were simultaneously classical conditioned. Chemotherapy, the UCS, caused both nausea and immune suppression, the UCRs. As the chemotherapy was repeatedly paired with the hospital, the hospital itself became the CS for the CRs of ANV and AIS. This seems like alphabet soup, but when you can read this through and understand it, you are getting a grasp of classical conditioning.

The importance of the research can be illustrated by one case. Among the group of women studied by Bovbjerg et al. (1990), one person showed a dramatic 50 percent decrease in one of the measures of immune function. A person who is immuno-compromised to this extent, even before the chemotherapy has been administered, is at considerable risk for contracting other diseases. In spite of sanitation procedures, hospitals are, after all, full of disease organisms waiting for people to come by. For people with AIS, the hospital might not merely make them nauseated, it might play a role in making them severely ill owing to poor immune function.

Understanding is the first step toward finding a remedy. Other classically conditioned responses, such as unreasonable fears—called *phobias*—have been successfully treated by programs designed to gradually expose the participant to the fear-producing object. It is not clear that this process of systematic desensitization would help the chemotherapy patients, but it is an illustration that understanding classical conditioning can lead to treatment. Perhaps further work in this area will assure that, in the future, there is no need for the hospital to make people any sicker than they already are.

REFERENCES

American Psychological Association (1994). *Publication manual of the American Psychological Association* (4th ed.). Washington DC: Author.

Anokhin, P. K. (1971, March). Three giants of Soviet psychology. *Psychology Today*, 43–78.

Babkin, B. P. (1940). *Pavlov: A biography*. Chicago: University of Chicago Press.

Bovbjerg, D. H., Redd, W. H., Maier, L. A., Holland, J. C., Lesko, L. M., Niedzwiecki, D., Rubin, S. C., & Hakes, T. B. (1990). Anticipatory immune suppression and nausea in women receiving cyclic chemotherapy for ovarian cancer. *Journal of Consulting and Clinical Psychology, 58*, 153–157.

Cella, D. F., Pratt, A., & Holland, J. C. (1986). Persistent anticipatory nausea, vomiting and anxiety in cured Hodgkin's disease patients after completion of chemotherapy. *American Journal of Psychiatry, 143*, 641–643.

DeVita, V. T., Hellman, S., & Rosenberg, S. A. (1985). *Cancer: Principles and practice of oncology*. Philadelphia, PA: Lippincott.

Frolov, Y. P. (1938). *Pavlov and his school*. London: Kegan, Paul, Tench, Trubner.

Gustafson, C. R., Garcia, J., Hawkins, W., & Rusinak, K. (1974). Coyote predation control by aversive conditioning. *Science, 184*, 581–583.

Kiecolt-Glaser, J. K., & Glaser, R. (1988). Psychological influences on immunity: Implications for AIDS. *American Psychologist, 43*, 892–898,

Redd, W. H. (1989). Anticipatory nausea and vomiting and their management. In J. Holland & J. Rowland (Eds.), *Psychooncology* (pp. 423–433). New York: Oxford University Press.

CHAPTER 12

YOKING SMOKING[1]

Material selected from:
Research Stories for Introductory Psychology,
Second Edition, by Lary Shaffer and Matthew R. Merrens

---

[1]Incorporating the research of J. M. Roll, S. T. Higgins, and G. J. Badger, "An Experimental Comparison of Three Different Schedules of Reinforcement of Drug Abstinence Using Cigarette Smoking as an Exemplar," 1996, *Journal of Applied Behavior Analysis, 29,* pp. 495–505.

B. F. Skinner (1904–1990) started his academic life wanting to be a writer with an academic major in English. By the time his career was over, he was the best-known empirical psychologist of his time. He was a confirmed behaviorist and had little use for things inside the body, including mental events. He believed that mental characteristics were unobservable and, therefore, beyond the reach of science. For Skinner, proper scientific psychology should center its attention on the manipulation and measurement of the frequency of behavior. A great deal of Skinnerian psychology, also known as *operant conditioning*, can be summarized by the statement, *behavior is maintained by its consequences.* Skinner believed that the events that followed a behavior played a significant role in the subsequent frequency of the behavior. If pleasant stimuli followed a behavior, the behavior would increase in frequency. On the other hand, if unpleasant events followed the behavior, its frequency would decrease. If the behavior actually produced the consequences, Skinner would say that the consequences were *contingent* on the behavior.

PULLING HABITS OUT OF A RAT

Skinner believed that control over consequences would mean control over behavior. Many of his studies were carried out in an apparatus that he called an *operant chamber*, but almost everyone else calls it a *Skinner box*. The steps in the development of this device were amusingly described by Skinner (1956) in a well-known article entitled "A Case History in Scientific Method."

The Skinner box was a chamber tailored to the size of the organism under study. For example, a typical Skinner box for a rat might have dimensions of a little less than 1 foot on a side. The walls and lid were usually made of clear plastic to facilitate observation of the animal. The floor was a series of closely spaced metal bars. Usually one wall of the box was a control panel with a device variously called a *bar* or *lever* protruding from it. This smooth metal object was the correct height so that a rat could push it down. The wall with the control panel also typically included an automatic food or water dispenser, which could be programmed to deliver water or food rewards to the animal in a manner controlled by the researcher (see Figure 12.1).

FIGURE 12.1 Skinner Box. An example of the sort of Skinner box that might be used in studies of learning with rats.

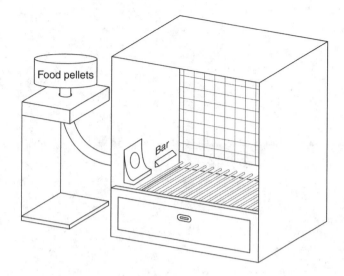

The researcher was able to program the Skinner box creating a contingency, or causal link, between a behavior (pressing the bar down) and a pleasant event (receiving food or water). Skinner devised operant chambers for many different types of organisms. Although design of the device might be different, the point would be the same: to alter the frequency of behavior by changing consequences. A Skinner box for pigeons might have a little window that the pigeon could peck and a feeder that delivered birdseed, but the idea, and the resulting behavior, were not much different from a rat in a Skinner box.

In a typical Skinnerian training situation the researcher would watch a hungry rat and, using a handheld switch, reward it for small movements, thereby coercing it nearer to the bar. At first the researcher might reward the rat for turning toward the bar. Each time the rat turned that way, it would be rewarded. The effect of this contingent consequence was that the rat would begin to turn toward the bar more frequently. Next, the experimenter would reward only steps in the direction of the bar. The rat would move successively nearer the bar. Following this, the criteria would be restricted, and only a lift of the paw in the direction of the bar would be rewarded. Next the rat would have to touch the bar for a reward, and finally it would have to push the bar down to get food. This procedure of training a rat to press the bar by rewarding successive approximations to the desired behavior is called *shaping*. In the space of two or three shaping sessions in a Skinner box, a hungry rat can learn to press the bar and feed itself. Skinner was not merely interested in teaching rats to feed themselves. He wanted to predict and control behavior. He found that changing the consequences of behavior rapidly changed the behavior itself.

REINFORCEMENTS AND PUNISHMENTS

Skinner believed that for humans, the world was like a big Skinner box. We usually experience consequences following behavior, and he expected that the nature of those consequences would determine the frequency of our behavior. Consequences that increased the frequency of behavior were called *reinforcements*, and those that decreased behavior frequency were called *punishments*. An additional complication is introduced by saying that both reward and punishment can be administered in one of two ways: a stimulus can be added to the situation or it can be taken away. When the consequences following a behavior involve adding a stimulus, we say that the reinforcement or punishment is *positive*. When the consequences involve removing a stimulus, we speak of negative reinforcement or negative punishment being applied to the behavior. Notice that the words *positive* and *negative* do not mean good or bad; they are only technical labels telling us that a stimulus has been added or removed.

This is best understood with a little patience and a few examples. In *positive reinforcement* there are two components: *positive* means that a stimulus is being added, *reinforcement* means that the frequency of the behavior is going to increase. If you mow someone's lawn and they give you 20 dollars, you have been positively reinforced. The consequences of the behavior were that a stimulus was added ($20) and the behavior frequency was likely to increase (you will do this again if you can). Here's another one: you are watching television and a particularly annoying commercial comes on with loud music of a sort you hate. You press the mute button on the remote control and find the silence to be a relief. You find that you do this more often when this commercial comes on. You have been negatively reinforced. A stimulus has been removed (annoying music), and the frequency of the behavior (pushing mute button) increases. It is very likely that the stimulus that is removed in negative reinforcement is something aversive or irritating. The removal of this unpleasant event is likely to increase the frequency of the behavior. People sometimes use the term *negative reinforcement* when they are really referring to *punishment*. This is a common error, and you should learn to discriminate between these two operant situations. Imagine that you catch your finger in the car door as you slam it. It hurts. It hurts a lot. You do not do that again. This is positive punishment. A stimulus (pain) has been added following the door-slamming behavior. The frequency of the behavior decreases. Negative punishment may be a bit difficult to picture, although there are a few common examples of it (Cautela & Kearney, 1986). Probably one of the best is the application of so called "time-out" to reduce various undesirable behaviors in children. It may help you to see this as negative punishment if we tell you that the original name of this procedure was *time-out from reinforcement*. A child does not get its way and throws a tantrum. The child is taken to some quiet place and told that he or she can return to the family when the crying stops. This is punishment because the goal is to decrease the frequency of the behavior (tantrum). It is negative punishment because a stimulus has been removed (interaction with family and toys). This will be easier to see if you understand that the child is being placed into a neutral environment that has few, if any, sources of reward or reinforcement. Schools sometimes have a room designed to be a time-out environment. It is quiet and ordinary, perhaps carpeted with a chair or two but it has no other source of entertainment or reinforcement. Because most kids prefer to be around other people, toys, and things to do, removing these things decreases the frequency of the behavior. This is negative punishment. In recent years negative punishment has largely replaced positive punishment in the management of child behavior. Positive punishment required adding a stimulus, generally a painful one. Spankings and other physical forms of positive punishment have been associated with undesirable outcomes, such as increased aggressive behavior toward others (Strassberg, Dodge, Pettit, & Bates, 1994). The four operant learning situations described above are diagrammed in Figure 12.2.

In trying to analyze behavior in Skinnerian or operant terms it is important to remember that the consequences must follow the behavior and must be seen to have a contingency with the behavior in order for reinforcement or punishment to be effective in behavior change.

In order to do an operant analysis of behavior, you must answer two questions: Is behavior going to increase or decrease following consequences (reinforcement or punishment)? Is a stimulus being added or taken away as a consequence of behavior (positive or negative)? Operant analysis of behavior into these

FIGURE 12.2 Positive and Negative Types of Reinforcement and Punishment

	Behavior frequency increases	Behavior frequency decreases
Add stimulus	Positive reinforcement	Positive punishment
Take stimulus away	Negative reinforcement	Negative punishment

four categories can be challenging and calls for precision. The target behavior and target organism must be clearly specified before this analysis can take place. For example, a child in a grocery store checkout line starts screaming because he or she wants some candy that is displayed next to the cash register. The parent eventually gives in and buys some candy. To do an operant analysis of this situation we first have to decide who is the target: parent or child. If it is the parent, then the situation is negative reinforcement. Immediately following candy buying, a stimulus (screaming) is removed. The parent is more likely to make this response in the future because it works. If the target organism is the child, then the situation is positive reinforcement. The response (screaming) is rewarded with candy. The screaming behavior is more likely to happen in the future. In this case, both individuals in the setting are receiving reinforcement, so it is easy to imagine more screaming and candy buying in their future.

SCHEDULES OF REINFORCEMENT

Skinner discovered quite early in his career that it was not necessary to reinforce every single response in order to maintain a high level of responding. There are a variety of ways to manipulate the frequency of rewarded responses. Collectively, these methods are called *intermittent* or *partial reinforcement*. Procedures of partial reinforcement can be seen to belong to one of four basic categories. In thinking about these, it is important to remember that reinforcement is an event that follows a response: the response must come first in operant conditioning. It is possible to issue reinforcements in some ratio to the number of responses. For example, every third response might be reinforced. This is what would happen if a rat in a Skinner box was given a food reward following three bar presses. This is partial reinforcement, because not every response is reinforced. The first two presses would not be followed by reinforcement, but the third would be. Correspondingly, the next two presses would not be rewarded but the third would, and so on. This kind of schedule is called a *fixed ratio* schedule, because every third response is rewarded. The ratio between responses and rewards does not change. Contrast this with a long operant session in which, *on the average*, one response in three is rewarded. Sometimes reinforcements occur close together, sometimes they do not, but, over time, the ratio *averages* to one in three. This is a type of partial reinforcement called a *variable ratio* schedule. The rat must make responses in order to receive reinforcements, but it is impossible for the rat to predict which particular response will be followed by food reward. A shorthand used for this situation is VR 3, or variable ratio three.

Instead for reinforcing on a ratio schedule, it is, alternatively, possible to reinforce responses after a particular *time* interval has passed. Partial reinforcement schedules that work this way are called *interval schedules*. If we continue to use a Skinner box example, the important thing to remember is that the rat in the Skinner box must still make a response. In an interval schedule the time interval since the last reward is what matters, not the number of responses the rat makes. In a *fixed interval* schedule, the first response after some period of time, for example 2 minutes, will be rewarded. The rat can do anything it likes during the interval, but only the first bar press after every 2-minute interval will be reinforced. The rat must make a response. Simply sitting and waiting will not be reinforced. However, only one response is required, and that has to occur at least 2 minutes after the previous reinforcement. This would be called an FI 2 schedule, meaning that there is a fixed interval of 2 minutes before another reinforcement can be obtained. After some experience of FI 2 schedules, rats will respond with few bar presses until the 2-minute interval approaches. There will be a burst of responses around the end of the interval until the reinforcement is delivered. Responding is then likely to decrease until the end of the interval again draws near. The last of the basic schedules is the variable interval schedule. In this schedule, over a long session the rat is rewarded after an *average* time interval, for example, 2 minutes. The Skinner box would be programmed to pay off after a series of time periods that, over the course of a long session would average to 2 minutes. In this situation the rat cannot figure out the length of the interval. Merely sitting and waiting will not be reinforced, the rat must continue to respond and, when one of the programmed variable intervals passes, the next response will be rewarded. As you will have

FIGURE 12.3   **Four Schedules of Reinforcement**

	Payoff	
	Predictable or regular	Unpredictable or irregular
Time	Fixed interval	Variable interval
Responses	Fixed ratio	Variable ratio

Reinforcement only after:

guessed, this schedule would be called a VI 2, indicating a variable interval averaging overall to 2 minutes. These schedules are diagrammed in Figure 12.3.

We have chosen three responses and 2 minutes for use in describing the ratio and interval schedules. Be aware that these were arbitrary choices for the purposes of example, and either schedule might have any reasonable number attached to it.

THE HUMAN SIDE OF REINFORCEMENT SCHEDULES

Skinner firmly believed that these schedules of reinforcement were part of everyday life. We have used Skinner box situations as examples, but we would not want you to think that these phenomena are restricted to rats in operant chambers. For example, imagine that a class you are in meets on Mondays, Wednesdays, and Fridays and has a quiz every Friday. You do well on the quizzes, and this reinforces your studying and hard work. You are on a fixed interval schedule. This is an interval schedule, because the reinforcement is issued only after a period of time (1 week) goes by. It is not dependent on your responses. In contrast, another Monday, Wednesday, Friday class has pop quizzes that can happen any time, during any day of class. The instructor has decided that the average frequency will be two each week, but you do not know when they will happen. There may be four of them the first week and none the second week. You are on a variable interval schedule. If you are like many students, these two schedules would influence your study patterns. The fixed interval schedule tends to make you put off studying until it is almost time for class on Friday. The variable interval schedule tends to result in more continual study patterns. These frequency differences in your behavior are similar to those that would be seen in a rat responding in a Skinner box. Skinner believed that the schedule would determine the behavior frequency, and the species of organism did not matter very much. If you were to work in a car salesroom where you were given a bonus for every five cars you sold, you would be operating on a fixed ratio schedule. You get the bonus after five sales. Time does not matter. If you sell five cars in a morning you get the same bonus you would get by selling five cars in two weeks. A variable ratio schedule is illustrated by a slot machine. It is programmed to pay off at some average low frequency but only after a varying number of responses. Time does not matter to a slot machine. It is not operating on an interval schedule, so waiting around does not make it more likely to pay off.

CHANGING THE FREQUENCY OF BEHAVIOR

The rather simple notions of reinforcement and punishment and the schedules of reinforcement have been shown to be powerful means of changing behavior. For many psychologists, Skinner's radical behaviorism has been tempered by cognitive approaches, yet it continues to provide a useful technology for implementing behavior change. John Roll, Stephen Higgins, and Gary Badger (1996) investigated the use of schedules of reinforcement to promote and sustain abstinence from cigarette smoking. Their study was not intended to be a treatment for people who wanted to quit smoking. Instead, they studied people who did not want to quit smoking in order to demonstrate the power of reinforcers to increase abstinence. Because none of the participants wanted to quit or was trying to quit, any cessation of smoking among the participants was probably a result of reinforcements, not other factors. Roll and his colleagues pointed out that use of addictive drugs is a kind of operant behavior. It is maintained by the reinforcing consequences of the drug effects. The researchers believed that alternate nondrug reinforcers should be able to increase drug abstinence if they were sufficiently attractive to the participants and if the reinforcers were delivered on an optimum schedule. The schedules of reinforcement used in this study were more complex than the basic examples we have described, but they are not difficult to understand once you have mastered the basics.

Participants

The participants were 60 adult smokers who responded to descriptions of the study in newspaper advertisements or flyers posted on bulletin boards. Twenty-one of them were females and 39 were males. The mean age was 30 years, and the mean number of years they had smoked was 13. On the average they smoked 26 cigarettes per day, with a range from 10 to 50. The extent of their addiction was measured with a scale called the Fagerstrom Tolerance Questionnaire (Fagerstrom & Schneider, 1989). The Fagerstrom Tolerance Questionnaire is scored from 0 to 11, with higher numbers representing more nicotine dependence. The participants had a mean Fagerstrom score of 6.5, with a range of 4 to 9. In order to be eligible for the study, participants had to be over 18 years of age and appear for the initial meeting with an initial exhaled carbon monoxide (CO) reading of at least 18 parts per million (ppm). This was assessed with a carbon monoxide meter that measured exhaled CO. Smokers have high levels of CO in their lungs, so this was one way of assessing whether or not a person was a smoker. To be included, participants also had to answer "no" to the question, "Are you currently trying to, or do you want to, quit smoking?" Lastly, people were allowed to participate only if they showed no signs of physical or psychiatric problems. Questionnaires were administered that collected information on drug use, as well as medical and psychiatric history. Following this initial interview, the study took 5 days to complete.

Procedure

All participants agreed to either visit the laboratory or to be visited by the researchers at a prearranged place three times a day for the duration of the study. These visits occurred between 9:00 and 11:00 A.M., 3:00 and 5:00 P.M., and 8:00 and 11:00 P.M. The first visit of the study took place on a Monday morning. Participants were told that they should stop smoking by the previous Friday night. On each of the visits a CO level was taken to assess whether or not the participant had remained abstinent from smoking. Abstinence was defined as having a CO level equal to, or less than, 11 ppm. Participants were given immediate feedback about their CO level at each visit. They were also offered a supply of their own brand of cigarettes at each visit. Presumably, this was to ensure that abstinence was a result of the reinforcement schedule, not merely lack of access to cigarettes.

Participants were randomly assigned to one of three reinforcement schedules:

Progressive reinforcement group: The first time the CO level indicated abstinence, the participant received $3.00. On each subsequent consecutive measurement indicating abstinence, the amount of money was increased by $.50. In addition, every third consecutive abstinent visit was rewarded with an extra $10.00 bonus. A participant in this group who remained abstinent for four visits would earn for those four visits respectively, $3.00, $3.50, $14.00 ($4.00 + $10.00 bonus), and $4.50. If a participant was over the 11 ppm level, indicating that smoking had taken place, payment was withheld for that visit. On the next visit in which abstinence was demonstrated, the reinforcement was reset to the initial $3.00 level. If the participant had three abstinent visits following a reset, the reinforcement level was restored to the high value that had been received before the reset occurred. It was felt that this would support efforts to achieve abstinence again following a reset because the early gains made in level of reinforcement would be given back to the participant after three abstinent visits.

Fixed reinforcement group: Participants were paid $9.80 each time they made an abstinent visit to the researchers. There was no bonus money and there were no resets. The reason why the amount $9.80 was chosen was that this made it possible for a completely abstinent individual in this group to earn the same amount of money overall as a completely abstinent participant in the progressive reinforcement group.

Control group: Payments to control participants were yoked to the average of payments to the first 10 participants to be assigned to the progressive reinforcement group. Yoking was described in the earlier chapter (Chapter 2, "Oh Rats!") where a control group was fed the same quantity of food as an experimental group ate. In the smoking study the concept was the same: the control group received the same payment as another group; however, the payment was not contingent upon the control group's behavior. The control group was paid no matter what CO level they had at any given visit. They were told to try to achieve a CO level at or below 11 ppm, but there were no reward contingencies attached to this request.

Each participant received a detailed oral and written explanation of his or her reinforcement schedule. It was made clear to them exactly what they would have to do in order to receive payment. Money was paid in cash immediately following each CO assessment. In addition, participants were given an additional $50.00 on completion of the study. This encouraged them to finish the study, even if they were having problems achieving abstinence.

Results

Reinforcement contingencies were found to make a difference in abstinence as measured by the mean percentage of visits with CO readings at or below 11 ppm. These data are shown in Figure 12.4.

Mean abstinence levels in the progressive and fixed group differed significantly from the control group ($p < .05$), but not from each other. This measure showed that contingent reinforcement could lead to abstinence from smoking. The control group showed that even noncontingent reinforcement had some effect, but less than with other groups. Using other measures, we can see a difference between the progressive and the fixed schedules. An immediate difference could be seen between the groups in their ability to achieve an initial period of abstinence indicated by three consecutive visits with CO levels under 11 ppm. These data are shown in Figure 12.5.

FIGURE 12.4   Abstinence by Group. Mean percentage of CO readings at 15 trials at which participants were abstinent during the course of the 5-day study.

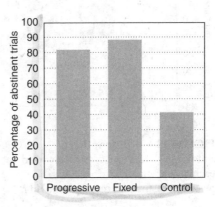

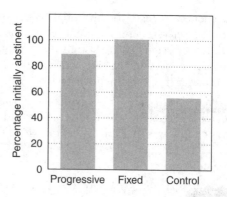

FIGURE 12.5 Achievement of Initial Abstinence. Percentage of participants from each group who achieved initial abstinence as defined by having the first three visits show levels of CO at or below 11 ppm.

The control group is significantly lower on this measure than the other two groups ($p < .01$). The fixed group appears to be a little higher in abstinence on this measure, although not statistically significantly so. The percentage of participants from each group who resumed smoking during any part of the study following an initial period of three abstinent visits is shown in Figure 12.6.

The progressive group had significantly fewer individuals resuming smoking than in the fixed or control groups ($p < .02$ and $p < .01$, respectively). Although they appear to be different in Figure 12.6, the fixed and control groups were not statistically significantly different on this measure. A last interesting measure was the percentage of individuals who remained abstinent through the entire course of the study. These data are shown in Figure 12.7.

The first thing to notice here is that the scale on the y-axis has changed. In order to think critically about data, it is important to look at the scales on graphs. Whereas on the previous figures, a bar reaching almost to the top would indicate 100 percent, on this graph it only indicates 60 percent. This does not diminish the importance of the findings shown in Figure 12.7, but it illustrates the importance of paying attention to the scaling. The progressive and fixed groups were each statistically significantly different from the control group ($p < .01$ and $p < .04$, respectively), but not from each other. Another question you might ask at this point is "How many people are we talking about?" Percentages do not, by themselves, tell you how many individuals are presented in each bar of the graph. Remembering that there were 20 participants in each group, you can figure out that the numbers abstaining throughout the

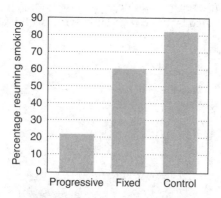

FIGURE 12.6 Resumption of Smoking. Percentage of participants in each group who, following an initial period of abstinence, resumed smoking.

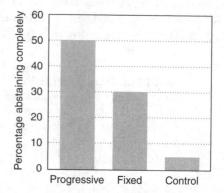

FIGURE 12.7 Abstaining throughout Study. Percentage of participants in each group who were abstinent on all 15 visits during the course of the 5-day study.

entire study were: 10 progressive group members, 6 fixed group members, and 1 control group member. These numbers are quite small for making sweeping generalizations about large populations, nevertheless, the differences between them are interesting.

DISCUSSION

This study was not intended to be a treatment program, but it provided information that might be useful in treatments for nicotine addiction. Often the most difficult part of quitting smoking is the first week or two. This study suggested that monetary rewards were effective in increasing abstinence during this period of time, at least with a progressive reinforcement schedule. Even small amounts of tobacco use during attempts to quit have been found to be a significant predictor of long-term failure to remain abstinent (Chornock, Stitzer, Gross, & Leischow, 1992; Hughes, Gulliver, Fenwick, Valliere, & Flynn, 1986). Progressive reinforcement might help people to remain abstinent, improving their chances of long-term abstinence. You might argue that this was an expensive program, costing about $150 per participant in reward money for only 5 days. This has to be put in the context that a two-pack-a-day smoker may be spending up to $2,000 a year on cigarettes. In this context, the money required to get through initial weeks of quitting is small. Although the study did not address this issue, it is also possible that people who want to quit would be more amenable to abstinence than the participants in this study and might find it easier to achieve and maintain. Further study will be required if the hopeful outcomes reported here are to become part of attempts to treat drug addictions.

REFERENCES

Cautela, J. R., & Kearney, J. A. (1986). *The covert conditioning handbook.* New York: Springer.

Chornock, W. M., Stitzer, M. L., Gross, J., & Leischow, S. (1992). Experimental model of smoking re-exposure: Effects on relapse. *Psychopharmacology, 108,* 495–500.

Fagerstrom, K. O., & Schneider, N. G. (1989). Measuring nicotine dependence: A review of the Fagerstrom tolerance questionnaire. *Journal of Behavioral Medicine, 12,* 159–182.

Hughes, J. R., Gulliver, S. B., Fenwick, J. W., Valliere, L. J., & Flynn, B. S. (1986). Smoking cessation among self-quitters. *Health Psychology, 11,* 331–334.

Roll, J. M., Higgins, S. T., & Badger, G. J. (1996). An experimental comparison of three different schedules of reinforcement of drug abstinence using cigarette smoking as an exemplar. *Journal of Applied Behavior Analysis, 29,* 495–505.

Skinner, B. F. (1956). A case history in scientific method. *American Psychologist, 11,* 221–233.

Strassberg, Z., Dodge, K. A., Pettit, G. S., & Bates, J. E. (1994). Spanking in the home and children's subsequent aggression toward kindergarten peers. *Development and Psychopathology, 6,* 445–461.

CHAPTER 13

STEREOTYPES:
A GOOD THING IN
THE COGNITIVE TOOLKIT[1]

Material selected from:
Research Stories for Introductory Psychology,
Second Edition, by Lary Shaffer and Matthew R. Merrens

---

[1]Incorporating the research of C. N. Macrae, A. B. Milne, and G. V. Bodenhausen, "Stereotypes as Energy Saving Devices: A Peek Inside the Cognitive Toolbox," 1994, *Journal of Personality and Social Psychology, 66,* pp. 37–47.

The term *stereotype* likely will evoke negative thoughts and feelings, perhaps even thoughts of prejudice or discrimination. In psychology however, stereotypes serve a different function. They are a group of characteristics believed to be shared by all individuals who belong to a group. A group might consist of a racial or ethnic group, an occupation, the neighborhood you live in, your gender, or formal membership in a club or organization. When we form opinions or beliefs about individuals based on a stereotype, we tend to ignore their individual qualities and conclude things about them based on the particular stereotype we are using. Furthermore, stereotypes can be seen as cognitive mechanisms that we use to save mental resources and assist in information processing (Allport, 1954; Andersen, Klatzky, & Murray, 1990; Fiske & Neuberg, 1990). Gilbert and Hixon (1991) describe stereotypes as cognitive tools that "jump out" of the mental toolkit "when there is a job to be done." Instead of having to make constant cognitive judgments, stereotypes allow us to rely on simple rules of categorization that can save cognitive energy (Hamilton, 1979; Hamilton, Sherman, & Ruvolo, 1990; Hamilton & Trolier, 1986). Stereotypes help us further by simplifying our perception of the world. In a very real sense, having stereotypes available for ready usage saves us from the difficulty of having to constantly make decisions in a changing, difficult environment (Lippman, 1922).

A number of research studies have shown that we tend to use stereotypes in situations that are difficult and energy draining (Bodenhausen, 1990, 1993; Pratto & Bargh, 1991; Stangor & Duan, 1991). The thinking emphasized in this research is that people under pressure to make a decision will rely on stereotypic thinking to facilitate the task and therefore save energy. It is also possible that stereotypic thinking may be used when people are too lazy or unmotivated to cognitively delve into the task in a critical manner. In summing up this research Macrae, Milne, and Bodenhausen (1994) state, "When the processing environment reaches a sufficient level of difficulty, and perceivers' resources are correspondingly depleted, stereotypes are likely to be activated, and applied in judgmental tasks." The research in this chapter describes more about the first kind of usage, stereotypes as energy misers (i.e., the use of stereotypes saves cognitive energy and resources that can be available for other assignments).

PROCEDURE

Macrae and his colleagues used a *dual-task experimental paradigm* in this investigation. In this procedure participants are placed in a situation in which they are required to handle two tasks at the same time. In a study by Wickens (1976) participants were required to observe the movement of an object on a computer monitor, while simultaneously responding to auditory stimuli. In this situation it is possible to manipulate the difficulty of each of the tasks so that researchers can estimate the amount of cognitive energy used on the primary and secondary tasks. Because the researcher can determine and manipulate characteristics of the primary task, the participant's performance on the secondary task can indicate the amount of excess mental processing capacity not used in carrying out the primary assignment. This is useful because if stereotypes serve to enhance and improve the efficiency of cognitive processing on a primary task, it should be observed in how well a participant performs on a secondary task. If stereotyped information enhances cognitive processing on the primary task, the task should be less difficult to accomplish and, therefore, save mental energy for better cognitive performance on the secondary task.

METHOD

The participants were 24 female college students from Cardiff, Wales, who were compensated with £2 for taking part in the study. The participants performed two tasks simultaneously. Task 1 required them to form impressions of four males based on trait descriptors provided. While they were engaged in Task 1 they were also required to listen to auditory information about an unfamiliar topic (Task 2). Participants were randomly assigned to stereotype present or stereotype absent group. The independent variable (IV) was whether or not the participants had access to a stereotype during Task 1, which presented them with impressions of four males. Participants were told that they would be assessed later on the trait impression they had formed (Task 1) as well as the information acquired in Task 2. The dependent variables were therefore the recall of the trait data (stereotyped and neutral traits) on Task 1 and scores on a multiple-choice exam regarding the auditory information provided in Task 2.

Participants were each seated in front of a computer monitor and told they would be asked to form impressions of a male individual whose name appeared on the monitor's screen. In order to form impressions, 10 trait descriptors were displayed one at a time beneath the name. A single trait appeared on the monitor at a time for approximately 3 seconds. Five of the 10 traits presented were previously determined to be consistent with a specific stereotype. This stereotype was the job description of the male name being presented on the monitor. In the stereotype-present group, the specific stereotype was given along with the male person's name; in the stereotype-absent group the stereotype label was absent. Both groups were asked to perform the same task, with the difference being the presence or absence of the stereotype label. The rationale was that the presence of the stereotype would simplify the task by giving them a focal point to guide their impressions. Table 13.1 provides the name, stereotype label, and traits used in Task 1. As you can see in Table 13.1, the stereotypes for doctor, artist, skinhead, and estate agent (real estate agent in U.S.) were different from one another. The italicized items beneath each stereotype are trait descriptors congruent with the stereotype. Although this research was done in Wales, the stereotypes are consistent with American stereotypes. In this research the selection of the stereotypes was based on a pilot study to insure the stereotypic traits were accurate and the neutral traits were indeed neutral with respect to all four stereotypes.

While the participants were engaged in Task 1, an audiotape describing the economy and geography of Indonesia was played. Participants were told they would be tested on the information contained in the tape. They also knew that they would be assessed on the traits presented by video monitor. The participants were in a situation that required them to pay attention to two completely different streams of information presented simultaneously. The audiotape (i.e., Task 2) and the video presentation of traits (i.e., Task 1) were synchronized so that both presentations occurred simultaneously and took exactly 2 minutes.

TABLE 13.1   The Impression Management Task: Names, Stereotypes, and Traits

NAME STEREOTYPE	NIGEL DOCTOR	JULIAN ARTIST	JOHN SKINHEAD	GRAHAM ESTATE AGENT
	caring	*creative*	*rebellious*	*pushy*
	honest	*temperamental*	*aggressive*	*talkative*
	reliable	*unconventional*	*dishonest*	*arrogant*
	upstanding	*sensitive*	*untrustworthy*	*confidant*
	responsible	*individualistic*	*dangerous*	*unscrupulous*
	unlucky	fearless	lucky	musical
	forgetful	active	observant	pessimistic
	passive	cordial	modest	humorless
	clumsy	progressive	optimistic	alert
	enthusiastic	generous	curious	spirited

Italic Text: stereotyped

Plain text: nonstereotyped

Dependent Variables

The ability of participants to recall traits characteristic of the male person was the dependent measure of Task 1. The participants were given a sheet of paper with each male person's name at the top and they were asked to list as many of each person's traits as possible. The dependent variable for Task 2 was a multiple-choice exam to measure the participant's knowledge about topics presented in the audiotape on Indonesia. For example, participants were asked about the official religion of Indonesia and where the capital of Jakarta was located. After both dependent measures were obtained, the participants were debriefed and compensated.

Findings

The experimenters expected that participants who had a stereotype label available would recall more traits than the group of participants who had no access to the stereotypic label. The data are shown in Table 13.2.

As can be seen in Table 13.2, the participants who had the stereotype available were able to recall more than twice as many traits than the participants without access to the stereotypic label. For Task 2, the multiple-choice data are also presented in Table 13.2. Remember that if stereotypes are useful to the

TABLE 13.2   Participants' Mean Scores on Tasks 1 and 2

TASK 1	STEREOTYPE PRESENT	STEREOTYPE ABSENT	
Recalling stereotype consistent traits	4.42	2.08	$p < .002$
Recalling neutral traits	1.83	.33	N.S.
TASK 2			
Correct multiple-choice responses	8.75	6.66	$p < .04$

participant in making the cognitive processing of information more efficient, then participants who had access to the stereotypic label would have more cognitive resources to handle the audio monitoring task about Indonesia. It would be expected therefore that the group of participants who had access to the stereotype would learn more about Indonesia and obtain higher multiple-choice test scores. The data in Table 13.2 provide confirmation of this hypothesis with the stereotype label group answering significantly more multiple-choice test items ($p < .04$).

The findings of this experiment provided confirmation that stereotypes can facilitate cognitive processing by conserving and economizing cognitive resources. Additional studies by the same researchers (Macrae, Milne, & Bodenhausen, 1994) indicate that the process of using stereotypes operates in an unintentional manner without the perceiver's awareness. Because the use of stereotypes operates in an automatic manner, it lends support for the viewpoint that stereotypic thinking contributes to cognitive efficiency. Our cognitive toolkit is set up, by default, to use stereotypes because they are efficient. We are cognitive misers. The presence of stereotypes does not mean that the person gives up all conscious, voluntary, and reasoned control of cognition. A person may choose to give up the advantages and savings associated with stereotypes to engage in an active, more complicated mode to cognitive processes in certain circumstances. There is no doubt that stereotypic thinking can lead to negative, prejudicial, and discriminatory beliefs, especially because of the automatic, default nature of its operation. However, one should recognize that the stereotypes are a major part of the cognitive toolkit and have benefits for cognitive functioning. To learn more about the implications of this "negative" aspect of stereotypic thinking, the work of Patricia Devine (1989) is an excellent source. Devine's research also points to solutions to reduce prejudice. The very automatic manner in which stereotypes operate imposes problems for the immediate elimination of prejudiced responses. Devine (1995) stated, "People are not always aware of when the stereotype affects their judgments. It (the stereotype) is so easily activated that one has to be extremely vigilant in detecting instances when judgments of others may be clouded by the stereotype." Devine's research supports the findings in this chapter that stereotypes get activated by default. Given this scenario, Devine stated that it will take considerable attention, energy, and vigilance to initiate our personal beliefs and values and to inhibit prejudicial stereotypic thinking.

REFERENCES

Allport, G. W. (1954). *The nature of prejudice*. Reading, MA: Addison-Wesley.

Andersen, S. M., Klatzky, R. L., & Murray, J. (1990). Traits and social stereotypes: Efficiency differences in social information processing. *Journal of Personality and Social Psychology, 59*, 192–201.

Bodenhausen, G. V. (1990). Stereotypes as judgmental heuristics: Evidence of circadian variations in discrimination. *Psychological Science, 1*, 319–322.

Bodenhausen, G. V. (1993). Emotion, arousal, and stereotypic judgments: A heuristic model of affect and stereotyping. In D. Mackie & D. Hamilton (Eds.), *Affect, cognition, and stereotyping: Interactive processes in group perception* (pp. 13–37). San Diego, CA: Academic Press.

Devine, P. G. (1989). Stereotypes and prejudice: Their automatic and controlled components. *Journal of Personality and Social Psychology, 56*, 5–18.

Devine, P. G. (1995). Getting hooked on research in social psychology: Examples from eyewitness identification and prejudice. In G. C. Brannigan & M. R. Merrens (Eds.), *The social psychologist: Research adventures* (pp. 160–184). New York: McGraw-Hill.

Fiske, S. T., & Neuberg, S. L. (1990). A continuum model of impression formation from category-based to individuating processes: Influences of information and motivation on attention and interpretation. In M. P. Zanna (Ed.), *Advances in experimental social psychology* (Vol. 3, pp. 1–74). San Diego, CA: Academic Press.

Gilbert, D. T., & Hixon, J. G. (1991). The trouble of thinking: Activation and application of stereotypic beliefs. *Journal of Personality and Social Psychology, 60*, 509–517.

Hamilton, D. L. (1979). A cognitive-attributional analysis of stereotyping. In L. Berkowitz (Ed.), *Advances in experimental social psychology* (Vol. 12, pp. 53–84). San Diego, CA: Academic Press.

Hamilton, D. L., Sherman, S. J., & Ruvolo, C. M. (1990). Stereotype-based expectancies: Effects on information processing and social behavior. *Journal of Social Issues, 46*, 35–60.

Hamilton, D. L., & Trolier, T. K. (1986). Stereotypes and stereotyping: An overview of the cognitive approach. In J. Dovidio & S. Gaerther (Eds.), *Prejudice, discrimination, and racism* (pp. 127–163). San Diego, CA: Academic Press.

Lippman, W. (1922). *Public opinion.* New York: Harcourt & Brace.

Macrae, C. N., Milne, A. B., & Bodenhausen, G. V. (1994). Stereotypes as energy saving devices: A peek inside the cognitive toolbox. *Journal of Personality and Social Psychology, 66*, 37–47.

Pratto F., & Bargh, J. A. (1991). Stereotyping based upon apparently individuating information: Trait and global components of sex stereotypes under attention overload. *Journal of Experimental Social Psychology, 27*, 26–47.

Stangor, C., & Duan, C. (1991). Effects of multiple task demands upon memory for information about social groups. *Journal of Experimental Social Psychology, 27*, 357–378.

Wickens, C. D. (1976). The effects of divided attention in information processing in tracking. *Journal of Experimental Psychology: Human Perception and Performance, 2*, 1–13.

SECTION IV
DEVELOPMENT

CHAPTER 14

INTRODUCTION

Material selected from:
Development Through the Lifespan,
Third Edition, by Laura E. Berk

Sofie Lentschner was born in 1908, the second child of Jewish parents who made their home in Leipzig, Germany, a city of thriving commerce and cultural vitality. Her father was a successful businessman and community leader. Her mother was a socialite well known for her charm, beauty, and hospitality. As a baby, Sofie displayed the determination and persistence that would be sustained throughout her life. She sat for long periods inspecting small objects with her eyes and hands. The single event that consistently broke her gaze was the sound of the piano in the parlor. As soon as Sofie could crawl, she steadfastly pulled herself up to finger its keys and marveled at the tinkling sound.

By the time Sofie entered elementary school, she was an introspective child, often ill at ease at the festive parties that girls of her family's social standing were expected to attend. She immersed herself in her schoolwork, especially in mastering the foreign languages that were a regular part of German elementary and secondary education. Twice a week, she took piano lessons from the finest teacher in Leipzig. By the time Sofie graduated from high school, she spoke English and French fluently and had become an accomplished pianist. Whereas most German girls of her time married by age 20, Sofie postponed serious courtship in favor of entering the university. Her parents began to wonder whether their intense, studious daughter would ever settle into family life.

Sofie wanted marriage as well as education, but her plans were thwarted by the political turbulence of her times. When Hitler rose to power in the early 1930s, Sofie's father feared for the safety of his wife and children and moved the family to Belgium. Conditions for Jews in Europe quickly worsened. The Nazis plundered Sofie's family home and confiscated her father's business. By the end of the 1930s, Sofie had lost contact with all but a handful of her aunts, uncles, cousins, and childhood friends, many of whom (she later learned) were herded into cattle cars and transported to the slave labor and death camps at Auschwitz-Birkenau. In 1939, as anti-Jewish laws and atrocities intensified, Sofie's family fled to the United States.

As Sofie turned 30, her parents concluded she would never marry and would need a career for financial security. They agreed to support her return to school, and Sofie earned two master's degrees, one in music and the other in librarianship. Then, on a blind date, she met Philip, a U.S. army officer. Philip's calm, gentle nature complemented Sofie's intensity and worldliness. Within 6 months they married. During the next 4 years, two daughters and a son were born. Soon Sofie's father became ill. The strain of uprooting his family and losing his home and business had shattered his health. After months of being bedridden, he died of heart failure.

When World War II ended, Philip left the army and opened a small men's clothing store, Sofie divided her time between caring for the children and helping Philip in the store. Now in her forties, she was a devoted mother, but few women her age were still rearing young children. As Philip struggled with the business, he spent longer hours at work, and Sofie often felt lonely. She rarely touched the piano, which brought back painful memories of youthful life plans shattered by war. Sofie's sense of isolation and lack of fulfillment frequently left her short-tempered. Late at night, she and Philip could be heard arguing.

As Sofie's children grew older and parenting took less time, she returned to school once more, this time to earn a teaching credential. Finally, at age 50, she launched a career. For the next decade, Sofie taught German and French to high school students and English to newly arrived immigrants. Besides easing her family's financial difficulties, she felt a gratifying sense of accomplishment and creativity. These years were among the most energetic and satisfying of Sofie's life. She had an unending enthusiasm for teaching—for transmitting her facility with language, her first hand knowledge of the consequences of hatred and oppression, and her practical understanding of how to adapt to life in a new land. She watched her children, whose young lives were free of the trauma of war, adopt many of her values and commitments and begin their marital and vocational lives at the expected time.

Sofie approached age 60 with an optimistic outlook. As she and Philip were released from the financial burden of paying for their children's college education, they looked forward to greater leisure. Their affection and respect for one another deepened. Once again, Sofie began to play the piano. But this period of contentment was short-lived.

One morning, Sofie awoke and felt a hard lump under her arm. Several days later, her doctor diagnosed cancer. Sofie's spirited disposition and capacity to adapt to radical life changes helped her meet the illness head on. She defined it as an enemy—to be fought and overcome. As a result, she lived 5 more years. Despite the exhaustion of chemotherapy, Sofie maintained a full schedule of teaching duties and continued to visit and run errands for her elderly mother. But as she weakened physically, she no longer had the stamina to meet her classes. Gradually, she gave in to the ravaging illness. Bedridden for the last few weeks, she slipped quietly into death with Philip at her side. The funeral chapel overflowed with hundreds of Sofie's students. She had granted each a memorable image of a woman of courage and caring.

One of Sofie's three children, Laura, is the author of the book from which this chapter is taken. Married a year before Sofie died, Laura and her husband, Ken, often think of Sofie's message, spoken privately to them on the eve of their wedding day: "I learned from my own life and marriage that you must build a life together but also a life apart. You must grant each other the time, space, and support to forge your own identities, your own ways of expressing yourselves and giving to others. The most important ingredient of your relationship must be respect."

Laura and Ken settled in a small midwestern city, near Illinois State University, where they continue to teach today—Laura in the Department of Psychology, Ken in the Department of Mathematics. They have two sons, David and Peter, to whom Laura has related many stories about Sofie's life and who carry her legacy forward. David shares his grandmother's penchant for teaching; he is a first-grade teacher in California. Peter practices law in Chicago; he shares his grandmother's love of music, playing violin, viola, and mandolin in his spare time.

Sofie's story raises a wealth of fascinating issues about human life histories:

- What determines the features that Sofie shares with others and those that make her unique—in physical characteristics, mental capacities, interests, and behaviors?

- What led Sofie to retain the same persistent, determined disposition throughout her life but to change in other essential ways?

- How do historical and cultural conditions—for Sofie, the persecution that destroyed her childhood home, caused the death of family members and friends, and engendered her flight to the United States—affect well-being throughout life?

- How does the timing of events—for example, Sofie's early exposure to foreign languages and her delayed entry into marriage, parenthood, and career—affect development?

- What factors—both personal and environmental—led Sofie to die sooner than expected?

These are central questions addressed by **human development**, a field of study devoted to understanding constancy and change throughout the lifespan. Great diversity characterizes the interests and concerns of investigators who study human development. But all share a single goal: to describe and identify those factors that influence consistencies and transformations in people from conception to death.

HUMAN DEVELOPMENT AS A SCIENTIFIC, APPLIED, AND INTERDISCIPLINARY FIELD

Look again at the questions just listed, and you will see that they are not just of scientific interest. Each is of *applied*, or practical, importance as well. In fact, scientific curiosity is just one factor that led human development to become the exciting field of study it is today. Research about development has also been stimulated by social pressures to better people's lives. For example, the beginning of public education in the early part of this century led to a demand for knowledge about what and how to teach children of different ages. The interest of the medical profession in improving people's health required an understanding of physical development, nutrition, and disease. The social service profession's desire to treat anxieties and behavior problems and to help people adjust to major life events, such as divorce, job loss, or the death of a loved one, required information about personality and social development. And parents have continually asked for expert advice about child-rearing practices and experiences that would foster happy and successful lives for their children.

Our large storehouse of information about human development is *interdisciplinary*. It grew through the combined efforts of people from many fields of study. Because of the need for solutions to everyday problems at all ages, researchers from psychology, sociology, anthropology, and biology joined forces in research with professionals from education, family studies, medicine, public health, and social service, to name just a few. Today, the field of human development is a melting pot of contributions. Its body of knowledge is not just scientifically important but also relevant and useful.

BASIC ISSUES

Research on human development is a relatively recent endeavor. Studies of children did not begin until the early part of the twentieth century. Investigations into adult development, aging, and change over the life course emerged only in the 1960s and 1970s (Elder, 1998). Nevertheless, ideas about how people grow and change have existed for centuries. As these speculations combined with research, they inspired the construction of *theories* of development. A **theory** is an orderly, integrated set of statements that describes, explains, and predicts behavior. For example, a good theory of infant-caregiver attachment would (1) *describe* the behaviors of babies of 6 to 8 months of age as they seek the affection and comfort of a familiar adult, (2) *explain* how and why infants develop this strong desire to bond with a caregiver, and (3) *predict* the consequences of this emotional bond for relationships throughout life.

Theories are vital tools for two reasons. First, they provide organizing frameworks for our observations of people. In other words, they *guide and give meaning to what we see*. Second, theories that are verified by research provide a sound basis for practical action. Once a theory helps us *understand* development, we are in a much better position to know *what to do* in our efforts to improve the welfare and treatment of children and adults.

Theories are influenced by the cultural values and belief systems of their times. But theories differ in one important way from mere opinion and belief: A theory's continued existence depends on *scientific verification*. This means that the theory must be tested with a fair set of research procedures agreed on by the scientific community and that its findings must endure, or be replicated, over time.

In the field of human development, there are many theories with very different ideas about what people are like and how they change. The study of development provides no ultimate truth because investigators do not always agree on the meaning of what they see. In addition, humans are complex beings; they change physically, mentally, emotionally, and socially. As yet, no single theory has explained all these aspects. However, the existence of many theories helps advance knowledge because researchers are continually trying to support, contradict, and integrate these different points of view.

This chapter introduces you to major theories of human development. Although there are many theories, we can easily organize them, since almost all take a stance on three basic issues: (1) Is the course of development continuous or discontinuous? (2) Does one course of development characterize all people, or are there many possible courses? (3) Are genetic or environmental factors more important in determining development? Let's look closely at each of these issues.

Continuous or Discontinuous Development?

How can we best describe the differences in capacities between small infants, young children, adolescents, and adults? As Figure 14.1 illustrates, major theories recognize two possibilities.

One view holds that infants and preschoolers respond to the world in much the same way as adults do. The difference between the immature and mature being is simply one of *amount or complexity*. For example, when Sofie was a baby, her perception of a piano melody, memory for past events, and ability to sort objects into categories may have been much like our own. Perhaps her only limitation was that she could not perform these skills with as much information and precision as we can. If this is so, then change in her thinking must be **continuous**—a process of gradually augmenting the same types of skills that were there to begin with.

A second view regards infants and children as having *unique ways of thinking, feeling, and behaving*, ones quite different from adults'. In other words, development is **discontinuous**—a process in which new and different ways of interpreting and responding to the world emerge at particular time periods. From this perspective, infant Sofie was not yet able to perceive and organize events and objects as a mature person could. Instead, she moved through a series of developmental steps, each with unique features, until she reached the highest level of functioning.

Theories that accept the discontinuous perspective regard development as taking place in **stages**—*qualitative changes* in thinking, feeling, and behaving that characterize specific periods of development. In stage theories, development is much like climbing a staircase, with each step corresponding to a more mature, reorganized way of functioning. The stage concept also assumes that people undergo

FIGURE 14.1   Is development continuous or discontinuous?
(a) Some theorists believe that development is a smooth, continuous process. Individuals gradually add more of the same types of skills. (b) Other theorists think that development takes place in discontinuous stages. People change rapidly as they step up to a new level and then change very little for a while. With each new step, the person interprets and responds to the world in a qualitatively different way.

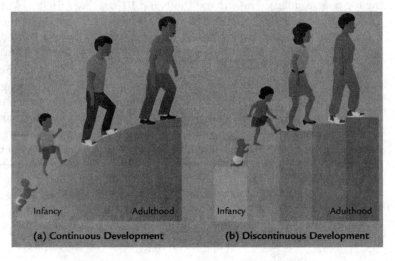

periods of rapid transformation as they step up from one stage to the next. In other words, change is fairly sudden rather than gradual and ongoing.

Does development actually take place in a neat, orderly sequence of stages? For now, let's note that this is a very ambitious assumption that has not gone unchallenged. We will review some very influential stage theories later in this chapter.

One Course of Development or Many?

Stage theorists assume that people everywhere follow the same sequence of development. Yet the field of human development is becoming increasingly aware that children and adults live in distinct **contexts**, or unique combinations of personal and environmental circumstances that can result in different paths of change. For example, a shy individual who fears social encounters develops in very different contexts from those of a social agemate who readily seeks out other people (Rubin & Coplan, 1998). Children and adults in non-Western village societies encounter experiences in their families and communities that differ sharply from those of people in large Western cities. These different circumstances foster different intellectual capacities, social skills, and feelings about the self and others (Shweder et al., 1998).

As we will see, contemporary theorists regard the contexts that shape development as many-layered and complex. On the personal side, they include heredity and biological makeup. One the environmental side, they include immediate settings, such as home, school, and neighborhood, as well as circumstances more remote from people's everyday lives—community resources, societal values, and historical time period. Finally, a special interest in culture has made researchers more conscious than ever before or diversity in development.

Nature or Nurture as More Important?

In addition to describing the course of human development, each theory takes a stance on a major question about its underlying causes: Are genetic or environmental factors more important in determining development? This is the age-old **nature-nurture controversy**. By *nature*, we mean inborn biological givens—the hereditary information we receive from our parents at the moment of conception. By *nurture*, we mean the complex forces of the physical and social world that influence our biological makeup and psychological experiences before and after birth.

Although all theories grant at least some role to both nature and nurture, they vary in emphasis. For example, consider the following questions: Is the developing person's ability to think in more complex ways largely the result of an inborn timetable of growth? Or is it primarily influenced by stimulation from parents and teachers? Do children acquire language rapidly because they are genetically predisposed to do so or because parents tutor them from an early age? And what accounts for the vast individual differences among people—in height, weight, physical coordination, intelligence, personality, and social skills? Is nature or nurture more responsible?

The stances theories take on nature versus nurture affect their explanations of individual differences. Some theorists emphasize *stability*—that individuals who are high or low in a characteristic (such as verbal ability, anxiety, or sociability) will remain so at later ages. These theorists typically stress the importance of *heredity*. If they regard environment as important, they usually point to *early experiences* as establishing a lifelong pattern of behavior. Powerful negative events in the first few years, they argue, cannot be fully overcome by later, more positive ones (Bowlby, 1980; Sroufe, Egeland, & Kreutzer, 1990). Other theorists take a more optimistic view (Chess & Thomas, 1984; Nelson, 2002; Werner & Smith, 2001). They emphasize *plasticity*—that change is possible and likely if new experiences support it.

Throughout this chapter we will see that investigators disagree, at times sharply, on the question of *stability or change*. Their answers often vary across *domains*, or aspects, of development. Think back to Sofie's story, and you will see that her linguistic ability and persistent approach to challenges were stable over the lifespan. In contrast, her psychological well-being and life satisfaction fluctuated considerably.

THE LIFESPAN PERSPECTIVE: A BALANCED POINT OF VIEW

So far, we have discussed basic issues of human development in terms of extremes—solutions on one side or the other. As we trace the unfolding of the field in the rest of this chapter, you will see that the positions of many theories have softened. Modern ones, especially, recognize the merits of both sides. Some theorists believe that both continuous and discontinuous changes occur and alternate with one another. And some acknowledge that development can have both universal features and features unique to the individual and his or her contexts. Furthermore, an increasing number of investigators regard heredity and environment as inseparably interwoven, each affecting the potential of the other to modify the child's traits and capacities (de Waal, 1999; Wachs, 2000).

These balanced visions owe much to the expansion of research from a nearly exclusive focus on the first two decades to include adulthood. In the first half of the twentieth century, it was widely assumed that development stopped at adolescence. Infancy and childhood were viewed as periods of rapid transformation, adulthood as a plateau, and aging as a period of decline. The changing character of the North American population awakened researchers to the idea that development is lifelong. Due to improvements in nutrition, sanitation, and medical knowledge, the *average life expectancy* (the number of years an individual born in a particular year can expect to live) gained more in the twentieth century than in the preceding five thousand years. In 1900, it was just under age 50; today, it is around age 77 in the United States and 79 in Canada. As a result, there are more older adults, a trend that has occurred in most of the world but is especially striking in industrialized nations. People age 65 and older accounted for about 4 percent of the North American population in 1900, 7 percent in 1950, and 12 percent in 2000. Growth in sheer numbers of elderly American and Canadian adults during the twentieth century has been even more dramatic, increasing more than eleven-fold, from 3 million to 34 million in the United States and from 290,000 to 4 million in Canada (U.S. Bureau of the Census, 2002; Statistics Canada, 2002).

Older adults are not just more numerous; they are also healthier and more active. They challenge the earlier stereotype of the withering person and have sparked a profound shift in our view of human development. Compared with other approaches, the **lifespan perspective** offers a more complex vision of change and the factors that underlie it. Four assumptions make up this broader view: (1) development as lifelong, (2) development as multidimensional and multidirectional, (3) development as highly plastic, and (4) development as embedded in multiple contexts (Baltes, Lindenberger, & Staudinger, 1998; Smith & Baltes, 1999).

Development as Lifelong

According to the lifespan perspective, no age period is supreme in its impact on the life course. Instead, events occurring during each major period, summarized in Table 14.1, can have equally powerful effects on the future path of change. Within each period, change occurs in three broad domains: *physical*, *cognitive*, and *social*, which we separate for convenience of discussion. Yet, as you are already aware from reading the first part of this chapter, the domains are not really distinct; they overlap and interact a great deal.

Every age period has its own agenda, bringing with it unique demands and opportunities that yield some similarities in development across many individuals. Nevertheless, throughout life, the challenges people face and the adjustments they make are highly diverse in timing and pattern, as the remaining assumptions make clear.

Development as Multidimensional and Multidirectional

Think back to Sofie's life and how she was continually faced with new demands and opportunities. The lifespan perspective regards the challenges and adjustments of development as *multidimensional*—affected by an intricate blend of biological, psychological, and social forces.

TABLE 14.1   Major Periods of Human Development

PERIOD	APPROXIMATE AGE RANGE	BRIEF DESCRIPTION
Prenatal	Conception to birth	The one-celled organism transforms into a human baby with remarkable capacities to adjust to life outside the womb.
Infancy and toddlerhood	Birth–2 years	Dramatic changes in the body and brain support emergence of a wide array of motor, perceptual, and intellectual capacities and first intimate ties to others.
Early childhood	2–6 years	The play years, in which motor skills are refined, thought and language expand at an astounding pace, a sense of morality is evident, and children begin to establish ties to peers.
Middle childhood	6–11 years	The school years, marked by advances in athletic abilities; logical thought processes; basic literacy skills; understanding of self, morality, and friendship; and peer-group membership.
Adolescence	11–20 years	Puberty leads to an adult-sized body and sexual maturity. Thought becomes abstract and idealistic and school achievement more serious. Adolescents focus on defining personal values and goals and establishing autonomy from the family.
Early adulthood	20–40 years	Most young people leave home, complete their education, and begin full-time work. Major concerns are developing a career; forming an intimate partnership; and marrying, rearing children, or establishing other lifestyles.
Middle adulthood	40–60 years	Many people are at the height of their careers and attain leadership positions. They must also help their children begin independent lives and their parents adapt to aging. They become more aware of their own mortality.
Late adulthood	60 years–death	People adjust to retirement, to decreased physical strength and health, and often to the death of a spouse. They reflect on the meaning of their lives.

Lifespan development is also *multidirectional*—in at least two ways. First, development is not limited to improved performance. Instead, at all periods, it is a joint expression of growth and decline. When Sofie directed her energies toward mastering languages and music as a school-age child, she gave up refining other skills to their full potential. When she chose to become a teacher in adulthood, she let go of other career options. Although gains are especially evident early in life, and losses during the final years, people of all ages can improve current skills and develop new skills, including ones that compensate for reduced functioning (Freund & Baltes, 2000). One elderly psychologist who noticed his difficulty remembering people's names devised graceful ways of explaining his memory failure. Often he flattered his listener by remarking that he tended to forget only the names of important people! Under these conditions, he reflected, "forgetting may even be a pleasure" (Skinner, 1983, p. 240).

Second, besides being multidirectional over time, change is multidirectional within the same domain of development. Although some qualities of Sofie's cognitive functioning (such as memory) probably declined in her mature years, her knowledge of English and French undoubtedly grew throughout her life. And she also developed new forms of thinking. For example, Sofie's wealth of experience and ability to cope with diverse problems led her to become expert in practical matters—a quality of reasoning called wisdom. Recall the wise advice that Sofie gave Laura and Ken on the eve of their wedding day. Notice, in these examples, how the lifespan perspective includes both continuous and discontinuous change.

Development as Plastic

Lifespan researchers emphasize that development is *plastic* at all ages. For example, consider Sofie's social reserve in childhood and her decision to study rather than marry as a young adult. As new opportunities arose, Sofie moved easily into marriage and childbearing in her thirties. And although parenthood and financial difficulties posed challenges to Sofie and Philip's happiness, their relationship gradually became richer and more fulfilling. Intellectual performance also remains flexible with advancing age. Elderly people respond to special training with substantial (but not unlimited) gains in a wide variety of mental abilities (Schaie, 1996).

Evidence on plasticity makes it clear that aging is not an eventual "shipwreck," as has often been assumed. Instead, the metaphor of a "butterfly"—of metamorphosis and continued potential—provides a far more accurate picture of lifespan change (Lemme, 2002). Still, development gradually becomes less plastic, as both capacity and opportunity for change are reduced. And plasticity varies greatly across individuals. Some children and adults experience more diverse life circumstances, and some adapt more easily to changing conditions than do others.

Development as Embedded in Multiple Contexts

According to the lifespan perspective, pathways of change are highly diverse because development is *embedded in multiple contexts*. Although these wide-ranging influences can be organized into three categories, they work together, combining in unique ways to fashion each life course.

- **Age-Graded Influences.** Events that are strongly related to age and therefore fairly predictable in when they occur and how long they last are called **age-graded influences**. For example, most individuals walk shortly after their first birthday, acquire their native language during the preschool years, reach puberty around ages 12 to 14, and (for women) experience menopause in their late forties or early fifties. These milestones are influenced by biology, but social customs can create age-graded influences as well. Starting school around age 6, getting a driver's license at age 16, and entering college around age 18 are events of this kind. Age-graded influences are especially prevalent during childhood and adolescence, when biological changes are rapid and cultures impose many age-related experiences to ensure that young people acquire the skills they need to participate in their society.

- **History-Graded Influences.** Development is also profoundly affected by forces unique to a particular historical era. Examples include epidemics, wars, and periods of economic prosperity or depression; technological advances, such as the introduction of television, computers, and the Internet; and changing cultural values, such as revised attitudes toward women and ethnic minorities. These **history-graded influences** explain why people born around the same time—called a *cohort*—tend to be alike in ways that set them apart from people born at other times.

- **Nonnormative Influences.** *Normative* means typical, or average. Age-graded and history-graded influences are normative because each affects large numbers of people in a similar way. **Nonnormative influences** are events that are irregular, in that they happen to just one or a few people and do not follow a predictable timetable. Consequently, they enhance the multidirectionality of development. Piano lessons in childhood with an inspiring teacher; a blind date with Philip; delayed marriage, parenthood, and career entry; and a battle with cancer are nonnormative influences that had a major impact on the direction of Sofie's life. Because they occur haphazardly, nonnormative events are among the most difficult for researchers to capture and study. Yet, as each of us can attest from our own experiences, they can affect us in powerful ways.

Lifespan investigators point out that nonnormative influences have become more powerful and age-graded influences less so in contemporary adult development. Compared with Sofie's era, the ages at which people finish their education, enter careers, get married, have children, and retire are much more diverse (Schroots & Birren, 1990). Indeed, Sofie's "off-time" accomplishments would have been less unusual had she been born a generation or two later! Age remains a powerful organizer of everyday experiences, and age-related expectations have certainly not disappeared. But age markers have blurred, and they vary across ethnic groups and cultures. The increasing role of nonnormative events in the life course adds to the fluid nature of lifespan development.

Notice that instead of a single line of development, the lifespan perspective emphasizes many potential pathways and outcomes—an image more like tree branches extending in diverse directions, which may undergo continuous and stagewise transformations. Now let's turn to the historical foundations of the field as a prelude to discussing major theories that address various aspects of change.

HISTORICAL FOUNDATIONS

Contemporary theories of human development are the result of centuries of change in Western cultural values, philosophical thinking, and scientific progress. To understand the field as it exists today, we must return to its early beginnings—to influences that long preceded scientific study. We will see that many early ideas linger on as important forces in current theory and research.

Philosophies of Childhood

In medieval Europe (the sixth through the fifteenth centuries), little importance was placed on childhood as a separate phase of life. Once children emerged from infancy, they were regarded as miniature, already-formed adults, a view called **preformationism** (Ariès, 1962). Certain laws did recognize that children needed protection from people who might mistreat them, and medical works provided special instructions for their care. However, despite practical awareness of the vulnerability of children, there were no philosophies of the uniqueness of childhood or separate developmental periods (Borstelmann, 1983).

In the sixteenth century, a revised image of children sprang from the Puritan belief in original sin. Harsh, restrictive parenting practices were recommended as the most efficient means of taming the depraved child. Although punitiveness was the prevailing child-rearing philosophy, affection for their children prevented most Puritan parents from using extremely repressive measures. Instead, they tried to promote reason in their sons and daughters so they could tell right from wrong and resist temptation (Clarke-Stewart, 1998).

• **John Locke.** The seventeenth-century Enlightenment brought philosophies that emphasized ideals of human dignity and respect. The writings of John Locke (1632–1704), a leading British philosopher, served as the forerunner of a twentieth-century perspective that we will discuss shortly: behaviorism. Locke viewed the child as a **tabula rasa,** or, translated from Latin, "blank slate." According to this idea, children are, to begin with, nothing at all, and all kinds of experiences can shape their characters. Locke (1690/1892) described parents as rational tutors who can mold the child in any way they wish through careful instruction, effective example, and rewards for good behavior. His philosophy led to a change from harshness toward children to kindness and compassion.

Look carefully at Locke's ideas, and you will see that he took a firm stand on basic issues discussed earlier in this chapter. Locke regarded development as *continuous;* adultlike behaviors are gradually built up through the warm, consistent teachings of parents. Furthermore, Locke's view of the child as a tabula rasa led him to champion *nurture*—the power of the environment to shape the child. And his faith in nurture suggests the possibility of *many courses of development* and *change at later ages* due to new experiences. Finally, Locke's philosophy characterizes children as passive—as doing little to shape their own destiny, which is written on blank slates by others. This vision has been discarded. All contemporary theories view the developing person as an active, purposeful being who contributes substantially to his or her own development.

• **Jean Jacques Rousseau.** In the eighteenth century, a new theory of childhood was introduced by French philosopher Jean Jacques Rousseau (1712–1778). Children, Rousseau (1762/1955) thought, were not blank slates to be filled by adult instruction. Instead, they were **noble savages**, naturally endowed with a sense of right and wrong and with an innate plan for orderly, healthy growth. Unlike Locke, Rousseau thought children's built-in moral sense and unique ways of thinking and feeling would only be harmed by adult training. His was a child-centered philosophy in which the adult should be receptive to the child's needs at each of four stages of development: infancy, childhood, late childhood, and adolescence.

Rousseau's philosophy includes two influential concepts. The first is the concept of *stage*, which we discussed earlier in this chapter. The second is the concept of **maturation,** which refers to a genetically determined, naturally unfolding course of growth. Unlike Locke, Rousseau saw children as determining their own destinies. And he took a different stand on basic developmental issues. He saw development as a discontinuous, *stagewise* process that follows a *single, unified course* mapped out by *nature*.

Philosophies of Adulthood and Aging

Shortly after Rousseau devised his conception of childhood, the first lifespan views appeared. In the eighteenth and early nineteenth centuries, two German philosophers—John Nicolaus Tetens (1736–1807) and Friedrich August Carus (1770–1808)—urged that attention to development be extended through adulthood. Each asked important questions about aging.

Tetens (1777) addressed the origins and extent of individual differences, the degree to which behavior can be changed in adulthood, and the impact of historical eras on the life course. He was ahead of his time in recognizing that older people can compensate for intellectual declines that, at times, may reflect hidden gains. For example, Tetens suggested that some memory difficulties are due to searching for a word or name among a lifetime of accumulated information—a possibility acknowledged by current research (Maylor & Valentine, 1992).

Carus (1808) moved beyond Rousseau's stages by identifying four periods that span the life course: childhood, youth, adulthood, and senescence. Like Tetens, Carus viewed aging not only as decline but also as progression. His writings reflect a remarkable awareness of multidirectionality and plasticity, which are at the heart of the lifespan perspective.

Scientific Beginnings

The study of development evolved quickly during the late nineteenth and early twentieth centuries. Early observations of human change were soon followed by improved methods and theories. Each advance contributed to the firm foundation on which the field rests today.

• **Darwin: Forefather of Scientific Child Study.** Charles Darwin (1809–1882), a British naturalist, is often considered the forefather of scientific child study. Darwin (1859/1936) observed the infinite variation among plant and animal species. He also saw that within a species, no two individuals are exactly alike. From these observations, he constructed his famous theory of evolution.

The theory emphasized two related principles: *natural selection* and *survival of the fittest*. Darwin explained that certain species survived in particular environments because they have characteristics that fit with, or are adapted to, their surroundings. Other species die off because they are not well suited to their environments. Individuals within a species who best meet the survival requirements of the environment live long enough to reproduce and pass their more favorable characteristics to future generations. Darwin's emphasis on the adaptive value of physical characteristics and behavior found its way into important developmental theories.

During his explorations, Darwin discovered that the early prenatal growth of many species is strikingly similar. Other scientists concluded from Darwin's observation that the development of the human child followed the same general plan as the evolution of the human species. Although this belief eventually proved inaccurate, efforts to chart parallels between child growth and human evolution prompted researchers to make careful observations of all aspects of children's behavior. Out of these first attempts to document an idea about development, scientific child study was born.

- **The Normative Period.** G. Stanley Hall (1846–1924), one of the most influential American psychologists of the early twentieth century, is generally regarded as the founder of the child study movement (Dixon & Lerner, 1999). He also foreshadowed lifespan research by writing one of the few books of his time on aging. Inspired by Darwin's work, Hall and his well-known student Arnold Gesell (1880–1961) devised theories of childhood and adolescence based on evolutionary ideas. These early leaders regarded development as a genetically determined process that unfolds automatically, much like a flower (Gesell, 1933; Hall, 1904).

Hall and Gesell are remembered less for their one-sided theories than for their intensive efforts to describe all aspects of development. They launched the **normative approach**, in which measures of behavior are taken on large numbers of individuals, and age-related averages are computed to represent typical development. Using this method, Hall constructed elaborate questionnaires asking children of different ages almost everything they could tell about themselves—interests, fears, imaginary playmates, dreams, friendships, everyday knowledge, and more (White, 1992). In the same fashion, Gesell collected detailed normative information on the motor achievements, social behaviors, and personality characteristics of infants and children (Gesell & Ilg, 1946/1949a, 1943/1949b).

Gesell was also among the first to make knowledge about child development meaningful to parents. If, as he believed, the timetable of development is the product of millions of years of evolution, then children are naturally knowledgeable about their needs. His child-rearing advice, in the tradition of Rousseau, recommended sensitivity to children's cues (Thelen & Adolph, 1992). Along with Benjamin Spock's *Baby and Child Care*, Gesell's books became a central part of a rapidly expanding popular literature for parents.

- **The Mental Testing Movement.** While Hall and Gesell were developing their theories and methods in the United States, French psychologist Alfred Binet (1857–1911) was also taking a normative approach to child development, but for a different reason. In the early 1900s, Binet and his colleague Theodore Simon were asked to find a way to identify children with learning problems who needed to be placed in special classes. The first successful intelligence test, which they constructed for this purpose, grew out of practical educational concerns.

In 1916, at Stanford University, Binet's test was adapted for use with English-speaking children. Since then the English version has been known as the Stanford-Binet Intelligence Scale. Besides providing a score that could successfully predict school achievement, the Binet test sparked tremendous interest in individual differences in development. Comparisons of the scores of people who vary in gender, ethnicity, birth order, family background, and other characteristics became a major focus of research. Intelligence tests also rose quickly to the forefront of the controversy over nature versus nurture that has continued to this day.

MID-TWENTIETH-CENTURY THEORIES

In the mid-twentieth century, human development expanded into a legitimate discipline. As it attracted increasing interest, a variety of mid-twentieth-century theories emerged, each of which continues to have followers today.

The Psychoanalytic Perspective

In the 1930s and 1940s, as more people sought help from professionals in dealing with emotional difficulties, a new question had to be addressed: How and why did people become the way they are? To treat psychological problems, psychiatrists and social workers turned to an emerging approach to personality development because of its emphasis on understanding the unique life history of each person.

According to the **psychoanalytic perspective**, people move through a series of stages in which they confront conflicts between biological drives and social expectations. The way these conflicts are resolved determines the individual's ability to learn, to get along with others, and to cope with anxiety. Although many individuals contributed to the psychoanalytic perspective, two were especially influential: Sigmund Freud founder of the psychoanalytic movement, and Erik Erikson.

- **Freud's Theory.** Freud (1856–1939), a Viennese physician, saw patients in his practice with a variety of nervous symptoms, such as hallucinations, fears, and paralyses, that appeared to have no physical basis. Seeking a cure for these troubled adults, Freud found that their symptoms could be relieved by having patients talk freely about painful events of their childhoods. On the basis of adult remembrances, he examined the unconscious motivations of his patients and constructed his **psychosexual theory**, which emphasized that how parents manage their child's sexual and aggressive drives in the first few years is crucial for healthy personality development.

Three Parts of the Personality. In Freud's theory, three parts of the personality—id, ego, and superego—become integrated during five stages, summarized in Table 14.2. The id, the largest portion of the mind, is the source of basic biological needs and desires. The ego—the conscious, rational part of personality—emerges in early infancy to redirect the id's impulses so they are discharged on appropriate objects at acceptable times and places. For example, aided by the ego, the hungry baby of a few months of age stops crying when he sees his mother unfasten her clothing for breast-feeding. And the more competent preschooler goes into the kitchen and gets a snack on her own.

Between 3 and 6 years of age, the *superego,* or conscience, develops from interactions with parents, who insist that children conform to the values of society. Now the ego faces the increasingly complex task of reconciling the demands of the id, the external world, and conscience (Freud, 1923/1974). For example, when the ego is tempted to gratify an id impulse by hitting a playmate to get an attractive toy, the superego may warn that such behavior is wrong. The ego must decide which of the two forces (id or superego) will win this inner struggle, or it must work out a compromise, such as asking for a turn with the toy. According to Freud, the relations established among the id, ego, and superego during the preschool years determine the individual's basic personality.

Psychosexual Development. Freud (1938/1973) believed that during childhood, sexual impulses shift their focus from the oral to the anal to the genital regions of the body. In each stage of development, parents walk a fine line between permitting too much or too little gratification of their child's basic needs. If parents strike an appropriate balance, then children grow into well-adjusted adults with the capacity for mature sexual behavior, investment in family life, and rearing of the next generation.

Freud's psychosexual theory highlighted the importance of family relationships for children's development. It was the first theory to stress the role of early experience. But Freud's perspective was eventually criticized. First, the theory overemphasized the influence of sexual feelings in development.

TABLE 14.2   **Freud's Psychosexual Stages**

PSYCHOSEXUAL STAGE	PERIOD OF DEVELOPMENT	DESCRIPTION
Oral	Birth–1 year	The new ego directs the baby's suckling activities toward breast or bottle. If oral needs are not met appropriately, the individual may develop such habits as thumb sucking, fingernail biting, and pencil chewing in childhood and overeating and smoking in later life.
Anal	1–3 years	Toddlers and preschoolers enjoy holding and releasing urine and feces. Toilet training becomes a major issue between parent and child. If parents insist that children be trained before they are ready or make too few demands, conflicts about anal control may appear in the form of extreme orderliness and cleanliness or messiness and disorder.
Phallic	3–6 years	Id impulses transfer to the genitals, and the child finds pleasure in genital stimulation. Freud's *Oedipus conflict* for boys and *Electra conflict* for girls arise, and young children feel a sexual desire for the other-sex parent. To avoid punishment, they give up this desire and, instead, adopt the same-sex parent's characteristics and values. As a result, the superego is formed, and children feel guilty each time they violate its standards. The relations among id, ego, and superego established at this time determine the individual's basic personality.
Latency	6–11 years	Sexual instincts die down, and the superego develops further. The child acquires new social values from adults outside the family and from play with same-sex peers.
Genital	Adolescence	Puberty causes the sexual impulses of the phallic stage to reappear. If development has been successful during earlier stages, it leads to marriage, mature sexuality, and the birth and rearing of children.

Second, because it was based on the problems of sexually repressed, well-to-do adults, it did not apply in cultures differing from nineteenth-century Victorian society. Finally, Freud had not studied children directly.

• **Erikson's Theory.** Several of Freud's followers took what was useful from his theory and improved on his vision. The most important of these neo-Freudians is Erik Erikson (1902–1994).

Although Erikson (1950) accepted Freud's basic psychosexual framework, he expanded the picture of development at each stage. In his **psychosocial theory**, Erikson emphasized that the ego does not just mediate between id impulses and superego demands. At each stage, it acquires attitudes and skills that make the individual an active, contributing member of society. A basic psychological conflict, which is resolved along a continuum from positive to negative, determines healthy or maladaptive outcomes at each stage. As Table 14.3 shows, Erikson's first five stages parallel Freud's stages, but Erikson added three adult stages.

Finally, unlike Freud, Erikson pointed out that normal development must be understood in relation to each culture's life situation. For example, among the Yurok Indians on the Northwest coast of the United States, babies are deprived of breast-feeding for the first 10 days after birth and instead are

TABLE 14.3   Erikson's Psychosocial Stages, with Corresponding Psychosexual Stages Indicated

PSYCHOSOCIAL STAGE	PERIOD OF DEVELOPMENT	DESCRIPTION
Basic trust versus mistrust (Oral)	Birth–1 year	From warm, responsive care, infants gain a sense of trust, or confidence, that the world is good. Mistrust occurs when infants have to wait too long for comfort and are handled harshly.
Autonomy versus shame and doubt (Anal)	1–3 years	Using new mental and motor skills, children want to choose and decide for themselves. Autonomy is fostered when parents permit reasonable free choice and do not force or shame the child.
Initiative versus guilt (Phallic)	3–6 years	Through make-believe play, children experiment with the kind of person they can become. Initiative—a sense of ambition and responsibility—develops when parents support their child's new sense of purpose. The danger is that parents will demand too much self-control, which leads to overcontrol, meaning too much guilt.
Industry versus diffusion (Latency)	6–11 years	At school, children develop the capacity to work and cooperate with others. Inferiority develops when negative experiences at home, at school, or with peers lead to feelings of incompetence.
Identity versus identity confusion (Genital)	Adolescence	The adolescent tries to answer the question, Who am I, and what is my place in society? Self-chosen values and vocational goals lead to a lasting personal identity. The negative outcome is confusion about future adult roles.
Intimacy versus isolation	Young adulthood	Young people work on establishing intimate ties to others. Because of earlier disappointments, some individuals cannot form close relationships and remain isolated.
Generativity versus stagnation	Middle adulthood	Generativity means giving to the next generation through child rearing, caring for other people, or productive work. The person who fails in these ways feels an absence of meaningful accomplishment.
Ego integrity versus despair	Old age	In this final stage, individuals reflect on the kind of person they have been. Integrity results from feeling that life was worth living as it happened. Older people who are dissatisfied with their lives fear death.

fed a thin soup from a small shell. At age 6 months, infants are abruptly weaned—if necessary, by having the mother leave for a few days. These experiences, from our cultural vantage point, might seem cruel. But Erikson explained that the Yurok live in a world in which salmon fill the river just once a year, a circumstance that requires considerable self-restraint for survival. In this way, he showed that child rearing can be understood only by making reference to the competencies valued and needed by the individual's society.

- **Contributions and Limitations of Psychoanalytic Theory.** A special strength of the psychoanalytic perspective is its emphasis on the individual's unique life history as worthy of study and understanding (Emde, 1992). Consistent with this view, psychoanalytic theorists accept the *clinical method*, which synthesizes information from a variety of sources into a detailed picture of the personality functioning of a single person. Psychoanalytic theory has also inspired a wealth of research on many aspects of emotional and social development, including infant–caregiver attachment, aggression, sibling relationships, child-rearing practices, morality, gender roles, and adolescent identity.

Despite its extensive contributions, the psychoanalytic perspective is no longer in the mainstream of human development research (Cairns, 1998). Psychoanalytic theorists may have become isolated from the rest of the field because they were so strongly committed to the clinical approach that they failed to consider other methods. In addition, many psychoanalytic ideas, such as psychosexual stages and ego functioning, are so vague that they are difficult or impossible to test empirically (Thomas, 2000; Westen & Gabbard, 1999).

Nevertheless, Erikson's broad outline of lifespan change captures the essence of personality development during each major period of the life course.

Behaviorism and Social Learning Theory

As psychoanalytic theory gained in prominence, human development was also influenced by a very different perspective. According to **behaviorism**, directly observable events—stimuli and responses—are the appropriate focus of study. American behaviorism began with the work of psychologist John Watson (1878–1958) in the early twentieth century. Watson wanted to create an objective science of psychology and rejected the psychoanalytic concern with the unseen workings of the mind (Horowitz, 1992).

- **Traditional Behaviorism.** Watson was inspired by studies of animal learning carried out by famous Russian physiologist Ivan Pavlov. Pavlov knew that dogs release saliva as an innate reflex when they are given food. But he noticed that his dogs were salivating before they tasted any food—when they saw the trainer who usually fed them. The dogs, Pavlov reasoned, must have learned to associate a neutral stimulus (the trainer) with another stimulus (food) that produces a reflexive response (salivation). As a result of this association, the neutral stimulus could bring about a response resembling the reflex. Eager to test this idea, Pavlov successfully taught dogs to salivate at the sound of a bell by pairing it with the presentation of food. He had discovered *classical conditioning*.

Watson wanted to find out if classical conditioning could be applied to children's behavior. In a historic experiment, he taught Albert, an 11-month-old infant, to fear a neutral stimulus—a soft white rat—by presenting it several times with a sharp, loud sound, which naturally scared the baby. Little Albert, who at first had reached out eagerly to touch the furry rat, began to cry and turn his head away when he caught sight of it (Watson & Raynor, 1920). In fact, Albert's fear was so intense that researchers eventually challenged the ethics of studies like this one. Consistent with Locke's tabula rasa, Watson concluded that environment is the supreme force in development. Adults can mold children's behavior, he thought, by carefully controlling stimulus-response associations. And development is a continuous process, consisting of a gradual increase in the number and strength of these associations.

Another form of behaviorism was B. F. Skinner's (1904–1990) *operant conditioning theory*. According to Skinner, behavior can be increased by following it with a wide variety of *reinforcers*, such as food, praise, or a friendly smile. It can also be decreased through *punishment*, such as disapproval or withdrawal of privileges. As a result of Skinner's work, operant conditioning became a broadly applied learning principle.

- **Social Learning Theory.** Psychologists quickly became interested in whether behaviorism might offer a more direct and effective explanation of the development of social behavior than the less precise concepts of psychoanalytic theory. This concern sparked the emergence of several approaches that built on the principles of conditioning that came before them, offering expanded views of how children and adults acquire new responses.

Several kinds of **social learning theory** emerged. The most influential, devised by Albert Bandura, emphasized *modeling*, otherwise known as *imitation* or *observational learning*, as a powerful source of development. Bandura (1977) recognized that children acquire many favorable and unfavorable responses simply by watching and listening to others around them. The baby who claps her hands after her mother does so, the child who angrily hits a playmate in the same way that he has been punished at home, and the teenager who wears the same clothes and hairstyle as her friends at school are all displaying observational learning.

Bandura's work continues to influence much research on social development. However, like the field of human development as a whole, today his theory stresses the importance of *cognition*, or thinking. In fact, the most recent revision of Bandura's (1989, 1992) theory places such strong emphasis on how we think about ourselves and other people that he calls it a *social-cognitive* rather than a social learning approach.

According to this view, children gradually become more selective in what they imitate. From watching others engage in self-praise and self-blame and through feedback about the worth of their own actions, children develop *personal standards* for behavior and a *sense of self-efficacy*—the belief that their own abilities and characteristics will help them succeed. These cognitions guide responses in particular situations (Bandura, 1999). For example, imagine a parent who often remarks, "I'm glad I kept working on that task, even though it was hard," who explains the value of persistence, and who encourages her child by saying, "I know you can do a good job on that homework!" Soon the child starts to view himself as hardworking and high achieving and selects people with these characteristics as models. In this way, as individuals acquire attitudes, values, and convictions about themselves, they control their own learning and behavior.

• **Contributions and Limitations of Behaviorism and Social Learning Theory.** Like psychoanalytic theory, behaviorism and social learning theory have been helpful in treating emotional and behavior problems. Yet the techniques are decidedly different. **Behavior modification** consists of procedures that combine conditioning and modeling to eliminate undesirable behaviors and increase desirable responses. It has been used to relieve a wide range of difficulties in children and adults, such as persistent aggression, language delays, and extreme fears (Pierce & Epling, 1995; Wolpe & Plaud, 1997).

Nevertheless, modeling and reinforcement do not provide a complete account of development. Many theorists believe that behaviorism and social learning theory offer too narrow a view of important environmental influences. These extend beyond immediate reinforcements and modeled behaviors to the richness of the physical and social worlds. Finally, behaviorism and social learning theory have been criticized for underestimating people's contributions to their own development. In emphasizing cognition, Bandura is unique among theorists whose work grew out of the behaviorist tradition in granting children an active role in their own learning.

Piaget's Cognitive-Developmental Theory

If one individual has influenced research on child development more than any other, it is Swiss cognitive theorist Jean Piaget (1896–1980). North American investigators had been aware of Piaget's work since 1930. However, they did not grant it much attention until 1960, mainly because his ideas were very much at odds with behaviorism, which dominated psychology during the middle of the twentieth century (Zigler & Gilman, 1998). Piaget did not believe that knowledge could be imposed on a reinforced child. According to his **cognitive-developmental theory**, children actively construct knowledge as they manipulate and explore their world.

• **Piaget's Stages.** Piaget's view of development was greatly influenced by his early training in biology. Central to his theory is the biological concept of *adaptation* (Piaget, 1971). Just as the structures of the body are adapted to fit with the environment, so the structures of the mind develop to better fit with, or represent, the external world. In infancy and early childhood, children's understanding is different from adults'. For example, Piaget believed that young babies do not realize that an object hidden from view—a favorite toy or even the mother—continues to exist. He also concluded that preschoolers' thinking is full of faulty logic. For example, children younger than age 7 commonly say that the amount of milk or lemonade changes when it is poured into a different-shaped container. According to Piaget, children eventually revise these incorrect ideas in their ongoing efforts to achieve an equilibrium, or balance, between internal structures and information they encounter in their everyday worlds.

In Piaget's theory, as the brain develops and children's experiences expand, they move through four broad stages, each characterized by qualitatively distinct ways of thinking. Table 14.4 provides a brief description of Piaget's stages. In the *sensorimotor stage*, cognitive development begins with the baby's use of the senses and movements to explore the world. These action patterns evolve into the symbolic but illogical thinking of the preschooler in the *preoperational stage*. Then cognition is transformed into the more organized reasoning of the school-age child in the *concrete operational stage*. Finally, in the *formal operational stage*, thought becomes the complex, abstract reasoning system of the adolescent and adult.

* **Piaget's Methods of Study.** Piaget devised special methods for investigating how children think. In the early part of his career, he carefully observed his three infant children and also presented them with everyday problems, such as an attractive object that could be grasped, mouthed, kicked, or searched for. From their reactions, Piaget derived his ideas about cognitive changes during the first 2 years. In studying childhood and adolescent thought, Piaget took advantage of children's ability to describe their thinking. He adapted the clinical method of psychoanalysis, conducting open-ended

TABLE 14.4   Piaget's Stages of Cognitive Development

STAGE	PERIOD OF DEVELOPMENT	DESCRIPTION
Sensorimotor	Birth–2 years	Infants "think" by acting on the world with their eyes, ears, hands, and mouth. As a result, they invent ways of solving sensorimotor problems, such as pulling a lever to hear the sound of a music box, finding hidden toys, and putting objects in and taking them out of containers.
Preoperational	2–7 years	Preschool children use symbols to represent their earlier sensorimotor discoveries. Development of language and make-believe play takes place. However, thinking lacks the logical qualities of the two remaining stages.
Concrete operational	7–11 years	Children's reasoning becomes logical. School-age children understand that a certain amount of lemonade or play dough remains the same even after its appearance changes. They also organize objects into hierarchies of classes and subclasses. However, thinking falls short of adult intelligence. It is not yet abstract.
Formal operational	11 years on	The capacity for abstraction permits adolescents to reason with symbols that do not refer to objects in the real world, as in advanced mathematics. They can also think of all possible outcomes in a scientific problem, not just the most obvious ones.

clinical interviews in which a child's initial response to a task served as the basis for the next question Piaget would ask. We will look more closely at this technique when we discuss research methods later in this chapter.

• **Contributions and Limitations of Piaget's Theory.** Piaget's cognitive-developmental perspective convinced the field that children are active learners whose minds consist of rich structures of knowledge. Besides investigating children's understanding of the physical world, Piaget explored their reasoning about the social world. His stages have sparked a wealth of research on children's conceptions of themselves, other people, and human relationships. Practically speaking, Piaget's theory encouraged the development of educational philosophies and programs that emphasize discovery learning and direct contact with the environment.

Despite Piaget's overwhelming contributions, his theory has been challenged. Research indicates that Piaget underestimated the competencies of infants and preschoolers. When young children are given tasks scaled down in difficulty, their understanding appears closer to that of the older child and adult than Piaget assumed. Furthermore, many studies show that children's performance on Piagetian problems can be improved with training. This finding raises questions about his assumption that discovery learning rather than adult teaching is the best way to foster development. Critics also point out that Piaget's stagewise account pays insufficient attention to social and cultural influences on development. Finally, some lifespan theorists take issue with Piaget's conclusion that no major cognitive changes occur after adolescence. Several have proposed accounts of postformal thought that stress important transformations in adulthood (Arlin, 1989; Labouvie-Vief, 1985).

Today, the field of human development is divided over its loyalty to Piaget's ideas. Those who continue to find merit in Piaget's stage approach accept a modified view—one in which changes in thinking are not sudden and abrupt but take place gradually (Case, 1992, 1998; Fischer & Bidell, 1998). Others have turned to an approach that emphasizes continuous gains in children's cognition: information processing. And still others have been drawn to theories that focus on the role of children's social and cultural contexts. We take up these approaches in the next section.

RECENT THEORETICAL PERSPECTIVES

New ways of understanding the developing person are constantly emerging—questioning, building on, and enhancing the discoveries of earlier theories. Today, a burst of fresh approaches and research emphases is broadening our understanding of the lifespan.

Information Processing

During the 1970s, researchers turned to the field of cognitive psychology for ways to understand the development of thinking. The design of digital computers that use mathematically specified steps to solve problems suggested to psychologists that the human mind might also be viewed as a symbol-manipulating system through which information flows—a perspective called **information processing** (Klahr & MacWhinney, 1998). From presentation to the senses at input to behavioral responses at output, information is actively coded, transformed, and organized.

Information-processing researchers often use flowcharts to map the precise series of steps individuals use to solve problems and complete tasks, much like the plans devised by programmers to get computers to perform a series of "mental operations." Let's look at an example to clarify the usefulness of this approach. In a study of problem solving, a researcher provided a pile of blocks varying in size, shape, and weight and asked school-age children to build a bridge across a "river" (painted on a floor mat) that was too wide for any single block to span (Thornton, 1999). Whereas older children easily built successful bridges, only one 5-year-old did. Careful tracking of her efforts revealed that she repeatedly tried unsuccessful strategies, such as pushing two planks together and pressing down on their ends to hold them in place. But eventually, her experimentation triggered the idea of using the blocks as counter-weights. Her mistaken procedures helped her understand why the counterweight approach worked.

A wide variety of information-processing models exist. Some, like the one just considered, track children's mastery of one or a few tasks. Others describe the human cognitive system as a whole (Atkinson & Shiffrin, 1968; Lockhart & Craik, 1990). These general models are used as guides for asking questions about broad changes in thinking. For example, does a child's ability to solve problems become more organized and "planful" with age? Why is information processing slower among older than younger adults? Are declines in memory during old age evident on only some or on all types of tasks?

Like Piaget's cognitive-developmental theory, information processing regards people as active, sense-making beings. But unlike Piaget's theory, there are no stages of development. Rather, the thought processes studied—perception, attention, memory, planning strategies, categorization of information, and comprehension of written and spoken prose—are regarded as similar at all ages but present to a lesser or greater extent. Therefore, the view of development is one of continuous change.

A great strength of the information-processing approach is its commitment to careful, rigorous research methods. Because it has provided precise accounts of how children and adults tackle many cognitive tasks, its findings have important implications for education (Geary, 1994; Siegler, 1998). But information processing has fallen short in some respects. Although good at analyzing thinking into its components, information processing has had difficulty putting them back together into a comprehensive theory. In addition, aspects of cognition that are not linear and logical, such as imagination and creativity, are all but ignored by this approach (Lutz & Sternberg, 1999). Finally, much information-processing research has been conducted in laboratories rather than in real-life situations. Recently, investigators have addressed this concern by studying conversations, stories, memory for everyday events, and academic problem solving.

An advantage of having many theories is that they encourage one another to attend to previously neglected dimensions of people's lives. A unique feature of the final three perspectives we will discuss is their focus on *contexts for development*. The first of these views emphasizes that development of many capacities is influenced by our long evolutionary history.

Ethology and Evolutionary Developmental Psychology

Ethology is concerned with the adaptive, or survival, value of behavior and its evolutionary history (Dewsbury, 1992; Hinde, 1989). Its roots can be traced to the work of Darwin. Two European zoologists, Konrad Lorenz and Niko Tinbergen, laid its modern foundations. Watching diverse animal species in their natural habitats, Lorenz and Tinbergen observed behavior patterns that promote survival. The best known of these is *imprinting*, the early following behavior of certain baby birds, such as geese, that ensures that the young will stay close to the mother and be fed and protected from danger. Imprinting takes place during an early, restricted time period of development. If the mother goose is not present during this time but an object resembling her in important features is, young goslings may imprint on it instead (Lorenz, 1952).

Observations of imprinting led to a major concept in human development: the *critical period*. It refers to a limited time span during which the individual is biologically prepared to acquire certain adaptive behaviors but needs the support of an appropriately stimulating environment. Many researchers have conducted studies to find out whether complex cognitive and social behaviors must be learned during certain time periods. For example, if children are deprived of adequate food or physical and social stimulation during their early years, will their intelligence be impaired? If language is not mastered during early childhood, is the capacity to acquire it reduced?

The term *sensitive period* applies better to human development than does the strict notion of a critical period (Bornstein, 1989). A **sensitive period** is a time that is optimal for certain capacities to emerge and in which the individual is especially responsive to environmental influences. However, its boundaries are less well defined than are those of a critical period. Development may occur later, but it is harder to induce.

Inspired by observations of imprinting, British psychoanalyst John Bowlby (1969) applied ethological theory to the understanding of the human infant-caregiver relationship. He argued that infant smiling, babbling, grasping, and crying are built-in social signals that encourage the parent to approach, care for, and interact with the baby. By keeping the mother near, these behaviors help ensure that the infant will be fed, protected from danger, and provided with the stimulation and affection necessary for healthy growth. The development of attachment in humans is a lengthy process involving changes in psychological structures that lead the baby to form a deep affectional tie with the caregiver. Bowlby (1979) believed that this bond has lifelong consequences, affecting relationships "from cradle to grave" (p. 129).

Observations by ethologists have shown that many aspects of social behavior, including emotional expressions, aggression, cooperation, and social play, resemble those of our primate relatives. Recently, researchers have extended this effort in a new area of research called **evolutionary developmental psychology**. It seeks to understand the adaptive value of species-wide cognitive, emotional, and social competencies as those competencies change with age. Evolutionary developmental psychologists ask such questions as, What role does the newborn's visual preference for facelike stimuli play in survival? Does it support older infants' capacity to distinguish familiar caregivers from unfamiliar people? Why do children play in sex-segregated groups? What do they learn from such play that might lead to adult gender-typed behaviors, such as male dominance and female investment in caregiving?

As these examples suggest, evolutionary psychologists are not just concerned with the biological basis of development. They are also interested in how individuals learn because learning lends flexibility and greater adaptiveness to behavior (Bjorklund & Pellegrini, 2000; Geary, 1999). The evolutionary selection benefits of behavior are believed to be strongest in the first half of life—to ensure survival, reproduction, and effective parenting. As people age, social and cultural factors become increasingly important in generating and maintaining high levels of functioning (Smith & Baltes, 1999). The next contextual perspective we will discuss, Vygotsky's sociocultural theory, serves as an excellent complement to ethology because it highlights social and cultural contexts for development.

Vygotsky's Sociocultural Theory

The field of human development has recently seen a dramatic increase in studies addressing the cultural context of people's lives. Investigations that make comparisons across cultures, and among ethnic groups within cultures, provide insight into whether developmental pathways apply to all people or are limited to particular environmental conditions. As a result, cross-cultural and multicultural research helps us untangle the contributions of biological and environmental factors to the timing, order of appearance, and diversity of children's and adults' behaviors (Greenfield, 1994).

In the past, cross-cultural studies focused on broad cultural differences in development—for example, whether children in one culture are more advanced in motor development or do better on intellectual tasks than children in another. However, this approach can lead us to conclude incorrectly that one culture is superior in enhancing development, whereas another is deficient. In addition, it does not help us understand the precise experiences that contribute to cultural differences in behavior.

Today, more research is examining the relationship of *culturally specific practices* to development. The contributions of Russian psychologist Lev Vygotsky (1896–1934) have played a major role in this trend. Vygotsky's (1934/1987) perspective is called **sociocultural theory**. It focuses on how *culture*—the values, beliefs, customs, and skills of a social group—is transmitted to the next generation. According to Vygotsky, *social interaction*—in particular, cooperative dialogues with more knowledgeable members of society—is necessary for children to acquire the ways of thinking and behaving that make up a community's culture (Wertsch & Tulviste, 1992). Vygotsky believed that as adults and more expert peers help children master culturally meaningful activities, the communication between them becomes part of children's thinking. As children internalize the essential features of these dialogues, they can use the language within them to guide their own thought and actions and to acquire new skills (Berk, 2001).

Vygotsky's theory has been especially influential in the study of cognitive development. Vygotsky agreed with Piaget that children are active, constructive beings. But unlike Piaget, who emphasized children's independent efforts to make sense of their world, Vygotsky viewed cognitive development as a *socially mediated process*—as dependent on the support that adults and more mature peers provide as children try new tasks.

In Vygotsky's theory, children undergo certain stagewise changes. For example, when they acquire language, their ability to participate in dialogues with others is greatly enhanced, and mastery of culturally valued competencies surges forward. When children enter school, they spend much time discussing language, literacy, and other academic concepts—experiences that encourage them to reflect on their own thinking. As a result, they show dramatic gains in reasoning and problem solving.

Although most research inspired by Vygotsky's theory focuses on children, his ideas apply to people of any age. A central theme is that cultures select tasks for their members, and social interaction surrounding those tasks leads to competencies essential for success in a particular culture. For example, in industrialized nations, teachers can be seen helping people learn to read, drive a car, or use a computer (Schwebel, Maher, & Fagley, 1990). Among the Zinacanteco Indians of southern Mexico, adult experts guide young girls as they master complicated weaving techniques (Childs & Greenfield, 1982). In Brazil, child candy sellers with little or no schooling develop sophisticated mathematical abilities as the result of buying candy from wholesalers, pricing it in collaboration with adults and experienced peers, and bargaining with customers on city streets (Saxe, 1988).

Vygotsky's theory, and the research stimulated by it, reveal that children in every culture develop unique strengths. At the same time, Vygotsky's emphasis on culture and social experience led him to neglect the biological side of development. Although he recognized the importance of heredity and brain growth, he said little about their role in cognitive change. Furthermore, Vygotsky's emphasis on social transmission of knowledge meant that he placed less emphasis than other theorists on children's capacity to shape their own development. Contemporary followers of Vygotsky grant the individual and society more balanced roles (Gauvain, 1999; Rogoff, 1998).

Ecological Systems Theory

Urie Bronfenbrenner, an American psychologist, is responsible for an approach to human development that has moved to the forefront of the field over the past two decades because it offers the most differentiated and thorough account of contextual influences on development. **Ecological systems theory** views the person as developing within a complex *system* of relationships affected by multiple levels of the surrounding environment. Since the child's biological dispositions join with environmental forces to mold development, Bronfenbrenner recently characterized his perspective as a *bioecological model* (Bronfenbrenner & Morris, 1998).

As Figure 14.2 shows, Bronfenbrenner envisions the environment as a series of nested structures that includes but extends beyond the home, school, neighborhood, and workplace settings in which people spend their everyday lives. Each layer of the environment is viewed as having a powerful impact on development.

● **The Microsystem.** The innermost level of the environment is the **microsystem**, which consists of activities and interaction patterns in the person's immediate surroundings. Bronfenbrenner emphasizes that to understand development at this level, we must keep in mind that all relationships are *bidirectional*. For example, adults affect children's behavior, but children's biologically and socially influenced characteristics—their physical attributes, personalities, and capacities—also affect adults' behavior. For example, a friendly, attentive child is likely to evoke positive and patient reactions from parents, whereas an active, distractible youngster is more likely to receive restriction and punishment. When

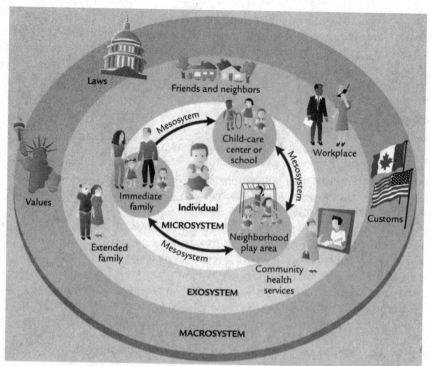

FIGURE 14.2 **Structure of the environment in ecological systems theory.** The *microsystem* concerns relations between the developing person and the immediate environment; the *mesosystem*, connections among immediate settings; the *exosystem*, social settings that affect but do not contain the developing person; and the *macrosystem*, the values, laws, customs, and resources of the culture that affect activities and interactions at all inner layers. The *chronosystem* (not pictured) is not a specific context. Instead, it refers to the dynamic, ever-changing nature of the person's environment.

these bidirectional interactions occur often over time, they have an enduring impact on development (Bronfenbrenner, 1995; Collins et al., 2000).

At the same time, other individuals in the microsystem affect the quality of any two-person relationship. If they are supportive, then interaction is enhanced. For example, when parents encourage one another in their child-rearing roles, each engages in more effective parenting (Cowan, Powell, & Cowan, 1998). In contrast, marital conflict is associated with inconsistent discipline and hostile reactions toward children. In response, children typically become hostile, and both parent and child adjustment suffers (Hetherington & Stanley-Hagen, 2002).

● **The Mesosystem.** The second level of Bronfenbrenner's model, the **mesosytem**, encompasses connections between microsystems. For example, a child's academic progress depends not just on activities that take place in classrooms. It is also promoted by parent involvement in school life and by the extent to which academic learning is carried over into the home (Connors & Epstein, 1996). Among adults, how well a person functions as spouse and parent at home is affected by relationships in the workplace, and vice versa (Gottfried, Gottfried, & Bathurst, 2002).

● **The Exosystem.** The **exosystem** refers to social settings that do not contain the developing person but nevertheless affect experiences in immediate settings. These can be formal organizations, such as the board of directors in the individual's workplace or health and welfare services in the community. For example, flexible work schedules, paid maternity and paternity leave, and sick leave for parents whose children are ill are ways that work settings can help parents rear children and, indirectly, enhance the development of both adult and child. Exosystem supports can also be informal, such as social networks—friends and extended-family members who provide advice, companionship, and even financial assistance. Research confirms the negative impact of a breakdown in exosystem activities. Families who are socially isolated because they have few personal or community-based ties or who are affected by unemployment show increased rates of marital conflict and child abuse (Emery & Laumann-Billings, 1998).

- **The Macrosystem.** The outermost level of Bronfenbrenner's model, the **macrosystem**, is not a specific context. Instead, it consists of cultural values, laws, customs, and resources. The priority that the macrosystem gives to the needs of children and adults affects the support they receive at inner levels of the environment. For example, in countries that require high-quality standards for child care and workplace benefits for employed parents, children are more likely to have favorable experiences in their immediate settings. And when the government provides a generous pension plan for retirees, it supports the well-being of the elderly.

- **A Dynamic, Ever-Changing System.** According to Bronfenbrenner, the environment is not a static force that affects people in a uniform way. Instead, it is dynamic and ever-changing. Whenever individuals add or let go of roles or settings in their lives, the breadth of their microsystems changes. These shifts in contexts, or ecological transitions, as Bronfenbrenner calls them, take place throughout life and are often important turning points in development. Starting school, entering the workforce, marrying, becoming a parent, getting divorced, moving, and retiring are examples.

Bronfenbrenner refers to the temporal dimension of his model as the **chronosystem** (the prefix *chrono* means "time"). Changes in life events can be imposed externally. Alternatively they can arise from within the person, since individuals select, modify, and create many of their own settings and experiences. How they do so depends on their age; their physical, intellectual, and personality characteristics; and their environmental opportunities. Therefore, in ecological systems theory, development is neither controlled by environmental circumstances nor driven by inner dispositions. Instead, people are products and producers of their environments, so both people and their environments form a network of interdependent effects. We will see many more examples of these principles in later chapters.

COMPARING AND EVALUATING THEORIES

In the preceding sections, we reviewed theoretical perspectives that are major forces in human development research. They differ in many respects. First, they focus on different domains of development. Some, such as the psychoanalytic perspective and ethology, emphasize emotional and social development. Others, such as Piaget's cognitive-developmental theory, information processing, and Vygotsky's sociocultural theory, stress changes in thinking. The remaining approaches—behaviorism, social learning theory, ecological systems theory, and the lifespan perspective—discuss many aspects of human functioning.

Second, every theory contains a point of view about development. As we conclude our review of theoretical perspectives, identify the stand each theory takes on the controversial issues presented at the beginning of this chapter. Then check your analysis against Table 14.5.

Finally, we have seen that theories have strengths and limitations. Perhaps you found that you were attracted to some theories, but you had doubts about others. As you read more about development, you may find it useful to keep a notebook in which you test your theoretical likes and dislikes against the evidence. Don't be surprised if you revise your ideas many times, just as theorists have done throughout this century.

TABLE 14.5   Stances of Major Theories on Basic Issues in Human Development

THEORY	CONTINUOUS OR DISCONTINUOUS DEVELOPMENT?	ONE COURSE OF DEVELOPMENT OR MANY?	NATURE OR NURTURE AS MORE IMPORTANT?
Psychoanalytic perspective	*Discontinuous:* Stages of psychosexual and psychosocial development are emphasized.	*One course:* Stages are assumed to be universal.	*Both nature and nurture:* Innate impulses are channeled and controlled through childrearing experiences. *The individual as stable:* Early experiences set the course of later development.
Behaviorism and social learning theory	*Continuous:* Development involves an increase in learned behaviors.	*Many possible courses:* Behaviors reinforced and modeled may vary from person to person.	*Emphasis on nurture:* Development is the result of conditioning and modeling. *Both early and later experiences* are important.
Piaget's cognitive-developmental theory	*Discontinuous:* Stages of cognitive development are emphasized.	*One course:* Stages are assumed to be universal.	*Both nature and nurture:* Development occurs as the brain matures and children exercise their innate drive to discover reality in a generally stimulating environment. *Both early and later experiences* are important.
Information processing	*Continuous:* Children and adults gradually improve in perception, attention, memory, and problem-solving skills.	*One course:* Changes studied characterize most or all children and adults.	*Both nature and nurture:* Children and adults are active, sense-making beings who modify their thinking as the brain matures and they confront new environmental demands. *Both early and later experiences* are important.
Ethology and evolutionary developmental psychology	*Both continuous and discontinuous:* Children and adults gradually develop a wider range of adaptive behaviors. Sensitive periods occur, in which qualitatively distinct capacities emerge fairly suddenly.	*One course:* Adaptive behaviors and sensitive periods apply to all members of a species.	*Both nature and nurture:* Evolution and heredity influence behavior, and learning lends greater flexibility and adaptiveness to it. In sensitive periods, *early experiences* set the course of later development.
Vygotsky's sociocultural theory	*Both continuous and discontinuous:* Language development and schooling lead to stagewise changes. Dialogues with more expert members of society also lead to continuous changes that vary from culture to culture.	*Many possible courses:* Socially mediated changes in thought and behavior vary from culture to culture.	*Both nature and nurture:* Heredity, brain growth, and dialogues with more expert members of society jointly contribute to development. *Both early and later experiences* are important.

(continued)

TABLE 14.5 Stances of Major Theories on Basic Issues in Human Development (continued)

THEORY	CONTINUOUS OR DISCONTINUOUS DEVELOPMENT?	ONE COURSE OF DEVELOPMENT OR MANY?	NATURE OR NURTURE AS MORE IMPORTANT?
Ecological systems theory	*Not specified.*	*Many possible courses:* Biological dispositions join with environmental forces at multiple levels to mold development in unique ways.	*Both nature and nurture:* The individual's characteristics and the reactions of others affect each other in a bidirectional fashion. *Both early and later experiences* are important.
Lifespan perspective	*Both continuous and discontinuous:* Continuous gains and declines, as well as discontinuous, stagewise emergence of new skills, occur during all age periods.	*Many possible courses:* Development is embedded in multiple contexts that vary from person to person, leading to diverse pathways of change.	*Both nature and nurture:* Development is multidimensional, affected by an intricate blend of biological and social forces. Emphasizes plasticity at all ages. *Both early and later experiences* are important.

ETHICS IN LIFESPAN RESEARCH

Research into human behavior creates ethical issues because, unfortunately, the quest for scientific knowledge can sometimes exploit people. For this reason, special guidelines for research have been developed by the federal government, funding agencies, and research-oriented associations, such as the American Psychological Association (1994). Table 14.6 presents a summary of basic research rights drawn from these guidelines. Once you have examined them, read the following research situations, each of which poses a serious ethical dilemma. What precautions do you think should be taken in each instance?

- In a study of moral development, an investigator wants to assess children's ability to resist temptation by videotaping their behavior without their knowledge. Seven-year-olds are promised a prize for solving difficult puzzles. They are also told not to look at a classmate's correct solutions, which are deliberately placed at the back of the room. Telling children ahead of time that cheating is being studied or that their behavior is being closely monitored will destroy the purpose of the study.

- A researcher wants to study the impact of mild daily exercise on the physical and mental health of elderly patients in nursing homes. He consults each resident's doctor to make sure that the exercise routine will not be harmful. But when he seeks the residents' consent, he finds that many do not comprehend the purpose of the research. And some appear to agree simply to relieve feelings of isolation and loneliness.

As these examples indicate, when children or the aged take part in research, the ethical concerns are especially complex. Immaturity makes it difficult or impossible for children to evaluate for themselves what participation in research will mean. And because mental impairment rises with very advanced age, some older adults cannot make voluntary and informed choices. The life circumstances of others make them unusually vulnerable to pressure for participation (Kimmel & Moody, 1990; Society for Research in Child Development, 1993).

Virtually every committee that has worked on developing ethical principles for research has concluded that conflicts arising in research situations often cannot be resolved with simple right or wrong

TABLE 14.6 **Rights of Research Participants**

RESEARCH RIGHTS	DESCRIPTION
Protection from harm	Participants have the right to be protected from physical or psychological harm in research. If in doubt about the harmful effects of research, investigators should seek the opinion of others. When harm seems possible, investigators should find other means for obtaining the desired information or abandon the research.
Informed consent	Participants, including children and the elderly, have the right to have explained to them, in language appropriate to their level of understanding, all aspects of the research that may affect their willingness to participate. When children are participants, informed consent of parents as well as of others who act on the child's behalf (such as school officials) should be obtained, preferably in writing. Older adults who are cognitively impaired should be asked to appoint a surrogate decision maker. If they cannot do so, then someone should be named by an ethics committee that includes relatives and professionals who know the person well. All participants have the right to discontinue participation in the research at any time.
Privacy	Participants have the right to concealment of their identity on all information collected in the course of research. They also have this right with respect to written reports and any informal discussions about the research.
Knowledge of results	Participants have the right to be informed of the results of research in language appropriate to their level of understanding.
Beneficial treatments	If experimental treatments believed to be beneficial are under investigation, participants in control groups have the right to alternative beneficial treatments if they are available.

Sources: American Psychological Association, 1994; Cassel, 1988; Society for Research in Child Development, 1993.

answers (Stanley & Seiber, 1992). The ultimate responsibility for the ethical integrity of research lies with the investigator. However, researchers are advised or, in the case of federally funded research, required to seek advice from others. Special committees exist in colleges, universities, and other institutions for this purpose. These committees weigh the costs of the research to participants in terms of inconvenience and possible psychological or physical injury against the study's value for advancing knowledge and improving conditions of life. If there are any risks to participants' safety and welfare that the worth of the research does not justify, then preference is always given to the interests of the participants.

The ethical principle of *informed consent* requires special interpretation when participants cannot fully appreciate the research goals and activities. Parental consent is meant to protect the safety of children whose ability to decide is not yet mature. For children 7 years and older, their own informed consent should be obtained in addition to parental consent. Around age 7, changes in children's thinking permit them to better understand simple scientific principles and the needs of others. Researchers should respect and enhance these new capacities by providing school-age children with a full explanation of research activities in language they can understand (Fisher, 1993; Thompson, 1992). Extra care must be taken when telling children that the information they provide will be kept confidential and that they can end their participation at any time. Children may not understand, and sometimes do not believe, these promises (Abramovitch et al., 1995; Ondrusek et al., 1998).

Most older adults require no more than the usual informed-consent procedures. Yet many investigators set upper age limits in studies relevant to the elderly, thereby excluding the oldest adults (Bayer & Tadd, 2000). Researchers should not stereotype the elderly as incompetent to decide about participation or to engage in the research activities. Nevertheless, extra measures must be taken to protect those who are cognitively impaired or in settings for care of the chronically ill. Sometimes these individuals may agree to participate simply to obtain rewarding social interaction. Yet participation should not be automatically withheld, since it can result in personal as well as scientific benefits (High & Doole, 1995). In these instances, potential participants should be asked to appoint a surrogate decision maker. If they cannot do so, then someone should be named by an ethics committee that includes relatives and professionals who know the person well. As an added precaution, if the elderly person is incapable of consenting and the risks of the research are more than minimal, then the study should not be done unless it is likely to directly benefit the participant (Cassel, 1988).

Finally, all ethical guidelines advise that special precautions be taken in the use of deception and concealment, as occurs when researchers observe people from behind one-way mirrors, give them false feedback about their performance, or do not tell them the truth regarding what the research is about. When these kinds of procedures are used, *debriefing*, in which the investigator provides a full account and justification of the activities, occurs after the research session is over. Debriefing should also take place with children, but it does not always work well. Despite explanations, children may come away from the situation with their belief in the honesty of adults undermined. Ethical standards permit deception if investigators satisfy institutional committees that such practices are necessary. Nevertheless, because deception may have serious emotional consequences for some youngsters, investigators should try to come up with other research strategies when children are involved.

REFERENCES

Abramovitch, R., Freedman, J. L., Henry, K., & Van Brunschot, M. (1995). Children's capacity to agree to psychological research: Knowledge of risks and benefits and voluntariness. *Ethics and Behavior, 5*, 25–48.

American Psychological Association. (1994). *Publication manual of the American Psychological Association.* Washington, DC: Author.

Arlin, P. K. (1989). Problem solving and problem finding in young artists and young scientists. In M. L. Commons, J. D. Sinnot, F. A. Richards, & C. Armon (Eds.), *Adult development: Vol 1. Comparisons and applications of developmental models* (pp. 197–216). New York: Praeger.

Atkinson, R. C., & Shiffrin, R. M. (1968). Human memory: A proposed system and its control processes. In K. W. Spence & J. T. Spence (Eds.), *Advances in the psychology of learning and motivation* (Vol. 2, pp. 90–195). New York: Academic Press.

Baltes, P. B., Lindenberger, U., & Staudinger, U. M. (1998). Lifespan theory in developmental psychology. In R. M. Lerner (Ed.), *Handbook of child psychology: Vol. 1. Theoretical models of human development* (5th ed., pp. 1029–1143). New York: Wiley.

Bandura, A. (1977). *Social learning theory.* Englewood Cliffs, NJ: Prentice-Hall.

Bandura, A. (1989). Social cognitive theory. In R. Vasta (Ed.), *Annals of child development* (Vol. 6, pp. 1–60). Greenwich, CT: JAI Press.

Bandura, A. (1992). Perceived self-efficacy in cognitive development and functioning. *Educational Psychologist, 28*, 117–118.

Bandura, A. (1999). Social cognitive theory of personality. In L. A. Pervin (Ed.), *Handbook of personality: Theory and research* (2nd ed., pp. 154–196). New York: Guilford.

Bayer, A., & Tadd, W. (2000). Unjustified exclusion of elderly people from studies submitted to research ethics committee for approval: Descriptive study. *British Medical Journal, 321*, 992–993.

Berk, L. E. (2001). *Awakening children's minds: How parents and teachers can make a difference.* New York: Oxford University Press.

Bjorklund, D. F., & Pellegrini, A. D. (2000). Child development and evolutionary psychology. *Child Development, 71*, 1687–1708.

Bornstein, M. H. (1989). Sensitive periods in development: Structural characteristics and causal interpretations. *Psychological Bulletin, 105*, 179–197.

Borstelmann, L. J. (1983). Children before psychology: Ideas about children from antiquity to the late 1800s. In W. Kessen (Ed.), *Handbook of child psychology: Vol. 1. History, theory, and methods* (pp. 1–40). New York: Wiley.

Bowlby, J. (1969). *Attachment and loss: Vol. 1. Attachment*. New York: Basic Books.

Bowlby, J. (1979). *The making and breaking of affectional bonds*. London: Tavistock.

Bowlby, J. (1980). *Attachment and loss: Vol. 3. Loss: Sadness and depression*. New York: Basic Books.

Bronfenbrenner, U. (1995). The bioecological model from a life course perspective: Reflections of a participant observer. In P. Moen, G. H. Elder, Jr., & K. Lüscher (Eds.), *Examining lives in context* (pp. 599–618). Washington, DC: American Psychological Association.

Bronfenbrenner, U., & Morris, P. A. (1998). The ecology of developmental processes. In R. M. Lerner (Ed.), *Handbook of child psychology: Vol. 1. Theoretical models of human development* (5th ed., pp. 535–584). New York: Wiley.

Cairns, R. B. (1998). The making of developmental psychology. In R. M. Lerner (Ed.), *Handbook of child psychology: Vol. 1. Theoretical models of human development* (5th ed., pp. 25–105). New York: Wiley.

Carus, F. A. (1808). *Psychologie. Sweiter Teil: Specialpsychologie*. Leipzig: Barth & Kummer.

Case, R. (1992). *The mind's staircase: Exploring the conceptual underpinnings of children's thought and knowledge*. Hillsdale, NJ: Erlbaum.

Case, R. (1998). The development of central conceptual structures. In D. Kuhn & R. Siegler (Eds.), *Handbook of child psychology: Vol. 2. Cognition, perception, and language* (5th ed., pp. 745–800). New York: Wiley.

Cassel, C. K. (1988). Ethical issues in the conduct of research in long-term care. *Gerontologist, 28* (Suppl.), 90–96.

Chess, S., & Thomas, A. (1984). *Origins and evolution of behavior disorders*. New York: Brunner/Mazel.

Childs, C. P., & Greenfield, P. M. (1982). Informal modes of learning and teaching: The case of Zinacanteco weaving. In N. Warren (Ed.), *Advances in cross-cultural psychology* (Vol. 2, pp. 269–316). London: Academic Press.

Clarke-Stewart, K. A. (1998). Historical shifts and underlying themes in ideas about rearing young children in the United States: Where have we been? Where are we going? *Early Development and Parenting, 7,* 101–117.

Collins, W. A., Maccoby, E. E., Steinberg, L., Hetherington, E. M., & Bornstein, M. H. (2000). Contemporary research on parenting: The case for nature and nurture. *American Psychologist, 55,* 218–232.

Connors, L. J., & Epstein, J. L. (1996). Parent and school partnerships. In M. H. Bornstein (Ed.), *Handbook of parenting: Vol. 4. Applied and practical parenting* (pp. 437–458). Mahwah, NJ: Erlbaum.

Cowan, P. A., Powell, D., & Cowan, C. P. (1998). Parenting interventions: A family systems perspective. In I. E. Sigel & K. A. Renninger (Eds.), *Handbook of child psychology: Vol. 4. Child psychology in practice* (5th ed., pp. 3–72). New York: Wiley.

Darwin, C. (1936). *On the origin of species by means of natural selection*. New York: Modern Library. (Original work published 1859)

de Waal, F. B. M. (1999). The end of nature versus nurture. *Scientific American, 281*(6), 94–99.

Dewsbury, D. A. (1992). Comparative psychology and ethology: A reassessment. *American Psychologist, 47,* 208–215.

Dixon, R. A., & Lerner, R. M. (1999). History and systems in developmental psychology. In M. H. Bornstein & M. E. Lamb (Eds.), *Developmental psychology: An advanced textbook* (4th ed., pp. 3–46). Mahwah, NJ: Erlbaum.

Elder, G., Jr. (1998). The life course and human development. In R. M. Lerner (Ed.), *Handbook of child psychology: Vol. 1. Theoretical models of human development* (5th ed., pp. 939–991). New York: Wiley.

Emde, R. N. (1992). Individual meaning and increasing complexity: Contributions of Sigmund Freud and René Spitz to developmental psychology. *Developmental Psychology, 28,* 347–359.

Emery, R. E., & Laumann-Billings, L. (1998). An overview of the nature, causes, and consequences of abusive family relationships: Toward differentiating maltreatment and violence. *American Psychologist, 53,* 121–135.

Erikson, E. H. (1950). *Childhood and society*. New York: Norton.

Fischer, K. W., & Bidell, T. R. (1998). Dynamic development of psychological structures in action and thought. In R. M. Lerner (Ed.), *Handbook of child psychology: Vol. 1. Theoretical models of human development* (5th ed., pp. 467–562). New York: Wiley.

Fisher, C. B. (1993, Winter). Integrating science and ethics in research with high-risk children and youth. *Social Policy Report of the Society for Research in Child Development, 4*(4).

Freud, S. (1973). *An outline of psychoanalysis*. London: Hogarth. (Original work published 1938)

Freud, S. (1974). *The ego and the id*. London: Hogarth. (Original work published 1923)

Freund, A. M., & Baltes, P. B. (2000). The orchestration of selection, optimization and compensation: An action-theoretical conceptualization of a theory of developmental regulation. In W. J. Perrig & A. Grob (Eds.), *Control of human behavior, mental processes, and consciousness* (pp. 35–58). Mahwah, NJ: Erlbaum.

Gauvain, M. (1999). Cognitive development in social and cultural context. *Current Directions in Psychological Science, 7,* 188–192.

Geary, D. C. (1994). *Children's mathematical development.* Washington, DC: American Psychological Association.

Geary, D. C. (1999). Evolution and developmental sex differences. *Current Directions in Psychological Science, 8,* 115–120.

Gesell, A. (1933). Maturation and patterning of behavior. In C. Murchison (Ed.), *A handbook of child psychology.* Worcester, MA: Clark University Press.

Gesell, A., & Ilg, F. L. (1949a). The child from five to ten. In A. Gesell & F. Ilg (Eds.), *Child development* (pp. 394–454). New York: Harper & Row. (Original work published 1946)

Gesell, A., & Ilg, F. L. (1949b). The infant and child in the culture of today. In A. Gesell & F. Ilg (Eds.), *Child development* (pp. 1–393). New York: Harper & Row.

Gottfried, A. E., Gottfried, A. W., & Bathurst, K. (2002). Maternal and dual-earner employment status and parenting. In M. H. Bornstein (Ed.), *Handbook of parenting. Vol. 2: Biology and ecology of parenting* (2nd ed., pp. 207–229). Mahwah, NJ: Erlbaum.

Greenfield, P. M. (1994). Independence and interdependence as developmental scripts: Implications for theory, research, and practice. In P. M. Greenfield & R. R. Cocking (Eds.), *Cross-cultural roots of minority child development* (pp. 1–37). Hillsdale, NJ: Erlbaum.

Hall, G. S. (1904). *Adolescence.* New York: Appleton.

Hetherington, E. M., & Stanley-Hagan, M. (2000). Diversity among stepfamilies. In D. H. Demo, K. R. Allen, & M. A. Fine (Eds.), *Handbook of family diversity* (pp. 173–196). New York: Oxford University Press.

Hetherington, E. M., & Stanley-Hagan, M. (2002). Parenting in divorced and remarried families. In M. H. Bornstein (Ed.), *Handbook of parenting* (2nd ed., Vol. 3, pp. 287–315). Mahwah, NJ: Erlbaum.

High, D. M., & Doole, M. M. (1995). Ethical and legal issues in conducting research involving elderly subjects. *Behavioral Sciences and the Law, 13,* 319–335.

Hinde, R. A. (1989). Ethological and relationships approaches. In R. Vasta (Ed.), *Annals of child development* (Vol. 6, pp. 251–285). Greenwich, CT: JAI Press.

Horowitz, F. D. (1992). John B. Watson's legacy: Learning and environment. *Developmental Psychology, 28,* 360–367.

Kimmel, D. C., & Moody, H. R. (1990). Ethical issues in gerontological research and services. In J. E. Birren & K. W. Schaie (Eds.), *Handbook of the psychology of aging* (3rd ed., pp. 489–501). San Diego, CA: Academic Press.

Klahr, D., & MacWhinney, B. (1998). Information processing. In D. Kuhn & R. S. Siegler (Eds.), *Handbook of child psychology: Vol. 2. Cognition, perception, and language* (5th ed., pp. 631–678). New York: Wiley.

Labouvie-Vief, G. (1985). Logic and self-regulation from youth to maturity: A model. In M. Commons, F. Richards, & C. Armon (Eds.), *Beyond formal operations: Late adolescent and adult cognitive development* (pp. 158–180). New York: Praeger.

Lemme, B. H. (2002). *Development in adulthood* (3rd ed.) Boston: Allyn and Bacon.

Locke, J. (1892). Some thoughts concerning education. In R. H. Quick (Ed.), *Locke on education* (pp. 1–236). Cambridge, U.K.: Cambridge University Press. (Original work published 1690)

Lockhart, R. S., & Craik, F. I. M. (1990). Levels of processing: A retrospective commentary on a framework for memory research. *Canadian Journal of Psychology, 44,* 87–112.

Lorenz, K. (1952). *King Solomon's ring.* New York: Crowell.

Lutz, D. J., & Sternberg, R. J. (1999). Cognitive development. In M. H. Bornstein & M. E. Lamb (Eds.), *Developmental psychology: An advanced textbook* (4th ed., pp. 275–311). Mahwah, NJ: Erlbaum.

Maylor, E., & Valentine, T. (1992). Linear and nonlinear effects of aging on categorizing and naming faces. *Psychology and Aging, 7,* 317–323.

Nelson, C. A. (2002). Neural development and lifelong plasticity. In R. M. Lerner, F. Jacobs, & D. Wertlieb (Eds.), *Handbook of applied developmental science* (Vol. 1, pp. 31–60). Thousand Oaks, CA: Sage.

Ondrusek, N., Abramovitch, R., Pencharz, P., & Koren, G. (1998). Empirical examination of the ability of children to consent to clinical research. *Journal of Medical Ethics, 24,* 158–165.

Piaget, J. (1971). *Biology and knowledge.* Chicago: University of Chicago Press.

Pierce, W. D., & Epling, W. F. (1995). *Behavior analysis and learning.* Englewood Cliffs, NJ: Prentice-Hall.

Rogoff, B. (1998). Cognition as a collaborative process. In D. Kuhn & R. S. Siegler (Eds.), *Handbook of child psychology: Vol. 2. Cognition, perception, and language* (5th ed., pp. 679–744). New York: Wiley.

Rousseau, J. J. (1955). *Emile*. New York: Dutton. (Original work published 1762)

Rubin, K. H., & Coplan, R. J. (1998). Social and nonsocial play in childhood: An individual differences perspective. In O. N. Saracho & B. Spodek (Eds.), *Multiple perspectives on play in early childhood education* (pp. 144–170). Albany: State University of New York Press.

Saxe, G. B. (1988, August–September). Candy selling and math learning. *Educational Research, 17(6),* 14–21.

Schaie, K. W. (1996). *Intellectual development in adulthood: The Seattle Longitudinal Study.* New York: Cambridge University Press.

Schroots, J., & Birren, J. (1990). Concept of time and aging in science. In J. E. Birren & K. W. Schaie (Eds.), *Handbook of the psychology of aging* (3rd ed., pp. 45–64). San Diego: Academic Press.

Schwebel, M., Maher, C. A., & Fagley, N. S. (1990). Introduction: The social role in promoting cognitive growth over the life span. In M. Schwebel, C. A. Maher, & N. S. Fagley (Eds.), *Promoting cognitive growth over the life span* (pp. 1–20). Hillsdale, NJ: Erlbaum.

Shweder, R. A., Goodnow, J., Hatano, G., LeVine, R. A., Markus, H., & Miller, P. (1998). The cultural psychology of development: One mind, many mentalities. In R. M. Lerner (Ed.), *Handbook of child psychology: Vol. 1. Theoretical models of human development* (5th ed., pp. 865–937). New York: Wiley.

Siegler, R. S. (1998). *Children's thinking* (3rd ed.). Upper Saddle River, NJ: Prentice-Hall.

Skinner, B. F. (1983). Intellectual self-management in old age. *American Psychologist, 38,* 239–244.

Smith, J., & Baltes, P. B. (1999). Life-span perspectives on development. In M. H. Bornstein & M. E. Lamb (Eds.), *Developmental psychology: An advanced textbook* (4th ed., pp. 275–311). Mahwah, NJ: Erlbaum.

Society for Research in Child Development (1993). Ethical standards for research with children. In *Directory of Members* (pp. 337–339). Ann Arbor, MI: Author.

Sroufe, L. A., Egeland, B., & Kreutzer, T. (1990). The fate of early experience following developmental change: Longitudinal approaches to individual adaptation. *Child Development, 61,* 1363–1373.

Stanley, B., & Seiber, J. E. (Eds.). (1992). *Social research on children and adolescents: Ethical issues.* Newbury Park, CA: Sage.

Statistics Canada. (2002). Population. Retrieved from http://www.statcan.ca

Tetens, J. N. (1777). *Philosophische Versuche über die menschliche Natur und ihre Entwicklung.* Leipzig: Weidmanns Erben & Reich.

Thelen, E., & Adolph, K. E. (1992). Arnold Gesell: The paradox of nature and nurture. *Developmental Psychology, 28,* 368–380.

Thomas, R. M. (2000). *Comparing theories of child development* (5th ed.). Belmont, CA: Wadsworth.

Thompson, R. A. (1992). Developmental changes in research risk and benefit: A changing calculus of concerns. In B. Stanley & J. E. Sieber (Eds.), *Social research on children and adolescents: Ethical issues* (pp. 31–64). Newbury Park, CA: Sage.

Thornton, S. (1999). Creating conditions for cognitive change: The interaction between task structures and specific strategies. *Child Development, 70,* 588–603.

U.S. Bureau of the Census. (2002). *IDB Summary Demographic Data.* Retrieved from http://www.census.gov/ipc/www/idbsum.html

Vygotsky, L. S. (1987). Thinking and speech. In R. W. Rieber, & A. S. Carton (Eds.), & N. Minick (Trans.), *The collected works of L. S. Vygotsky: Vol. 1. Problems of general psychology* (pp. 37–285). New York: Plenum. (Original work published 1934)

Wachs, T. D. (2000). *Necessary but not sufficient: The respective roles of single and multiple influences on individual development.* Washington, DC: American Psychological Association.

Watson, J. B., & Raynor, R. (1920). Conditioned emotional reactions. *Journal of Experimental Psychology, 3,* 1–14.

Werner, E. E., & Smith, R. S. (2001). *Journeys from childhood to midlife: Risk, resilience, and recovery.* Ithaca, NY: Cornell University Press.

Wertsch, J. V., & Tulviste, P. (1992). L. S. Vygotsky and contemporary developmental psychology. *Developmental Psychology, 28,* 548–557.

Westen, D., & Gabbard, G. O. (1999). Psychoanalytic approaches to personality. In L. A. Pervin & O. P. John (Eds.), *Handbook of personality: Theory and research* (2nd ed.). New York: Guilford.

Wolpe, J., & Plaud, J. J. (1997). Pavlov's contributions to behavior therapy: The obvious and not so obvious. *American Psychologist, 52,* 966–972.

Zigler, E. F., & Gilman, E. (1998). The legacy of Jean Piaget. In G. A. Kimble & M. Wertheimer (Eds.), *Portraits of pioneers in psychology* (Vol. 3, pp. 145–160). Washington, DC: American Psychological Association.

CHAPTER 15

THE WOLF IN SHEEPDOG'S CLOTHING[1]

Material selected from:
Research Stories for Introductory Psychology,
Second Edition, by Lary Shaffer and Matthew R. Merrens

---

[1]Incorporating previously unpublished observations of L. C. Shaffer and N. Tinbergen. Adapted from research presented in L. C. Shaffer, "Man Bites Dog," 1976, *Discovery.* Leeds, UK: Yorkshire Television.

The research in this chapter is an example of two research methods, the *case study* and the *naturalistic observation*. A case study collects data or observations on one or a few individuals. It is often a rather weak method of investigation. In the research reported here, a case study was used to develop means of data collection about behavior and to support systematic observations on a new research question that might lead to testable hypotheses. Naturalistic observation qualifies for inclusion as a scientific method because it can be used as a means of hypothesis testing. This method is a sort of a maverick within the study of behavior. Some psychologists consider it to be the weakest possible approach to research, a last resort to be used only when all other methods have been ruled out. Others might celebrate this method because it examines real behavior in real settings. Opinions differ widely about the value of naturalistic observations because this label is used to describe a variety of actual research procedures. The common factor is the observation of behavior within a natural context. This description hinges on something difficult to define: a *natural context*. It is probably not productive to try to create a strict definition for this term, but usually natural contexts are considered to be the places where animals are typically found. For wild animals, it is the wild, but it might also be a zoo. The natural environment of a farm animal is, we suppose, a farm. For humans, it might be homes, workplaces, cars, recreational sites, and shopping areas. With humans, it is easier to say what a naturalistic observation is *not:* it is not a contrived lab setting in which people are randomly assigned to various experimental groups. It is not a survey, it is not an interview, and it is not a psychological test. Could a naturalistic observation of people be done in a lab? Maybe. If people were behaving without any particular instruction from the researcher, we might consider lab observations to be naturalistic. There are several examples like this in the chapters that follow. Even though they take place in labs, we believe they qualify as naturalistic observations. Naturalistic observations are sometimes used as one of the outcome measures in a study that employs other research methods as well.

At one extreme, naturalistic observations can be totally descriptive, producing only narrative text about behavior. Early studies of animal behavior were often like this: the animal was watched and actions were described (Lorenz, 1952). More recently, Dian Fossey's work on mountain gorillas was largely descriptive (Fossey, 1983). However, it is also possible to produce numerical data from naturalistic observations, sometimes including making alterations in the natural environment and watching to see how behavior is affected. Early examples, which still make compelling reading, can be found in the work of Tinbergen (1958, 1974), who studied a wide variety of animals in outdoor settings. Although many people associate naturalistic observation with the study of nonhuman animals, sometimes it can be a very good way of finding things out about people as well. Let us presume you wanted to know whether men or women drivers are more likely to wear seat belts. You could observe cars going underneath a highway overpass, while making recordings of sex of driver and seat belt wearing. We believe these data might be better than those you could collect in an interview or survey, because surveys are susceptible to errors from faulty memories or purposeful attempts to misrepresent behavior. A published example of this method can be found in the work of Hoxie and Rubenstein (1994), who observed that traffic lights did not stay red long enough to allow elderly people to cross a busy street safely. An example from a different area of study can be found in the work of Martin and Ross (1996) who went to people's homes to make observations of parents responding to aggression in children.

A STUDY OF SHEEPDOGS

The researchers for this chapter, Lary Shaffer and Niko Tinbergen, worked in the north of England, near the Scottish border, making science documentaries for British television. In addition to being filmmakers, both of them had degrees in zoology, specializing in animal behavior. Indeed, during the course of the study to be described, Tinbergen was awarded a Nobel Prize for his enduring contributions to the study of animal behavior. While traveling in the rolling green farmland of northern England, they had numerous opportunities to observe border collie sheepdogs at work herding vast flocks of sheep. On distant hillsides the white mass of sheep looked like a single organism, stretching out, bunching up, and forming into strings while being forced through gates in the stone walls. If Shaffer and Tinbergen looked carefully, they could sometimes see the single dog that was responsible for all this activity: a black and white speck, darting this way and that, rounding up errant branches of the flock. Thinking this behavior might be worthy of a research study, they asked a friend, Jimmy Rose, for help. Jimmy lived in the Pennine Hills, where there are many sheep farms, and he said he knew just the place to do a study of dogs. This was a lucky break for Shaffer and Tinbergen. They were fortunate to know someone who could make some introductions.

Two weeks later, Shaffer and Tinbergen, in the company of Jimmy, found themselves on their way to Dufton Village for an introduction to the Dargues, a family who had been farming the hills around Dufton for almost 1,000 years. The farms in that area were mostly family farms, staffed by sprawling extended families of parents, offspring, aunts, uncles, cousins, and grandparents, all living under one roof and all working, in some capacity, at the daily chores of the farm. Jimmy had known the Dargues for years and, following the customs of the area, he drove up to the farmhouse and went right in without knocking. Shaffer and Tinbergen followed shyly behind. The Dargues were having their midday meal, seated around a big oak table covered with steaming mountains of food. After a one-sentence introduction from Jimmy, all three guests were invited to pull up to the table and "have a bit of dinner." No one paid any particular attention to the newly arrived guests, and food was shoveled down while the talk centered on cattle feed prices and the weather. Almost as an aside, Jimmy said, "Oh, by the way, Lary and Niko would like to hang about here in the next year or two, watch you work with your sheepdogs, and make a film about it." The head of the family, old John Dargue, slowly looked up from his plate. Chewing along without missing a beat he gazed first at Shaffer, then at Tinbergen, then at Shaffer again and softly said "Aye" between bites. That was all it took to seal the deal. Permission from "Boss" John Dargue meant that the whole farm would be at Shaffer and Tinbergen's disposal for as long as was necessary to complete the project. Shaffer shot a questioning glance at Tinbergen, who returned a meek little shrug and forked a roast potato into his mouth.

Jimmy Rose was correct in thinking that the Dargue's farm would be a good place to watch sheep and dogs. As with most of the farms in the area, their farm was too small to easily provide both food and pasture space for the number of sheep they owned. This fact necessitated a considerable amount of moving sheep from one place to another. Although the entire Dargue family would pitch in when needed, Edwin did most of the shepherding. At 50 years old, Edwin Dargue was short, stoutish, and strong as an ox. He had a quick wit and enjoyed the company afforded by Shaffer and Tinbergen on his rambles around the hills, shepherding his flock. At first, Shaffer and Tinbergen spent a great deal of time just watching the dogs. Sometimes naturalistic observations have a hypothesis immediately but, in this case, hypotheses grew out of weeks of initial observations. Tinbergen was one of the pioneers in the use of naturalistic observation, and he strongly believed that the way to approach a new research project was to "observe, observe, and observe again." As the researcher became acquainted with the behavior, questions would begin to appear. At first these might be small questions or puzzles, but, over numerous observations, they would gradually form into more specific and important questions. This research method required faith that sufficient observations of behavior in a natural setting could be counted on to lead to testable hypotheses. Naturalistic observations are also used by many scientists to suggest hypotheses that will later be tested by other research methods, such as experiments.

Although there were no specific and testable hypotheses at the start of the investigation, Shaffer and Tinbergen both believed that the spectacular performances of the sheepdogs were not merely a matter of training. Dogs are closely related to wolves, and good scientific studies of wolves were beginning to appear (Mech, 1970). Shaffer and Tinbergen suspected that much of the herding behavior was really thinly disguised pack hunting behavior. In the domestication of the dog, humans had created breeds by selective mating that emphasized different characteristics. In the sheepdog, Shaffer and Tinbergen believed that aspects of ancestral wolflike hunting behavior, which might have been useful in herding flock animals, had been retained through generations of selective breeding.

GETTING STARTED

Their first unsystematic observations seemed to confirm the idea that at times the dogs were behaving as a wolf pack. When groups of dogs worked together, a clear dominance hierarchy could be seen among the dogs. The same kinds of status arrangements are found in wolf packs. The dog who seemed to be in the role of the alpha male, or the head of the pack, was always out in front of the others as they trotted to the fields where they would work. If another dog tried to pass him, he would charge at it, chasing it back with the others. In particular, the lead dog spent a great deal of time rebuffing one particular challenger, who usually seemed to be in second place. The alpha male frequently urinated on rocks and tufts of grass. The number two dog would stop, sniff and urinate in the same places, followed by the other male dogs in a predictable order. Female dogs played no obvious part in this scent marking. One day, the dog who had been running second in the dog pack picked a fight with the lead male, which turned into a ferocious battle of flashing teeth and flying fur. The other dogs gathered around to watch. Shaffer and Tinbergen were surprised that Edwin did nothing to break up this fight, which looked as if it would certainly end in injury for both dogs, and maybe death for one. Edwin said, "If you let them fight, they will sort it out for themselves. If you break it up, they will be trying for a rematch every time they see each other. This way, both dogs may get hurt but when it is over they will know who is boss and will be able to work together without any more fighting." After a few minutes of fierce combat, the number two dog went squealing away from the fight. It was over, and the alpha male was still in charge. Edwin was correct about the reestablishment of order. Shaffer and Tinbergen saw no further fighting between these dogs. These observations further convinced Shaffer and Tinbergen that, at times, the dogs were behaving as a wolf pack.

After initial observations and discussions, Tinbergen returned to his busy professorship at Oxford University, reluctantly leaving much of the daily observation to Shaffer. At regular intervals, Tinbergen returned to Dufton to have some days among the dogs, discuss the work, generate new ideas, and debate interpretations.

Shaffer gradually got used to the routine of farm life. After a few weeks, he ceased to notice the smell of farm animals and hardly noticed when running sheep kicked up a spray of liquid manure, which flew in all directions, landing on his clothes and face. As Tinbergen predicted, he began to notice things about the dogs. For most ordinary work around the farm, Edwin used only one dog, a 5-year-old male named Spot. Most border collies have large patches of black and white on their backs, but Spot was almost all black with a white nose, a white bib, and a white spot just behind his ears.

Shaffer marveled at how Spot seemed to know just what to do, requiring very few commands from Edwin. They worked together like a well-rehearsed ballet when moving large flocks or isolating single sheep for specific purposes. When Shaffer asked Edwin about Spot's training, the response was, "They either have it in them, or they don't—you work them and they soon figure out what to do." As Shaffer observed, he was struck by the sorts of commands that Edwin was giving. There seemed to be many more commands telling Spot to *stop* doing some behavior than there were to tell him to *start* doing a particular behavior. Once Shaffer had this idea, it was easy to do the empirical checking. In his little notebook, Shaffer began to record the circumstances of Edwin's commands. The original intention had been to study the dogs, but Shaffer was coming to the realization that the dog behavior made no sense without some understanding of the shepherd and the sheep. For 3 weeks in ordinary work around the farm, Shaffer noted each of Edwin's commands and scored it as a command either to stop a behavior or start a behavior. Other utterances, such as "Good lad, Spot," were not scored because they did not tell the dog to do anything specific. The overall frequencies of these commands are shown in Figure 15.1.

Although the data here only involve one dog and one shepherd, Shaffer's hunch that most of the commands were *stop* commands was confirmed. Shaffer was excited about this because it was the beginning of systematic observations and the start of an emerging story about sheepdog behavior. Although 3 weeks might seem to be a long time to spend confirming such a small point, at the same time Shaffer was beginning work on a documentary film about sheepdogs that was paying for the project, and the film work limited the amount of time each day that could be spent in unencumbered observation.

Having convinced himself that most commands were *stop* commands, the next question seemed to appear automatically: Stop doing what? Another bout of research was launched with Edwin and Spot. Shaffer tried, over a series of days, to find a way to put Spot's behavior into meaningful categories. Initially, this proved to be a challenge. The behaviors of sheep and dog seemed chaotic at first. There seemed to be so many completely different kinds of situations in which Spot had to be stopped by a stream of shouted invective. Tinbergen gave Shaffer a lot of encouragement to keep watching, waiting, and thinking. Patience is more than a virtue in naturalistic observation; it has to be an obsession. Shaffer persevered and, rather suddenly, the clouds of confusion began to clear.

FIGURE 15.1   Frequency of Stop and Start Commands

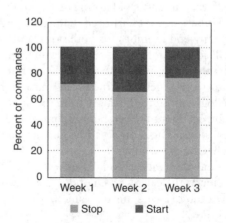

MISTAKES AND INSIGHTS

For a few days Edwin and Spot had been moving sheep from one field to another, down a narrow road with high stone walls on both sides. Edwin's Uncle Joss was helping with this using his dog, Meg, as was Cousin John with a dog called Moss. Moss was just over a year old and was still a big, shaggy, good-natured pup. He would bound around, dividing his time between getting in trouble and working in useful ways. The high stone walls and gates on each side of the roadway focused the errors that a dog could make by squeezing the sheep from both sides. Unlike an open field, the sheep could only go forward or back. At some point, this constriction from the sides, combined with the large number of errors made by Moss, resulted in a flash of insight for Shaffer about the herding behavior of dogs. Moss, Meg, and Spot really had very little work to do in order to keep the sheep moving. The dogs would dart back and forth behind the last row of sheep. If any sheep from the last row tried to turn around and run away from the flock the dogs would charge at these individuals, causing them to turn around and rejoin the flock. If the sheep did not act quickly enough, it was likely to get a little bite on one of its hind legs, causing it to launch into the air and land among the flock. While the dogs were working at this, it became obvious that Moss was also often moving around the side of the flock, pushing in between the sheep and the stone wall, as if he were going to work his way to the front of the flock and stop them. Each time he did this, John would yell at him to stop and come back where he belonged. Shaffer noticed that this was also a common error for Spot, and even for old Meg. These were more than random errors of an untrained puppy: the older dogs were doing the same thing.

Shaffer had been reading about the hunting of wolves and other pack-hunting carnivores, and the reading suggested a reason for this "error." The breakthrough came when Shaffer realized that the dog was acting as a social hunter, treating the shepherd as the head of the hunting pack. In a carnivore pack hunt, the hunters will try to isolate one or a few animals from a large flock. In the early phases, pack hunters split up and spread around the prey trying to make a grab for an individual.

Shaffer believed that this was the situation in which the dogs found themselves. They had moved in close to a small flock and if they were to use patterns of ancestral hunting behavior, the sensible thing to do first would be to spread out around the sheep. The farmers needed to have the sheep driven down the road. However, for a hunting pack, nothing is gained by endlessly driving prey in one direction with all the pack members close together. In the narrow lane, the dogs appeared to be reverting to an ancestral hunting strategy in the tendency to surround the sheep. In order to understand this, you have to remember that although the dogs had their own dominance hierarchy within the pack, they also treated the shepherd as the ultimate pack member.

Shaffer's head began to whirl as he tried to think about the other mistakes he had seen the dogs make. Had most or all of these "mistakes" really been pack-hunting maneuvers that happened to interfere with the dog's role as a sheepdog? Were the dogs depending upon a pack-hunting ancestry in the mistakes they made as well as in their successes? Shaffer thought so, but needed to confirm this hunch with new observations.

Much of sheepdog work involves handling sheep in close quarters in small fields. On other occasions, however, the dog has to run distances of a mile or more away from the shepherd to bring a distant flock back down to the shepherd. As Shaffer reflected upon this, it occurred to him that there were four basic kinds of interactions involving shepherds, dogs, and sheep. These are shown in Figure 15.2, top and bottom.

Figure 15.2 shows that there are two elements in the observed situations that closely resemble a pack hunt: pack members surrounding the sheep and pack members being close to the sheep. The plus and minus signs in the top part of Figure 15.2 became the hypothesis for further observations. The logic of the pack hunt is that it is important for the pack members, in this case shepherd and dogs, to surround the prey, preparatory to catching one of them. This is found in the upper left cell, and it has a double plus, because Shaffer thought it was very like a pack-hunting situation and, therefore something the dogs should do well. Shepherds typically use this arrangement when it is necessary to surround and catch one sheep from a flock so that it can be given some medicine or other treatment.

(a)

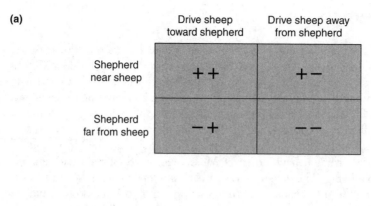

(b)

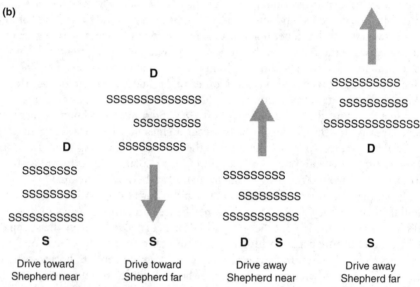

S = shepherd, S = sheep, **D** = dog.
Arrows indicate direction in which shepherd would like sheep to move.

FIGURE 15.2   Categories of Sheepdog Behavior with Sheep and Shepherd.
(a) Shepherd, sheepdog, and sheep maneuvers reduced to basic examples. The plus signs
indicate Shaffer's guess that the situation is something the dog would do readily based on
hunting ancestry: driving toward the shepherd and being near the sheep. The minus
signs suggest that a dog would be expected to have trouble performing well in the situation, as in driving sheep away and being far from the shepherd. Mixed signs predict
mixed success. (b) Schematic representations of the maneuvers in (a).

Moving across the top of Figure 15.2, the upper right cell is the situation that the dogs had
encountered in the narrow lane. "Pack members" were all near the sheep, but the shepherd wanted the
sheep driven away from themselves and the dogs. This has a mixed sign because it is like the hunt in having pack members near the sheep, but it also has the nonhunting element in that the goal is to drive the
sheep away from the pack members.

The lower left cell has one hunting element: the pack has the sheep surrounded. The shepherd is a
long way away from the dog and the sheep. In hunting terms, the head of the pack is too far away to help
with the hunt. This is the situation that can occur when the dog is sent up a hillside to fetch sheep back
to the shepherd.

The remaining cell in Figure 15.2 is an unlikely event in which the shepherd is far away from the flock and wants the dog to show itself and chase the sheep further away. Neither element of this, being far from the pack or chasing sheep farther from the pack, would have any obvious role in a pack hunt. As Shaffer worked out this theoretical scheme, he could not remember seeing any actual field situations that would fit in the lower right cell.

The next step was to go to the field and try to do observations that would support the model. The best times for getting observations of a number of different dogs was during the gathering days when sheep were brought down from the high moors where they shared common grazing during the summer. Because the sheep from many farms had been been grazing on hundreds of square miles of open moorland, gathering is a big job, requiring shepherds and dogs from all the farms in the area. Shaffer took this opportunity to observe behavior of several different dogs and to rate the overall success of each individual maneuver. The outcome was judged to be successful if fewer than 10 percent of commands given by the shepherd were attempts to get the dog to stop doing behaviors. This is a fairly high standard for success, and you should know that it was chosen somewhat arbitrarily. There are no established rules for observing and rating behavior. This leaves it up to the researcher to make a decision. Needless to say, Shaffer tried to avoid introducing bias into the data. Several different operational definitions of the successful maneuver did not produce very different patterns of results. The results of these observations are shown in Figure 15.3.

The data offer some confirmation of the initial observation that closely surrounding the sheep, dog on one side of the sheep and shepherd on the other, was something that the dogs did readily and well. In this figure, the last column for each dog is the situation on the right at the bottom of Figure 15.2 that rarely, if ever, occurred: the dog is sent by the shepherd to approach a distant flock and chase them further away. This had no application for a pack hunter and made little sense in sheepherding. Shaffer asked Edwin if he had ever done this and, after some thought, Edwin responded that occasionally he needed a dog to run at distant intruding neighbor sheep and move them out of the way in order to prevent mixing with his own flock. Zeros have been entered as data for this column in Figure 15.3, because Shaffer asked each of the shepherds to try to get their dogs to do it, and the result was a complete failure. The dogs refused to do this in spite of a barrage of commands from the red-faced, arm-waving shepherd. The dogs were practically incapable of this behavior.

It is important to make a distinction between these rough working farm dogs and the polished and trained dogs who perform in the spectator events called sheepdog trials. Dog trials are local and national competitions that are held to show off the peak achievements of herding dogs who have been meticulously taught to follow instructions. The training of these dogs is so intense and thorough that they appear to be radio controlled. The dogs trained for exhibition in sheepdog trials demonstrate that

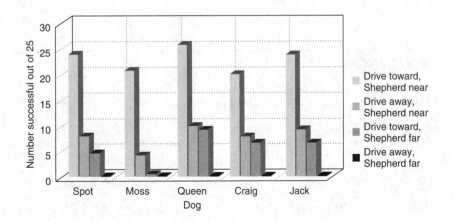

FIGURE 15.3 Success in Maneuvers for Several Dogs. Number of successful maneuvers of four different types by five different dogs. Success was defined as a herding event in which less than 10 percent of commands were telling the dog to *stop* a particular behavior.

it is possible to teach these dogs to do exactly what the shepherd wants. For Shaffer and Tinbergen, however, the rough farm dogs provided a better window into the workings of canine behavior.

The observations described here illustrated an important, but rarely appreciated, aspect of learning. People sometimes think of learning as adding a new behavior to a list of behaviors that can already be performed. For example, as a child, you learned to do arithmetical operations such as multiplication. It might be easy to conclude that this learning only involved adding new responses to a behavior repertoire. What is less obvious is that learning also includes eliminating responses: learning *not* to perform certain behaviors. To perform multiplication, we must learn to put the numbers in straight columns above each other, but this includes learning to avoid having the response of having columns so misaligned that arithmetic becomes impossible. Much of the sheepdog behavior involved learning *not* to do things. Remember that most of the commands given to the dogs were "stop" commands.

Shaffer and Tinbergen were also interested in the development of sheepdog behavior. During their work with Edwin, they had an opportunity to watch him raise a pup, Jill. At first Jill seemed to have no particular interest in sheep. When she was around 8 months old, she rather suddenly started to run along beside Spot, doing what he was doing. It seemed to Shaffer and Tinbergen that Jill was learning as much from Spot as she was from Edwin. By the time she was a year and a half old, she was able to work on her own and be useful in herding the sheep. Years ago, Jill's behavior might have been described as a herding instinct, suggesting that it was caused by her genetic endowment. We now believe that this sort of label is too simple to be of any use. Herding behavior certainly has some genetic components. This becomes clear if, facetiously, we ask why *dogs* are used for herding? Why not cats? *Sheepcats*? Shaffer and Tinbergen believed that the dogs carried a genetic package that predisposed them to perform many of the behaviors needed by the farmer. These behaviors were thinly disguised hunting behaviors, and probably this genetic component had come to the dogs through ancestral lines. The spectacular levels of performance in sheep trial dogs clearly showed that learning was involved. Much of this learning was the elimination of undesirable responses. Immediate situational components such as nutrition, time of day, and the behavior of other dogs also made a difference. One of the recurrent themes of contemporary psychological research is that a behavior does not have a single cause. All behaviors have genetic, biological, experiential, and situational components. As you will see in subsequent chapters, these components, and the interactions among them, are the primary topic for psychological investigations today.

People who know little about contemporary psychology may consider that most human behavior is learned: we use misleading phrases such as "the child learned to walk." Although learning is certainly a component of walking, other factors are also involved. For example, research by Esther Thelen (1992) has shown that the appearance of walking is delayed by the leg muscle strength of babies. The legs of young babies are so heavy that their underdeveloped muscles cannot move the legs in walking motions without assistance. Walking does not simply appear as the result of learning. Much as with the sheepdog behavior described in this article, human walking has many components, not a single cause.

REFERENCES

Fossey, D. (1983). *Gorillas in the mist*. Boston: Houghton Mifflin.

Hoxie, R., & Rubenstein, L. (1994). Are older pedestrians allowed enough time to cross intersections safely? *The Journal of the American Geriatrics Society, 42,* 241–244.

Lorenz, K. (1952). *King Solomon's ring*. London: Crowell.

Martin, J., & Ross, H. (1996). Do mitigating circumstances influence family reactions to physical aggression? *Child Development, 67,* 1455–1466.

Mech, L. D. (1970). *The wolf*. New York: Natural History Press.

Thelen, E. (1992). Development as a dynamic system. *Current Directions in Psychological Science, 1,* 189–193.

Tinbergen, N. (1958). *Curious naturalists*. London: Country Life.

Tinbergen, N. (1974). *Curious naturalists* (rev. ed.). Amherst: University of Massachusetts Press.

CHAPTER 16

NOW YOU SEE IT,
NOW YOU DON'T[1]

Material selected from:
Research Stories for Introductory Psychology,
Second Edition, by Lary Shaffer and Matthew R. Merrens

---

[1]Incorporating the research of R. Baillargeon & J. DeVos, "Object Permanence in Young Infants: Further Evidence," 1991, *Child Development, 62,* pp. 1227–1246.

Jean Piaget (1896–1980) was one of the founding fathers of modern developmental psychology. Most of his life work involved studying the cognitive processes of children. Probably his most important discovery was that children think differently from adults. Piaget first noticed this while he was giving individually administered intelligence tests to children. Because this task involved having to ask the same questions over and over, he began to notice that different children independently and repeatedly came up with the same wrong answers to questions on the test. For example, children would repeatedly fail to understand the abstract point that objects can belong to two classes at once: a marble may be both red and round. Over time, Piaget came to see that these answers were only "wrong" from the adult perspective. Children think differently than adults do and, from the perspective of the children, their answers were right.

Later, Piaget did a number of classic demonstrations of childhood thought processes using his own children as participants (Piaget, 1954). He recounted his interpretations of these demonstrations in his early and important books about cognitive development in children. Piaget's books were very influential because his work was a new approach to understanding the development of mental processes. Many researchers were soon working hard to find solid empirical confirmation for the charming observations he reported.

Piaget turned his observations into a stage theory of cognitive development in which a child progresses through a number of stages as childhood thinking comes to resemble adult thinking. In summary, this cognitive development consists of two major components: (1) the child being able to understand the viewpoints of others and (2) the child coming to deal with abstract ideas. One way to think about these abstract ideas is to contrast them with concrete ideas. *House* is a concrete word, *beauty* is an abstract word. Small children have difficulty grasping the meaning of ideas that are not tied to observable objects and events. The central idea of a stage theory is that the transition between stages is quite rapid compared to the longer time spent within the stage. Much of the research on this topic attempted to evaluate the timetables Piaget proposed for the stages of development.

It may seem a bit strange, but part of the fun of science consists of taking on the established notions or theories of others and finding problems with them. This is an adult version of the giggle that a child might get when a feared authority figure gets a pie in the face. Although many textbooks correctly stress the value of science, few of them point out the fun. The most stolid scientists might not want to admit this, but it can be great fun, even for adults, to throw a pie at the establishment. The scientific way to do this is to conduct carefully designed research that contradicts long-held and widely believed notions. Often this involves replication of earlier research. You can see one reason why science is self-correcting: a flawed theory is likely to be attacked from a number of directions. If these attacks find problems for the theory, then the theory is likely to be modified. In extreme cases, a theory may be found to be so badly flawed that it is discarded completely.

CONSERVATION

Piaget's entire theory is not exactly spinning around the drain, but it has been successfully attacked by a number of contemporary researchers. These attacks have occurred on a number of Piagetian fronts. For example Samuel and Bryant (1984) studied a well-known Piagetian task called *conservation*. The classic conservation task is designed to show that young children are unable to mentally manipulate ideas about concrete events. In the classic demonstration of conservation, a child is presented with two balls of clay that are identical in size and shape and asked if they are the same. The child responds that they are. Next, while the child watches, one of the balls is rolled into some obviously different shape, such as a pizza or a hot dog. Then the child is asked again whether the two objects still have the same amount of clay. Piaget found that children younger than about 5 years old tended to answer "no" to this question, indicating that one lump of clay or the other now contained more clay. He believed that the child could not grasp the transformation that the clay had undergone and was misled by the obvious visual difference between the two portions of clay.

Samuel and Bryant wondered if, perhaps, the children were also responding to being asked the same question twice in a row. Children learn that when they are asked a question twice, often it is because they are expected to change their answer. For example, if a child is being interrogated about some misdeed and the adult does not get an admission of guilt, the child is asked the same question again and is expected to change the answer. "Now I want you to tell me the truth, *did you scratch your initials in the side of the piano?*" Standard Piagetian conservation testing asked the same question twice and the "correct" outcome was to change the answer. Samuel and Bryant examined this by asking the question only once. The children were shown two objects that were equivalent and, without any questions being asked of them, watched while one was changed. Only then were they asked the question about equivalence. The children in this situation made fewer errors than children who were asked the question twice, in the usual Piagetian manner. This suggested that being asked the question twice played a role in the changed answer.

Winer, Craig, and Weinbaum (1992) studied the classic conservation task with college students as participants and found that the wording of the question also played a role in correct responses. Remember: Piaget expected children to be fully conservational by about age 6. He also expected that once people were fully conservational, they would stay that way. This is an important issue because the conservation task was considered by Piaget to be a hallmark achievement defining the boundary between two major stages of cognitive development. A stage theory suggests a one-way progression of development, and Piaget did not expect cognitive achievement to come and go depending upon factors such as the number and nature of the questions being asked.

One of the more successful of the scientists leading commando raids into Piagetian territory has been Renée Baillargeon (pronounced *bay-r-jon*). One of the focuses of her research has been the timing of another important cognitive achievement, *object permanence*.

OBJECT PERMANENCE

Object permanence is the name given to the ability of children to understand that objects continue to exist, or are permanent, even when they are out of sight. Piaget believed that children younger than about

9 months did not yet have object permanence. His conclusions were based on observations of his young son and daughter. Piaget took an attractive toy away from his kids and hid it under a piece of cloth while they watched. At ages younger than 9 months, they would make no effort to recover it. Piaget concluded that his kids did not try to recover the toy because they thought that it ceased to exist when it was out of sight (Piaget, 1954).

It is easy to jump to wrong conclusions based on simple observations where the researcher is emotionally involved with the observation. If you have ever tried to change a baby's diaper and had the infant use the instant of nakedness to urinate, you could probably convince yourself that the infant had planned this as a way to frustrate you. Your conclusion would have some of the same problems that Piaget's research had—you only made one observation, and you were a part of the event you were trying to observe. You might come to different conclusions if you were to observe a large number of caregivers diapering infants. Case studies should be confined to unusual situations in which the study of larger groups is not possible.

Sometimes students wonder why object permanence is given such prominence in the research literature. Much research energy has been devoted to object permanence because it is an early, clear, and important indication that a child is beginning to think the way an adult does. It is not possible to think rationally about the world if you believe that anything you cannot see no longer exists and that when things reappear to you, they have suddenly started to exist again.

HABITUATION

It is always a problem to know what an infant has heard or seen. Inability to use language is a defining characteristic of infancy. One of the most common research methods for getting babies to show us what they know is a strategy called *habituation*. In habituation, a baby is exposed to the same stimulus—for example, a visual event—over and over until it shows significant decreases in responding to the stimulus. Although we do not know what the baby is actually thinking, if you were to watch a baby becoming habituated, it would be easy to conclude that the baby has just become bored with the repetitious event. Then the visual event is changed. Typically when the baby first sees the change, strong responding will reappear. The return of responding indicates that the baby can tell something new has happened. Several different infant responses have been used by researchers to indicate that a baby is reacting to a new event. These have included staring at the new visual stimulus, as well as more subtle measures such as pupil dilation or heart rate changes. As long as the baby does something different when the event is changed, we know that the baby has noticed the change.

In 1991, Baillargeon and DeVos published an article that questioned Piaget's notions about the age at which object permanence first appeared. Baillargeon and DeVos used much more sophisticated methodology than Piaget and, unlike Piaget, they went to great lengths to ensure that their own beliefs and other uncontrolled factors were unlikely to bias their results. Baillargeon and DeVos believed that Piaget's observations may have misled him because in his demonstration the child was required to do at least two things at once. Piaget's children had to understand (1) that objects continued to exist when hidden *and* (2) to be able to plan and execute a search for the object. Planning a search involves knowing what to do first, what to do next, and so on. It is a fairly complex task that we, as adults, take for granted. A young child might know that an object continues to exist but may be unable to plan an orderly search for it—these are different tasks. Piaget's situation was even more complex because his kids had to plan the search as well as have the cognitive and motor skills to carry it out.

In order to disentangle object permanence from other cognitive and motor skills, a number of researchers have simplified the tasks children must perform to demonstrate early object permanence. For example, infants have been given tests requiring only visual responses, which can be much easier for an infant than the crawling and reaching required by Piaget's tasks.

Baillargeon and DeVos studied object permanence with a habituation situation called, in the developmental psychology literature, the *possible event* and the *impossible event*. Special effects in the movies have trained us to think that no visual event is impossible. However, for a baby, disappearing and reappearing objects should be surprising any time after object permanence develops. For example, imagine a simple visual test of object permanence in which a child watches while a toy car is rolled down a ramp. At one point the car rolls behind a piece of cardboard that momentarily blocks the child's view of the car. On some trials, while the car is behind the cardboard screen, the researcher, unseen, grabs it off the ramp and hides it. Unaware of this, the infant continues to turn its eyes as if tracking the car behind the screen and then, perhaps, shows some surprise that the car has not reappeared at the downhill side of the cardboard screen. The little car failing to appear on the other side of the cardboard screen is called the *impossible event*. It is "impossible" because the car disappears into thin air. You should be able to figure out why showing surprise at this would be an indication of object permanence. The infants with object permanence show surprise because they are wondering, as we might, where the car has gone. In contrast, if these children did not have object permanence, if they thought objects ceased to exist when not visible, there would be no reason for them to show any particular surprise when a car vanished behind a screen and did not reappear: the car has ceased to exist.

You might make the argument that a disappearing and reappearing car is a surprising event in itself and that even children without object permanence would show surprise as cars come and go. This is why it is important to compare impossible event responses to those of a child watching the *possible event*: a car rolls down a ramp, behind a screen, and out the other side. If a child did not have object permanence, the reaction to these events should be the same—cars here and there, coming and going. However, if the child has object permanence, then the reaction to the possible and impossible events should be different. The impossible event should be a surprise. The possible event, which does not contradict object permanence, should be less interesting and maybe even boring. Because you have object permanence yourself (or you are going to have trouble in life), you can imagine the surprise of the impossible event compared to the ordinary nature of the possible event.

Baillargeon and DeVos (1991) presented a well-controlled series of studies that used visual tasks such as this in an attempt to find the youngest age at which children could demonstrate the achievement of object permanence in visual tasks. Several related studies were presented in the main article. This kind of presentation can be interesting because we can see the evolution of the researcher's ideas. Usually later studies are done to fix methodological oversights or to extend findings from earlier studies. We will present one of their studies in some detail and refer to the findings of two others.

OBJECT PERMANENCE STUDIES

A primary method used in the research to be discussed here is the *experiment*. Remember, although that word is often used very loosely in everyday parlance, within psychology it refers to a specific set of operations that can lead to confident conclusions about cause and effect. In the most basic kind of experiment, there is an experimental group that gets some particular kind of experience or treatment. There is also a control group, which does not get the special experience. By comparing the outcomes of the two groups, one can see the effect of the special treatment. The experiment described here involved a within-subjects comparison similar to those described in earlier chapters. The participants were their own control group. There are also some quasiexperimental outcomes.

Participants

The participants were 32 healthy, full-term infants ranging in age from 3 months, 23 days to 4 months, 13 days old (mean = 3 months, 24 days). The names of the infants were found in the birth announcements in a newspaper. Parents were contacted and offered some money for travel expenses, but they were not otherwise paid. This may be important because it suggests that all the parents had some interest in the study itself. They were not merely doing it for the money.

Procedures

Baillargeon and DeVos described the apparatus and procedures in great detail. This was done so that other researchers could replicate the study. Think of this apparatus as being like a small stage upon which infants could observe events. The infants were held on the parent's lap in front of the apparatus during the trials. The parent was asked to close his or her eyes and not to interact with the child during the experimental procedures. In this way the parent could not transmit his or her own reactions to the infant. The infants were watched by two observers looking through peepholes in cloth-covered frames on each side of the apparatus. The observers could not see each other nor, presumably, hear each other in any way. Additionally, they could not see the events on the little stage from where they were and they did not know the order in which the events were presented. These arrangements prevented them from unknowingly biasing the data in some way. Each observer had a button that was wired to a computer. The observer's job was to watch the baby and to push the button when the baby showed interest or surprise by attending to the events presented. The computer could record whether the two observers agreed on the direction of the infant's gaze. Agreement averaged 91 percent or more, suggesting that they were both observing quite accurately. There is no minimum level of observer agreement that is universally accepted in psychology. However, it is not possible to place much confidence in results unless the agreement between observers is quite high. In practice, studies are published with agreements ranging upward from about 80 percent. If the event being observed is relatively unimportant to the main point of the study, one might accept slightly lower levels. If the event is central to the study, higher levels might be sought.

The habituation event in this study consisted of the infants seeing a little ramp that had a track on it with additional track extending from the base of the ramp along the floor. A screen blocked the view of part of the track. The screen was lifted for a short period of time so that the infants could see the whole track set up. The screen was lowered, and a little car rolled down the track, passed behind the screen, and reappeared rolling along the track on the other side of the screen (see Figure 16.1).

The impossible test event in this study was like the habituation event, except that before the car was rolled down the ramp, the screen was raised to reveal a large plastic mouse sitting directly on the tracks. The screen was then lowered and, unseen to the infants, the mouse was removed from behind. The car was then rolled down the ramp and appeared rolling at the far side of the screen. The mouse was then quickly replaced so that when the screen was raised, the mouse appeared to the infant to have been sitting on the track all along.

The possible test event was like the impossible one, except that the mouse was placed 10 cm behind the track. Although the mouse was behind the track and it would not have impeded the rolling of the car, it was removed during the time when the screen was down so that any small noises associated with mouse removal would be the same for both the possible and the impossible event (see Figure 16.2).

Before they were repeatedly presented with the habituation event, each infant was given a chance to see the mouse on the tracks and off the tracks in order to become familiar with the two positions. Half of the infants saw mouse-on-the-tracks first and half saw mouse-off-the-tracks first. Following these familiarization trials, the infants were habituated to the event shown in Figure 16.1 in which the car merely rolled down the track. Habituation was operationally defined as a 50 percent decrease in time attending the event or nine full trials. Once one of these criteria had been reached, infants were presented with the impossible and possible mouse events in alternating trials.

FIGURE 16.1   The Habituation Event. Infants are shown the ramp and track, the cardboard screen is lowered, and the little car rolls down the track, behind the screen, and out the other side.

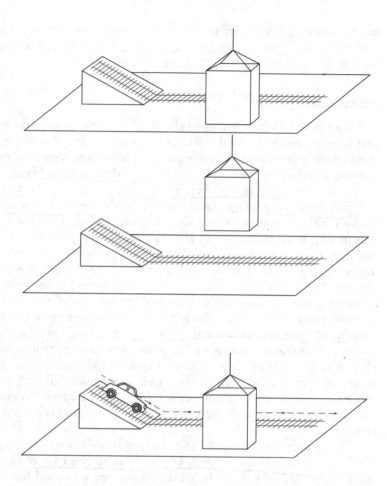

During these tests, some infants became fussy and one started to fall asleep. Their data were included—as far as they went—even if they did not finish the experiment. It is possible to bias data by leaving participants in or by dropping them out. In this case, there is no reason to think that including data from these individuals had any adverse effect on the outcome of the study.

Results

As shown in Figure 16.3, both male and female infants showed decreases in looking at the event, which defined habituation.

Following habituation, infants were presented with the possible and impossible events. When all infants were considered together, the statistical analysis of the data for the test trials indicated that infants did not look longer at the impossible event (mean = 27.4 sec) than at the possible event (mean = 25.8 sec). However, when the group was divided by sex, female infants looked longer ($p < .05$) at the impossible event (mean = 31.1 sec) than at the possible event (mean = 23.7 sec), but males did not seem to notice the difference (possible mean = 27.6 sec, impossible mean = 24.1 sec, $p > .05$). The data for male and female test trials are presented in Figure 16.4.

It is easy to see the female differences in this figure. The males seemed to look longer at the possible event early in the trials, but ended up looking about equally at possible and impossible events. There

FIGURE 16.2   The Possible and Impossible Test Events. In the possible event, the mouse is shown behind the track. In the impossible event it is on the track. In both cases, the cardboard screen is lowered before the car rolls behind the block and out the other side.

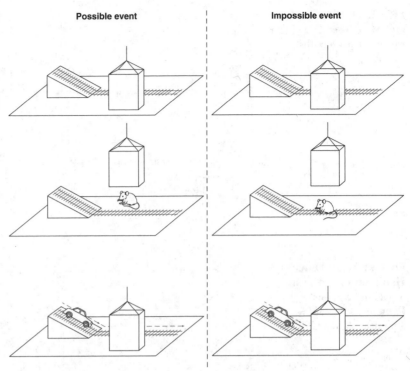

Possible event   Impossible event

were no significant sex differences in looking times on the familiarization or habituation trials, only on the test trials. Studies by other researchers have shown that male infants lag several weeks behind females in some visual skills such as depth perception (Gwiazda, Bauer, & Held, 1989), and this may be the reason why the males seemed to be developmentally behind in the mouse studies of object permanence. The visual displays used by Baillargeon and DeVos require depth perception as well as object permanence.

Baillargeon and DeVos ran this study again with other infants. The only change was that the possible event had the mouse placed in front of the tracks, not behind the tracks. This was done to eliminate the possibility that the females who responded most strongly were merely more interested in the mouse when it was nearer to them. This rival explanation of the data was not supported. The results showed the same finding as in the first study: female infants looked longer than male infants at the impossible event. When the study was done one more time with younger females (3 months, 6 days to 3 months, 22 days, mean = 3 months, 16 days) the effect disappeared, as can be seen in Figure 16.5.

FIGURE 16.3   Female and Male Habituation Trials. Mean age = 3 months, 29 days.

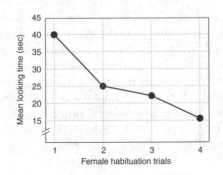

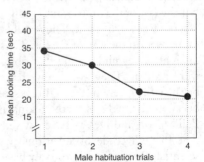

FIGURE 16.4 Female and Male Test Trial Data. Mean age = 3 months, 29 days.

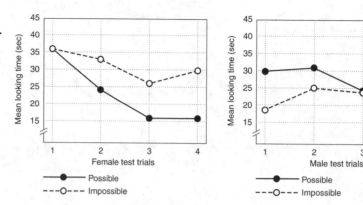

FIGURE 16.5 Female Habituation and Test Trials in Younger Females. Mean age = 3 months, 16 days.

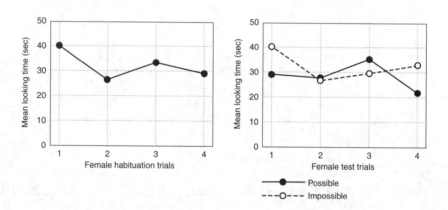

Probably these infants were too cognitively immature to figure this out or too visually immature to see the differences in the mouse positions. Through repeated testing, Baillargeon and DeVos pushed the envelope of this study design as far as it would go and demonstrated the age boundary for object permanence, at least when tested in this situation. It is worth a reminder that Piaget did not find object permanence in his children until they were 8 or 9 months old.

The carefully planned and conducted experiments of Baillargeon and DeVos demonstrate striking abilities in children as young as 3.5 months old. We doubt that many parents, even those having considerable experience with infants, would have predicted this level of reasoning in such young children. All but the last of the mouse studies gives evidence that at least young females knew the mouse existed even when it was out of sight. They could figure out the trajectory of the car, understanding that, at times, the mouse was in the way of the car. These children knew that objects continued to exist when they were out of sight. They understood that objects retained their solidity and other physical properties when they were hidden. They also knew that the interactions between physical objects did not change merely because they were out of sight. It seems likely that Piaget did not notice these things in young children because his methods were lacking in adequate experimental procedures and controls. Even though Baillargeon and DeVos have revised Piaget's view of cognition in childhood, it must be remembered that Piaget's crude observations pointed the way to more sophisticated analyses of behavior. As a scientist, Piaget would probably have been well pleased with this outcome.

REFERENCES

Baillargeon, R., & DeVos, J. (1991). Object permanence in young infants: Further evidence. *Child Development, 62,* 1227–1246.

Gwiazda, J., Bauer, J., & Held, R. (1989). Binocular function in human infants: Correlation of stereoscopic and fusion-rivalry discriminations. *Journal of Pediatric Ophthalmology and Strabismus, 26,* 128–132.

Piaget, J. (1954). *The construction of reality in the child.* New York: Basic Books.

Samuel, J., & Bryant, P. (1984). Asking only one question in the conservation experiment. *Journal of Child Psychology and Psychiatry, 25,* 315–318.

Winer, G., Craig, R., & Weinbaum, E. (1992). Adults' failure on misleading weight-conservation tests: A developmental analysis. *Developmental Psychology, 28,* 109–120.

CHAPTER 17

KIDS SAY THE DARNDEST THINGS[1]

Material selected from:
Research Stories for Introductory Psychology,
Second Edition, by Lary Shaffer and Matthew R. Merrens

---

[1]Incorporating the research of M. D. Leichtman and S. J. Ceci, "The Effects of Stereotypes and Suggestions on Preschoolers' Reports," 1995, *Developmental Psychology, 31,* pp. 568–578.

Memory was a topic of research within psychology before the beginning of scientific psychology over 100 years ago. One of the most surprising findings of recent decades is the extent to which memories can be modified by events that happen subsequently. You will have some hint of this if you have ever heard a friend relating a past incident that included you as a participant. As you listen to your friend's account, you find yourself thinking, "That isn't what happened, that's not the way I remember it."

RECALLING AN ACCIDENT

One of the most formative classic pieces of research about the manipulation of memory was done by Loftus and Palmer (1974). This study demonstrated that memory was unlike a video recorder; it was not a faithful or objective record of what happened. Instead, they found that memory was reconstructive: some aspects of our memory were shown to be accurate, but later events were merged with some existing memories, changing their content.

In an experiment, Loftus and Palmer showed adults a film of a car accident. Following this, participants wrote a description of what they had seen and answered some questions about it. One key question was: "About how fast were the cars going when they *contacted* each other?" Different groups of participants were given different versions of this question. Although some were asked the question with *contacted* as the verb, for other participants this word was replaced with one of the following: *hit, bumped, collided,* or *smashed.* The speed estimates given by the participants as answers to the question were a dependent variable. These estimates varied depending on the word that had been used in the question. Participants who were asked about the speed as the cars *contacted* each other gave an average speed estimate of 32 miles per hour. Other words resulted in successively faster estimates, culminating in *smashed,* which resulted in a 41 mph average estimate.

A week later, participants were asked to recall the film and to answer another group of questions. Memory was operationally defined as the responses that participants made to questions about past events. One of the questions asked was, "Did you see any broken glass?" There was no broken glass in the film, but most participants who had heard the word *smashed* in the initial phase of the study also remembered broken glass that was not really there. This nicely illustrates what is meant by reconstructive memory. When we refer back to memories of past events, what we retrieve is a patchwork composed of things that really happened, things that have been changed a bit, and things that were added later. Memory is not like a photograph, unchanged in storage across time. Rather, it is a project constantly under reconstruction.

PRESUPPOSITIONS

In a subsequent study, Loftus (1975) further investigated memory reconstruction as a function of additional information tucked into questions. This extra information was called a presupposition. For example, in the sentence "Did it hurt when the vicious dog bit you?" the question is *"Did it hurt?"* but there is also a presupposition that the dog was vicious. You are not being *asked* if the dog was vicious, you are being *told* this. You are asked about being hurt. Loftus (1975) showed participants a film involving a car hitting a baby carriage. Some participants were asked if they had seen a barn, although there was no barn in the film. Other participants were asked if there was a station wagon parked in front of the barn. In this latter case, the question asked directly about a station wagon and the barn was a presupposition: these participants were not asked about the barn—they were told about it.

When asked a week later, 29.2 percent of the participants who were given false presuppositions, such as the barn, claimed that they actually remembered the nonexistent object. In comparison, surprisingly, only 15.6 percent of people who had false objects introduced as direct questions—for example, "Did you see a barn?"—remembered false objects. Lastly, only 8.7 percent of a control group, which had not been given any false information, remembered false objects. The wider implications of these findings ought to be of great interest to a society that depends on testimony from memory.

These are among many clear research demonstrations of the reconstructive nature of memory. We observe events, but the memory we have of them includes more than perfectly stored observations. Even completely false information can be included merely because it happened to be available around the time of the event. We all feel that there are some things we *know*; things that we remember so clearly that we have no doubt about the objectivity or truthfulness of our memory. The studies of Loftus and others indicate that we should not be so sure of ourselves. What does this say about objectivity? If we accept these research findings as having external validity, it becomes nonsense to instruct someone to "be objective" about past events, as if objectivity were something that could be turned on or off at will. The studies of memory suggest quite different conclusions: the memories in which we put so much stock are mosaics of real and false information.

These observations ought to undermine some of our confidence in the truth of our memories. Usually this does not matter very much. Who cares if we remember that there was potato salad at the family picnic last summer when, in fact, it was a fruit salad? Aunt Mildred may care when you rave about the potato salad she never made. The worst-case scenario might have you remembering a salad as good when it was not and, as a result, Aunt Mildred makes it "especially for you" every time there is a family gathering.

Setting the salads aside, there are cases where memory and confidence in memory can be a matter of life or death. When we take account of research findings, this becomes a scary proposition. Courts of law often consider that eyewitness testimony is a truthful account of events, particularly if it holds up under grueling cross-examination. In the time since the memory studies of the 1970s, psychologists have increasingly questioned this assumption. In the studies discussed above, the participants were adults. However, in the past decade there have been a number of high-profile cases in which the recollections of children have played a pivotal role. If the accuracy of adult memory is questionable, what about the memories of children? The research literature in this area shows, unsurprisingly, that memories of younger kids are even more vulnerable to false information than those of older kids (see Ceci & Bruck, 1993, for a review of the literature).

Michelle Leichtman and Stephen Ceci (1995) identified two classes of reasons for false memories in children: cognitive factors and social factors. Children have difficulty in distinguishing the sources of their stored memories. Younger children are particularly likely to remember performing an act when, in reality, they only repeatedly imagined performing it. This is called *source misattribution*, and it is an example of a cognitive factor. Social factors include bribes, threats, or feeling pressured to respond in ways that will please certain adults. When children are required to testify in court, both cognitive and social influences may be present, setting the stage for false memories. Cognitive factors will operate in court, where it is routine that children are questioned in detail and at great length. It is easy to imagine that some of the questions will contain presuppositions or will be leading questions. Repeated leading questions can make particular scenarios so familiar to children that they become incorporated into the child's memory. In one case involving child sexual abuse, a mother indicated that her daughter had been interviewed between 30 and 50 times by county officials (Humphrey, 1985). It is also easy to imagine a role for social factors: a child might figure out which responses please the adults. The child may give those responses at higher frequencies. A key child witness in a Texas murder case changed her testimony saying, "Originally I think I told police just what I saw. But the more questions I was asked, the more confused I became. I answered questions I wasn't certain about because I wanted to help the adults" (quoted in Leichtman & Ceci, 1995).

Leichtman and Ceci (1995) conducted an experiment in which they studied the recollections of children about a prearranged event. This has become known as the *Sam Stone Study*, because an enactment was staged for the children in which a man called Sam Stone visited their day-care center.

Participants

The participants were 176 preschool children who were enrolled in private day-care centers. The children represented a wide range of socioeconomic status and ethnic groups. The children belonged to one of two age groups: early preschoolers (3- and 4-year-olds) and later preschoolers (5- and 6-year-olds). They spent their days in classrooms consisting of eight children each. Whole classrooms, not individual children, were randomly assigned to an experimental condition. This was done to prevent children within a single class from talking with each other and discovering that different things were going on for different children.

Procedures

There were eight different groups of kids in the study. There was a control group and three experimental groups for the young preschoolers and the same four groups for the older preschoolers. The procedure for the actual visit of Sam Stone was repeated in each of the eight classrooms. A confederate acted the role of Sam. *Confederate*, in this context, means someone who works for the researcher as an actor, pretending to be someone else. You will see this again in later chapters where, for example, confederates pretend to be additional participants in studies. These confederates are sometimes making behavior observations of the real participants. By pretending to be participants themselves, they are able to do so without the awareness of the real participants. In this study the confederate, Sam, was not collecting data, but was playing the role of a classroom visitor. Sam entered the classroom during a story reading session and said hello to the adult in charge. He was introduced to the children. He commented upon the story being read by saying, "I know that story; it's one of my favorites!" He walked around the perimeter of the room, waved to the children, and left. His visit lasted about 2 minutes.

Neither the young nor the older control group had prior knowledge of Sam Stone's visit. Following the visit they were interviewed once a week for 4 weeks. In these interviews they were asked questions about what Sam had done during the visit to their school, but they were given no suggestions or additional information about Sam or his visit.

The *stereotype* experimental groups, one younger and one older, were told about Sam Stone before his visit in a manner designed to create a stereotype of Sam's personality. A research assistant went to these groups once a week for a month before the visit and, while playing with the children, told three different scripted stories about Sam. Over the course of the four visits, these children heard 12 stories that presented a consistent stereotype of Sam. In each story Sam was shown to be a kind person, but somewhat accident prone. In one of these stories, for example, the children were told that Sam Stone had visited the research assistant the previous night and asked to borrow a Barbie doll. On the way down the stairs he tripped and broke the doll, but he was having it fixed. In other versions of the story Sam did other things. They were told he lost a borrowed pen and replaced it; spilled soda on the research assistant but cleaned it up, and accidentally took some board game pieces home but brought them back. After 4 weeks of stereotype building, this group had a 2-minute visit from Sam Stone in which he behaved as he did in all groups: he walked around doing nothing remarkable. Following Sam Stone's visit, this group was treated like the control group in being asked neutral, suggestion-free questions at 1-week intervals for 4 weeks.

For the *suggestion* experimental groups, no attempt was made to create a stereotype of Sam Stone in the month before his visit. Instead, following the visit, at 1-week intervals, the children were asked questions that contained two false suggestions about Sam Stone's visit: that he had ripped a book and that he had gotten dirt on a teddy bear. Children were asked, for example, "When Sam got the bear dirty, did he do it on purpose or was it an accident?" and "Was Sam Stone happy or sad that he got the bear dirty?"

The children in the remaining experimental condition received both the stereotyping information about Sam's clumsiness before his visit and the leading questions once a week after the event. They were called the *stereotype-plus-suggestion* groups. These children were exposed to a stereotypical expectation about Sam for the month before the visit as well as misinformation planted in the month following the visit.

At the completion of the experimental conditions described above, all children were exposed to a final interview conducted by a new person who was not present during Sam's visit or the experimental procedures. The quality of their memory for events was operationally defined as the accuracy of their responses to interview questions. In this interview, the same questions were asked of all children. In this test of memory, the children were first asked to describe, in their own words, the happenings on the day of Sam's visit to their class. Once this free narrative was done, children were asked specific probing questions about whether they had "heard something" about the book or the teddy bear or had seen Sam dealing with either of these objects. If children indicated that they had seen Sam do something, which, in fact, he had not done, other questions were asked to test the strength of belief in the memory, such as "You didn't really see him do this, did you?"

Results

The final interviews were videotaped, and data were produced by having the children's responses coded. The coders were people who did not know which condition the children had been in. Twenty percent of the tapes were randomly selected and recoded by another rater to check for rater reliability. Agreement between raters was found to be 90 percent, certainly high enough to indicate that raters were sufficiently reliable. The coders were looking to see if individual children made false statements either during free narrative or pointed questioning.

As can be seen from Figure 17.1, there were striking differences in the extent to which children made false allegations in their unguided recall about what happened during Sam Stone's visit.

No children from the control group or from the stereotype group made any false statements about the visit in free recall. However, the group that had been given after-the-fact suggestions about tearing the book and soiling the teddy bear did include these events in their free narrative. It is important to remember that these suggestions were presuppositions inserted in questions that were, ostensibly, asking about something else. A stereotype was established for two groups in which Sam was clumsy,

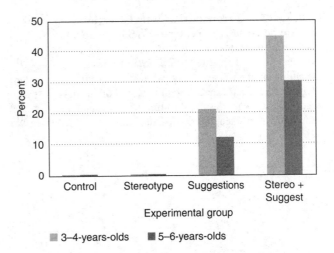

FIGURE 17.1   Percentage of Children Making False Allegations. Statements were made during the free recall narrative at the beginning of the fifth interview.

likely to spill and break things. It is interesting that the stereotype alone was not enough to result in false events being reported in free recall. Yet, Figure 17.1 shows that in the *stereotype-plus-suggestion* group, it had an additive effect: levels of false allegations were higher than in the *suggestion-only* group. The stereotype procedure did not have an effect on its own but it made a difference when combined with subsequent suggestions. In these latter two groups there was also a difference between the younger and the older children, with the younger ones being more likely to include false stories in their narratives.

Figure 17.2 shows the control group outcomes for the procedures that followed free narratives in the final interview. These were responses to probing questions about (1) whether the child believed that the book or the teddy bear incidents had occurred, (2) whether they had seen either of them, and (3) whether they would insist on the reality of the events. Because the control group had been given no formal exposure to any of the false events, the expectation was that they would not make false assertions, even when pointed questions were asked. As expected, only a few such responses were seen in this group. Although these children had not been previously exposed to false information about the book and the teddy bear, a few of them were prepared to say they remembered these false events. They had first heard about the book and the bear minutes before, in final interview questions.

Even though the stereotype group did not mention false events during free recall, Figure 17.3 shows that they became likely to assert the reality of false events under pointed questioning. As in all these data, there is an age trend favoring better memory for the older children.

FIGURE 17.2   Erroneous Answers Given by Control Group (No Stereotype; No Suggestions). *1 or 2 errors* indicates that the child asserted that a false event really happened. *Witnessed* indicates that the child claimed to have observed the false event. *Maintained* indicates that the child insisted on having observed the event, despite the attempt at dissuading: "You didn't really see him do this, did you?"

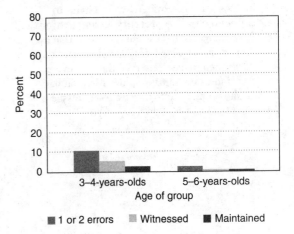

FIGURE 17.3 Erroneous Answers Given by Stereotype Group (Stereotype; No Suggestions). *1 or 2 errors* indicates that the child asserted that a false event really happened. *Witnessed* indicates that the child claimed to have observed the false event. *Maintained* indicates that the child insisted on having observed the event, despite the attempt at dissuading: "You didn't really see him do this, did you?"

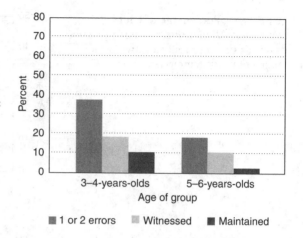

In the suggestion group the levels were even higher as shown in Figure 17.4. Over half of the 3- and 4-year-olds reported one or two false memories under pointed questioning, and there was a noticeable increase in the percentage of younger children who claimed to have witnessed a false event.

Lastly, Figure 17.5 shows the effects of having some training in a stereotype about Sam's personality and then, over time, having a number of embedded suggestions made that are congruent with the stereotype. As in the other groups, there is an age trend when the two age groups are compared. Particularly in the younger children, there are strikingly high levels of reporting false beliefs, claiming to have witnessed the event, and maintaining this stance under gentle, but adverse, questioning.

These are important findings. We know, from earlier studies, that even adult memory can be influenced by presuppositions, but this study presents clear evidence that the memory of a child, particularly a young child, can be greatly influenced especially when previously held stereotypes are supported by subsequent suggestions. The design of the study is very clever in being able to create stereotypes about a person previously unknown to the children and in being able to follow this up with congruent suggestions. These findings are not only important for what they tell us about reconstructive memory; they also bear directly on the issue of children testifying in courtrooms. Children quickly pick up stereotypes. Imagine a child who witnesses a crime committed by a person of an ethnic group different from the child itself. Further imagine that the child has grown up in a home where there is substantial prejudice against other ethnic groups. In addition, imagine that, following the crime, the child is

FIGURE 17.4 Erroneous Answers Given by Suggestion Group (No Stereotype; Suggestions). *1 or 2 errors* indicates that the child asserted that a false event really happened. *Witnessed* indicates that the child claimed to have observed the false event. *Maintained* indicates that the child insisted on having observed the event, despite the attempt at dissuading: "You didn't really see him do this, did you?"

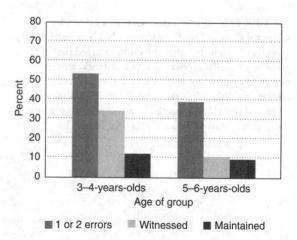

FIGURE 17.5   Erroneous Answers Given by Stereotype Plus Suggestion Group (Stereotype; Suggestions). *1 or 2 errors* indicates that the child asserted that a false event really happened. *Witnessed* indicates that the child claimed to have observed the false event. *Maintained* indicates that the child insisted on having observed the event, despite the attempt at dissuading: "You didn't really see him do this, did you?"

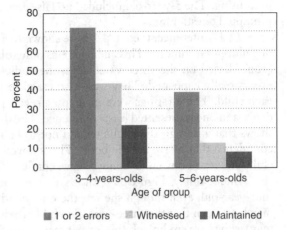

repeatedly questioned by all sorts of people: parents, police, and prosecuting attorneys. Unless these interrogators are extraordinarily careful in the wording of questions, it would be easy for them to unknowingly make presuppositions or suggestions such as, "Did the long-haired man with the knife yell at the store clerk?" In this question there are presuppositions about the man having long hair and a knife, yet the child has not been asked about either of these. It takes little imagination to apply the findings of the Leichtman and Ceci (1995) research to the real world. It creates a chilling picture.

This research suggests what should be avoided with child witnesses, but it also suggests what should be done to maximize the value of their recollections. As can be seen in Figure 17.1, the free narratives of children in the stereotype group are factually accurate, in spite of experience with stereotypical information. Although the stereotype in this study may be weaker than real-life stereotypes embedded by repeated expression in a child's daily environment, the data here indicated that stereotypes play no role in false allegations during free narrative. The problems begin to occur when suggestions are made. A conclusion that might be drawn by police and prosecutors is that evidence from the free narrative might be more accurate than evidence under pointed questioning. Free narratives of child witnesses should be solicited and carefully recorded at the earliest possible time following a crime. At the least, any additional questions should be carefully structured, and court officials should caution parents and others against questioning the child further, possibly inadvertently adding suggestions that become part of memory.

CAN ADULTS DETECT INACCURATE REPORTS FROM CHILDREN?

Leichtman and Ceci (1995) were interested in applications of their research to real-world settings. They believed that adults who had no knowledge of the history of Sam Stone's visit would be unable to determine the extent to which children were giving accurate accounts. In contrast to their beliefs, they cited Goodman (1990) as having stated that adults can easily detect false reports in the narratives of young children.

As noted above, the final interview responses of the children experiencing free recall, probing questions, and challenging questions had been videotaped. Leichtman and Ceci (1995) showed some of these tapes to adults, asking them to try to detect false statements. The videos chosen were of a 3-year-old, a 4-year-old, and a 5-year-old. Each of these children was selected from the *stereotype-plus-suggestion* group. The particular children were chosen because they were coherent and seemed engaged by the interviewer. On the tape, the 3-year-old spontaneously asserted that Sam had done the false acts. The 4-year-old was a soft-spoken child who made no false allegations in her narrative or in subsequent prompting. The 5-year-old included no false acts in his narrative, but assented to false memories under prompted questioning.

At a conference, these tapes were shown to 119 researchers and clinicians who worked in the area of children's testimony. This audience was only told that each child had witnessed the same visit by Sam Stone. Based on the three videotapes, the audience was asked to rate their confidence about which events really happened. They were also asked to rate their confidence in the overall account given by each child. These ratings were made on a seven-point scale, where seven represented the most confidence and one represented least confidence. The data are presented in Figures 17.6 and 17.7. Figure 17.6 shows that although the adults tended not to believe that Sam soiled the bear, they had considerable confidence that he ripped the book. This showed that even skilled professionals who are interested in children's testimony could come to have confidence in some false memories reported by children.

Interestingly, Figure 17.7 shows that the adults had the least confidence in the reports of the four-year-old, even though she was the only child giving accurate reports. One of the reasons for this may have been that the three-year-old child provided the most detail in her story. A story rich in detail may seem more credible. If this is so, it may be useful for school children to give more detail with the old excuse about how the dog ate their homework. What kind of dog was it? How long did it take him to eat it? Did he spit out the staple? Although details may not have formed the entire basis for audience judgment of credibility, it was probably part of it. Whatever the reason, the data suggested that adults, even interested and motivated adults, are not very good at determining the accuracy of reports by children.

We hope that you will bear the findings of this study in mind as you watch media accounts of children in courtrooms. It would be nice to think that results of carefully conducted research, such as that presented by Leichtman and Ceci (1995), will find their way into the daily practice of people who are professionally involved with children's testimony. Media depictions suggest to us that the scientific studies concerning eyewitness testimony have not yet resulted in standardized procedures for dealing with eyewitness accounts. Maybe the general public, even members of the educated general public such as police, judges, and lawyers, do not understand research about behavior. *Psychology* means many things to different people, but few people associate it with a cautious, empirical approach to understanding behavior. In reading these articles, you are coming to see that no research study is perfect. Those who are ignorant about psychological research may use this fact to conclude that psychology is useless and meaningless. It is our contention that a person with adequate skills in understanding psychological research can assess and evaluate studies, making decisions about when and how results can be applied to daily life. We believe that this is the point of learning about psychology. We hope that you agree.

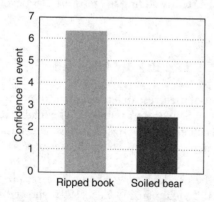

FIGURE 17.6 Mean Confidence Levels That Events Occurred. Confidence ratings of professional adults that events occurred, based on videotapes of children (1 = sure it didn't, 7 = sure it did).

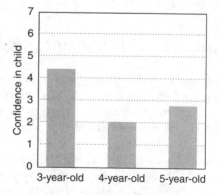

FIGURE 17.7 Mean Confidence Levels in Accounts Given. Confidence ratings of professional adults in the accounts given by three children.

REFERENCES

Ceci, S. J., & Bruck, M. (1993). Suggestibility of the child witness: A historical review and synthesis. *Psychological Bulletin, 113,* 403–439.

Goodman, G. S. (1990). Media effects and children's testimony. In D. Singer (Chair), *The impact of the media on the judicial system.* Symposium conducted at the 98th Annual Convention of the American Psychological Association, Boston.

Humphrey, H. H., III (1985). *Report on Scott County Investigations.* Minneapolis, MN: Attorney General's Office.

Leichtman, M. D., & Ceci, S. J. (1995). The effects of stereotypes and suggestions on preschoolers' reports. *Developmental Psychology, 31,* 568–578.

Loftus, E. F. (1975). Leading questions and the eyewitness report. *Cognitive Psychology, 7,* 560–572.

Loftus, E. F., & Palmer, J. C. (1974). Reconstruction of automobile destruction: An example of the interaction between language and memory. *Journal of Verbal Learning and Verbal Behavior, 13,* 585–589.

CHAPTER 18

ARE YOUR PROFESSORS LOSING IT? NOT IF THEY'RE USING IT[1]

Justin M. Joffe

---

[1]Incorporating the research of A. P. Shimamura, J. M. Berry, J. A. Mangels, C. L. Rusting, and P. J. Jurica (1995).

"Use it or lose it" is an expression we have all come across. As far as I can ascertain, it comes from the world of budgets: in many organizations, a department that did not spend its allocated budget by the end of the fiscal year would lose the balance of the money—they didn't use it so they lost it.

The expression is now used in a variety of areas far removed from annual budgets including, in effect, the research described in this chapter. Shimamura and his colleagues looked at the question of whether using your brain as you age protects you from the decline in many cognitive skills that are found as people get older. Their hypothesis, roughly stated, was that if you use it (your brain, that is), you won't lose it (or at least not so much of it or not as rapidly).

"I'm not getting older I'm getting better," is a statement people sometimes make. Well, how true is it of skills as we age? If we look at changes over the entire lifespan, it is clear that initially we do get better as we age, at least up to a certain point. A teenager, for example, will be able to outrun almost any five-year-old, will have a larger vocabulary, be better at math, and so on. But what happens after that? Motor skills continue to improve with practice, and athletes in many fields reach their peak in their 20s and maintain their outstanding skills, in some cases into their mid and even late thirties. There is some consensus that the decline in physiological capacity that underlies changes in performance is due in part to disuse, and indeed there is a decline in exercise with age that accounts for some of the decline in the average performance of the population. In other words, there is some of the "use it or lose it" factor at work here.

Bortz and Bortz (1993) have termed the effects of lack of exercise in aging "the disuse syndrome." In addition, however, it seems likely that genetically determined biological factors, and disease, play a role, and even the most dedicated exercisers are not going to maintain their best performance as the years accumulate. Yes, they will almost certainly be fitter, faster, more energetic than contemporaries who are couch potatoes, but they won't be the athletes they were 20 or even 10 years previously when they get into their forties and fifties.

RESEARCH DESIGNS

What do we see when we look at cognitive performance over time as people get older? What happens to skills like learning new information, memory, reasoning, and so on? The consensus here is that "declines in memory and cognitive abilities are a normal consequence of aging in humans. . . . This is true across cultures and, indeed, in virtually all mammalian species" (American Psychological Association, 1998).

But the news is better than it used to be. This is not because people have stopped aging, of course, but partly because the poorer scores of older people in earlier studies seem to have been influenced by something other than age (something we call a "confound," which is a variable other than the one we are interested in that may influence the outcome). And in this area of research the variable is one that comes into play in a particular kind of research method, the so-called "cross-sectional" developmental study is used.

Think about how you might go about doing research to answer the question of whether there are changes in performance due to age. You cannot do a true experiment, of course, because that would require you to assign people randomly to the groups to which you applied different amounts of the independent variable. In other words you would have to assign people randomly to different age groups. You would immediately realize that this is impossible, and obviously simply seek out people of different ages to test (making do with a quasi-experimental design). Perhaps you would recruit groups of 25 year-olds, 50 year-olds, and 75 year-olds and test them on the cognitive task you were interested in. Let us assume you did this and found that the 75 year-olds performed significantly worse than the 50 year-olds who, in turn, were significantly less able than the 25 year-olds.

Conclusion? "There are age-related declines in performance on Task X." Yes, perhaps, but are the changes due to aging itself, or are there other possibilities?

In this kind of study, where there are differences between people of different ages tested at the same time, there is the likelihood of what is known as a "cohort effect." This is where the people of different ages differ not only in how old they are but in something else they have in common on account of their age. Is age the only difference between you and one of your grandparents? What was the world like when she or he was your age? In most cases, our grandparents will have had different experiences in just about every imaginable aspect of their lives, including nutrition, medical and dental care, parental and school discipline, school curricula, incomes, national events such as recessions and wars, and so on and on.

Results of research using cross-sectional designs showed big drops in many measures of cognitive performance with age. Realizing that the confounds that are almost inevitable in cross-sectional research leave us unsure about the effects of aging itself, researchers turned to longitudinal studies, where the same people are studied over long periods of time. Such an approach is not without problems: among other things, a longitudinal study is likely to be more expensive than a cross-sectional study, it is difficult to keep contact with people studied over long periods, and it takes a long time, sometimes a very long time, to get data.

Despite the difficulties, a large number of longitudinal research studies have been carried out on aging and cognitive function (and many are still in progress, sometimes outliving the researchers who started the work!). These have given more reason to be optimistic about retaining a good deal of our ability as we get older. For example, overall declines in IQ are not replicated in longitudinal studies. Rather it appears that what is termed "crystallized" intelligence (vocabulary, recollection of historical events, etc.) increases, while "fluid" intelligence (deductive reasoning, problem solving, etc.) declines—leaving us with about the same overall score. We may not have the *same* pattern of intellectual strengths and weaknesses at 70 as we had at 30, but overall we may be just as smart. Not everything stays the same, and there are declines in scores on reasoning tests, memory tests, and so on, but they occur later than was once assumed to be the case.

In short, there are declines in skills with age but (a) the decline due to age alone is not as great as cross-sectional studies sometimes indicate and (b) some skills may not decline at all, or even increase throughout life: Baltes (1993) summarizes research on "wisdom" and reports that (just as we might have guessed from positive stereotypes) it shows no decline with age—just as many 60 and

70 year-olds performed in the top 20 percent as 30 year-olds. Speed and accuracy, memory, and such processes, probably more heavily dependent on biological, genetic, and health-related factors, show a decline with age, but wisdom, which Baltes conceptualizes as more dependent on cultural and social factors, may increase with age and the associated opportunities to acquire more knowledge and experience.

In attempts (among other things) to obtain information on the role of knowledge in cognitive performance across the lifespan, professors and other special populations, such as business executives and pilots, have been studied. Over 50 years ago, Sward (1945) studied 45 younger (25–35 years of age) and 45 older (60–80 years of age) professors. The older group included retired (emeriti) faculty members, which adds a potential confound. He devised eight tests, deliberately designed to be difficult, that took 3–4 hours in all to complete. The older professors were outperformed by the younger ones on seven of the eight tests (significantly so on six of the eight); only on one of the vocabulary tests (involving synonyms and antonyms) did the older professors have better average scores than the younger ones. On the two tests where speed was important because of time limits, the differences in favor of the younger men was particularly marked: over 95% of the younger professors scored at or above the median score of the older professors. (This was true also of the total scores on all eight tests). Surprisingly, perhaps, Sward concluded that "at least within the upper ranges of ability, an impairment of the 'higher mental processes' is by no means an invariable concomitant of the years beyond sixty" (p. 479). He believed that lower scores on six of the tests were "a by-product of disuse" (p. 478) and that "old age acts selectively and most decisively on those functions which have suffered for want of practice and sustained interest, all depending upon the older man's field of interest and his specialized knowledge and occupation" (p. 479). The older men, he argued, might be rusty and losses on speed tests could probably be explained by "disuse or by mere lack of exercise" (p. 479). Roughly translated, he is saying that those who used it didn't lose it—unfortunately the data then suggest that quite a lot of the old professors hadn't been using it!

Less contentious is Sward's conclusion that individual differences in performance are very considerable, "far more impressive than age differences" (p. 478). Indeed, one of the intriguing and puzzling aspects of research findings on cognitive function and aging is the variability that is found. Even in the absence of factors like ill health and medication that can adversely affect cognition, there are big differences between people of the same age. This variability makes the interpretation of age-related declines in performance more difficult to interpret, since one has to consider whether the drop (if there is one) in average scores is due to serious declines in some individuals (perhaps due to age-related diseases like Alzheimer's) rather than to decrements in all or most aging people. It is clear that some people could maintain all or most of their skills but that the presence in the group of people with serious deterioration could lower the group's average to make it appear that there is a general decline due to age alone. This seems to have been the case in the Seattle Longitudinal Study, a major study, started in 1957, of intellectual change and aging. Almost two-thirds of the older participants showed no decline in performance on five tests (including spatial orientation, inductive reasoning, and word fluency) on each of which the average score declined with age quite substantially from age 60 on (Cox, 2001, Ch. 6).

This variability in changes in cognitive skills with age was one of the starting points for Shimamura and colleagues' investigation of memory and cognitive abilities in university professors. Education, or remaining cognitively active, or high intelligence (or all three factors) may protect against some of the decline in intellectual performance as one gets older. Comparing younger professors to older ones ("middle-aged") to even older ones (who Shimamura et al. politely term "senior" professors) and comparing the scores to non-professors of different ages may give insight into some of the variables associated with "successful aging." (This latter term means something like growing old gracefully; in the context of cognitive performance it means showing less of a decline in performance on tests of cognitive function than other people show).

TABLE 18.1 **Participants (Acronyms for each group indicated in parentheses: "P" = professors, "N" = non-professors, "Y" = young, "M" = middle-aged, "O" = old)**

| | PROFESSORS[1] | | | OTHER PARTICIPANTS[2] | |
	YOUNG (YP)	MIDDLE AGED (MP)	OLD (OP)	YOUNG (YN)[3]	OLD (ON)
Number of men	16	24	19	—	—
Number of women	6	4	3	—	—
Total number	22	28	22	40	17
Average age (years)	38.4	52.2	64.7	19.8	66.5
Age range (years)	30–44	45–59	60–71	18–23	60–71
Average years of education	22	21	21	14	16

Notes:
1. From various disciplines, University of California at Berkeley
2. Not specified how many were men or women
3. Undergraduates. Between 12 and 40 completed particular tests

METHOD

Participants

The people studied by Shimamura et al. are shown in Table 18.1, where you can see how many people were in each category, their average age (and range of ages), and years of education.

The professors were recruited through publicity in a campus newsletter for faculty and staff, by mailings to individual faculty, and by telephone calls requesting volunteers; (in the paper about this research the researchers do not tell us how they decided who they would phone or send a letter). Participants were paid $15 for completing a set of tests (or "test battery") that took 90 minutes to do. Shimamura et al. do not say how the other participants were recruited (nor if they were paid), but note that these people should not be compared statistically with the professors from whom they differ in ways other than age, notably years of education, as you can see in Table 18.1.

Tests

The tests used (in the order they were given) are shown in Table 18.2.

RESULTS

The results are shown in Figures 18.1–18.4. Let us look at each set of data in turn.

TABLE 18.2 Tests

TEST	PROCEDURE	EARLIER FINDINGS
1.A. Reaction Time Words	Participants had to press one of four keys on a computer keyboard as soon as a particular stimulus appeared onthe screen. 32 trials given in each condition.	Older people have slower reaction times than younger ones. The difference increases as the task becomes more difficult.
a. 1 Choice	They had to press a designated key (e.g., the letter "h") when they saw the word "go."	
b. 2 Choices	When the word "left" appeared on the screen they had to press the key to the left (g) and when the word right appeared, the key to the right (j) of the center key.	
c. 4 Choices	Now the words could be "left," "right," "up," or "down," and participants had to press the appropriate key.	

1.B. Reaction Time, Symbols
  a. 1 Choice
  b. 2 Choices
  c. 4 Choices
	As for Words, except that instead of "go" a traffic light symbol appeared, and instead of "left," "right," "up," and "down" an arrow pointing in the corresponding direction appeared.	

2. Paired-Associate Learning	Participants are presented with pairs of stimuli and then shown the first member of the pair and asked which stimulus was paired with it. Pairings and testings were carried out three times for faces and for names.	People with brain damage of certain kinds do very poorly on this kind of test. These regions of the brain are often implicated in neurological deterioration that occurs in some diseases associated with aging (e.g., Alzheimer's) and so older groups may show poorer performance.
a. Faces	Line drawings of 6 pairs of faces were used; each pair contained one female face and one male, and each was shown once for 4 seconds. Then each female face was shown in turn and participants asked to select the male face that had been paired with it.	
b. Names	10 pairs of names were used, each pair containing one male name and one female name, and each pair was shown once. Then each male name was presented and participants asked to select the female name that had been paired with it.	

(continued)

TABLE 18.2   Tests (continued)

TEST	PROCEDURE	EARLIER FINDINGS
3. Working Memory	Participants were shown a computer-generated array of 16 patterns, with the patterns randomly arranged differently on each of 16 trials. On each trial they were asked to point to a different pattern on each trial. They then did a further 16 trials requiring the same response of pointing to a different pattern on each trial.	"Working memory" (a broader term than short-term memory) is that cognitive function that enables us to monitor what we are doing from moment to moment, so we can (for example) dial a phone number we have just looked up or do mental arithmetic. People with brain damage in areas that atrophy (waste away) with age show declines in tasks involving short-term memory.
4. Prose Recall	Participants listened to three tape-recorded prose passages, one a story about a woman who was robbed, one about the elements making up the earth's atmosphere, and the third with anthropological and historical information about tribal cultures. Each contained 25 conceptual segments, and participants were scored on how many of these they recalled correctly immediately after the passage was heard.	Accuracy of recall of information recently read or heard has been found to decline with age, but less so in people with high verbal ability.

1. REACTION TIME RESULTS

Figure 18.1 summarizes reaction times to words and to symbols on tasks involving one, two, or four choices.

A number of differences are apparent:

a. Reactions to symbols were significantly faster than reactions to words. This was true for all groups of participants and for all three reaction-time tasks.

b. Reactions are slower when choices have to be made about how to respond, and reactions are slower when there are two choices rather than one and slower again when there are four choices.

c. On all tasks older people show slower reactions than younger ones, whether we compare professors alone (OP times are longer than MP times which in turn are longer than YP times) or other participants (YN vs. ON). If we compare young professors (YP) with other young participants (YN), or older professors with other participants of a similar age (OP vs. ON) we find little difference, suggesting that education is not an important determinant of reaction time.

The slowing with age occurs whether the stimuli are words or symbols, but the differences between younger and older participants are greater when the number of choices is larger. The

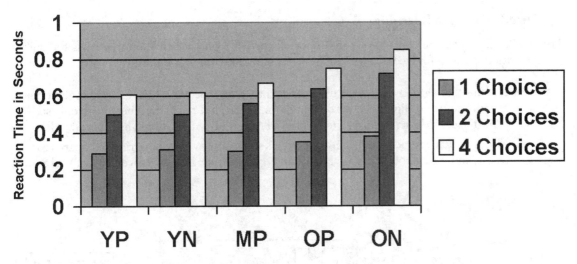

FIGURE 18.1A   Reaction Times to Words

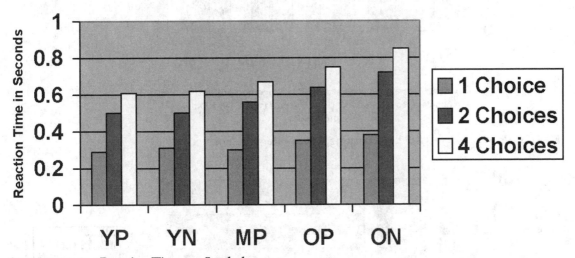

FIGURE 18.1B   Reaction Times to Symbols

researchers also reported a correlation between age and reaction time for professors; there was a significant correlation of 0.53 between these two variables, and they estimate that there is a slowing of reaction time of 3.9 milliseconds (0.0039 seconds) per year between the ages of 30 and 70.

How important is this change? It would mean that an average 70 year-old might respond to the flash of the brake lights of a car ahead 0.156 seconds later than the average 30 year-old would respond. A car traveling at 40 m.p.h. travels a little over 9 feet in that time. The biggest difference between younger people and older people is on the 4-choice task with words as stimuli. This difference of 0.24 seconds would mean a car at 60 m.p.h. traveling about 21 feet further before the driver braked. You can make up your own mind about the importance of this. Personally I'd rather see an old person driving the car behind me than someone talking on a phone.

2. Paired-Associate Learning

Figure 18.2 shows the percentage of pairs reported correctly on each of the three trials for the five groups, with the results for faces shown in Figure18.2a and for names in Figure 18.2b.

    a. It seems that pairing names is a little easier than remembering which faces go together: overall people do slightly better on names than faces, but recall that there were only six pairs of faces to learn compared to 10 pairs of names, so names should have been harder.

    b. Also note that practice is relevant—all groups show improvement on trial 2 compared to trial 1, and most show some further, though generally smaller, improvement on trial 3.

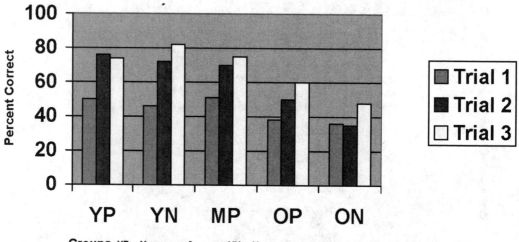

FIGURE 18.2A   Paired-Associate Learning, Faces—Percent Correct

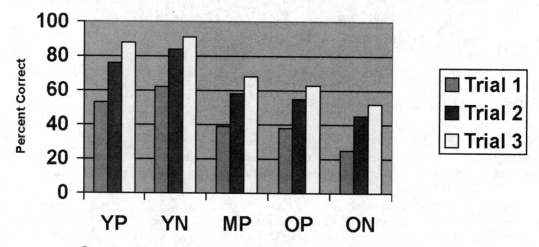

FIGURE 18.2B   Paired-Associate Learning, Names—Percent Correct

c. The effects attributable to age are less clear than in the case of reaction times. As far as the participants who were not professors are concerned, the younger ones (YN) remembered both kinds of pairings better than the older ones (ON). Among the professors, the younger ones (YP) outperformed the older ones (OP) on both kinds of pairings, but the middle-aged ones (MP) significantly outperformed the old professors only when learning face pairings and the young ones outperformed middle-aged ones only when learning name pairings.

3. Working Memory

The mean errors made by each group on both blocks of trials are shown in Figure 18.3.

a. On the first block of trials the two younger groups of professors (YP and MP) make fewer errors than the participants in the other three groups (old professors and both younger and older non-professors). These three groups do not differ from one another.

b. The picture changes on the second block of trials. Young professors show the largest decrease in errors and outperform everyone else. All the other groups show a small decrease in errors except the older non-professors (ON) who actually show a fairly large increase in errors, which makes them by far the worst performing group on this block of trials.

c. On both block of trials old professors perform as well as young non-professors (YN), making it look as if both age and education affect performance on this task.

4. Prose Recall

a. All groups recalled information from the fiction passage at least slightly better than the information from either of the other two passages (Figure 18.4).

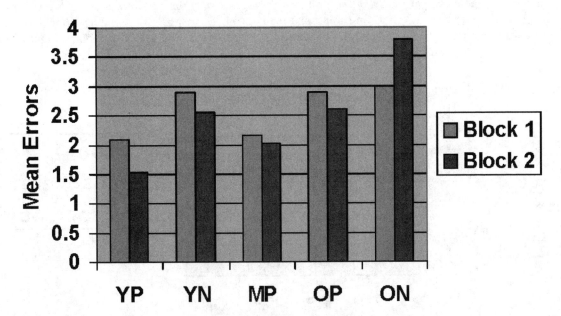

FIGURE 18.3   Working Memory—Errors on Each Block of Trials

    b. An age-related difference is seen in the non-professor participants, with the older participants (ON) recalling less than the younger ones (YN).

    c. Among professors, however, there are no significant differences attributable to age, and old professors recalled as much information about all three prose passages as middle-aged or young professors.

DISCUSSION

As Shimamura et al. point out, professors show declines in performance similar to those found in the non-professorial older people on two of the sets of tests used, namely reaction time and paired-associate learning (Figures 18.1 and 18.2). This is similar to findings in earlier research on older people, and supports the more general conclusion of earlier research that there are age-related declines in "fluid" skills, those perhaps more dependent on biology than experience. (It might be interesting to study people who spend a lot of time playing computer-games that necessitate rapid responses to unexpected stimuli, both now and when they get older. It may be that using it may to some extent protect against later losses, a finding that would make one more cautious about stating too strongly that the slowing of reaction time with age is biologically inevitable.). Sward (1945) also found that older professors performed less well on tests requiring speed of performance. One of his conclusions, over half a century ago, was that "other things equal, age has the effect of impairing the rate far more than the quality or accuracy of the mental operations . . ." (p. 479).

    The findings on the other two sets of tests, however, provide some support for the "use it or lose it" notion and consequently for the general notion that some aspects of cognitive functioning are less vulnerable to the effects of aging. On the test of working memory (see Figure 18.3), older professors do not show the decline in performance on the second block of trials that we see in non-professors of a similar age. The increase in errors on the second block is attributed by the researchers to a process known as "proactive interference," a term meaning that material we learned previously interferes with something we are currently trying to learn. It is common for this to happen in tasks where one is required to

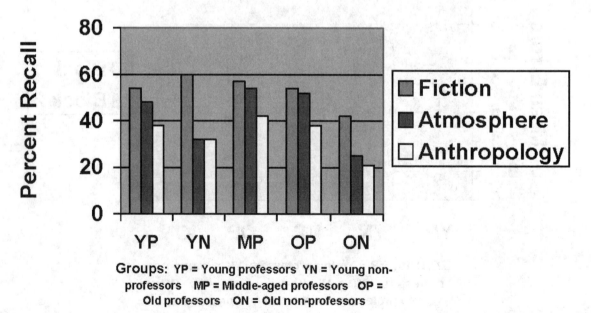

FIGURE 18.4 Recall of Prose of different kinds

learn very similar material in a short space of time. Remember that the second block of trials in the working memory test required the participants to point to a different pattern on each of 16 trials. Having just done the same thing on the first block of trials, it is not easy to remember which patterns you have pointed to before during the second block of trials (you score an error if you do point to the same pattern again) and which you pointed to before on the first block of trials. In other words, memory of the first block can interfere with performance on the second block, and this proactive interference is worse in older than younger participants—unless they are older professors: these participants showed better performance on Block 2 (and on both blocks performed as well as younger non-professors, although not as well as young or middle-aged professors).

In addition, where older non-professors were not as good at remembering prose as younger people, older professors performed just as well as younger ones.

Shimamura et al. point out that the two tests where little or no age effect is seen are similar in requiring "planning, organization, and the manipulation of information in memory" (p. 276) and they speculate that perhaps professors are better at these kinds of things because of daily practice in doing them. The researchers are not (of course) suggesting that professors do tasks like those in the working memory and prose recall tests on a daily basis, but rather that their normal work requires them to use cognitive strategies that exercise the kinds of skills that facilitate performance on the tasks the researchers asked them to do. They also point out that it is these kinds of planning and organizing skills that are often most affected in older people, so their results are unusual and although they do not say so, encouraging.

Shimamura et al. suggest that the better performance of older professors than of other old people on certain cognitive tasks is attributable to continued mental activity—"using it"—and could occur in either of two ways: it could be that mental activity protects cognitive function or that their better performance is due to their having developed better ability to compensate for the impairments due to aging. "For example, efficient use of memory strategies developed during adulthood may compensate for biological aging effects, such as generalized slowing" (p. 276).

Because older people, including professors, perform less well on tests of reaction time and in paired-associate learning, Shimamura think it more likely that "using it" has resulted in better ways of compensating for the losses rather than in protecting against the loss altogether. I may be getting older—*and* getting better, at least at finding ways of compensating for my decline!

REFERENCES

American Psychological Association, Presidential Task Force on the Assessment of Age-Consistent Memory Decline and Dementia (1998). *Guidelines for the evaluation of dementia and age-related cognitive decline*. Washington, DC: American Psychological Association.

Baltes, P. B. (1992). The aging mind: Potential and limits. *The Gerontologist, 33,* 580–594.

Bortz, W. M., IV & W. M. Bortz, II. (1993). Aging and the disuse syndrome—effect of lifetime exercise. In: S. Harris, R. Harris, & W. S. Harris (Eds), *Physical Activity, Aging and Sports, Vol. II: Practice, Program and Policy* (pp. 44–50). Albany, N. Y.: Center for the Study of Aging (pp. 44–50).

Cox, H. G. (2001). *Later Life: The Realities of Aging* (5th Ed.). New Jersey: Prentice Hall.

Craik, F. I. M., & T. A. Salthouse (1992). *Handbook of aging and cognition*. Hillsdale, N J: Erlbaum.

Shimamura, A. P., J .M. Berry, J. A. Mangels, C. L. Rusting, and P. J. Jurica (1995). Memory and cognitive abilities in university professors: Evidence for successful aging. *Psychological Science, 6,* 271–277.

Sward, K. (1945). Age and mental abilities in superior men. *American Journal of Psychology, 58,* 443–479.

SECTION V

SOCIAL AND PERSONALITY

CHAPTER 19

INTRODUCTION

Material selected from:
Mastering the World of Psychology,
by Wood, Wood & Boyd

SOCIAL PSYCHOLOGY

In the 1960s, an advertisement appeared in newspapers in New Haven, Connecticut, and other communities near Yale University. It read, "Wanted: Volunteers to serve as subjects in a study of memory and learning at Yale University." Many people responded to the ad, and 40 male participants between the ages of 20 and 50 were selected. Yet, instead of a memory experiment, a staged drama was planned. The cast of characters consisted of the experimenter, a 31-year-old high school biology teacher dressed in a gray laboratory coat, who assumed a stern and serious manner; the learner, a middle-aged man (an actor and accomplice of the experimenter); and, the teacher, one of the volunteers.

The experimenter led the teacher and the learner into one room, where the learner was strapped into a chair wired to deliver shocks. The teacher was given a sample shock of 45 volts, supposedly for the purpose of testing the equipment and showing the teacher what the learner would feel. Next, the script called for the learner to complain of a heart condition and say that he hoped the electric shocks would not be too painful. The experimenter admitted that the stronger shocks would hurt but added, "Although the shocks can be extremely painful, they cause no permanent tissue damage" (Milgram, 1963, p. 373).

The experimenter took the teacher to an adjoining room and seated him in front of an instrument panel with 30 lever switches arranged horizontally across the front. The first switch on the left, he was told, delivered only 15 volts, but each successive switch was 15 volts stronger than the last, up to the final switch, which carried 450 volts. The switches on the instrument panel were labeled with designations ranging from "Slight Shock" to "Danger: Severe Shock." The experimenter instructed the teacher to read a list of word pairs to the learner and then test his memory. When the learner made the right choice, the teacher was supposed to go on to the next pair. If the learner missed a question, the teacher was told to flip a switch and shock him, moving one switch to the right—delivering 15 additional volts— each time the learner missed a question.

The learner performed well at first but then began missing about three out of every four questions. The teacher began flipping the switches. When he hesitated, the experimenter urged him to continue. If he still hesitated, the experimenter ordered him, "The experiment requires that you continue," or, more strongly, "You have no other choice, you must go on" (Milgram, 1963, p. 374). At the 20th switch, 300 volts, the script required the learner to pound on the wall and scream, "Let me out of here, let me out, my heart's bothering me, let me out!" (Meyer, 1972, p. 461). From this point on, the learner answered no more questions. If the teacher expressed concern or a desire to discontinue the experiment, the experimenter answered, "Whether the learner likes it or not, you must go on" (Milgram, 1963, p. 374). At the flip of the next switch—315 volts—the teacher heard only groans from the learner. Again, if the teacher expressed reluctance to go on, the experimenter told him, "You have no other choice, you must go on" (p. 374). But if the teacher insisted on stopping at this point, the experimenter allowed him to do so.

How many of the 40 participants in the Milgram study do you think obeyed the experimenter to the end—450 volts? Not a single participant stopped before the 20th switch, supposedly 300 volts, when the learner began pounding the wall. Amazingly, 26 participants—65% of the sample—obeyed the experimenter to the bitter end. But this experiment took a terrible toll on the participants. They "were observed to sweat, tremble, stutter, bite their lips, groan, and dig their fingernails into their flesh. These were characteristic rather than exceptional responses to the experiment" (Milgram, 1963, p. 375).

You have just read a description of a classic experiment in **social psychology,** the area of study that attempts to explain how the actual, imagined, or implied presence of others influences the thoughts, feelings, and behaviors of individuals. A study like Milgram's could not be performed today because it would violate the American Psychological Association's code of conduct governing ethics in research. Still, deception has traditionally played a prominent part in social psychologists' research. To accomplish this deception, the researcher often must use one or more **confederates**—people who pose as participants in a psychology experiment but who are actually assisting the experimenter, such as the learner in the Milgram experiment. A **naive subject**—like the teacher in Milgram's study—is an actual participant who has agreed to participate but is not aware that deception is being used to conceal the real purpose of the experiment. You will continue to see why it is often necessary to conceal the purpose of an experiment as you read about other classic studies in social psychology.

SOCIAL PERCEPTION

Other people can be puzzling, but our ability to understand others is important because we live in a social world. The process we use to obtain critically important social information about others is known as *social perception* (Allison et al., 2000).

Impression Formation

When we meet people for the first time, we begin forming impressions about them right away, and, of course, they are busily forming impressions of us. Naturally, we notice the obvious attributes first—gender, race, age, dress, and how physically attractive or unattractive someone appears (Shaw & Steers, 2001). We may wonder: What's her occupation? Is he married? Answers to such questions, combined with people's verbal and nonverbal behavior, play a part in forming first impressions. Research shows that a firm handshake still makes a positive first impression (Chaplin et al., 2000). It conveys that a person is confident and outgoing, not shy or weak-willed. Moods also play a part—when we are happy, our impressions of others are usually more positive than when we are unhappy.

A number of studies reveal that an overall impression or judgment of another person is influenced more by the first information received about the person than by information that comes later (Luchins, 1957). This phenomenon is called the **primacy effect.** It seems that we attend to initial information more carefully, and once an impression is formed, it provides the framework through which we interpret later information (Gawronski et al., 2002). Any information that is consistent with the first impression is likely to be accepted, thus strengthening the impression. Information that does not fit with the earlier information is more likely to be disregarded. Remember, any time you list your personal traits or qualities, always list your most positive qualities first. It pays to put your best foot forward—first.

Attribution

Why do people do the things they do? To answer this question, we all make **attributions**—that is, we assign, or attribute, causes to explain the behavior of others and to explain our own behavior as well. One kind of attribution is called a **situational attribution** (an external attribution), in which we attribute a person's behavior to some external cause or factor operating within the situation. After failing an exam, you might say, "The test was unfair" or "The professor didn't give us enough time." Another kind of attribution is a **dispositional attribution** (an internal attribution)—attributing a person's behavior to some internal cause such as a personal trait, motive, or attitude. You might attribute failing the exam to lack of ability or to a poor memory.

We tend to use situational attributions to explain our own failures, because we are aware of factors in the situation that influenced us to act as we did (Jones, 1976, 1990; Jones & Nisbett, 1971). When we explain others' failures, we focus more on personal factors than on the factors operating within the situation (Gilbert & Malone, 1995; Leyens et al., 1996). For example, in the United States, the plight of individuals who are homeless or receiving welfare payments is often attributed to laziness, an internal attribution, rather than to factors in their situation that might explain their condition.

The tendency to attribute our own shortcomings primarily to situational factors and those of others to internal or dispositional factors is known as the **actor-observer effect.** Members of both Catholic and Protestant activist groups in Northern Ireland are subject to the actor-observer effect. Each group attributes the violence of the other group to internal or dispositional characteristics (they are murderers, they have evil intentions, etc.). And each group attempts to justify its own violence by attributing it to external or situational causes (we were protecting ourselves, we were retaliating for their actions, etc.) (Hunter et al., 2000).

There is one striking inconsistency in the way we view our own behavior: the self-serving bias. We use the **self-serving bias** when we attribute our successes to internal, or dispositional, causes and blame our failures on external, or situational, causes (Baumgardner et al., 1986; Brown & Rogers, 1991; Pansu & Gilibert, 2002). If you interview for a job and get it, it is probably because you have the right qualifications. If someone else gets the job, it is probably because he or she knew the right people. The self-serving bias allows us to take credit for our successes and shift the blame for our failures to the situation. Research examining the attributions of professional athletes, for example, has shown that they attribute victories to internal traits, such as ability and effort, and losses to situational factors, such as poor officiating and the like (Roesch & Amirkhan, 1997). Interestingly, too, managers prefer job applicants who make dispositional attributions during their interview, especially when the attributions focus on effort rather than natural ability (Pansu & Gilibert, 2002).

ATTRACTION

Think for a moment about your friends. What makes you like, or even fall in love with, one person and ignore or react negatively to someone else?

Factors Influencing Attraction

There are several factors that influence attraction. One is physical **proximity,** or geographic closeness. Obviously, it is much easier to make friends with people who are close at hand. One reason proximity matters is the **mere-exposure effect,** the tendency to feel more positively toward stimuli with repeated exposure. People, food, songs, and styles become more acceptable the more we are exposed to them. Advertisers rely on the positive effects of repeated exposure to increase people's liking for products and even for political candidates.

Our own moods and emotions, whether positive or negative, can influence how much we are attracted to people we meet. We may develop positive or negative feelings toward others simply because they are present when very good or very bad things happen to us. And we tend to like the people who also like us—or who we *believe* like us—a phenomenon called *reciprocity* or *reciprocal liking*.

Beginning in elementary school and continuing through life, people are also more likely to pick friends of the same age, gender, race, and socioeconomic class. We are likely to choose friends and lovers who hold similar views on most things that are important to us. Having similar interests and attitudes toward leisure-time activities makes it more likely that time spent together is rewarding.

Physical Attractiveness

Perhaps no other factor influences attraction more than physical attractiveness. People of all ages have a strong tendency to prefer physically attractive people (Langlois et al., 2000). Even 6-month-old infants, when given the chance to look at a photograph of an attractive or an unattractive woman, man, or infant, will spend more time looking at the attractive face. How people behave, especially the simple act of smiling, influences our perceptions of their attractiveness (Reis et al., 1990). But physical appearance matters as well.

Based on studies involving computer-generated faces, researchers Langlois and Roggman (1990) reported that perceptions of attractiveness are based on features that approximate the mathematical average of the features in a given general population. But Perrett and others (1994) found that simply averaging facial features only partially accounted for facial beauty. These researchers generated two composite images, one of 60 Caucasian female faces and another of the most attractive 15 of the 60 faces. Then, by exaggerating the differences between the two composite images, they derived the most attractive image, with larger eyes, higher cheekbones, and a thinner jaw. Averaging faces tends to make them more symmetrical. And symmetrical faces and bodies are seen as more attractive and sexually appealing (Singh, 1995; Thornhill & Gangestad, 1994).

Cross-cultural research shows that males and females in many cultures have similar ideas about the physical attractiveness of members of the opposite sex (Langlois et al., 2000). For example, when native Asian, Hispanic, and Caucasian American male students rated photographs of Asian, Hispanic, African American, and Caucasian females on attractiveness, Cunningham and others (1995) reported a very high mean correlation (.93) among the groups in attractiveness ratings. When African American and Caucasian American men rated photos of African American women, their agreement on facial features was also very high—the correlation was .94. Evolutionary psychologists suggest that this cross-cultural similarity is because of a tendency, shaped by natural selection, to look for indicators of health in potential mates (Fink & Penton-Voak, 2002).

Why does physical attractiveness matter? When people have one trait or quality that we either admire or dislike very much, we often assume that they also have other admirable or negative traits—a phenomenon known as the **halo effect** (Nisbett & Wilson, 1977). Dion and others (1972) found that people generally attribute other favorable qualities to those who are attractive. Attractive people are seen as more exciting, personable, interesting, and socially desirable than unattractive people. As a result, job interviewers are more likely to recommend highly attractive people (Dipboye et al., 1975).

Does this mean that unattractive people don't have a chance? Fortunately not. Eagly and her colleagues (1991) suggest that the impact of physical attractiveness is strongest in the perception of strangers. Once we get to know people, other qualities assume more importance. In fact, as we come to like people, they begin to look more attractive to us, and people with undesirable personal qualities begin to look less attractive.

Romantic Attraction and Mating

Even though most of us may be attracted to handsome or beautiful people, the **matching hypothesis** suggests that we are likely to end up with someone similar to ourselves in attractiveness and other assets (Berscheid et al., 1971; Feingold, 1988; Walster & Walster, 1969). Furthermore, couples mismatched in attractiveness are more likely to end the relationship (Cash & Janda, 1984). It has been suggested that most people estimate their social assets and realistically expect to attract someone with approximately equal assets. In terms of physical attractiveness, some people might consider a movie star or supermodel to be the ideal man or woman, but they do not seriously consider the ideal to be a realistic, attainable possibility. Fear of rejection keeps many people from pursuing those who are much more attractive than they are. But instead of marrying an extremely handsome man, a very beautiful woman may base her choice not on physical attractiveness but on money and social status. Extremely handsome men have been known to make similar "sacrifices." The matching hypothesis is generally applicable to friendships as well as romantic relationships (Cash & Derlega, 1978), although it is more true of males than of females (Feingold, 1988).

But is a virtual "clone" of oneself the most desirable life partner? Not necessarily. Robert Winch (1958) proposes that men and women tend to choose mates with needs and personalities that are complementary rather than similar to their own. Winch sees complementary needs as not necessarily opposite, but as supplying what the partner lacks. A talkative person may seek a quiet mate who prefers to listen. There is some support for this view (Dryer & Horowitz, 1997).

Most research, however, indicates that similarity in needs is mainly what attracts (Buss, 1984; Phillips et al., 1988). Similarity in personality, physical traits, intellectual ability, education, religion, ethnicity, socioeconomic status, and attitudes are all related to partner choice (O'Leary & Smith, 1991). And similarity in needs and in personality appears to be related to marital success as well as to marital choice (O'Leary & Smith, 1991). Similarities wear well.

If you were to select a marriage partner, what qualities would attract you?

Generally, men and women across cultures rate these four qualities as most important in mate selection: (1) mutual attraction/love, (2) dependable character, (3) emotional stability and maturity, and (4) pleasing disposition (Buss et al., 1990). Aside from these four first choices, however, women and men differ somewhat in the attributes they prefer. According to Buss (1994), "Men prefer to mate with beautiful young women, whereas women prefer to mate with men who have resources and social status" (p. 239). These preferences, he claims, have been adaptive in human evolutionary history. To a male, beauty and youth suggest health and fertility—the best chance to pass his genes onto the next generation. To a female, resources and social status provide security for her and her children (Buss, 2000).

Sternberg's Theory of Love

In Western culture, affection is an important part of most relationships, including friendships, and being "in love" is the most important factor in the formation of a long-term romantic relationship. But what is love? Robert Sternberg (1986, 1987) proposes a **triangular theory of love.** Its three components are *intimacy*, *passion*, and *commitment*. Sternberg explains intimacy as "those feelings in a relationship that promote closeness, bondedness, and connectedness" (1987, p. 339). Passion refers to those drives in a loving relationship "that lead to romance, physical attraction, [and] sexual consummation" (1986, p. 119). The commitment, or decision/commitment, component consists of (1) a short-term aspect (the decision that one loves another person) and (2) a long-term aspect (a commitment to maintaining that love over time).

Sternberg proposes that these three components, singly and in various combinations, produce seven different kinds of love:

- *Liking* has only one of the love components—intimacy. In this case, liking is not used in a trivial sense. Sternberg says that liking characterizes true friendships.
- *Infatuated love* consists solely of passion and is often what is felt as "love at first sight."

- *Empty love* consists of the decision/commitment component without intimacy or passion. Sometimes a stronger love deteriorates into empty love. In cultures in which arranged marriages are common, relationships often begin as empty love.

- *Romantic love* is a combination of intimacy and passion. Romantic lovers are bonded emotionally (as in liking) and physically through passionate arousal.

- *Fatuous love* has the components of passion and decision/commitment but not intimacy. This type of love can be exemplified by a whirlwind courtship and marriage in which a commitment is motivated largely by passion without the stabilizing influence of intimacy.

- *Companionate love* consists of intimacy and commitment. This type of love is often found in marriages in which the passion has gone out of the relationship, but a deep affection and commitment remain.

- *Consummate love* is the only type that has all three components—intimacy, decision/commitment, and passion. It represents the ideal love relationship for which many people strive.

SOCIAL INFLUENCE

Conformity

Conformity is changing or adopting a behavior or an attitude in order to be consistent with the social norms of a group or the expectations of other people. **Social norms** are the standards of behavior and the attitudes that are expected of members of a group. Some conformity is necessary if there is to be any social order at all. We cannot drive on either side of the street at whim, for example. And we conform to other people's expectations in order to have their esteem, their love, or even their company. Moreover, there are times when conformity is beneficial to us. Researchers have found that teenagers who attend schools where the majority of students are opposed to smoking, drinking, and drug use are less likely to use these substances than peers who attend schools where the majority approves of these behaviors (Kumar et al., 2002).

The best-known experiment on conformity was conducted by Solomon Asch (1951, 1955), who designed the simple test shown in Figure 19.1. Eight male participants were seated around a large table and were asked, one by one, to tell the experimenter which of the three lines matched the standard line. But only one of the eight was an actual participant; the others were confederates assisting the

FIGURE 19.1 Asch's Classic Study of Conformity. If you were one of eight participants in the Asch experiment who were asked to pick the line (1, 2, or 3) that matched the standard line shown at the top, which line would you choose? If the other participants all chose line 3, would you conform and answer line 3? (Based on Asch, 1955.)

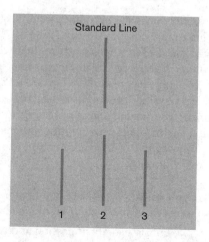

experimenter. There were 18 trials—18 different lines to be matched. During 12 of these trials, the confederates all gave the same wrong answer, which of course puzzled the naive participant. Remarkably, Asch found that 5% of the subjects conformed to the incorrect, unanimous majority all of the time, 70% conformed some of the time, and 25% remained completely independent and were never swayed by the group.

Varying the experiment with groups of 2, 3, 4, 8, and 10–15, Asch found that the tendency to "go along" with the majority opinion was operating, even when there was a unanimous majority of only 3 confederates. Surprisingly, unanimous majorities of 15 produced no higher conformity rate than did those of 3. Asch also discovered that if just one other person voiced a dissenting opinion, the tendency to conform was not as strong. When just one confederate in the group disagreed with the incorrect majority, the naive participants' errors dropped drastically, from 32% to 10.4%.

Other research on conformity reveals further interesting aspects. For instance, people who are high in three of the Big Five personality dimensions—emotional stability, Agreeableness, and Conscientiousness—are more likely to conform than those who are low in these factors (DeYoung et al., 2002). Contrary to conventional wisdom, women are no more likely to conform than men (Eagly & Carli, 1981). But conformity is greater for everyone if the sources of influence are perceived as belonging to one's own group (Abrams et al., 1990). And with respect to nonconformity, those who hold minority opinions on an issue have more influence in changing a majority view if they present a well-organized, clearly stated argument and if they are especially consistent in advocating their views (Wood et al., 1994).

Obedience

Some obedience is necessary if civilized society is to function, but unquestioned obedience can cause humans to commit unbelievably horrible acts. One of the darkest chapters in human history was due to the obedience of officials in Nazi Germany in carrying out Adolph Hitler's orders to exterminate Jews and other "undesirables."

The study you read about at the beginning of this chapter demonstrated how far ordinary citizens would go to obey orders; remember, more than 60% of Milgram's participants went all the way to 450 volts despite the pleading and eventual collapse of the "learner." Another researcher repeated the experiment in a three-room office suite in a run-down building rather than at prestigious Yale University. Even there, 48% of the participants administered the maximum shock (Meyer, 1972).

Milgram (1965) conducted a variation of the original experiment in which each trial involved three teachers, two of whom were confederates and the other, a naive participant. One confederate was instructed to refuse to continue after 150 volts, and the other confederate after 210 volts. In this situation, 36 out of 40 naive participants (90%) defied the experimenter before the maximum shock could be given, compared with only 14 participants in the original experiment (Milgram, 1965). In Milgram's experiment, as in Asch's conformity study, the presence of another person who refused to go along gave many of the participants the courage to defy the authority.

Compliance

There are many times when people act not out of conformity or obedience, but in accordance with the wishes, suggestions, or direct requests of another person. This type of action is called **compliance.** One strategy people use to gain the compliance of others, the **foot-in-the-door technique,** is designed to gain a favorable response to a small request first. The intent is to make the person more likely to agree later to a larger request (the result desired from the beginning).

In a classic study of the foot-in-the-door technique, a researcher claiming to represent a consumers' group called a number of homes and asked whether the people answering the phone would mind answering a few questions about the soap products they used. Then, a few days later, the same person called those who had agreed to the first request and asked if he could send five or six of his assistants to conduct an inventory of the products in their home. The researcher told the people that the inventory would take about 2 hours, and that the inventory team would have to search all drawers, cabinets, and closets in the house. Nearly 53% of those who had earlier answered the questions agreed to the second request, compared with 22% of a control group who were contacted only once, with that request (Freedman & Fraser, 1966).

With the **door-in-the-face technique,** a large, unreasonable request is made first. The expectation is that the person will refuse but will then be more likely to respond favorably to a later, smaller request (the result desired from the beginning). In one of the best-known studies on the door-in-the-face technique, college students were approached on campus. They were asked to agree to serve without pay as counselors to juvenile delinquents for 2 hours each week for a minimum of 2 years. As you would imagine, not a single person agreed (Cialdini et al., 1975). Then, the experimenters countered with a much smaller request, asking if the students would agree to take a group of juveniles on a 2-hour trip to the zoo. Half the students agreed, a fairly high compliance rate. The researchers used another group of college students as controls, asking them to respond only to the smaller request, the zoo trip. Only 17% agreed when the smaller request was presented alone.

Another method used to gain compliance is the **low-ball technique.** A very attractive initial offer is made to get people to commit themselves to an action, and then the terms are made less favorable. In a frequently cited study of this technique, college students were asked to enroll in an experimental course for which they would receive credit. Only after the students had agreed to participate were they informed that the class would meet at 7:00 a.m. Control group participants were told of the time when first asked to enroll. More than 50% of the low-balled group agreed to participate, but only 25% of control participants agreed to take the class (Cialdini et al., 1978).

GROUP INFLUENCE

It is obvious that being in a group influences our behavior and our performance. We behave differently in a variety of ways when we are alone and when we are part of a group, small or large.

Social Facilitation

In certain cases, individual performance can be either helped or hindered by the mere physical presence of others. The term **social facilitation** refers to any effect on performance, whether positive or negative, that can be attributed to the presence of others. Research on this phenomenon has focused on two types of effects: (1) **audience effects,** or the impact of passive spectators on performance; and (2) **co-action effects,** or the impact on performance caused by the presence of other people engaged in the same task.

In one of the first studies in social psychology, Norman Triplett (1898) looked at co-action effects. He had observed in official bicycle records that bicycle racers pedaled faster when they were pedaling against other racers than when they were racing against the clock. Was this pattern of performance peculiar to competitive bicycling? Or was it part of a more general phenomenon in which people worked faster and harder in the presence of others than when performing alone? Triplett set up a study in which he told 40 children to wind fishing reels as quickly as possible under two conditions: (1) alone and (2) in the presence of other children performing the same task. He found that the children worked faster when other reel turners were present than when they performed alone. But later studies on social facilitation found that, in the presence of others, performance improves on tasks that can be done easily, but suffers on difficult tasks (Michaels et al., 1982). See Figure 19.2.

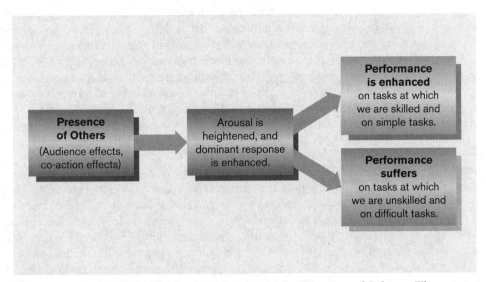

FIGURE 19.2   Social Facilitation: Performing in the Presence of Others. The presence of others (either as an audience or as co-actors engaged in the same task) may have opposite effects, either helping or hindering an individual's performance. Why? Robert Zajonc explained that (1) the presence of others heightens arousal and (2) heightened arousal leads to better performance on easier tasks and worse performance on more difficult tasks. (Based on Zajonc & Sales, 1966.)

Social Loafing

Researcher Bibb Latané used the term **social loafing** to refer to people's tendency to exert less effort when working with others on a common task than when working alone. Social loafing occurs in situations where no one person's contribution to the group can be identified and individuals are neither praised for a good performance nor blamed for a poor one (Williams et al., 1981). Social loafing is a problem in many workplaces, especially where employees have unlimited access to the Internet (Lim, 2002). Employees tend to justify "cyberloafing" in terms of perceived injustices committed by their supervisors.

In one experiment, Latané and others (1979) asked male students to shout and clap as loudly as possible, first alone and then in groups. In groups of two, individuals made only 71% of the noise they had made alone; in groups of four, each person put forth 51% of his solo effort; and with six persons each made only a 40% effort. But Harkins and Jackson (1985) found that social loafing disappeared when participants in a group were led to believe that each person's output could be monitored and his or her performance evaluated. Even the possibility that the group performance may be evaluated against some standard can be sufficient to eliminate the loafing effect (Harkins & Szymanski, 1989).

Some 80 experimental studies have been conducted on social loafing in diverse cultures, including those of Taiwan, Japan, Thailand, India, China, and the United States. Social loafing on a variety of tasks was evident to some degree in all of the cultures studied. But it appears to be more common in individualistic Western cultures such as the United States (Karau & Williams, 1993).

Group Polarization and Groupthink

It is commonly believed that groups tend to make more moderate decisions than individuals. However, research shows that group discussion often causes members of a group to shift to a more extreme position in whatever direction the group was leaning initially—a phenomenon known as **group polarization** (Isenberg, 1986; Lamm, 1988). Group members, it seems, will decide to take a greater risk if they were leaning in a risky direction to begin with, but they will shift toward a more cautious position if they were, on average, somewhat cautious at the beginning of the discussion (Myers & Lamm, 1975). Myers and Bishop (1970) found that as a result of group polarization, group discussions of racial issues can either increase or decrease prejudice. However, group members do not always all lean in the same direction at the beginning of a discussion. When evidence both for and against a particular stand on a given topic is presented, group polarization occurs infrequently (Kuhn & Lao, 1996). Moreover, when subgroups within a larger group hold opposing views, compromise rather than polarization is the likely outcome (Vinokur & Burnstein, 1978).

Groupthink is the term social psychologist Irving Janis (1982) applies to the decisions often reached by tightly knit groups. When a tightly knit group is more concerned with preserving group solidarity and uniformity than with evaluating all possible alternatives objectively, individual members may hesitate to voice any dissent. The group may also discredit opposing views from outsiders and begin to believe it is incapable of making mistakes. To guard against groupthink, Janis suggests that the group encourage an open discussion of alternative views and encourage the expression of any objections and doubts. He further recommends that outside experts sit in and challenge the views of the group. At least one group member should take the role of devil's advocate whenever a policy alternative is evaluated. Finally, to avoid groupthink in the workplace, managers should withhold their own opinions when problem-solving and decision-making strategies are being considered (Bazan, 1998).

Social Roles

Social roles are socially defined behaviors that are considered appropriate for individuals occupying certain positions within a given group. Roles can shape people's behavior, sometimes quickly and dramatically. Consider a classic experiment in which psychologist Philip Zimbardo (1972) simulated a prison experience. College student volunteers were randomly assigned to be either guards or prisoners. The guards, wearing uniforms and carrying small clubs, strictly enforced harsh rules. The prisoners were stripped naked, searched, and deloused. Then they were given prison uniforms, assigned numbers, and locked away in small, bare cells. The guards quickly adopted their role, some even to the point of becoming heartless and sadistic. One guard remembered forcing prisoners to clean toilets with their bare hands. Prisoners began to behave like real prisoners, acting debased and subservient. The role playing became all too real—so much so that the experiment had to be ended in only 6 days.

Of course, social roles can have positive effects on behavior as well. In classic research involving adolescents with learning disabilities, Palinscar and Brown (1984) reported that students' learning behaviors were powerfully affected by their being assigned to play either the "teacher" or "student" role in group study sessions. Participants summarized reading assignments more effectively and, as a result, learned more from them when functioning as teachers than when functioning as students.

ATTITUDES AND ATTITUDE CHANGE

Attitudes

Essentially, **attitudes** are relatively stable evaluations of persons, objects, situations, or issues along a continuum ranging from positive to negative (Petty et al., 1997). Most attitudes have three components: (1) a cognitive component consisting of thoughts and beliefs about the attitudinal object, (2) an emotional component composed of feelings toward the attitudinal object, and (3) a behavioral component made up of predispositions concerning actions toward the object (Breckler, 1984). Figure 19.3 shows these three components of an attitude. Attitudes enable us to appraise people, objects, and situations and provide structure and consistency in the social environment (Fazio, 1989). Attitudes also help us

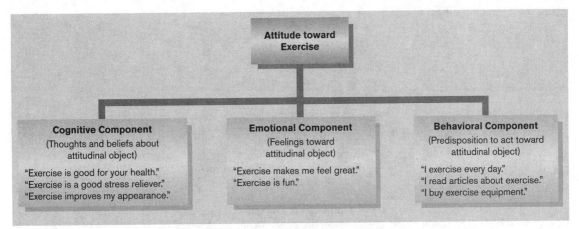

FIGURE 19.3   The Three Components of an Attitude. An attitude is a relatively stable evaluation of a person, object, situation, or issue. Most of our attitudes have (1) a cognitive component, (2) an emotional component, and (3) a behavioral component.

process social information (Pratkanis, 1989), guide our behavior (Sanbonmatsu & Fazio, 1990), and influence our social judgments and decisions (Jamieson & Zanna, 1989).

Some attitudes are acquired through firsthand experience with people, objects, situations, and issues. Others are acquired when children hear parents, other family members, friends, and teachers express positive or negative attitudes toward certain issues or people. The mass media, including advertising, influence people's attitudes and reap billions of dollars annually for their efforts. As you might expect, however, the attitudes that people form through their own direct experience are stronger than those they acquire vicariously and are also more resistant to change (Wu & Shaffer, 1987). And, despite ageist stereotypes, many studies have found that older adults are more likely than middle-aged adults to change their attitudes (Visser & Krosnick, 1998).

We often hear that attitude change is the key to behavior change. However, a number of early studies showed that attitudes predict behavior only about 10% of the time (e.g., Wicker, 1969). People, for example, may express strong attitudes in favor of protecting the environment and conservation of resources, yet not take their aluminum cans to a recycling center or join carpools. However, attitudes are better predictors of behavior if they are strongly held, are readily accessible in memory (Bassili, 1995; Fazio & Williams, 1986; Kraus, 1995), and vitally affect the holder's interests (Sivacek & Crano, 1982).

If people discover that some of their attitudes are in conflict with others or that their attitudes are not consistent with their behavior, they are likely to experience an unpleasant state. Leon Festinger (1957) called this state **cognitive dissonance.** People usually try to reduce this dissonance by changing the behavior or the attitude or by somehow explaining away the inconsistency or reducing its importance (Aronson, 1976; Festinger, 1957). A change in attitude does seem to reduce the discomfort caused by cognitive dissonance (Elliot & Devine, 1994).

Smoking is a perfect behavior for illustrating cognitive dissonance. Faced with a mountain of evidence linking smoking to a number of diseases, what are smokers to do? The healthiest, but perhaps not the easiest, way to reduce the cognitive dissonance is to change the behavior—quit smoking. Another way is to change the attitude—to convince themselves that smoking is not as dangerous as it is said to be. Smokers might also tell themselves that they will stop smoking long before any permanent damage is done, or that medical science is advancing so rapidly that a cure for cancer or emphysema is just around the corner. Figure 19.4 illustrates the methods a smoker might use to reduce cognitive dissonance.

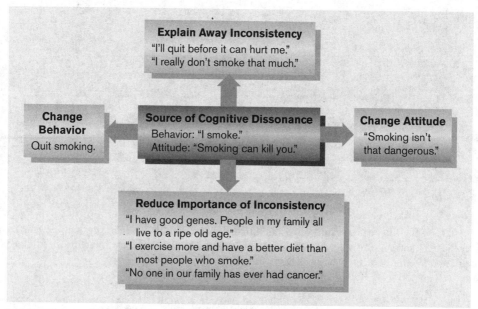

FIGURE 19.4   Methods of Reducing Cognitive Dissonance. Cognitive dissonance can occur when people become aware of inconsistencies in their attitudes or between their attitudes and their behavior. People try to reduce dissonance by (1) changing their behavior, (2) changing their attitude, (3) explaining away the inconsistency, or (4) reducing its importance. Here are examples of how a smoker might use these methods to reduce the cognitive dissonance created by his or her habit.

Expanding the applicability of the concept of cognitive dissonance, Aronson and Mills (1959) argued that the more people have to sacrifice, give up, or suffer to become a member of an organization—say, a fraternity or sorority—the more positive their attitudes are likely to become toward the group, in order to justify their sacrifice. Members of cults are often required to endure hardships and make great sacrifices, such as severing ties with their families and friends and turning over their property and possessions to the group. Such extreme sacrifice can then be justified only by a strong and radical defense of the cult, its goals, and its leaders.

Persuasion

Persuasion is a deliberate attempt to influence the attitudes and/or the behavior of another person. Attempts at persuasion are pervasive parts of work experience, social experience, and even family life. Researchers have identified four elements of persuasion: (1) the source of the communication (who is doing the persuading), (2) the audience (who is being persuaded), (3) the message (what is being said), and (4) the medium (the means by which the message is transmitted).

Some factors that make the source (the communicator) more persuasive are credibility, attractiveness, and likability. A credible communicator is one who has expertise (knowledge of the topic at hand) and trustworthiness (truthfulness and integrity). Other characteristics of the source—such as physical attractiveness, celebrity status, and similarity to the audience—also contribute to audience responses to the sources of persuasive messages.

Audience characteristics influence responses to persuasion as well. In general, people with low intelligence are easier to persuade than those who are highly intelligent (Rhodes & Wood, 1992). Evidence suggests that a one-sided message is usually most persuasive if the audience is not well informed on the issue, is not overly intelligent, or already agrees with the point of view. A two-sided message (where both sides of an issue are mentioned) works best when the audience is well informed on the issue, is fairly intelligent, or is initially opposed to the point of view. A two-sided appeal will usually sway more people than a one-sided appeal (Hovland et al., 1949; McGuire, 1985). And people tend to scrutinize arguments that are contrary to their existing beliefs more carefully and exert more effort refuting them; they are also more likely to judge such arguments as weaker than those that support their beliefs (Edwards & Smith, 1996).

A message can be well reasoned, logical, and unemotional ("just the facts"); a message can be strictly emotional ("scare the hell out of them"); or it can be a combination of the two. Arousing fear seems to be an effective method for persuading people to quit smoking and wear seat belts. Appeals based on fear are most effective when the presentation outlines definite actions the audience can take to avoid the feared outcomes (Buller et al., 2000; Stephenson & Witte, 1998). By contrast, nutritional messages are more effective when framed in terms of the benefits of dietary change than in terms of the harmful effects of a poor diet (van Assema et al., 2001).

Another important factor in persuasion is repetition. The more often a product or a point of view is presented, the more people will be persuaded to buy it or embrace it. Advertisers apparently believe in this *mere-exposure effect*, for they repeat their messages over and over (Bornstein, 1989). But messages are likely to be less persuasive if they include vivid elements (colorful language, striking examples) that hinder the reception of the content (Frey & Eagly, 1993).

PROSOCIAL BEHAVIOR

Reasons for Helping

There are many kinds of **prosocial behavior**—behavior that benefits others, such as helping, cooperation, and sympathy. Such impulses arise early in life. Researchers agree that young children respond sympathetically to companions in distress, usually before their second birthday (Hay, 1994; Kochanska, 1993). The term **altruism** is usually reserved for behavior that is aimed at helping others and requires some self-sacrifice but is not performed for personal gain. Batson and colleagues (1989) believe that we help out of *empathy*—the ability to take the perspective of others, to put oneself in their place.

Cultures vary in their norms for helping others—that is, their *social responsibility norms*. According to Miller and others (1990), people in the United States tend to feel an obligation to help family, friends, and even strangers in life-threatening circumstances, but only family in moderately serious situations. In contrast, in India, the social responsibility norm extends to strangers whose needs are only moderately serious or even minor.

The Bystander Effect

There are a variety of social circumstances that contribute to the decision to help another person. One such circumstance involves the **bystander effect**: As the number of bystanders at an emergency increases, the probability that the victim will receive help from them decreases, and the help, if given, is likely to be delayed. In now-classic research, Darley and Latané (1968a) placed research participants one at a time in a small room and told them that they would be participating in a discussion group by means of an intercom system. Some participants were told that they would be communicating with only one other participant, some believed that two other participants would be involved, and some were told that five other people would participate. There really were no other participants in the study—only the prerecorded voices of confederates assisting the experimenter.

Shortly after the discussion began, the voice of one confederate was heard over the intercom calling for help, indicating that he was having an epileptic seizure. Of the participants who believed that

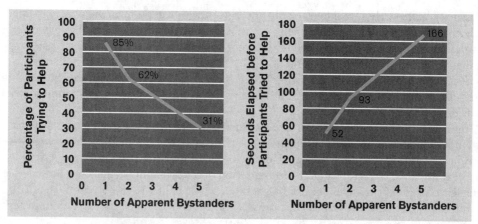

FIGURE 19.5   The Bystander Effect. In their intercom experiment, Darley and Latané showed that the more people a participant believed were present during an emergency, the longer it took the participant to respond and help a person in distress. (Data from Darley & Latané, 1968a.)

they alone were hearing the victim, 85% went for help before the end of the seizure. When participants believed that one other person heard the seizure, 62% sought help. But when they believed that four other people were aware of the emergency, only 31% tried to get help before the end of the seizure. Figure 19.5 shows how the number of bystanders affects both the number of people who try to help and the speed of response.

Latané and Darley suggest that, when bystanders are present in an emergency, they generally feel that the responsibility for helping is shared by the group, a phenomenon known as **diffusion of responsibility.** Consequently, each person feels less compelled to act than if she or he were alone and felt the total responsibility. Each thinks that "somebody else must be doing something" (Darley & Latané, 1968a). Another reason for the bystander effect, according to Darley & Latané, is the influence of other calm-appearing bystanders. When others appear calm, people may conclude that nothing is really wrong and no intervention is necessary (Darley & Latané, 1968b).

Interestingly, during catastrophes such as those on September 11, 2001, the bystander effect is greatly reduced. In fact, people are likely to put forth extraordinary effort to help others in such situations. This phenomenon was evidenced by the countless individual acts of altruism that occurred in both Washington, DC, and New York City immediately after the terrorist attacks. And those who couldn't help directly contributed millions of dollars to the families of 9/11 victims within hours after the events. Research examining public responses to large-scale disasters would predict just such a level of response (Shepperd, 2001).

AGGRESSION

Aggression is the intentional infliction of physical or psychological harm on others. Aggression may form and take place in a variety of locations—at home, at work, or even among drivers on the road. Acts of aggression against others' person or property take place frequently in the United States. But why does one person intentionally harm another?

Biological Factors in Aggression

Sigmund Freud believed that humans have an aggressive instinct that can be turned inward as self-destruction or outward as aggression or violence toward others. While rejecting this view, many psychologists do concede that biological factors are involved. A review of 24 twin and adoption studies of several personality measures of aggression revealed a heritability estimate of about .50 for aggression (Miles & Carey, 1997). Twin and adoption studies have also revealed a genetic link for criminal behavior (DiLalla & Gottesman, 1991). Cloninger and others (1982) found that adoptees with a criminal biological parent were four times as likely as members of the general population to commit a crime, adoptees with a criminal adoptive parent were at twice the risk of committing a crime, but adoptees with both a biological and an adoptive parent who had a criminal record were fourteen times as likely to commit a crime. This finding indicates the power of the combined influences of nature and nurture.

One biological factor that seems closely related to aggression is a low arousal level of the autonomic nervous system (Raine, 1996). Low arousal level (low heart rate and lower reactivity) has been linked to antisocial and violent behavior (Brennan et al., 1997). People with low arousal levels tend to seek stimulation and excitement and often exhibit fearlessness, even in the face of danger.

Men are more physically aggressive than women (Green et al., 1996), and the male hormone testosterone is partly the cause. In fact, the primary biological variable related to domestic violence (both verbal and physical abuse) appears to be high testosterone levels, which are highly heritable (Soler et al., 2000). A correlation between high testosterone level and aggressive behavior has been found in males (Archer, 1991; Dabbs & Morris, 1990), and Harris and others (1996) found testosterone levels in both male *and* female college students to be positively correlated with aggression and negatively correlated with prosocial behavior. And violent behavior has been associated with low levels of the neurotransmitter serotonin (Gartner & Whitaker-Azimitia, 1996; Mitsis et al., 2000).

Brain damage, brain tumors, and temporal lobe epilepsy have all been related to aggressive and violent behavior (Mednick et al., 1988; van Elst et al., 2000). A study of 15 death row inmates revealed that all had histories of severe head injuries (Lewis et al., 1986). According to Eronen and others (1996), homicide rates are eight times higher in men with schizophrenia and ten times higher in men with antisocial personality disorder. The risk of violence is even greater when individuals with these disorders abuse alcohol (Hodgins et al., 1996; Tiihonen et al., 1997). In children, high levels of lead exposure (Needleman et al., 1996) and low IQ and problems paying attention (Loeber & Hay, 1997) are related to aggressive behavior and delinquency.

Alcohol and aggression are also frequent partners. A review of 30 experimental studies indicated that alcohol is related to aggression (Bushman & Cooper, 1990). Alcohol and other drugs that affect the brain's prefrontal cortex lead to aggressive behavior in humans and other animals by disrupting normal emotional and behavioral control functions (Lyvers, 2000). Ito and others (1996) found that alcohol intoxication is particularly likely to lead to aggression in response to frustration. People who are intoxicated commit the majority of murders, spouse beatings, stabbings, and acts of physical child abuse.

Aggression in Response to Frustration and Aversive Events

The **frustration-aggression hypothesis** suggests that frustration produces aggression (Dollard et al., 1939; Miller, 1941). If a traffic jam delayed you and you were frustrated, would you lean on your horn, shout obscenities out of your window, or just sit patiently and wait? Frustration doesn't always cause aggression, but it is especially likely to if it is intense and seems to be unjustified (Doob & Sears, 1939; Pastore, 1950). Berkowitz (1988) points out that even if frustration is justified and not aimed specifically at an individual, it can cause aggression if it arouses negative emotions.

Aggression in response to frustration is not always aimed at the people causing it. If the preferred target is too threatening or not available, the aggression may be displaced. For example, children who are angry with their parents may take out their frustrations on younger siblings. Sometimes members of minority groups or others who have not been responsible for a frustrating situation become targets of displaced aggression, a practice known as **scapegoating** (Koltz, 1983).

People often become aggressive when they are in pain (Berkowitz, 1983) or are exposed to loud noise or foul odors (Rotton et al., 1979). Extreme heat has also been linked to aggression in several studies (Anderson & Anderson, 1996; Rotton & Cohn, 2000). These and other studies lend support to the *cognitive-neoassociationistic model* proposed by Berkowitz (1990). He has suggested that anger and aggression result from aversive events and from unpleasant emotional states such as sadness, grief, and depression. The cognitive component of Berkowitz's model involves the angered person's appraising the aversive situation and making attributions about the motives of the people involved. As a result of the cognitive appraisal, the initial reaction of anger can be intensified or reduced or suppressed. This process makes the person either more or less likely to act on the aggressive tendency.

Personal space is an area surrounding each individual, much like an invisible bubble, that the person considers part of himself or herself and uses to regulate the closeness of interactions with others. Personal space serves to protect personal privacy and to regulate the level of intimacy with others. The size of personal space varies according to the person or persons with whom an individual is interacting and the nature of the interaction. And when personal space is reduced, aggression can result.

Crowding—the subjective judgment that there are too many people in a confined space—often leads to higher physiological arousal. Males typically experience the effects of crowding more negatively than females do, and those effects also vary across cultures and situations. Researchers have studied the effects of crowding on such diverse populations as male heads of households in India and middle-class male and female college students in the United States (Evans & Lepore, 1993). In both of these studies, psychological distress was linked to household crowding. And studies in prisons have shown that the more inmates per cell, the greater the number of violent incidents (Paulus et al., 1988). However, keep in mind that a prison is an atypical environment with a population some of whose members have been confined precisely because they tend to be aggressive.

The Social Learning Theory of Aggression

The *social learning theory of aggression* holds that people learn to behave aggressively by observing aggressive models and by having their aggressive responses reinforced (Bandura, 1973). It is well known that aggression is higher in groups and subcultures that condone violent behavior and accord high status to aggressive members. A leading advocate of the social learning theory of aggression, Albert Bandura (1976), claims that aggressive models in the subculture, the family, and the media all play a part in increasing the level of aggression in society.

Abused children certainly experience aggression and see it modeled day after day. And the rate of physical abuse is seven times greater in families in which there is a step-parent (Daly & Wilson, 1996). "One of the most commonly held beliefs in both the scholarly and popular literature is that adults who were abused as children are more likely to abuse their own children" (Widom, 1989, p. 6). There is some truth to this belief. On the basis of original research and an analysis of 60 other studies, Oliver (1993) concludes that one-third of people who are abused go on to become abusers, one-third do not, and the final third may become abusers if their lives are highly stressful.

Most abusive parents, however, were not abused as children (Widom, 1989). Although abused and neglected children are at higher risk of becoming delinquent, criminal, or violent, the majority do not (Widom & Maxfield, 1996). Several researchers suggest that the higher risk for aggression may not be due solely to an abusive family environment but may be partly influenced by the genes (DiLalla & Gottesman, 1991). Some abused children become withdrawn and isolated rather than aggressive and abusive (Dodge et al., 1990).

The research evidence overwhelmingly supports a relationship between TV violence and viewer aggression (Huesmann & Moise, 1996; Singer et al., 1999). And the negative effects of TV violence are even worse for individuals who are, by nature, highly aggressive (Bushman, 1995). According to Eron

(1987, p. 438), "One of the best predictors of how aggressive a young man would be at age 19 was the violence of the TV programs he preferred when he was 8 years old." A longitudinal study conducted in Finland also found that the viewing of TV violence was related to criminality in young adulthood (Viemerö, 1996). And a review of 28 studies of the effects of media violence on children and adolescents revealed that "media violence enhances children's and adolescents' aggression in interactions with strangers, classmates, and friends" (Wood et al., 1991, p. 380). It may stimulate physiological arousal, lower inhibitions, cause unpleasant feelings, and decrease sensitivity to violence and make it more acceptable to people.

Researchers have also found a correlation between playing violent video games and aggression (Anderson & Dill, 2000). Moreover, aggressiveness increases as more time is spent playing such games (Colwell & Payne, 2000). However, researchers in the Netherlands found that boys who chose aggressive video games tended to be more aggressive, less intelligent, and less prosocial in their behavior (Weigman & van Schie, 1998). So the link between aggression and video games may reflect the tendency of individuals who are more aggressive to prefer entertainment media that feature aggression.

PREJUDICE AND DISCRIMINATION

Prejudice consists of (usually negative) attitudes toward others based on their gender, religion, race, or membership in a particular group. Prejudice involves beliefs and emotions (not actions) that can escalate into hatred. **Discrimination** consists of behavior—actions (usually negative) toward members of a group. Many Americans have experienced prejudice and discrimination—minority racial groups (racism), women (sexism), the elderly (ageism), the handicapped, homosexuals, religious groups, and others. What are the roots of prejudice and discrimination?

The Roots of Prejudice and Discrimination

One of the oldest explanations of how prejudice arises is that it comes from competition among various social groups who must struggle against one another for scarce resources—good jobs, homes, schools, and so on. Commonly called the **realistic conflict theory,** this view suggests that as competition increases, so do prejudice, discrimination, and hatred among the competing groups. Some historical evidence supports the realistic conflict theory. Prejudice and hatred were high between the early settlers and the Native Americans who struggled over land during the westward expansion. The multitudes of Irish and German immigrants who came to the United States in the 1830s and 1840s felt the sting of prejudice and hatred from other Americans who were facing economic scarcity. But prejudice and discrimination are attitudes and actions too complex to be explained solely by economic conflict and competition.

Prejudice can also spring from the distinct social categories into which people divide the world—us versus them (Turner et al., 1987). An **in-group** is a social group in which there is a strong feeling of togetherness and from which others are excluded. Members of college fraternities and sororities often exhibit strong in-group feelings. An **out-group** consists of individuals or groups specifically identified by an in-group as not belonging. Us-versus-them thinking can lead to excessive competition, hostility, prejudice, discrimination, and even war. Prejudiced individuals who most strongly identify with their racial in-group are most reluctant to admit others to the group if there is the slightest doubt about their racial purity (Blascovich et al., 1997).

A famous study by Sherif and Sherif (1967) shows how in-group/out-group conflict can escalate into prejudice and hostility rather quickly, even between groups that are very much alike. The researchers set up their experiment at the Robber's Cave summer camp. Their subjects were 22 bright, well-adjusted, 11- and 12-year-old Caucasian middle-class boys from Oklahoma City. Divided into two groups and housed in separate cabins, the boys were kept apart for all their daily activities and games. During the first week, in-group solidarity, friendship, and cooperation developed within each of the groups.

During the second week of the study, competitive events were purposely scheduled so that the goals of one group could be achieved "only at the expense of the other group" (Sherif, 1958, p. 353). The groups were happy to battle each other, and intergroup conflict quickly emerged. Name-calling began, fights broke out, and accusations were hurled back and forth. During the third week of the experiment, the researchers tried to put an end to the hostility and to turn rivalry into cooperation. They simply brought the groups together for pleasant activities such as eating meals and watching movies. "But far from reducing conflict, these situations only served as opportunities for the rival groups to berate and attack each other. . . . They threw paper, food and vile names at each other at the tables" (Sherif, 1956, pp. 57–58).

Finally, the researchers manufactured a series of crises that could be solved only if all the boys combined their efforts and resources and cooperated. The water supply, sabotaged by the researchers, could be restored only if all the boys worked together. After a week of several activities requiring cooperation, cut-throat competition gave way to cooperative exchanges. Friendships developed between groups, and before the end of the experiment, peace was declared. Working together toward shared goals had turned hostility into friendship.

According to social learning theory, people learn attitudes of prejudice and hatred the same way they learn other attitudes. If children hear their parents, teachers, peers, and others openly express prejudices toward different racial, ethnic, religious, or cultural groups, they may be quick to learn such attitudes. And if parents, peers, and others reward children with smiles and approval for parroting their own prejudices (operant conditioning), children may learn these prejudices even more quickly. Phillips and Ziller (1997) suggest that people learn to be nonprejudiced in the same way.

Emotion- and learning-based views help explain how prejudice develops. But a more recent view suggests that social cognition plays a role in giving birth to prejudice. **Social cognition** refers to the ways in which people typically process social information—the natural thinking processes used to notice, interpret, and remember information about the social world. The very processes we use to simplify, categorize, and order the social world are the same processes that distort our views of it. So prejudice may arise not only from heated negative emotions and hatred toward other social groups, but also from cooler cognitive processes that govern how we think and process social information (Kunda & Oleson, 1995).

One way people simplify, categorize, and order the world is by using stereotypes. **Stereotypes** are widely shared beliefs about the characteristics of members of various social groups (racial, ethnic, religious), which include the assumption that "they" are usually all alike. Macrae and colleagues (1994) suggest that people apply stereotypes in their interactions with others because doing so requires less mental energy than trying to understand others as individuals. Stereotyping allows people to make quick, automatic (thoughtless) judgments about others and apply their mental resources to other activities (Forgas & Fiedler, 1996). Research by Anderson and others (1990) showed that participants could process information more efficiently and answer questions faster when they were using stereotypes.

Some research has revealed that people tend to perceive more diversity—more variability—within the groups to which they belong (in-groups), but they see more similarity among members of other groups (out-groups) (Ostrom et al., 1993). Caucasian Americans see more diversity among themselves but more sameness within groups of African or Asian Americans. This tendency in stereotypical thinking can be based on race, gender, age, or any other characteristic. Another study showed that young college students believed that there was much more variability in 100 of them than in a group of 100 elderly Americans, whom the students perceived to be much the same (Linville et al., 1989). And a study involving elderly adults showed that they perceived more variability within their own age group than among college students. Age stereotypes can be even more pronounced and negative than gender stereotypes (Kite et al., 1991).

Some research indicates that prejudice and stereotyping (whether conscious or not) may be means of bolstering one's self-image by disparaging others (Fein & Spencer, 1997). Moreover, some minority group members may protect their self-esteem by attempting to minimize discrimination or by denying its significance (Ruggiero & Taylor, 1997).

Discrimination in the Workplace

Research conducted at Princeton University by Word and others (1974) indicates that stereotypic thinking can govern people's expectancies. And often what we expect is what we get, regardless of whether our expectancies are high or low. Participants in one study were Caucasian American undergraduates who were to interview Caucasian and African American job applicants (actually confederates of the researchers). The researchers secretly videotaped the interviews and studied the tapes to see if the student interviewers had treated the African American and Caucasian American applicants differently. The researchers found substantial differences in the interviews based on the race of the applicants. The interviewers spent less time with the African American applicants, maintained a greater physical distance from them, and generally were less friendly and outgoing. During interviews with these applicants, the interviewers' speech deteriorated—they made more errors in grammar and pronunciation.

In a followup study, the same researchers trained Caucasian American confederates to copy the two different interview styles used in the first study (Word et al., 1974). The confederates then used the different styles to interview a group of Caucasian American job applicants. These interviews were videotaped as well, and later a panel of judges evaluated the tapes. The judges agreed that applicants who were subjected to the interview style for African Americans were more nervous and performed more poorly than applicants interviewed according to the "Caucasian" style. The experimenters concluded that, as a result of the interview style they experienced, the African American job applicants from the first study were not given the opportunity to demonstrate their skills and qualifications to the best of their ability. Thus, they were subjected to a subtle form of discrimination in which their performance was hampered by the expectancies of their interviewers.

Even though federal legislation forbids hiring, promoting, laying off, or awarding benefits to workers on the basis of sex, race, color, national origin, or religion, studies continue to show that workplace discrimination exists (Renzetti & Curran, 1992). A considerable body of research refutes the notion that deficiencies due to gender or race explain why so few women and minorities are in upper management (Morrison & Von Glinow, 1990). Nevertheless, the mere perception of deficiencies, if held by the dominant corporate leaders, is sufficient to produce bias and discrimination.

Morrison and Von Glinow (1990) claim that "discrimination occurs in part because of the belief by Caucasian men that women and people of color are less suited for management than white men" (p. 202). The dominant group's belief that customers, employees, and others are more comfortable dealing with or working for Caucasian male managers may lead to discrimination. In such cases, these managers may be less willing to promote women and minorities to sensitive, responsible management positions.

Tokenism is a subtle form of discrimination in which people are hired or promoted primarily because they represent a specific group or category rather than strictly on the basis of their qualifications. Female and minority employees may be perceived by the White male majority as "tokens," especially as they move up in the ranks of management. But "tokens" are interchangeable. If placed in a position solely to meet a company's affirmative action goals, one token is as good as another, as long as he or she represents the right category. No matter how eminently qualified an employee may be, if the employee perceives that he or she is a token, the individual suffers and so does the organization.

Is Prejudice Increasing or Decreasing?

Few people would readily admit to being prejudiced. Gordon Allport (1954), a pioneer in research on prejudice, said, "Defeated intellectually, prejudice lingers emotionally" (p. 328). Even those who are sincerely intellectually opposed to prejudice may still harbor some prejudiced feelings (Devine, 1989). However, most people feel guilty when they catch themselves having prejudiced thoughts or engaging in discriminatory behavior (Volis et al., 2002).

Is there any evidence that prejudice is decreasing in U.S. society? Gallup polls revealed that Caucasian Americans became more racially tolerant over the final decades of the 20th century

(Gallup & Hugick, 1990). When Caucasian Americans were asked in 1990 whether they would move if African Americans were to move next door to them, 93% said no, compared with 65% in 1965. Even if African Americans were to move into their neighborhood in great numbers, 68% of Caucasians still said they would not move. Moreover, both Caucasian and African Americans overwhelmingly agree that conditions have improved for minorities in the United States over the past several decades (Public Agenda Online, 2002). However, there are still marked differences of opinion among ethnic and racial groups as to whether racism continues to be a problem in the United States.

Recall, too, that attitudes do not always predict behavior. In a recent study, researchers asked participants to judge whether a fictitious woman was qualified to be the president of a parent-teacher organization (Lott & Saxon, 2002). Participants were provided with information about the woman's occupation and education. In addition, they were told, based on random assignment, that the woman's ethnic background was Hispanic, Anglo-Saxon, or Jewish. The experimenters found that participants who believed the woman to be Hispanic were more likely than those who thought her to be Anglo-Saxon or Jewish to say that she was not qualified for the position. Moreover, researchers have learned that teachers are more likely to attribute Caucasian children's behavior problems to situational variables and those of minority children to dispositional factors (Jackson, 2002).

PERSONALITY

In 1924, two young Chicago men, 18-year-old Nathan Leopold and 19-year-old Richard Loeb, brutally killed a 13-year-old boy in an effort to prove their intellectual superiority. They believed that their superior cognitive abilities exempted them from society's rules. Moreover, they thought that their intelligence would enable them to murder at will, without risk of detection by the presumably intellectually inferior authorities. However, the police were able to trace a pair of glasses Leopold carelessly left at the murder scene and arrested the pair a few days after the crime.

Leopold and Loeb confessed, and their wealthy families hired well-known attorney Clarence Darrow to try to save them from the death penalty. Arguing from several books and articles authored by Sigmund Freud, Darrow tried to convince the judge who would pass sentence that Leopold and Loeb's parents were at least partially responsible for the crime because they had deprived the young men of emotional warmth when they were children (Higdon, 1975). Darrow hired psychologists to testify that the two murderers were emotionally equivalent to young children and should not be put to death for their crime. At the end of the trial, the judge sided with Darrow and sentenced the two young men to life in prison.

Publicity surrounding the Leopold and Loeb trial was how Freud's theory first became widely known among the general public in the United States (Torrey, 1992). The claim that two murderers' parents might be morally responsible for their heinous crime caused many people to see Freud's theory as repugnant. But it was Darrow, not Freud, who turned the theory into a "blame your parents" legal defense. Indeed, Freud's assertion that early childhood experiences contribute to adult behavior is accepted by both psychologists and nonpsychologists and may be his most enduring contribution. But can early childhood experiences alone account for variations among adults?

Psychologists use the term *personality* to capture what we mean when we talk about the ways in which one person is different from another. **Personality** is formally defined as an individual's characteristic patterns of behaving, thinking, and feeling (Carver & Scheier, 1996). This chapter explores some of the theories, including Freud's, that have been proposed to explain personality.

SIGMUND FREUD AND PSYCHOANALYSIS

When you hear the term *psychoanalysis*, you may picture a psychiatrist treating a troubled patient on a couch. But **psychoanalysis** refers not only to a therapy for treating psychological disorders devised by

Sigmund Freud, but also to the influential personality theory he proposed. The central idea of psychoanalytic theory is that unconscious forces shape human thought and behavior.

The Conscious, the Preconscious, and the Unconscious

Freud believed that there are three levels of awareness in consciousness: the conscious, the preconscious, and the unconscious. The **conscious** consists of whatever a person is aware of at any given moment—a thought, a feeling, a sensation, or a memory. Freud's **preconscious** is very much like long-term memory. It contains all the memories, feelings, experiences, and perceptions that an individual is not consciously thinking about at the moment, but that may be easily brought to consciousness.

The most important of the three levels is the **unconscious,** which Freud believed to be the primary motivating force of human behavior. The unconscious holds memories that once were conscious but were so unpleasant or anxiety-provoking that they were repressed (involuntarily removed from consciousness). The unconscious also contains all of the instincts (sexual and aggressive), wishes, and desires that have never been allowed into consciousness. Freud traced the roots of psychological disorders to these impulses and repressed memories.

The Id, the Ego, and the Superego

Freud proposed three systems of personality. Figure 19.6 shows these three systems and how they relate to the conscious, preconscious, and unconscious levels. These systems do not exist physically; they are only concepts, or ways of looking at personality.

According to Freud, the **id** is the only part of the personality that is present at birth. It is inherited, primitive, inaccessible, and completely unconscious. The id contains (1) the life instincts, which are the sexual instincts and the biological urges such as hunger and thirst; and (2) the death instinct, which accounts for aggressive and destructive impulses (Freud, 1933/1965). The id operates according to the *pleasure principle*; that is, it tries to seek pleasure, avoid pain, and gain immediate gratification of its wishes. The id is the source of the *libido*, the psychic energy that fuels the entire personality; yet the id can only wish, imagine, fantasize, or demand.

The **ego** is the logical, rational, realistic part of the personality. The ego evolves from and draws its energy from the id. One of the ego's functions is to satisfy the id's urges. But the ego, which is mostly conscious, acts according to the *reality principle*. It must consider the constraints of the real world in

FIGURE 19.6 Freud's Conception of Personality
According to Freud, personality, which may be conceptualized as a giant iceberg, is composed of three structures: the id, the ego, and the superego. The id, completely unconscious, is wholly submerged, floating beneath the surface. The ego is largely conscious and visible, but partly unconscious. The superego also operates at both the conscious and unconscious levels.

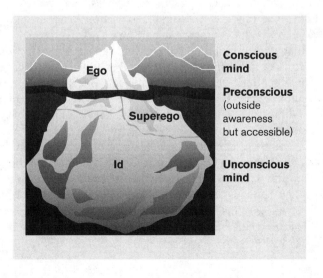

determining appropriate times, places, and objects for gratification of the id's wishes. The art of the possible is its guide, and sometimes compromises must be made—for example, when you settle for a McDonald's hamburger instead of steak or lobster.

When a child is 5 or 6 years old, the **superego**—the moral component of the personality—is formed. The superego has two parts: (1) behaviors for which the child has been punished and about which he or she feels guilty constitute the *conscience*; (2) behaviors for which the child has been praised and rewarded and about which he or she feels pride and satisfaction make up the *ego ideal*. At first, the superego reflects only the parents' expectations of what is good and right, but it expands over time to incorporate broader social and cultural values. In its quest for moral perfection, the superego sets guidelines that define and limit the ego's flexibility. A harsher judge than any external authority, including one's parents, the superego governs not only behavior, but also thoughts, feelings, and wishes.

Defense Mechanisms

All would be well if the id, the ego, and the superego had compatible aims. But the id's demands for pleasure are often in direct conflict with the superego's desire for moral perfection. At times, the ego needs some way to defend itself against the anxiety created by the excessive demands of the id and the harsh judgments of the superego. When it cannot solve problems directly, the ego may use a **defense mechanism,** a means of fighting anxiety and maintaining self-esteem. All people use defense mechanisms to some degree, but research supports Freud's view that the overuse of defense mechanisms can adversely affect mental health (Watson, 2002).

According to Freud, *repression* is the most frequently used defense mechanism. Repression can remove painful or threatening memories, thoughts, ideas, or perceptions from consciousness and keep them in the unconscious. It may also prevent unconscious sexual and aggressive impulses from breaking into consciousness. Several studies have shown that people do indeed try to repress unpleasant thoughts (Koehler et al., 2002). Freud believed that repressed thoughts lurk in the unconscious and can cause psychological disorders in adults. He thought that the way to cure such disorders was to bring the repressed material back to consciousness. This was what he tried to accomplish through his system of therapy, psychoanalysis.

The Psychosexual Stages of Development

The sex instinct, Freud said, is the most important factor influencing personality. It is present at birth and then develops through a series of **psychosexual stages.** Each stage centers on a particular part of the body that provides pleasurable sensations and around which a conflict arises (1905/1953b, 1920/1963b). If the conflict is not resolved relatively easily, the child may develop a **fixation.** This means that a portion of the libido (psychic energy) remains invested at that stage, leaving less psychic energy to meet the challenges of later stages. Overindulgence at a stage may leave a person psychologically unwilling to move on to the next stage. But too little gratification may leave the person trying to make up for previously unmet needs. Freud believed that certain personality characteristics develop as a result of difficulty at one or another of the stages. Table 19.1 provides a summary of Freud's psychosexual stages.

One of the most controversial features of Freud's theory is called the **Oedipus complex** (after the central character in the Greek tragedy *Oedipus Rex*, by Sophocles). Freud claimed that, during the phallic stage (age 3 to 6), "boys concentrate their sexual wishes upon their mother and develop hostile impulses against their father as being a rival" (1925/1963a, p. 61). The boy usually resolves the Oedipus complex by identifying with his father and repressing his sexual feelings for his mother. Through identification, the child takes on his father's behaviors, mannerisms, and superego standards, thus developing a superego (Freud, 1930/1962).

TABLE 19.1   Freud's Psychosexual Stages of Development

STAGE	PART OF THE BODY	CONFLICTS/ EXPERIENCES	ADULT TRAITS ASSOCIATED WITH PROBLEMS AT THIS STAGE
Oral (birth to 12–18 months)	Mouth	Weaning Oral gratification from sucking, eating, biting	Optimism, gullibility, dependency, pessimism, passivity, hostility, sarcasm, aggression
Anal (12–18 months to 3 years)	Anus	Toilet training Gratification from expelling and withholding feces	Excessive cleanliness, orderliness, stinginess, messiness, rebelliousness, destructiveness
Phallic (3 to 5-6 years)	Genitals	Oedipal conflict Sexual curiosity Masturbation	Flirtatiousness, vanity, promiscuity, pride, chastity
Latency (5–6 years to puberty)	None	Period of sexual calm Interest in school, hobbies, same-sex friends	
Genital (puberty onward)	Genitals	Revival of sexual interests Establishment of mature sexual relationships	

When girls in the phallic stage discover they have no penis, they develop "penis envy," Freud claimed, and they turn to their father because he has the desired organ (1933/1965). They feel sexual desires for him and develop jealousy and rivalry toward their mother. But eventually, girls, too, experience anxiety as a result of their hostile feelings. They repress their sexual feelings toward the father and identify with the mother, leading to the formation of their superego (Freud, 1930/1962).

According to Freud, failure to resolve these conflicts can have serious consequences for both boys and girls. Freud thought that tremendous guilt and anxiety could be carried over into adulthood and cause sexual problems, great difficulty relating to members of the opposite sex, and even homosexuality.

Evaluating Freud's Contribution

Psychology is indebted to Freud for introducing the idea that unconscious forces may motivate behavior and for emphasizing the influence of early childhood experiences on later development. Moreover, psychoanalysis is still viewed as a useful therapeutic technique (Bartlett, 2002). And Freud's concept of defense mechanisms provides a useful way of categorizing the cognitive strategies people use to manage stress (Fauerbach et al., 2002; Tori & Bilmes, 2002). Critics charge, however, that much of Freud's theory defies scientific testing. In too many cases, any behavior or even a lack of behavior can be interpreted as supporting Freud's theory. How, for instance, can psychologists ever test the idea that little boys are in love with their mothers and want to get rid of their fathers? How can researchers verify or falsify the idea that one component of personality is motivated entirely by the pursuit of pleasure? Chiefly because of the difficulty involved in finding scientific answers to such questions, there are very few strict Freudians left today.

THE NEO-FREUDIANS

Several personality theorists, referred to as *neo-Freudians*, started their careers as followers of Freud but began to disagree on certain basic principles of psychoanalytic theory. One of the most important of the neo-Freudians, Carl Jung (1875–1961), did not consider the sexual instinct to be the main factor in personality; nor did he believe that the personality is almost completely formed in early childhood. For Jung (1933), middle age was an even more important period for personality development. Jung conceived of the personality as consisting of three parts: the ego, the personal unconscious, and the collective unconscious. He saw the ego as the conscious component of personality, which carries out normal daily activities. Like Freud, he believed the ego to be less important than the unconscious.

The **personal unconscious** develops as a result of individual experience and is therefore unique to each person. It contains all the experiences, thoughts, and perceptions accessible to the conscious, as well as repressed memories, wishes, and impulses. The **collective unconscious** contains the universal experiences of humankind throughout evolution. Jung believed that this part of the personality accounts for the similarity of certain myths, dreams, symbols, and religious beliefs in cultures widely separated by distance and time. Moreover, the collective unconscious contains what Jung called **archetypes**—inherited tendencies to respond to universal human situations in particular ways. Jung would say that the tendencies of people to believe in a god, a devil, evil spirits, and heroes all result from inherited archetypes that reflect the shared experience of humankind.

Another neo-Freudian, Alfred Adler (1870–1937), emphasized the unity of the personality rather than separate warring components of id, ego, and superego. Adler (1927, 1956) also maintained that the drive to overcome feelings of inferiority acquired in childhood motivates most adult behavior. He (1956) claimed that people develop a "style of life" at an early age—a unique way in which the child and later the adult will go about the struggle to achieve superiority. Sometimes inferiority feelings are so strong that they prevent personal development, and Adler originated a term to describe this condition—the "inferiority complex" (Dreikurs, 1953). Because Adler's theory stressed the uniqueness of each individual's struggle to achieve superiority and referred to the "creative self," a conscious, self-aware component of the individual's personality, it is known as *individual psychology*.

The work of neo-Freudian Karen Horney (1885—1952) centered on two main themes: the neurotic personality (Horney, 1937, 1945, 1950) and feminine psychology (Horney, 1967). Horney did not accept Freud's division of personality into id, ego, and superego, and she flatly rejected his psychosexual stages and the concepts of the Oedipus complex and penis envy. Furthermore, Horney thought that Freud overemphasized the role of the sexual instinct and neglected cultural and environmental influences on personality. Although she did stress the importance of early childhood experiences, Horney (1939) believed that personality could continue to develop and change throughout life.

Horney argued forcefully against Freud's notion that a woman's desire to have a child and a man is nothing more than a conversion of the unfulfilled wish for a penis. Horney (1945) believed that many of women's psychological difficulties arise from failure to live up to an idealized version of themselves. To be psychologically healthy, she claimed, women—and men, for that matter—must learn to overcome irrational beliefs about the need for perfection. Her influence may be seen in modern cognitive-behavioral therapies.

LEARNING THEORIES AND PERSONALITY

Using principles such as those associated with B. F. Skinner's operant conditioning, learning theories explain personality as a function of environmental influences rather than unconscious thoughts and feelings. For this reason, many psychologists regard these theories as more scientific and easily tested than Freud's psychoanalysis. However, learning theories are often criticized for paying too little attention to emotions and other internal processes.

One learning theory that does take internal factors into account is the social-cognitive approach of Albert Bandura (1977a, 1986). He maintains that cognitive factors (such as a child's or adult's stage of cognitive development), behavior, and the external environment all influence and are influenced by one another (Bandura, 1989). Bandura calls this mutual relationship **reciprocal determinism** (see Figure 19.7).

One of the cognitive factors Bandura (1997a, 1997b) considers especially important is **self-efficacy**—the perception people hold of their ability to perform competently in whatever they attempt. According to Bandura, people high in self-efficacy approach new situations confidently, set high goals, and persist in their efforts because they believe success is likely. People low in self-efficacy, on the other hand, expect failure; consequently, they avoid challenges and typically give up on tasks they find difficult. Bandura's research has shown that people with high self-efficacy are less likely than those with low self-efficacy to experience depression (Bandura, 1997a, 1997b).

Julian Rotter proposes a similar cognitive factor called **locus of control.** Some people see themselves as primarily in control of their behavior and its consequences. This perception Rotter (1966, 1971, 1990) defines as an *internal* locus of control. Others perceive that whatever happens to them is in the hands of fate, luck, or chance. They exhibit an *external* locus of control and may claim that it does not matter what they do, because "whatever will be, will be." Rotter contends that people with an external locus of control are less likely to change their behavior as a result of reinforcement, because they do not see reinforcers as being tied to their own actions. Students who have an external locus of control tend to be procrastinators and, thus, are less likely to be academically successful than those with an internal locus of control (Janssen & Carton, 1999).

HUMANISTIC PERSONALITY THEORIES

In *humanistic psychology*, people are assumed to have a natural tendency toward growth and the realization of their fullest potential. As a result, humanistic personality theories are more optimistic than Freud's psychoanalysis and give greater weight to emotional experiences than the learning theories do. However, like Freud's theory, these perspectives are often criticized as being difficult to test scientifically.

For humanistic psychologist Abraham Maslow (1908–1970), motivational factors were at the root of personality. Maslow constructed a hierarchy of needs, ranging from physiological needs at the bottom up through safety needs, belonging and love needs, esteem needs, and finally to the highest need—the need for self-actualization. **Self-actualization** means developing to one's fullest potential. A healthy person is ever growing and becoming all that he or she can be. In his research, Maslow found

FIGURE 19.7 Albert Bandura's Reciprocal Determinism
Albert Bandura takes a social-cognitive view of personality. He suggests that three components—the environment, behavior, and personal/cognitive factors such as beliefs, expectancies, and personal dispositions—play reciprocal roles in determining personality and behavior.

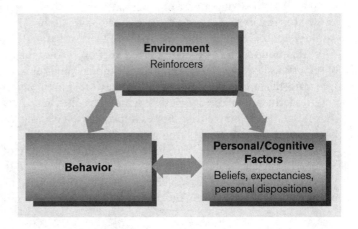

self-actualizers to be accurate in perceiving reality—able to judge honestly and to spot quickly the fake and the dishonest. Most of them believe they have a mission to accomplish or feel the need to devote their life to some larger good. Self- actualizers tend not to depend on external authority or other people but seem to be inner-driven, autonomous, and independent. Finally, the hallmark of self-actualizers is frequently occurring *peak experiences*—experiences of deep meaning, insight, and harmony within and with the universe. Current researchers have modified Maslow's definition of self-actualization to include effectiveness in personal relationships, as well as peak experiences (Hanley & Abell, 2002).

According to another humanistic psychologist, Carl Rogers (1902–1987), our parents set up **conditions of worth**—conditions on which their positive regard hinges. Conditions of worth force us to live and act according to someone else's values rather than our own. In our efforts to gain positive regard, we deny our true self by inhibiting some of our behavior, denying and distorting some of our perceptions, and closing ourselves to parts of our experience. In so doing, we experience stress and anxiety, and our whole sense of self may be threatened.

For Rogers, a major goal of psychotherapy is to enable people to open themselves up to experiences and begin to live according to their own values rather than according to the values of others in order to gain positive regard. He called his therapy *person-centered therapy*, preferring not to use the term *patient*. Rogers believed that the therapist must give the client **unconditional positive regard**—that is, show positive regard no matter what the client says, does, has done, or is thinking of doing. Unconditional positive regard is designed to reduce threat, eliminate conditions of worth, and bring the person back in tune with his or her true self. If successful, the therapy helps the client become what Rogers called a *fully functioning person*—one who is functioning at an optimal level and living fully and spontaneously according to his or her inner value system.

TRAIT THEORIES

Traits are the qualities or characteristics that make it possible for us to face a wide variety of situational demands and deal with unforeseen circumstances (De Raad & Kokkonen, 2000). *Trait theories* attempt to explain personality and differences between people in terms of personal characteristics that are stable across situations.

Early Trait Theories

Gordon Allport (1897–1967) claimed that each person inherits a unique set of raw materials for given traits, which are then shaped by experiences (Allport & Odbert, 1936). A *cardinal trait* is "so pervasive and so outstanding in a life that . . . almost every act seems traceable to its influence" (Allport, 1961, p. 365). It is so strong a part of a person's personality that he or she may become identified with or known for that trait. *Central traits* are those, said Allport (1961), that one would "mention in writing a careful letter of recommendation" (p. 365), such as being decisive or industrious.

Raymond Cattell (1950) referred to observable qualities of personality as *surface traits*. Using observations and questionnaires, Cattell studied thousands of people and found certain clusters of surface traits that appeared together time after time. He thought these were evidence of deeper, more general, underlying personality factors, which he called *source traits*. People differ in the degree to which they possess each source trait. For example, Cattell claimed that intelligence is a source trait: Everyone has it, but the amount varies from person to person.

Cattell found 23 source traits in normal individuals, 16 of which he studied in great detail. Cattell's Sixteen Personality Factor Questionnaire, commonly called the *16 PF*, yields a personality profile (Cattell et al., 1950, 1977). This test continues to be widely used in research (e.g., Brody et al., 2000) and for personality assessment in career counseling, schools, and employment settings.

Factor Models of Personality

The early trait theories represented the beginning of a movement that continues to be important in personality research. Cattell's notion of personality "factors" has been especially influential. One factor model that has shaped much personality research is that of British psychologist Hans Eysenck (1990). Eysenck places particular emphasis on two dimensions: Extraversion (extraversion versus introversion) and Neuroticism (emotional stability versus instability). Extraverts are sociable, outgoing, and active, whereas introverts are withdrawn, quiet, and introspective. Emotionally stable people are calm, even-tempered, and often easygoing; emotionally unstable people are anxious, excitable, and easily distressed.

Extraversion and Neuroticism are also important in today's most talked-about personality theory—the **five-factor theory,** also known as the *Big Five* (Wiggins, 1996). According to Robert McCrae and Paul Costa (1987; McCrae, 1996), the most influential proponents of the five-factor theory, the Big Five dimensions are as follows:

1. *Extraversion.* This dimension contrasts such traits as sociable, outgoing, talkative, assertive, persuasive, decisive, and active with more introverted traits such as withdrawn, quiet, passive, retiring, and reserved.

2. *Neuroticism.* People high on Neuroticism are prone to emotional instability. They tend to experience negative emotions and to be moody, irritable, nervous, and inclined to worry. Neuroticism differentiates people who are anxious, excitable, and easily distressed from those who are emotionally stable and thus calm, even-tempered, easygoing, and relaxed.

3. *Conscientiousness.* This factor differentiates individuals who are dependable, organized, reliable, responsible, thorough, hard-working, and persevering from those who are undependable, disorganized, impulsive, unreliable, irresponsible, careless, negligent, and lazy.

4. *Agreeableness.* This factor is composed of a collection of traits that range from compassion to antagonism toward others. A person high on Agreeableness would be pleasant, good-natured, warm, sympathetic, and cooperative; one low on Agreeableness would tend to be unfriendly, unpleasant, aggressive, argumentative, cold, and even hostile and vindictive.

5. *Openness to Experience.* This factor contrasts individuals who seek out varied experiences and who are imaginative, intellectually curious, and broad-minded with those who are concrete-minded and practical and whose interests are narrow. Researchers have found that being high on Openness to Experience is a requirement for creative accomplishment (King et al., 1996).

To measure the Big Five dimensions of personality, Costa and McCrae (1985, 1992, 1997) developed the NEO Personality Inventory (NEO-PI) and, more recently, the Revised NEO Personality Inventory (NEO-PI-R). Their test is currently being used in a wide variety of personality research studies. For example, psychologists in the Australian army have used the test to measure personality differences between effective and ineffective leaders (McCormack & Mellor, 2002). And all five factors have been found in cross-cultural studies involving participants from Canada, Finland, Poland, Germany, Russia, Hong Kong, Croatia, Italy, South Korea, and Portugal (McCrae et al., 2000; Paunonen et al., 1996).

But how important are the Big Five in everyday behavior? A 3-year longitudinal study among university students revealed that Neuroticism, Extraversion, and Conscientiousness were correlated with reported high levels of frustration due to daily hassles. There was only a small correlation of hassled feelings with Openness to Experience and none at all with Agreeableness (Vollrath, 2000). The Big Five have also proved useful in predicting job performance in the United States (Costa, 1996) and Europe (Salgado, 1997).

The Situation-versus-Trait Debate

One of the severest critics of trait theories, Walter Mischel (1968), initiated the situation-versus-trait debate over the relative importance of factors within the situation and factors within the person that account for behavior (Rowe, 1987). For instance, you probably wouldn't steal money from a store, but what if you see a stranger unknowingly drop a five-dollar bill? Mischel and those who agree with him say that characteristics of the two situations dictate your behavior, not a trait such as honesty. Stealing from a store might require devising and carrying out a complicated plan, and it would carry a heavy penalty if you were caught, so you opt for honesty. Picking up a five-dollar bill is easy and may only result in embarrassment if you get caught, so you are likely to do it. Mischel (1973, 1977) later modified his original position and admitted that behavior is influenced by both the person and the situation. Mischel views a *trait* as a conditional probability that a particular action will occur in response to a particular situation (Wright & Mischel, 1987).

Advocates of the trait side of the debate point out that support for trait theories has come from many longitudinal studies (McCrae, 2002). McCrae and Costa (1990) studied people's personality traits over time and found them to be stable for periods of 3 to 30 years. Typically, personality changes very little with age. As McCrae (1993) puts it, "stable individual differences in basic dimensions are a universal feature of adult personality" (p. 577). An extensive recent review found that the consistency of personality traits increased from .31 in childhood to .54 for college students, rose to .64 by age 30, and peaked at .74 between the ages of 50 and 70 (Roberts & DelVecchio, 2000).

The weight of evidence supports the view that internal traits strongly influence behavior across situations (Carson, 1989; McAdams, 1992). However, many situations in life call forth similar behavior from most people, even though their internal traits differ drastically. Even the most talkative and boisterous among us tend to be quiet during a religious service, a funeral, or another solemn occasion. Characteristic traits, say the trait theorists, determine how we behave most of the time, not all of the time. Even the most optimistic, happy, and outgoing people have "down" days, fall ill, and frown occasionally.

NATURE, NURTURE, AND PERSONALITY

Recall that twin studies are often used to assess the degree to which psychological traits may be inherited. One of the best known of these studies, the Minnesota twin study, revealed that the IQ scores of identical twins are strongly correlated regardless of whether they are raised in the same or in different environments. Using data from the same participants, Tellegen and others (1988) found that identical twins are also quite similar on several personality factors, again regardless of whether they are raised together or apart.

In another twin study, Rushton and colleagues (1986) found that nurturance, empathy, and assertiveness are substantially influenced by heredity. Even altruism and aggressiveness, traits one would expect to be strongly influenced by parental upbringing, were more heavily influenced by heredity. A review by Miles and Carey (1997) revealed that the heritability of aggressiveness may be as high as .50 (50%). Moreover, a number of longitudinal studies indicate that heredity makes a substantial contribution to individual differences in the Big Five personality factors (Bouchard, 1994; Caspi, 2000; Loehlin, 1992; Pesonen et al., 2003).

Adoption studies have also shown that heredity strongly influences personality. Loehlin and others (1987) assessed the personalities of 17-year-olds who had been adopted at birth. When the adopted children were compared with other children in their adoptive families, the researchers found that the shared family environment had virtually no influence on their personalities. In another study, Loehlin and colleagues (1990) measured change in personality of adoptees over a 10-year period and found that children tended "to change on the average in the direction of their genetic parents' personalities" (p. 221). The prevailing thinking in behavioral genetics, then, is that the shared environment plays a negligible role in the formation of personality (Loehlin et al., 1988), although there have been a few dissenting voices (Rose et al., 1988).

Despite the evidence supporting the role of heredity, most psychologists agree that heredity and environment interact in personality development. For example, a child who has a genetic tendency towards shyness may be gently encouraged by parents to be more sociable. But in another family, parents may reject and ridicule a shy child. In either case, how parents respond to a child's inborn tendencies will influence how those characteristics are manifested later in life.

Personality and Culture

Important among environmental influences on personality are the diverse cultures in which humans live and work. Hofstede (1980, 1983) analyzed responses to a questionnaire measuring the work-related values of more than 100,000 IBM employees in 53 countries around the world. Factor analysis revealed four separate dimensions related to culture and personality, but one factor, the **individualism/collectivism dimension,** is of particular interest.

"Individualist cultures emphasize independence, self-reliance, [and] creativity" (Triandis et al., 1993, p. 368). Individualists "see themselves as more differentiated and separate from others, and place more importance on asserting their individuality" (Bochner, 1994, p. 274). More emphasis is placed on individual achievement than on group achievement. High-achieving individuals are accorded honor and prestige in individualist cultures. People in collectivist cultures, on the other hand, tend to be more interdependent and to define themselves and their personal interests in terms of their group membership. Asians, for example, have highly collectivist cultures, and collectivism is compatible with Confucianism, the predominant religion of these Eastern cultures. In fact, according to the Confucian values, the individual finds his or her identity in interrelatedness—as a part of, not apart from, the larger group. Moreover, this interrelatedness is an important ingredient of happiness for Asians (Kitayama & Markus, 2000).

Hofstede rank-ordered the 53 countries on each of the four dimensions. It should not be surprising that the United States ranked as the most individualist culture in the sample, followed by Australia, Great Britain, Canada, and the Netherlands. At the other end of the continuum were the most collectivist, or least individualist, cultures—Guatemala, Ecuador, Panama, Venezuela, and Colombia, all Latin American countries.

Although, according to Hofstede, the United States ranks first in individualism, there are many distinct minority cultural groups in the United States that may be decidedly less individualistic. Native Americans number close to 2 million, but even within this relatively small cultural group, there are over 200 different tribes and no single language, religion, or culture (Bennett, 1994). Yet Native Americans have many shared values—collectivist values—such as the importance of family, community, cooperation, and generosity. Native Americans value a generous nature as evidenced by gift giving and helpfulness. Such behaviors bring more honor and prestige than accumulating property and building individual wealth.

Hispanic Americans, who number almost 28.3 million (U.S. Bureau of the Census, 1997), also tend to be more collectivist than individualist. Although there are significant cultural differences among various Hispanic American groups, there are striking similarities as well. The clearest shared cultural value is a strong identification with and attachment to the extended family. Another important value is *simpatía*—the desire for smooth and harmonious social relationships, which includes respect for the dignity of others, avoidance of confrontation, and avoidance of words or actions that might hurt the feelings of another (Marín, 1994).

But to observe that Native American and Hispanic American cultures are more collectivist than individualist does not mean that any one member of these cultures is necessarily less individualistic than any given member of the majority American culture. Moreover, many people could value both orientations, being individualistic at work, for example, and collectivistic in the home and community (Kagitcibasi, 1992).

PERSONALITY ASSESSMENT

Various ways of measuring personality are used by clinical and counseling psychologists, psychiatrists, and counselors in the diagnosis of patients and in the assessment of progress in therapy. Personality assessment is also used by personnel managers to aid in hiring decisions and by counselors to give vocational and educational assessments.

Observation, Interviews, and Rating Scales

Psychologists use observation in personality assessment in a variety of settings—hospitals, clinics, schools, and workplaces. Behaviorists, in particular, prefer observation to other methods of personality assessment. Using an observational technique known as *behavioral assessment*, psychologists can count and record the frequency of particular behaviors. This method is often used in behavior modification programs in settings such as mental hospitals, where psychologists may chart the patients' progress in reducing aggressive acts or other undesirable or abnormal behaviors. However, behavioral assessment is time-consuming, and behavior may be misinterpreted. Probably the most serious limitation is that the very presence of the observer can alter the behavior being observed.

Clinical psychologists and psychiatrists use interviews to help in the diagnosis and treatment of patients. Counselors use interviews to screen applicants for admission to colleges or other special programs, and employers use them to evaluate job applicants and employees for job promotions. Interviewers consider not only a person's answers to questions, but also the person's tone of voice, speech, mannerisms, gestures, and general appearance. Interviewers often use a *structured interview*, in which the content of the questions and the order and manner in which they are asked are preset. The interviewer tries not to deviate in any way from the structured format so that more reliable comparisons can be made between different people being interviewed.

Sometimes examiners use *rating scales* to record data from interviews or observations. Rating scales are useful because they provide a standardized format, including a list of traits or behaviors to evaluate. A rating scale helps to focus the rater's attention on the relevant traits to be considered so that none is overlooked or weighed too heavily. The major limitation of rating scales is that the ratings are often subjective. Another problem in evaluation is the *halo effect*—the tendency of raters to be excessively influenced in their overall evaluation of a person by one or a few favorable or unfavorable traits. Often traits or attributes that are not even on the rating scale, such as physical attractiveness or similarity to the rater, heavily influence a rater's perception of an individual. To overcome these limitations, it is often necessary to have individuals rated by more than one interviewer.

Personality Inventories

One objective method for measuring personality, in which the personal opinions and ratings of observers or interviewers do not unduly influence the results, is the **personality inventory,** a paper-and-pencil test with questions about an individual's thoughts, feelings, and behaviors, which measures several dimensions of personality and is scored according to a standard procedure. Psychologists favoring the trait approach prefer to use a personality inventory because it reveals where people fall on various dimensions of personality and yields a personality profile.

The most widely used personality inventory is the *Minnesota Multiphasic Personality Inventory (MMPI)* and its revision, the MMPI-2. The MMPI is the most heavily researched personality test for diagnosing psychiatric problems and disorders and for use in psychological research (Butcher & Rouse, 1996). There have been more than 115 authorized translations of the MMPI, and it is used in more than 65 countries (Butcher & Graham, 1989).

Published in 1943 by J. C. McKinley and Starke Hathaway, the MMPI was originally intended to identify tendencies toward various types of psychiatric disorders. The researchers administered over 1,000 questions about attitudes, feelings, and specific psychiatric symptoms to selected groups of psychiatric patients who had been clearly diagnosed with various specific disorders and to a control group of normal men and women. They retained the 550 items that differentiated the specific groups of psychiatric patients from the group of participants considered to be normal.

Because the original MMPI had become outdated, the MMPI-2 was published in 1989 (Butcher et al., 1989). Most of the original test items were retained, but new items were added to more adequately cover areas such as alcoholism, drug abuse, suicidal tendencies, eating disorders, and Type A behavior. New norms were established to reflect national census data and thus achieve a better geographical, racial, and cultural balance (Ben-Porath & Butcher, 1989).

Table 19.2 shows the 10 clinical scales of the MMPI-2. Following are examples of items on the test, which are to be answered "true," "false," or "cannot say."

- I wish I were not bothered by thoughts about sex.
- When I get bored I like to stir up some excitement.
- In walking I am very careful to step over sidewalk cracks.
- If people had not had it in for me, I would have been much more successful.

A high score on any of the scales does not necessarily mean that a person has a problem or symptoms of a psychiatric disorder. Rather, the psychologist looks at the individual's MMPI profile—the pattern of scores on all the scales—and then compares it to the profiles of normal individuals and those with various psychiatric disorders.

TABLE 19.2   The Clinical Scales of the MMPI-2

SCALE NAME	INTERPRETATION
1. Hypochondriasis (Hs)	High scorers exhibit an exaggerated concern about their physical health.
2. Depression (D)	High scorers are usually depressed, despondent, and distressed.
3. Hysteria (Hy)	High scorers complain often about physical symptoms that have no apparent organic cause.
4. Psychopathic deviate (Pd)	High scorers show a disregard for social and moral standards.
5. Masculinity/femininity (Mf)	High scorers show "traditional" masculine or feminine attitudes and values.
6. Paranoia (Pa)	High scorers demonstrate extreme suspiciousness and feelings of persecution.
7. Psychasthenia (Pt)	High scorers tend to be highly anxious, rigid, tense, and worrying.
8. Schizophrenia (Sc)	High scorers tend to be socially withdrawn and to engage in bizarre and unusual thinking.
9. Hypomania (Ma)	High scorers are usually emotional, excitable, energetic, and impulsive.
10. Social introversion (S)	High scorers tend to be modest, self-effacing, and shy.

But what if someone lies on the test in order to appear mentally healthy? Embedded in the test to provide a check against lying are items such as these:

- Once in a while I put off until tomorrow what I ought to do today.
- I gossip a little at times.
- Once in a while, I laugh at a dirty joke.

Most people would almost certainly have to answer "true" in response to such items—unless, of course, they were lying. Another scale controls for people who are faking psychiatric problems, such as someone who is hoping to be judged not guilty of a crime by reason of insanity. Research seems to indicate that the validity scales in the MMPI-2 are effective in detecting test takers who were instructed to fake psychological disturbance or to lie to make themselves appear more psychologically healthy (Bagby et al., 1994; Butcher et al., 1995). Even when given specific information about various psychological disorders, test takers could not produce profiles similar to those of people who actually suffered from the disorders (Wetter et al., 1993).

The MMPI-2 is reliable, easy to administer and score, and inexpensive to use. It is useful in the screening, diagnosis, and clinical description of abnormal behavior, but does not reveal differences among normal personalities very well. The MMPI had been somewhat unreliable for African Americans, women, and adolescents (Levitt & Duckworth, 1984). But this problem has been addressed by establishing norms for the MMPI-2 that are more representative of the national population. A special form of the test, the MMPI-A, was developed for adolescents in 1992. The MMPI-A has some items that are especially relevant to adolescents, referring to eating disorders, substance abuse, and problems with school and family.

The MMPI-2 has been translated for use in Belgium, Chile, China, France, Hong Kong, Israel, Italy, Japan, Korea, Norway, Russia, Spain, and Thailand (Butcher, 1992). Lucio and others (1994) administered the Mexican (Spanish) version of MMPI-2 to more than 2,100 Mexican college students. They found the profiles of these students "remarkably similar" to those of U.S. college students.

An important limitation of the MMPI-2, though, is that it is designed to assess abnormality. By contrast, the *California Psychological Inventory (CPI)* is a highly regarded personality test developed especially for normal individuals aged 13 and older. The CPI has many of the same questions as the MMPI, but it does not include any questions designed to reveal psychiatric illness (Gough, 1987). The CPI is valuable for predicting behavior, and it has been "praised for its technical competency, careful development, cross-validation and follow-up, use of sizable samples and separate sex norms" (Domino, 1984, p. 156). The CPI was revised in 1987, to make it provide "a picture of the subject's life-style and the degree to which his or her potential is being realized" (McReynolds, 1989, p. 101). The CPI is particularly useful in predicting school achievement in high school and beyond; leadership and executive success; and effectiveness of police, military personnel, and student teachers (Gregory, 1996).

The *Myers-Briggs Type Indicator (MBTI)* is another personality inventory that is useful for measuring normal individual differences. This test is based on Jung's theory. The MBTI is a forced-choice, self-report inventory that is scored on four bipolar dimensions:

Extraversion (E) —————— Introversion (I)
Sensing (S) —————— Intuition (N)
Thinking (T) —————— Feeling (F)
Judging (J) —————— Perceptive (P)

A person can score anywhere along each continuum, and the four individual scores are usually summarized according to a typology. Sixteen types of personality profile can be derived from the possible combinations of the four bipolar dimensions. For example, a person whose scores were more toward Extraversion, Intuition, Feeling, and Perceptive would be labeled an ENFP personality type, which is described as follows:

> Relates more readily to the outer world of people and things than to the inner world of ideas (E); prefers to search for new possibilities over working with known facts and conventional ways of doing things (N); makes decisions and solves problems on the basis of personal values and feelings rather than relying on logical thinking and analysis (F); and prefers a flexible, spontaneous life to a planned and orderly existence (P). (Gregory, 1996)

The MBTI is growing in popularity, especially in business and industry and in schools. Critics point to the absence of rigorous, controlled validity studies of this test (Pittenger, 1993). And it has been criticized for being interpreted too often by unskilled examiners, who may make overly simplistic interpretations (Gregory, 1996). Sufficiently sophisticated methods for interpreting the MBTI do exist, however, as revealed by almost 500 research studies to date. And interest in this tool continues to be strong (Allen, 1997).

Projective Tests

Responses on interviews and questionnaires are conscious responses and, for this reason, are less useful to therapists who wish to probe the unconscious. Such therapists may choose a completely different technique called a projective test. A **projective test** is a personality test consisting of inkblots, drawings of ambiguous human situations, or incomplete sentences for which there are no obvious correct or incorrect responses. People respond by projecting their own inner thoughts, feelings, fears, or conflicts into the test materials.

One of the oldest and most popular projective tests is the *Rorschach Inkblot Method*, developed by Swiss psychiatrist Hermann Rorschach (ROR-shok) in 1921. It consists of ten inkblots, which the test taker is asked to describe. To develop his test, Rorschach put ink on paper and then folded the paper so that symmetrical patterns would result. Earlier, psychologists had used standardized series of inkblots to study imagination and other variables, but Rorschach was the first to use inkblots to investigate personality. He experimented with thousands of inkblots on different groups of people and found that ten of the inkblots could be used to discriminate among different diagnostic groups, such as manic depressives, paranoid schizophrenics, and so on. These ten inkblots—five black-and-white, and five with color—were standardized and are still widely used.

The Rorschach can be used to describe personality, make differential diagnoses, plan and evaluate treatment, and predict behavior (Ganellen, 1996; Weiner, 1997). For the last 20 years, it has been second in popularity to the MMPI for use in research and clinical assessment (Butcher & Rouse, 1996). The test taker is shown the ten inkblots and asked to tell everything he or she thinks about what each inkblot looks like or resembles. The examiner writes down the test taker's responses and then goes through the cards again, asking questions to clarify what the test taker has reported. In scoring the Rorschach, the examiner considers whether the test taker uses the whole inkblot in the description or only parts of it. The test taker is asked whether the shape of the inkblot, its color, or something else prompted the response. The examiner also considers whether the test taker sees movement, human figures or parts, animal figures or parts, or other objects in the inkblots.

Until the 1990s, the main problem with the Rorschach was that the results were too dependent on the interpretation and judgment of the examiner. In response to such criticisms, Exner (1993) developed the Comprehensive System—a more reliable system for scoring the Rorschach. It provides some normative data so that the responses of a person taking the test can be compared to those of others with known personality characteristics. Using this system, some researchers have found high agreement among different raters interpreting the same responses (interrater agreement) (McDowell & Acklin, 1996). Others believe that more research is necessary before it can be concluded that the Comprehensive System yields reliable and valid results (Wood et al., 1996). However, a number of research reviews indicate that the Rorschach Inkblot Method has "psychometric soundness and practical utility" (Weiner, 1996).

Another projective test is the *Thematic Apperception Test (TAT)* developed by Henry Murray and his colleagues in 1935 (Morgan & Murray, 1935; Murray, 1938). Researchers have used the TAT to study the need for achievement, but it is also useful for assessing other aspects of personality. The TAT consists of 1 blank card and 19 other cards showing vague or ambiguous black-and-white drawings of human figures in various situations. If you were tested on the TAT, this is what you would be told:

> This is a test of your creative imagination. I shall show you a picture, and I want you to make up a plot or story for which it might be used as an illustration. What is the relation of the individuals in the picture? What has happened to them? What are their present thoughts and feelings? What will be the outcome? (Morgan & Murray, 1962, p. 532)

What does the story you write have to do with your personality or your problems or motives? Murray (1965) stresses the importance of "an element or theme that recurs three or more times in the series of stories" (p. 432). For example, if many of a person's story themes are about illness, sex, fear of failure, aggression, power, or interpersonal conflict, such a recurring theme is thought to reveal a problem in the person's life. Murray (1965) also claims that the strength of the TAT is "its capacity to reveal things that the patient is unwilling to tell or is unable to tell because he [or she] is unconscious of them" (p. 427).

The TAT is time-consuming and difficult to administer and score. Although it has been used extensively in research, it suffers from the same weaknesses as other projective techniques: (1) It relies heavily on the interpretation skills of the examiner, and (2) it may reflect too strongly a person's temporary motivational and emotional state and not reveal the more permanent aspects of personality.

REFERENCES

Abrams, D., Wetherell, M., Cochrane, S., Hogg, M. A., & Turner, J. C. (1990). Knowing what to think by knowing who you are: Self-categorization and the nature of norm formation, conformity and group polarization. *British Journal of Social Psychology, 29* (Pt. 2), 97–119.

Adler, A. (1927). *Understanding human nature.* New York: Greenberg.

Adler, A. (1956). In H. L. Ansbacher & R. R. Ansbacher (Eds.), *The individual psychology of Alfred Adler: A systematic presentation in selections from his writings.* New York: Harper & Row.

Allen, B. P. (1997). *Personality theories: Development, growth, and diversity* (2nd ed.). Boston: Allyn & Bacon.

Allison, T. Puce, A., & McCarthy, G. (2000). Social perception from visual cues: Role of the STS region. *Trends in Cognitive Sciences, 4,* 267–278.

Allport, G. W. (1954). *The nature of prejudice.* Reading, MA: Addison-Wesley.

Allport, G. W. (1961). *Pattern and growth in personality.* New York: Holt, Rinehart & Winston.

Allport, G. W., & Odbert, J. S. (1936). Trait names: A psycho-lexical study. *Psychological Monographs, 47*(1, Whole No. 211), 1–171.

American Psychiatric Association. (1994). *Diagnostic and statistical manual of mental disorders* (4th ed.). Washington DC: Author.

Anderson, C. A., & Anderson, K. B. (1996). Violent crime rate studies in philosophical context: A destructive testing approach to heat and southern culture of violence effects. *Journal of Personality and Social Psychology, 70,* 740–756.

Anderson, C. A., & Dill, K. E. (2000). Video games and aggressive thoughts, feelings, and behavior in the laboratory and in life. *Journal of Personality & Social Psychology, 78,* 772–790.

Anderson, S. M., Klatzky, R. L., & Murray, J. (1990). Traits and social stereotypes: Efficiency differences in social information processing. *Journal of Personality and Social Psychology, 59,* 192–201.

Archer, J. (1991). The influence of testosterone on human aggression. *British Journal of Social Psychology, 82*(Pt. 1), 1–28.

Aronson, E. (1976). Dissonance theory: Progress and problems. In E. P. Hollander & R. C. Hunt (Eds.), *Current perspectives in social psychology* (4th ed., pp. 316–328). New York: Oxford University Press.

Aronson, E. (1988). *The social animal* (3rd ed.). San Francisco: W. H. Freeman.

Aronson, E. (1990). Applying social psychology to desegregation and energy conservation. *Personality and Social Psychology Bulletin, 16,* 118–132.

Aronson, E., & Mills, J. (1959). The effect of severity of initiation on liking for a group. *Journal of Abnormal and Social Psychology, 59,* 177–181.

Aronson, E., Stephan, W., Sikes, J., Blaney, N., & Snapp, M. (1978). *Cooperation in the classroom,* Beverly Hills, CA: Sage.

Asch, S. E. (1951). Effects of group pressure upon the modification and distortion of judgments. In H. Guetzkow (Ed.), *Groups, leadership, and men.* Pittsburgh, PA: Carnegie Press.

Asch, S. E. (1955). Opinions and social pressure. *Scientific American, 193,* 31–35.

Bagby, R. M., Rogers, R., & Buis, T. (1994). Detecting malingered and defensive responding on the MMPI-2 in a forensic impatient sample. *Journal of Personality Assessment, 62,* 191–203.

Bandura, A. (1973). *Aggression: A social learning analysis.* Englewood Cliffs, NJ: Prentice-Hall.

Bandura, A. (1976). On social learning and aggression. In E. P. Hollander & R. C. Hunt (Eds.), *Current perspectives in social psychology* (4th ed., pp. 116–128). New York: Oxford University Press.

Bandura, A. (1977a). *Social learning theory.* Englewood Cliffs, NJ: Prentice-Hall.

Bandura, A. (1986). *Social functions of thought and action: A social-cognitive theory.* Englewood Cliffs, NJ: Prentice-Hall.

Bandura, A. (1989). Social cognitive theory. *Annals of Child Development, 6,* 1–60.

Bandura, A. (1977a, March). Self-efficacy. *Harvard Mental Health Letter, 13*(9), 4–6.

Bandura, A. (1997b). *Self-efficacy: The exercise of control.* New York: Freeman.

Bartlett, A. (2002). Current perspectives on the goals of psychoanalysis. *Journal of the American Psychoanalytic Association, 50,* 629–638.

Bassili, J. N. (1995). Response latency and the accessibility of voting intentions: What contributes to accessibility and how it affects vote choice. *Personality and Social Psychology Bulletin, 21,* 686–695.

Batson, C. D., Batson, J. G., Griffitt, C. A., Barrientos, S., Brandt, J. R., Sprengelmeyer, P., & Bayly, M. J. (1989). Negative-state relief and the empathy-altruism hypothesis. *Journal of Personality and Social Psychology, 56,* 922–933.

Baumgardner, A. H., Heppner, P. P., & Arkin, R. M. (1986). Role of causal attribution in personal problem solving. *Journal of Personality and Social Psychology, 50,* 636–643.

Bazan, S. (1998). Enhancing decision-making effectiveness in problem-solving teams. *Clinical Laboratory Management Review, 12,* 272–276.

Ben-Porath, Y. S., & Butcher, J. N. (1989). The comparability of MMPI and MMPI-2 scales and profiles. *Psychological Assessment: A Journal of Consulting and Clinical Psychology, 1,* 345–347.

Berkowitz, L. (1983). Aversively stimulated aggression: Some parallels and differences in research with animals and humans. *American Psychologist, 38,* 1135–1144.

Berkowitz, L. (1988). Frustrations, appraisals, and aversively stimulated aggression. *Aggressive Behavior, 14,* 3–11.

Berkowitz, L. (1990). On the formation and regulation of anger and aggression: A cognitive-neoassociationistic analysis. *American Psychologist, 45,* 494–503.

Berscheid, E., Dion, K., Walster, E., & Walster, G. W. (1971). Physical attractiveness and dating choice: A test of the matching hypothesis. *Journal of Experimental Social Psychology, 7,* 173–189.

Blascovich, J., Wyer, N. A., Swart, L. A., & Kibler, J. L. (1997). Racism and racial categorization. *Journal of Personality and Social Psychology, 72,* 1364–1372.

Bochner, S. (1994). Cross-cultural differences in the self concept: A test of Hofstede's individualism/collectivism distinction. *Journal of Cross-Cultural Psychology, 25,* 273–283.

Bornstein, R. F. (1989). Exposure and affect: Overview and meta-analysis of research, 1968–1987. *Psychological Bulletin, 106,* 265–289.

Bouchard, T. J., Jr. (1994). Genes, environment, and personality. *Science, 264,* 1700–1701.

Breckler, S. J. (1984). Empirical validation of affect, behavior, and cognition as distinct attitude components. *Journal of Personality and Social Psychology, 47,* 1191–1205.

Brennan, P. A., Raine, A., Schulsinger, F., Kirkegaard-Sorensen, L., Knop, J., Hutchings, B., Rosenberg, R., & Mednick, S. A. (1997). Psychophysiological protective factors for male subjects at high risk for criminal behavior. *American Journal of Psychiatry, 154,* 853–855.

Brody, A., Saxena, S., Fairbanks, L., Alborzian, S., Demaree, H., Maidment, K., & Baxter, L. (2000). Personality changes in adult subjects with major depressive disorder or obsessive-compulsive disorder treated with paroxetine. *Journal of Clinical Psychiatry, 61*, 349–355.

Brown, J. D., & Rogers, R. J. (1991). Self-serving attributions: The role of physiological arousal. *Personality and Social Psychology Bulletin, 17*, 501–506.

Buller, D. B., Burgoon, M., Hall, J. R., Levine, N., Taylor, A. M., Beach, B. H., Melcher, C., Buller, M. K., Bowen, S. L., Hunsaker, F. G., & Bergen, A. (2000). Using language intensity to increase the success of a family intervention to protect children from ultraviolet radiation: Predictions from language expectancy theory. *Preventive Medicine, 30*, 103–113.

Bushman, B. J. (1995). Moderating role of trait aggressiveness in the effects of violent media on aggression. *Journal of Personality and Social Psychology, 69*, 950–960.

Bushman, B. J., & Cooper, H. M. (1990). Effects of alcohol on human aggression: An integrative research review. *Psychological Bulletin, 107*, 341–354.

Buss, D. M. (1984). Marital assortment for personality dispositions: Assessment with three different data sources. *Behavioral Genetics, 14*, 111–123.

Buss, D. M. (1994). The strategies of human mating. *American Scientist, 82*, 238–249.

Buss, D. M. (2000). Desires in human mating. *Annals of the New York Academy of Sciences, 907*, 39–49.

Buss, D. M., Abbott, M., Angleitner, A., Asherian, A., Biaggio, A., Blanco-Villasenor, A., Bruchon-Schweitzer, M., et al. (1990). International preferences in selecting mates: A study of 37 cultures. *Journal of Cross-Cultural Psychology, 21*, 5–47.

Butcher, J. N. (1992, October). International developments with the MMPI-2. *MMPI-2 News & Profiles, 3*, 4.

Butcher, J. N., Dahlstrom, W. G., Graham, J. R., Tellegen, A., & Kaemmer, B. (1989). *Manual for the restandardized Minnesota Multiphasic Personality Inventory: MMPI-2. An administrative and interpretive guide.* Minneapolis: University of Minnesota Press.

Butcher, J. N., & Graham, J. R. (1989). *Topics in MMPI-2 interpretation.* Minneapolis: Department of Psychology, University of Minnesota.

Butcher, J. N., Graham, J. R., & Ben-Porath, Y. S. (1995). Methodological problems and issues in MMPI, MMPI-2, and MMPI-A research. *Psychological Assessment, 7*, 320–329.

Butcher, J. N., & Rouse, S. V. (1996). Personality: Individual differences and clinical assessment. *Annual Review of Psychology, 47*, 89–111.

Carson, R. C. (1989). Personality. *Annual Review of Psychology, 40*, 227–248.

Carver, C. S., & Scheier, M. F. (1996). *Perspectives on personality* (3rd ed.). Boston: Allyn & Bacon.

Cash, T. F., & Derlega, V. J. (1978). The matching hypothesis: Physical attractiveness among same-sexed friends. *Personality and Social Psychology Bulletin, 4*, 240–243.

Cash, T. F., & Janda, L. H. (1984, December). The eye of the beholder. *Psychology Today*, pp. 46–52.

Caspi, A. (2000). The child is father of the man: Personality continuities from childhood to adulthood. *Journal of Personality & Social Psychology, 78*, 158–172.

Cattell, R. B. (1950). *Personality: A systematic, theoretical, and factual study.* New York: McGraw-Hill.

Cattell, R. B. (1993). *16PF® fifth edition profile sheet.* Champaign, IL: Institute for Personality and Ability Testing.

Cattell, R. B., Eber, H. W., & Tatsuoka, M. M. (1977). *Handbook for the 16 personality factor questionnaire.* Champaign, IL: Institute of Personality and Ability Testing.

Cattell, R. B., Saunders, D. R., & Stice, G. F. (1950). *The 16 personality factor questionnaire.* Champaign, IL: Institute of Personality and Ability Testing.

Chaplin, W. F., Philips, J. B., Brown, J. D., Clanton, N. R., & Stein, J. L. (2000). Handshaking, gender, personality, and first impressions. *Journal of Personality and Social Psychology, 19*, 110–117.

Cialdini, R. B., Cacioppo, J. T., Basset, R., & Miller, J. A. (1978). Low-ball procedure for producing compliance: Commitment then cost. *Journal of Personality and Social Psychology, 36*, 463–476.

Cialdini, R. B., Vincent, J. E., Lewis, S. K., Catalan, J., Wheeler, D., & Darby, B. L. (1975). Reciprocal concessions procedure for inducing compliance: The door-in-the-face technique. *Journal of Personality and Social Psychology, 31*, 206–215.

Cloninger, C. R., Sigvardsson, S., Bohman, M., & von Knorring, A. L. (1982). Predispositions to petty criminality in Swedish adoptees, II. Cross-fostering analysis of gene-environment interaction. *Archives of General Psychiatry, 39*, 1242–1249.

Colwell, J., & Payne, J. (2000). Negative correlates of computer game play in adolescents. *British Journal of Psychology, 91* (Pt. 3), 295–310.

Costa, P. T., Jr. (1996). Work and personality: Use of the NEO-PI-R in industrial/organisational psychology. *Applied Psychology: An International Review, 45,* 225–241.

Costa, P. T., Jr., & McCrae, R. R. (1985). *The NEO Personality Inventory.* Odessa, FL: Psychological Assessment Resources.

Costa, P. T., Jr., & McCrae, R. R. (1992). *NEO-PI-R: Revised NEO Personality Inventory (NEO-PI-R).* Odessa, FL: Psychological Assessment Resources.

Costa, P. T., Jr., & McCrae, R. R. (1997). Stability and change in personality assessment: The Revised NEO Personality Inventory in the year 2000. *Journal of Personality Assessment, 68,* 8694.

Cunningham, M. R., Roberts, A. R., Barbee, A. P., Druen, P. B., & Wu, C-H. (1995). "Their ideas of beauty are, on the whole, the same as ours": Consistency and variability in the cross-cultural perception of female physical attractiveness. *Journal of Personality and Social Psychology, 68,* 261–279.

Dabbs, J. M., Jr., & Morris, R. (1990). Testosterone, social class, and antisocial behavior in a sample of 4,462 men. *Psychological Science, 1,* 209–211.

Daly, M., & Wilson, M. I. (1996). Violence against stepchildren. *Current Directions in Psychological Science, 5,* 77–81.

Darley, J. M., & Latané, B. (1968a). Bystander intervention in emergencies: Diffusion of responsibility. *Journal of Personality and Social Psychology, 8,* 377–383.

Darley, J. M., & Latané, B. (1968b, December). When will people help in a crisis? *Psychology Today,* pp. 54–57, 70–71.

De Raad, B., & Kokkonen, M. (2000). Traits and emotions: A review of their structure and management. *European Journal of Personality, 14,* 477–496.

Devine, P. G. (1989). Stereotypes and prejudice: Their automatic and controlled components. *Journal of Personality and Social Psychology, 56,* 5–18.

DeYoung, C., Peterson, J., & Higgins, D. (2002). Higher-order factors of the Big Five predict conformity: Are there neuroses of health? *Personality & Individual Differences, 33,* 533–552.

DiLalla, L. F., & Gottesman, I. I. (1991). Biological and genetic contributors to violence—Widom's untold tale. *Psychological Bulletin, 109,* 125–129.

Dion, K., Berscheid, E., & Walster, E. (1972). What is beautiful is good. *Journal of Personality and Social Psychology, 24,* 285–290.

Dipboye, R. L., Fromkin, H. L., & Wilback, K. (1975). Relative importance of applicant sex, attractiveness, and scholastic standing in evaluation of job applicant resumes. *Journal of Applied Psychology, 60,* 39–43.

Dodge, K. A., Bates, J. E., & Pettit, G. S. (1990). Mechanisms in the cycle of violence. *Science, 250,* 1678–1683.

Dollard, J., Doob, L. W., Miller, N., Nowrer, O. H., & Sears, R. R. (1939). *Frustration and aggression.* New Haven: Yale University Press.

Domino, G. (1984). California Psychological Inventory. In D. J. Keyser & R. C. Sweetland (Eds.), *Test Critiques* (Vol. 1, pp. 146–157). Kansas City: Test Corporation of America.

Doob, L. W., & Sears, R. R. (1939). Factors determining substitute behavior and the overt expression of aggression. *Journal of Abnormal and Social Psychology, 34,* 293–313.

Dreikurs, R. (1953). *Fundamentals of Adlerian psychology.* Chicago: Alfred Adler Institute.

Dryer, D. C., & Horowitz, L. M. (1997). When do opposites attract? Interpersonal complementarity versus similarity. *Journal of Personality and Social Psychology, 72,* 592–603.

Eagly, A. H., Ashmore, R. D., Makhijani, M. G., & Longo, L. C. (1991). What is beautiful is good . . . : A meta-analytic review of research on the physical attractiveness stereotype. *Psychological Bulletin, 110,* 109–128.

Eagly, A. H., & Carli, L. (1981). Sex of researchers and sex-typed communications as determinants of sex differences in influence-ability: A meta-analysis of social influence studies. *Psychological Bulletin, 90,* 1–19.

Edwards, K., & Smith, E. E. (1996). A disconfirmation bias in the evaluation of arguments. *Journal of Personality and Social Psychology, 71,* 5–24.

Elliot, A. J., & Devine, P. G. (1994). On the motivational nature of cognitive dissonance: Dissonance as psychological discomfort. *Journal of Personality and Social Psychology, 67,* 382–394.

Eron, L. D. (1987). The development of aggressive behavior from the perspective of a developing behaviorism. *American Psychologist, 42,* 435–442.

Eronen, M., Hakola, P., & Tiihonen, J. (1996). Mental disorders and homicidal behavior in Finland. *Journal of Personality and Social Psychology, 53*, 497–501.

Evans, G. W., & Lepore, S. J. (1993). Household crowding and social support: A quasiexperimental analysis. *Journal of Personality and Social Psychology, 65*, 308–316.

Exner, J. E. (1993). *The Rorschach: A comprehensive system: Vol. 1. Basic foundations* (3rd ed.). New York: Wiley.

Eysenck, H. J. (1990). Genetic and environmental contributions to individual differences: The three major dimensions of personality. *Journal of Personality, 58*, 245–261.

Fauerbach, J., Lawrence, J., Haythornthwaite, J., & Richter, L. (2002). Coping with the stress of a painful medical procedure. *Behaviour Research & Therapy, 40*, 1003–1015.

Fazio, R. H. (1989). On the power and functionality of attitudes: The role of attitude accessibility. In A. R. Pratkanis, S. J. Breckler, & A. G. Greenwald (Eds.), *Attitude structure and function* (pp. 153–179). Hillsdale, NJ: Erlbaum.

Fazio, R. H., & Williams, C. J. (1986). Attitude accessibility as a moderator of the attitude perception and attitude-behavior relations: An investigation of the 1984 presidential election. *Journal of Personality and Social Psychology, 51*, 505–514.

Federal Bureau of Investigation. (1999). United States crime rates 1960–1998 [On-line]. Retrieved from http://www.disaster center.com/crime/uscrime.htm

Fein, S., & Spencer, S. J. (1997). Prejudice as self-image maintenance: Affirming the self through derogating others. *Journal of Personality and Social Psychology, 73*, 31–44.

Feingold, A. (1988). Matching for attractiveness in romantic partners and same-sex friends: A meta-analysis and theoretical critique. *Psychological Bulletin, 104*, 226–235.

Festinger, L. (1957). *A theory of cognitive dissonance.* Evanston, IL: Row, Peterson.

Finchilescu, G. (1988). Interracial contact in South Africa within the nursing context. *Journal of Applied Social Psychology, 18*, 1207–1221.

Fink, B., & Penton-Voak, I. (2002). Evolutionary psychology of facial attractiveness. *Current Directions in Psychological Science, 11*, 154–158.

Forgas, J. P., & Fiedler, K. (1996). Us and them: Mood effects on intergroup discrimination. *Journal of Personality and Social Psychology, 70*, 28–40.

Freedman, J. L., & Fraser, S. C. (1966). Compliance without pressure: The foot-on-the-door technique. *Journal of Personality and Social Psychology, 4*, 195–202.

Freud, S. (1953b). Three essays on the theory of sexuality. In J. Strachey (Ed. and Trans.), *The standard edition of the complete psychological works of Sigmund Freud* (Vol. 7). London: Hogarth Press. (Original work published 1905).

Freud, S. (1962). *Civilization and its discontents* (J. Strachey, Trans.). New York: W. W. Norton. (Original work published 1930).

Freud, S. (1963a). *An autobiographical study* (J. Strachey, Trans.). New York: W. W. Norton. (Original work published 1925).

Freud, S. (1963b). *A general introduction to psycho-analysis* (J. Riviere, Trans.). New York: Simon & Schuster. (Original work published 1920).

Freud, S. (1965). *New introductory lectures on psychoanalysis* (J. Strachey, Trans.). New York: W. W. Norton (Original work published 1933).

Frey, K. P., & Eagly, A. H. (1993). Vividness can undermine the persuasiveness of messages. *Journal of Personality and Social Psychology, 65*, 32–44.

Gallup, G., Jr., & Hugick, L. (1990). Racial tolerance grows, progress on racial equality less evident. *Gallup Poll Monthly, No. 297*, 23–32.

Ganellen, R. J. (1996). Comparing the diagnostic efficiency of the MMPI, MCMI-II, and Rorschach: A review. *Journal of Personality Assessment, 67*, 219–243.

Gartner, J., & Whitaker-Azimitia, P. M. (1996). Developmental factors influencing aggression: Animal models and clinical correlates. *Annals of the New York Academy of Sciences, 794*, 113–119.

Gawronski, B., Alshut, E., Grafe, J., Nespethal, J., Ruhmland, A., & Schulz, L. (2002). Processes of judging known and unknown persons. *Zeitschrift fuer Sozialpsychologie, 33*, 24–34.

Gilbert, D. T., & Malone, P. S. (1995). The correspondence bias. *Psychological Bulletin, 117*, 21–38.

Green, L. R., Richardson, D. R., & Lago, T. (1996). How do friendship, indirect, and direct aggression relate? *Aggressive Behavior, 22*, 81–86.

Gregory, R. J. (1996). *Psychological testing: History, principles, and applications* (2nd ed.). Boston: Allyn & Bacon.

Hanley, S., & Abell, S. (2002). Maslow and relatedness: Creating an interpersonal model of self-actualization. *Journal of Humanistic Psychology, 42,* 37–56.

Harkins, S. G., & Jackson, J. M. (1985). The role of evaluation in eliminating social loafing. *Personality and Social Psychology Bulletin, 11,* 456–465.

Harkins, S. G., & Szymanski, K. (1989). Social loafing and group evaluation. *Journal of Personality and Social Psychology, 56,* 941–943.

Harris, J. A., Rushton, J. P., Hampson, E., & Jackson, D. N. (1996). Salivary testosterone and self-report aggressive and pro-social personality characteristics in men and women. *Aggressive Behavior, 22,* 321–331.

Hay, D. F. (1994). Prosocial development. *Journal of Child Psychology and Psychiatry, 35,* 29–71.

Higdon, H. (1975). *The crime of the century.* New York: Putnam.

Hill, M., & Augoustinos, M. (2001). Stereotype change and prejudice reduction: Short- and long-term evaluation of a cross-cultural awareness programme. *Journal of Community & Applied Social Psychology, 11,* 243–262.

Hodgins, S., Mednick, S. A., Brennan, P. A., Schulsinger, F., & Engberg, M. (1996). Mental disorder and crime: Evidence from a Danish birth cohort. *Journal of Personality and Social Psychology, 53,* 489–496.

Hofstede, G. (1980). *Culture's consequences: International differences in work-related values.* Beverly Hills, CA: Sage.

Hofstede, G. (1983). Dimensions of national cultures in fifty countries and three regions. In J. Deregowski, S. Dzuirawiec, and R. Annis (Eds.), *Explications in cross-cultural psychology.* Lisse: Swets and Zeitlinger.

Horney, K. (1939). *New ways in psychoanalysis.* New York: W. W. Norton.

Horney, K. (1937). *The neurotic personality of our time.* New York: W. W. Norton.

Horney, L. (1945). *Our inner conflicts.* New York: W. W. Norton.

Horney, K. (1950). *Neurosis and human growth.* New York: W. W. Norton.

Horney, K. (1967). *Feminine psychology.* New York: W. W. Norton.

Hovland, C. I., Lumsdaine, A. A., & Sheffield, F. D. (1949). *Experiments on mass communication.* Princeton, NJ: Princeton University Press.

Huesmann, L. R., & Moise, J. (1996, June). Media violence: A demonstrated public health threat to children. *Harvard Mental Health Letter, 12*(12), 5–7.

Hunter, J. A., Reid, J. M., Stokell, N. M., & Platow, M. J. (2000). Social attribution, self-esteem, and social identity. *Current Research in Social Psychology, 5,* 97–125.

Isenberg, D. J. (1986). Group polarization: A critical review and meta-analysis. *Journal of Personality and Social Psychology, 50,* 1141–1151.

Ito, T. A., Miller, N., & Pollock, V. E. (1996). Alcohol and aggression: A meta-analysis on the moderating effects of inhibitory cues, triggering events, and self-focused attention. *Psychological Bulletin, 120,* 60–82.

Jackson, S. (2002). A study of teachers' perceptions of youth problems. *Journal of Youth Studies, 5,* 313–322.

Jamieson, D. W., & Zanna, M. P. (1989). Need for structure in attitude formation and expression. In A. R. Pratkanis, S. J. Breckler, & A. G. Greenwald (Eds.), *Attitude structure and function* (pp. 383–406). Hillsdale, NJ: Erlbaum.

Janis, I. L. (1982). *Groupthink: Psychological studies of policy decisions and fiascoes* (2nd ed.). Boston: Houghton Mifflin.

Janssen, T., & Carton, J. (1999). The effects of locus of control and task difficulty on procrastination. *Journal of Genetic Psychology, 160,* 436–442.

Jones, E. E. (1976). How do people perceive the causes of behavior? *American Scientist, 64,* 300–305.

Jones, E. E. (1990). *Interpersonal perception.* New York: Freeman.

Jones, E. E., & Nisbett, R. E. (1971). *The actor and the observer: Divergent perceptions of the causes of behavior.* New York: General Learning.

Jung, C. G. (1933). *Modern man in search of a soul.* New York: Harcourt Brace Jovanovich.

Kagitcibasi, C. (1992). A critical appraisal of individualism-collectivism: Toward a new formulation. In U. Kim, H. C. Triandis, and G. Yoon (Eds.), *Individualism and collectivism: Theoretical and methodological issues.* Newbury Park, CA: Sage.

Karau, S. J., & Williams, K. D. (1993). Social loafing; a meta-analytic review and theoretical integration. *Journal of Personality and Social Psychology, 65,* 681–706.

King, L. A., Walker, L. M., & Broyles, S. J. (1996). Creativity and the five-factor model. *Journal of Research on Personality, 30,* 189–203.

Kitayama, S., & Markus, H. R. (2000). The pursuit of happiness and the realization of sympathy: Cultural patterns of self, social relations, and well-being. In E. Diener & E. M. Suh (Eds.), *Subjective well-being across cultures.* Cambridge, MA: MIT Press.

Kite, M. E., Deaux, K., & Mieled, M. (1991). Stereotypes of young and old: Does age outweigh gender? *Psychology and Aging, 6,* 19–27.

Kochanska, G. (1993). Toward a synthesis of parental socialization and child temperament in early development of conscience. *Child Development, 64,* 325–347.

Koehler, T., Tiede, G., & Thoens, M. (2002). Long and short-term forgetting of word associations: An experimental study of the Freudian concepts of resistance and repression. *Zeitschrift fuer klinische Psychologie, Psychiatrie und Psychotherapie, 50,* 328–333.

Koltz, C. (1983, December). Scapegoating. *Psychology Today,* pp. 68–69.

Kraus, S. J. (1995). Attitudes and the prediction of behavior: A meta-analysis of the empirical literature. *Personality and Social Psychology Bulletin, 21,* 58–75.

Kuhn, D., & Lao, J. (1996). Effects of evidence on attitudes: Is polarization the norm? *Psychological Science, 7,* 115–120.

Kumar, R., O'Malley, P., Johnston, L., Schulenberg, J., & Bachman, J. (2002). Effects of school-level norms on student substance abuse. *Prevention Science, 3,* 105–124.

Kunda, Z., & Oleson, K. C. (1995). Maintaining stereotypes in the face of disconfirmation: Construction grounds for subtyping deviants. *Journal of Personality and Social Psychology, 68,* 565–579.

Lamm, H. (1988). A review of our research on group polarization: Eleven experiments on the effects of group discussion on risk acceptance, probability estimation, and negotiation positions. *Psychological Reports, 62,* 807–813.

Langlois, J. H., Kalakanis, L., Rubenstein, A. J., Larson, A., Hallam, M., & Smoot, M. (2000). Maxims or myths of beauty? A meta-analytic and theoretical review. *Psychological Bulletin, 126,* 390–423.

Langlois, J. H., & Roggman, L. A. (1990). Attractive faces are only average. *Psychological Science, 1,* 115–121.

Latané, B., Williams, K., & Harkins, S. (1979). Many hands make light the work: The causes and consequences of social loafing. *Journal of Personality and Social Psychology, 37,* 822–832.

Levitt, E. E., & Duckworth, J. C. (1984). Minnesota Multiphasic Personality Inventory. In D. J. Keyser & R. C. Sweetland (Eds.), *Test critiques* (Vol. 1, pp. 466–472). Kansas City: Test Corporation of America.

Lewis, D. O., Pincus, J. H., Feldman, M., Jackson, L., & Bard, B. (1986). Psychiatric, neurological, and psychoeducational characteristics of 15 death row inmates in the United States. *American Journal of Psychiatry, 143,* 838–845.

Leyens, J-P., Yzerbyt, V., & Olivier, C. (1996). The role of applicability in the emergence of the overattribution bias. *Journal of Personality and Social Psychology, 70,* 219–229.

Lim, V. (2002). The IT way of loafing on the job: Cyberloafing, neutralizing and organizational justice. *Journal of Organizational Behavior, 23,* 675–694.

Linville, P. W., Fischer, G. W., & Salovey, P. (1989). Perceived distributions of the characteristics of in-group and out-group members: Empirical evidence and a computer simulation. *Journal of Personality and Social Psychology, 57,* 165–188.

Loeber, R., & Hay, D. (1997). Key issues in the development of aggression and violence from childhood to early adulthood. *Annual Review of Psychology, 48,* 371–410.

Lott, B., & Saxon, S. (2002). The influence of ethnicity, social class and context on judgments about U.S. women. *Journal of Social Psychology, 142,* 481–499.

Luchins, A. S. (1957). Experimental attempts to minimize the impact of first impressions. In C. I. Hovland (Ed.), *Yale studies in attitude and communication: Vol. 1. The order of presentation in persuasion* (pp. 62–75). New Haven, CT: Yale University Press.

Lucio, E., Reyes-Lagunes, I., & Scott, R. L. (1994). MMPI-2 for Mexico: Translation and adaptation. *Journal of Personality Assessment, 63,* 105–116.

Lyvers, M. (2000). Cognition, emotion, and the alcohol-aggression relationship: Comment on Giancola. *Experimental Clinical Psychopharmacology, 8,* 612–617.

Macrae, C. N., Milne, A. B., & Bodenhausen, G. V. (1994). Stereotypes as energy-saving devices: A peek inside the cognitive toolbox. *Journal of Personality and Social Psychology, 66,* 37–47.

Marín, G. (1994). The experience of being a Hispanic in the United States. In W. J. Lonner & R. Malpass (Eds.), *Psychology and culture* (pp. 23–27). Boston: Allyn & Bacon.

McAdams, D. P. (1992). The five-factor model in personality: A critical appraisal. *Journal of Personality, 60*, 329–361.

McCormack, L., & Mellor, D. (2002). The role of personality in leadership: An application of the five-factor model in the Australian military. *Military Psychology, 14*, 179–197.

McCrae, R. (2002). The maturation of personality psychology: Adult personality development and psychological well-being. *Journal of Research in Personality, 36*, 307–317.

McCrae, R. R. (1993). Moderated analyses of longitudinal personality stability. *Journal of Personality and Social Psychology, 65*, 577–583.

McCrae, R. R. (1996). Social consequences of experiential openness. *Psychological Bulletin, 120*, 323–337.

McCrae, R. R., & Costa, P. T., Jr. (1987). Validation of the five-factor model of personality across instruments and observers. *Journal of Personality and Social Psychology, 52*, 81–90.

McCrae, R. R., & Costa, P. T., Jr. (1990). *Personality in adulthood.* New York: Guilford.

McCrae, R. R., Costa, P. T., Jr., Ostendorf, F., Angleitner, A., Hrebickova, M., Avia, S. J., Sanchez-Bernardos, M. L., Kusdil, M. E., Woodfield, R., Saunders, P. R., & Smith, P. B. (2000). Nature over nurture: Temperament, personality, and life span development. *Journal of Personality and Social Psychology, 78*, 173–186.

McDowell, C., & Acklin, M. W. (1996). Standardizing procedures for calculating Rorschach interrater reliability: Conceptual and empirical foundations. *Journal of Personality Assessment, 66*, 308–320.

McGuire, W. J. (1985). Attitudes and attitude change. In G. Lindzey & E. Aronson (Ed.), *Handbook of social psychology* (Vol. 2, 3rd ed.). New York: Random House.

McReynolds, P. (1989). Diagnosis and clinical assessment: Current status and major issues. *Annual Review of Psychology, 40*, 83–108.

Mednick, S. A., Brennan, P., & Kandel, E. (1988). Predisposition to violence. *Aggressive Behavior, 14*, 25–33.

Meyer, P. (1972). If Hitler asked you to electrocute a stranger, would you? In R. Greenbaum & H. A. Tilker (Eds.), *The challenge of psychology* (pp. 456–465). Englewood Cliffs, NJ: Prentice-Hall.

Michaels, J. W., Bloomel, J. M., Brocato, R. M., Linkous, R. A., & Rowe, J. S. (1982). Social facilitation and inhibition in a natural setting. *Replications in Social Psychology, 2*, 21–24.

Miles, D. R., & Carey, G. (1997). Genetic and environmental architecture of human aggression. *Journal of Personality and Social Psychology, 72*, 207–217.

Milgram, S. (1963). Behavioral study of obedience. *Journal of Abnormal and Social Psychology, 67*, 371–378.

Milgram, S. (1965). Liberating effects of group pressure. *Journal of Personality and Social Psychology, 1*, 127–134.

Miller, J. G., Bersoff, D. M., & Harwood, R. L. (1990). Perceptions of social responsibilities in India and in the United States: Moral imperatives or personal decisions? *Journal of Personality and Social Psychology, 58*, 33–47.

Miller, N. E. (1941). The frustration-aggression hypothesis. *Psychological Review, 48*, 337–342.

Mischel, W. (1968). *Personality and assessment.* New York: Wiley.

Mischel, W. (1973). Toward a cognitive social learning reconceptualization of personality. *Psychological Review, 80*, 252–283.

Mischel, W. (1977). The interaction of person and situation. In D. Magnusson & N. S. Endler (Eds.), *Personality at the crossroads: Current issues in interactional psychology.* Hillsdale, NJ: Lawrence Erlbaum.

Mitsis, E. M., Halperin, J. M., & Newcorn, J. H. (2000). Serotonin and aggression in children. *Current Psychiatry Reports, 2*, 95–101.

Morgan, C. D., & Murray, H. A. (1935). A method for investigating fantasies: The Thematic Apperception Test. *Archives of Neurology and Psychiatry, 34*, 289–306.

Morgan, C. D., & Murray, H. A. (1962). Thematic Apperception Test. 530–545. In H. A. Murray et al. (Eds.), *Explorations in personality: A clinical and experimental study of fifty men of college age.* New York: Science Editions.

Morrison, A. M., & Von Glinow, M. S. (1990). Women and minorities in management. *American Psychologist, 45*, 200–208.

Murray, H. (1938). *Explorations in personality.* New York: Oxford University Press.

Murray, H. A. (1965). Uses of the Thematic Apperception Test. In B. I. Murstein (Ed.), *Handbook of projective techniques* (pp. 425–432). New York: Basic Books.

Myers, D. G., & Bishop, G. D. (1970). Discussion effects on racial attitudes. *Science, 169*, 778–779.

Myers, D. G., & Lamm, H. (1975). The polarizing effect of group discussion. *American Scientist, 63*, 297–303.

Needleman, H. L., Riess, J. A., Tobin, M. J., Biesecker, G. E., & Greenhouse, J. B. (1996). Bone lead levels and delinquent behavior. *Journal of the American Medical Association, 275*, 363–369.

Nisbett, R. E., & Wilson, T. D. (1977). The halo effect: Evidence for unconscious alteration of judgments. *Journal of Personality and Social Psychology, 35*, 250–256.

O'Leary, K. D., & Smith, D. A. (1991). Marital interactions. *Annual Review of Psychology, 42*, 191–212.

Oliver, J. E. (1993). Intergenerational transmission of child abuse: Rates, research, and clinical implications. *American Journal of Psychiatry, 150*, 1315–1324.

Ostrom, T. M., Carpenter, S. L., Sedikides, C., & Li, F. (1993). Differential processing of in-group and out-group information. *Journal of Personality and Social Psychology, 64*, 21–34.

Palinscar, A. S., & Brown, A. L. (1984). Reciprocal teaching of comprehension-fostering and comprehension-monitoring activities. *Cognition and Instruction, 1*, 117–175.

Pansu, P., & Gilbert, D. (2002). Effect of causal explanations on work-related judgments. *Applied Psychology: An International Review, 51*, 505–526.

Pastore, N. (1950). The role of arbitrariness in the frustration-aggression hypothesis. *Journal of Personality and Social Psychology, 47*, 728–731.

Paulus, P. B., Cox, V. C., & McCain, G. (1988). *Prison crowding: A psychological perspective.* New York: Springer-Verlag.

Paunonen, S. V., Keinonen, M., Trzebinski, J., Fosterling, F., Grishenko-Roze, N., Kouznetsova, L., & Chan, D. W. (1996). The structure of personality in six cultures. *Journal of Cross-Cultural Psychology, 27*, 339–353.

Perrett, D. I., May, K. A., & Yoshikawa, S. (1994). Facial shape and judgments of female attractiveness. *Nature, 368*, 239–242.

Pesonen, A., Raeikkoenen, K., Keskivaara, P., & Keltikangas-Jaervinen, L. (2003). Difficult temperament in childhood and adulthood: Continuity from maternal perceptions to self-ratings over 17 years. *Personality & Individual Differences, 34*, 19–31.

Petty, R. E., Wegener, D. T., & Fabrigar, L. R. (1997). Attitudes and attitude change. *Annual Review of Psychology, 48*, 609–647.

Phillips, K., Fulker, D. W., Carey, G., & Nagoshi, C. T. (1988). Direct marital assortment for cognitive and personality variables. *Behavioral Genetics, 18*, 347–356.

Phillips, S. T., & Ziller, R. C. (1997). Toward a theory and measure of the nature of nonprejudice. *Journal of Personality and Social Psychology, 72*, 420–434.

Pittenger, D. J. (1993). The utility of the Myers-Briggs Type Indicator. *Review of Educational Research, 63*, 467–488.

Pratkanis, A. R. (1989). The cognitive representation of attitudes. In A. R. Pratkanis, S. J. Breckler, & A. G. Greenwald (Eds.), *Attitude structure and function* (pp. 71–93). Hillsdale, NJ: Erlbaum.

Public Agenda Online. (2002). *The Issues: Race.* [Online report] Retrieved November 13, 2002, from http://www.public-agenda.com/issues/overview.dfm?issue_type=race

Raine, A. (1996). Autonomic nervous system factors underlying disinhibited, antisocial, and violent behavior: Biosocial perspectives and treatment implications. *Annals of the New York Academy of Sciences, 794*, 46–59.

Reis, H. T., Wilson, I. M., Monestere, C., Bernstein, S., Clark, K., Seidl, E., Franco, M., Gioioso, E., Freeman, L., & Radoane, K. (1990). What is smiling is beautiful and good. *European Journal of Social Psychology, 20*, 259–267.

Renzetti, C. M., & Curran, D. J. (1992). *Women, men, and society.* Boston: Allyn & Bacon.

Rhodes, N., & Wood, W. (1992). Self-esteem and intelligence affect influenceability: The mediating role of message reception. *Psychological Bulletin, 111*, 156–171.

Roberts, B. W., & DelVecchio, W. F. (2000). The rank-order consistency of personality traits from childhood to old age: A quantitative review of longitudinal studies. *Psychological Bulletin, 126*, 3–25.

Roesch, S. C., & Amirkhan, J. H. (1997). Boundary condition for self-serving attributions: Another look at the sports pages. *Journal of Applied Social Psychology, 27*, 245–261.

Rose, R. J., Koskenvuo, M., Kaprio, J., Sarna, S., & Langinvainio, H. (1988). Shared genes, shared experiences, and similarity of personality: Data from 14,288 adult Finnish co-twins. *Journal of Personality and Social Psychology, 54*, 161–171.

Rotton, J., & Cohn, E. G. (2000). Violence is a curvilinear function of temperature in Dallas: A replication. *Journal of Personality and Social Psychology, 78*, 1074–1082.

Rotton, J., Frey, J., Barry, T., Milligan, M., & Fitzpatrick, M. (1979). The air pollution experience and physical aggression. *Journal of Applied Social Psychology, 9*, 397–412.

Rowe, D. C. (1987). Resolving the person-situation debate: Invitation to an interdisciplinary dialogue. *American Psychologist, 42*, 218–227.

Rudman, L., Ashmore, R., & Gary, M. (2001). "Unlearning" automatic biases: The malleability of implicit prejudice and stereotypes. *Journal of Personality and Social Psychology, 81,* 856–868.

Ruggiero, K. M., & Taylor, D. M. (1997). Why minority group members perceive or do not perceive the discrimination that confronts them: The role of self-esteem and perceived control. *Journal of Personality and Social Psychology, 72,* 373–389.

Rushton, J. P., Fulker, D. W., Neale, M. C., Nias, D. K. B., & Eysenck, H. J. (1986). Altruism and aggression: The heritability of individual differences. *Journal of Personality and Social Psychology, 50,* 1192–1198.

Salgado, J. F. (1997). The five factor model of personality and job performance in the European community. *Journal of Applied Psychology, 82,* 30–43.

Sanbonmatsu, D. M., & Fazio, R. H. (1990). The role of attitudes in memory-based decision making. *Journal of Personality and Social Psychology, 59,* 614–622.

Seligman, M. E. P. (1990). *Learned optimism: How to change your mind and your life.* New York: Simon & Schuster.

Shaw, J. I., & Steers, W. N. (2001). Gathering information to form an impression: Attribute categories and information valence. *Current Research in Social Psychology, 6,* 1–21.

Shepperd, J. (2001). The desire to help and behavior in social dilemmas: Exploring responses to catastrophes. *Group Dynamics, 5,* 304–314.

Sherif, M. (1956). Experiments in group conflict. *Scientific American, 195,* 53–58.

Sherif, M. (1958). Superordinate goals in the reduction of intergroup conflict. *American Journal of Sociology, 63,* 349–358.

Sherif, M., & Sherif, C. W. (1967). The Robbers' Cave study. In J. F. Perez, R. C. Sprinthall, G. S. Groser, & P. J. Anastasiou, *General psychology: Selected readings* (pp. 411–421). Princeton, NJ: D. Van Nostrand.

Singer, M. I., Miller, D. B., Guo, S., Flannery, D. J., Frierson, T., & Slovak, K. (1999). Contributors to violent behavior among elementary and middle school children. *Pediatrics, 104*(Pt. 1), 878–884.

Singh, B. (1991). Teaching methods for reducing prejudice and enhancing academic achievement for all children. *Educational Studies, 17,* 157–171.

Singh, D. (1995). Female health, attractiveness, and desirability for relationships: Role of breast asymmetry and waist-hip ratio. *Ethology and Sociobiology, 16,* 445–481.

Sivacek, J., & Crano, W. D. (1982). Vested interest as a moderator of attitude-behavior consistency. *Journal of Personality and Social Psychology, 43,* 210–221.

Soler, H., Vinayak, P., & Quadagno, D. (2000). Biosocial aspects of domestic violence. *Psychoneuroendocrinology, 25,* 721–739.

Stephenson, M. T., & Witte, K. (1998). Fear, threat, and perceptions of efficiency from frightening skin cancer messages. *Public Health Review, 26,* 147–174.

Sternberg, R. J. (1986). A triangular theory of love. *Psychological Review, 93,* 119–135.

Sternberg, R. J. (1987). Liking versus loving: A comparative evaluation of theories. *Psychological Bulletin, 102,* 331–345.

Tellegen, A., Lykken, D. T., Bouchard, T. J., Jr., Wilcox, K. J., Segal, N. L., & Rich, S. (1988). Personality similarity in twins reared apart and together. *Journal of Personality and Social Psychology, 54,* 1031–1039.

Thornhill, R., & Gangestad, G. W. (1994). Human fluctuating asymmetry and sexual behavior. *Psychological Science, 5,* 297–302.

Tiihonen, J., Isohanni, M., Räsänen, P., Koiranen, M., & Moring, J. (1997). Specific major mental disorders and criminality: A 26-year prospective study of the 1966 northern Finland birth cohort. *American Journal of Psychiatry, 154,* 840–845.

Tori, C., & Bilmes, M. (2002). Multiculturalism and psychoanalytic psychology: the validation of a defense mechanisms measure in an Asian population. *Psychoanalytic Psychology, 19,* 701–721.

Torrey, E. (1992). *Freudian fraud: The malignant effect of Freud's theory on American thought and culture,* New York: Harper Collins.

Triandis, H. C., McCusker, C., Betancourt, H., Iwao, S., Leung, K., Salazar, J. M., Setiadi, B., Sinha, J. B. P., Touxard, H., & Zaleski, Z. (1993). An etic-emic analysis of individualism and collectivism. *Journal of Cross-Cultural Psychology, 24,* 366–383.

Triplett, N. (1898). the dynamogenic factors in pacemaking and competition. *American Journal of Psychology, 9,* 507–533.

Turner, J. C., Hogg, M. A., Oakes, P. J., Reicher, S. D., & Wetherell, M. S. (1987). *Rediscovering the social group: A self-categorization theory.* Oxford, England: Blackwell.

U.S. Bureau of the Census. (1997). *Statistical abstract of the United States 1997* (117th ed.). Washington, DC: U.S. Government Printing Office.

van Assema, P., Martens, M., Ruiter, A., & Brug, J. (2001). Framing of nutrition education messages in persuading consumers of the advantages of a healthy diet. *Journal of Human Nutrition & Dietetics, 14,* 435–442.

van Elst, L. T., Woermann, F. G., Lemieux, L., Thompson, P. J., & Trimble, M. R. (2000). Affective aggression in patients with temporal lobe epilepsy. *Brain, 123,* 234–243.

Viemerö, V. (1996). Factors in childhood that predict later criminal behavior. *Aggressive Behavior, 22,* 87–97.

Vinokur, A., & Burnstein, E. (1978). Depolarization of attitudes in groups. *Journal of Personality and Social Psychology, 36,* 872–885.

Visser, P. S., & Krosnick, J. A. (1998). Development of attitude strength over the life cycle: Surge and decline. *Journal of Personality and Social Psychology, 75,* 1389–1410.

Vollrath, M. (2000). Personality and hassles among university students: A three-year longitudinal study. *European Journal of Personality, 14,* 199–215.

Walker, I., & Crogan, M. (1998). Academic performance, prejudice and the Jigsaw classroom: New pieces to the puzzle. *Journal of Community & Applied Social Psychology, 8,* 381–393.

Walster, E., & Walster, G. W. (1969). The matching hypothesis. *Journal of Personality and Social Psychology, 6,* 248–253.

Watson, D. (2002). Predicting psychiatric symptomatology with the Defense Style Questionnaire-40. *International Journal of Stress Management, 9,* 275–287.

Weigman, O., & van Schie, E. G. (1998). Video game playing and its relations with aggressive and prosocial behaviour. *British Journal of Social Psychology, 37*(Pt. 3), 367–378.

Weiner, I. B. (1996). Some observations on the validity of the Rorschach Inkblot Method. *Psychological Assessment, 8,* 206–213.

Weiner, I. B. (1997). Current status of the Rorschach Inkblot Method. *Journal of Personality Assessment, 68,* 5–19.

Wetter, M. W. Baer, R. A., Berry, T. R., Robison, L. H., & Sumpter, J. (1993). MMPI-2 profiles of motivated fakers given specific symptom information: A comparison to matched patients. *Psychological Assessment, 5,* 317–323.

Wicker, A. W. (1969). Attitudes versus action: The relationship of verbal and overt behavioral responses to attitude objects. *Journal of Social Issues, 25,* 41–78.

Widom, C. S. (1989). Does violence beget violence? A critical examination of the literature. *Psychological Bulletin, 106,* 3–28.

Widom, C. S., & Maxfield, M. G. (1996). A prospective examination of risk for violence among abused and neglected children. *Annals of the New York Academy of Sciences, 794,* 224–237.

Wiggins, J. S. (Ed.) (1996). *The five-factor model of personality: Theoretical perspectives.* New York: Guilford.

Williams, K., Harkins, S. G., & Latané, B. (1981). Identifiability as a deterrent to social loafing: Two cheering experiments. *Journal of Personality and Social Psychology, 40,* 303–311.

Winch, R. F. (1958). *Mate selection: A study of complementary needs.* New York: Harper & Row.

Wood, J. M., Nezworski, M. T., & Stejskal, W. J. (1996). The Comprehensive System for the Rorschach: A critical examination. *Psychological Science, 7,* 3–10.

Wood, W., Lundgren, S., Ovellette, J. A., Busceme, S., & Blackstone, T. (1994). Minority influence: A meta-analytic review of social influence processes. *Psychological Bulletin, 115,* 323–345.

Wood, W., Wong, F. Y., & Chachere, J. G. (1991). Effects of media violence on viewers' aggression in unconstrained social interaction. *Psychological Bulletin, 109,* 371–383.

Word, C. O., Zanna, M. P., & Cooper, J. (1974). The nonverbal mediation of self-fulfilling prophecies in interracial interaction. *Journal of Experimental Social Psychology, 10,* 109–120.

Wright, J. C., & Mischel, W. (1987). A conditional approach to dispositional constructs: The local predictability of social behavior. *Journal of Personality and Social Psychology, 53,* 1159–1177.

Wu, C., & Shaffer, D. R. (1987). Susceptibility to persuasive appeals as a function of source credibility and prior experience with the attitude object. *Journal of Personality and Social Psychology, 52,* 677–688.

Zajonc, R. B., & Sales, S. M. (1966). Social facilitation of dominant and subordinate responses. *Journal of Experimental Social Psychology, 2,* 160–168.

Zimbardo, P. G. (1972). Pathology of imprisonment. *Society, 9,* 4–8.

CHAPTER 20

PANTS ON FIRE[1]

Material selected from:
Research Stories for Introductory Psychology,
Second Edition, by Lary Shaffer and Matthew R. Merrens

---

[1]Incorporating the research of M. G. Frank and P. Ekman, "The Ability to Detect Deceit Generalizes across Different Types of High-Stake Lies," 1997, *Journal of Personality and Social Psychology*, 72, pp. 1429–1439.

Lives can depend on the ability to detect lies. Police and customs officers use this ability on a day-to-day basis. In most other occupations the detection of falsehoods may not be a life or death matter but, in one way or another, all of us hope that we are successful as lie detectors, particularly when it really matters. For example, we hope that we can tell that real estate agents, car dealers, and significant others are telling the truth.

As you might expect, this topic has drawn the attention of a number of psychological researchers. Most of the research in psychology has suggested that lie detection ability is not a stable trait. When we are in different situations or trying to detect lies from different people, our accuracy in lie detection may vary from good to poor (Kraut, 1978, 1980).

If a liar is under emotional strain, facial expressions of emotion might betray the lie. Paul Ekman and his coworkers have long been interested in the relationship between facial expression and emotions (Ekman & Friesen, 1971, 1975). In their 1971 study, they demonstrated that emotions could be recognized across cultures. In this study, pictures of facial emotions from Western societies were shown to people living in an isolated area of New Guinea. These people were asked to identify the emotion depicted. It was found that the research participants were usually more than 80 percent accurate in making these judgments, even though they had not had any extensive contact with Western people.

Ekman (1985) reasoned that so-called high-stake lies, where detection of the lie can result in major negative consequences for the liar, would be accompanied by facial expressions of emotion recognizable to many people. High-stake lies might, for example, be told by criminals attempting to avoid incarceration. If a jury believes the lie, a guilty person escapes penalties. The liar has a high stake in being believed, and Ekman expected the lie to be accompanied by signs of emotion on the face. Individuals who could detect these emotions through observation of facial expressions ought to be accurate high-stake lie detectors. Ekman further argued that people who are accurate high-stake lie detectors should be able to reliably detect lies across different situations, or different liars. This was expected because if an individual was good at detecting details of facial expressions, the emotions behind expressions should be noticeable whenever there were high-stake lies. Much of the previous research in psychology investigated the detection of trivial lies that made little or no real difference to the person who was lying. The liar was a confederate of the experimenter who had been told to lie about some small matter so that research participants could be presented with lies to detect. Ekman believed that these low-stake lies were less likely to be accompanied by strong emotion and, as a result, would be more difficult to detect. If this were correct, it would offer an explanation why past psychology studies had not found that lie detection generalized across situations. These trivial lies might be more likely to be detected through verbal behavior than facial expression of strong emotions. Ekman suspected that it is easier to lie with words than with genuine, strong emotions.

STIMULUS MATERIALS

Frank and Ekman (1997) did a carefully designed piece of research to investigate these issues. The first step in this investigation was the construction of videotapes depicting some people telling high-stake lies and some people telling the truth. Much of the first part of this chapter involves the method for constructing the stimulus tapes. Usually the term *participant* is used to refer to the people whose behaviors provide the outcome data for the research. In this study there were two sorts of participants: those involved in creating the stimulus materials and those whose responses were recorded as the data in the study. To avoid confusion, we will adopt the language of Frank and Ekman in calling the people who helped in the creation of stimulus materials *participants*. The people who viewed the stimulus tapes and made the ratings that became the outcome data, will be called *observers*. As will become obvious, the work in this study was divided into two parts: creation of stimulus videotapes and subsequent data collection using these tapes. Because Ekman believed that the facial expressions of emotion accompanying high-stake lies were difficult to fake, the creation of stimulus materials for the experiment required putting people in situations where they really wanted their lies to be believed. This required considerable human engineering.

Creation of the Stimulus Tapes

Twenty male participants age 18 to 28 were involved in the creation of stimulus videotapes. They were recruited from the San Francisco area and were told that they would be paid $10 an hour for participation, but that they might be able to make more. A first engineered situation, called the *crime scenario*, involved a mock theft of money. The "crime" in which they might participate involved taking $50 dollars from an envelope in a briefcase while they were alone in a lab room. They knew that it was not a real crime. They understood that the researchers planned to lose the money. They knew that the researchers expected some other participant to take the money if they did not. This "other participant" was a fictitious person only introduced because pilot testing had suggested that participants became very suspicious about the purpose of the entire procedure if they thought they were the only "suspect." Although the actual instructions to these participants were fairly complex (see Frank & Ekman, 1997), for our purposes it is only important to know that there was a role-play theft in which some of the participants took the money and some did not. Participants believed that the researchers could not be sure if the "thief" was them or the "other participant."

All participants were instructed to deny they had taken the money. Participants were told that if they chose to take the money and were able to convince an interrogator that they had *not* done so, they could keep the $50. If a participant took the money and the interrogator detected the lie, the participant was told he would lose not only the "stolen" $50, but also the $10 per hour that he was being paid for participating in the research. This created the high-stake situation—a successful lie could result in finishing participation with a tidy sum of money. Some participants chose not to take the $50. These participants were, of course, telling the truth when they were interrogated and denied taking the missing money. They were told that if their truthful denials were believed, they would get a $10 bonus in addition to the $10 per hour that they had been promised for being in the research. This was not as much money as the successful liars would get, but it was thought to be an easier task. However, if the interrogator did not believe their truthful denials, they were told they would not get the bonus and would lose their $10 hourly payment as well.

The same participants were also given a second situation in which they could lie or tell the truth. This one was called the *opinion scenario*. Participants were given a questionnaire that asked their opinion about various social issues and allowed them to rate their strength of feeling on the issue from 1 (strongly agree) to 7 (definitely disagree). The issues were things such as the death penalty and the banning of smoking in public places. The opinion that the participant felt most strongly about was selected as the one to be lied about or to be described truthfully. Participants could choose whether they would lie or tell the truth, and the reward structure was the same as in the crime scenario described above. Truth tellers who were believed received a $10 dollar bonus; liars who were believed received a $50 bonus. Liars or truth tellers who were disbelieved lost all money. All participants were instructed to claim that they were being honest in describing their beliefs.

All participants took part in the crime scenario first. They were told that the interrogator knew the money had been taken, but did not know who had taken it. After having the opportunity to take the money or not, they were taken to a small interrogation room. There were two chairs in that room: an uncomfortable metal one that was anchored to the floor and a comfortable padded chair. The participant was led to the metal chair and introduced to the interrogator, who had been described as an expert in deception. The interrogator did not know if the participant had taken the money. The participant was interrogated for 5 to 7 minutes on a series of 20 questions from a printed list.

At this point, the interrogator left and the researcher reentered and described the opinion scenario. The participant was told that he should choose whether he wanted to lie or tell the truth about his opinion. He was then told that he would have about 2 minutes to think about what he was going to say. After 2 minutes, the interrogator returned and asked another 20 scripted questions, similar to those asked in the crime interrogation. When this was complete, the participant was given a questionnaire that asked about his suspicions concerning the research, how good he felt he had been at convincing the interrogator, and the extent to which he feared the consequences of being judged as a liar.

After this, the participants were told that their part in the research was over. They were informed of the interrogator's judgment concerning whether they had been lying about each scenario. Any bonus money that had been promised was paid. Those accurately judged as having lied were reminded they would not receive any bonus money but, in contrast to expectations, all participants were paid the $10 per hour that they had been promised at the time they volunteered for the research. This was probably part of an effort to restore positive feelings about the research: the promise made during recruitment was kept. They were debriefed about the details of the research and dismissed.

Two videotapes were created, one containing men being interrogated about the crime scenario and one featuring men being interrogated about the opinion scenario. The tapes were assembled using the first six questions a participant answered. For the crime scenario, these were questions such as, "Describe exactly what happened, what you saw and did when you were in that room." "Did you take the money from the envelope?" and "Are you lying to me now?" For the opinion scenario, questions included, "What is your position on this current event issue?" "Is this your true opinion?" and "You didn't just make up this opinion a few minutes ago?" These tapes were edited down so that, in the end, each tape contained five men telling the truth and five men lying. No participant appeared more than once on each tape. For the opinion video, a few specific social issues were selected for inclusion and equal numbers of men were lying and telling the truth about these issues.

Stakes Confirmation

Frank and Ekman believed that the threatened loss of $50 and the $10 hourly fee would be enough to induce strong emotions in the liars. In order to establish that this high-stakes situation was associated with emotion, they had a person trained in scoring emotions look at both of the final edited videotapes. This rater scored the tapes using the Facial Action Coding System (FACS), (Ekman & Friesen, 1978). This is a standardized system that records all visible facial muscle movements, not only those presumed to be involved with emotion. Past research had established that each basic emotion was associated with particular patterns of muscle movements (Ekman, 1985). Based on these findings, it was predicted that the high-stake liars on these videos should show specific facial muscle movements associated with the emotions *fear* (of getting caught) and *disgust* (at oneself for lying). When scores of both videos were combined, the scorer found that 90 percent of the participants could be correctly identified as liars based on facial muscle movements associated with fear and disgust. Seventy percent of the truth tellers could be correctly identified by the absence of facial indicators of fear and disgust. A second FACS trained rater rescored 20 percent of the videos as a reliability check and the agreement between them was 76 percent.

The presence or absence of facial expressions of emotion in the men confirmed two important things. First, it indicated that the liars were, indeed, in a high-stake situation because they displayed empirical evidence of strong emotions. Second, this finding indicated that there was an observable difference when the facial expressions of high-stake liars were compared to those of people telling the truth. The difference had been captured in the participants on the two videotapes. This enabled Frank and Ekman to proceed to their primary research question: How reliable are ordinary people— presumably responding to these differences—at detecting high-stake lies? Their hypothesis was that some people would be consistently better at high-stake lie detection than others. Frank and Ekman were also interested in the overall level of accuracy of lie detection, but made no particular prediction about this before the data were collected.

STUDY 1

The most important outcome measure was the observer's accuracy for each videotape. It might seem that whether the person was lying or not should be considered the independent variable. In a strict technical sense this is not an independent variable because the experimenter did not create it: people chose for themselves whether they were going to lie or tell the truth. Nevertheless it was an important variable and was associated with the most interesting findings in the study. As you know by now, the only reason why this is an issue is that one should be cautious about asserting a cause-and-effect relationship unless dealing with a real, randomly assigned, independent variable. To help you understand this, imagine that all the people who chose to tell the truth were also personally more confident and secure than those who chose to lie. Observers watching the tapes might have responded to the display of confidence, not to the lie. Because this is possible, it is not correct to call lying or being truthful an independent variable in this study. The usual way to solve this in research design is to randomly assign some people to lie and some people to be truthful. Probably Frank and Ekman thought they would get higher quality performances if participants could choose to lie or be truthful. In designing the study the way they did, our confidence about cause-and-effect relationships was undermined. It is our judgment that this study should be considered a quasi-experiment because of the lack of a real independent variable.

Compromise is common in the design of scientific studies. In this case it was necessitated because the participant's performance was the real priority. It may seem that we are worrying too much about a small matter, but we want you to be able to think critically and clearly about study outcomes. Researchers will sometimes consider, for example, gender to be an independent variable. Gender is not a characteristic that is randomly assigned by an experimenter and as a critical thinker you should exercise caution in drawing cause-and-effect conclusions when it is a variable in a study. Some statistical techniques routinely call one variable an *independent variable*, even though it is not really *independent*. For the purposes of this book, we have tried to be consistent, using this term only when the study is a true experiment. We are aware that this degree of caution is unusual, but we think it is important. We want you to be able to think clearly about research findings regardless of the terms that are used by a particular author.

The Judgment Procedure

Forty-nine observers were recruited, and they viewed the videotapes in an attempt to detect lies. They were 32 females and 17 males who were students at San Francisco State University. They received course credit for being observers. They watched the tapes in groups with seven to ten other observers. They were told that they would be seeing 10 men who were being interrogated about a crime and 10 men who were being interrogated about their opinion on a current event topic. Observers were given a form that permitted them to circle the word *truthful* or *lying* after viewing each participant's segment of the tape. Ability to detect lies was operationally defined as success on this task. The observers were told that between one fourth and three fourths of the men they would see were lying. This was done to prevent observers from merely assuming that all the participants were either lying or truthful. Before and after the videotapes were viewed, observers were asked to rate their own ability to detect lying in other people. These ratings were done on a five point scale where 1 = *very poor* and 5 = *very good*. One observer did not follow instructions and was dropped from the study.

Results of Study 1

Accuracy scores of observers were calculated by counting the number of correct judgments, out of 10 possible, for each video. Each video had been constructed to contain five men who were lying and five who were telling the truth. Because there were two choices, lying or truth, an observer who only guessed would average 50 percent correct. Frank and Ekman divided the observers into two groups: high accuracy: those getting 60 percent or more correct and low accuracy, those getting 50 percent or fewer correct. The number of high and low scorers for each scenario is shown in Table 20.1.

As this table shows, people who scored high on the crime scenario were also likely to score high on the opinion scenario. Although less pronounced, the same trend can be seen for low scorers. You can see this by looking at the diagonally positioned cells on the table: the high/high cell in the upper left and the low/low cell in the lower right. In contrast, looking at the diagonal cells in the other direction—the high/low and low/high—there were not too many observers who scored high on one scenario and low on the other. Although it may take a bit of study to understand this table, it is worth your time to do so, because this is a standard method for presenting data assessing two levels of behavior in two situations.

There were also some interesting correlational findings among the results. There was a significant positive correlation ($r = .48$, $p < .001$) between the performance of an observer on the crime scenario and on the opinion scenario. This indicated that many of those who performed well on one performed well on the other. Those who achieved about the chance level on one did about the same on the other, and those who were poor at lie detection on one videotape were also poor lie detectors when watching the other tape. These accuracy scores for individual observers ranged from 10 percent to 90 percent for

TABLE 20.1   Number of Observers Scoring High and Low on Each of the Scenarios in Study 1

		OPINION SCENARIO SCORE	
		High	*Low*
CRIME SCENARIO SCORE	*High*	21	6
	Low	9	12

the opinion video and from 10 percent to 80 percent for the crime video. These data can be used to illustrate the difference between the detection of ordinary and high-stake lies. In other psychology research, where lies were not high stake, it was unusual for any measured accuracy to surpass 60 percent (DePaulo, Zuckerman, & Rosenthal 1980). Neither the gender of the observer nor the order of videotape presentation had any effect on the results.

No relationship was found between observer's pretest or posttest ratings of *confidence* in their detection ability and their *actual* detection ability. People do not know how good or bad they have been, or are going to be, when it comes to actually detecting lies. Even though these assessments had no relationship to actual detection they did have a relationship to each other: observers who thought they were good lie detectors before seeing the tapes continued to think they were good lie detectors after the tape, even though confidence was, in fact, unrelated to accuracy. This is a good example of a situation in which reliability is not evidence of validity.

STUDY 2

Study 2 was similar to Study 1, but it was also an attempt to directly demonstrate that observers who were good at recognizing facial expressions of emotions would also be good at detecting high-stake lies. In addition, Study 2 provided a replication of Study 1.

The observers in Study 2 were 13 male and 17 female undergraduates from San Jose State University who received course credit for taking part in the research. These observers saw the two deception videotapes developed for Study 1. As in Study 1, they were asked to rate pretest and posttest confidence in their ability to detect lying. Study 2 differed because after judging the videotapes, participants were all given a test of accuracy in judging facial expressions of emotion, called the *microexpression test*.

The 40-item microexpression test consisted of slides of facial expressions of emotions. The emotions depicted were anger, contempt, disgust, fear, happiness, sadness, and surprise. These slides were presented using an apparatus called a tachistoscope, which is essentially a slide projector with a shutter-like device that controls duration of presentation of the slide. In this case, the pictures of facial emotions were on the screen for $\frac{1}{25}$ of a second. Although this may not seem very long, it is easily long enough to see the facial expression. This slide show was videotaped for presentation to the observers. After each picture of an emotion was briefly flashed on the screen, the observer was given the opportunity to identify the emotion by circling the answer from a list of the seven emotions. Presenting the emotions for such a short period of time made the task more challenging and presumably helped to separate those who were good at identifying emotions from those who were not.

As in Study 1, a hypothesis in this study was that observers who were good at finding liars in the crime tape would also be good at finding liars in the opinion tape. Frank and Ekman further predicted that there would be a positive correlation between performance on the microexpression test and the successful detection of lies in the crime and opinion scenarios. As in Study 1, they also expected to find no relationship between confidence in lie detection ability and accuracy at lie detection.

Results of Study 2

As had been found in Study 1, neither the gender of the observer nor the order of videotape presentation had any effect on the results. As in Study 1, observers who were 60 percent accurate or higher were classified as high scorers and those 50 percent and below were considered to be low scorers. Table 20.2 shows the number of observers who were high and low scorers for each tape in Study 2.

A statistically significant positive correlation ($r = .31$, $p < .05$) was found between the detection of lies in the opinion video and the detection of lies in the crime video. There was a significant positive correlation ($r = .34$, $p < .04$) between the successful identification of emotions on the microexpression test and the successful detection of lies in the crime video. The relation between microexpression

TABLE 20.2 Number of Observers Scoring High and Low on Each of the Scenarios in Study 2

		OPINION SCENARIO SCORE	
		High	*Low*
CRIME SCENARIO SCORE	*High*	15	4
	Low	4	7

accuracy and opinion video accuracy was a positive correlation, but it was not statistically significant ($r = .20$, $p = .15$). It is not obvious why this happened, but unanticipated variation from one version of a study to another is not highly unusual. As in Study 1, observer's ratings of pretest and posttest confidence indicated, in Frank and Ekman's words, that "observers seem to have fairly reliable beliefs about their abilities to detect deception, independent of their actual ability" (p. 1436).

DISCUSSION AND CONCLUSIONS

The results of these two studies suggest that the ability to detect high-stake lies may not vary much from one lie to the next, but may, instead, be a more general trait that some people possess and some people do not. The ability to accurately read emotions from facial expressions seems to be related to this ability and may well be an important component of it. This kind of cautious language is required here because the data were correlational, so although a relationship was established, there was no evidence for a cause-and-effect relationship between emotion recognition and lie detection. There may, of course, *be* a cause-and-effect relationship here, but a correlation is not sufficient evidence to confirm it.

Given the findings of these studies, it is possible to imagine a true experiment that might help to determine if recognition of emotions is a cause of lie detection. An approach might be to identify a group of people who were not good at emotion recognition, randomly assign them to two groups and train one group to recognize emotions. This presumes that it is possible to train this skill, which, by itself, is another interesting question. Once training had been attempted, both groups could be given an appropriate lie detection task to see if the group that was taught the emotion detection skill would do better at lie detection. This design could be strengthened if these groups were given a lie detection assessment before training to assure that the groups were not different in lie detection before one group received training. It is easy to *imagine* further research, but we would not want the ease of this interesting activity to distract you from an appreciation of the vast amount of work involved in actually conducting such a study. Aside from the hard work involved in creating the stimulus videotapes, the study that we imagine would also involve a long-term commitment from observers through the training program.

Frank and Ekman showed appropriate caution in the interpretation of their results. Although they believed that the identification of emotions was a component of the detection of deceit, they also stated that lie detection probably involves a number of skills and abilities, some closely related to each other and some not. Because there is no one characteristic that is always present in people who are lying, there can be no one strategy that will always result in successful lie detection. It is highly probable that some people can tell lies, even high-stake lies, while exhibiting no outward evidence of emotional responses. It seems clear from this study, however, that many liars do give themselves away, at least to the skilled observer. The significant correlations in this study are of moderate strength, being in the range of .30 to the middle .40s. Although they have some predictive power, it is clear that other, unknown, factors also play a role in lie detection.

Frank and Ekman noted that there are two rather different approaches that might be used in the application of these findings to professional high-stake lie detection in agencies. One approach would be to attempt training using facial emotion recognition. The other would be to identify those people within the organization who are already reliably good at lie detection and have these individuals take responsibility for this task, saving the investment that would be required for training programs. Either way, the future practical application of this important area of research is obvious.

REFERENCES

DePaulo, B. M., Zuckerman, M., & Rosenthal, R. (1980). Humans as lie detectors. *Journal of Communication, 30,* 129–139.

Ekman, P. (1985). *Telling lies: Clues to deceit in the marketplace, politics and marriage.* New York: Norton.

Ekman, P., & Friesen, W. V. (1971). Constants across cultures in the face and emotion. *Journal of Personality and Social Psychology, 17,* 124–129.

Ekman, P., & Friesen, W. V. (1975). *Unmasking the face: A guide to recognizing emotions from facial cues.* Upper Saddle River, NJ: Prentice Hall.

Ekman, P., & Friesen, W. V. (1978). *The facial action coding system.* Palo Alto, CA: Consulting Psychologists Press.

Frank, M. G., & Ekman, P. (1997). The ability to detect deceit generalizes across different types of high-stake lies. *Journal of Personality and Social Psychology, 72,* 1429–1439.

Kraut. R. E. (1978). Verbal and nonverbal cues in the perception of lying. *Journal of Personality and Social Psychology, 36,* 380–391.

Kraut, R. E. (1980). Humans as lie detectors: Some second thoughts. *Journal of Communication, 30,* 209–216.

CHAPTER 21

AGGRESSION BREEDS AGGRESSION[1]

Material selected from:
Research Stories for Introductory Psychology,
Second Edition, by Lary Shaffer and Matthew R. Merrens

---

[1]Incorporating the research of B. J. Bushman, R. F. Baumeister, and A. Stack, "Catharsis, Aggression, and Persuasive Influence: Self-Fulfilling or Self-Defeating Prophecies?" 1999, *Journal of Personality and Social Psychology*, 76, pp. 367–376.

Popular culture, self-help books, and pop psychology foster the belief that externalizing anger, hostility, or aggression is therapeutic. This process of catharsis or venting feelings, often on inanimate objects, is proposed as a healthy way to reduce the impact of negative emotions. Striking a pillow or hitting a punching bag are advocated as cathartic release techniques. Lee (1993), in a mass market self-help book, advocates that "If you are angry at a particular person, imagine his or her face on the pillow or punching bag, and vent your rage physically and verbally . . . you are not hitting a person. You are hitting the ghost of that person—a ghost from the past, . . . that must be exorcised in a concrete, physical way" (p. 96). The catharsis hypothesis is endorsed widely and has led people to believe that venting anger is a positive, healthy strategy that will make you feel better. The research presented in this chapter focuses on the following questions: (1) Can media endorsement of catharsis lead people to engage in cathartic activities such as venting anger? and (2) If people believe in the benefits of catharsis, will acting in an aggressive manner lead to reduced feelings of aggression?

WHAT IS CATHARSIS AND DOES IT HAVE SUPPORT?

Catharsis has a long history and has a great deal of contemporary mass media support. Aristotle advocated viewing tragic plays as a means of catharsis to cleanse personal emotional issues. Freud's views, which certainly dominated early-twentieth-century thinking, suggest that the internal build-up of pent-up emotions is responsible for conversion and anxiety disorders. Freud's thinking is often referred to as the *plumbing or hydraulic model;* as negative emotions build up internally the "hydraulic" pressure inside the person increases, like water behind a dam.

Because this pressure represents an uncomfortable state, an external release is proposed as being adaptive for the person (Geen & Quantry, 1977). The self-help book by Lee (1993) mentioned above cites a number of ways to focus your hostilities on inanimate objects including breaking glass, twisting a towel, and using a plastic baseball bat to strike a couch. Exploring the catharsis data from empirical studies, Tavris (1988) determined that there has been almost no research support for the value of catharsis in getting rid of negative feelings. On the other hand, it is very possible that venting anger through a cathartic process can lead to higher levels of feelings of aggression (Berkowitz, 1984; Tice & Baumeister, 1993).

In spite of this, however, catharsis continues to be seen in our culture, as a remedy for anger and hostility, and the belief remains resistant to modification.

THE CURRENT SITUATION

Popular Media: Endorses the catharsis hypothesis as truth and produces books, tapes, and articles in support. Because popular media is pervasive, the general public believes this view is fact.

Scientific Psychology: Does not validate catharsis and supports just the opposite—acting in a violent manner leads to more violence.

SELF-FULFILLING AND SELF-DEFEATING PROPHECIES

In the first experiment, participants were evaluated to see if pro- or anti-catharsis messages influenced their decision to select a method to cope with anger. The researchers hypothesized that participants exposed to pro-catharsis messages would elect to vent their anger by engaging in aggressive acts against inanimate objects. A second experiment explored the after effects of a participant's choice. Participants were exposed to one of three catharsis messages: pro-catharsis, anti-catharsis, or a control message that said nothing about catharsis. After being encouraged to engage in aggression by striking a punching bag, they were given the chance to engage in aggressive behavior toward a person who has angered them. Would the prepunching message they received be a factor in determining later aggressive behavior? Bushman et al. (1999) suggested that a *self-fulfilling prophecy* viewpoint (a person's beliefs lead to outcomes consistent with expectations) would lead to low aggression after the participants engaged in the physical aggression of hitting the punching bag. On the other hand, a *self-defeating prophecy* (a person's beliefs lead to outcomes opposite to expectations) would lead to higher levels of aggression after engaging in slugging the punching bag. This is not a socially desirable outcome.

First Experiment

The participants in this experiment were 180 male and 180 female introductory psychology students who volunteered and also received additional class credit. They were given a cover story that the investigators were studying people's perceptions in a variety of situations. Participants were assigned randomly to one of three message conditions: pro-catharsis, anti-catharsis, and a control condition. The participants in all conditions were asked to write a brief essay on the topic of abortion, taking either a pro-choice or pro-life position. Half of the participant's essays were assigned to receive very negative evaluations regardless of the quality of the essay, and the other half were assigned to receive very positive evaluations. This was accomplished by comments such as "This is one of the worst essays I have read" in the negative condition or "No suggestions, great essay" in the positive condition. Previous research by Bushman and Baumeister (1998) supported the view that the above manipulation does, in fact, create significantly more anger in the group receiving the negative evaluation than in the group receiving positive evaluations. Next the participants were given 10 activities to place in rank order based on their desire to engage in these activities later in the experiment. Activities in the rank ordering included reading, playing cards, playing computer games, and hitting a punching bag.

This research is an experiment with two independent variables, *media message* (pro-catharsis, anti-catharsis, control), and *anger level* (angered or not angered by feedback). The dependent variable was the participants' preference ranking of "hitting a punching bag" among nine other activities.

FIGURE 21.1   Bag Punching Preferences as a Function of Anger and Media Message. Preferences are displayed as standardized scores with positive scores indicating greater aggressive preferences, and negative scores indicating lower preferences for aggressive action.

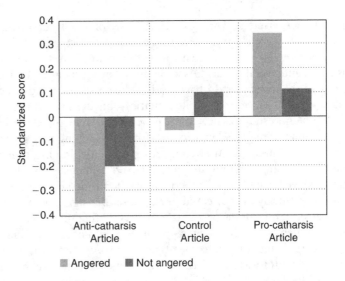

Results of Experiment 1

The major results of this experiment are presented in Figure 21.1. Participants who were angry as a result of their essay evaluations and who received the pro-catharsis message ranked hitting the punching bag significantly higher than angry participants who received the anti-catharsis message or those participants who were in the control condition. In the groups of participants that were not angered by the essay grading, the anti-catharsis and pro-catharsis messages played no role in their rank of interest in hitting a punching bag. Overall, participants who received the anti-catharsis message were significantly less likely to want to hit the punching bag than participants who received the pro-catharsis message ($p < .05$). Lastly, sex of participants played a role in wanting to hit the punching bag, with males participants having significantly higher rankings than females ($p < .05$). This experiment shows that messages from such popular media as self-help books, segments on the evening television news, and talk shows can impact an individual's choice to behave in an aggressive manner or not when provoked to anger. The researchers, Bushman, Baumeister, and Strack, thought it was conceivable that demand characteristics found in the experiment may have been responsible for the findings. *Demand characteristics* are environmental or situational stimuli that guide our behavior. Small, seemingly insignificant messages and stimuli can play a major role in determining our behavior. For example, if you are led to believe (even in the mildest way) that a course exam in college will be very difficult, it may affect your test-taking style and performance. This is true even if the exam is quite easy. Similarly, the sanctuary for a religious service contains demand characteristics for being quiet, reverent, and serious. An important interview in your senior year in college for a great job contains demand characteristic for formal dress and formal manners.

Second Experiment

In this experiment participants were given the chance to actually express anger toward an individual who had angered them. In the initial experiment, the outcome measure was a self-reported ranking; in this experiment the outcome measure was behavioral. In addition, the researchers were able to determine how cathartic aggressive behavior might impact a person's anger level. Would such actions lower one's anger as the catharsis hypothesis suggests, or not?

The participants were similar to the first experiment with 350 males and 357 females. Participants were evaluated individually and were told that the research project involved the accuracy of perceptions of people in various interactions. Participants were randomly assigned to one of three conditions; pro-catharsis, anti-catharsis, or control condition with no relevancy to catharsis. The next step was similar to the first experiment, with participants writing a brief pro-life or pro-choice essay on abortion. Participants were led to believe that another participant would evaluate the essays. In fact, the essays were *all* given very poor assessments with comments describing poor organization, style, clarity, persuasiveness, and overall quality. As in the initial experiment there was a written comment stating that "This is one of the worst essays I have read." The same ranking procedure used in the initial experiment was used, with one of the 10 possible activities, "hitting a punching bag."

The next step was new to the procedure and involved participants actually hitting a punching bag. Participants were placed in a room with the punching bag, given boxing gloves, and encouraged to hit the bag for 2 minutes. After completing the punching bag exercise participants were asked to indicate their level of enjoyment in slugging the bag. The next step involved having participants engage in what they believed would be a competitive reaction time task. Participants were given instructions to press a button as quickly as they could in response to a signal because they were in competition with another participant. Some of the participants were told that their competitor was the person who evaluated their essay (remember all participants received very negative evaluations designed to induce anger), while other participants were informed that their competitor was unknown to them. The information about their competitor was transmitted to the participants before the bag punching exercise. This was done so that participants could "use" the bag punching exercise as a chance to "vent" their anger *or* to hold on to the anger and direct it against the person who made them angry by insulting them with a negative essay evaluation. The slowest of the pair in the competitive reaction time task would be subjected to a noise blast administered by the winner. The intensity of the noise could be set at one of 10 levels ranging from 60 decibels to 105 decibels. Participants could also select a no-noise condition. A second variable of the noise choice was the duration of the noise to the loser by the winner. The winner administered the noise by holding down a button. The longer the button was depressed the longer the noise was administered. Participants could therefore effectively "punish" other participants by selecting the level and duration of the aversive sound. In summary, the trial winner had control of a "noise gun" that could zap the other competitor. The competitive reaction time task had an initial trial followed by 24 succeeding trials. On the initial trial the "real participant" always won, and on the succeeding 24 trials the "real participant" won half the time. Because the experimental procedure is somewhat complex, the following procedural summary is provided.

- Participants randomly assigned to one of three conditions (pro-catharsis, anti-catharsis, control)
- Participants write pro-life or pro-choice essays
- All essays given very negative written feedback to induce anger
- Ranking list of activities, which included punching a bag
- Some participants informed they would engage in competitive reaction task later with grader of their essay
- Participants engage in 2-minute punching bag session with enjoyment level measured by self-rating
- Participants engage in competitive reaction task (competitor is believed to be essay grader or non-essay grader)
- Participants could inflict various levels of noise "pain" for various time duration

Results of Experiment 2

Sex of Participants.   Male participants showed a trend toward higher levels of aggressive behavior across all measures.

Angry Pro-Catharsis Participants.   Participant rankings for the 10 activities were quite similar to Experiment 1, with participants who were made angry and exposed to the pro-catharsis message showing significantly more desire to hit the bag than participants made angry who were exposed to the anti-catharsis message ($p < .05$). In addition, participants showed a trend to hit the punching bag more (but not significantly so) when they were aware they would be interacting later with the person who made them angry by evaluating their essay unfavorably ($p < .10$).

Zapping Your Competitor.   An additional component of Experiment 2 was to observe whether or not participants from various conditions, if given the opportunity, would show more hostility in punishing the person who made them angry. The dependent measures to determine this were level of noise intensity chosen and duration of exposure chosen. Both were seen as measures of anger toward the source or the aggression. Since these measures correlated significantly with each other a single *composite intensity + duration measure* was used to assess aggressive interpersonal behavior. The researchers thought that the initial trial (out of 25) represented the best test of aggressive behavior. They reasoned that on the next 24 trials the participant's aggressiveness response would be affected by how aggressive their competitor had been toward them. The results of aggressivity on trial 1 showed a trend for participants who received the pro-catharsis message to be more aggressive than both the anti-catharsis and control message groups ($p < .05$). On the remaining trials the pro-catharsis message group behaved in a significantly more aggressive manner than did the anti-catharsis message group participants do ($p < .05$).

People Like to Punch.   Seventy-two percent of participants liked to hit the punching bag with no differences observed between message conditions. Male participants enjoyed slugging the bag more than females.

Does Hitting the Bag Lead to Catharsis?   Further analyses of pro-catharsis participants who hit the punching bag show higher aggressive levels in the *composite intensity + duration measure* than participants who did not hit the bag. These findings are contrary to the catharsis hypothesis.

These findings from Experiment 2 supported the results of the initial experiment. Hitting a punching bag does not appear to yield a cathartic effect. On the contrary, it increases aggressive behavior. Experiment 2 also provided a replication of the finding that desire to hit a punching bag ranked higher among the pro-catharsis participants than other groups.

This research shows that messages from the media can impact behavior. Most importantly it showed that interpersonal aggression is heightened by a pro-catharsis message even after participants have been given a chance to supposedly let off steam by hitting a punching bag. The findings support the viewpoint that a belief in catharsis appears to initiate a self-defeating prophecy.

CONCLUSIONS

The researchers in this experiment could not see any beneficial cathartic effect even when participants were given positive messages about its benefits. Catharsis leads to aggressivity rather than dampens it. Why then does the catharsis model retain its current popularity, prestige, and power? Bushman et al. (1999) suggested that the pop media endlessly promotes the catharsis as therapeutic, and people may believe it is a natural, normal process to lower one's anger level. In addition, because it has a long history, people may have come to believe it must be correct.

It is frequently the case that old ideas take a long time to die out, especially in psychology. The Rorschach inkblot technique for personality assessment and clinical diagnosis has consistently been found to have low validity and reliability when scored by traditional methods. However it is still in wide usage among clinicians. This data from this research suggests that pro-catharsis actions are not effective in reducing aggressive behavior. In fact, catharsis promotes aggressive behavior and, therefore, is a hazard to personal, social, and community life. Alternatives to the catharsis hypothesis such as self-control and nonaggressive behavior should be promoted widely.

REFERENCES

Berkowitz, L. (1984). Some effects of thoughts on anti-social and pro-social influences of media effects: A cognitive-neoassociation analysis. *Psychological Bulletin, 95,* 410–427.

Bushman, B. J., & Baumeister, R. F. (1998). Threatened egotism, narcissism, self-esteem, and direct and displaced aggression: Does self-love or self-hate lead to violence? *Journal of Personality and Social Psychology, 75,* 219–229.

Bushman, B. J., Baumeister, R. F., & Stack, A. (1999). Catharsis, aggression, and persuasive influence: Self-fulfilling or self-defeating prophecies? *Journal of Personality and Social Psychology, 76,* 367–376.

Geen, R. G., & Quantry, M. B. (1977). The catharsis of aggression: An evaluation of a hypothesis. In L. Berkowitz (Ed.), *Advances in experimental social psychology* (Vol. 10, pp. 1–37). New York: Academic Press.

Lee, J. (1993). *Facing the fire: Experiencing and expressing anger appropriately.* New York: Bantam.

Tavris, C. (1988). Beyond cartoon killings: Comments on two overlooked effects of television. In S. Oskamp (Ed.), *Television as a social issue* (pp. 189–197). Newbury Park, CA: Sage.

Tice, D. M., & Baumeister, R. F. (1993). Controlling anger: Self-induced emotion change. In D. M. Wegner & J. W. Pennebaker (Eds.), *Handbook of mental control* (pp. 393–409). Upper Saddle River, NJ: Prentice Hall.

CHAPTER 22

I'M OKAY, YOU'RE NOT[1]

Material selected from:
Research Stories for Introductory Psychology,
Second Edition, by Lary Shaffer and Matthew R. Merrens

[1]Incorporating the research of S. Fein and S. J. Spencer, "Prejudice as Self-Image Maintenance: Affirming the Self through Derogating Others," 1997, *Journal of Personality and Social Psychology*, *73*, pp. 31–44.

Prejudice, as the word is usually used, is an irrational attitude of hostility directed against an individual, group, or race. It is an ugly thing. It is also very common. When this irrational attitude is directed against the supposed characteristics of a group, it is a kind of prejudice called *stereotyping*. Prejudice has been studied for a long time in psychology (see, for example, Miller & Bugelski, 1948), and during the past decade there have been many studies on this important issue (see Hilton & von Hippel, 1996, for a review).

It takes some courage to do these studies because in order to study prejudice and stereotypes, we have to admit that they exist. Moreover, the study of these attitudes often involves exposure to the distasteful details of prejudicial beliefs that may be held by those around us, maybe even by people we like, or love. This can make us uncomfortable, and rightly so. One reason why the study of prejudice is undertaken in psychology is because researchers are horrified by it. They believe that achieving understanding of prejudice may be one pathway to eliminating it. Sometimes the researchers themselves are members of the stereotyped group under study. You can imagine it is not easy for them to receive constant reminders of negative stereotypes about their own group.

We take the time to introduce this topic in this way because the study to be reviewed in this chapter examines stereotyping and other prejudice against two groups: young Jewish women and gay men. Some students are members of one of these groups, and many of you will have friends or family members included in these groups. It may upset you to read aspects of the stereotypes that are held about these people. It upsets us. Psychologists study many topics that are deeply and personally upsetting to some people including such things as racism, sexuality, religious practices, social class, and child abuse. We believe it is better to study sensitive topics than to ignore them. Ignorance has always been a poor solution to human problems.

Steven Fein and Steven Spencer (1997) did three related investigations to test different aspects of a hypothesis that prejudice is linked to a person's own self-image. As we have seen in previous chapters, it is not unusual that several small studies are reported in one journal article. If the studies are closely related, there is some economy for the reader. The introduction to the topic is likely to be the same for all of them, and the conclusions can summarize all the study findings at once. Fein and Spencer believed that, ironically, prejudice results from inherent attempts of people to maintain their own feelings of self-worth and self-integrity. People like to feel good about themselves. When something threatens positive feelings about the self, probably the best way to deal with the resulting discomfort is to confront the source. We do not always do that. If, for example, you have done something that later does not appear very smart—such as sitting on the plate of pizza (with extra toppings) that you left on a kitchen stool— you might rationalize it by saying that you were tired and not thinking too clearly. This permits you to remove the threatening idea that you were stupid, replacing it with the idea that you were merely tired. Your sense of self-worth and self-integrity has been maintained or restored.

Steel, Spencer, and Lynch (1993) pointed out that threats to self-worth do not always have to be addressed directly. Sometimes people will accept one set of negative implications about themselves and turn elsewhere to bolster some other aspect of their self-image, increasing their overall total sense of self-adequacy. For example, a person who feels that he is not particularly intelligent might accept and ignore that feeling, while taking particular pride in some other sort of personal achievement.

Unfortunately, making negative assessments of others is another tactic people use to feel better about themselves. Threats to a person's self-image can result in that person becoming more prejudiced. When people make disparagements in order to feel better, they avoid having to do anything about the sources of threat that lowered their self-image in the first place. The ability of prejudice to restore positive feelings about the self in prejudiced people has been called the *self-affirming* nature of prejudice. Self-affirmation is the name given to our own reassurance that we have overall personal worth and integrity.

STUDY 1

Fein and Spencer (1997) believed that increased self-affirmation ought to lead to decreased prejudice. A good way to think about this proposition is to imagine that each person needs to maintain a certain pool or supply of feelings of self-worth. Unfortunately, prejudice has been shown to boost self-worth and adds to this supply. If the self-worth supply is increased by having people do other, nonprejudicial, self-affirming things, self-worth levels will be high, and prejudice will be less necessary. Fein and Spencer set up a situation in which one group of people had the opportunity to review some aspect of their lives that they particularly valued and to remind themselves of the reasons why this value was important. This was the self-affirmation manipulation. Another group performed a task involving similar amounts of time, but did not engage in self-affirmation.

Participants and Procedure for Study 1

The participants in Study 1 were 54 students from an introductory psychology course at the University of Michigan who received course credit for being in the study.

They were told that they were going to be in two pieces of research. The first was described as a study of values and the second was supposed to be an investigation of how people evaluate job applicants. Really, the "values study" was a manipulation, or set of created conditions, within the investigation designed to create or boost self-affirmation in half the participants. *Self-affirmation* and *no-affirmation* were operationally defined by the manipulation in the so-called values study. Half of the participants received the self-affirmation manipulation. The participants in the self-affirmation group were given a list of words such as *social life, business, pursuit of knowledge,* and *art.* They were asked to choose the topic from the list that had the most value to them and write a paragraph about why it was important. This was considered self-affirmation because it gave the participants a chance to feel good about their beliefs. In contrast, the participants in the no-affirmation control group were asked to choose a value that was least important to them and write a paragraph about why this value might be important to someone else. This no-affirmation procedure was conducted so both groups would have a somewhat parallel lab experience with the exception that one group was self-affirmed and one was not.

For the second part of Study 1, the participants were told their task was to evaluate a woman who was applying for a job as personnel manager in an organization. They were told to assess the fit between this individual and the job as accurately as possible. They were given a job description and a fictitious job application. The application was constructed by the researchers to make the candidate appear fairly well qualified for the position, but not an excellent match. There was a photograph on the application. After examining the application, the participants were asked to view an 8-minute videotape that showed an interview with the applicant. The woman playing the applicant put on an adequate performance, but was not outstandingly positive or negative.

All research participants saw the same videotape. The application materials shown to all participants were the same except a few modifications had been made to imply that the woman belonged to one of two different ethnic groups: Jewish or Italian. These groups were chosen because at that time on the Michigan campus there was a prejudicial stereotype that was widely held among the student body about young Jewish women. These women were the target of racist jokes about what was called the Jewish American Princess, or JAP, stereotype. This particular prejudice was chosen for study because many students openly believed it and seemed to see nothing racist in its endorsement. Italian ethnicity was chosen for comparison because pilot testing indicated that there was no widely held stereotype of any sort associated with Italian ethnicity on this campus.

In order to manipulate the ethnicity of the woman who was supposed to be the job candidate, some applications had different details than others. Half of the applications had the name Julie Goldberg, but on the others the name was Maria D'Agostino. Julie's application showed her volunteering for a Jewish organization and Maria's listed volunteer work for a Catholic organization. On the application, Julie belonged to a sorority that consisted predominantly of Jewish women, whereas Maria belonged to a sorority that had mainly non-Jewish women as members. All the other printed material was identical. The photograph was varied slightly so that Julie was wearing a Star of David necklace and Maria was wearing a cross. Julie had her hair clipped up with what was known on the campus as a "JAP clip," whereas Maria had her hair down. Because the participants viewed the same video, a sweater was arranged to cover the necklace and the woman's hair was arranged to be intermediate between clipped up and let down.

Outcome Measures for Study 1

Participants rated the job applicants in terms of overall personality on a 7-point scale. Twenty-one specific traits were rated including *intelligent, friendly, trustworthy, arrogant, materialistic, cliquish, happy, warm, superficial,* and *vain*. The extent to which applicants were qualified for the job was also rated. *Prejudice* was operationally defined as high scores given on negative personality traits in this procedure.

Results of Study 1

Fein and Spencer predicted that participants who had not been self-affirmed and who thought the job applicant was Jewish would be more negative towards her. The data are presented in Figure 22.1.

The prediction was supported; although there were no significant differences among the personality ratings from the two self-affirmed groups and the non–self-affirmed group who believed the candidate was ethnically Italian, the nonaffirmed people who thought she was Jewish rated her personality significantly more negatively ($p < .05$). As you can see in Figure 22.1, the same pattern was found for evaluation of the candidate's qualifications for the job. The data presented in Figure 22.1 consist of the total ratings given by each participant, averaged with the total ratings for all other participants. Because there were 21 traits rated, it appears that, most typically, participants rated traits around 3 or 4, using the middle of the 7-point rating scale. Ratings of about 3 or 4 on each of 21 traits would result in the kinds of totals found in Figure 22.1. We mention this because as part of your critical thinking, you should always try to discover what is being scaled when interpreting graphic material.

The nonaffirmed participants rated the Jewish woman as significantly less qualified ($p < .001$). The data shown for qualifications consisted of the average of the total ratings given by each participant

FIGURE 22.1   Ratings from Study 1. Affirmed and nonaffirmed participant's ratings of candidate's personality (a) and qualifications (b) for Italian and Jewish applicant conditions.

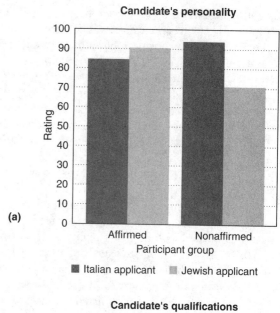

(a)

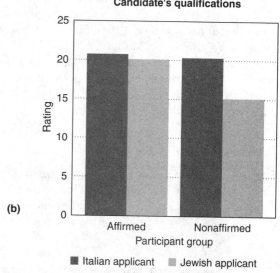

(b)

on each of four statements, using a 7-point scale. An example of one these statements was "I feel this person would make an excellent candidate for the position in question."

STUDY 2

In Study 2, Fein and Spencer asked if posing a threat to self-image would make people more likely to use stereotypes to describe a member of a group. To return to the analogy of a pool or supply of self-worth discussed in Study 1, threatening self-worth ought to lower the supply, forcing people to behave in ways that would rebuild self-worth. In a way, this was the opposite question from that posed in Study 1: this second study set people up to feel negatively about themselves and predicted this would make them more likely to stereotype others. This was expected because, as was shown in Study 1, self-affirmation decreased prejudice. It would make sense, therefore, that a lowered self-affirmation would be associated with more prejudice, demonstrated in this case by increased stereotyping.

Participants and Procedure for Study 2

The participants were 61 male undergraduates from Williams College who were given either extra credit in their introductory psychology course or an opportunity to win money in a lottery. Allowing research participants to take part in a drawing for cash is one way to attract willing participants without having to spend as much money as would be required to pay each one of them a significant sum.

Half of the participants received a bogus intelligence test given on a desktop computer. They were told that this was "a new form of intelligence test that is given on the computer. It measures both verbal and reasoning abilities." They were told it was a valid way to measure intelligence. In fact, the fake test had been constructed so there were no possible correct answers to some questions, and the time limits given were so short that some items could not possibly be done in the time allotted. At the end of the test, the computer gave these participants a fake score for each part of the test. These scores ranged from the 56th percentile down to the 33rd percentile. The percentile rating of a score tells what percent of scores are typically found below the score in question. At best, these students were being told that they were barely in the top half of the population of people who had taken this intelligence test. Williams College is a very selective college, and these scores were disappointing to the experimental group participants, who were accustomed to doing well on other standardized tests, such as the SAT. The other half of the participants, the control group, were given the same test, but were told that it was a fake intelligence test. They were also told they were in the control group of a study and that although they should do the test, they should not work too hard because some of the questions were impossible. They were told not to worry about the phony scores they would receive at the end. In short, they were told the truth about what was going on.

Following the testing experience, both groups were given what was described as a social judgment task. They were told they would be read some information about a man and then would make some judgments about him. The story they were told was of a man, Greg, who was trying to make it as an actor while living in the East Village in New York City. He got a part in a controversial play directed by a young director. He was eager to work with this particular director. The pronouns indicated that the director was a man. After some rehearsals, Greg asked the director if he wanted to get "a drink or something" so they could talk more about Greg's part in the play. There were more details in the story, but this was the substance. The intelligence test procedure had created two groups: those who were told the truth about the test (neutral self-image group) and those who thought the test was real (negative self-image group). These two groups were divided in half. Half of each group received an additional implication about Greg: that he was gay. The other half was led to believe that he was straight. This was accomplished by small changes to the story of Greg. In the *straight-implied condition*, participants were told that Greg had a girlfriend named Anne with whom he had been living for several years. She was mentioned several times in the story. In the *gay-implied condition*, participants were told Greg had "a partner," but no name or gender was specified. With these two variables: *IQ test feedback* and *Greg's implied sexual orientation*, four groups could be constructed:

Neutral test feedback/Gay implied
Neutral test feedback/Straight implied
Negative test feedback/Gay implied
Negative test feedback/Straight implied

Outcome Measures in Study 2

Following the story about Greg, participants were asked to rate Greg's personality on a number of measures using an 11-point scale ranging from 0—*not at all like Greg*, to 11—*extremely like Greg*. Three of the dimensions rated were not considered to be part of a gay stereotype: intelligent, funny, and boring. The stereotype-relevant traits included sensitive, assertive/aggressive, considerate, feminine, strong, creative, and passive. If participants endorsed the gay stereotype they scored Greg high for some of these traits (e.g., sensitive, feminine) and low for others (e.g., assertive/aggressive, strong). This was done on purpose so that participants would pay attention to their ratings and not merely mark all traits high or low, without thinking about them.

Results for Study 2

The results of this study are shown in Figure 22.2. Remember that some individuals had been given a negative self-image through thinking that they had done poorly on a real intelligence test. Others had an experience that had little or no effect, called here *a neutral effect*, on self-image: they had taken a test that they had been told in advance was a fake.

As Fein and Spencer predicted, participants who had experienced an attack to their self-image on the intelligence test were significantly ($p < .001$) more likely to use stereotypically gay descriptions when their information implied that Greg was gay.

PARTICIPANTS AND PROCEDURE FOR STUDY 3

Study 3 combined some procedures of Study 1 and Study 2. Participants were 126 introductory psychology students from University of Michigan who participated as partial fulfillment of a requirement in an introductory psychology course. Seventeen students were excluded because they were Jewish and 7 because they were foreign students, unlikely to be familiar with the stereotype about Jewish American women. Two more were eliminated during participation because they refused to believe the false feedback about their supposed intelligence test.

All participants were given the bogus intelligence test used in Study 2. In this study, however, all participants were told that the intelligence test was real, but half of them were told they had done very well and half were told they had done poorly. Next they were given a scale developed by Heatherton and

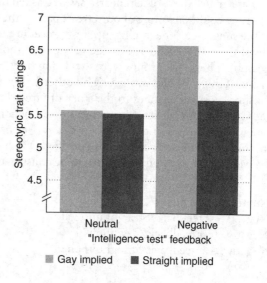

FIGURE 22.2 Findings from Study 2. Amount of stereotypical gay trait ratings of Greg by neutral and negative feedback participants in the gay-implied and straight-implied groups.

Polivy (1991) that measured their self-esteem. *Self-esteem* was operationally defined as the score on this instrument. On this scale, self-esteem scores could fall between 20 and 100. After completion of this scale, they were sent on to what they believed to be a second study in "social evaluation." This second study was the same procedure as in Study 1, requiring evaluation of a supposed job candidate who was either Jewish or Italian. Following this, self-esteem was measured again.

Results of Study 3

The personality ratings that participants gave the supposed job applicant are shown in Figure 22.3. When individuals received negative feedback on their intelligence test performance and the candidate was Jewish, the personality ratings were significantly lower ($p < .01$). Self-esteem was measured twice: after receiving information about their intelligence test scores and after rating the job applicant. After the second measurement, the change in self-esteem was calculated by subtracting the first measurement from the second for each candidate. Figure 22.4 shows the average self-esteem change in each group.

Participants who evaluated the Jewish candidate and who received low scores on the fake intelligence test had a significantly greater increase in self-esteem ($p < .05$). There is a statistically significant difference, but it is not as dramatic as it may appear if you consider the scale on the y-axis of Figure 22.4. In this study, self-esteem could range from 20 to 100, and the maximum change seen here is a bit more than 3 points. In evaluating graphic presentations of data, there is no substitute for being a careful consumer. It is important to look at the graph to discern the overall trends in the data, but it is also important to look carefully at the y-axis. Differences between groups can be made to appear striking if the data range is stretched out or if only part of the whole data range is shown. This is illustrated in Figure 22.5, using the self-esteem data from Figure 22.4 plotted in two different ways.

When part of the range is shown, the graph should indicate this with a "break line" that is either two little hash marks or a little squiggle in the otherwise straight vertical axis. The break line is there to help alert you that part of the data range is missing. In sources other than scientific journals, for example in advertising, the y-axis is often distorted and break lines are missing in a deliberate attempt to mislead.

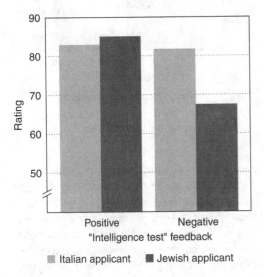

FIGURE 22.3   Results from Study 3. Ratings of candidate's personality from positive and negative feedback participants for Italian and Jewish applicant conditions.

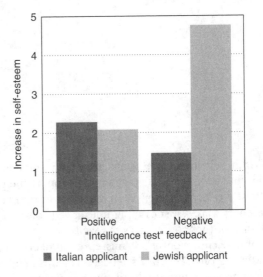

FIGURE 22.4   Increases in Reported Self-Esteem Following Ratings of Italian-Appearing or Jewish-Appearing Applicant for Negative and Positive Feedback Applicants.

FIGURE 22.5 What a Difference a Scale Makes.
The top (a) and bottom (b) graph both show the same data taken from the Fein & Spencer study: the self-esteem levels before and after rating the Jewish applicant. Although the numbers are the same in both graphs, on the *y*-axis of graph (b) a small section of the range was selected and stretched to make the differences appear to be bigger.

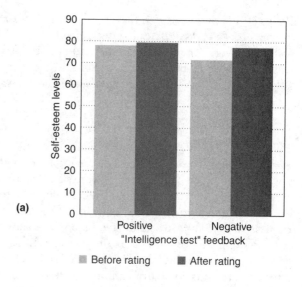

(a)

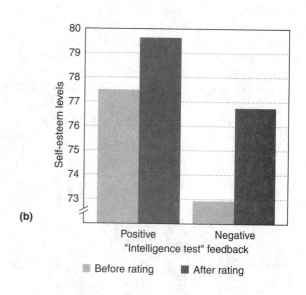

(b)

Within scientific publications, the data presented in graphs are also described in the results, where you can find statistical tests that should support the graphic depictions of data. For example, even though the self-esteem differences in the study were small in absolute terms, the results indicated that the differences were statistically significant. Of course, Fein and Spencer pointed out the small but significant nature of these differences. As we have mentioned before, we would not want you to think that reputable scientists purposely misrepresent data. Exaggeration of data is, however, common practice in the realm beyond reputable science. As a consumer of information, you should protect yourself by paying attention to important details, such as the ways in which data are presented.

DISCUSSION

The results of this study supported the overall hypotheses of Fein and Spencer. Study 1 showed that participants who were self-affirmed were less likely to be prejudiced than those who were in a neutral state. Study 2 showed that participants who had been given negative feedback were more likely to stereotype an individual than those in a neutral state. Study 3 showed that negative self-esteem not only leads to prejudice but that prejudiced ratings, in turn, raised the self-esteem of the raters.

Aside from its important main findings, this study also illustrates the shallowness of stereotyping and other prejudice. Although prejudicial beliefs may be considered by bigots to be great truths and may be deeply held, it is noteworthy that this study showed how little was required in order for prejudice to be invoked resulting in negative ratings of other people. A necklace, hairstyle, and social group activities were enough to decrease ratings of job suitability for Julie. A residence in the East Village, living with a partner, as well as a few other nonspecific descriptors were adequate to make college men apply existing gay stereotypes to Greg. Clearly it does not take anything substantial to unleash the mechanisms of prejudice.

It is important to notice that the prejudice displayed here, particularly following a lowering of self-esteem, was not broadly aimed, shotgun fashion, at anybody and everybody. If that were so, in Study 3 Maria would also have been rated lower in personality and job-suitability by individuals who received negative feedback from the fake intelligence test. The prejudice seen here seems to be turned on in response to an attack to self-esteem, but only when participants thought that the applicant belonged to a group for which there was a preexisting negative stereotype. This research also casts doubt on the view that bigotry is a personality characteristic that is stable over time and across conditions. At least in this study, students were not as likely to act in a biased manner until their own self-esteem was threatened. Are there students who would not act prejudiced even in the face of severe threats to self-esteem? This is a question for future research.

This study is part of a traditional view within social psychology that sees behavior largely as the outcome of a particular context, rather than viewing it as a result of ingrained and stable personality traits as we have seen in other chapters. These two views are not really contradictory, and there is some evidence that both of them operate together. As you have seen in earlier chapters, situations can be powerful determinants of behavior but probably only within the limits set by more stable traits. The cautionary tale is that given a sufficiently powerful setting, many of us might become bigots. An understanding of what is going on here might help to decrease prejudice. We hope most people would feel worse, not better, if they realized that they had disparaged another person only to raise their own feelings of self-worth. It is an empirical question.

REFERENCES

Fein, S., & Spencer, S. J. (1997). Prejudice as self-image maintenance: Affirming the self through derogating others. *Journal of Personality and Social Psychology, 73*, 31–44.

Heatherton, T. F., & Polivy, J. (1991). Development and validation of a scale for measuring state self-esteem. *Journal of Personality and Social Psychology, 60*, 895–910.

Hilton, J. L., & von Hippel, W. H. (1996). Stereotypes. *Annual Review of Psychology, 47*, 237–271.

Miller, N. E., & Bugelski, R. (1948). The influence of frustrations imposed by the in-group on attitude expressed toward the out-group. *Journal of Psychology, 25*, 437–442.

Steel, C. M., Spencer, S. J., & Lynch, M. (1993). Self-image resilience and dissonance: the role of affirmational resources. *Journal of Personality and Social Psychology, 64*, 885–896.

CHAPTER 23

JUST WHAT I EXPECTED, YOU FLIRT![1]

Julianne Krulewitz

---

[1]Incorporating the research of R. D. Ridge, and J. S. Reber (2002).

If you are a fan of musicals, you have probably seen *My Fair Lady*, the tale of an unrefined young woman who is turned into a genteel lady by a proper Englishman. But even if this kind of theatrical performance is not your cup of tea, the plot is one you are likely to be familiar with. This theme has been rehashed countless times in works as diverse as Greek mythology and contemporary reality television. In each depiction, a character undergoes a *self-fulfilling prophecy* in which an expectation leads to action that causes that expectation to come true (Merton, 1948). Take the example of the aforementioned musical. Here, a man sees a flower peddler who he believes has the potential to rise in social class. Encouraged by a wager from an incredulous friend, the man takes this girl under his wing and schools her in the art of etiquette. As a result, she eventually accepts that she does in fact possess the ability to be a fair lady. In time, she fulfills her benefactor's prophecy and, with much musical fanfare, is accepted as a member of high society.

Like the young woman in *My Fair Lady*, we are all greatly influenced by the people we encounter and the events we observe. In fact, our actions are guided by how we focus on, interpret, judge, and remember the people and events that make up our social worlds in a fundamental way. This process in which we think about ourselves and our surrounding environment is referred to as *social cognition*.

SOCIAL COGNITION

In order to understand ourselves as "social thinkers" we must recognize four core processes. Kenrick, Neuberg, and Cialdini (2002) provide a through explanation of these processes. First, we *select information to attend to*. Because, as described in the chapter *Stereotypes: A good thing in the cognitive toolkit*, we are only able to concentrate on a limited portion of our environment as a result of time and energy constraints, the way we choose to divvy up our time and energy is often very different from the way another individual in a similar situation might. As a consequence of the decisions we make at this first step, we each see our worlds from at least a slightly different perspective than others do. For instance, imagine you and a friend attend a musical performance at a local coffeehouse. Think about how differently you and other members of the audience might select information to attend to. You, a psychology major, watch how the musician engages the audience by using nonverbal gestures like making eye contact with individuals. Your friend, majoring in music, pays close attention to the musician's reworking of traditional tunes. The coffeehouse owner, notices neither the musician's facial expressions nor her playing, instead focusing on the high percentage of customers taking advantage of the free coffee refills he offers.

After we have focused our attention, we *attempt to understand the meaning* of the information at hand. Take the example of your visit to the coffeehouse. Is the musician purposely trying to draw spectators in with her gaze or is this a natural process? Is her interpretation of the music paying homage to its originators or a cheap steal? Are the coffee drinkers just being greedy or will they become loyal customers now that they see how nice the owner can be?

How we go on to *make judgments* about this information may depend on our previous experiences with similar situations, our particular goals, the cognitive resources we have available, as well as on a number of other factors. For example, if you just learned about people's unconscious use of nonverbal gesturing in your psychology class, you might think her eye contact was natural. Conversely, if you had learned that some people use nonverbal actions to persuade and manipulate others, you might be more skeptical of the meaning of her body language. Similarly, if your friend loves covers and remixes of old songs, her impression is likely to be very different than if she only likes original music. And imagine how the coffeehouse owner's decision to continue or discontinue the free refill promotion would differ if it had been suggested by his new wife or by the one he had recently divorced!

However, the impressions we form and the decisions we make affect our more general understanding of our social world only if we remember them. If we *store information in our memory*, we will have it as a resource in the future. But how well do you think you, your friend, and the coffeehouse owner would each remember your momentary musings if, as your friend stood up, she dumped her free refill all over you and the owner's newly upholstered chair?

BEHAVIORAL CONFIRMATION

As described in earlier chapters, our decisions are often based on a variety of heuristics (see chapter 10) and are apt to be influenced by the norms of our surrounding community (see chapter 20). One way we conserve mental effort is by thinking back over our own experiences as well as those of others in apparently similar situations to determine a course of action or to predict what someone else's attitudes and behaviors will be. In many cases, this thought process leads us to develop a set of expectancies about the individual we are about to encounter. When it actually comes time to interact with this individual, we are likely to treat him or her in a way that fits with our expectations. In many cases, he or she senses our expectations and behaves accordingly; often coming to the conclusion that his or her action was not only appropriate but also self-generated. When this individual appears to behave how we expect him or her to, our expectations have been confirmed (Darley and Fazio, 1980; Jones, 1986). And when our expectations have actually caused the other individual's behavior, a true self-fulfilling prophecy has occurred (Darley and Fazio, 1980).

Examples of *expectancy* or *behavioral confirmation* have been documented to occur in a number of situations (Rosenthal, 2002). For instance, in one series of early studies, some experimenters were led to believe they would be working with highly intelligent rats and other experimenters were led to believe they would be working with unintelligent ones. Even though the rats were in fact all the same genetically, the rats believed to be intelligent by their experimenters outperformed the rats believed to be unintelligent on a number of tasks (as cited in Rosenthal, 2002).

The difference in the rat's performance was attributed to the way they had been treated; experimenters working with supposedly superior rats described both their attitudes and behaviors towards their rats as being more positive than experimenters who thought they had been assigned the inferior rats. As a consequence of experimenters' beliefs and following actions, rats behaved as anticipated and experimenters' expectancies were confirmed.

Intrigued by the results of these animal experiments, researchers began to wonder if similar examples of behavioral confirmation could be found in humans. In an article for the *American Scientist*, young researcher Robert Rosenthal asked such a question (Rosenthal, 1963). He hypothesized that a teacher's expectations for his or her pupils might influence those students' performance just as the experimenter had influenced his or her rat's. This hypothesis led to the "Pygmalion Experiment[2]," the collaborative effort of Rosenthal and a San Franciscan elementary school principal to determine the effect of teachers' expectations on students' achievement (Rosenthal and Jacobson, 1966).

After receiving all of the necessary approvals, each of the students in Principal Jacobson's school was given a written intelligence test that supposedly predicted intellectual "blooming." Rosenthal and Jacobson then randomly assigned 20% of the students from each of the elementary school's 18 classrooms to the experimental group. Teachers were told that each of these students' test scores indicated that they would show "surprising gains in intellectual competence" over the course of the school year (Rosenthal and Jacobson, 1966). They were not told anything in particular about the remaining students. Because the students had been randomly assigned to either the experimental or control group, any differences between the two groups would necessarily be a result of what their teachers thought they knew about them.

When students were retested eight months later, the experimental group as a whole showed greater gains in intelligence than the control group did. When questioned, teachers described their "bloomers" as being more socially adjusted and more likely to succeed too. In other words, teachers' expectations about their students' intelligence had not only been confirmed, teachers also used this information to make positive generalizations about their students' personalities and behaviors.

Over the years, these concepts have been scrutinized by countless researchers. Behavioral confirmation has been documented as occurring among managers and workers in business (McNatt, 2000), judges and defendants in the courtroom (Halverson, Halahan, Hart, and Rosenthal, 1997), caretakers and residents in nursing homes (Learman, Avorn, Everitt, and Rosenthal, 1990) as well as in a number of other situations. Despite evidence that behavioral confirmation is the result of many interactions, certain personal and situational factors often mitigate the occurrence of this phenomenon. For instance, the motivation behind an interaction and the way in which it is conducted may each affect the degree to which expectancies affect behaviors (Moblio and Snyder, 1996 as cited in Ridge and Reber, 2002; Snyder and Haugen, 1994, 1995).

Research has also determined that as a culture we share sets of beliefs about humans' interactions in many different kinds of situations. These shared beliefs are referred to as *normative expectations* (Ridge and Reber, 2002). We have a basic understanding of who we will meet in different situations, how they will act, and what we should be doing in return. Although there are sure to be exceptions, we know, at least in general, what to expect when entering an office, our home, a party, and so on.

For instance, it is normal to expect that a meeting between a student and a professor will differ from that between two classmates. The student-professor discussion might stick more closely to specific topic and might reference more scholarly works than that between classmates. Differences could also be evident in the way the two individuals sit, the body language they use, and in their facial expressions. Imagine that you are this student and the person you are talking to asks you out on a date. Or asks you why you are not doing better in class. How would your reaction to each question differ depending on if you were talking to your professor or another student? And what if the person said he or she didn't know where his or her life was going? Or asked you where you thought yours was going? Although it is impossible to pinpoint exactly what your answers to these questions would be, it is probably safe to say you might feel and act differently depending on who was doing the asking.

In situations where our initial observations match our expectations, we will probably follow suit. But what will we do if we encounter a person that does something that we do not expect him or

---

[2]According to Greek mythology, Pygmalion was a man who fell in love with an ivory statue of a woman. So moved by his adoration for the statue, Aphrodite, goddess of love and beauty, brought life to his ivory love. Based on this self-fulfilling prophecy, playwright Bernard Shaw's *Pygmalion* was later adapted into the musical *My Fair Lady*.

her to do in that situation? And how will this break from the norm affect our interpretation of potentially behaviorally confirming interactions? This is exactly the question that Ridge and Reber (2002) set out to answer in their study of undergraduates' flirtatious behaviors in job interview situation.

Specifically, Ridge and Reber (2002) wondered how young men would react to seemingly flirtatious young women in a situation where flirtatiousness was both unexpected and inappropriate. Would normative expectations to act professional and courteous guide men's actions or would they instead be influenced by their intrinsic interest in investigating their female partner's intentions? To test this, Ridge and Reber designed an experiment in which some men were led to believe that their partner was attracted to them and other men were not led to this conclusion. Participants were randomly assigned to one of the two conditions and both men and women were unaware of the manipulation.

Ridge and Reber (2002) hypothesized that when the men believed that they were being flirted with, in part because they figured they could always deny their own behaviors if challenged, they would flirt in return. They also predicted that when led to believe that their female partner was attracted to them, men would actually elicit more flirtatious behavior from their partner than when they were not led to believe she had initiated the flirtatiousness. However, because the women were not expecting to be flirted with and the men's flirtatiousness was likely to be subtle, Ridge and Reber did not expect women's impressions of their own and their partner's behaviors to differ between groups. In other words, they expected men who thought their partner was attracted to them to flirt with them just enough to encourage flirtatiousness and thus have their expectations confirmed, but not enough that their partner would be aware of the situation-inappropriate behaviors.

METHOD

Participants

In order to determine if behavioral confirmation is likely to occur in a situation between men and women in a job interview situation, equal numbers of male and female participants were recruited from introductory psychology courses. A majority of the 120 participants were single, Caucasian first-year students. Participants received extra credit for their participation.

Procedures

Participants were told that they would be taking part in a study comparing how students and faculty assess undergraduates who are applying for teaching assistant (TA) positions. To do this, they would be taking part in an interaction with another student where one of them would be the interviewer and the other would be the TA applicant. These interviews would then be compared with those between professors and students to understand any similarities and differences that exist. Participants were told that in addition to receiving extra credit, they might be offered a position as a TA if they performed well during the interaction. The researchers hoped this possibility might motivate participants to perform as they would during an actual interview.

To decrease the likelihood that participant pairs (often referred to as "dyads" in psychological research) knew each other, participants were matched with someone from a different section of introductory psychology. The members of each dyad were scheduled to arrive 10 minutes apart and were sent to different rooms so they would not meet before their interaction. All participants were told that they had been randomly assigned to the opposite sex interview condition and that because real TA interviews are likely to occur over the phone, they would be using a "telephone-like system" (a combination of a microphone and headphones) to communicate with their partner.

Male participants were greeted by a male researcher. Each was told that he had been randomly assigned to be the interviewer and that the other participant would be the TA applicant. They were then told that they and their partners would be asked to provide each other a few facts about themselves since in real interviews it was likely that the interviewer and applicant would know a little about each other. Each male participant was then informed that soon after he and the applicant had exchanged these self-descriptions, the interview would begin. The researchers also let them know that they would be asked to evaluate their own performance as well as that of the applicant after the interview was finished. After receiving these instructions and consenting to participate, the interviewers proceeded to answer the questions about their academic standing and personal interests that made up the biographical information sheet.

Once an interviewer had completed the questions about himself, the researcher took the interviewer's answers and gave him what he was led to believe was the applicant's real biographical sheet in return. However, what the interviewer really received was a bogus set of generic answers that had been created by the researchers in order to eliminate the potentially confounding effects of her real background and interests. The answers that interviewer read were very general and could have fit the profile of most any female college student.

After reading over the applicant's information sheet, interviewers were told that even if interviewers and applicants did not know each other well before an interview; they were likely to have already formed preliminary impressions about the person they would be interacting with. Because this was supposedly one of the things the researcher were interested in studying, interviewers were told to use the information they had learned about the applicant to answer a series of questions about what they thought the applicant would be like. Within this large battery of questions were items that asked the interviewer to preconceive the applicant's professional job skills, her interpersonal style, and how attracted he was towards her in general.

Once these questions had been answered, the researcher returned with what he said was the preinteraction impression questionnaire that the applicant had filled out. Interviewers were told that because previous research had determined that knowing this information was useful to interviewers, they were being provided with the impressions that the applicant had formed about them. After being informed that the applicant was unaware that he would be reading her impressions, interviewers were left to read over them.

In fact, the interviewers were left with one of two preinterview questionnaires that had been written by the researchers as a way of manipulating how attractive the interviewer believed the applicant thought he was. Half of the interviewers were randomly assigned to the attraction condition. These interviewers read that the applicant thought he was, among other things, rather desirable and someone they would like to get to know more personally. The remaining interviewers read that the woman they would be interviewing found them fairly undesirable and had no interest in getting to know them more. After learning whether the applicant was attracted to them or not, interviewers were told to put their headphones on and to prepare for the interview they were about to conduct.

Meanwhile, a female researcher greeted female participants and described the study's procedures to them. This description was the same as the one that the male participants had received with one exception; female participants were all told that they had randomly been assigned to the TA applicant role. After signing a consent form, applicants filled out the biographical information sheet and gave it to the researcher. Because the researchers were not trying to manipulate what the applicant knew about the interviewer, and because they wanted the applicants to realistically react to how their interviewer was treating them, each applicant received her interviewer's real information sheet in return. After the applicant had read over the interviewer's biographical information, the researcher took it back and explained how to use the headphones and microphone.

Once both the interviewer and applicant completed these preinterview tasks, the male researcher turned on the headphones and microphones and prompted the interviewer to begin interviewing the applicant for the hypothetical TA position.

After ten minutes, the interview ended and each researcher returned to his or her participant's room with a postinterview questionnaire. Interviewers were asked how much they tried to adhere to their role as an interviewer, how they thought their applicant had behaved, how they felt about her, and how they thought she felt about them. Items on the questionnaire ranged from questions about her personality (e.g., enthusiastic) to her athleticism (e.g., physically active), to her faith (e.g., devout). Embedded in these questions were items that got at how flirtatious (e.g., sexually warm, intimate) and professional (e.g., competent, responsible) the applicant seemed to be as well as how good the interviewer thought she would be as a TA (e.g., suitability as a teaching assistant). Interviewers were also asked how attracted they were to their applicant and conversely, how attracted they thought she was to them. Participants were asked to respond to each of these questions using a 7-point scale (e.g., where 1 is not at all interested and 7 is very interested, "how romantically interested is the applicant in you now?").

Applicants were asked how hard they had tried to act like TA applicants and how well they though they had done in the interview. To rate their behavior, they were asked the same questions that the interviewer had been asked. They were also asked how well they thought their interviewer had done as well as what they thought about him. Applicants were also asked to report on their general motivations during the interview, perceptions of their own flirtatiousness, and on how attracted they thought their interviewer was to them. Once participants had finished their postinterview questionnaires, their respective researchers returned and asked them about the procedures they had undergone to determine if they were suspicious of any of the deception that had taken place. Finally participants were fully debriefed and excused. See Table 23.1 for an outline of Ridge and Reber's (2002) procedures.

TABLE 23.1   Overview of procedures

OVERVIEW OF PROCEDURES	
Males (Interviewer)	**Female (Applicant)**
Preinterview	*Preinterview*
Fill out biographical information sheet	Fill out biographical information sheet
Receive TA applicant's (bogus) information sheet	Receive interviewer's information sheet
Asked to form an opinion of applicant's job skills, interpersonal style, and his attraction to her.	—
Receive applicant's opinions of him (attraction manipulation)	—
Interview	*Interview*
Postinterview	*Postinterview*
Fill out questionnaire about their behaviors and applicant's behaviors.	Fill out questionnaire about their behaviors and interviewer's behaviors

RESULTS

To understand if behavioral confirmation had occurred, Ridge and Reber (2002) first looked to see if the interviewers and applicants adhered to their roles. All participants appeared to have tried hard to portray the role they had been given. The belief condition (attraction or no-attraction) had no affect on this portrayal. The researchers then investigated whether applicants' preinterview feedback influenced interviewers' perceptions of their applicants' attraction to them. As seen in Figure 23.1, interviewers receiving attraction feedback thought their applicant was significantly more attracted to him than interviewers receiving no-attraction feedback. These analyses are referred to as *manipulation checks*. A manipulation check is a way of looking to see if participants have followed your directions and if your manipulation of the independent variable has worked.

Since their manipulation worked, Ridge and Reber (2002) continued their analyses and investigated whether interviewers who were led to believe that the applicant was attracted to them were in turn more attracted to the applicant than interviewers who were led to believe that the applicant was not attracted to them were. They also looked to see if interviewers in the attraction condition thought they had treated the applicant more flirtatiously and/or more professionally than interviewers in the no-attraction condition.

As expected, interviewers who thought their applicant was attracted to them felt more attraction back and thought they had flirted more with her than interviewers in the no-attraction condition (see Figures 23.2a and 23.2b). Interviewers evidently did not think this attraction affected their professionalism as there was no difference between the two groups on this measure. Even though interviewers thought they were acting more flirtatiously in the attraction condition, applicants did not. Applicants rated interviewers as being equally flirtatious, skilled as an interviewer, and professional across belief conditions.

The information that interviewers had learned about their applicants interest in getting to know them had no effect on how either interviewers or applicants felt the applicant would do as a TA. However, in support of behavioral confirmation theory, interviewers who had been led to believe they were interviewing someone who was attracted to them thought their applicants liked and flirted with them more during the interview than interviewers who thought they were interviewing an indifferent applicant (see Figure 23.3a and 23.3b). Applicants' assessment of their interviewer's behavior, as well as their responses to him, were unaffected by his beliefs.

To answer the question of whether the expectations interviewers had about their applicants actually influenced interviewers' and applicants' behaviors, the researchers had several independent raters listen to recordings of the interviews. To ensure raters' responses would not be influenced by their expectations, they were not told which group the participants they were listening to were in. These raters judged both interviewer and applicant's level of professionalism as being equal across conditions.

FIGURE 23.1   Male participants' perceptions of female participants' attraction to them as a function of feedback

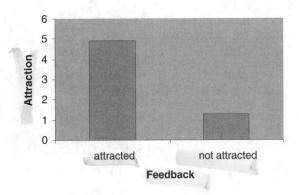

FIGURE 23.2a   Male
participants' perceptions of their
own attraction

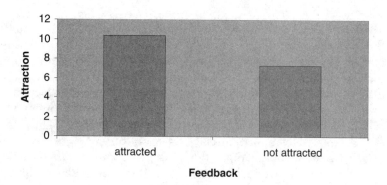

FIGURE 23.2b   Male
participants' perceptions
of their own flirtatiousness

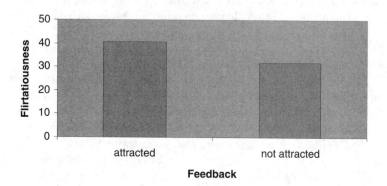

They did not notice any differences in the interviewers' levels of flirtatiousness between the attraction
and no-attraction condition either. They did however perceive a difference between the behaviors of
the applicants in the two groups. As seen in Figure 23.4, raters thought applicants who were interacting
with an interviewer who had been led to believe she found him attractive were behaving more
flirtatiously than applicants whose interviewers did not have this belief. In other words, applicants
were apparently "behaviorally confirming" interviewers' expectations. Additional statistical analyses
supported this claim.

FIGURE 23.3a   Males'
perceptions of females'
attraction to them

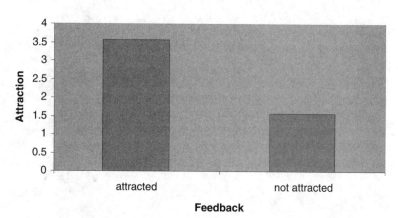

FIGURE 23.3b Males' perceptions of females' flirtatiousness

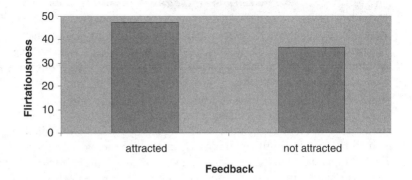

Feedback

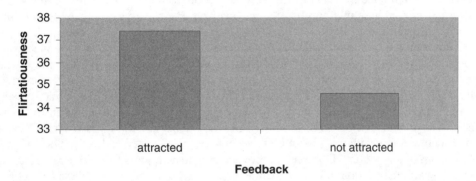

Feedback

FIGURE 23.4 Independent raters' assessment of female participants' flirtatiousness as a function of feedback

DISCUSSION

Ridge and Reber (2002) set out to understand how young men would act when their desire to flirt was at odds with their professional relationship and how women would react to the men's chosen behavior. What they found was a clear example of behavioral confirmation. If a male believed that his female partner was attracted to him, he defied normative expectations and flirted with her, and in turn, elicited flirtatiousness from his partner. Both the men and independent raters observed heightened flirtatiousness in women whose partners had been told they were attracted to them compared to the group in which women's partners had not been given this information. Of particular interest, was how subtle the difference was between the men's treatment of women in the two conditions. Even though the men who believed their partners were attracted to them thought they had treated their partners more flirtatiously than men who believed their partners were not attracted to them, neither the women nor the independent raters picked up on any differences in the men's flirtatiousness. Evidently, the men were able to flirt just enough to make the women return their gestures but not enough to alert them (or the independent raters) that their actions were inappropriate for the job interview situation that they were taking part in.

Because this was a laboratory-based investigation of college students, it is difficult to determine how men and women would act in a real employment situation. There is certainly a chance that these men and women would be less likely to disregard situational norms at the risk of appearing inappropriate in a "real-life" situation than they were in this experiment. For instance, knowing that acting on women's flirtatiousness, even when initiated by her, might have detrimental effects on employment, men taking part in an actual interview might choose to ignore information incongruent with normative expectations for a job interview situation. Knowing that they were only taking part in an experiment, men might have felt more comfortable defying norms. In the same vein, women might not have been as aware of the inappropriateness of men's behaviors as they would have been if being interviewed for a real job. Female participants may have viewed their partners primarily as peers rather than as interviewers. Because mild flirtation between college-aged men and women is often a normative expectation, women might have accepted their partners' behavior without giving it much conscious thought.

However, both the men and women participating in Ridge and Reber's experiment appeared to understand what kind of behaviors are expected, as well as the ones that are prohibited, in job interviews. Participants in both conditions reported trying to adhere to their roles as interviewers and applicants and rated themselves and their partners as being highly professional. The independent raters also described the men and women in both conditions as acting professionally and exhibiting little inappropriate behavior. Therefore, although it's true that men and women might have behaved differently in a real job interview, there is little indication that they were not taking their participation seriously.

Instead, the results of this experiment suggest that men engaged in unprofessional behaviors in order to initiate women's behavioral confirmation even though they knew it might come at a cost to them or their partners. These men might have rationalized that this was not an actual job interview and therefore conforming to real job interview tactics was not necessary, but more realistically they took the actions they did because they believed they would be able to investigate the meaning of the women's behaviors without being caught acting inappropriately. And since neither the women nor the independent raters recognized their flirtatiousness, this assessment would have been correct.

In the present study, the sequence of events that led women to confirm men's expectations was set in motion by information surreptitiously planted by the experimenter. But is there reason to believe that women might start this chain of events themselves? Ridge and Reber (2002) suggest there is. Women, just trying to be friendly, could inadvertently lead men to believe their interest is deeper. They may also use flirtation as a means of ingratiation. Observing these cues, men may respond with similar behaviors, and in doing so, elicit even more flirtatiousness from their female partners. Unfortunately, these seemingly harmless interactions may escalate into unwanted attention and harassment. Although at odds with workplace regulations and normative expectations, the desire to confirm behaviors is evidently so strong in certain situations that individuals are willing to risk the repercussions of appearing inappropriate. Understanding more about the underlying processes that lead to behavioral confirmation will enable researchers to potentially help make important changes in employee education programs and policy decisions.

Ridge and Reber's study provides just a glimpse into the influence that other individuals have on us and that in return, we have on them. As evidenced by their study, expected behaviors are likely to be confirmed, whether we are aware of them or not. Although as "social thinkers" we select, construe, and remember the information that we believe will be most beneficial, this study shows these interpretations may come at some cost to ourselves or others. It is important to remember the ramifications of our behaviors; not everyone wants to be transformed into a fair lady.

REFERENCES

Darley, J. M. & Fazio, R. H. (1980). Expectancy confirmation processes arising in the social interaction sequence. *American Psychologist, 35*, 867–881.

Halverson, A. M., Hallahan, M., Hart, A. J., & Rosenthal, R. (1997). Reducing the biasing effects of judges' nonverbal behavior with simplified jury instruction. *Journal of Applied Psychology, 82*, 590–598.

Jones, E. E. (1986). Interpreting interpersonal behavior: The effects of expectancies. *Science, 234*, 41–46.

Kenrick, D. T., Neuberg, S. L., & Cialdini, R. B. (2002). Social psychology: Unraveling the mystery (2nd ed.). Boston: Allyn & Bacon.

Learman, L. A., Avorn, J., Everitt, D. E., & Rosenthal, R. (1990). Pygmalion in the nursing home: The effects of caregiver expectations on patient outcomes. *Journal of the American Geriatrics Society, 38*, 797–803.

Merton, R. (1948). The self-fulfilling prophecy. *Antioch Review, 8,* 193–210.

McNatt, D. B. (2000). Ancient Pygmalion joins contemporary management: A meta-analysis of the result. *Journal of Applied Psychology, 85,* 314–322.

Ridge, R. D. and Reber, J. S. (2002). "I think she's attracted to me": The effect of men's beliefs on women's behavior in a job interview scenario. *Basic and Applied Social Psychology, 24,* 1–14.

Rosenthal, R. (1963). On the social psychology of the psychological experiment: the experimenter's hypothesis as unintended determinant of experimental results. *American Scientist, 51,* 268–283.

Rosenthal, R. & Jacobson, L. (1966). Teachers' expectancies: Determinants of pupils' IQ gains. *Psychological Reports, 19,* 115–118.

Rosenthal, R. (2002). Covert communication in classrooms, clinics, courtrooms, and cubicles. *American Psychologist, 57,* 838–849.

Snyder, M. & Haugen, J. A. (1994). Why does behavioral confirmation occur? A functional perspective on the role of the perceiver. *Journal of Experimental Social Psychology, 30,* 218–246.

Snyder, M. & Haugen, J. A. (1995). Why does behavioral confirmation occur? A function al perspective on the role of the target. *Personality and Social Psychology Bulletin, 21,* 963–974.

CHAPTER 24

YOU *WILL* DO WHAT YOU'RE TOLD! STUDIES OF OBEDIENCE[1]

Justin M. Joffe

[1]Incorporating the research of S. Milgram (1963, 1974).

In 1963 a young assistant professor at Yale University published an eight-page paper with the unexciting title "Behavioral study of obedience" in the *Journal of Abnormal Psychology* (Milgram, 1963).

This experiment and Milgram's further research on the topic of obedience were to make him the 12th most frequently cited author in introductory psychology textbooks published 35 to 37 years later (1998–2000) and the 46th "most eminent" psychologist of the 20th Century (Haggbloom et al., 2002)[2]. His research has been enormously controversial since the first report appeared, and has been heavily criticized on both methodological and ethical grounds. The ethical controversy that it triggered was probably a major reason why many more constraints are now placed on psychological research than was the case in the middle of the 20th Century—one measure of Milgram's impact is that it would be virtually impossible to obtain clearance from a human subjects' review committee to repeat his research today.

So why all the fuss?

Partly it is because Milgram's data apparently reveal a feature of ourselves that we prefer not to face, a willingness to cause serious harm to others simply because we are instructed to do so. And partly because concerns were raised about the ethical acceptability of deceiving people and causing them considerable stress in order to collect research data.

A brief look at the historical context from which Milgram derived the questions he was posing gives some insight into the reason he and many others considered the work of great relevance and importance.

> Obedience, as a determinant of behavior, is of particular relevance to our time. It has been reliably established that from 1933 to 1945 millions of innocent people were systematically slaughtered on command. Gas chambers were built, death camps were guarded, daily quotas of corpses were produced with the same efficiency as the manufacture of appliances. These inhumane policies may have originated in the mind of a single person, but they could only have been carried out on a massive scale if a very large number of people obeyed orders.
>
> (Milgram, 1974, p. 1)

When Germany surrendered in May 1945, ending World War II in Europe, the world was astonished and horrified by the revelation of the scope and brutality of the systematic extermination of millions

---

[2]The top three, if you are curious, were Skinner, Piaget, and Freud, in that order.

of men, women, and children. People were haunted by the images of the near-dead skeletal figures released from the death camps and of the stacks of naked emaciated corpses not yet incinerated when the Allied forces arrived.

The question that Milgram and many many others found so immensely troubling was, in effect, "How could this have happened in a sophisticated, educated, Christian society whose ethics and values were not dissimilar to our own?" How could people like you and me come to participate in such events? What leads people to obey orders even when the results are horrifying, and contrary to our principles and beliefs? The Nuremberg trials of Nazi leaders for war crimes and crimes against humanity did not help to answer the question. Many of the defendants "explained" their involvement by saying that they had simply been obeying orders.

Most of us would probably respond that we would never collaborate in acts of such horror, but Milgram and others believed that the question required investigation and that simply denying that we might do it would leave us in ignorance—and thus in danger of being unable to prevent it from happening again.

Milgram's research findings, showing that normal Americans—people just like you and me—could indeed be induced to commit acts that they thought were causing considerable pain and distress in an innocent person, were shocking in part because they forced people to take their heads out of the sand. A good deal of the controversy the findings engendered reads like an attempt to avoid the conclusion that we too might just "obey orders," even if the orders were to harm or even kill innocent people.

MILGRAM'S (1963) FIRST EXPERIMENT

Participants

Forty men in the New Haven area were recruited to participate in a "study of memory" by way of a newspaper ad and direct mail; they ranged in age from 20–50, were from a variety of occupations (not including students), and were paid a modest amount for participating. They were explicitly told that the payment was "simply for coming to the laboratory, and that the money was theirs no matter what happened after they arrived" (p. 372).

Procedures

On arrival at the lab, they were met by an "experimenter" (a confederate of Milgram's) and another man who appeared to be another participant but was in fact a second confederate. After the experimenter told them they were there to participate in an experiment on the effects of punishment on learning, they drew lots to determine which of the two would be the "learner" and which the "teacher." Both slips of paper had the word teacher on them, but the real participant had no idea that his role as teacher was due to anything but chance.

The "learner" was then taken to a room and strapped into a chair, with the experimenter claiming that this was to reduce excessive movement when he was given the electric shocks that would be used to punish him when he gave incorrect answers in the "learning experiment." Electrode paste was applied to the learner's wrist (and both teacher and learner told that this was "to avoid blisters and burns").

The teacher was located in another room and asked the learner questions over an intercom. The teacher's job was to read a list of word pairs (e.g., blue-sky, wild-duck, etc.) to the learner and then test recall by saying the first word in each pair and giving the learner four choices; this is called paired associate learning. When all 10 pairs had been tested the list would be repeated, until the learner got all 10 pairs right; each time the learner gave an incorrect answer the teacher gave him an electric shock. The learner responded to each multiple-choice question by pressing one of four switches in front of him, and this action lit a bulb on a panel in front of the teacher.

The shock generator was a key component in the deception practiced on the teacher. It had a horizontal panel of 30 switches labeled in 15 volt increments from 15 volts to 450 volts and each set of four had a verbal label as well; the verbal labels were "Slight Shock" (levels 15–60 volts), "Moderate Shock" (75–120), "Strong Shock" (135–180), "Very Strong Shock" (195–240), "Intense Shock" (255–300), "Extreme Intensity Shock" (315–360), and "Danger: Severe Shock" (375–420). The 435 and 450-volt switches were under a label that simply said "XXX." When a switch was thrown a red pilot light above it came on, the needle on the voltage meter would swing, etc.

To add further realism, before the start of the learning trials the teacher was given a sample shock (a real one), set at the 45-volt level.

The teacher was told to give the learner an electric shock as punishment if the learner answered incorrectly—and he was instructed to "move one level higher . . . each time the learner flashes a wrong answer." The major deception, of course, is that the learner never receives any shocks, but the teacher (the only true participant of three men involved in the drama) thinks he is administering shock, and the situation is manipulated to make him believe that the shocks he is administering reach an extremely painful level and might even be fatal.

When the shock level reached 300 volts, the teacher heard the learner (in the adjoining room) pound on the wall. After this, the learner stopped responding to questions entirely. If the teacher asked the experimenter what he should do, he was told that the absence of an answer within 5 to 10 seconds of asking a question should be treated as a wrong answer and shock administered. The wall pounding was repeated after the 315-volt shock, and then nothing further was heard.

Most participants found the process extremely stressful and unpleasant and many questioned the experimenter about continuing. Whenever this occurred the experimenter responded with "commands" to continue, in a graduated sequence of verbal prods:

1.   "Please continue" or "Please go on;"

2.   "The experiment requires that you continue;"

3.   "It is absolutely essential that you continue;"

4.   "You have no other choice, you must go on." (Milgram, 1963, p. 374)

The experimenter would use statement 2 only if the teacher continued to balk after statement 1, statement 3 only if statement 2 did not work, and so on. If a teacher expressed concern about causing injury they were told that there would be no permanent tissue damage, and if they said the learner did not want to go on were told to please go on until the learner had learned all the word pairs.

After the teacher had administered the 450-volt shock—the operational definition of obedience: administering the maximum shock possible—or refused to continue, he was debriefed. He was told the truth about the experiment and efforts were made to insure that the teacher did not continue to feel stressed by having him meet the obviously unharmed learner. Teachers were questioned also about whether they were convinced of the reality of the experiment and how painful they thought the shocks were.

Results

And how many were "obedient"? People who were asked to guess the answer to this question before the research became famous guessed that very few participants would administer the 450-volt shock. When Milgram described the situation in detail to 110 people (psychiatrists, college students, and middle-class adults), not one of them thought they themselves would administer a 450-volt shock and only four thought they would go as high as 300 volts. When various groups of people, including psychiatrists, were asked how *other people* would respond, they predicted that most people would not go beyond 150 volts, only about 4 percent would go as high as 300 volts, and only about one in a thousand would go all the way up to 450 volts.

Well, is that what happened? Regrettably, no! Not a single participant refused to increase the shock level every time the learner gave the wrong answer until the learner pounded on the wall (at 300 volts, the highest of the "intense shock" settings). At this point five of the 40 stopped, despite the experimenter's urgings to go on. Four more quit at 315 volts (more wall pounding), a few more later (at levels when there was no response at all from the learner), but 26 participants—65 percent, or nearly two of every three—went past the "Extreme Intensity Shock" levels, past the "Danger: Severe Shock" settings, past the first "XXX" (435 volts) label, and all the way to the second "XXX" (450 volts) label.

Conclusions

On the basis of these results and others (which we will look at soon), Milgram (1974, p. 123) concluded:

> . . . we have witnessed a level of obedience to authority that is disturbing. With numbing regularity good people were seen to knuckle under to the demands of authority and perform actions that were callous and severe. Men who are in everyday life responsible and decent were seduced by the trappings of authority, by the control of their perceptions, and by the uncritical acceptance of the experimenter's definition of the situation into performing harsh acts. . . . Submission to authority is a powerful and prepotent condition in man.

Are these conclusions reasonable? What questions might you have about Milgram's research that might cast doubt on his conclusions?

Before you continue reading, jot down some alternative possibilities that might explain the results. Then we will look at some of the additional experiments Milgram carried out and see if they address your questions and concerns and leave you more (or less) convinced that he is right.

Alternatives

A variety of reasons have been advanced to explain why so many people in Milgram's first experiment obeyed orders. Suggestions about the reasons for obedience were addressed in a series of 17 additional experiments, involving an additional 580 participants (Milgram, 1974). These experiments address a range of questions about what accounts for the high level of obedience seen in the first experiment, each in turn posing a question about a variable that might influence obedience. We will look at four possibilities in detail:

- Participants believed that the learner not really being hurt (or they wouldn't have obeyed)
- Participants were not like the rest of us ("normal" people wouldn't do what they did)
- Obedience was due to the prestige of Yale (and thus would not occur in "real life")
- The learner had agreed to be shocked—thus he was obliged to go on (otherwise participants would not have gone to high shock levels)

Did the participants not really believe that the learner was being hurt?

Data collected in the first experiment itself is relevant here. In the first place, participants demonstrated considerable agitation and the signs of stress are incompatible with their believing the shock was not real. A substantial majority of participants rated themselves as moderately or extremely tense and nervous at the end of the experiment. Participants rated the level of pain they believed the learner experienced at 12.4 on a scale where 14 was the maximum; only two (of 40) did not think the learner was receiving painful shocks. When participants in the first experiment and several others were sent a questionnaire a year after the experiment, 56 percent indicated that they fully believed that the learner was receiving painful shocks, 24 percent that he probably was. Only one was certain that the learner was not getting shocks.

And when participants heard reactions of the learner, expressions of pain and distress, it had little effect on their willingness to administer ever-increasing levels of shock. The procedures in this second experiment are summarized in Table 24.1.

TABLE 24.1   Protocol in Experiment 24.2 (Milgram, 1974)

SHOCK LEVEL (VOLTS)	"LEARNER'S" RESPONSE
75, 90, 105	Grunt
120	Shout: "Shocks are becoming painful"
135	Painful groans
150	"Experimenter, get me out of here. I won't be in the experiment any more. I refuse to go on"
165–255	Similar to 150 volts, with increasing intensity and, at 180 volts, "I can't stand the pain"
270	Agonized scream
300	Says he won't give answers
315	Violent scream; refusal to continue; no answer
330–450	No answer; silence

The results of both experiments are summarized in Table 24.2. You can see that the addition of clear indications of pain and distress made no difference to participants' willingness to shock learners. (Table 24.2 also shows the percentage of participants who were obedient in a similar study by Meuss and Raaijmakers [1986]. This will be described later).

TABLE 24.2   Learner Not Being Hurt

MILIGRAM STUDY	CONDITIONS	PERCENT OBEDIENT	
		Milgram	Meuss & Raaijmakers
1	"Baseline"[1]	65	83–92
2	Voice Feedback (see Table 24.1)	63	--

1. Experimenter present, orders participant to continue when necessary; learner in another room providing limited auditory feedback

Were the participants unrepresentative of the general population? Were they unusually aggressive?

In other words, were they in some way unlike us, weird in some way—perhaps highly aggressive—that would account for so many of them obeying orders to hurt an innocent person? After all, the participants were volunteers rather than a random selection of people from the general population.

We get some answers to these questions in Experiment 11, and to some extent in Experiment 8.

Until Experiment 11 was conducted, there had been no clear demonstration that the instructions to continue increasing the level of shock are responsible for the compliance observed. Perhaps participants would have been happy to inflict pain and simply needed permission to do so. Milgram tested this possibility: he told participants that they were *free to select any shock level they wished* when the learner made an error; the experimenter stressed the point that they could use the highest level available if they chose. The learner's protests were geared to shock levels, as before (Table 24.1).

In these circumstances, only one participant (of 40) administered a 450-volt shock (see Table 24.3). All but two went no higher than 150 volts, 23 no higher than 60 volts (a level at which no grunts or other feedback from the leaner had been heard). As Milgram (1974) notes, "It is not enough to say that the situation provided a setting in which it was acceptable for the subject to hurt another person. . . . Whatever leads to shocking the victim at the highest level cannot be explained by autonomously generated aggression but needs to be explained by the transformation of behavior that comes about through obedience to orders" (p. 72).

TABLE 24.3   Participants Not Representative

MILIGRAM STUDY	CONDITIONS	PERCENT OBEDIENT	
		Milgram	Meuss & Raaijmakers
11	Teacher chooses shock level	3	0
8	Women participants ("teachers")	65	--

Well, perhaps men in Connecticut are different from people in general. One thing we could ask is, are women different? Would they be less likely than men to harm someone else?

Social stereotypes, criminal records, and research indicate that women behave less aggressively than men. Would this make them more resistant to harming an innocent victim? When the question was put to the test (Experiment 8) the results indicated that obedience has more to do with the situation than with personal characteristics, and exactly the same proportion of women as men went up to the maximum voltage shock (Table 24.3). Other research has indicated that women are more likely to be compliant than men, and this may offset their lower levels of aggression.

Furthermore, when Milgram's experiment was carried out in five other places (Princeton, Munich, Rome, South Africa, and Australia), participants demonstrated even higher levels of obedience than Milgram found in Connecticut.

Is obedience all due to the prestige of the institution where the research was done?

In other words, do participants perhaps feel that a prestigious and highly respected institution would not allow something unethical to take place under its auspices? Milgram looked at this issue in two experiments: in one the research still took place at Yale but in much less sumptuous surroundings, in the other there was no connection at all with Yale.

Experiment 5 was carried out in far more modest surroundings, the basement of the building where earlier experiments had been done in an "elegant" laboratory. And perhaps more importantly, the learner mentioned in advance that he had some concerns that the shocks might be dangerous because he had been diagnosed as having a "slight" heart condition. The learner's responses were similar to those shown in Table 24.1, and, in addition, at 150 volts, he started protesting that his heart was bothering him, something he continued to do at various higher shock levels, often accompanied by "agonized screams" and hysterical shouting to be let out.

As you can see in Table 24.4, neither change reduced obedience, with 26 of 40 participants administering the maximum shock, exactly the same number as in Experiment 1.

TABLE 24.4   Obedience Due to Yale's Prestige

MILIGRAM STUDY	CONDITIONS	PERCENT OBEDIENT
5	More modest premises and learner concerned about heart condition	65
10	Research in downtown office building, not at Yale	48

So to what degree do participants obey because the research is taking place in a prestigious institution, a place with considerable authority and the kind of place in which people do not really subject innocent people to serious harm?

Experiment 10 looked at this question directly: it was run as before, but in a sparsely furnished suite in a somewhat rundown office building in Bridgeport CT, under the auspices of a fictitious organization ("Research Associates of Bridgeport") with no prestigious associations or institutional authority.

Was it the prestige of Yale that accounted for the high levels of obedience in earlier studies? Apparently not, 48 percent of participants obeyed (compared to 65 percent in the corresponding experiment at Yale; see Table 24.4). As Milgram (1974) notes, although some sort of institutional structure may be needed, compliance does not much depend on the distinction of the institution.

Do participants see the learner as willing to be shocked?

Perhaps this seems to be an unlikely explanation for participants continuing to increase shock levels when the learner is screaming in pain and demanding to be let out, but the suggestion has been made that the learner is seen to have entered into an implicit contract to be shocked as much as the experimenter requires: he has volunteered to participate, is getting paid, his getting the shocks rather than giving them appears to be a matter of luck. He may be seen as having surrendered the right to ask for the experiment to be terminated and to renege.

Two experiments suggest this is not the case. In one (Experiment 9) Milgram examined the question by asking if there would be less obedience if the learner were to be seen *not* to relinquish his rights. This time, before agreeing to participate, the learner said that because of his heart condition, he could only agree to participate if the experimenter agreed to let him out when he says so. In other words, his "contract" now is to participate only until he chooses to stop.

The participant is, as usual, urged to continue shocking the learner even when the learner protests that he has had enough. Now the experimenter's instructions violate not only the participants' beliefs but also the contract they have heard negotiated. The result is some decrease in obedience, but not much: In Table 24.5 you can see that 40 percent were obedient, compared to 50 percent in the comparable experiment without the advance agreement (Experiment 6).

TABLE 24.5   **Learner Agreed To Be Shocked**

MILIGRAM STUDY	CONDITIONS	PERCENT OBEDIENT
9	Learner specifies ahead of time that he must be allowed to quit	40
12	Learner demands higher shock levels, experimenter prohibits them	0

Experiment 12 looked at the issue in a different and clever way, asking whether or not the participant would obey the learner if the learner *wanted* to be shocked.

In this experiment, the learner indicated the usual discomfort, but when the experimenter called a halt to proceedings after the 150-volt shock had been given (due, he said, to the learner's heart condition and his "unusually severe" reaction to shock) the learner demanded that they go on. The reason the learner gave was that a friend of his had gone all the way and it would be "an affront to his manliness" not to do the same. Despite this argument and repeated demands that the teacher continue, not one participant continued; they all terminated shocks at that point (see Table 24.5). Clearly the obedience is to the authority figure, the experimenter, not to the wishes of the learner whether these are for the participant to stop (as in the earlier experiments) or to continue (as in Experiment 12).

CAN WE DECREASE OBEDIENCE?

The experiments described thus far do not really demonstrate a decrease in obedience. Where we see decreases in numbers of participants administering the 450-volt shock we are usually seeing obedience to different orders (as when the experimenter himself demands that the teacher stop).

Milgram also identified circumstances in which participants were likely to be less obedient, including ones where the closeness to the victim was increased and where other participants (once again, confederates) disobeyed the experimenter.

Pilot studies carried out prior to Experiment 1 had shown that with no feedback at all from the learner all participants raised the shock level to 450 volts, and the number dropped from 100 percent only when participants had feedback from the learner indicating he was distressed. Milgram postulated that increasing the degree to which participants were aware of (close to) the participant might decrease their willingness to inflict pain, and he varied the degree of closeness.

Milgram varied proximity along a continuum from very distant in Experiment 18 (participant and learner in separate rooms, someone other than the participant administers the shocks), to physically fairly distant in Experiment 1 (participant and learner in separate rooms, little heard from learner) to increasing closeness in Experiment 3 (participant and learner in the same room, considerable protesting done), to very close (participant has to touch the learner) in Experiment 4.

The effects of these variations are shown in Table 24.6, and the results support the notion that increasing proximity decreases obedience.

Many participants in these studies administered the highest level of shock even though they found it very stressful and repugnant to them to do so. Milgram investigated the question of whether seeing other people defy the experimenter would make it easier for the participant to rebel too.

In Experiment 17 there were three teachers, one of whom read the word pairs, another who told the learner whether the answer was right or wrong and the third (the participant) who gave the shocks.

TABLE 24.6   How to Decrease Obedience

MILIGRAM STUDY	CONDITIONS	PERCENT OBEDIENT	
		Milgram	Meuss & Raaijmakers
18	Confederate teacher administers shock to learner in different room; participant data	93[1]	
1, 2, 5	Learner in different room (with or without voice feedback)	63–65	83–92
3	Teacher and learner in same room	40	
4	Teacher has to force learner's hand onto shock plate	30	
7	Experimenter leaves lab and gives orders by telephone	21	36
17	Three "teachers." Two (confederates) refuse to go on	10	16

1 Percentage of participants who did not interfere with man administering the maximum shock

When the learner protested at 150 volts, teacher 1 refused to continue despite the experimenter's insistence, and moved to a chair away from the shock generator. The experimenter told the participant to read the word pairs (in addition to continuing to give shocks). At 210 volts, teacher 2 refused to continue despite the experimenter's insistence, and also moved to a chair in another part of the room, leaving the participant doing his tasks as well.

A majority of participants (25 of 40) refused to continue at or before the withdrawal of the second teacher (210 volts), and only four continued to administer shocks up to 450 volts (Table 24.6). Milgram believed that a number of factors were operating to produce this much lower level of obedience, including the following:

- Seeing others disobey reassures participants that their refusal is not bizarre;
- Continuing giving shocks in the presence of those who have refused to continue may make them feel that their behavior is disapproved of;
- Seeing the experimenter unable to make two other people obey him may undermine the perceived power of the experimenter.

WOULD PEOPLE DO THE SAME IN "REAL LIFE"?

This is a question we frequently ask of findings from laboratory research, done in circumstances that often strike us as somewhat artificial. Even if we are satisfied that the internal validity is satisfactory, we should still ask questions about external validity—that is, to what extent the findings reflect what might happen in the world outside the laboratory.

The role of authority

Four studies that identify where authority stems from offer insights into applicability of the findings outside the laboratory.

In Experiments 1–12, orders were given by an authority figure, the "experimenter" in the lab coat. What happens if the orders are given by someone with less authority?

In Experiment 13, the question was addressed by having a second confederate: now three people arrive at the lab and in a rigged drawing one confederate is assigned to be the learner (as before), the second to record times, and the real participant to read the word pairs and administer shocks. The other procedures are as before, except that the experimenter does not say anything about what shock levels should be administered. The experimenter is then called away by a phony phone call, and tells them to continue the research in his absence.

After he is gone, the confederate doing the timing says he has a good idea—they should increase the shock level each time the learner makes an error. The results indicate that a person without full authority is far less likely to be obeyed (see Table 24.7).

TABLE 24.7   Role of Authority

MILIGRAM STUDY	CONDITIONS	PERCENT OBEDIENT
13	Experimenter leaves and "ordinary man" gives orders[1]	20
14	Experimenter is learner, ordinary man is experimenter	0
16	Experimenter is learner, second experimenter gives orders	65
15	Two experimenters: one says "go on," the other "no"	0

1 Increasing shock seems to be his idea

In Experiment 14, the authority figure (the experimenter) became the learner; the ruse was to have the learner claim that he is afraid of shocks and will only agree to participate if he sees someone else go through the whole process first. The experimenter says they need as many volunteers as they can get and agrees to be the learner first. The real participant once again is the teacher, the second confederate does the experimenter's job, and everything else is as before.

As Table 24.7 indicates, none of the participants administered a 450-volt shock. In fact, they all stopped at 150 volts, the first time the "learner" refuses to go on. It appears that the "real" experimenter retains his authority in the face of instructions from the stand-in experimenter, and is obeyed absolutely when he says he wants to quit. Interestingly, when the participants were asked what they would do if someone other than the experimenter were being shocked, they all "denied vehemently" that they would continue after the learner asked them to stop.

Experiment 16 posed the question of what it is that gives "authority:" is it the title ("experimenter") alone or is it the actual position occupied. Milgram sees this question as analogous to a situation where "a king may possess enormous authority while on his throne, yet not be able to command when cast into prison" (1974, p. 108).

In this experiment there are two experimenters and the ruse takes the form of a phony phone call indicating that the fourth participant is unable to get there, and so one of the two experimenters (picked by a coin toss) draws lots to determine whether he or the genuine participant will be the teacher; as usual, the participant gets to be teacher, leaving the experimenter to be the learner. The remaining scenario is as before, with protests as shown in Table 24.1.

We now have a situation in which one experimenter urges the participant to continue, while the second experimenter demands that he stop—but the demands that he stop are made by the experimenter playing the learner's role. 65 percent of participants go all the way to 450 volts, the same percentage as in experiments where the learner is just an "ordinary" man. Milgram's interpretation is that undertaking the role of the learner temporarily lowers the second experimenter's level of authority relative to the experimenter who remains in his original role; the experimenter in the learner's role is "the king in the dungeon".

These data are in striking contrast to the results of Experiment 15. Here there were also two experimenters, taking turns to give instructions, but with both acting as experimenters throughout. When the participant wants to stop shocking the learner, one urges him to continue (as in earlier experiments) while the other tells him to stop. Not a single participant went above 165 volts, and 18 of 20 stopped at 150 volts, in striking contrast to the 65 percent who went to the maximum shock level in Experiment 16.

When orders come from an ordinary man they are disobeyed (Experiments 13 and 14), when two experimenters of apparently equal authority contradict each other (Experiment 15) actions stop (no shocks are given), but when there are cues as to who has more authority, they obey the person of higher rank (Experiment 16).

"These studies [and Experiment 12, in which the learner's demands to be shocked are ignored] confirm an essential fact: the decisive factor is the response to authority, rather than the response to the particular order to administer shocks. Orders originating outside authority lose all force" (Milgram, 1974, p. 104).

And in the "real world"?

These findings are helpful, but Milgram's research provides no direct empirical answer to the question of whether people would do the same thing in "real life," so we need to address it in other ways. One would be to point to the bloodcurdling list of atrocities, torture, and violence inflicted by people (usually men) on their fellows throughout history including, on an even wider scale, the last century. People of many nations have "obeyed orders," with horrifying consequences.

Another approach to the question is to ask, is the laboratory all that different in essential features from "real life"? Milgram (1974) argues that the essential features of the laboratory situation are the same as those in Nazi Germany, at My Lai, at Andersonville—they all have in common the central psychological process: a "situation in which a man is told by a legitimate authority to act against a third individual" (p. 177). There are, of course, important differences too, but a case could be made that obedience is *more* likely to occur in real life, since there are often implicit of explicit threats of dire consequences for failure to obey; in Milgram's experiments there was no suggestion of personal consequences for refusing to continue.

The "experiment," like the military, the organization we work for, and many other institutions in our society, is an entity that defines roles (including indicating who has authority over whom) and thus responsibility for what occurs, implies rules. The rule may be something like "I've entered into an agreement or contract—and thus have an obligation—to do as I'm told." And the situation controls rewards and punishments ("I'm rewarded for doing well what I agreed to do, punished for rocking the boat").

And a third set of information on external validity comes from other research on obedience, research done in a laboratory once again, but using procedures very different from Milgram's. Meeus and Raaijmakers (1986, 1995) did a number of studies in Utrecht (Holland) that parallel many of Milgram's conceptually but where the harm inflicted on the victim and the entire set-up was very different.

Meuss and Raaijmakers believed there were two aspects of Milgram's situation that could be improved upon to make the procedure more realistic: first, they wished to avoid the ambiguity inherent in the process whereby learner is screaming in pain while a responsible authority figure is unperturbed and somewhat reassuring ("the shocks will cause no tissue damage"); although they rejected the view that participants did not believe that the learner was being shocked (see data on this issue presented earlier), they believed they could improve on the credibility (and hence the ecological validity) of the experimental situation.

Second, the method of harming the victim—giving electric shocks—was very far from anything most people do in everyday life. Modern violence, they argue, is more often what they call "mediated;" that is, it is violence where the relationship with the victim is less direct, where we cause harm at second-hand, rather than directly.

Therefore they set up a very different situation to investigate obedience. Participants were recruited to administer a 32-item multiple-choice test to people they believed were job candidates. They were told that that the applicant would not get the job if he failed the test. They were also told that without the applicant's knowledge the psychology department wanted to study the effects of stress on test performance, so the participants administering the test were to make negative remarks about performance, causing the applicant to believe he was at risk of failing the test and thus causing him considerable stress.

The participants were told that ability to perform well under stress had no relevance to the job, but was simply to assist the experimenter gather data for an unrelated research project. The participant saw and heard the experimenter tell the job applicant that his stress levels would be measured using skin electrodes, but not that he would be subjected to negative remarks to increase stress; he also heard the experimenter reassure the job applicant that his chances of success would not be affected by the stress experiment, whereas the participant was told that it would. The participants were made aware that the applicant was under considerable stress by viewing feigned indications of the level of tension indicated, allegedly, by the electrodes.

The negative remarks, like Milgram's shocks, progressively increased in severity, as did the applicant's protests: remarks proceeded along a 15-point continuum from (1) "Your answer to question 9 was wrong," through (8) "If you continue like this, you will fail the test," to (15) "According to the test, it would be better for you to apply for lower functions" (Meuss and Raaijmakers, 1986, p. 323). Protests ranged from mild ("But surely my answer wasn't wrong?") to nervous, to angry, including demands that the tester stop making remarks.

The parallels to Milgram are clear, and Meuss and Raaijmakers conducted a series of studies, some of which replicate Milgram's, but using a very different experimental situation and method of inflicting harm. The results of these parallel experiments are shown in Tables 2, 3, and 6[3]. In all cases the levels of obedience with this "mediated violence" are the same as, or higher than, levels found with Milgram's more direct violence. The similarity of the findings in this conceptual replication of Milgram's research lends weight to arguments that the processes captured in the laboratory may be very similar to those that occur in the outside world, and that Milgram's (1974, p. 189) pessimistic conclusion is correct:

---

[3]Meuss and Raaimakers conducted a variety of additional experiments that do not parallel Milgram's and thus are not represented in the Table, including studies of Personnel Officers (who should have a professional ethical commitment to testing job applicants fairly—(93 percent obeyed) and of situations where participants were told they would be legally liable for the consequences of their actions (obedience decreased).

The results . . . raise the possibility that . . . the kind of character produced in American democratic society, cannot be counted on to insulate its citizens from brutality and inhumane treatment at the direction of malevolent authority. A substantial proportion of people do what they are told to do, irrespective of the content of the act and without limitations of conscience, so long as they perceive that the command comes from a legitimate authority."

REFERENCES

Haggbloom, S. J., R. Warnick, J. E. Warnick, V. K. Jones, G. L. Yarbrough, T. M. Russell, C. M. Borecky, R. McGahhey. J. L. Powell, III, J. Beavers, & E. Monte (2002). The 100 most eminent psychologists of the Twentieth Century. *Review of General Psychology, 6,* 139–152.

Meeus, W. H. J. & Q. A. W. Raaijmakers (1986). Administrative obedience: Carrying out orders to use psychological-administrative violence. *European Journal of Social Psychology, 16,* 311–324.

Meeus, W. H. J. and Q. A. W. Raaijmakers (1995). Obedience in modern society: The Utrecht studies. *Journal of Social Issues, 51,* 155–175.

Milgram, S. (1963). Behavioral study of obedience. *Journal of Abnormal and Social Psychology, 67,* 371–378.

Milgram, S. (1974). *Obedience to authority: An experimental view.* New York, NY: Harper & Row.

SECTION VI

ABNORMAL BEHAVIOR AND THERAPY

CHAPTER 25

INTRODUCTION

Material selected from:
Abnormal Psychology: Integrating Perspectives,
by Wilson, Nathan, O'Leary, & Clark
Mastering the World of Psychology,
by Wood, Wood, & Boyd

PERSPECTIVES ON ABNORMAL BEHAVIOR

The young woman called at dinnertime. After giving her name, she said she was calling people in Saint Louis and asking them to participate in a national survey on mental health and mental illness, sponsored by the National Institute of Mental Health (NIMH), an agency of the federal government. Elizabeth H. had been randomly selected to participate in a face-to-face interview. The young woman went on to explain that the federal government wanted to get a clear picture of the mental health needs of healthy, functioning people in order to decide whether the nation's mental health dollars were being spent as efficiently as possible.

Although she was a little apprehensive about talking about such personal things with a stranger, Elizabeth decided it was in the country's best interest to know more about mental health and mental illness. And besides, her family would clearly come across as being normal. As far as she knew, no one in the family had ever gone to a psychiatrist or to a mental hospital.

Sure, over the years, her husband had been drinking heavily, and he'd occasionally been abusive to her and the children. And Elizabeth still had her "spells" every once in a while, when she couldn't get out of bed and didn't have the energy to go to work or care for her children as well as she usually did. All these problems seemed to be getting better, though. So Elizabeth told the young woman she'd see her, and they set up an appointment for the following Friday, after work.

Throughout history, we've been fascinated by the abnormal behavior of others and preoccupied with signs of abnormality in ourselves. So it's not surprising that today, many of us are interested in studying the subject, as undergraduate students of abnormal behavior or as graduate or professional students of clinical psychology, psychiatry, psychiatric nursing, or social work. Our fascination with this subject also plays a role in the design of surveys like the NIMH study in which Elizabeth H. was asked to participate. (We'll review some of the NIMH findings and Elizabeth's role in the study later in the chapter.)

This chapter puts the subject *abnormal behavior* into proper perspective. We'll look at the many ways in which abnormality has been defined and review findings from recent epidemiologic surveys, including the NIMH study that Elizabeth participated in. You may be surprised to find that mental health problems are even more prevalent and impactful than you had imagined. The next section is an overview of the history of efforts to understand, describe, and treat mental disorders.

WHY STUDY ABNORMAL BEHAVIOR?

Human beings have always noticed abnormality and wanted to understand it better. The ancient Greeks developed elaborate scientific theories to explain abnormality, and the ancient Romans and Chinese tried to treat it. During the Inquisition, people who were insane were tortured and scorned because they presumably conversed with the devil. Shakespeare wrote plays in the seventeenth century in which characters exhibit mental disorders recognizable to us today. In the nineteenth century, composers of operas wrote scenes in which their heroines were insane—screaming and sobbing hysterically—which allowed these performers to show off their voices. And in this century, television programs and movies regularly portray such disorders as multiple personality, paranoia, autism, schizophrenia, and depression. Abnormal behavior is so commonly discussed now that the technical language of psychology has become pervasive in everyday speech. We might say, "He's a sadist" or "She's neurotic," knowingly using terms such as *narcissistic, paranoid, compulsive,* and *phobic*.

We've all asked ourselves, usually during periods of stress, whether we're going to "lose it" or "go off the deep end." And who hasn't wondered whether an aunt, a cousin, or even a rock star is abnormal, eccentric, or just plain weird? The normal strains of life inevitably create situations that cause us pain and anxiety. Despite the turmoil we may be in, though, our bouts with depression, anxiety, and fear usually play out and then disappear, without leaving significant effects or meriting formal diagnoses. Even when we decide to seek help during particularly troublesome periods—for instance, when we end important relationships, have difficulties with our parents or friends, or make tough vocational choices—we're often surprised later to realize that living through the distress was a necessary step toward greater self-understanding and maturity.

Perhaps you've witnessed firsthand the impact of mental disorder on a close friend or relative. Alcoholism and drug abuse, depression and anxiety, and even the serious mental disorder we call **psychosis** (which is synonymous with **insanity**) are sufficiently common that most of us know someone who suffers from one or another of them. Psychosis involves an actual break with reality; it's typically accompanied by **delusions** (i.e., false beliefs) and **hallucinations** (i.e., false perceptions).

Learning about these conditions will give you some understanding of how they originate, are diagnosed, and can be treated. You'll also develop a better sense of whether the circumstances of your life, as well as your family's history of medical or psychiatric disorders, increase or decrease your chances of developing a mental disorder. By learning about these conditions, you'll likely come to appreciate that definitions of abnormality can vary with time and culture.

We also hope that by studying this material you'll come to appreciate—perhaps for the first time—the vital interplay of biology, psychology, and the environment in determining behavior. We stress repeatedly throughout this book that all behavior—normal and abnormal—is affected by many influences. We think it's important to share with you this **biopsychosocial perspective.** This term is used throughout to highlight the simultaneous impact on behavior of:

* *biological factors*—normal biology and disease processes as well as genetic influences
* *psychological factors*—our thoughts, feelings, and perceptions
* *social and environmental factors*—features of the social environments we live in

To understand psychopathology, we believe you must understand the biopsychosocial perspective.

WHAT IS ABNORMAL BEHAVIOR?

How do we decide whether our own behavior or that of others is normal or abnormal? In some cases, the symptoms are so dramatic or unusual that there's little doubt that a person is no longer behaving normally. For instance, a young man who believes that his thoughts are being broadcast by the local radio station or that a fraternity brother plans to wire his car with explosives is clearly no longer thinking normally. Similarly, a young woman who regularly converses aloud with deceased members of her family as she sits in class has, to some degree, lost touch with reality.

But other cases are more subtle. What about the individual who becomes so upset over a supervisor's criticism that she quits her job, causing her and her family great financial hardship? What about someone who's firmly convinced that a fortune-teller can predict the future? What about the man who occasionally enjoys dressing up in women's clothing, although he's happily married and seems, in all other respects, an average, well-adjusted person? For that matter, what about people who continue to smoke cigarettes or athletes who continue to take steroids, even though they know the substantial health risks they're running? As these examples suggest, it's not always easy to decide when behavior is abnormal.

The case material that follows makes the same point. In reading about Billy Ainsworth, you'll find yourself asking whether he suffered from mental illness at all or just had a few rough months. Was his behavior abnormal or just troubled for a brief period?

> Billy Ainsworth was a 21-year-old senior at a university in the southwestern United States when he came to the university's counseling center following the end of a relationship three months earlier with a young woman, Jill, with whom he had had a lengthy relationship. Even though, in his words, they had shared a real love relationship, they had ultimately decided to date other people. After doing so for a time, Jill had found someone else she preferred to Billy.
>
> After their breakup, life at the university changed dramatically for Billy. His interest in his schoolwork, previously very high, diminished substantially, in part because he began finding it harder and harder to concentrate properly, both during class and when he wanted to study. Billy also found it more and more difficult to get to sleep; and even when he was able to do so, he would often awaken early in the morning, unable to fall back to sleep. His waking thoughts centered on his role in the loss of his relationship with Jill. Interestingly, though he felt sad when he thought about what they had had together, there were times when he could enjoy himself with friends and get involved again in politics and sports, his special interests.
>
> Compounding his turmoil and adding to his reasons for coming to the counseling center were Billy's problems making choices among his career options. Although he was within a few months of graduating from the university, he had still not decided what he wanted to do after graduation. Should he find a job and begin a business career or, instead, remain a student for a few additional years? And, if he chose the graduate school route, should it be law school or business school?
>
> This was the agenda Billy brought to his first appointment with a counselor at the university counseling center. (adapted from Spitzer, Skodol, Gibbon, & Williams, 1983, p. 195)

Billy's problems interfered enough with living a normal life that he sought professional help to deal with them. One of the most common reasons people seek help for psychological problems is that their problems have begun to interfere with their school, job, or family life. (As a general rule, if and when you come to believe you need help with emotional problems, you probably do!)

Billy Ainsworth's behavior raises a number of questions: Is it abnormal to be so sad following the loss of a valued relationship that it interferes with regular functioning? When do sadness and the experience of loss become depression? When should someone who's depressed seek help, and who should he turn to? Since we all experience periods of depression (most of them, fortunately, of brief duration), it's clear that only some depressive experiences merit professional attention. Finally, when should someone seek professional help for other emotional or psychological problems, either for himself or for a friend or loved one?

How Should We Judge Behavior?

We use a variety of standards to judge whether behavior—our own and that of others—is normal or abnormal, healthy or pathological. These judgments are important to us. During times of stress, grief, or illness, for example, we may worry that our behavior has become so disturbed or unusual that taking care of ourselves, receiving solace from friends, or just letting time pass may not be enough. Professional consultation may be required. Billy Ainsworth came to this conclusion, but only after several months of suffering.

Judgments of behavior (including our own) are difficult to make because the standards we use to determine adequacy or appropriateness vary a lot from person to person and group to group within our multifaceted society. These standards vary even more between societies, cultures, and nations that are separated by time, climate, and distance. Consider how much things have changed in the United States over the past few generations. For example, today, we consider the harsh physical punishments once routinely imposed on children to be child abuse. And although divorce is common today, only a couple of generations ago, it was considered shockingly deviant. Similarly, in the 1940s and 1950s, the idea of a coed dormitory would have been considered scandalous. In light of these changes in what's considered *normal*, no wonder it's so difficult to label someone's actions *abnormal*.

The fourth edition of the ***Diagnostic and Statistical Manual of Mental Disorders (DSM-IV)*** (American Psychiatric Association, 1994)—the current, authoritative listing of mental disorders used by U.S. mental health professionals—solves the problem of judging what's abnormal by adopting a very broad definition. The *DSM-IV* conceptualizes *mental disorder* as "a clinically significant behavioral or psychological syndrome or pattern . . . associated with either a painful symptom or impairment in one or more important areas of functioning."

Billy Ainsworth's condition meets this definition. The individuals who drafted this instrument and its immediate predecessors were criticized for adopting an overinclusive definition of mental disorder, which means that the *DSM* includes some behaviors that not everyone agrees should be considered mental disorders. For example, these critics would claim that Billy Ainsworth's reaction to the loss of his relationship with Jill doesn't warrant inclusion because its impact on his life was likely to be brief and of little long-term consequence.

Seven Views of Abnormal Behavior

Wakefield (1992) describes seven different views of abnormal behavior. Even though each is thought provoking, none completely defines the concept *abnormal behavior*. Collectively, however, these definitions nicely establish the limits of the concept.

Mental Disorder as Myth   More than thirty years ago, psychiatrist Thomas Szasz (1960) expressed the idea that schizophrenia is not a disease. Even today, Szasz is considered psychiatry's best-known critic for his belief that mental disorders don't exist and that the concept *mental disorder* was invented by psychiatrists to justify their exercise of power and social control over others. Critiquing this view that mental disorders are myths, Wakefield cites a wide range of data that demonstrate the real, undoubted existence of mental conditions that harm individuals and interfere with their ability to function in society. Wakefield and most other authorities, including the authors of this text, now accept the very substantial empirical evidence that mental disorders do exist.

Mental Disorder as Violation of Social Norms   Can mental disorders be the product of social norms? Can those behaviors a group considers unacceptable be labeled abnormal? In fact, some of the behaviors a group chooses to condemn might be defined as mental disorders, even though groups with different norms might not define them this way. As an example, some groups in U.S. society still consider homosexuality a form of mental disorder, even though most behavioral and biological scientists have rejected this view.

In suggesting this view of mental disorder, Wakefield acknowledges that social norms do play an important role in defining certain behaviors as normal or abnormal. Previous generations would certainly have found a great deal in contemporary society to take issue with. Nonetheless, as Wakefield also notes, many of the most serious mental disorders have been considered problems by people of every society, regardless of when they lived or what values they had, which suggests that social values must yield to objective reality in these instances.

Mental Disorder as Whatever Professionals Treat   Perhaps mental disorder should be defined as whatever professionals decide to treat (assuming, of course, that professionals know best what mental disorder is and how it should be treated). This suggestion has an obvious flaw, however, since mental health professionals are often called on to treat troubling behavior that clearly does not represent mental disorder. Difficulties with marriage, childrearing, and finding meaning in life are all troubling issues, but they aren't mental disorders.

Mental Disorder as Statistical Deviance   Defining mental disorder as statistical deviance would have us consider only behaviors that are statistically deviant (that is, unusual and rare). However, many conditions that are generally agreed to be mental disorders aren't unusual. Suicide is all too common—in fact, it's the third-leading cause of death among young people—but it's not normal. Moreover, as Wakefield points out, exceptional levels of intelligence, energy, and talent are rare, but no one thinks they're signs of mental disorder.

Mental Disorder as Biological Disadvantage   It's also tempting to define mental disorder in terms of its impact on reproduction, given the great personal importance reproduction has to us, as well as its significance to our species from an evolutionary perspective. Defining mental disorder as biological disadvantage labels as mental disorders those behaviors that interfere seriously with an individual's reproductive capacities. A number of serious mental disorders affect their victims' reproductive capacity adversely (including schizophrenia, some mood disorders, and developmental disabilities), even though many others do not. Homosexuality also affects reproduction, even though few psychologists or psychiatrists today consider it a mental disorder.

Mental Disorder as Unexpectable Distress or Disability   Defining mental disorder as unexpectable distress or disability is attractive because doing so comes reasonably close to the *DSM-IV* definition. According to this view, if your behavior causes you distress or disability that you don't expect, it meets the definition of mental disorder. However, as Wakefield observes, many conditions that simply can't be anticipated also cause distress or disability but are clearly not disorders (for example, extreme ignorance and plain misfortune, as well as poverty and discrimination).

Mental Disorder as Harmful Dysfunction   The view of mental disorder as harmful dysfunction is Wakefield's choice as the most accurate and helpful definition. It also happens to come closer than any of the other six to the definition of mental disorder in the *DSM-IV.*

There are two crucial elements in this definition. The first is that the concept *harmful* is a value term based on social norms. That is, what's considered harmful behavior varies from society to society. Some societies consider behaviors such as premarital sex, drug use, and certain antisocial actions to be harmful, whereas other societies consider them harmless. The second crucial element in this definition is *dysfunction*, which Wakefield considers to be a scientific term that refers to the failure of our "mental mechanism" (responsible for our emotional and cognitive selves) to perform the function it was designed for.

In sum, Wakefield values this definition of mental disorder above the others because it requires both scientific validation and consideration of social values.

Because of the complexity of judging behavior, most modern societies depend on mental health professionals to differentiate psychopathology from eccentricity, cultural deviance, or lifestyle variations. On their clinical judgments rest such vital decisions as whether someone ought to receive psychological or psychiatric treatment, where it should occur, and what it should consist of.

ABNORMAL BEHAVIOR IN THE CONTEMPORARY UNITED STATES

How many people in the United States suffer from mental disorders? What are the most common forms of mental illness? Is psychopathology increasing or decreasing in U.S. society? Do age, gender, race, income, lifestyle, or living conditions influence abnormal behavior? What about creativity or artistic temperament? How is abnormal behavior affected by natural catastrophes, such as floods and hurricanes, or environmental disasters, like the *Exxon Valdez* oil spill?

In March 1989, the supertanker *Exxon Valdez* spilled 11 million gallons of crude oil into the waters of Prince William Sound in Alaska, killing millions of sea birds, mammals, and fish; despoiling one of the nation's most pristine natural settings; and disrupting the economy of a large region of southern Alaska. A year later, an epidemiologic survey investigated the social and psychological consequences the event and its cleanup had on 599 residents of 13 communities in the region surrounding Prince William Sound (Palinkas, Petterson, Russell, & Downs, 1993).

Although significantly higher rates of both physical and psychiatric disorders have been reported following other disasters, the *Exxon Valdez* calamity was different in that its victims were never in physical danger or felt physically threatened. Nonetheless, the psychiatric consequences caused by this event and its cleanup were formidable. Of the residents who participated in the study, 30 percent met the diagnostic criteria for anxiety disorder, including posttraumatic stress, and 15 percent met the criteria for depressive disorder. These rates were between two and three times higher than those for Alaskans who had not been exposed to the oil spill and its consequences.

Women in the sample reported higher rates of depression and anxiety than men, whereas Inuits (Native Alaskans) reported higher rates of depression than non-Inuits. Previous research has reported women to be more vulnerable than men to the psychological consequences of disasters (Breslau, Davis, Andreski, & Peterson, 1991), but the reasons for this difference aren't obvious. Palinkas et al. (1993) speculate that the increased psychological vulnerability of Native Alaskans to the oil spill may reflect high rates of alcohol abuse before the spill as well as the traumatic effects of seeing these special lands spoiled. As the authors point out, "When the *Exxon Valdez* ran aground in Prince William Sound, it spilled oil into a social as well as a natural environment" (p. 1522).

Determining what impacts environmental events have on behavior is one of the primary tasks of mental health professionals. Much of the training of clinical psychologists, psychiatrists, psychiatric social workers, and psychiatric nurses is devoted to learning how to evaluate and diagnose (as shown in our overview of professional education, later in this chapter). Yet only in the last two decades have standardized diagnostic interviews enabled clinicians to achieve diagnostic agreement. These new, more reliable diagnostic tools have made it possible to reach greater consensus on the **incidence** and **prevalence** of psychopathology in the United States. The prevalence of a disorder is the total number of people within a given population who suffer from it, and the incidence is the number of people within a given population who have acquired the disorder within a specific time period (usually, a year).

It's surprising that agreement on the extent of psychopathology in the United States has only been reached so recently, given that five landmark **epidemiological surveys** of psychiatric disorder have been conducted since World War II, along with many smaller-scale epidemiologic investigations, such as the *Exxon Valdez* study. An epidemiological survey examines a carefully defined group of people to answer questions relating to the incidence, prevalence, and causation of disorder. The landmark surveys of psychiatric epidemiology include the Stirling County Study (Hughes, Tremblay, Rapaport, & Leighton, 1960), the Baltimore Morbidity Survey (Pasamanick, Toberts, Lemkau, & Krueger, 1962), the Midtown

Manhattan Study (Srole, Langner, Michael, Opler, & Rennie, 1962), the New Haven Study (Weissman, Myers, & Harding, 1978), and the NIMH Epidemiologic Catchment Area (ECA) Study (Eaton, Anthony, Tepper, & Dryman, 1992; Regier et al., 1984). Each is considered a landmark study because its authors drew on the best survey methodology of their day to design a study that would yield data that could be generalized to populations across the United States.

The comparison that follows of data from the two most recent large-scale epidemiologic surveys of mental health and mental disorder in the United States (the Midtown and ECA surveys), as well as data from a more restricted survey of depression (Blazer, Kessler, McGonagle, & Swartz, 1994), shows the overall scope of the problem of mental disorder in this country.

Abnormal Behavior in Midtown Manhattan: 1952–1960

The **Midtown Manhattan Study** surveyed the mental health problems and resources in New York City between 1952 and 1960 (Srole et al., 1962). At the time, it was the most ambitious survey ever undertaken of mental health and mental illness in the United States. Interviews, based on a 200-item questionnaire, were given to 1,660 residents of mid-Manhattan who were selected to represent the 750,000 residents of the area as closely as possible in age, sex, race, ethnicity, and socioeconomic status.

The mental health of Midtown residents was categorized on a 6-point scale. Figure 25.1 shows the percentages of Midtown residents who fell into each category. These judgments were made by two psychiatrists after reading the completed interviews.

Only 18.5 percent of the persons surveyed were considered "well," or free from psychopathology. By contrast, more than 23 percent fell into one of the three severity categories: "marked," "severe," and "incapacitated." An individual given one of these ratings had at least some difficulty working, going to school, meeting ordinary family obligations, and the like. Since these interviewees were representative

FIGURE 25.1   Prevalence of psycho-pathology in Midtown Manhattan
To almost everyone's surprise, only 18.5 percent of the people interviewed in the Midtown survey were considered to be free from psychopathology (those in the "well" category). More than 23 percent (those in the "marked," "severe," and "incapacitated" categories) were considered to have significant impairment.

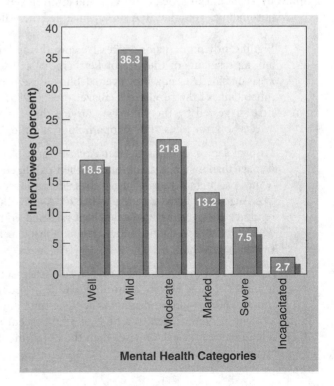

Source: From *Mental Health in the Metropolis: The Midtown Manhattan Study* by L. Srole et al., 1962. New York: McGraw-Hill. Reprinted by permission of the author.

of the entire New York metropolitan area, the study's unexpected major finding was that almost one-quarter of the several million people living and working there were emotionally impaired.

The Midtown study generated additional controversy when subsequent analysis of its findings showed that lower-class, or poor, Midtown residents were much more likely to be judged impaired than middle- or upper-middle-class residents. Since a principal aim of the study was to examine the effects of urban stress on psychopathology, the obvious conclusion from these findings was that urban stress disproportionately burdens people who are poor. Publication of these findings brought charges ranging from racism on the part of the interviewers, because the poor in Midtown were mainly African American and Hispanic, to insensitivity on the part of the politicians, who were accused of systematically ignoring the plight of these people.

Similar findings have emerged from subsequent epidemiological studies, leading to the conclusion that racism and discrimination against people who are poor appear to have a disproportionate impact on psychopathology in American society.

Abnormal Behavior in Five U.S. Cities: 1981–1983

The **NIMH Epidemiologic Catchment Area (ECA) Study** surveyed the psychiatric status of more than 20,000 persons residing in five U.S. cities and towns in the early 1980s (Eaton et al., 1992; Regier et al., 1984). The ECA study assessed rates of specific mental disorders, rather than the more general rates of impairment the Midtown study reported (Regier & Burke, 1987). The development of a standardized interview schedule, the Diagnostic Interview Schedule (DIS) (Robins, Helzer, Croughan, & Ratcliff, 1981), enabled interviewers to make diagnostic judgments this specific. The DIS could also be administered by trained nonprofessionals, making a large-scale diagnostic study economically feasible.

The size, diversity, and representativeness of the ECA sample population was an additional strength. Drawn from five sites (Baltimore, Maryland; Durham, North Carolina; Los Angeles, California; New Haven, Connecticut; and Saint Louis, Missouri), survey subjects were almost as diverse geographically, economically, socioculturally, and ethnically as the United States as a whole.

Major findings from the ECA survey included the following:

- Significantly more major depressive episodes and drug abuse/dependence were found among residents of the city of Durham, North Carolina, than those living in rural areas outside Durham. However, alcohol abuse/dependence was a greater problem for inhabitants of the rural areas (Blazer et al., 1985). These findings reinforce the idea, first suggested by the Midtown survey, that the social environment people live in affects both the rates of psychopathology and the forms it takes.

- Hispanics, most of them Mexican Americans, displayed significantly higher rates of brain damage than non-Hispanic whites in the Los Angeles sample. By contrast, non-Hispanic whites had higher rates of drug abuse/dependence than either Mexican Americans in Los Angeles or interviewees at other ECA sites (Burnam et al., 1987). These findings reinforce the growing conviction that race and ethnicity play an important role in the development of psychopathology, a finding that data from the Midtown study implied but couldn't confirm.

- As Table 25.1 indicates, about one-third of the persons studied in the three ECA communities of New Haven, Baltimore, and Saint Louis met interview criteria for one or more of nine common diagnoses at some time during their lives—from a low of 28.8 percent in New Haven to a high of 38.0 percent in Baltimore (Robins et al., 1984). These figures are even higher than the impairment figures reported by the Midtown study.

TABLE 25.1   Lifetime Prevalence Rates of DIS/DSM-III Disorders (in percent)

DISORDERS	NEW HAVEN	BALTIMORE	SAINT LOUIS
Any disorder	28.8	38.0	31.0
• Substance use disorders	15.0	17.0	18.1
• Schizophrenic/schizophreniform	2.0	1.9	1.1
• Affective disorders	9.5	6.1	8.0
• Anxiety/somatoform disorder	10.4	25.1	11.1
• Eating disorder	0.0	0.1	0.1
• Antisocial personality	2.1	2.6	3.3
• Cognitive impairment—severe	1.3	1.3	1.0

SOURCE: From Robins et al. (1984), "Lifetime Prevalence Rates of DIS/DSM-III Disorders," *Archives of General Psychiatry, 41*, p. 952. Copyright 1984 American Medical Association.

Overall, the ECA study confirms that many Americans suffer significant impairment from stress, distress, and emotionally related problems. Men and women demonstrate comparable prevalence rates, which vary with age, socioeconomic status, race, ethnicity, and environment. Relatively few individuals, however, seek treatment for their disorders, and of those who do, even fewer go to adequately trained mental health professionals.

Remember Elizabeth H. from the scenario at the beginning of the chapter? She'd been asked to participate in an ECA study conducted by NIMH. Let's take a look at Elizabeth H.'s interview.

Elizabeth's interview didn't begin exactly as she thought it would. Because she arrived back home late from work, the young woman who was to interview her was waiting by her door when she got off the elevator. So Elizabeth had no time to get her children settled or to change into more comfortable clothes before sitting down in the living room for the interview.

Most of the questions were what Elizabeth expected (it helped that she'd been a psychology major in college!), but there were more of them and they covered a broader range of thoughts, feelings, and behaviors than she'd anticipated. They also got pretty personal at times, such as when she was asked about her sexual preferences and drug and alcohol use. The only times Elizabeth actually got flustered, though, were when she was asked about her husband's drinking (along with the anger that sometimes accompanied it) and her "spells" of lethargy and sadness.

Although she may have been especially sensitive to these questions, Elizabeth thought the interviewer pushed a bit more about these subjects, asking a few more probing questions than she had to. But later that evening and then several more times during the days that followed, when Elizabeth reflected on the interview, she began to feel differently. Maybe those issues were ones she hadn't ever been able to view objectively. Maybe she'd been fooling herself a bit. The interviewer, with her objectivity and established interview style, was only doing what she was supposed to be doing.

Elizabeth concluded that the experience had been interesting, worthwhile, a bit daunting, but ultimately valuable. She thought some more about her "spells" and her husband's drinking and decided that she should come to better terms with them. She wondered whether she ought to ask a friend at work for the name of a counselor she could talk to about them.

Depression in a National Sample: 1990–1992

Depression is a very common, sometimes disabling psychiatric condition. Based on results of a recent survey, involving a national sample of 8,098 persons, 15 to 54 years of age, from the 48 mainland U.S. states, Blazer and his colleagues report a current rate of major depression of about 5 percent (Blazer et al., 1994). Women, young adults, and individuals with less than a college education showed the highest rates. Lifetime prevalence for major depression was about 17 percent, with the same groups (women, young adults, and individuals with less than a college education) demonstrating the highest lifetime prevalences.

When called on to explain these rates, which are substantially higher than estimates from the ECA and Midtown studies (which were themselves surprisingly high), Blazer and his co-workers point to a more sensitive diagnostic questionnaire and a younger sample, from which higher rates of major depression could be expected. As the product of a methodologically sound, large-scale epidemiologic study, these findings confirm that depression, in its several forms, has become one of the major mental health problems in the United States, especially among women.

Speculating on reasons for women's heightened vulnerability to depression, Strickland (1992) concludes that because both biological and psychosocial factors are involved, a biopsychosocial perspective on the problem makes the most sense. She cites three factors relevant to the biological side of the equation: (1) gender differences in neurophysiological functioning, (2) the premenstrual mood changes some women experience, and (3) the use of oral contraceptives by some women. Psychosocial factors include gender-role socialization patterns, the economic realities that face most single mothers, and the high levels of sexual and physical violence against women in this country. The heightened risk of depression for women is a highly important clinical and methodological issue.

ABNORMAL BEHAVIOR THROUGH HISTORY

Our earliest ideas about abnormal behavior have been lost in prehistory. We have no way of knowing whether our distant ancestors attributed strange behavior to **natural forces**, such as sickness or a blow to the head, or to **supernatural forces**, like demonic possession or punishment from the gods. Perhaps they accepted both kinds of explanation, as some people still do today.

Throughout recorded history, natural and supernatural explanations for abnormal behavior have competed for acceptance. Only during the last century have most people come to recognize that mental disorders are caused by natural forces, rather than supernatural ones. Today, we know these natural forces include biological, psychological, and social factors. But even in the relatively recent and enlightened past, people believed that the gods caused every event beyond human understanding or control, including natural events (such as earthquakes, hurricanes, pestilence, famine, eclipses, and seasons) as well as personal disorders (such as psychosis, mental retardation, and epilepsy).

Many of the disorders that ancient and medieval peoples attributed to supernatural forces were psychotic disorders, or psychoses. We can easily understand why ancient peoples were frightened by such behavior, which they couldn't understand. Since they lacked the knowledge provided by modern science, they created mythic explanations to account for abnormal behavior and employed harsh measures to treat it. In like manner, the behavioral abnormalities associated with **mental retardation** and **epilepsy** caused people with these conditions to be socially isolated and even persecuted.

The Ancient World

Not all ancient societies accepted the prevailing supernatural explanations for psychiatric and behavioral disorders. During the seventh century B.C., for example, Chinese physicians concluded that an imbalance in the essential natural forces they called *yin* and *yang* shared responsibility for physical and mental illness.

The ancient Greeks held a similarly naturalistic view of the causes of disease. Hippocrates (460–377 B.C.), the father of medicine, suggested that disease (mainly brain disease) was responsible for mental disorders. He believed that most common mental disorders were due to an imbalance in the four essential fluids, or *humors*, circulating through the body: blood, phlegm, yellow bile, and black bile. For example, too much black bile caused depression, and too much yellow bile caused anxiety and irritability. Hippocrates prescribed natural treatments for these conditions, including rest, solitude, good food and drink, and abstinence from sexual activity.

Hippocrates' theory of imbalance in the body's chemistry foreshadowed the discovery of biological components of mental disorders made centuries later by modern science. Hippocrates also recognized other natural causes of abnormality—including stress, diet, heredity, head injury, and family problems—and contributed to the diagnoses of medical and psychiatric disorders. Although the most rudimentary diagnostic instruments had not yet been invented and knowledge of human anatomy was extremely primitive, Hippocrates described a number of mental disorders that are familiar to us today, including mania, melancholia (depression), and paranoia. His careful observation of patients, which was by itself innovative, permitted him to describe these conditions with great accuracy.

Although Plato (429–347 B.C.) and Aristotle (384–322 B.C.) were philosophers, not physicians, they were influential in promoting a naturalistic approach to treating mental disorders. They also believed that people with mental disturbances were ill; accordingly, they were to be treated humanely and not to be held accountable for their actions. In addition, the ancient Greeks recognized the behavioral effects of pathological aging, describing the symptoms of what we now call Alzheimer's disease as well as the psychological and behavioral effects of alcohol abuse.

The Middle Ages

Greek views of mental disorder persisted into Roman times, but after the fall of the Roman empire in the fifth century, efforts such as those by Hippocrates and Galen (c. A.D. 130–200) to discover natural causes for abnormal behavior virtually stopped. During the Middle Ages, religion dominated all aspects of European life, and people explained episodes of mental disorder in supernatural terms. Persons who were troubled were supposedly being punished for their sins or possessed by demons. Although some of these individuals were considered to be sick and were humanely cared for at home, others were horribly persecuted. Exorcisms were performed on some disturbed individuals, in an attempt to drive out the devils possessing them, and others were shouted at, deprived of food, flogged, or tortured.

During the late years of the Middle Ages, the stable medieval world began to change. Wars, peasant revolts, and finally the Black Death convinced people of the idea that powerful evil forces existed. One result of this thinking was the phenomenon known as the *witch craze*.

The Renaissance

During the Renaissance (1400s–1600s), people who were insane, poor, and epileptic were treated more humanely. Swiss physician and philosopher Paracelsus (1493–1541) criticized the notion that demons possess people. He proposed instead that the stars and planets affect the actions of the brain—specifically, that the phases of the moon play an important role in the development of abnormal behavior. This idea is preserved today in the word *lunatic*, which refers to an insane person. (*Luna* is the Latin word for *moon*.)

After personally witnessing the torture and death of several supposed witches, German physician Johann Weyer (1515–1588) wrote a treatise published in 1563, in which he argued that many of the people put to death were mentally unbalanced and thus couldn't be held responsible for their actions. Although the Catholic Church banned his work, a few academics and intellectuals shared Weyer's skepticism. One such individual was Englishman Reginald Scot (1538–1595), who published *Discovery of Witchcraft* in 1584, arguing that mental disorders were caused by illness, rather than demons and devils.

Asylums and Reforms

The earliest institutional care for people who were mentally disturbed was provided by religious orders, who sometimes sheltered them in monasteries. Hospitals occasionally accepted mental patients, too. By the mid–sixteenth century, institutions known as *asylums*, or madhouses, were established specifically to house the mentally ill. Perhaps the best known was London's Bethlehem Hospital, whose name was commonly contracted to *Bedlam*, a term that has come to mean chaos and confusion. Residents were chained to walls and otherwise subjected to a variety of mistreatments; the public purchased tickets to see them, as if they were animals in a zoo. "Bedlam" and other contemporary asylums were more like prisons than hospitals. In the United States, the first asylums were established in the mid-1700s. Conditions in these institutions weren't much better than those in Europe.

Reform in the care of mental patients followed the American (1776) and French (1789) Revolutions, which both spread ideas about individual rights and human dignity. The first notable reform occurred at La Bicêtre, a large asylum in Paris. Conditions improved through the efforts of Philippe Pinel (1745–1826), physician-in-chief at La Bicêtre, and his staff. Pinel unchained patients, allowed them outdoor exercise, ordered their cells cleaned, and prohibited attendants from beating them.

While Pinel was instituting his reforms, Englishman William Tuke (1732–1822) set up York Retreat, an asylum in a country house in northern England. A Quaker, Tuke believed that a haven of rural quiet and considerate treatment would benefit mental patients. At York Retreat, patients prayed and worked together, took walks, and rested. Many apparently recovered and went home.

In America, the most prominent mental health reformer was Benjamin Rush (1745–1813), who's known as "the father of American psychiatry." While associated with the Pennsylvania Hospital in Philadelphia, Rush wrote the first American treatise on psychiatry and established the first medical course in psychiatry. His medical theories were primitive; for instance, he believed that the positions of the stars influenced the brain and regularly employed bloodletting, believing that too much blood in the brain caused disturbed behavior. But Rush's interest in the scientific study of his patients and his insistence on humane treatment were positive influences on the field.

Another American reformer, Dorothea Dix (1802–1887), was a Massachusetts schoolteacher. Her work teaching women inmates in prison made her aware of the conditions in the asylums of her day. Hoping to improve conditions inside mental institutions and to raise money to build new ones, Dix began to travel around her state and then across the country. Through her efforts, more than 30 mental hospitals were built.

The Rise of the Scientific Model

The founding of insane asylums toward the end of the eighteenth century meant that, for the first time, sizable groups of mental patients were brought together. In addition to providing humane conditions for patients, asylums also gave physicians their first opportunity to observe, contrast, and study the behavior of large groups of individuals with serious disorders. These studies laid the groundwork for the scientific model of mental disorder, which was soon to follow.

Pinel's Classification System   Philippe Pinel was one of the first to take advantage of this new opportunity for research. After making detailed observations of patients, he divided their disorders into the following categories:

- **melancholia** (severe depression)
- **mania** (marked agitation, grandiose thinking, and elation) without **delirium** (lost awareness of the environment, time, and self)
- **mania with delirium**

- **dementia** (a chronic disabling disorder marked by memory loss, personality change, and deterioration in judgment and personal habits)
- **idiotism** (mental retardation)

This classification system, based on Pinel's careful clinical observations, was one of the first modern psychiatric nomenclatures.

Kraepelin and the German Classifiers German physicians working in the latter half of the nineteenth century, about 60 years after Pinel's reforms, led a growing effort to develop more systematic methods for classifying and categorizing mental disorders. The availability of large groups of patients in mental hospitals made the effort possible.

The most influential of these workers was Emil Kraepelin (1856–1926). He combined previously separate diagnostic conditions into a single diagnostic category, which he called *dementia praecox* (literally, "premature dementia"). Kraepelin used this term to describe the decline in cognitive functioning he saw in adolescents suffering from the disorder, which resembled the decline found in some elderly people. Kraepelin described this common disorder in detail and carefully described its subtypes. Swiss psychiatrist Eugen Bleuler (1857–1939) subsequently renamed the condition **schizophrenia**, which it's known as today.

The emergence of dementia praecox, or schizophrenia, as a single, recognized disorder constituted a great advance. It marked the first time that a clinician taking a scientific approach had investigated in detail a common and serious psychiatric disorder. In his *Psychiatry: A Textbook* (1913), Kraepelin argued persuasively that many of the most common mental disorders are disorders of the brain—for instance, dementia praecox, manic-depressive psychosis (now called *bipolar affective disorder*), and disorders of the central nervous system. Kraepelin's views on the causes of mental disorders were revolutionary. In fact, his views and practices continue to influence mental health professionals today, including his detailed medical and psychiatric histories of patients, his development of the mental status examination (to assess more completely the patient's mental state), his emphasis on thorough behavioral observation of patients' symptoms to establish diagnoses, and his consideration of the psychoses as, first and foremost, diseases of the brain.

Also during the mid-nineteenth century, French physician Louis Pasteur (1822–1895) postulated the germ theory of disease. He was the first to prove that tiny organisms and viruses infect the body, ultimately producing physical symptoms. Ultimately, bacterial diseases with behavioral consequences received scientific attention; syphilis, a sexually transmitted disease with many serious consequences, was among the first to be studied. The causal agents of these diseases were identified and effective antibacterial treatments were found for some of them, with discoveries continuing well into the present century. Acceptance of the idea that bodily diseases had identifiable, biological causes supported the notion that mental problems might also prove to be diseases, with known causes and effective treatments.

Freud's Psychoanalytic Revolution

Another influential view on mental illness emerged at the end of the nineteenth century and, like that of Emil Kraepelin, still affects us today. Psychoanalytic theory was developed by Viennese physician Sigmund Freud (1856–1939). As a young man, Freud studied in Paris with the famous neurologist Jean-Martin Charcot (1825–1893), who was interested in the role of emotional factors in neurological disorders. Charcot and his associates found that patients lost their neurological symptoms when they were hypnotized. Freud concluded that patients lost their symptoms during hypnosis because psychological factors, not bodily disease, had caused them.

Returning to Vienna, Freud began working with neuropsychiatrist Josef Breuer (1842–1925), who had begun to treat psychiatric patients with hypnosis. Breuer revealed to Freud that even very disturbed patients recovered when they talked about their problems under hypnosis. He called this approach the *cathartic method,* or "talking cure," since hysterical patients seemed to undergo an emotional catharsis, or cleansing, while talking about their problems under hypnosis (Jones, 1953). After trying Breuer's method for a time, Freud abandoned hypnosis and began to simply encourage his patients to talk freely in his presence. He believed that the emotional conflicts behind patients' problems would eventually reveal themselves during verbal free association, when patients were asked to talk about whatever came to mind.

Together, Breuer and Freud wrote *Studies in Hysteria,* published in 1895, and launched the psychoanalytic revolution. Their book put forth several revolutionary ideas:

- Psychological factors affect behavior in powerful ways.
- "Talking treatments" could be more effective for treating disordered behavior than the harsh physical and moral treatments then in use.
- Behavior is influenced by thought patterns, impulses, and wishes that individuals are largely unaware of.
- Nonpsychotic behavioral disorders, such as anxiety and phobic behavior, are worthy of attention and treatment by psychiatrists.

These tenets of psychoanalytic theory dominated the treatment of mental disorders in the early and mid–twentieth century. That's no longer the case, largely because a variety of other views of psychopathology have been developed since that time. Nonetheless, psychoanalytic theory continues to influence the views of mental health professionals regarding some conditions.

Adolf Meyer's Psychobiology

During the 1920s and 1930s, clinicians jarred by the horrors of World War I and its psychiatric casualties began to play a significant role in the development of psychiatry. One such figure was Adolf Meyer (1866–1950), a German psychiatrist who had emigrated to the United States. His conviction that organic, psychological, and environmental factors all contribute to psychopathology greatly influenced the clinical methods and procedures of his era. Meyer succinctly summarized his primary thesis as follows: "All life is a reaction, either to stimuli of the outside world or of the various parts of the organism. We recognize death by the absolute absence of these reactions" (Meyer, 1994, p. 44).

At the time, Meyer's *psychobiology* influenced generations of psychiatrists in training and countered the emphasis that psychoanalytic theory placed on the primacy of unconscious factors in determining behavior. Today, the influence of psychobiology (called the *biopsychosocial perspective* in this book) can be seen in a number of developments: in the nearly universal practice of clinicians, who take detailed personal, social, psychiatric, and family histories of all patients; in the multiaxial, biopsychosocial approach of the *DSM-IV* to diagnosis; and in the increasingly prevalent idea that one-dimensional perspectives on etiology (for instance, entirely biological or entirely psychological) are less productive than biopsychosocial views.

Contemporary Developments

Research on Etiology Kraepelin, Freud, and Meyer all proposed theories of **etiology,** or explanations of the causes, of psychiatric disorders. These theories still influence many mental health workers.

The advances made in recent decades in understanding the etiology of mental disorder have outpaced those of any other time. Making these advances required the development of new investigative techniques and procedures, such as neuroimaging, genetics, molecular biology, and longitudinal research. Consequently, the etiologies of such common, profoundly disabling disorders as schizophrenia, bipolar affective disorder, alcoholism, and some cognitive disorders are now much better understood.

Etiologic understanding, in turn, will almost certainly lead at some point to more effective prevention and treatment.

Advances in Treatment   Psychiatric patients have been offered treatment, rather than punishment, only since the late 1700s, when Pinel brought reform to psychiatric institutions. During most of the 1800s, however, until Freud's time, treatment consisted mainly of ineffective physical measures, such as special diets, baths, and bloodletting, even in mental hospitals that prided themselves on their humane care of patients. Dr. Samuel Woodward described one such treatment for mania in 1850:

> As a means of exciting nausea, in violent cases of mania, the circular swing was recommended by the highest medical authority. Dr. Darwin speaks well of it and Dr. Cox relies upon it almost exclusively to remove maniacal excitement. It is a very effective means of producing sickness, vertigo, and vomiting, and usually prostrates the system remarkably. It is not always a safe remedy. It is extremely unpleasant to the patient, and always regarded as a punishment, rather than a means of cure. (Woodward, 1994, p. 222)

Following Freud's development of the "talking therapies," psychological treatments were more widely used. After Freud proposed his psychoanalytic theory, a continuing stream of theorists and clinicians modified this theory and its techniques.

Recent advances in pharmacotherapy (the use of drugs to treat psychopathology) have restored many persons suffering from psychoses to independent living. Newly developed drug treatments for schizophrenia, bipolar affective disorder, and major depression have permitted some patients to leave the hospital permanently after years of institutionalization. Also promising is the use of psychoactive drugs to treat less severe disorders, including nonpsychotic but troubling conditions like mild and moderate depressive disorders and attention-deficit, obsessive-compulsive, and anxiety disorders. Used in combination with brief, intensive, inpatient treatment lasting two or three weeks, these new drugs help patients return far more quickly to their families and jobs than was possible before. Overall, the average length of a hospital stay for treating a mental disorder has been shortened dramatically, in part because of advances in drug therapy and in part because lengthy stays are too costly. Contemporary approaches to the physical treatment of psychiatric and behavioral disorders have been developed mainly during the last 30 years.

Another exciting development, even more recent than the development of effective physical treatments for psychiatric and behavioral disorders, has been the emergence of health psychology and its effort to find effective psychological treatments for physical disorders. Although still in its relative youth, the field of health psychology holds great promise for the fuller understanding and more effective treatment of some of our most burdensome physical disorders, including cancer and heart disease (Chesney, 1993).

Developments in Diagnosis and Classification   As mentioned earlier, advances in treating patients with mental disorders were made following the recognition that some of these individuals behaved differently from others in predictable ways. Based on careful observations, patients could be classified according to which symptoms they showed. With the realization that distinctive psychological disorders existed came awareness of the value of careful diagnosis. Accurate diagnosis is crucial, since, as with physical disease, proper treatment depends on correct identification and evaluation of the problem.

A psychiatric classification system designed specifically for use in the United States was first developed in the mid-1930s by an association of state hospital superintendents. Previously, almost every hospital that cared for psychiatric patients had its own diagnostic system. The lack of a standard system created enormous communication difficulties among professionals working in different hospitals. The new system predictably served the pressing needs of the large state psychiatric hospitals, which cared for most of the country's mental patients.

After the United States entered World War II in 1941, the need for a new classification system became clear, as many American soldiers developed behavioral symptoms under the profound stress of combat that couldn't be diagnosed by the existing system. A system was needed to categorize the psychiatric casualties of war, one that emphasized disorders reactive to the stress of combat rather than chronic psychosis. The U.S. War Department undertook the task.

In 1946, shortly after the end of World War II, representatives of the state hospitals, the War Department, and the Veterans Administration met to discuss creating a contemporary diagnostic system—a system that would be as useful for diagnosing people whose disorders seemed to be reactions to the stresses of modern life as it was for diagnosing long-term psychotic patients. The result was publication of the first edition of the *Diagnostic and Statistical Manual of Mental Disorders (DSM-I)* by the American Psychiatric Association in 1952. The *DSM-I* has been followed by the *DSM-II* (1968), *DSM-III* (1980), *DSM-III-R* (1987), and, most recently, *DSM-IV* (1994).

All four editions of the *DSM* show Kraepelin's influence. Each calls for the careful observation of signs and symptoms of psychiatric disorder, assumes that many of these disorders derive from central nervous system damage, and separates the major psychotic disorders into subtypes based on the same signs and symptoms Kraepelin identified. Meyer's psychobiology has also influenced the *DSM*.

By introducing a diagnostic system that enabled all mental health professionals in the United States to employ a common language, the first two editions of the *DSM* represented a great step forward. But once in use, its serious deficiencies became obvious. These slim volumes provided only a brief description of each disorder, together with one or two short paragraphs listing distinguishing signs and symptoms. This information wasn't detailed enough to enable clinicians to make reliable diagnoses. The third edition of the *DSM*, published in 1980, made marked advances in diagnoses (M. Wilson, 1993), giving clinicians and researchers a more reliable diagnostic system.

THE MENTAL HEALTH PROFESSIONS

Four distinct professions—clinical psychology, psychiatry, psychiatric social work, and psychiatric nursing—provide care for patients suffering from mental disorders. Differences in education, training, and experience ensure that each of these professions makes a unique contribution to the understanding and care of people with mental disorders.

Clinical Psychology

The first work in clinical psychology was conducted in the early 1900s by experts on the assessment of intelligence and personality. But it wasn't until the psychiatric casualties of World War II overwhelmed existing mental health resources that the field of clinical psychology began to grow in earnest. Beginning with a handful of clinical psychologists in 1945, the field had grown to more than 60,000 members by 1994.

Although men still make up the majority of clinical psychologists, increasing numbers of women have been attracted to the field during the past 20 years; in fact, more than half the graduate students in clinical psychology are now women. Historically, the clinical psychologist's major contributions to the mental health team have been skills in the assessment of intelligence, personality, and psychopathology as well as research skills. Clinical psychologists in training now receive more extensive education than other mental health professionals in psychotherapy and behavior therapy, so in many clinical settings, they have become authorities on the "talking therapies."

Because clinical psychologists have responded to the growing body of research that points to psychological and environmental factors in the etiology of a number of physical disorders, they have played an important role in establishing the new field of **health psychology** (Carmody & Matarazzo, 1991). Health psychologists assess the role of psychological factors in physical diseases and apply psychological treatments to people with those diseases. Health psychologists also carry out research on the relationship between psychological and biological factors in specific physical diseases in an effort to develop more effective psychological assessment and treatment methods.

Neuropsychology is another recently developed branch of clinical psychology (Jones & Butters, 1991). Neuropsychologists study, evaluate, and diagnose patients with suspected or actual brain injury, using the neuropsychological test batteries and, increasingly, imaging techniques. Neuropsychologists have also begun to develop remediation strategies to help patients with these types of injuries regain as many of their cognitive abilities as possible.

Like all health professionals, clinical psychologists have been challenged by the profound changes in health care delivery patterns currently under way in the United States, in which the goal is to provide a broader range of services at lower costs (Dial et al., 1992). For clinical psychologists, whose traditional roles are as mental health assessment and treatment specialists, this means shorter, more focused, more intensive assessment and treatment. One new role involves directly admitting psychiatric patients to hospitals and assuming primary responsibility for them while they're in the hospital (Dorken, 1993). Another role change calls for the clinical psychologist to develop a close working relationship with the family physician; in this role, the psychologist becomes the primary resource to diagnose, evaluate, and treat the psychological problems that influence patients' decisions to consult their family doctors (Schmittling, 1993; Wiggins, 1994).

On graduating from a four-year college, usually with a major in psychology or another social or natural science, the clinical psychologist-to-be enters a Ph.D. (doctorate in philosophy) or Psy.D. (doctorate in psychology) program in clinical psychology. Both require four or five years of academic work, plus a minimum one-year clinical internship. Programs awarding the Ph.D. provide more extensive training in research, while those awarding the Psy.D. offer more comprehensive training in practice.

Psychiatry

The special contributions psychiatrists make to the mental health team stem from their education and training as physicians, which gives them special skills in recognizing the impact of physical health and disease on both normal behavior and psychopathology. Since physical disorders masquerade as behavioral or psychiatric conditions and behavioral and psychiatric disorders share symptoms with some physical illnesses, these diagnostic skills are essential. Moreover, psychiatrists study **psychopharmacology** (the use of drugs to treat psychopathology) as part of their training as physicians and with special emphasis during their psychiatric residencies. During the past 30 years, effective drug treatments for several serious psychiatric disorders have been developed. The ability to prescribe the right drug for a certain condition, as well as knowing when a drug is not the treatment of choice, is an invaluable part of the psychiatrist's role and an essential element in the contemporary treatment of psychiatric patients.

A recent survey of the professional practice patterns of psychiatrists (Olfson, Pincus, & Dial, 1994) revealed that psychiatry, unlike the other three mental health professions, remains predominantly a private, rather than public, practice profession. More than 75 percent of psychiatrists now work primarily in private hospitals, clinics, and offices. In comparison, a substantially larger percentage of clinical psychologists work primarily in public service settings, and relatively few psychiatric social workers and psychiatric nurses work independently in private settings.

Psychiatry is a branch of medicine. As a result, the person intent on becoming a psychiatrist must first complete four years of college, followed by four years of medical school, a year of internship in a medical setting, and then three or more years in a psychiatric residency. During their residencies, psychiatrists-in-training assume increasing responsibility for the care of both inpatients, most of them seriously disturbed, and outpatients. As part of their residencies, psychiatrists learn how to diagnose psychiatric disorders, differentiate them from physical disorders they may share symptoms with, and treat them both psychotherapeutically and somatically (by physical means, including drugs). Psychiatric residents are also trained extensively in consultation skills, because consultation has become an increasingly important part of the role of the psychiatrist. Consultation involves conferring with other physicians and health professionals on the diagnosis and treatment of patients with physical disorders influenced by psychological factors.

Psychiatric Social Work

Psychiatric social workers bring strengths in group work to the mental health team—specifically, in assessing and treating the problems experienced by families, married couples, and groups in the urban United States. Psychiatric social workers trained in group psychotherapy devote much of their workday to providing psychotherapeutic services to couples, families, and groups. Not surprisingly, psychiatric social workers in poor, inner-city neighborhoods frequently suffer from burnout from having to care for too many patients with few individual resources.

Social workers also use their detailed knowledge of resources available in the community to help bring people badly in need of those resources to the mental health team. This knowledge enables psychiatric social workers to make sure that their patients receive the financial and social support from community programs that they may qualify for. Given their involvement in the community, it's not surprising that psychiatric social workers are often experts on the impact of environmental factors (such as substance abuse, poverty, crime, and homelessness) on patients' abilities to benefit from treatment.

Psychiatric social workers must complete four years of college and then two additional years at a university-based school of social work, from which they receive the master of social work (M.S.W.) degree. During their two years of graduate training, social work students learn about group and social processes and development, public policy and social organization, research methods, and the various kinds of programs federal, state, and local governments develop to help persons who can't help themselves. While in training, social workers may also study psychology, sociology, and other social science disciplines.

Psychiatric Nursing

Nurses trained in university settings generally receive a B.S. (bachelor of science) degree and a diploma in nursing upon graduation from the four-year nursing curriculum. After passing the required examination, graduates of these programs are then licensed as registered nurses. Psychiatric nursing students spend an additional two years in college pursuing a master's degree in psychiatric nursing, during which time they study psychopathology, diagnosis, and treatment. Special emphasis is given to psychopharmacology; nurses are usually responsible for ensuring that the powerful medications given to psychiatric inpatients are both effective and as free from side-effects as possible.

Extensive practicum training during the master's program, frequently with patients in inpatient settings, ensures that psychiatric nursing students acquire therapeutic skills. Psychiatric nurses have contributed to family therapy substantially. Another contribution has been to the *therapeutic milieu*, also termed the *therapeutic community*. Helped and supported by the nursing staff, psychiatric patients in a therapeutic community establish and enforce the rules governing their unit and regulating their interactions with each other. Many professionals believe that this approach helps even seriously disturbed patients to start reassuming responsibility for their own behavior and reestablishing social relations. Psychiatric nurses frequently have the task of ensuring the smooth functioning of the inpatient unit; for this reason, more and more psychiatric nurses are obtaining the management skills necessary for their roles as unit administrators.

THERAPIES

Bill, a 21-year-old college student, suffered from a debilitating phobia—an intense fear of any kind of sudden loud noise. He had become so anxious about possible exposure to noises that he had almost no social life. Balloons were especially frightening (they might pop!), so he avoided birthday parties, weddings, and other events where balloons might be present. Bill's girlfriend insisted that he get help.

On the first day of his therapy, two people led Bill—with his permission—into a small room filled with 100 large balloons. One person stood close to Bill, while the other person explained that he was going to begin popping the balloons. While some 50 balloons were popped with a pin, Bill shook uncontrollably, tears streaming down his face. Bill had to endure the popping of another 50 balloons before he was allowed to leave. And he returned for the next 2 days for still more balloon popping.

During the course of the 3 days, Bill became progressively less fearful and was eventually able to join in, stepping on hundreds of balloons and popping them. A year later, in a follow-up interview, Bill reported that he experienced no distress in the presence of balloons and no longer avoided situations where he might encounter them. Neither was he ill at ease when he sat relatively near a fireworks display on the Fourth of July. (Adapted from Houlihan et al., 1993.)

Bill's therapists were using a rapid treatment technique known as *flooding*, a form of behavior therapy in which the patient agrees to be instantly and totally immersed in the feared situation or surrounded by the feared object. Flooding is known to be effective in treating various types of phobias (Coles & Heinberg, 2000). But flooding is only one of the many effective therapies you will learn about in this chapter.

Psychotherapy uses psychological, rather than biological, means to treat emotional and behavioral disorders. The practice of psychotherapy has grown and changed enormously in the more than 100 years that have passed since Freud and his colleagues began using it.

INSIGHT THERAPIES

Some forms of psychotherapy are collectively referred to as **insight therapies** because their assumption is that psychological well-being depends on self-understanding—understanding of one's own thoughts, emotions, motives, behavior, and coping mechanisms.

Psychodynamic Therapies

Psychodynamic therapies attempt to uncover childhood experiences that explain a patient's current difficulties. The techniques associated with the first such therapy, Freud's **psychoanalysis,** are still used by psychodynamic therapists today (Epstein et al., 2001). One such technique is **free association,** in which the patient is asked to reveal whatever thoughts, feelings, or images come to mind, no matter how trivial, embarrassing, or terrible they might seem. The analyst then pieces together the free-flowing associations, explains their meaning, and helps the patient gain insight into the thoughts and behavior that are troubling him or her. But some patients avoid revealing certain painful or embarrassing thoughts while engaging in free association, a phenomenon Freud called *resistance*. Resistance may take the form of halting speech during free association, "forgetting" appointments with the analyst, or even arriving late.

Dream analysis is another technique used by psychoanalysts. Freud believed that areas of emotional concern repressed in waking life are sometimes expressed in symbolic form in dreams. And Freud claimed that patient behavior may have a symbolic quality as well. At some point during psychoanalysis, Freud said, the patient reacts to the analyst with the same feelings that were present in another significant relationship—usually that with the patient's mother or father. This reaction he called **transference.** Freud believed that encouraging patients to achieve transference was an essential part of psychotherapy. He claimed that transference allows the patient to relive troubling experiences from the past with the analyst as parent substitute, thereby resolving any hidden conflicts.

Many therapists today practice *brief psychodynamic therapy* in which the therapist and patient decide on the issues to explore at the outset rather than waiting for them to emerge in the course of treatment. The therapist assumes a more active role and places more emphasis on the present than in traditional psychoanalysis. Brief psychodynamic therapy may require only one or two visits per week for as few as 12 to 20 weeks. In a review of 11 well-controlled studies, Crits-Christoph (1992) found brief psychodynamic therapy to be as effective as other psychotherapies. And more recent research has also supported this evaluation (Hager et al., 2000).

Humanistic Therapies

Humanistic therapies assume that people have the ability and freedom to lead rational lives and make rational choices. **Person-centered therapy,** developed by Carl Rogers (1951), is one of the most frequently used humanistic therapies. According to this view, people are innately good and, if allowed to develop naturally, will grow toward *self-actualization*—the realization of their inner potential. The humanistic perspective suggests that psychological disorders result when a person's natural tendency toward self-actualization is blocked either by the person or by others. In the 1940s and 1950s, person-centered therapy enjoyed a strong following among psychologists.

The person-centered therapist attempts to create an accepting climate—based on unconditional positive regard for the client. The therapist also empathizes with the client's concerns and emotions. When the client speaks, the therapist follows by restating or reflecting back the client's ideas and feelings. Using these techniques, the therapist allows the direction of the therapy sessions to be controlled by the client. Rogers rejected all forms of therapy that cast the therapist in the role of expert and the client in the role of a patient who expects the therapist to prescribe something that "cures" his or her problem. Thus, person-centered therapy is called **nondirective therapy.**

Gestalt Therapy

Gestalt therapy, developed by Fritz Perls (1969), emphasizes the importance of clients' fully experiencing, in the present moment, their feelings, thoughts, and actions and then taking responsibility for them. The goal of Gestalt therapy is to help clients achieve a more integrated self and become more authentic and self-accepting. In addition, they must learn to assume personal responsibility for their behavior, rather than blaming society, past experiences, parents, or others.

Gestalt therapy is a **directive therapy,** one in which the therapist takes an active role in determining the course of therapy sessions. The well-known phrase "getting in touch with your feelings" is an ever-present objective of the Gestalt therapist. Perls suggested that individuals who are in need of therapy carry around a heavy load of unfinished business, which may be in the form of resentment toward or conflicts with parents, siblings, lovers, employers, or others. If not resolved, these conflicts are carried forward into the person's present relationships. One method for dealing with unfinished business is the "empty chair" technique (Paivio & Greenberg, 1995). The client sits facing an empty chair and imagines, for example, that a wife, husband, father, or mother sits there, and then proceeds to tell the chair what he or she truly feels about that person. Next, the client trades places and sits in the empty chair and role-plays what the imagined person's response would be to what the client has said.

RELATIONSHIP THERAPIES

Relationship therapies look not only at the individual's internal struggles but also at his or her interpersonal relationships. Some deliberately create new relationships for people, relationships that can support them in their efforts to address psychological problems.

Interpersonal Therapy

Interpersonal therapy (IPT) is a brief psychotherapy that has proven very effective in the treatment of depression (Elkin et al., 1989, 1995; Klerman et al., 1984). This type of therapy is designed specifically to help patients cope with four types of problems commonly associated with major depression:

1. *Unusual or severe responses to the death of a loved one.* The therapist and patient discuss the patient's relationship with the deceased person and feelings (such as guilt) that may be associated with the death.

2. *Interpersonal role disputes.* The therapist helps the patient understand others' points of view and explore options for bringing about change.

3. *Difficulty in adjusting to a role transition such as divorce, a career change, or retirement.* The patient is helped to see the change not as a threat but rather as a challenge and an opportunity for growth that can be mastered.

4. *Deficits in interpersonal skills.* Through role-playing and analysis of the patient's communication style, the therapist tries to help the patient develop the interpersonal skills necessary to initiate and sustain relationships.

Interpersonal therapy is relatively brief, consisting of 12 to 16 weekly sessions. A large study conducted by the National Institute of Mental Health found this type of psychotherapy to be an effective treatment, even for severe depression, and one with a low dropout rate (Elkin et al., 1989, 1995). Research also indicates that patients who recover from major depression can enjoy a longer period without relapse when they continue with monthly sessions of interpersonal therapy (Frank et al., 1991).

Couple and Family Therapy

There are therapists who specialize in treating the troubled family. Some therapists work with couples in *couple therapy* to help them resolve their difficulties. In **family therapy,** parents and children enter therapy as a group. The therapist pays attention to the dynamics of the family unit—how family members communicate, how they act toward one another, and how they view each other. The goal of the therapist is to help the family members reach agreement on certain changes that will help heal the wounds of the family unit, improve communication patterns, and create more understanding and harmony within the group.

Couple or family therapy appears to have positive effects in treating a number of disorders and clinical problems (Lebow & Gurman, 1995). When used along with medication, family therapy can be beneficial in the treatment of schizophrenia and can reduce relapse rates (Carpenter, 1996). Patients with schizophrenia are more likely to relapse if their family members express emotions, attitudes, and behaviors that involve criticism, hostility, or emotional overinvolvement (Linszen et al., 1997). This pattern is labeled *high in expressed emotion,* or *high EE* (Falloon, 1988; Jenkins & Karno, 1992). Family therapy can help other family members modify their behavior toward the patient. Family therapy also seems to be the most favorable setting for treating adolescent drug abuse (Lebow & Gurman, 1995).

Group Therapy

Group therapy is a form of therapy in which several clients (usually seven to ten) meet regularly with one or more therapists to resolve personal problems. Besides being less expensive than individual therapy, group therapy gives the individual a sense of belonging, an opportunity to express feelings, to get feedback from others in the group, and to give and receive help and emotional support. Learning that others share their problems leaves people feeling less alone and ashamed. A review of studies comparing prisoners who participated in group therapy to those who did not found that group participation was helpful for a variety of problems, including anxiety, depression, and low self-esteem (Morgan & Flora, 2002).

A variant of group therapy is the *self-help group.* About 12 million people in the United States participate in roughly 500,000 self-help groups, most of which focus on a single problem such as substance abuse or depression. Self-help groups usually are not led by professional therapists. They are simply groups of people who share a common problem and meet to give and receive support. One of the oldest and best-known self-help groups is Alcoholics Anonymous (AA), which claims 1.5 million members worldwide. Self-help groups patterned after Alcoholics Anonymous have been formed to help individuals overcome many other addictive behaviors, from overeating (Overeaters Anonymous) to gambling (Gamblers Anonymous). One study indicated that people suffering from anxiety-based problems were helped by a commercial multimedia self-help program called "Attacking Anxiety." Of the 176 individuals who participated in the study, 62 were reported to have achieved clinically significant improvement, and another 40 reported some improvement (Finch et al., 2000).

BEHAVIOR THERAPIES

A **behavior therapy** is a treatment approach consistent with the learning perspective on psychological disorders—that abnormal behavior is learned. Instead of viewing the maladaptive behavior as a symptom of some underlying disorder, the behavior therapist sees the behavior itself as the disorder. If a person comes to a therapist with a fear of flying, that fear of flying is seen as the problem. Behavior therapies use learning principles to eliminate inappropriate or maladaptive behaviors and replace them with more adaptive ones, an approach referred to as **behavior modification.** The goal is to change the troublesome behavior, not to change the individual's personality structure or to search for the origin of the problem behavior.

Behavior Modification Techniques Based on Operant Conditioning

Behavior modification techniques based on operant conditioning seek to control the consequences of behavior. *Extinction* of an undesirable behavior is accomplished by terminating, or withholding, the reinforcement that is maintaining that behavior (Lerman & Iwata, 1996). Behavior therapists also seek to reinforce any desirable behavior in order to increase its frequency. Institutional settings such as hospitals, prisons, and school classrooms are well suited to these techniques, because they provide a restricted environment in which the consequences of behavior can be more strictly controlled.

Some institutions use **token economies,** which reward appropriate behavior with tokens (such as poker chips, play money, or gold stars). These tokens can later be exchanged for desired goods (such as candy, gum, or cigarettes) and/or privileges (such as weekend passes, free time, or participation in desirable activities). Sometimes individuals are fined a given number of tokens for undesirable behavior. For decades, mental hospitals have successfully used token economies with chronic schizophrenics to improve their self-care skills and social interaction (Ayllon & Azrin, 1965, 1968).

Another effective method used to eliminate undesirable behavior, especially in children and adolescents, is **time out** (Brantner & Doherty, 1983). Children are told in advance that if they engage in certain undesirable behaviors, they will be removed from the situation and will have to pass a period of time (usually no more than 15 minutes) in a place containing no reinforcers (no television, books, toys, friends, and so on). Theoretically, the undesirable behavior will stop if it is no longer followed by attention or any other positive reinforcers.

Behavior therapies based on operant conditioning have been particularly effective in modifying some behaviors of seriously disturbed people. Although these techniques do not cure schizophrenia, autism, or mental retardation, they can increase the frequency of desirable behaviors and decrease the frequency of undesirable behaviors in individuals who suffer from these conditions. For example, a large proportion of people who suffer from schizophrenia smoke cigarettes. Monetary reinforcement has been found to be as effective as nicotine patches for the reduction of smoking among them (Tidey et al., 2002). Sometimes, modifying such behaviors enables the family members of people with schizophrenia to accept and care for them more easily.

Behavior modification techniques can also be used by people who want to break bad habits such as smoking and overeating or to develop good habits such as a regular exercise regime. If you want to modify any of your behaviors, devise a reward system for desirable behaviors, and remember the principles of shaping. Reward gradual changes in the direction of your ultimate goal. If you are trying to develop better eating habits, don't try to change a lifetime of bad habits all at once. Begin with a small step such as substituting frozen yogurt for ice cream. Set realistic weekly goals that you are likely to be able to achieve.

Therapies Based on Classical Conditioning

Therapies based on classical conditioning can be used to rid people of fears and other undesirable behaviors. One of the pioneers of this approach, psychiatrist Joseph Wolpe (1958, 1973), reasoned that if he could get people to relax and stay relaxed while they thought about a feared object, person, place, or situation, they could conquer their fear or phobia. In Wolpe's therapy, **systematic desensitization,** clients are trained in deep muscle relaxation. Then they confront a hierarchy of fears—a graduated series of anxiety-producing situations—either *in vivo* (in real life) or in imagination, until they can remain relaxed even in the presence of the most feared situation. The technique can be used for everything from fear of animals to claustrophobia, test anxiety, and social and other situational fears.

Many experiments, demonstrations, and case reports confirm that systematic desensitization is a highly successful treatment for eliminating fears and phobias in a relatively short time (Kalish, 1981; Rachman & Wilson, 1980). This technique has proved effective for specific problems such as test anxiety, stage fright, and anxiety related to sexual disorders.

Flooding, a behavior therapy used in the treatment of phobias, was the type of therapy used to help Bill, who was featured in this chapter's opening story. It involves exposing clients to the feared object or event (or asking them to vividly imagine it) for an extended period until their anxiety decreases. Clients are exposed to the fear all at once, not gradually as in systematic desensitization. An individual with a fear of heights, for example, might have to go onto the roof of a tall building and remain there until the fear subsided.

Flooding sessions typically last from 30 minutes to 2 hours and should not be terminated until patients are markedly less afraid than they were at the beginning of the session. Additional sessions are required until the fear response is extinguished or reduced to an acceptable level. It is rare for a patient to need more than six treatment sessions (Marshall & Segal, 1988). *In vivo* flooding, the real-life experience, works faster and is more effective than simply imagining the feared object or event (Chambless & Goldstein, 1979; Marks, 1972). For example, a person who fears flying would be better off taking an actual plane trip than just thinking about one.

Exposure and Response Prevention

Exposure and response prevention has been successful in treating obsessive-compulsive disorder (Baer, 1996; Foa, 1995; Rhéaume & Ladouceur, 2000). The first component of this therapy involves *exposure*—confronting patients with objects or situations they have been avoiding because those things trigger obsessions and compulsive rituals. The second component is *response prevention*, in which patients agree to resist performing their compulsive rituals for progressively longer periods of time.

Initially, the therapist identifies the thoughts, objects, or situations that trigger the compulsive ritual. For example, touching a doorknob, a piece of unwashed fruit, or garbage might ordinarily send people with a fear of contamination to the nearest bathroom to wash their hands. Patients are gradually exposed to stimuli they find more and more distasteful and anxiety-provoking. They must agree not to perform the normal ritual (hand washing, bathing, or the like) for a specified period of time after exposure. A typical treatment course—about ten sessions over a period of 3 to 7 weeks—can bring about considerable improvement in 60–70% of patients (Jenike, 1990). And patients treated with exposure and response prevention are less likely to relapse after treatment than those treated with drugs alone (Greist, 1992). This therapy has also proved useful in the treatment of posttraumatic stress disorder (Cloitre et al., 2002).

Aversion Therapy

Aversion therapy is used to rid clients of a harmful or socially undesirable behavior by pairing it with a painful, sickening, or otherwise aversive stimulus. Electric shock, emetics (substances that cause nausea and vomiting), or other unpleasant stimuli are paired with the undesirable behavior time after time until a strong negative association is formed and the person comes to avoid that behavior, habit, or substance. Treatment continues until the bad habit loses its appeal and becomes associated with pain or discomfort.

Alcoholics are sometimes given a nausea-producing substance such as Antabuse, which reacts violently with alcohol in a person's stomach, causing retching and vomiting. But for most problems, aversion therapy need not be so intense as to make a person physically ill. A controlled comparison of treatments for chronic nail biting revealed that mild aversion therapy—painting a bitter-tasting substance on the fingernails—yielded significant improvement (Allen, 1996).

Participant Modeling

Therapies derived from Albert Bandura's work on observational learning are based on the belief that people can overcome fears and acquire social skills through modeling. The most effective type of therapy based on observational learning theory is called **participant modeling** (Bandura, 1977; Bandura et al., 1975, 1977). In this therapy, a model demonstrates the appropriate response in graduated steps, and the client attempts to imitate the model step by step, while the therapist gives encouragement and support. Most specific phobias can be extinguished in only 3 or 4 hours with participant modeling.

COGNITIVE THERAPIES

Cognitive therapies, based on the cognitive perspective toward psychological disorders, assume that maladaptive behavior can result from irrational thoughts, beliefs, and ideas, which the therapist tries to change.

Rational-Emotive Therapy

Clinical psychologist Albert Ellis (1961, 1977, 1993) developed **rational-emotive therapy** in the 1950s. Rational-emotive therapy is based on Ellis's *ABC theory*. The A refers to the activating event; the B, to the person's belief about the event; and the C, to the emotional consequence that follows. Ellis claims that it is not the event itself that causes the emotional consequence, but rather the person's belief about the event. In other words, A does not cause C; B causes C. If the belief is irrational, then the emotional consequence can be extreme distress, as illustrated in Figure 25.2.

Rational-emotive therapy is a directive, confrontational form of psychotherapy designed to challenge clients' irrational beliefs about themselves and others. With this form of therapy, most clients see a therapist individually, once a week, for 5 to 50 sessions. In Ellis's view, as clients begin to replace irrational beliefs with rational ones, their emotional reactions become more appropriate, less distressing, and more likely to lead to constructive behavior. One review of 28 studies showed that patients receiving rational-emotive therapy did better than those receiving no treatment or a placebo and about the same as those undergoing systematic desensitization (Engles et al., 1993).

Cognitive Therapy

Psychiatrist Aaron T. Beck (1976) claims that much of the misery endured by a depressed and anxious person can be traced to *automatic thoughts*—unreasonable but unquestioned ideas that rule the person's life ("To be happy, I must be liked by everyone"; "If people disagree with me, it means they don't like me"). Beck (1991) believes that depressed persons hold "a negative view of the present, past, and future experiences" (p. 369). These persons notice only negative, unpleasant things and jump to upsetting conclusions.

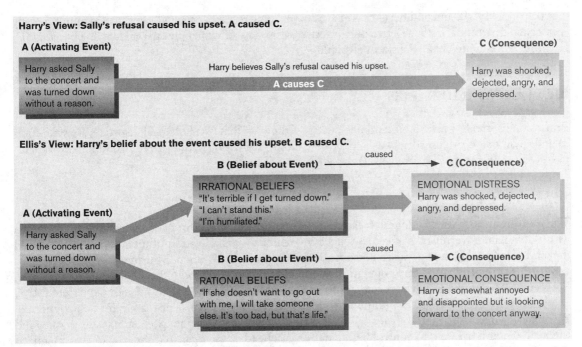

Harry's View: Sally's refusal caused his upset. A caused C.

A (Activating Event)

Harry asked Sally to the concert and was turned down without a reason.

Harry believes Sally's refusal caused his upset.
A causes C

C (Consequence)

Harry was shocked, dejected, angry, and depressed.

Ellis's View: Harry's belief about the event caused his upset. B caused C.

B (Belief about Event) —— caused ——▶ **C (Consequence)**

IRRATIONAL BELIEFS
"It's terrible if I get turned down."
"I can't stand this."
"I'm humiliated."

EMOTIONAL DISTRESS
Harry was shocked, dejected, angry, and depressed.

A (Activating Event)

Harry asked Sally to the concert and was turned down without a reason.

B (Belief about Event) —— caused ——▶ **C (Consequence)**

RATIONAL BELIEFS
"If she doesn't want to go out with me, I will take someone else. It's too bad, but that's life."

EMOTIONAL CONSEQUENCE
Harry is somewhat annoyed and disappointed but is looking forward to the concert anyway.

FIGURE 25.2   The ABCs of Rational-Emotive Therapy. Rational-emotive therapy teaches clients that it is not the activating event (A) that causes the upsetting consequences (C). Rather, it is the client's beliefs (B) about the activating event. Irrational beliefs cause emotional distress, according to Albert Ellis. Rational-emotive therapists help clients identify their irrational beliefs and replace them with rational ones.

The goal of **cognitive therapy** is to help patients stop their negative thoughts as they occur and replace them with more objective thoughts. After identifying and challenging patients' irrational thoughts, the therapist sets up a plan and guides patients so that their own experience can provide actual evidence from the real world to refute their false beliefs. Patients are given homework assignments, such as keeping track of automatic thoughts and the feelings evoked by them and substituting more rational thoughts. When cognitive therapy is combined with behavioral techniques such as relaxation training or exposure, it is called *cognitive-behavioral therapy.*

Cognitive therapy is brief, usually lasting only 10 to 20 sessions (Beck, 1976). This therapy has been researched extensively and is reported to be highly successful in the treatment of mild to moderately depressed patients (Holloa et al., 2002; Thase et al., 1991). There is some evidence that depressed people who have received cognitive therapy are less likely to relapse than those who have been treated with antidepressant drugs (Evans et al., 1992; Scott, 1996).

Cognitive therapy has also been shown to be effective for treating panic disorder (Barlow, 1997; Power et al., 2000). Cognitive therapy teaches patients to change the catastrophic interpretations of their symptoms and thereby prevent the symptoms from escalating into panic. Studies have shown that about 90% of patients with panic disorder are panic-free after 3 months of cognitive therapy (Robins & Hayes, 1993). Not only does cognitive therapy have a low dropout rate and a low relapse rate, but patients often continue to improve even after the treatment is completed (Öst & Westling, 1995). Also, cognitive therapy has proved effective as a treatment for generalized anxiety disorder (Beck, 1993; Wetherell et al., 2003), obsessive-compulsive disorder (OCD) (Abramowitz, 1997), cocaine addiction

(Carroll et al., 1994), and bulimia (Agras et al., 2000). Some research even indicates that cognitive therapy is effective in treating both negative and positive symptoms of schizophrenia (Bach & Hayes, 2002; Lecomte & Lecomte, 2002; Sensky et al., 2000).

BIOLOGICAL THERAPIES

Professionals who favor the biological perspective—the view that psychological disorders are symptoms of underlying physical disorders—usually favor a **biological therapy.** The three main biological therapies are drug therapy, electroconvulsive therapy, and psychosurgery.

Drug Therapy

The most frequently used biological treatment is drug therapy. Breakthroughs in drug therapy, coupled with the federal government's effort to reduce involuntary hospitalization of mental patients, reduced the mental hospital patient population from about 559,000 in 1955, when the drugs were introduced, to about 100,000 by 1990. And that population continued to drop throughout the 1990s. (See Figure 25.3.) Furthermore, the average stay of patients who do require hospitalization is now usually a matter of days.

Antipsychotic drugs, also known as *neuroleptics,* are prescribed primarily for schizophrenia. You may have heard of these drugs by their brand names—Thorazine, Stelazine, Compazine, and Mellaril. Their purpose is to control hallucinations, delusions, disorganized speech, and disorganized

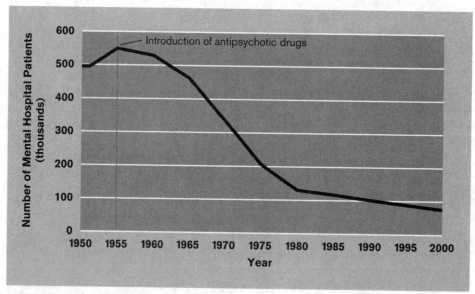

FIGURE 25.3   Decrease in Patient Populations in State and County Mental Hospitals (1950–2000). State and county mental hospital patient populations peaked at approximately 560,000 in 1955. In the same year, the antipsychotic drugs were introduced. The drugs, coupled with the federal government's efforts to reduce involuntary hospitalization of mental patients, resulted in a dramatic decrease in the patient population—down to about 100,000 in 1990 and lower than that in 2000. (Data from Manderscheid & Henderson, 2000.)

behavior (Andreasen et al., 1995). The neuroleptics work primarily by inhibiting the activity of the neurotransmitter dopamine. About 50% of patients have a good response to the standard antipsychotic drugs (Kane, 1996). But many patients, particularly those with an early onset of schizophrenia, are not helped by them (Meltzer et al., 1997), and others show only slight or modest improvement in symptoms. The long-term use of these antipsychotic drugs carries a high risk of a severe side effect, *tardive dyskinesia*—almost continual twitching and jerking movements of the face and tongue and squirming movements of the hands and trunk (Glazer et al., 1993).

Newer antipsychotic drugs, called *atypical neuroleptics* (clozapine, risperidone, olanzipine), can treat both the positive symptoms and the negative symptoms of schizophrenia, leading to marked improvement in patients' quality of life (Worrel et al., 2000). Atypical neuroleptics target both dopamine receptors and seratonin receptors in the brain (Kawanishi et al., 2000). About 10% of patients who take clozapine find the results so dramatic that they almost feel as though they have been reborn. Clozapine produces fewer side effects than typical neuroleptics, and patients taking it are less likely to develop tardive dyskinesia (Casey, 1996). However, clozapine is extremely expensive, and without careful monitoring, it can cause a fatal blood defect in 1–2% of patients who take it. Risperidone appears to be effective and safe and has fewer side effects than typical neuroleptics (Marder, 1996; Tamminga, 1996). Yet another advantage is that risperidone is much more effective than other neuroleptics in treating the negative symptoms of schizophrenia (Marder, 1996).

Antidepressants act as mood elevators for people who are severely depressed (Elkin et al., 1995), and they are also helpful in treating certain anxiety disorders. About 65–75% of patients who take antidepressants find themselves significantly improved, and 40–50% of those essentially recover completely (Frazer, 1997). The first generation of antidepressants are known as the *tricyclics* (amitriptyline, imipramine) (Nutt, 2000). The tricyclics work against depression by blocking the reuptake of norepinephrine and serotonin into the axon terminals, thus enhancing the action of these neurotransmitters in the synapses. But tricyclics can have some unpleasant side effects—sedation, dizziness, nervousness, fatigue, dry mouth, forgetfulness, and weight gain (Frazer, 1997). Progressive weight gain (an average of more than 20 pounds) is the main reason people stop taking tricyclics, in spite of the relief these drugs provide from distressing psychological symptoms.

The second-generation antidepressants, the *selective serotonin reuptake inhibitors (SSRIs)*, block the reuptake of the neurotransmitter serotonin, increasing its availability at the synapses in the brain (Nutt, 2000; Vetulani & Nalepa, 2000). SSRIs (fluoxetine, clomipramine) have fewer side effects (Nelson, 1997) and are safer in overdose than tricyclics (Thase & Kupfer, 1996). SSRIs have been found to be promising in treating obsessive-compulsive disorder (Goodwin, 1996), social phobia (Jefferson, 1995), panic disorder (Coplan et al., 1997; Jefferson, 1997), and binge eating (Hudson et al., 1996). However, SSRIs can cause sexual dysfunction, although normal sexual functioning returns when the drug is discontinued. Early publicity that SSRIs, especially fluoxetine (Prozac), increase the risk of suicide has not been substantiated (Warshaw & Keller, 1996).

Another drug treatment for depression involves the *monoamine oxidase (MAO) inhibitors* (sold under the names Marplan, Nardil, and Parnate). By blocking the action of an enzyme that breaks down norepinephrine and serotonin in the synapses, MAO inhibitors increase the availability of norepinephrine and serotonin. MAO inhibitors are usually prescribed for depressed patients who do not respond to other antidepressants (Thase et al., 1992). They are also effective in treating panic disorder (Sheehan & Raj, 1988) and social phobia (Marshall et al., 1994). But MAO inhibitors have many of the same unpleasant side effects as tricyclic antidepressants, and patients taking MAO inhibitors must avoid certain foods or run the risk of stroke.

Lithium, in the form of a naturally occurring salt, is considered a wonder drug for 40–50% of patients suffering from bipolar disorder (Thase & Kupfer, 1996). It is said to begin to quiet the manic state within 5 to 10 days. This is an amazing accomplishment, because the average episode, if untreated, lasts about 3 to 4 months. A proper maintenance dose of lithium yields reductions in depressive episodes as well as manic ones. Published reports over a period of three decades show that the clinical effectiveness of lithium for treating depression and bipolar disorder is unmatched (Ross et al., 2000). But 40–60% of those who take a maintenance dose will experience a recurrence (Thase & Kupfer, 1996). Also, careful measurement of the lithium level in the patient's system is necessary every 2 to 6 months to guard against lithium poisoning and permanent damage to the nervous system (Schou, 1997). Recent research suggests that *anticonvulsant drugs*, such as divalproex, may be just as effective as lithium for managing bipolar symptoms (Bowden et al., 2000; Kowatch et al., 2000). Moreover, the best treatment outcomes occur when a mood stabilizer (lithium or divalproex) is combined with an antipsychotic drug (Sachs et al., 2002).

The family of minor tranquilizers, called *benzodiazepines*, includes, among others, the well-known drugs sold as Valium and Librium and the newer high-potency drug Xanax (pronounced ZAN-ax). Used primarily to treat anxiety, benzodiazepines are prescribed more often than any other class of psychiatric drugs (Medina et al., 1993). They have been found to be an effective treatment for panic disorder (Davidson, 1997; Noyes et al., 1996) and generalized anxiety disorder (Lydiard et al., 1996).

Xanax, the largest-selling psychiatric drug (Famighetti, 1997), appears to be particularly effective in relieving anxiety and depression. Xanax is effective in the treatment of panic disorder (Noyes et al., 1996), and it works faster and has fewer side effects than antidepressants (Ballenger et al., 1993; Jonas & Cohon, 1993). However, if patients discontinue treatment, relapse is likely (Rickels et al., 1993). And there is a downside to Xanax: Many patients, once they are panic-free, find themselves unable to discontinue the drug because they experience moderate to intense withdrawal symptoms, including intense anxiety (Otto et al., 1993). Valium seems to be just as effective as Xanax for treating panic disorder, and withdrawal is easier. Although withdrawal is a problem with benzodiazepines, the abuse and addiction potential of these drugs is fairly low (Romach et al., 1995).

It's important to note that antipsychotics, antidepressants, and lithium do not cure psychological disorders, so patients usually experience a relapse if they stop taking the drugs when their symptoms fade. Maintenance doses of antidepressants following a major depression reduce the probability of recurrence (Prien & Kocsis, 1995). Maintenance doses are usually required with anxiety disorders as well, or symptoms are likely to return (Rasmussen et al., 1993).

Electroconvulsive Therapy

Antidepressant drugs are relatively slow-acting: A severely depressed patient needs at least 2 to 6 weeks to obtain relief, and 30% don't respond at all. This can be too risky for suicidal patients. **Electroconvulsive therapy (ECT),** in which an electric current is passed through the brain, causing a seizure, is sometimes used with such patients. ECT has a bad reputation because it was misused and overused in the 1940s and 1950s. Nevertheless, when used appropriately, ECT is a highly effective treatment for major depression (Folkerts, 2000). And depressed patients who are 75 and older tolerate the procedure as well as younger patients do and reap comparable therapeutic benefits (Tew et al., 1999).

For many years, ECT involved passing an electric current through both cerebral hemispheres, a procedure known as *bilateral ECT.* Today, electric current is administered to the right hemisphere only, and the procedure is called *unilateral ECT.* Research suggests that unilateral ECT is as effective as the more intense bilateral ECT while producing milder cognitive effects (Sackeim et al., 2000). Also, a patient undergoing ECT today is given anesthesia, controlled oxygenation, and a muscle relaxant.

Experts think that ECT changes the biochemical balance in the brain, which in turn results in a lifting of depression. When ECT is effective, cerebral blood flow in the prefrontal cortex is reduced, and delta waves (usually associated with slow-wave sleep) appear (Sackeim et al., 1996). Some psychiatrists and neurologists have spoken out against the use of ECT, claiming that it causes pervasive brain damage and memory loss. But advocates of ECT say that claims of brain damage are based on animal studies in which dosages of ECT were much higher than those now used in human patients.

No structural brain damage from ECT has been revealed in studies comparing MRI or CT scans of human patients before and after a series of treatments (Devanand et al., 1994).

There are other methods of physically stimulating the brain. Toward the end of the 20th century, a new therapy known as *rapid transcranial magnetic stimulation (rTMS)* appeared. This magnetic therapy is not invasive in any way. It is performed on patients who are not sedated; it causes no seizures or memory loss and has no known side effects. Its therapeutic value is similar to that of ECT, and it is much more accepted by the public (Vetulani & Nalepa, 2000). This therapy has also been used effectively in conjunction with SSRIs in treating depressed patients (Conca et al., 2000).

Psychosurgery

An even more drastic treatment than ECT is **psychosurgery**—brain surgery performed strictly to alleviate serious psychological disorders, such as severe depression, severe anxiety, and obsessions, or to provide relief from unbearable chronic pain. The first experimental brain surgery for human patients was developed by Portuguese neurologist Egas Moniz in 1935 to treat severe phobias, anxiety, and obsessions. In his technique, the *lobotomy*, surgeons severed the neural connections between the frontal lobes and the deeper brain centers involved in emotion. But no brain tissue was removed. At first the procedure was considered a tremendous contribution, and Moniz won the Nobel Prize in Medicine in 1949 for developing it. Eventually, it became apparent, however, that this treatment left patients in a severely deteriorated condition.

Modern psychosurgery procedures result in less intellectual impairment because, rather than using conventional surgery, surgeons deliver electric currents through electrodes to destroy a much smaller, more localized area of brain tissue. In one procedure, called a *cingulotomy*, electrodes are used to destroy the cingulum, a small bundle of nerves connecting the cortex to the emotional centers of the brain. Several procedures, including cingulotomy, have been helpful for some extreme cases of obsessive-compulsive disorder (Baer et al., 1995; Trivedi, 1996). But the results of psychosurgery are still not predictable, and the consequences—whether good or bad—are irreversible. For this reason, the treatment is considered experimental and absolutely a last resort.

EVALUATING THE THERAPIES

How effective are the various therapies summarized in Table 25.2? Research results are mixed. In a classic study of therapeutic effectiveness, researchers Smith and others (1980) reanalyzed the results of 475 studies, which involved 25,000 patients. Their review revealed that psychotherapy was better than no treatment, but no one type of therapy was more effective than another. A subsequent reanalysis of the same data by Hans Eysenck (1994), however, showed a slight advantage for behavioral therapies over other types. And a study by Holloa and others (2002) found that cognitive and interpersonal therapies have an advantage over psychodynamic approaches for depressed patients.

But how do the patients themselves rate the therapies? To answer this question, *Consumer Reports* (1995) conducted the largest survey to date on patient attitudes toward psychotherapy. Martin Seligman (1995, 1996), a consultant for the study, summarized its findings:

- Overall, patients believed that they benefited substantially from psychotherapy.
- Patients seemed equally satisfied with their therapy, whether it was provided by a psychologist, a psychiatrist, or a social worker.
- Patients who were in therapy for more than 6 months did considerably better; generally, the longer patients stayed in therapy, the more they improved.
- Patients who took a drug such as Prozac or Xanax believed that it helped, but overall, psychotherapy alone seemed to work about as well as psychotherapy plus drugs.

TABLE 25.2   Summary and Comparison of the Therapies

TYPE OF THERAPY	PERCEIVED CAUSE OF DISORDER	PRIMARY DISORDERS GOALS OF THERAPY	METHODS USED	TREATED
Psycho-analysis	Unconscious sexual and aggressive urges or conflicts; fixations; weak ego	Help patient bring disturbing, repressed material to consciousness and work through unconscious conflicts; strengthen ego functions	Psychoanalyst analyzes and interprets dreams, free associations, resistances, and transference.	General feelings of unhappiness; unresolved problems from childhood
Person-centered therapy	Blocking of normal tendency toward self-actualization; incongruence between real and desired self; overdependence on positive regard of others	Increase self-acceptance and self-understanding; help patient become more inner-directed; increase congruence between real and desired self; enhance personal growth	Therapist shows empathy, unconditional positive regard, and genuineness, and reflects client's expressed feelings back to client.	General feelings of unhappiness; interpersonal problems
Inter-personal therapy	Difficulty with relationships and/or life transitions, as well as possible biological causes	Adjust to bereavement; overcome interpersonal role disputes; improve interpersonal skills; adjust to role transitions such as divorce, career change, and retirement	Therapist helps patient (1) release the past and become actively interested in the present, (2) explore options for changing excessive role expectations (often involving other family members), (3) view change as a challenge rather than a threat, and/or (4) improve interpersonal skills, using techniques such as role-playing.	Depression

(continued)

    Choosing a therapist with the type of training best suited to your problem can be a key factor in how helpful the therapy turns out to be. Table 25.3 lists the various types of mental health professionals.

    One important difference among professionals that confuses many people is that a **psychologist** has an advanced degree, usually at the doctoral level, in psychology, while a **psychiatrist** is a medical doctor. Historically, drug therapy has been available only from psychiatrists. At present, however, there is a movement in the United States to allow psychologists with special training in psychopharmacology to prescribe drugs. To date, only the U.S. military and a couple of states have authorized prescribing privileges for psychologists. But the movement is gaining momentum.

TABLE 25.2 Summary and Comparison of the Therapies (continued)

TYPE OF THERAPY	PERCEIVED CAUSE OF DISORDER	PRIMARY DISORDERS GOALS OF THERAPY	METHODS USED	TREATED
Family and couple therapy	Problems caused by faulty communication patterns, unreasonable role expectations, drug and/or alcohol abuse, and so on	Create more understanding and harmony within the relationships; improve communication patterns; adjust to the emotional turmoil of divorce	Therapist sees clients individually or several family members at a time and explores such things as communication patterns, power struggles, and unreasonable demands and expectations.	Family problems such as marriage or relationship problems, troubled or troublesome teenagers, abusive relationships, drug or alcohol problems, schizophrenic family member
Behavior therapy	Learning of maladaptive behaviors or failure to learn appropriate behaviors	Extinguish maladaptive behaviors and replace with more adaptive ones; help patient acquire needed social skills	Therapist uses methods based on classical and operant conditioning and modeling, which include systematic desensitization, flooding, exposure and response prevention, and aversion therapy.	Fears, phobias, panic disorder, obsessive-compulsive disorder, bad habits
Cognitive therapy	Irrational and negative assumptions and ideas about self and others	Change faulty, irrational, and/or negative thinking	Therapist helps client identify irrational and negative thinking and substitute rational thinking.	Depression, anxiety, panic disorder, general feelings of unhappiness
Biological therapies	Underlying physical disorder caused by structural or biochemical abnormality in the brain; genetic inheritance	Eliminate or control biological cause of abnormal behavior; restore balance of neurotransmitters	Physician prescribes drugs such as antipsychotics, antidepressants, lithium, or tranquilizers; ECT; or psychosurgery.	Schizophrenia, depression, bipolar disorder, anxiety disorders

CULTURALLY SENSITIVE AND GENDER-SENSITIVE THERAPY

Among many psychotherapists, there is a growing awareness of the need to consider cultural variables in diagnosing and treating psychological disorders (Bernal & Castro, 1994). According to Kleinman and Cohen (1997), people experience and suffer from psychological disorders within a cultural context that may dramatically affect the meaning of symptoms, outcomes, and responses to therapy. Consequently, cultural differences between therapist and client may undermine the *therapeutic alliance*, the bond between therapist and client that is known to be a factor in the effectiveness of psychotherapy (Blatt et al., 1996). Thus, many experts advocate an approach called **culturally sensitive psychotherapy** in

TABLE 25.3   Mental Health Professionals

PROFESSIONAL TITLE	TRAINING	SERVICES PROVIDED
Psychiatrist	Medical degree (M.D. or O.D.); residency in psychiatry	Psychotherapy; drug therapy; hospitalization for serious psychological disorders
Psychoanalyst	M.D., Ph.D., or Psy.D.; additional training in psychoanalysis	Psychodynamic therapy
Clinical psychologist	Ph.D. or Psy.D.; internship in clinical psychology	Diagnosis and treatment of psychological disorders; can prescribe drugs in some settings after additional training; psychological testing
Counseling psychologist	Ph.D. or Ed.D.; internship in counseling psychology	Assessment and therapy for normal problems of life (e.g., divorce); psychological testing
School psychologist	Ph.D., Ed.D., or master's degree; internship in school psychology	Assessment and treatment of school problems in children and adolescents; psychological testing
Clinical or psychiatric social worker (M.S.W.)	Master's degree; internship in psychiatric social work	Diagnosis and treatment of psychological disorders; identification of supportive community services
Licensed professional counselor (L.P.C.)	Master's degree; internship in counseling	Assessment and therapy for normal problems of life; some psychological testing
Licensed marriage and family therapist (L.M.F.T.)	Master's degree; internship in couple and family therapy	Assessment and therapy for relationship problems
Licensed chemical dependency counsleor (L.C.D.C.)	Educational requirements vary from one state to another; often former addicts	Treatment and education for substance abuse problems

which knowledge of a client's cultural background guides the choice of therapeutic intervention (Kumpfer et al., 2002).

Culturally sensitive therapists recognize that language differences between therapists and patients can pose problems (Santiago-Rivera & Altarriba, 2002). For example, a patient who speaks both Spanish and English but is more fluent in Spanish may exhibit hesitations, back-tracking, and delayed responses to questions when being interviewed in English. Consequently, he or she may be thought to be suffering from the kind of disordered thinking that is often displayed by people with schizophrenia (Martinez, 1986). Such language differences may also affect patients' results on standardized tests used by clinicians. In one frequently cited study, researchers found that when a group of Puerto Rican patients took the Thematic Apperception Test (TAT) in English, their pauses and their choices of words were incorrectly interpreted as indications of psychological problems (Suarez, 1983). Thus, culturally sensitive therapists become familiar with patients' general fluency in the language in which they will be assessed prior to interviewing and testing them.

When working with recent immigrants to the United States, culturally sensitive therapists take into account the impact of the immigration experience on patients' thoughts and emotions (Lijtmaer, 2001; Smolar, 1999). Some researchers who have studied the responses of recent Asian immigrants to psychotherapy recommend that, prior to initiating diagnosis and treatment, therapists encourage patients who are immigrants to talk about feelings of sadness they have experienced as a result of leaving their native culture. Discussions of the patients' anxieties about adapting to life in a new society may also be helpful. Using this strategy, therapists may be able to separate depression and anxiety related to the immigration experience from true psychopathology.

Some advocates of culturally sensitive therapy point out that there are culture-specific practices that can be used as models for therapeutic interventions. Traditional Native American *healing circles*, for example, are being used by many mental health practitioners who serve Native Americans (Garrett et al., 2001). Members of a healing circle are committed to promoting the physical, mental, emotional, and spiritual well-being of one another. The members engage in group activities such as discussion, meditation, and prayer. Sometimes, a recognized Native healer leads the group in traditional healing ceremonies.

Culturally sensitive therapists also attempt to address group differences that can affect the results of therapy. For example, many studies have found that African Americans with mental disorders show less compliance with instructions about medication than do White Americans with the same diagnoses (Fleck et al., 2002; Hazlett-Stevens et al., 2002). A culturally sensitive approach to this problem might be based on a therapist's understanding of the importance of kinship networks and community relationships among African Americans. A therapist might increase an African American patient's medication compliance by having the patient participate in a support group with other African Americans suffering from the same illness and taking the same medications (Muller, 2002). In addition, researchers and experienced therapists recommend that non–African American therapists and African American patients openly discuss their differing racial perspectives prior to beginning therapy (Bean et al., 2002).

Many psychotherapists also note the need for **gender-sensitive therapy**— therapeutic techniques that take into the account the effects of gender on both the therapist's and the client's behavior (Gehart & Lyle, 2001). First, therapists must examine their own gender-based prejudices. They may assume men to be more analytical and women to be more emotional, for example. Or they may place too much emphasis on gender issues and misinterpret clients' problems. In one study, researchers found that therapists expect people who are working in nontraditional fields—female engineers and male nurses, for instance— to have more psychological problems (Rubinstein, 2001). Thus, therapists working with clients pursuing careers in nontraditional fields may assume that the clients' difficulties arise from conflicts about gender roles when, in reality, their problems may have an altogether different origin.

REFERENCES

Abramowitz, J. S. (1997). Effectiveness of psychological and pharmacological treatments for obsessive-compulsive disorder: A quantitative review. *Journal of Consulting and Clinical Psychology, 65,* 44–52.

Agras, W. S., Walsh, T., Fairburn, C. G., Wilson, T., & Kraemer, H. C. (2000). A multicenter comparison of cognitive-behavioral therapy and interpersonal psychotherapy for bulimia nervosa. *Archives of General Psychiatry, 57,* 459–466.

Ainsworth, M. (2000). ABCs of "internet therapy." *Metanoia* [On-line]. Retrieved from http://www.metanoia.org

Allen, K. W. (1996). Chronic nailbiting: A controlled comparison of competing response and mild aversion treatments. *Behaviour Research and Therapy, 34,* 269–272.

American Psychiatric Association. (1952). *Diagnostic and statistical manual of mental disorders*. Washington, DC: American Psychiatric Association.

American Psychiatric Association. (1968). *Diagnostic and statistical manual of mental disorders* (2nd ed.). Washington, DC: American Psychiatric Association.

American Psychiatric Association. (1980). *Diagnostic and statistical manual of mental disorders* (3rd ed.). Washington, DC: American Psychiatric Association.

American Psychiatric Association. (1987). *Diagnostic and statistical manual of mental disorders* (3rd ed., rev.). Washington, DC: American Psychiatric Association.

American Psychiatric Association. (1994). *Diagnostic and Statistical Manual of Mental Disorders* (4th ed.) Washington, DC: American Psychiatric Association.

Andreasen, N. C., Arndt, S., Alliger, R., Miller, D., & Flaum, M. (1995). Symptoms of schizophrenia: Methods, meanings, and mechanisms. *Archives of General Psychiatry, 52,* 341–351.

Ayllon, T., & Azrin, N. H. (1965). The measurement and reinforcement of behavior of psychotics. *Journal of the Experimental Analysis of Behavior, 8,* 357–383.

Ayllon, T., & Azrin, N. (1968). *The token economy: A motivational system for therapy and rehabilitation.* New York: Appleton-Century-Crofts.

Bach, P., & Hayes, S. (2002). The use of acceptance and commitment therapy to prevent the rehospitalization of psychotic patients: A randomized controlled trial. *Journal of Consulting and Clinical Psychology, 70,* 1129–1139.

Baer, L. (1996). Behavior theory: Endogenous serotonin therapy? *Journal of Clinical Psychiatry, 57*(6, Suppl.), 33–35.

Baer, L., Rauch, S. L., Ballantine, T., Jr., Martuza, R., Cosgrove, R., Cassem, E., Giriunas, I., Manzo, P. A., Dimino, C., & Jenike, M. A. (1995). Cingulotomy for intractable obsessive-compulsive disorder. *Archives of General Psychiatry, 52,* 384–392.

Ballenger, J. C., Pecknold, J., Rickels, K., & Sellers, E. M. (1993). Medication discontinuation in panic disorder. *Journal of Clinical Psychiatry, 54*(10, Suppl.), 15–21.

Bandura, A. (1977). *Social learning theory.* Englewood Cliffs, NJ: Prentice-Hall.

Bandura, A., Adams, N. E., & Beyer, J. (1977). Cognitive processes mediating behavioral change. *Journal of Personality and Social Psychology, 35,* 125–139.

Bandura, A., Jeffery, R. W., & Gajdos, E. (1975). Generalizing change through participant modeling with self-directed mastery. *Behaviour Research and Therapy, 13,* 141–152.

Barlow, D. H. (1997). Cognitive-behavioral therapy for panic disorder: Current status. *Journal of Clinical Psychiatry, 58*(6, Suppl.), 32–36.

Bean, R., Perry, B., & Bedell, T. (2002). Developing culturally competent marriage and family therapists: Treatment guidelines for non-African American therapists working with African American families. *Journal of Marital & Family Therapy, 28,* 153–164.

Beck, A. T. (1976). *Cognitive therapy and the emotional disorders.* New York: New American Library.

Beck, A. T. (1991). Cognitive therapy: A 30-year retrospective. *American Psychologist, 46,* 368–375.

Beck, A. T. (1993). Cognitive therapy: Past, present, and future. *Journal of Consulting and Clinical Psychology, 61,* 194–198.

Bernal, M. E., & Castro, F. G. (1994). Are clinical psychologists prepared for service and research with ethnic minorities? Report of a decade of progress. *American Psychologist, 49,* 797–805.

Blazer, D. G., George, L. K., Landerman, R., Pennybacker, M., Melville, M. L., Woodbury, M., Manton, K. G., Jordan, K., & Locke, B. Z. (1985). Psychiatric disorders: A rural urban comparison. *Archives of General Psychiatry, 42,* 651–656.

Blazer, D. G., Kessler, R. C., McGonagle, K. A., & Swartz, M. S. (1994). The prevalence and distribution of major depression in a national community sample: The National Comorbidity Survey. *American Journal of Psychiatry, 151,* 979–986.

Blatt, S. J., Sanislow, C. A., III, Zuroff, D. C., & Pinkonis, P. A. (1996). Characteristics of effective therapists: Further analyses of data from the National Institute of Mental Health Treatment of Depression Collaborative Research Program. *Journal of Consulting and Clinical Psychology, 64,* 1276–1284.

Bowden, C., Lecrubier, Y., Bauer, M., Goodwin, G., Greil, W., Sachs, G., & von Knorring, L. (2000). Maintenance therapies for classic and other forms of bipolar disorder. *Journal of Affective Disorders, 59* (Suppl. 1), S57–S67.

Brantner, J. P., & Doherty, M. A. (1983). A review of time out: A conceptual and methodological analysis. In S. Axlerod & J. Apsche (Eds.), *The effects of punishment on human behavior* (pp. 87–132). New York: Academic Press.

Breslau, N., Davis, G. C., Andreski, P., & Peterson, E. (1991). Traumatic events and posttraumatic stress disorder in an urban population of young adults. *Archives of General Psychiatry, 48*, 216–222.

Breuer, J., & Freud, S. (1895). Studies on hysteria. In J. Strachey (Ed.), *The standard edition of the complete psychological works of Sigmund Freud* (Vol. 2). London, England: Hogarth Press.

Burnam, M. A., Hough, R. L., Escobar, J. I., Karno, M., Timbers, D. M., Telles, C. A., & Locke, B. Z. (1987). Six-month prevalence of specific psychiatric disorders among Mexican Americans and non-Hispanic whites in Los Angeles. *Archives of General Psychiatry, 44*, 687–694.

Carmody, T. P., & Matarazzo, J. D. (1991). Health psychology. In M. Hersen, A. E. Kazdin, & A. S. Bellack (Eds.), *The clinical psychology handbook* (2nd ed.) (pp. 695–723). New York: Pergamon Press.

Carpenter, T., Jr. (1996). Maintenance therapy of persons with schizophrenia. *Journal of Clinical Psychiatry, 57*(9, Suppl.), 10–18.

Carroll, K. M., Rounsaville, B. J., Nich, C., Gordon, L. T., Wirtz, P. W., & Gawin, F. (1994). One-year follow-up of psychotherapy and pharmacotherapy for cocaine dependence: Delayed emergence of psychotherapy effects. *Archives of General Psychiatry, 51*, 989–997.

Casey, D. E. (1996). Side effect profiles of new antipsychotic agents. *Journal of Clinical Psychiatry, 57*(11, Suppl.), 40–45.

Chambless, D. L., & Goldstein, A. J. (1979). Behavioral psychotherapy. In R. J. Corsini (Ed.), *Current psychotherapies* (2nd ed., pp. 230–272). Itasca, IL: F. E. Peacock.

Chesney, M. A. (1993). Health psychology in the 21st century: Acquired immunodeficiency syndrome as a harbinger of things to come. *Health Psychology, 12*, 259–268.

Cloitre, M., Koenen, K., Cohen, L., & Han, H. (2002). Skills training in affective and interpersonal regulation followed by exposure: A phase-based treatment for PTSD related to childhood abuse. *Journal of Consulting and Clinical Psychology, 70*, 1067–1074.

Coles, M. E., & Heinberg, R. G. (2000). Patterns of anxious arousal during exposure to feared situations in individuals with social phobia. *Behaviour Research & Therapy, 38*, 405–424.

Conca, A., Swoboda, E., König, P., Koppi, S., Beraus, W., Künz, A., et al. (2000). Clinical impacts of single transcranial magnetic stimulation (sTMS) as an add-on therapy in severely depressed patients under SSRI treatment. *Human Psychopharmacology: Clinical and Experimental, 15*, 429–438.

Consumer Reports. (1995, November) Mental health: Does therapy help? pp. 734–739.

Coplan, J. D., Papp, L. A., Pine, D., Marinez, J., Cooper, T. Rosenblum, L. A., Klein, D. F., & Gorman, J. M. (1997). Clinical improvement with fluoxetine therapy and noradrenergic function in patients with panic disorder. *Archives of General Psychiatry, 54*, 643–648.

Crits-Christoph, P. (1992). The efficacy of brief dynamic psychotherapy: A meta-analysis. *American Journal of Psychiatry, 149*, 151–158.

Davidson, J. R. T. (1997). Use of benzodiazepines in panic disorder. *Journal of Clinical Psychiatry, 58*(2, Suppl.), 26–28.

Day, S., & Schneider, P. (2002). Psychotherapy using distance technology: A comparison of face-to-face, video, and audio treatment. *Journal of Counseling Psychology, 49*, 499–503.

Devanand, D. P., Dwork, A. J., Hutchinson, M. S. E., Bolwig, T. G., & Sackeim, H. A. (1994). Does ECT alter brain structure? *American Journal of Psychiatry, 151*, 957–970.

Dial, T. H., Pion, G., Cooney, B., Kohout, J., Kaplan, K., Ginsberg, L., Merwin, E., Fox, J., Ginsberg, M., Staton, J., Clawson, T., Wildermuth, V., Blankertz, L., & Hughes, R. (1992). Training of mental health providers. In R. Manderscheid & M. Sonnenschein (Eds.), *Mental health, United States, 1992* (pp. 142–162). Rockville, MD: U.S. Department of Health and Human Services.

Dorken, H. (1993). The hospital private practice of psychology: CHAMPUS 1981–1991. *Professional Psychology: Research and Practice, 24*, 409–417.

Eaton, W. W., Anthony, J. C., Tepper, S., & Dryman, A. (1992). Psychopathology and attrition in the Epidemiologic Catchment Area Study. *American Journal of Epidemiology, 135*, 1051–1059.

Elkin, I., Gibbons, R. D., Shea, M. T., Sotsky, S. M., Watkins, J. T., Pikonis, P. A., & Hedeker, D. (1995). Initial severity and differential treatment outcome in the National Institute of Mental Health Treatment of Depression Collaborative Research Program. *Journal of Consulting and Clinical Psychology, 63*, 841–847.

Elkin, I., Shea, M. T., Watkins, J. T., et al. (1989). National Institute of Mental Health Treatment of Depression Collaborative Research Program: General effectiveness of treatments. *Archives of General Psychology, 46*, 971–982.

Ellis, A. (1961). *A guide to rational living*. Englewood Cliffs, NJ: Prentice-Hall.

Ellis, A. (1977). The basic clinical theory of rational-emotive therapy. In A. Ellis & R. Grieger (Eds.), *Handbook of rational-emotive therapy* (pp. 3–33). New York: Springer.

Ellis, A. (1993). Reflections on rational emotive therapy. *Journal of Consulting and Clilnical Psychology, 61*, 199–201.

Engles, G. I., Garnefski, N., & Diekstra, R. F. W. (1993). Efficacy of rational-emotive therapy: A quantitative analysis. *Journal of Consulting and Clinical Psychology, 61*, 1083–1090.

Epstein, J., Stern, E., & Silbersweig, D. (2001). Neuropsychiatry at the millennium: The potential for mind/brain integration through emerging interdisciplinary research strategies. *Clinical Neuroscience Research, 1*, 10–18.

Evans, M. D., Hollon, S. D., DeRubeis, R. J., Piasecki, J. M., Grove, W. M., Garvey, M. J., & Tuason, V. B. (1992). Differential relapse following cognitive therapy and pharmacotherapy for depression. *Archives of General Psychiatry, 49*, 802–808.

Eysenck, H. J. (1994). The outcome problem in psychotherapy: What have we learned? *Behaviour Research and Therapy, 32*, 477–495.

Falloon, I. R. H. (1988). Expressed emotion: Current status. *Psychological Medicine, 18*, 269–274.

Famighetti, R. (Ed.). (1997). *The world almanac and book of facts 1998*. Mahwah, NJ: World Almanac Books.

Finch, A. E., Lambert, M. J., & Brown, G. (2000). Attacking anxiety: A naturalistic study of a multimedia self-help program. *Journal of Clinical Psychology, 56*, 11–21.

Fleck, D., Hendricks, W., DelBellow, M., & Strakowski, S. (2002). Differential prescription of maintenance antipsychotics to African American and White patients with new-onset bipolar disorder. *Journal of Clinical Psychiatry, 63*, 658–664.

Florian, V., Mikulincer, M., & Taubman, O. (1995). Does hardiness contribute to mental health during a stressful real-life situation? The roles of appraisal and coping. *Journal of Personality and Social Psychology, 68*, 687–695.

Foa, E. B. (1995). How do treatments for obsessive-compulsive disorder compare? *Harvard Mental Health Letter, 12*(1), 8.

Folkerts, H. (2000). Electroconvulsive therapy of depressive disorders. *Ther. Umsch, 57*, 290–294.

Frank, E., Kupfer, D. J., Wagner, E. F., McEachran, A. B., & Cornes, C. (1991). Efficacy of interpersonal psychotherapy as a maintenance treatment of recurrent depression: Contributing factors. *Archives of General Psychiatry, 48*, 1053–1059.

Frazer, A. (1997). Antidepressants. *Journal of Clinical Psychiatry, 58*(6, Suppl.), 9–25.

Garrett, M., Garrett, J., & Brotherton, D. (2001). Inner circle/outer circle: A group technique based on Native American healing circles. *Journal for Specialists in Group Work, 26*, 17–30.

Gehart, D., & Lyle, R. (2001). Client experience of gender in therapeutic relationships: An interpretive ethnography. *Family Process, 40*, 443–458.

Glazer, W. M., Morgenstern, H., & Doucette, J. T. (1993). Predicting the long-term risk of tardive dyskinesia in outpatients maintained on neuroleptic medications. *Journal of Clinical Psychiatry, 54*, 133–139.

Goodwin, G. M. (1996). How do antidepressants affect serotonin receptors? The role of serotonin receptors in the therapeutic and side effect profile of the SSRIs. *Journal of Clinical Psychiatry, 57*(4, Suppl.), 9–13.

Greist, J. H. (1992). An integrated approach to treatment of obsessive compulsive disorder. *Journal of Clinical Psychiatry, 53*(4, Suppl.), 38–41.

Hager, W., Leichsenring, F., & Schiffler, A. (2000). When does a study of different therapies allow comparisons of their relative efficacy? *Psychother. Psychosom. Med. Psychol., 50*, 251–262.

Hazlett-Stevens, H., Craske, M., Roy-Byrne, P., Sherbourne, C., Stein, M., & Bystritsky, A. (2002). Predictors of willingness to consider medication and psychosocial treatment for panic disorder in primary care patients. *General Hospital Psychology, 24*, 316–321.

Holloa, S., Thase, M., & Marches, J. (2002). Treatment and prevention of depression. *Psychological Science in the Public Interest, 3*, 39–77.

Houlihan, D., Schwartz, C., Miltenberger, R., & Heuton, D. (1993). The rapid treatment of a young man's balloon (noise) phobia using in vivo flooding. *Journal of Behavior Therapy and Experimental Psychiatry, 24*, 233–240.

Hudson, J. I., Carter, W. P., & Pope, H. G., Jr. (1996). Antidepressant treatment of binge-eating disorder: Research findings and clinical guidelines. *Journal of Clinical Psychiatry, 57*(8, Suppl.), 73–79.

Hughes, C. C., Tremblay, M., Rapaport, R. N., & Leighton, A. H. (1960). *People of cove and woodlot*. New York: Basic Books.

Jefferson, J. W. (1995). Social phobia: A pharmacologic treatment overview. *Journal of Clinical Psychiatry, 56*(5, Suppl.), 18–24.

Jefferson, J. W. (1997). Antidepressants in panic disorder. *Journal of Clinical Psychiatry, 58*(2, Suppl.), 20–24.

Jenike, M. A. (1990, April). Obsessive-compulsive disorder. *Harvard Medical School Health Letter, 12*, 4–8.

Jenkins, J. H., & Karno, M. (1992). The meaning of expressed emotion: Theoretical issues raised by cross-cultural research. *American Journal of Psychiatry, 149*, 9–21.

Jonas, J. M., & Cohon, M. S. (1993). A comparison of the safety and efficacy of alprazolam versus other agents in the treatment of anxiety, panic, and depression: A review of the literature. *Journal of Clinical Psychiatry, 54*(10, Suppl.), 25–45.

Jones, B. P., & Butters, N. (1991). Neuropsychological assessment. In M. Hersen, A. E. Kazdin, & A. S. Bellack (Eds.), *The clinical psychology handbook* (2nd ed.) (pp. 406–429). New York: Pergamon Press.

Jones, E. (1953). *The life and work of Sigmund Freud, Vol. 1: The formative years and the great discoveries.* New York: Basic Books.

Kalish, H. I. (1981). *From behavioral science to behavior modification.* New York: McGraw-Hill.

Kane, J. M. (1996). Treatment-resistant schizophrenic patients. *Journal of Clinical Psychiatry, 57*(9, Suppl.), 35–40.

Kawanishi, Y., Tachikawa, H., & Suzuki, T. (2000). Pharmacogenomics and schizophrenia. *European Journal of Pharmacology, 410*, 227–241.

Kleinman, A., & Cohen, A. (1997, March). Psychiatry's global challenge. *Scientific American, 276*, 86–89.

Klerman, G. L., Weissman, M. N., Rounsaville, B. J., & Chevron, E. S. (1984). *Interpersonal therapy of depression.* New York: Academic Press.

Kowatch, R., Suppes, T., Carmody, T., Bucci, J., Hume, J., Kromelis, M., Emslie, G., Weinberg, W., & Rush, A. (2000). Effect size of lithium, divalproex sodium, and carbamazepine in children and adolescents with bipolar. *Journal of the American Academy of Child & Adolescent Psychiatry, 39*, 713–720.

Kraepelin, E. (1913). *Psychiatry: A textbook.* Leipzig, Germany: Barth.

Kumpfer, K., Alvarado, R., Smith, P., & Ballamy, N. (2002). Cultural sensitivity and adaptation in family-based prevention interventions. *Prevention Science, 3*, 241–246.

Lebow, J. L., & Gurman, A. S. (1995). Research assessing couple and family therapy. *Annual Review of Psychology, 46*, 27–57.

Lecomte, T., & Cecomte, C. (2002). Toward uncovering robust principles of change inherent to cognitive-behavioral therapy for psychosis. *American Journal of Orthopsychiatry, 72*, 50–57.

Lerman, D. C., & Iwata, B. A. (1996). Developing a technology for the use of operant extinction in clinical settings: An examination of basic and applied research. *Journal of Applied Behavior Analysis, 29*, 345–382.

Lijtmaer, R. (2001). Splitting and nostalgia in recent immigrants: Psychodynamic considerations. *Journal of the American Academy of Psychoanalysis, 29*, 427–438.

Linszen, D. H., Dingemans, P. M., Nugter, M. A., Van der Does, J. W., Scholte, W. F., & Lenior, M. A. (1997). Patient attributes and expressed emotion as risk factors for psychotic relapse. *Schizophrenia Bulletin, 23*, 119–130.

Lydiard, R. B., Brawman-Mintzer, O., & Ballenger, J. C. (1996). Recent developments in the psychopharmacology of anxiety disorders. *Journal of Consulting and Clinical Psychology, 64*, 660–668.

Manderscheid, R., & Henderson, M. (2001). *Mental health, United States, 2000* [Online version]. Rockville, MD: Center for Mental Health Services. Retrieved January 14, 2003, from http://www.mentalhealth.org/publications/allpubs/SMA01-3537/

Manhal-Baugus, M. (2001). E-therapy: Practical, ethical, and legal issues. *CyberPsychology and Behavior, 4*, 551–563.

Marder, S. R. (1996). Clinical experience with risperidone. *Journal of Clinical Psychiatry, 57*(9, Suppl.), 57–61.

Marks, I. M. (1972). Flooding (implosion) and allied treatments. In W. S. Agras (Ed.), *Behavior modification.* New York: Little, Brown.

Marshall, R. D., Schneier, F. R., Fallon, B. A., Feerick, J., & Liebowitz, M. R. (1994). Medication therapy for social phobia. *Journal of Clinical Psychiatry, 56*(6, Suppl.), 33–37.

Marshall, W. L., & Segal, Z. (1988). Behavior therapy. In C. G. Last & M. Hersen (Eds.), *Handbook of anxiety disorders* (pp. 338–361). New York: Pergamon.

Martinez, C. (1986). Hispanics: Psychiatric issues. In C. B. Wilkinson (Ed.), *Ethnic psychiatry* (pp. 61–88). New York: Plenum.

Medina, J. H., Paladini, A. C., & Izquierdo, I. (1993). Naturally occurring benzodiazepines and benzodiazepine-like molecules in brain. *Behavioural Brain Research, 58*, 1–8.

Meltzer, H. Y., Rabinowitz, J., Lee, M. A., Cola, P. A., Ranjan, R., Findling, R. L., & Thompson, P. A. (1997). Age at onset and gender of schizophrenic patients in relation to neuroleptic resistance. *American Journal of Psychiatry, 154*, 475–482.

Meyer, A. (1994). A short sketch of the problems of psychiatry. *American Journal of Psychiatry, 151*(June Suppl.), 42–47. (Original work published in 1897)

Morgan, R., & Flora, D. (2002). Group psychotherapy with incarcerated offenders: A research synthesis. *Group Dynamics: Theory, Research, and Practice, 6,* 203–218.

Muller, L. (2002). Group counseling for African American males: When all you have are European American counselors. *Journal for Specialists in Group Work, 27,* 299–313.

Nelson, J. C. (1997). Safety and tolerability of the new antidepressants. *Journal of Clinical Psychiatry, 58*(6, Suppl.), 26–31.

Noyes, R., Jr., Burrows, G. D., Reich, J. H., Judd, F. K., Garvey, M. J., Norman, T. R., Cook, B. L., & Marriott, P. (1996). Diazepam versus alprazolam for the treatment of panic disorder. *Journal of Clinical Psychiatry, 57,* 344–355.

Nutt, D. (2000). Treatment of depression and concomitant anxiety. European *Neuropsychopharmacology, 10*(Suppl. 4), S433–S437.

Olfson, M., Pincus, H. A., & Dial, T. H. (1994). Professional practice patterns of U.S. psychiatrists. *American Journal of Psychiatry, 151,* 89–95.

Öst, L.-G., & Westling, B. E. (1995). Applied relaxation vs. cognitive behavior therapy in the treatment of panic disorder. *Behavior Research and Therapy, 33,* 145–158.

Otto, M. W., Pollack, M. H., Sachs, G. S., Reiter, S. R., Meltzer-Brody, S., & Rosenbaum, J. F. (1993). Discontinuation of benzodiazepine treatment: Efficacy of cognitive-behavioral therapy for patients with panic disorder. *American Journal of Psychiatry, 150,* 1485–1490.

Paivio, S. C., & Greenberg, L. S. (1995). Resolving "unfinished business": Efficacy of experiential therapy using empty-chair dialogue. *Journal of Consulting and Clinical Psychology, 63,* 419–425.

Palinkas, L. A., Petterson, J. S., Russell, J., & Downs, M. A. (1993). Community patterns of psychiatric disorders after the *Exxon Valdez* oil spill. *American Journal of Psychiatry, 150,* 1517–1523.

Pasamanick, B., Toberts, D. W., Lemkau, P. V., & Krueger, D. E. (1962). A survey of mental disease in an urban population. *American Journal of Public Health, 47,* 923–929.

Perls, F. S. (1969). *Gestalt therapy verbatim.* Lafayette, CA: Real People Press.

Power, K. G., Sharp, D. M., Swanson, V., & Simpson, R. J. (2000). Therapist contact in cognitive behaviour therapy for panic disorder and agoraphobia in primary care. *Clinical Psychology & Psychotherapy, 7,* 37–46.

Prien, R. F., & Kocsis, J. H. (1995). Long-term treatment of mood disorders. In F. E. Bloom & D. J. Kupfer (Eds.), *Psychopharmacology: The fourth generation of progress* (pp. 1067–1079). New York: Raven.

Rachman, S. J., & Wilson, G. T. (1980). *The effects of psychological therapy* (2nd ed.). New York: Pergamon.

Rasmussen, S. A., Eisen, J. L., & Pato, M. T. (1993). Current issues in the pharmacologic management of obsessive compulsive disorder. *Journal of Clinical Psychiatry, 54*(6, Suppl.), 4–9.

Regier, D. A., & Burke, J. D. (1987). Psychiatric disorders in the community: The Epidemiologic Catchment Area study. In R. E. Hales & A. J. Frances (Eds.), *American Psychiatric Association Annual Review* (Vol. 6). Washington, DC: American Psychiatric Press.

Regier, D. A., Myers, J. K., Kramer, M., Robins, L. N., Blazer, D. G., Hough, R. L., Eaton, W. W., & Locke, B. Z. (1984). The NIMH epidemiologic catchment area program. *Archives of General Psychiatry, 41,* 934–941.

Rhéaume, J., & Ladouceur, R. (2000). Cognitive and behavioural treatments of checking behaviours: An examination of individual cognitive change. *Clinical Psychology & Psychotherapy, 7,* 118–127.

Rickels, K., Schweizer, E., Weiss, S., & Zavodnick, S. (1993). Maintenance drug treatment for panic disorder II. Short- and long-term outcome after drug taper. *Archives of General Psychiatry, 50,* 61–68.

Riedel, G. (1996). Function of metabotropic glutamate receptors in learning and memory. *Trends in Neurosciences, 19,* 219–224.

Roan, S. (2000, March 6). Cyber analysis. *L.A. Times.*

Robins, C. J., & Hayes, A. M. (1993). An appraisal of cognitive therapy. *Journal of Consulting and Clinical Psychology, 61,* 205–214.

Robins, L. N., Helzer, J. E., Croughan, H., & Ratcliff, K. S. (1981). National Institute of Mental Health Diagnostic Interview Schedule: Its history, characteristics, and validity. *Archives of General Psychiatry, 38,* 381–389.

Robins, L. N., Helzer, J. E., Weissman, M. M., Orvaschel, H., Gruenberg, E., Burke, J. D., & Regier, D. A. (1984). Lifetime prevalence of specific psychiatric disorders in three sites. *Archives of General Psychiatry, 41,* 949–958.

Rogers, C. R. (1951). *Client-centered therapy: Its current practice, implications, and theory.* Boston: Houghton Mifflin.

Romach, M., Busto, U., Somer, G., et al. (1995). Clinical aspects of chronic use of alprazolam and lorazepam. *American Journal of Psychiatry, 152,* 1161–1167.

Ross, J., Baldessarini, R. J., & Tondo, L. (2000). Does lithium treatment still work? Evidence of stable responses over three decades. *Archives of General Psychiatry, 57,* 187–190.

Rubinstein, G. (2001). Sex-role reversal and clinical judgment of mental health. *Journal of Sex & Marital Therapy, 27,* 9–19.

Sachs, G., Grossman, F., Ghaemi, S., Okamoto, A., & Bosden, C. (2002). Combination of a mood stabilizer with risperidone or haloperidol for treatment of acute mania: A double-blind, placebo-controlled comparison of efficacy and safety. *American Journal of Psychiatry, 159,* 1146–1154.

Sackeim, H. A., Luber, B., Katzman, G. P., Moeller, J. R., Prudic, J., Devanand, D. P., & Nobler, M. S. (1996). The effects of electroconvulsive therapy on quantitative electroencephalograms. *Archives of General Psychiatry, 53,* 814–824.

Sackeim, H. A., Prudic, J., Devanand, D. P., Nobler, M. S., Lisanby, S. H., Peyser, S., Fitzsimons, L., Moody, B. J., & Clark, J. (2000). A prospective, randomized, double-blind comparison of bilateral and right unilateral electroconvulsive therapy at different stimulus intensities. *Archives of General Psychiatry, 57,* 425–434.

Santiago-Rivera, A., & Altarriba, J. (2002). The role of language in therapy with the Spanish-English bilingual client. *Professional Psychology: Research & Practice, 33,* 30–38.

Schmittling, G. (Ed.). (1993). *Facts about family practice.* Kansas City, MO: American Academy of Family Physicians.

Schou, M. (1997). Forty years of lithium treatment. *Archives of General Psychiatry, 54,* 9–13.

Scott, J. (1996). Cognitive therapy of affective disorders: a review. *Journal of Affective Disorders, 37,* 1–11.

Seligman, M. E. P. (1995). The effectiveness of psychotherapy: The Consumer Reports Study. *American Psychologist, 50,* 965–974.

Sensky, T., Turkington, D., Kingdon, D., Scott, J. L., Scott, J., Siddle, R., O'Carroll, M., & Barnes, T. R. E. (2000). A randomized controlled trial of cognitive-behavioral therapy for persistent symptoms in schizophrenia resistant to medication. *Archives of General Psychiatry, 57,* 165–172.

Sheehan, D. V., & Raj, A. B. (1988). Monoamine oxidase inhibitors. In C. G. Last & M. Hersen (Eds.), *Handbook of anxiety disorders* (pp. 478–506). New York: Pergamon.

Smith, M. L., Glass, G. V., & Miller, T. I. (1980). *The benefits of psychotherapy.* Baltimore: Johns Hopkins University Press.

Smolar, A. (1999). Bridging the gap: Technical aspects of the analysis of an Asian immigrant. *Journal of Clinical Psychoanalysis, 8,* 567–594.

Spitzer, R. L., Skodol, A. E., Gibbon, M., & Williams, J. B. W. (1981). DSM-III *case book.* Washington, DC: American Psychiatric Association.

Spitzer, R. L., Skodol, A. E., Gibbon, M., & Williams, J. B. W. (1983). *Psychopathology: A case book.* New York: McGraw-Hill.

Srole, L., Langner, T. S., Michael, S. T., Opler, M. K., & Rennie, T. A. C. (1962). *Mental health in the metropolis: The midtown Manhattan study.* New York: McGraw-Hill.

Strickland, B. R. (1992). Women and depression. *Current Directions in Psychological Science, 1,* 132–135.

Suarez, M. G. (1983). Implications of Spanish-English bilingualism in the TAT stories. Unpublished doctoral dissertation, University of Connecticut.

Szasz, T. S. (1960). The myth of mental illness. *American Psychologist, 15,* 113–118.

Tamminga, C. A. (1996, Winter). The new generation of antipsychotic drugs. *NARSAD Research Newsletter,* pp. 4–6.

Tew, J. D., Mulsant, B. H., Haskett, R. F., Prudic, J., Thase, M. E., Crowe, R. R., Dolata, D., Begley, A. E., Reynolds, C. F., III, & Sackeim, H. A. (1999). Acute efficacy of ECT in the treatment of major depression in the old-old. *American Journal of Psychiatry, 156,* 1865–1870.

Thase, M. E., Frank, E., Mallinger, A. G., Hammer, T., & Kupfer, D. J. (1992). Treatment of imipramine-resistant recurrent depression, III: Efficacy of monoamine oxidise inhibitors. *Journal of Clinical Psychiatry, 53*(2, Suppl.), 5–11.

Thase, M. E., & Kupfer, D. J. (1996). Recent developments in the pharmacotherapy of mood disorders. *Journal of Consulting and Clinical Psychology, 64,* 646–659.

Tidey, J., O'Neill, S., & Higgins, S. (2002). Contingent monetary reinforcement of smoking reductions, with and without transdermal nicotine, in outpatients with schizophrenia. *Experimental and Clinical Psychopharmacology, 10,* 241–247.

Trivedi, M. J. (1996). Functional neuroanatomy of obsessive-compulsive disorder. *Journal of Clinical Psychiatry, 57*(8, Suppl.), 26–36.

Vetulani, J., & Nalepa, I. (2000). Antidepressants: Past, present and future. *European Journal of Pharmacology, 405,* 351–363.

Wakefield, J. C. (1992). The concept of mental disorder: On the boundary between biological facts and social values. *American Psychologist, 47,* 373–388.

Walker, D. (2000). Online therapy? Not yet. *CBS News.* New York: CBS.

Warshaw, M. G., & Keller, M. B. (1996). The relationship between fluoxetine use and suicidal behavior in 654 subjects with anxiety disorders. *Journal of Clinical Psychiatry, 57,* 158–166.

Weissman, M. M., Myers, J. K., & Harding, P. S. (1978). Psychiatric disorders in a U.S. urban community: 1975–1976. *American Journal of Psychiatry, 135,* 459–462.

Wetherell, J., Gatz, M., & Craske, M. (2003). Treatment of generalized anxiety disorder in older adults. *Journal of Consulting and Clinical Psychology, 71,* 31–40.

Wiggins, J. G. (1994). Would you want your child to be a psychologist? *American Psychologist, 49,* 485–492.

Wilson, M. (1993). DSM-III and the transformation of American psychiatry: A history. *American Journal of Psychiatry, 150,* 399–410.

Woodward, S. B. (1994). Observations on the medical treatment of insanity. *American Journal of Psychiatry, 151*(June suppl.), 220–230. (Original work published in 1850)

Wolpe, J. (1958). *Psychotherapy by reciprocal inhibition.* Stanford, CA: Stanford University Press.

Wolpe, J. (1973). *The practice of behavior therapy* (2nd ed.). New York: Pergamon.

Worrel, J. A., Marken, P. A., Beckman, S. E., & Ruehter, V. L. (2000). Atypical antipsychotic agents: A critical review. *American Journal of Health System Pharmacology, 57,* 238–255.

CHAPTER 26

THE SADDEST TIME OF THE YEAR[1]

Lawrence P. Rudiger

---

[1]Incorporating the research of Lam, R. W. et al. (2006).

Most people can imagine what depression must be like. That's because at times we all experience the two most prominent aspects of clinical depression: sadness, and an inability to enjoy the parts of life that usually bring us pleasure. Magnify the intensity of those common feelings. Add some other symptoms, things like problems with sleep, or crying over trivial matters. Then make it go on for a while (2 weeks or longer) so that it really interferes with your life. Basically, that is major depressive disorder (for a more precise, technical definition, see the Diagnostic and Statistical Manual of the American Psychiatric Association).

Depression is quite common. About 15% of people would qualify for this diagnosis at some point during their life (Moore, 2004). For a subset of people with major depressive disorder (between 0.4% and 2.7% of the general population), there's also a strong correlation between their most debilitating symptoms and the calendar (Levitt, Boyle, Joffe, and Baumal, 2000). This is known as major depressive disorder with a seasonal (winter)[2] pattern, or by its apt acronym SAD, for *Seasonal Affective Disorder.* People with SAD endure a cluster of unappealing problems. In addition to depressed mood, they also report having little or no energy. They want to sleep more than usual and eat more as well, particularly carbohydrate-rich foods. Is this sounding (depressingly) familiar? For those of us who live up north, the short, often cloudy days of winter conspire to keep us indoors (and inactive). It's too cold to go out-side and get some exercise, even though we know it would make us feel better, so why not just stay inside and eat a bag of cookies, then take a nap? But SAD is much more serious than just the occasional round of couch-and-carb therapy. Given that the seasonal fluctuations are basically the same, year after year; this is a serious public-health challenge, a problem affecting millions of people. For these reasons (as you might expect), SAD researchers are clustered in the northern part of the United States. UVM's Dr. Kelly Rohan is an expert on the topic and has a research program looking at ways to treat SAD that do not rely on prescription drugs. We will look at that research a bit later. This chapter will focus on the main results from a SAD research project conducted in Canada, a major center of research on the topic. We will examine this study for a few reasons. It is an interesting example of how to conduct a particular type of research: the randomized controlled trial. It is also a good example of the advantages of conducting this kind of project over a reasonable period of time (eight weeks) and making multiple measurements of the variables of interest (five times).

---

[2]Some people experience the opposite, and feel more depressed when it is warm and sunny, but most research, including the paper summarized in this chapter, focuses on the more common type, where the problems are worse in the winter (Eisendrath & Lichtmacher, 2006).

Statistical Power

Yes, it's a lot of bother, and expensive, too. But this approach gave the researchers a lot of what's known as "statistical power," and it will give us a chance to discuss that concept as well. Power is a factor in all research where the results are analyzed with inferential statistical techniques, which is true of most of the research we cover in this book. A statistician's definition of power would be "the probability of correctly rejecting a false null hypothesis" (Howell, 1987). In other words, if there really is no difference between your comparison groups (something you would only know with any certainty by running the same study many times), when your research design affords adequate power, you'll be able to detect that something really happened and the difference you observed is likely to hold up if the study is repeated.

On a more basic level, power is a function of three aspects of a study.

- First, the number of measurements, which usually means the number of participants being observed (more measurements/participants means more power).
- Second, there is the size of the difference you hope to find. In experimental designs, that is the effect of the independent variable. Bigger differences are easier to detect and harder to miss because they don't look like random variation.
- The third power ingredient isn't something researchers can mess with, really: the statistical threshold of what constitutes a "significant" difference. As you've already learned, that cut point is usually a one-in-twenty chance ($p < .05$, and the p means *probability*). It's a matter of history and convention (though some research traditions in psychology relax that a bit to one-in-ten). The one-in-twenty threshold, though, represents a trade-off, a compromise of sorts. If we made it, say, one-in-fifty, then we increase the odds of mislabeling a real difference as one that was just due to chance, which we also want to avoid.

Researchers try and maximize power by increasing the number of participants and the size of the effect. Sure, it's easy to imagine that you would just get as many participants as possible. But that's expensive, often labor-intensive, and potentially wasteful. There are also limits on efforts to maximize the effect of your independent variable. Many are not really open to manipulation, including the ones in this study. There was nothing the researchers could do to enhance the antidepressant effects of light therapy or fluoxetine, other than implement a protocol that would minimize the influence of anything else that might diminish the therapeutic properties of the interventions. We'll come back to the topic of power at the end of the chapter.

TREATING SAD: LIGHT THERAPY AND MEDICATION

Most of the research on treating SAD has looked at two treatments, which this study compared. **Light therapy** involves intense artificial light, offering a sort of replacement when sunlight is in short supply as day length decreases. There are various light-therapy devices, including a range of floor and table lamps as well as visors and goggles that put the light near your eyes. In addition, various "doses" have been studied, in terms of the time of day and the amount of time under the lamp (including some suggestive results of shining the light at the back of people's knees, but that approach never became the standard for treating SAD). Light therapy alone has been found to be an effective treatment, both for SAD (Moore, 2004) and, interestingly, for nonseasonal depression as well (Tuunainen, Kripke, & Endo, 2004). When used as directed, it appears to be very safe, which makes it an appealing option.

Prescription antidepressant drugs also appear to be effective for treating SAD (Butler et al., 2006; Eisendrath & Lichtmacher, 2006; Moore, 2004). In addition, most people who watch television or read magazines (or the internet) know about them through *direct-to-consumer marketing*. These ads first appeared in the early 1980's, which was about the time the new types of antidepressant drugs were made available (U. S. Food and Drug Administration, 2005). The first of these, the selective serotonin-reuptake inhibitor fluoxetine (initially marketed as Prozac), was used in this chapter's study. Psychiatric drugs are quite controversial (Valenstein, 1998) but a detailed discussion of that matter is beyond the scope of this chapter. Part of the controversy stems from the conclusions drawn by summarizing all the relevant research. Overall, these drugs are no more effective than psychotherapy, except for the most severely depressed patients—people who would usually be hospitalized (Butler et al., 2006). Also a recent study (Szegedi, Kohnen, Dienel, & Kieser, 2005) found that the prescription antidepressant paroxetine was no more effective than the herbal preparation known as St. John's wort in treating even severe depression.

In addition to questions about how much they actually help patients, recent changes to these drugs' federally mandated package information reflects the accumulating evidence on their serious risks (U. S. Food and Drug Administration, 2004). Some people taking them go on to experience problems, including an increase in strong urges to commit suicide, although cause-effect relationships have not been conclusively demonstrated. In spite of this complicated situation psychiatric organizations recommend prescription drugs as an option for treating major depression (American Psychiatric Association, 2006; Kennedy, Lam, Cohen, & Ravindran, 2001).

THE CAN-SAD STUDY

This situation—one accepted therapy that involves taking drugs, one that does not—presents an excellent research opportunity. Comparing them might yield results that could become part of the bigger picture and offer practical guidance. As you'll see, the researchers used a clever technique to study the effects of each treatment while maximizing their statistical power and using a manageable (but sufficient) number of participants.

Participants

Female and male participants, aged 18–65, were recruited at four different clinical-research centers in Canada. Eligibility was determined based on a standardized clinical interview as well as with the Hamilton Rating Scale for Depression, which is described below. Many of the exclusionary criteria that are used in this sort of study were followed: women who were pregnant, lactating, or might become pregnant; people with additional medical or psychiatric conditions, those who had recently received psychotherapy or were planning to start, or people taking other drugs known to affect behavior. Other exclusion criteria were more specific to this study: prior use of light therapy or fluoxetine, shift work (so they had changes to their sleep-wake patterns as a result of work demands), or plans to travel south during the study period.

Starting with an initial group of 117, a total of 21 were excluded early on for various reasons, 3 of them because, during a week of observation, they simply got better. This is a common event in this sort of research. Depression fluctuates and some people improve spontaneously[3]. The remaining 96 were

---

[3]In addition to spontaneous remission, there are often many patients in depression-treatment research who get better even though they got a placebo, and some studies detect only a small difference between the placebo and treatment groups (Wampold, Minami, Tierney, Baskin, & Bhati, 2005). But because this study did not have a placebo-only condition, it is impossible to know what might have happened to participants who took an inert pill and used a fake light-therapy device.

then randomly assigned to one of two conditions: bona fide light-therapy treatment with a placebo pill (48 participants, 8 of whom did not complete the study); or a fake light therapy and the real drug, fluoxetine (the other 48, with seven dropping out for various reasons). In this manner, both groups could serve as the statistical control group for comparing the antidepressant effect of each treatment. Also, the participants and the researchers who dealt with them directly did not know who got what. Thus, this was a *double-blind, placebo-controlled trial.*

Light Therapy and Antidepressant Drug Therapy

The researchers employed a bit of deception to create a cover story about the light therapy. All participants were told that this aspect of the study was meant to research different *wavelengths* of light. Well, not quite. The real light therapy was at a level of *intensity* that has been shown to be effective: 10,000 lux, as strong as the light of 10,000 candles. They are impressively bright. The placebo-version light therapy was only 100 lux. Yes, 100 candles, so also pretty bright. The authors compared it "ordinary kitchen lighting" (Lam et al., 2006). But that is not intense enough to improve mood. All participants were instructed to sit near their light-therapy devices for a half hour session between 7:00 a.m. and 8:00 a.m. Once the study was completed, all participants were debriefed and all were offered real light therapy. As to the medication aspect of the study, participants in the real-drug/fake-light group took 20 mg/day of fluoxetine; the others took an inert pill that looked exactly the same. Everybody was instructed to take the pills in the morning.

Measures

All measures were administered five times over an eight-week period: at baseline, and again at weeks one, two, four, and eight. The researchers used the most popular method of tracking change in depression symptoms, the Hamilton Rating Scale for Depression (or HAM-D). Psychiatrists, who did not know which treatment each participant was getting, administered the HAM-D to quantify the various aspects of clinical depression: depressed mood, feelings of guilt, problems with sleep, feeling slowed down or agitated, and so on. Each problem is rated on a scale of severity. Higher scores suggest relatively more severe depression. For this study, the researchers also computed a subscale that focused on the symptoms that seem to predominate the SAD pattern: eating a lot, sleeping a lot, and weight gain. In addition, the participants completed a self-report questionnaire, the Beck Depression Inventory II. They were also asked detailed questions about adverse events – things like gastrointestinal problems, sexual dysfunction, fainting spells, or dry mouth.

Results

Before analyzing the dependent variable (or variables), researchers usually compare the treatment groups to see if they were systematically different on anything that might cloud the results. When that is the case, then those between-group differences can be factored into the statistical tests. Luckily for these researchers, none of these preliminary comparisons suggested that the two groups differed from each other, including participants' expectations for the treatments. Overall, there were significantly higher expectations for light therapy, which participants rated after being shown the light-therapy devices they would be using. But there were no differences in light therapy-expectation ratings between the two groups, which may suggest that the deception worked. Also, as mentioned earlier, about the same number of participants dropped out of both groups. These so-far, so-good results let the researchers go on to look at their main dependent variable: change on the overall HAM-D. In Figure 26.1, decrease in HAM-D scores is plotted on the vertical axis; week of treatment is on the horizontal axis.

There were two main research questions. First, did participants get better? Yes. For both groups, there was statistically significant improvement at each visit, compared to ratings at the prior visit, and (as you might assume), overall, from the beginning to the end of the study period. Second question: did the two groups differ from each other? The simple answer is *no,* but with one exception. At the first week (the second measure), the light-treatment group was significantly (but slightly) more improved than the

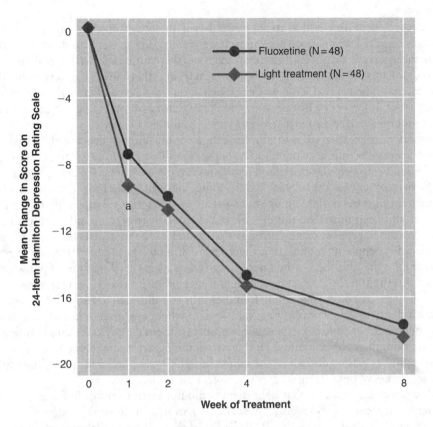

FIGURE 26.1   Change in HAM-D Scale Scores in Participants with SAD Randomly Assigned to Receive 8 Weeks of Double-Blind Treatment With Light Therapy Plus Placebo Capsules or Fluoxetine Plus Placebo Light. (Copyright, American Psychiatric Association. Reproduced by permission)

[a]Significantly greater imrovement in the first week of treatment for those receiving light therapy relative to those receiving fluoxetine (t = 2.1, df = 94, $p < 0.05$).

fluoxetine group. This is a case where the "intra-ocular analysis" (just look at it and guess) does not mislead. Keep looking. Sure, the fluoxetine group is always higher, which in this figure means less improvement. But the difference is trivial, both in the statistical and the clinical sense. Overall, light therapy and fluoxetine were equally effective from beginning to end. This same pattern emerged on the HAM-D items that asked about SAD-specific symptoms (eating and sleeping more, weight gain). Finally, an additional comparison focused in on the 49 participants who were more severely depressed. Even for them, there was no significant difference in the treatments. Light therapy was as effective as fluoxetine.

People might prefer a nondrug approach to avoid the bad things that seem to happen after treatment starts. The most precise term is *treatment-emergent adverse events*, though other labels are probably more familiar: *side effects, adverse effects,* or just *adverse events*. Interestingly, though, the overall rates for these problems were not significantly different between the two groups. At least one adverse event was reported by 77% of the participants who got the real light therapy and 75% of those who took fluoxetine. However, the rates for three specific problems (sleep disturbance, palpitations, and agitation) were significantly higher in the fluoxetine group.

Discussion

One of researchers' primary responsibilities is to state their predictions honestly, plan their tests, run them, and report them (Howell, 1987). It all sounds so simple. It gets complicated, though, when the results are unexpected or impossible to interpret based on the planned analyses. These fortunate researchers, however, had straightforward, interesting results. There were no differences between the groups before the intervention phase. Both treatments worked comparably well. Recall the single difference, obvious to the trained (after nearly a whole semester) eye: there was a bit more improvement with light therapy after the first week. This was unexpected, and the researchers used the proper analytic technique to test the difference. They also resisted the urge to turn this single difference into a big deal by drawing in a lot of after-the-fact explanations.

The authors were in a strong position, though, to point out the advantages of their design, the so-called *double-dummy* technique, where both groups were able to serve as treatment (or experimental) and control. In addition, their clever method let them keep the experience of being in the study consistent across the two conditions: the pills looked the same, the light boxes looked the same, and the cover story about the various types of light being study was always the same. It helped them to maximize their statistical power and keep down the number of participants, because they didn't need to again divide their sample into more groups, namely groups that would only get a placebo. The researchers also pointed out that, for people who think that there's something to the slight difference in response that seemed to favor light therapy, there would need to be observations on thousands of participants for that difference to reach the threshold of statistical significance (you can readily estimate these things, after the data are collected, based on your results). And even if you did such a study, the difference favoring light therapy was far below the conventional threshold of what constitutes clinically meaningful differences. It may not have been due to chance, but it probably doesn't support a claim that light therapy is superior. In addition, their clever method let them keep the experience of being in the study consistent across the two conditions: the pills looked the same, the light boxes looked the same, and the cover story about the various types of light being studies was always the same.

It may be surprising, though, that light therapy did not seem to result in fewer (we'll use the big term) treatment-emergent adverse events. After all, the narrators in those television advertisements for prescription drugs always seem to rattle off a long list of them. The similar rates, though, should give one pause about concluding that drugs *cause* the bad things that happen once people start taking them. Undoubtedly, they do, sometimes. However, in studies where a drug is compared to just a placebo, the rates of adverse events are sometimes quite similar. This may, in part, be due to the events' character. A percentage of people experience abdominal pain, rash, dry mouth, and all the other so-called "side effects" all the time. They are just part of the background noise of life.

Other Treatments for SAD

The researchers acknowledged that some of their instructions might have enhanced the antidepressant effect of both treatments (perhaps even introducing a bit of a confound). Participants were asked to take their pills and sit near their light-therapy devices early in the morning. If they followed instructions, then they may have been getting up earlier, and more consistently, which could have helped them fight the common SAD symptom of wanting to sleep a lot. Pills, light box, or nothing, it could just be some sound advice, particularly when the morning sun is weak, and rises late. Paradoxically, though, the instruction to sit near one of these expensive contraptions may serve to encourage the sort of hibernating that could make SAD worse (I can't go outside because I need to stay indoors to get my dose of fake sunlight). And the daily light-therapy regimen may be hard to maintain, as only 41% of participants in one study kept at it after initial research phase (Schwartz, Brown, Wehr, & Rosenthal, 1996).

These are some of the issues behind UVM psychology researcher Kelly Rohan's recent research (Reidel, 2005). She and her colleagues wondered why SAD wasn't being treated with cognitive-behavior therapy, which is an increasingly popular approach to helping people reduce their psychological distress by changing how they think about their problems. In addition, looking for alternatives is motivated by several factors that are not obvious from the Can-SAD study: nearly half of people with SAD do not appear to respond to light therapy (Rohan, Lindsey, Roecklein, & Lacy, 2004) and antidepressant drugs don't work for everybody, either (Saeed & Bruce, 1998).

Rohan's research compared cognitive-behavior therapy alone or in combination with light therapy. After six weeks, participants who got the combination therapy to achieve full remission of their SAD symptoms. In addition, though, a year later, of those who got the psychotherapy—with or without the light therapy—only 6% met the criteria for depression, compared to 40% of the group who got the light therapy alone. Given the cost of light-therapy devices (often several hundred dollars) and the difficulty of sticking with it, the preventative effects of cognitive-behavior therapy merit further study.

Professor Rohan offered a suggestion that is probably sensible for those who may feel like they endure the north country's winters in order to get to the next summer (Reidel, 2005). Go for a 30-minute walk each day once the sun is up. That is probably sound advice, year around, no matter what your latitude.

REFERENCES

American Psychiatric Association. (2006). *American Psychiatric Association practice guidelines for the treatment of psychiatric disorders. Compendium 2006.* Arlington, Va.: American Psychiatric Association.

Butler, R., Carney, S., Cipriani, A., Geddes, J., Hatcher, S., Price, J., et al. (2006). Depressive Disorders. In *Clinical Evidence* (15 ed.). London: BMJ Publishing Group.

Eisendrath, S. J., & Lichtmacher, J. E. (2006). Psychiatric Disorders. In L. M. Tierney, S. J. McPhee & M. A. Papadakis (Eds.), *Current Medical Diagnosis & Treatment* (pp. 1038–1097). New York: Lange Medical Books.

Howell, D. C. (1987). *Statistical methods for psychology* (2nd ed.). Boston, Mass.: PWS-Kent.

Kennedy, S. H., Lam, R. W., Cohen, N. L., & Ravindran, A. V. (2001). Clinical guidelines for the treatment of depressive disorders. IV. Medications and other biological treatments. *Can J Psychiatry, 46 Suppl 1*, 38S–58S.

Lam, R. W., Levitt, A. J., Levitan, R. D., Enns, M. W., Morehouse, R., Michalak, E. E., et al. (2006). The Can-SAD study: a randomized controlled trial of the effectiveness of light therapy and fluoxetine in patients with winter seasonal affective disorder. *Am J Psychiatry, 163*(5), 805–812.

Levitt, A. J., Boyle, M. H., Joffe, R. T., & Baumal, Z. (2000). Estimated prevalence of the seasonal subtype of major depression in a Canadian community sample. *Can J Psychiatry, 45*(7), 650–654.

Moore, D. P. (2004). *Handbook of medical psychiatry.* Retrieved October 1, 2006.

Reidel, J. (2005). SAD Conversation. Retrieved October 9, 2006, from http://www.uvm.edu/theview/article.php?id=1794

Rohan, K. J., Lindsey, K. T., Roecklein, K. A., & Lacy, T. J. (2004). Cognitive-behavioral therapy, light therapy, and their combination in treating seasonal affective disorder. *Journal of Affective Disorders, 80*(2–3), 273–283.

Saeed, S. A., & Bruce, T. J. (1998). Seasonal affective disorders. *American Family Physician, 57*(6), 1340–1346, 1351–1342.

Schwartz, P. J., Brown, C., Wehr, T. A., & Rosenthal, N. E. (1996). Winter seasonal affective disorder: a follow-up study of the first 59 patients of the National Institute of Mental Health Seasonal Studies Program. *Am J Psychiatry, 153*(8), 1028–1036.

Szegedi, A., Kohnen, R., Dienel, A., & Kieser, M. (2005). Acute treatment of moderate to severe depression with hypericum extract WS 5570 (St John's wort): randomised controlled double blind non-inferiority trial versus paroxetine. *Bmj, 330*(7490), 503.

Tuunainen, A., Kripke, D., & Endo, T. (2004). Light therapy for non-seasonal depression: John Wiley & Sons.

U. S. Food and Drug Administration. (2004). Worsening Depression and Suicidality in Patients.

Being Treated With Antidepressant. Retrieved October 3, 2006, from http://www.fda.gov/cder/drug/antidepressants/AntidepressantPHA.htm

U. S. Food and Drug, Administration. (2005). Statement of Rachel E. Behrman, M.D., M.P.H. Deputy Director, Office of Medical Policy Center for Drug Evaluation and Research. Retrieved October 3, 2006, from http://www.fda.gov/ola/2005/idcda0929.html

Valenstein, E. S. (1998). *Blaming the brain: the truth about drugs and mental health.* New York: Free Press.

Wampold, B. E., Minami, T., Baskin, T. W., & Callen Tierney, S. (2002). A meta-(re)analysis of the effects of cognitive therapy versus 'other therapies' for depression. *Journal of Affective Disorders, 68*(2–3), 159–165.

Wampold, B. E., Minami, T., Tierney, S. C., Baskin, T. W., & Bhati, K. S. (2005). The placebo is powerful: estimating placebo effects in medicine and psychotherapy from randomized clinical trials. *Journal of Clinical Psychology, 61*(7), 835–854.

CHAPTER 27

BETTING ON THE WINNERS[1]

Material selected from:
Research Stories for Introductory Psychology,
Second Edition, by Lary Shaffer and Matthew R. Merrens

[1]Incorporating the research of C. Sylvain, R. Ladouceur, and J. M. Boisvert, "Cognitive and Behavioral Treatment of Pathological Gambling: A Controlled Study," 1997, *Journal of Consulting and Clinical Psychology, 65*, pp. 727–732.

GAMBLING AS A PSYCHOLOGICAL DISORDER

Probably most of us, many times a week, offer to bet on something: "I bet it rains this afternoon; I bet we get a quiz in psychology today; I bet we end up being late for lunch. . . ." Most of our little wagers are not taken up by those around us and are forgotten. However, for some people, placing bets and other forms of gambling are a recognized psychological disorder. Starting in 1980, the *Diagnostic and Statistical Manual*, 3rd edition (*DSM-III*) (American Psychiatric Association, 1980) recognized a set of symptoms that defined pathological gambling. DSM is updated regularly, and it is taken by many to be the definitive list of disorders and symptoms within psychology, as well as in the medical specialty called psychiatry. This manual listed pathological gambling as "a chronic and progressive failure to resist impulses to gamble and gambling behavior that compromises, disrupts or damages personal, family or vocational pursuits." It is a preoccupation and urge that increases when people are stressed. The financial problems it creates lead to even more intense gambling. The debts incurred can also lead to various types of crime, such as embezzlement, theft, and knowingly writing bad checks. It includes the attitude that money is the cause of all one's problems; at the same time, money is the solution for all life's problems. People who have this disorder often lie to obtain more money. They are overconfident and energetic, but at times show signs of anxiety and depression. In males, it typically begins in adolescence, whereas in females, it appears later in life. It is estimated to be a problem for at least 2 to 3 percent of the adult population.

Notice that within the symptoms listed previously there are two different kinds of things: cognitive patterns and behavioral patterns. Concepts such as *urge*, *preoccupation*, and *attitude* refer to thoughts or cognitions, whereas *telling lies to obtain money* and *intense gambling* are behaviors. Often symptoms of psychological disorders include both thoughts and behaviors because disordered thinking is likely to be accompanied by problem actions.

APPROACHES TO TREATMENT OF PATHOLOGICAL GAMBLING

Various approaches have been tried as means of treating pathological gambling. For example, Dickerson and Weeks (1979) described a case study of a program that included *controlled gambling* in which an individual was allowed to make only small bets once a week. This manipulation was coupled with additional behavioral management and therapy. Behavior changes persisted over 15 months. This was a single-participant case study, and there was no control individual or group. Although it may serve as a pilot study suggesting treatment, caution should be exercised in generalizing the findings to other individuals. The case study is a weak research method for generalizing to large populations. Although psychological therapy is a common treatment, unfortunately it is fairly rare that some types of psychological therapies are evaluated to see if they are effective. One reason for this is that not all psychotherapists value science or have scientific training. Without an understanding of the power that a scientific approach has to evaluate new knowledge, assessment of therapeutic outcomes can be a matter of opinion. If treatment programs are to be evaluated successfully, they must be designed from the beginning with evaluation in mind. In order to be evaluated, treatment programs must make the assumption that psychological problems can be operationalized into measurable behavior. Participants should be randomly assigned into treatment and no-treatment control groups. Behavior problems should be assessed before treatment begins, after it has ended, and again after a longer period of time has passed.

A great deal of work and planning is required to design good research on efficacy of psychological treatment programs. Often the numbers of people being treated are small, and the treatment is not sufficiently standardized or quantified to permit numerical data to be collected. Probably one reason for this is that an individual therapist is unlikely to have a large number of clients with a single disorder, such as pathological gambling. Additionally, unless the therapist is interested in scientific data collection, treatment of individuals is likely to be the only goal. To make matters more difficult, following treatment, people can be hard to find, disrupting assessment of long-term outcomes. In most studies of gambling previous to the one discussed in this chapter, the only outcome measured was the frequency of gambling behavior. This seems narrow, given the multiple symptoms described in *DSM-III*.

CONTROL GROUPS IN THERAPY EVALUATION

It is usual, but poor practice, to have no control groups in studies of treatment for pathological gambling (Lesieur & Blume, 1987). Having a control group that receives no treatment is very important in studies of therapy because it is the only way to know that the treatment itself, and not mere passage of time, is making a difference. To do a scientific evaluation, ideally, a group of pathological gamblers would be randomly assigned either to the treatment group or to a no-treatment group. Following treatment, the two groups could be compared to determine the efficacy of the program. You may have some concern about the ethics of purposely withholding treatment from people identified as having a psychological disorder. One of the solutions to this ethical dilemma has been to put the no-treatment control group on a wait list, so that they are promised therapy eventually. They do not get it while the study is in progress but it is given to them, at no charge, as soon as possible after the study has ended. Although this may help to answer the ethical dilemma, it means that researchers have to assure themselves that wait-listed control participants do not seek therapy elsewhere while they are waiting.

THE GAMBLER'S FALLACY

Sylvain, Ladouceur, and Boisvert (1997) conducted a controlled study of a treatment program for compulsive gamblers. Sylvain and her colleagues argued that treatment should be based on cognitions as well as behaviors specific to gambling. These were specified in *DSM-III* and were the target of treatment. Ladouceur and Walker (1996) found that erroneous ideas about the concept of randomness were a primary cognitive component of the mistaken beliefs of gamblers. Gamblers believe and act as if they could predict, and maybe control, events that are not predictable or controllable. According to Ladouceur and Walker (1996), even though gamblers may not expect to win any particular gamble, they have mistaken beliefs that lead to continued gambling. They believe that they have found, or can find, ways to predict events that are governed by chance. These researchers also noted that gambling is frequently associated with superstitious behaviors. Within psychology, this term refers to a mistaken belief that there is a real causal link, called a *contingency*, between two events, when, in reality, there is no contingency at all. Gamblers are likely to think their chance of winning is increased if they use their lucky dice, bet their birthday as a lottery number, or hold a gold coin in one hand while betting with the other. In actuality, of course, there is no contingency between any of these specific behaviors and winning. One of these erroneous ways of thinking is so common that it has become a technical term: *the gambler's fallacy*. One version of the gambler's fallacy is the idea that independent or random events are linked: if you lose a game of chance 30 times in a row, this means your number is about to come up, and you will win. In fact, your chances do not change. If you repeatedly toss an unbiased coin and, by chance, happen to toss 10 heads in a row, the probability of a head on the 11th toss is still 50 percent. The string of head tosses does not affect the next independent random event.

Participants

The participants in this study were gamblers who were seeking help for gambling problems. There were 56 men and 2 women among them. They were evaluated by a clinical psychologist who was experienced in working with people diagnosed as pathological gamblers. All of the participants met the criteria for pathological gambling found in *DSM-III-R* (American Psychiatric Association, 1987), which was the current edition of *DSM* at the time the study commenced. Their most common mode of gambling was playing video poker, but others bet on horse races or played casino games. Some were recruited for the study either through advertisements in the newspaper or announcements on radio or TV. Others were referred by a professional care provider such as a physician, psychologist, or social worker. The study was conducted in the Province of Quebec in Canada. All 58 potential participants underwent a preliminary evaluation and 18 of them refused treatment following this evaluation. The remaining 40 individuals were randomly assigned to the treatment group or control group. Eight participants subsequently dropped out from the treatment group and 3 from the control group, leaving 29 individuals. These were reassigned so that 14 received treatment and 15 were left in the control group. Other studies of addictive behavior have shown similar proportions of participant attrition (Stark, 1992). This number of refusals and dropouts is high, but you should remember that these people are adults with complicated lives who were about to be involved in a rigorous program aimed at changing a problem behavior. They could not be required or coerced to remain in the study. The participants who completed treatment were significantly different from the dropouts and refusers on two variables: those completing the program began gambling at an older age ($p < .05$) and their *problem* gambling appeared later in life ($p < .05$). Does this invalidate the study as a whole? We do not believe so. Clearly part of your skill in thinking critically about scientific studies includes careful consideration of problems such as the characteristics of participants who drop out. In this case, at worst, these differences might limit our ability to apply these study findings to problem gamblers who had gambling problems early in life. People who do not understand science may be more likely to categorically dismiss an entire study because of a limitation such as this. In contrast, an educated critical thinker knows that there will always be some imperfections in studies. The important thing is to evaluate their effect on whatever conclusions may be drawn. Scientific researchers do not try to hide the problems that appear in the course of research; they point out problems that can be seen in the design of the study or in the data and discuss them in their publications. If the problem is sufficiently large, the study will not be published. With smaller blemishes, researchers expect the reader to be critical. Researchers give their readers the information required to make a cautious, realistic interpretation of the results.

In the treatment group the mean age was 37.6 years and in the control group it was 42.6 years. Half of the participants in each group were evaluated by a second clinician to check the reliability of the diagnosis. There was a 100 percent agreement between the evaluators. In other types of studies, the reliability of one rater is often checked by another observer who is unaware of the original ratings.

You can appreciate that this was probably not possible here; clients who see a clinical psychologist do not expect the psychologist to be unaware of the problems they are having. In this case the participants described these problems, and the nature of the reliability check was to see if the second clinician agreed that the symptoms indicated the same diagnosis.

Procedure

At the beginning of the study, all participants were made aware that because of random assignment to groups, some individuals would not be receiving treatment immediately. Once random assignment had taken place, participants in the control group were contacted and told that they would be on a waiting list. They were assured that they would receive treatment as soon as possible and that it was expected that all participants would receive treatment within 4 months. During this wait, they were phoned monthly as a way of keeping in contact with them. Two control participants felt that they could not wait any longer and were immediately assigned to the treatment group. None of the wait-listed patients reported receiving other therapy for this problem while they were waiting for treatment.

Cognitive-behavioral therapy was administered by two female psychologists who had, respectively, 4 and 5 years of clinical experience. They were supervised by Robert Ladouceur, a psychologist with 20 years of experience in cognitive-behavioral therapy. In the first session, treatment group participants were asked the question, "Are you willing to make an effort to reduce or stop gambling?" In order to continue in the study they had to answer in the affirmative. They also rated, on a scale of 1 to 10, their motivation to change the problem behavior.

The experience and training of the therapist are very important to the success of cognitive-behavioral therapy, but we would like to be clear that nothing magical or mystical is involved. By "nothing magical or mystical," we mean that the entire therapeutic process can be understood by ordinary people. It is a concrete teaching process in which a client learns to do new things and to think different thoughts. Unfortunately, popular media often depict psychological therapy as being a version of psychoanalysis, the approach developed 100 years ago by Sigmund Freud (see, for example, Freud, 1935). Freud believed that problems were rooted in unconscious desires and childhood problems. His therapy was supposed to dig deep into an unconscious mind using arcane and symbolic interpretations of the patient's verbal responses. Classically, the patient would lie on a couch and say anything that came into his or her head, while the therapist listened and attached florid interpretations to what was said. It was believed that as the contents of the unconscious came into the conscious mind, people could become aware of urges, often socially unacceptable urges, with sexual overtones. The patient's growing awareness of the unconscious was thought to be part of the cure. This kind of therapy was an art, not a science.

We took this little aside to illustrate what cognitive-behavioral therapy is *not*: it is not psychoanalysis or anything particularly like it. It does require a therapist with sharp clinical skills, but the skills are used to discuss the client's conscious thoughts and viewpoints about the world. The client is made aware that changing patterns of thinking can help to change behavior. The reverse is also important: changing one's behavior can change thinking. It is a rational and empirical approach that has no use for unconscious childhood trauma, hidden sexual urges, or couches. In some kinds of therapy, empirical evaluation is impossible, or nearly so. In contrast, the ultimate goal of cognitive-behavioral therapy is behavior change that can be observed and measured. As a result, cognitive-behavioral therapy can be evaluated through scientific means.

Cognitive-behavioral therapy was administered to the treatment group participants, or *clients*, in individual sessions. Sessions occurred once or twice a week and lasted between 60 and 90 minutes. This group received an average of 16.7 hours of treatment, with the maximum being 30 hours. They did not receive any additional therapy for this or other problems during the course of the study.

The cognitive-behavioral therapy had four main components. We describe these in some detail because we want you to understand the direct and sensible nature of this therapeutic approach. It has a strong empirical basis as well as a singular and determined goal to change behavior.

1. Cognitive correction. This component was aimed at correcting the misunderstanding of randomness. It included direct teaching about the concept. Random, by definition, means *not predictable*. Control is impossible. Erroneous beliefs commonly held by gamblers, including the gambler's fallacy, were exposed as misconstruals and explained. A recording was made of the participant pretending to gamble. The participant reviewed this with the therapist, and the therapist offered detailed corrections of the faulty beliefs indicated by the participant's verbalizations. An example of one of these was "if I lose four times in a row, I will win for sure the next time."

2. Problem-solving training. Participants were taught some specific strategies for dealing with problems in their lives. Obviously, the primary application of these tactics was to deal with some of the symptoms of gambling. They were taught to define the problems in unambiguous terms, collect information about the problems, generate alternative solutions listing the advantages and disadvantages of each, and to implement the solution, subsequently evaluating their effectiveness. These are the same processes that most of us use daily in a somewhat haphazard way, but the participants were taught to go through the steps in a careful and rational way. An example of one of the problems that was approached in this way was the need to get better control over spending to pay off debts incurred from past gambling. This was designed to help break the cycle of gambling to pay off debts.

3. Social skills training. Some of the individuals in the program suffered from links between poor social skills and gambling. For example, some of them needed assertiveness training because even if they did not want to gamble, friends would persuade them to do so. These people needed to be taught how to resist social pressure from people they liked. Role-playing was an important part of this training. Through role-play, gamblers could practice and learn the communication skills necessary to steer them through social situations that might, otherwise, lead to gambling.

4. Relapse prevention. As part of the therapy, participants discussed the possibility of relapsing and described their past relapses. Risk factors for relapse were identified, and participants were taught specific ways to avoid the creation of high relapse-risk situations. For the gamblers, these included events such as carrying cash, loneliness, stress, and lack of alternate social activities.

Dependent Variables

The dependent variables, or outcome measures, included the number of *DSM-III-R* criteria for pathological gambling that still described the participant. If the program was successful, there would be a decrease in this variable. Another dependent variable, or *D.V.*, was the outcome of the South Oaks Gambling Screen (SOGS), a valid self-report instrument. A total score of 5 or more on SOGS interview questions has been found to be indicative of pathological gambling (Lesieur & Blume, 1987). Beyond this threshold, higher scores indicate more problems with gambling. As an additional measure, participants rated their perception of their own control over gambling on a scale from 1—*no control*, to 10—*all control*. They also rated their desire to gamble on a 1 to 10 scale. Several measures were taken of self-reported frequency of gambling including the number of gambling sessions, the number of hours spent gambling, and the total amount of money spent on gambling during the previous week.

Pretreatment Scores

In order to assure themselves that the treatment and wait list control groups were not different with respect to some dimension of gambling, the dependent measures described above were assessed on both groups before treatment began in order to obtain a pretreatment baseline. Because participants had been randomly assigned to the groups, there was no reason to think groups would be different, but, of course, by chance, it is possible for random assignment to produce groups that are different with respect to the primary characteristic under investigation: in this case, gambling. For example, if, by chance, all the heaviest gamblers had ended up in the wait list control group, and no pretreatment measure had been taken, differences in dependent measures at the end of the study might suggest program success, when, in fact, the program had made little difference in changing behavior. For this reason, baseline measures were taken before any treatment began. No statistically significant differences were found between the groups in any of those measures of gambling.

Results

The changes between pretreatment and posttreatment for the treatment group and the same period of time for the wait list control group are found in Table 27.1. The control group received no treatment between these measures, so any changes in their scores must be a result of other things that were happening in their lives. Statistical analysis showed that the treatment group and the control group were statistically significantly different at the posttreatment measure for each of the five dependent variables, all at $p < .01$. As a result of the therapy, the treatment group had fewer of the pathological gambling diagnostic criteria from *DSM-III-R*, reported less desire to gamble, and had a lower South Oaks

TABLE 27.1   Means of the Main Variables at Pretreatment, Posttreatment, and 6-Month Follow-Up Measurements for the Treatment Group and the (Wait List) Control Group

	PRETREATMENT	POSTTREATMENT	6-MONTH FOLLOW-UP*
DSM-III-R			
Treatment	7.3	1.1	1.3
Control	7.1	5.7	
PERCEPTION OF CONTROL			
Treatment	1.4	8.0	8.6
Control	2.7	3.6	
DESIRE TO GAMBLE			
Treatment	5.7	2.0	0.5
Control	6.3	6.1	
BELIEVE CAN RESIST GAMBLING			
Treatment	2.8	8.4	8.8
Control	3.4	3.7	
SOGS			
Treatment	12.6	2.7	2.7
Control	13.1	13.0	

Note: *DSM-III-R* refers to the number of diagnostic criteria found in the Diagnostic and Statistical Manual that were met and SOGS refers to the scores obtained on the questionnaire.

*At 6-month follow-up only 10 participants were included.

Gambling Screen score (SOGS). They reported a higher perception of control over gambling and a higher belief that they could refrain from gambling.

Table 27.2 shows the data for self-report frequency-of-gambling variables during pretreatment, posttreatment, and 6-month follow-up. Initially, it might seem that some of the numbers reported in Table 27.2 are going to make it difficult to interpret the findings of the study with respect to frequency of gambling. A glance at the means might suggest that, even though the groups were formed by random assignment, the unusual has happened: frequency of gambling appears to be quite a bit lower in the treatment group compared to the control group, even in the pretreatment measures. Arithmetic means can be misleading. There was a great deal of variability in these data, with a few individuals gambling either a great deal more than the mean or a great deal less. In this particular case, the mean is an inadequate one-number summary of the entire data set because there is so much variability. Probably the median, which is the middle score in the distribution, would be a better summary, but when scores are widely variable, no single number is likely to represent them very well. Remember, when the treatment and control group means for frequency of gambling were compared statistically before treatment began, there were no statistically significant differences.

As you think critically about this issue you also need to see that the treatment groups and the control groups should be compared with themselves. The magnitude of group means is less important than the amount of change in them. If the program was effective we should see a statistically significant decrease between pretreatment and posttreatment within the treatment group. We do. If we want to conclude that this change is a result of the therapy, not just time passing by, we should not see a significant decrease between pretreatment and posttreatment in the control group, as, indeed, we do not.

Six months after the end of therapy, measures were taken again on the 10 participants from the treatment group who were available. Four of the original participants were not included in the 6-month

TABLE 27.2   Means of the Three Frequency-of-Gambling Variables at Pretreatment, Posttreatment, and 6-Month Follow-Up Measurements for the Treatment Group and the (Wait List) Control Group When Asked About the Previous Week

	PRETREATMENT	POSTTREATMENT	6-MONTH FOLLOW-UP*
NO. OF GAMBLING SESSIONS			
Treatment	0.8	0.2	0
Control	1.5	1.7	
NO. HOURS SPENT GAMBLING			
Treatment	1.4	0.9	0
Control	3.3	4.6	
MONEY SPENT ON GAMBLING			
Treatment	23.29	8.57	0
Control	99.67	188.00	

*At 6-month follow-up only 10 participants were included.

follow-up data. Three of them could not be located despite numerous attempts, and the other participant had probably relapsed. As can be seen from Table 27.1 and Table 27.2, 6 months later, the changes in gambling persisted among the 10 remaining participants. All pretreatment measures shown in Table 27.1 for the treatment group were significantly different from their 6-month follow-up scores ($p < .01$). Table 27.2 shows that at 6 months, those remaining in the study had no gambling activity.

Twelve months after the end of therapy, it was possible to reach nine of the participants from the original treatment group either by telephone or in interview. For eight of the nine, therapeutic gains persisted, and they were no longer considered pathological gamblers according to *DSM-III-R* criteria. One of these nine had relapsed and was still considered a pathological gambler.

DISCUSSION

The results of this study suggest that cognitive-behavioral therapy can effectively treat pathological gambling for some individuals. Their attitudes changed and so did their behavior. The success of this program has to be evaluated in the light of the initial dropouts and refusals. At this point, there is no evidence that this approach would work for everyone, even though it may have been successful for those who completed the program. In addition, it was a requirement that participants be willing to consider behavior change. There are probably many people who are classifiable under *DSM* criteria who are not willing to change their behavior. There is no therapy that is likely to be effective for people who make hard-line refusals.

Part of the success of this program may have been a result of its multifaceted approach to the problem. These individuals received help in changing erroneous beliefs about gambling. This cognitive component was linked to problem solving and relapse prevention in this program, helping people to develop the skills required to decrease or eliminate problem behavior. As we noted at the beginning of this chapter, the approach here was based on learning and, as you have seen, the therapy consisted of a variety of efforts to teach new skills, cognitive and behavioral. There was no hidden magic here. The therapy involved a skilled teacher, the therapist, working with a willing learner to change behavior. The process was not basically different from what might happen in learning to play tennis from an expert coach: behavior is changed. This was an important study because, although the final numbers were small, it was a careful and concerted attempt to evaluate the outcome of psychotherapy. If therapy had been seen as a probing of the unconscious in an attempt to repair primal forces, rather than an attempt to change behavior, there would be no outcome to measure. It is difficult for us to understand how a therapeutic approach can have any claim to success in the absence of observable and measurable outcomes.

REFERENCES

American Psychiatric Association (1980). *Diagnostic and statistical manual of mental disorders* (3rd ed.). Washington, DC: Author.

Dickerson, M. G., & Weeks, D. (1979). Controlled gambling as a therapeutic technique for compulsive gamblers. *Journal of Behavior Therapy and Experimental Psychiatry, 10,* 139–141.

Freud, S. (1935). *An autobiographical study.* New York: Norton.

Ladouceur, R., & Walker, M. (1996). A cognitive perspective on gambling. In P. M. Salkovskis (Ed.), *Trends in cognitive and behavioral therapies* (pp. 89–120). New York: Wiley.

Lesieur, H. R., & Blume, S. B. (1987). The South Oaks Gambling Screen (The SOGS): A new instrument for the identification of pathological gamblers. *American Journal of Psychiatry, 144,* 1184–1188.

Stark, M. J. (1992). Dropping out of substance abuse treatment: A clinically oriented review. *Clinical Psychology Review, 12,* 93–116.

Sylvain, C., Ladouceur, R., & Boisvert, J. M. (1997). Cognitive and behavioral treatment of pathological gambling: A controlled study. *Journal of Consulting and Clinical Psychology, 65,* 727–732.

CHAPTER 28

SHOW ME THE EVIDENCE[1]

Material selected from:
Research Stories for Introductory Psychology,
Second Edition, by Lary Shaffer and Matthew R. Merrens

---

[1]Incorporating the research of R. E. Drake, G. J. McHugo, D. R. Becker, W. A. Anthony, and R. E. Clark, "The New Hampshire Study of Supported Employment for People with Severe Mental Illness," 1996, *Journal of Clinical and Consulting Psychology, 64,* pp. 391–399.

SEVERE MENTAL ILLNESS AND EVIDENCE-BASED PRACTICE

Severe mental illness refers to the existence of a severe psychiatric disorder (typically schizophrenia, schizoaffective disorder, major depression, or bipolar disorder). In severe mental illness the disorder is accompanied by significant functional impairment, disruption of normal life tasks, periods of hospitalization, and the need for psychotropic medication. With the exception of medication (typically antipsychotic or antidepressant drugs), there has been little progress in offering psychosocial interventions for clients with mental illness that are effective and promote a more adaptive life style.

A major development to remedy this lack of effective psychosocial treatment options has been the emergence of evidence-based practices (EBP) for people with severe mental illness. Reviews of treatments for severe mental illness from the research literature (Drake et al., 2001) have found a number of treatment interventions that have demonstrated reduced symptoms, higher levels of functioning, and better quality of life. There are five psychosocial interventions that we refer to as EBPs: Illness Management and Recovery, Assertive Community Treatment, Family Psycho-Education, Supported Employment, and Integrated Dual Diagnosis Treatment.

The process of how a practice gets credentialed as evidence-based is described by Mueser, Torrey, Lynde, Singer, & Drake (in press). The initial steps include planning and discussion by mental health researchers, clinicians, and administrators as well as clients and family members. By having all the stakeholders involved at an early stage of EBP development, issues from each group's perspective can be discussed and an overall consensus among stakeholders can be achieved. EBPs were reviewed and approved by panels of researchers according to clear standards (Drake et al., 2001). At present the five psychosocial EBPs are being field-tested in community mental health centers in eight states. After the evaluation of this implementation data, the EBP material will be revised and made available for national use.

In medicine the term randomized controlled trial refers to an experiment that represents the best evaluation of the efficacy of a treatment. If you read reports in this area you often see RCT as the shorthand for randomized controlled trial. Repeated randomized controlled trials by different research programs with consistently favorable outcomes make a very compelling case for the designation of EBP. Some research uses a quasi-experimental design (no random assignment to condition). This is frequently the case when an entire mental health center adopts the same treatment practice so that all clients receive the designated treatment without random assignment. Engaging in research in clinical settings often does not allow the researcher to impose the same degree of control that one sees in laboratory studies. However, research in a genuine treatment center with actual clients provides strong external or ecological validity in comparison to the potential artificiality that is often seen in laboratory investigations even though there is greater control.

Research has shown that merely offering an intervention that is an EBP does not ensure that it will be effective. It is critically important that the EBP be implemented in a manner as faithful to the practice model as possible. Fidelity is the term used to define how faithful or close a practice is to the established EBP model. Research has demonstrated that only high-fidelity (programs that closely follow the EBP model) programs yield effective treatment outcomes (Jerrel & Ridgely, 1999; McHugo, Drake, Teague, & Xie, 1999). This should not really be too surprising. Think of cooking using a great recipe. If you follow it faithfully you are likely to have an excellent outcome. If, however, you are casual about measuring amounts and modifying ingredients, the results are likely to be less certain. EBPs represent models with excellent outcomes that have evolved as a result of research. For a practice to attain success it is important that the model be followed with high fidelity. In order to ensure that this happens, toolkits have been developed, as manuals that describe in detail how to initiate and maintain the EBP. These toolkits, combined with training, consultation and a focus on measuring and attaining high fidelity, are all aimed at promoting an effective EBP (Bond et al., 2000). Table 28.1 will give you an idea of how fidelity is measured. The table presents fidelity items from the Supported Employment EBP. Examining this table will give you an idea of the procedures necessary to establish and maintain a high-fidelity EBP. On this fidelity scale each of the 15 criteria is rated on a five-point scale. The higher the overall score, the greater the fidelity. Using this scale gives you a way to operationally define the concept of fidelity. The identified EBPs have all focused on the objectives and desires of the consumers of treatment. People with severe mental illness want to have jobs, meaningful relationships, be productive and happy, lead independent lives, and be free of symptoms (Mead & Copeland, 2000).

THE EBPS FOR PEOPLE WITH SEVERE MENTAL ILLNESS

From a mental health policy viewpoint it is essential that EBPs be implemented and offered to consumers throughout the national mental health treatment system. Researchers have documented evidence that these treatment interventions are effective, and failure to implement these EBPs represents negligence toward clients with severe mental illness.

Assertive Community Treatment

This EBP represents a new approach to case management. Assertive Community Treatment involves providing treatment to consumers in their own natural environments rather than in a mental health center or clinic. In Assertive Community Treatment the clinician caseloads are reduced, and a multi-disciplinary team of professionals shares caseloads. Consumers are not sent to other agencies for treatment, employment, or other services. Assertive Community Treatment teams deal with all the clients' issues in an active, integrated, intensive manner.

Family Psycho-Education

This EBP recognizes the importance of family members in assisting in the recovery of persons with severe mental illness. Family Psycho-education furnishes information to families about severe mental illness and how to assist in its management. Family Psycho-education aims to reduce tension and stress among family members, offers support and empathy for family members, helps the family to shift

TABLE 28.1   Brief Supported Employment Fidelity Scale (Bond, Becker, Drake, & Vogler, 1997)

Each of the criteria in the three major categories is rated on a five-point scale ranging from 1 representing poor implementation to 5 representing excellent implementation. This table shows the criteria for the end points 1 & 5. The actual scale operationally defines all points including 2, 3, & 4.

STAFFING

1. **Caseload Size:** 1 = 81 or more clients/employment specialist; 5 = 25 or fewer clients/employment specialist.
2. **Vocational Services Staff:** 1 = employment specialists provide non-vocational services 80% or more of the time; 5 = employment specialists provide only vocational services.
3. **Vocational Generalists:** 1 = employment specialists only provide vocational services to vendors and other programs; 5 = employment specialists are involved in all phases of the vocational service process to the client (engagement, assessment, development, placement, coaching, and support maintenance).

ORGANIZATION

1. **Integration of Rehabilitation with Mental Health Treatment:** 1 = Vocational specialists are separate from mental health treatment staff; 5 = Vocational specialists are part of treatment teams and client meetings.
2. **Vocational Unit:** 1 = Employment specialists don't meet as group but have same supervisor; 5 = employment specialists interact with each other, have group supervision and provide help and for each others cases.
3. **Zero Exclusion Criteria:** 1 = Clients are not offered job services because of substance abuse, violence, low functioning or other criteria; 5 = All clients are solicited and encouraged to participate in employment services.

SERVICES

1. **Ongoing, Work-Based Assessment:** 1 = vocational evaluation is based on standardized testing, work samples and is conducted prior to job placement; 5 = vocational assessment occurs on the job and is on-going; with focus on environmental assessments and job accommodations.
2. **Rapid Search for Competitive Job:** 1 = Initial contact with employer is typically one year or more after being in program; 5 = Initial contact with employer is typically within a month of entering program.
3. **Individualized Job Search:** 1 = Employer contacts made by vocational specialist and based on job market; 5 = Employer contacts based on client strengths, preferences, symptoms and other individual characteristics.
4. **Diversity of Jobs Developed:** 1 = Vocational specialists provide options within a limited job category; 5 = Vocational specialists provide diverse job options in various settings.
5. **Permanence of Jobs Developed:** 1 = Vocational specialists don't focus on options for permanent, competitive employment; 5 = Vocational specialists focus on competitive jobs that are permanent.
6. **Jobs as Transitions:** 1 = Vocational specialists prepare clients for a single job and don't always assist them if this placement fails; 5 = Vocational specialists help clients in all aspects of job process—finding work, ending work, and looking for new jobs.
7. **Follow-Along Supports:** 1 = supports for employers and clients do not exist; 5 = Employers are offered educational and guidance and clients are given coaching, crisis intervention, counseling, etc. on an on-going basis.
8. **Community-Based Services:** 1 = Vocational specialists spend 10% or less time in community; 5 = Vocational specialists spend 70% or more time in community.
9. **Assertive Engagement and Outreach:** 1 = Vocational specialists don't provide outreach in engagement or to those clients who terminate vocational services; 5 = Vocational specialists provide outreach in engagement, at least monthly, and to those clients who terminate vocational services.

its focus to the future, and attempts to improve communication and interactions between all family members, including the client. A major goal of family psycho-education is to establish an effective working relationship between the treatment providers and the family unit.

Supported Employment

Supported Employment offers vocational services geared toward securing competitive jobs for clients in the community in which they live, earning wages comparable to those of workers without disabilities. Supported Employment does not utilize the traditional prevocational strategies of assessment, psychometric testing, work trials, counseling, and so on. Instead, Supported Employment attempts to quickly place clients in jobs and then offers supportive services to facilitate the clients' job performances. Clients are not penalized for quitting jobs. They are, instead, helped to find new positions in which they might find greater success. Finally, clients' vocational and mental health services are integrated and managed in one program along with any additional services they might require.

Illness Management and Recovery

The practice emphasizes that clients should be actively involved in guiding their own treatment. Mueser et al. (in press) state that "illness management and recovery is aimed at helping consumers acquire the information and skills needed to collaborate effectively with professional and significant others in their treatment, to minimize the effects of mental illness on their lives, and to be able to pursue personally meaningful goals." An important focus of this EBP is informing consumers about mental illness, treatment options, the appropriate use of psychotropic medication, and dealing with symptoms and setbacks.

Integrated Dual-Diagnosis Treatment

This EBP recognizes that consumers with mental illness have high rates of substance abuse disorders. These consumers with dual diagnoses demonstrate significantly higher rates for poor treatment outcomes, hopelessness, acts of violence, imprisonment, relapse, HIV, and hepatitis (Drake and Brunette, 1998; Drake, Mueser, Clark, & Wallach, 1996). This EBP recognizes that dual-diagnosis clients often find it difficult to navigate treatment in two different centers and they fail to continue treatment. If they stay in treatment, they are likely to have poor outcomes (Ridgely, Goldman, & Willenbring, 1990). The key, as in all of the EBPs, is to provide integrated treatment including counseling, medication, vocational assistance, and other services in a coordinated manner with assertive, engaging strategies.

SUPPORTED VERSUS BROKERED EMPLOYMENT: AN EXPERIMENT

Now that you have some background information regarding severe mental illness and evidence-based practices, we would like to focus on an experiment that compared supported to brokered employment. Working at a competitive job is a major goal for people with severe mental illness (Rogers, Walsh, Mascotta, & Daniels, 1991). Research (Black, 1988; Palmer, 1989) has indicated that working at "real" jobs facilitates social contact and community integration, facilitates the ability to self-manage illness, increases self-esteem, and generally enhances quality of life. However, there are many obstacles for persons with severe mental illness who want to work at competitive jobs. These include incentives offered by insurance programs to not work, the cultural stigma of mental illness that limits job opportunities, and the attitudes and opinions of family members, mental health workers, and others who counsel to avoid seeking a competitive job. Therefore, job opportunities and help in securing jobs are inadequate.

The most favorable approach in assisting mental health consumers to obtain a competitive job has been the EBP of Supported Employment. This EBP focuses on getting clients with severe mental illness competitive jobs in work environments that allow for the necessary support to attain success.

The traditional approach to providing vocational services to mental health consumers has been to send them to a vocational service agency for assistance. In this model vocational services to clients are not handled as part of their mental health treatment but rather are brokered to another agency. Indeed, brokering has been the traditional way in which mental health centers have handled alcohol and drug treatment, housing issues, education options, and other aspects of the consumer's life. Research has shown that collaboration between various agencies in attempting to manage a consumer's overall care can be problematic. The interaction between agencies with different personnel and different rules and practices and at different geographic locations can lead to less than optimal treatment for the consumer. The result of the brokered approach can be a fragmented approach to care. Because of these issues there has been a movement to integrate vocational services with the clinical treatment at the mental health center. The purpose of this research (Drake, McHugo, Becker, Anthony, & Clark, 1996) was to investigate the effectiveness of the brokered or traditional model of vocational services in comparison to the integrated model of consumer services in which vocational and clinical services are combined in the same program at the same clinical center.

Participants

The participants were 143 volunteers with severe mental illness from two mental health centers. Participants were required to have a major mental illness of at least two years' duration, be out of the hospital for at least one month, be unemployed for longer than one month, be interested in seeking competitive employment, and be lacking in cognitive memory problems, medical illness, or substance abuse issues that would impede job training. All participants signed informed consent statements. The participants were generally similar to people in their community and state. There were approximately the same number of males and females, almost all Caucasian, generally young, and with reasonably good job records but currently unemployed.

Supported and Brokered Employment

The employment practices compared in this research were an excellent brokered employment model and an evidence-based supported employment intervention. The brokered employment program provided personalized intake services, group preemployment training, job placement and continuing job support, and ongoing contact with the client's mental health provider. The supported employment model used a team strategy to integrate the provision of vocational services with ongoing mental health treatment, and with vocational employment workers as an integral part of the treatment group providing services to the client. In Supported Employment, the employment specialists began to help the clients secure jobs and with the acquisition of a job, immediately instituted job-related training and support services as warranted by the client situation. A major assumption of the Supported Employment is that the client is placed in the position first and then expected to learn the skills and behaviors on the job rather than through the more conventional preemployment service model.

Research Design

The basic research design was an experiment with random assignment to either Supported Employment or Brokered Employment. The primary dependent variable, assessed weekly, was competitive employment, operationally defined as working at prevailing wages in a competitive job. In addition, instruments were used for assessment of psychiatric symptoms, diagnostic status, self-esteem, and quality of life.

Results and Discussion

After random assignment, the researchers checked the group equivalence in terms of demographic variables, psychiatric status, employment history and job status, quality of life, and self-esteem. These comparisons showed that the Supported Employment and Brokered Employment groups did not significantly differ from one another prior to the employment interventions. Figure 28.1 shows the percentage of each group employed on a monthly basis over the 18-month course of investigation. With the exception of months 12 through 15, there was a significant difference between groups, with the Supported Employment participants demonstrating a higher percentage of competitive employment. Therefore, the major outcome measure indicated that Supported Employment was a more advantageous approach to assist clients with severe mental illness secure competitive jobs. The data indicate that clients in the Supported Employment group secured jobs more quickly, and in month-to-month comparisons over the 18-month study, the Supported Employment group always maintained a lead over brokered employment clients in employment. There were no significant differences between Supported Employment and Brokered Employment groups in any of the measured nonemployment aspects (e.g., symptoms, quality of life, self-esteem) of their functioning. Both groups of clients showed positive growth in global functioning and financial satisfaction, with little modification on other assessed domains.

The researchers attribute the success of Supported Employment over Brokered Employment in vocational areas primarily to the fact that employment and mental health services are integrated so that clients don't have to manage the task of going to different agencies for services. Indeed, integration of services is a basic tenet of all of the evidence-based practices. In addition, the researchers noted that because clients immediately began to secure jobs through Supported Employment, they did not become unmotivated and uninvolved. Brokered Employment had a significant period of preplacement training that may have served as a barrier to job success. The detailed data analysis confirms that clients in the Brokered Employment group did find difficulty in navigating between mental health and vocational training agencies. Also, failures in interagency communication were typical.

The researchers note that nonvocational outcomes were not significantly different between Supported Employment and Brokered Employment groups. This finding was unexpected because prevalent thinking assumes better vocational adjustment is likely to lead to better nonvocational adjustment. This study indicated improvement in these areas by both Supported and Brokered Employment participants. The researchers note that it is possible that vocational outcomes are simply not related to other factors in the client's adjustment or that it may take longer to see changes in those areas than this investigation permitted.

FIGURE 28.1   Percent in Each Treatment Group Employed from Month 1 to Month 18

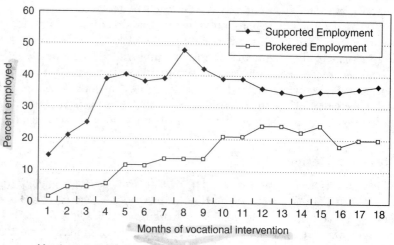

Months 1, 2, 7, 10, 11, 16, 18: $p < .05$
Months 3, 4, 5, 6, 8, 9: $p < .001$

REFERENCES

Black, B. J. (1988). *Work and mental illness: Transitions to employment.* Baltimore: Johns Hopkins Press.

Bond, G. R., Becker, D. R., Drake, R. E., & Vogler, K. (1997). A fidelity scale for the Individual Placement and Support model of supported employment. *Rehabilitation Counseling Bulletin, 40,* 265–284.

Bond, G. Williams, J., Evans, L., Salyers, M., Kim, H., Sharpe, H., & Leff, H. S. (2000). *Psychiatric rehabilitation fidelity toolkit.* Cambridge, MA, Evaluation Center @ HSRI.

Drake, R. E., Mueser, K. T., Clark, R. E., & Wallach, M. A. (1996). The course, treatment, and outcome of substance abuse disorder in persons with severe mental illness. *American Journal of Orthopsychiatry, 66,* 42–51.

Drake, R. E., McHugo, G. J., Becker, D. R., Anthony, W. A., & Clark, R. E. (1996). The New Hampshire study of supported employment for people with severe mental illness. *Journal of Clinical and Consulting Psychology, 64,* 391–399.

Drake, R. E., & Brunette, M. F. (1998). Complications of severe mental illness related to alcohol and other drug use disorders. In M. Galanter (Ed.), *Recent Developments in Alcoholism* (Vol. XIV, Consequences of Alcoholism, pp. 285–299). New York: Plenum Publishing Company.

Drake, R. E., Goldman, H. H., Leff, H. S., Lehman, A. F., Dixon, L., Mueser, K. T., & Torrey, W. C. (2001). Implementing evidence-based practices in routine mental health service settings. *Psychiatric Services, 52,* 179–182.

Jerrel, J. M., & Ridgely, M. S. (1999). Impact of robustness of program implementation on outcomes of clients in dual diagnosis programs. *Psychiatric Services, 50,* 109–112.

McHugo, G. J., Drake, R. E., Teague, G. B., & Xie, H. (1999). Fidelity to assertive community treatment and client outcomes in the New Hampshire Dual Disorders Study. *Psychiatric Services, 50,* 818–824.

Mead, S., & Copeland, M. E. (2000). What recovery means to us: Consumers' perspectives. *Community Mental Health Journal, 36,* 315–328.

Mueser, K. T., Torrey, W. C., Lynde, D., Singer, P., & Drake, R. E. (in press). Implementing evidence-based practices for people with severe mental ill. *Behavior Modification.*

Palmer, F. (1989). The place of work in psychiatric rehabilitation. *Hospital and Community Psychiatry, 40,* 222–224.

Ridgely, M. S., Goldman, H. H., & Willenbring, M. (1990). Barriers to the care of persons with dual diagnoses: Organizational and financing issues. *Schizophrenia Bulletin, 16,* 123–132.

Rogers, E. S., Walsh, D., Masotta, L., & Daniels, K. (1991). *Massachusetts survey of client preferences for community support services (Final Report).* Boston: Center for Psychiatric Rehabilitation.

CHAPTER 29

TO CATCH A COLD[1]

Material selected from:
Research Stories for Introductory Psychology,
Second Edition, by Lary Shaffer and Matthew R. Merrens

---

[1]Incorporating the research of S. Cohen, D. A. J. Tyrell, and A. P. Smith, "Negative Life Events, Perceived Stress, Negative Affect, and Susceptibility to the Common Cold," 1993, *Journal of Personality and Social Psychology, 64*, pp. 131–140.

There is an increasing evidence that stress in life may contribute to the development of organic illness. The field of psychoneuroimmunology, a branch of behavioral medicine, deals with life and environmental stress, as well as psychological events that increase susceptibility to disease. Until recently it was largely assumed that organic disease could only have organic origins. Current thinking is that excessive environmental stress, which exceeds the person's coping ability, can have negative physical consequences, such as disease (Lazarus & Folkman, 1984). It is thought that high stress may lead to negative cognitive and emotional reactions that, in turn, may alter the effectiveness of the immune system. The immune system can be adversely affected by autonomic and central nervous system activation (Felten & Olshchowka, 1987), release of hormones (Shavit, Lewis, Terman, Gale, & Liebeskind, 1984), and maladaptive lifestyle changes such as drug usage, smoking, or alcohol (Cohen & Williamson, 1991).

Although there is a belief that stress leads to illness, the research findings are not clear as to whether immune system breakdowns could be of such magnitude as to increase susceptibility to infection (Jemmott & Locke, 1984). Previous research on the current topic, catching a cold, is also unclear on the relationship between stress and the development of illness. The research reported in this chapter focuses on this question—Can stress increase the likelihood of catching a cold? In the research described in this chapter healthy participants were assessed on their level of stress, personality features, and health practices. They were then intentionally exposed to a cold virus or a placebo. Placebo groups are commonly used in research in order to create a control condition in which participants receive exactly the same treatment as the experimental condition, but do not receive the active ingredient under study. In a drug study a placebo pill mimics the actual medication under investigation in size, color, taste, and even side effects, but the pill does not have the active therapeutic ingredient. In this study the placebo group was treated identically to the viral exposure group except that the solution the placebo groups received contained no cold virus, but rather a saline solution. The importance of having a placebo group is to determine if factors other than the variable under study, in this case cold viruses, had any impact on viral infection and disease. We are likely to respond to placebos due to prior learning. For example, if someone has a history of going to a physician and getting medication that relieves pain and symptoms, it is probable that he or she may develop pain and symptom relief by being exposed to talking to a physician. If this occurs, it is an example of classical conditioning in which the medication was the unconditioned stimulus and relief of pain and symptoms was the unconditioned response. Talking to the physician, without treatment, was the conditioned stimulus for the conditioned response of symptom relief. You can review the classical conditioning paradigm in Chapter 11, "Being Sick of the Hospital."

PARTICIPANTS

The participants were 154 male and 266 female volunteers, with 394 randomly assigned to the virus infection group and 26 randomly assigned to the saline control group. The study was conducted at a medical research center in Salisbury, England. According to clinical evaluation and laboratory findings, all participants were judged to be in good health at the start of the investigation. Participants ranged in age from 18 to 54, with a mean age of 33.

PROCEDURE

The initial phase of the study consisted of a complete medical exam, administration of self-reported instruments including psychological stress, personality, and health practices questionnaires. Blood samples were obtained for immunity measurement and to check nicotine intake. Following these initial assessments participants were exposed to cold viruses using nasal drops. The placebo group was administered a saline solution.

For 2 days preceding the administration of nose drops and continuing for 6 days after exposure the participants were evaluated each day using a standard medical protocol. Protocol items included frequency of sneezing, eye tearing, nasal congestion, nasal blockage, postnasal discharge, sinus pain, sore throat, and coughing. In addition an objective count of number of paper tissues (e.g., Kleenex) used by the participants and twice-daily report of body temperature were made. Twenty-eight days after the viral exposure another blood sample was obtained. In all phases of this study, the researchers were purposely kept unaware as to the psychological status (based on the three measures used in the study) of participants and also whether or not they received a virus or were in the saline control group.

MEASURING PSYCHOLOGICAL STRESS

Psychological stress was assessed by the these measures:

- Selected items from the *List of Recent Experiences* (Henderson, Byrne, & Duncan-Jones, 1981). The number of major stressful life events rated by the participants as having a negative impact.
- *10-item Perceived Stress Scale* (Cohen & Williamson, 1988). This scale was used to measure the extent to which life circumstances are seen to be stressful. Items measured anxiety, sadness, anger, guilt, irritation, and related concepts.
- *Affect Intensity Measure.* A 5-point scale was used to assess affect (emotional) intensity experienced during the past week.

Previous research by Cohen, Tyrell, and Smith (1991) using the same measures suggested that the three scales were assessing a common underlying concept. Because these three measures are focusing on a single dimension, the researchers combined them into a single composite measure that was used to assess stress.

HOW WE CATCH A COLD

The growth and action of microorganisms is responsible for the development of the common cold. Infection results in the intensification of the attacking microorganism. It is possible for a person to be infected with the invading cold virus without developing clinical symptoms. In this investigation the researchers operationally defined whether a person was infected with a cold virus and also whether a person demonstrated clinical symptoms of a cold. Infection was determined by the presence of a virus found in fluid samples (cultures of nasal secretions) or a rise in cold virus specific antibodies found in blood samples. The presence of cold symptoms was determined by clinical rating on a four-point scale ranging from complete absence of symptoms (0) to severe symptoms (3). A rating of a mild cold (2) or higher was operationally defined as a positive diagnosis of a clinical cold. In this study clinical diagnosis of colds agreed with participants' self-diagnosis in 94 percent of cases. Participants were operationally defined as having a cold if *both* infection and symptoms were detected. Thirty-eight percent (148 participants) of the total infected sample ($N = 394$) developed colds. In the saline control group no participants became infected.

MEASURING BODY TEMPERATURE AND MUCUS WEIGHTS

In order to obtain additional, objective measures of a cold, the investigators measured body temperature and mucus weights. These additional measurements provided objective assessments not influenced by how an individual participant presented symptoms or how a clinician completed a rating scale. Mucus weights were calculated by weighing the paper tissues used by participants. Body temperatures and mucus weights were taken on the day before "infection" and on each succeeding day.

HEALTH PRACTICES OF PARTICIPANTS

Participants' health practices are important to evaluate because they may serve as important connections between stress and susceptibility to infection. Therefore smoking, alcohol consumption, exercise activity, sleep quality, and dietary habits were considered part of this study. Smoking was assessed objectively by reviewing cotinine levels in participants' blood samples. Cotinine is a biochemical indicator of nicotine intake that avoids the subjectivity of participants' self-report. However, in this study the correlation of self-reported smoking and cotinine levels was found to be +.96, indicating that both measures were assessing smoking behavior accurately. Alcohol consumption was measured by self-reports of the number of drinks per day with each drink (bottle of beer, glass of wine, shot of liquor) counting equally. Exercise was assessed by tabulating the self-reported frequency of engaging in walking, running, swimming, and other aerobic activities. Sleep was measured by a questionnaire tapping the various sleep qualities (e.g., feeling rested, difficulty falling asleep). Diet was measured by self-report items assessing participants' eating habits (e.g., dietary balance, eating vegetables and fruits).

PERSONALITY ASSESSMENT

Three personality dimensions were measured because the investigators thought it likely that psychological stress might be a result of more fundamental aspects of personality. Therefore they assessed self-esteem, personal control, and introversion-extroversion by using a variety of established scales. Self-esteem refers to the views that people hold about their own competencies. Personal control focuses on whether or not people believe that they control and are in charge of their lives and can determine outcomes. People with an internal personal control orientation feel in charge of their own destiny, whereas an external personal control would represent the view that things in life are a matter of chance and there is little personal control of how things turn out. Introversion represents a need for privacy and a lack of need for interpersonal relationships; extroverts are outgoing and social.

RESULTS

None of the saline control participants, the placebo group, became infected or developed colds and, therefore, the following data presented represent only the participants who were exposed to the genuine virus. For each of the four stress measure participants above the median score were considered high stress; those below the median were considered low stress. Table 29.1 presents the percentages of virally exposed participants in low and high groups on the four stress measures who became infected and of those who developed clinical colds.

As can be seen in Table 29.1, the rates of actual infection resulting from exposure are significantly higher for participants in the high groups for stress index (an overall composite score), perceived stress, and negative affect. The high stress group in the life events measure had greater levels of infection, but it was not statistically significant. In reviewing the data on those who actually developed a cold, the life events measure was the only assessment instrument to attain statistical significance between high- and low-stress participants. Therefore, while the life events measure did not differ significantly between high and low groups in determining infection, it did significantly differ for participants who actually became ill with a cold. Participants with high numbers of negative life events had higher percentages of

TABLE 29.1 Percentages of Virally Exposed Participants in Low- and High-Stress Groups Who Became Infected and Developed Clinical Colds Symptoms

	% INFECTED (n = 394)	% DEVELOPING COLD SYMPTOMS AMONG THOSE INFECTED (n = 325)
COMBINED STRESS INDEX		
Low	78.7	43.2
High	86.3*	47.7
LIFE EVENTS		
Low	80.9	40.1
High	84.6	52.5*
PERCEIVED STRESS		
Low	78.4	44.2
High	86.7*	46.8
NEGATIVE AFFECT		
Low	76.9	45.8
High	88.2*	45.4

*p < .05 between low and high Groups.

clinical colds than participants with low life events scores. This finding does suggest that the life events assessment is measuring something different from the other two measures (i.e., perceived stress and negative affect). The diagnosis of clinical cold in the data presented in Table 29.1 was made by clinical judgment. The data from the two other more objective sources of the presence of a cold, mucus weight in paper tissues and body temperature, provided mixed findings. Life events were not found to be associated with mucus weight changes in paper tissues (a good attempt at objective measurement that did not work). Participants with high numbers of life events did have correspondingly higher body temperature after infection than those participants with low numbers of life events. Figure 29.1 presents the average body temperature of high (more than 2 stressful events) and low (2 or fewer stressful events) groups over the initial 5 days after being infected.

As you can see by the vertical axis scaling, the displayed centigrade temperature ranges from 36.4 to 36.55. The differences between high and low groups are quite small, but in all daily comparisons the high group always has a significantly higher body temperature than the low group ($p < .02$).

In analyzing the data among the three measured personality variables (self-esteem, personal control, and introversion-extroversion) and development of the common cold, no significant relationships were found. This suggests that these three broad personality measures had little to do with the development of the common cold. In addition the data analysis did not find that the many health practices investigated played a role in the development of colds.

CONCLUSIONS

It is important to distinguish between being infected and the development of clinical illness. Infection and the development of illness as indicated by clinical symptoms may be the result of different processes. Cohen and his research team note that infection is linked to viral replication, whereas becoming ill with a cold may be due to an inflammation in the immune response system, which leads to the release of chemicals (e.g., histamines, prostaglandins) that produce cold symptoms. Cohen's research program showed that high-stress participants have significantly higher rates of infection compared to low-stress participants in three of the four major measures. However, when it comes to the development of clinical symptoms of a cold it is only with the life events measures that we see a significant difference between high- and low-stress groups. On this measure, high-stress people developed cold symptoms at significantly higher rates than their low-stress counterparts.

FIGURE 29.1   Postinfection Body Temperature for High- and Low-Stress Groups (Life Events Measure)

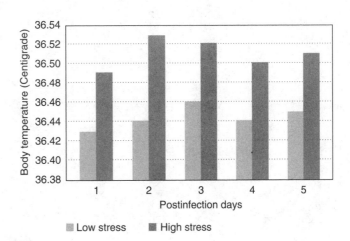

This investigation provides evidence for a link between the psychological and environmental factors that play an important role in understanding a disease process. Simply focusing on organic, biochemical origins in understanding the development of illness may just reveal part of the picture. This research suggests that clinical medicine should focus attention on stress factors in understanding patient illness.

REFERENCES

Cohen, S., Tyrrell, D. A. J., & Smith, A. P. (1991). Psychological stress and susceptibility to the common cold. *New England Journal of Medicine, 325*, 606–612.

Cohen, S., Tyrrell, D. A. J., & Smith, A. P. (1993). Negative life events, perceived stress, negative affect, and susceptibility to the common cold. *Journal of Personality and Social Psychology, 64*, 131–140.

Cohen, S., & Williamson, G. (1988). Perceived stress in a probability sample of the United States. In S. Spacapan & S. Oskamp (Eds.), *The social psychology of health* (pp. 31–67). Newbury Park, CA: Sage.

Cohen, S., & Williamson, G. (1991). Stress and infectious disease in humans. *Psychological Bulletin, 109*, 5–24.

Felten, S. Y., & Olschowka, J. A. (1987). Noradrenergic sympathetic innervation of the spleen: II. Tyrosine hydroxylase (TH)-positive nerve terminals from synaptic-like contacts on lymphocytes in the splenic white pulp. *Journal of Neuroscience Research, 18*, 37–48.

Henderson, S., Byrne, D. G., & Duncan-Jones, P. (1981). *Neurosis and the social environment.* San Diego, CA: Academic Press.

Jemmott, J. B., III, & Locke, S. E. (1984). Psychosocial factors, immunologic mediation, and human susceptibility to infectious diseases: How much do we know? *Psychological Bulletin, 95*, 78–108.

Lazarus, R. S., & Folkman, S. (1984). *Stress, appraisal, and coping.* New York: Springer.

Shavit, Y., Lewis, J. W., Terman, G. S., Gale, R. P., & Liebeskind, J. C. (1984). Opioid peptides mediated the suppressive effect of stress on natural killer cell cytotoxicity. *Science, 223*, 188–190.